AN ANTHOLOGY OF SPANISH LITERATURE

IN ENGLISH TRANSLATION

AN ANTHOLOGY OF
SPANISH LITERATURE

IN ENGLISH TRANSLATION

EDITED BY

SEYMOUR RESNICK, Ph.D.

AND

JEANNE PASMANTIER, M.A.

THE MEDIEVAL PERIOD
THE RENAISSANCE
THE GOLDEN AGE
EIGHTEENTH CENTURY
NINETEENTH CENTURY
TWENTIETH CENTURY

JOHN CALDER

LONDON

PUBLISHED IN GREAT BRITAIN BY
JOHN CALDER [PUBLISHERS] LTD.
17 SACKVILLE STREET . LONDON . W.3

PRINTED IN GREAT BRITAIN BY
THE GARDEN CITY PRESS LIMITED
LETCHWORTH . HERTFORDSHIRE

ACKNOWLEDGMENTS

The editors and the publishers are grateful for the co-operation of those individuals and publishers who granted permission to use their copyrighted material. Every effort has been made to trace and to acknowledge properly all copyright owners. If any acknowledgment has been inadvertently omitted, the publishers will be pleased to make the necessary correction in the next printing.

George Allen and Unwin, Ltd. For the selection from *Invertebrate Spain* by José Ortega y Gasset.

Burns, Oates & Washbourne, Ltd. For the translations by E. Allison Peers of poems by San Juan de la Cruz, from *Poems of Saint John of the Cross*.

The Clarendon Press. For the following selections from *Spanish Prose and Poetry* by Ida Farnell: Santillana, 'Serranilla VIII'; Luis de León, 'Ode to Salinas'; Rioja, 'To the Rose'; Campoamor, 'If Only I Could Write!'; Núñez de Arce, 'Dejection'; Azorín, 'Clouds'; Machado, 'Fields of Soria' and 'To Don Francisco Giner.' For the ballad 'The Prisoner' from *European Balladry* by W. J. Entwistle.

Harcourt, Brace and Company, Inc. For the 'Sonata of Spring' from *The Pleasant Memories of the Marquis of Bradomin* by Ramon del Valle-Inclan, copyright 1924 by Harcourt, Brace and Company, Inc.

Harvill Press Ltd. and Pantheon Books. For a translation by Roy Campbell of 'Verses written after an Ecstasy of High Exaltation' from *Poems of St. John of the Cross*.

Hispanic Society of America. For several selections from *Translations from Hispanic Poets* appearing on the stated pages in this *Anthology*: 'Song' p. 60; 'Sonnet' p. 47; 'The Lovely Infanta' p. 68; 'Cassandra's Song' p. 105; 'To a Nose' p. 272; the poems on pp. 377 and 415; 'Oriental' p. 428; the poems on pp. 587 and 588; 'Songs' p. 583; the poems on pp. 590 and 592; 'Slender Spring' p. 596; 'The Guitar' p. 598.

The Hogarth Press, Ltd. For selections from *Selected Poems* by Federico García Lorca (1943).

Henry Holt and Co., Inc. For 'King Don Sancho,' 'Count Arnaldos,' and 'Clear Eyes' from *The Heritage of Spain* by Nicholson B. Adams. Copyright 1943 by Henry Holt and Company, Inc. For Bécquer's 'Rima II,' and Campoamor's 'Boredom,' 'After Twenty Years,' and 'The Great Banquet' from *Main Currents of Spanish Literature* by J. M. D. Ford. Copyright 1919 by Henry Holt and Company.

The Johns Hopkins Press. For the following poems from *Contemporary Spanish Poetry*, translated by Eleanor Turnbull: Salinas, 'Soil,' 'How Gently You Rock,' and 'Swimmer of Night'; Guillén, 'Names' and 'Perfection'; García Lorca, 'Rider's Song' and 'Six Strings'; Alberti, 'The Sea,' 'Street Cry Under the Sea,' 'Street Cry,' and 'Angel of Numerals.'

Elisha K. Kane. For quotations from his translation of *The Book of Good Love*.

Alfred A. Knopf, Inc. For selections from *The Tree of Knowledge* by Pío Baroja and from *Mist* by Miguel de Unamuno, each copyright 1928 by Alfred A. Knopf, Inc., renewal copyright 1956 by Alfred A. Knopf, Inc. For the selection from *The Cabin* by V. Blasco Ibáñez, copyright 1919 by Alfred A. Knopf, Inc., renewal copyright 1947 by Alfred A. Knopf, Inc.

W. W. Norton & Company, Inc. For the selection from *Invertebrate Spain* by José Ortega y Gasset, copyright 1937 by W. W. Norton & Company, Inc.

Penguin Books Ltd. For the translation by J. M. Cohen of selections from Cervantes' 'Don Quixote,' copyright 1950 by Penguin Books Ltd.

Princeton University Press. For the selection 'The Judge of the Divorce Court' from *The Interludes of Cervantes* translated by S. Griswold Morley.

Routledge and Kegan Paul, Ltd. For the selection from chapter 3 of 'Paul, the Spanish Sharper' and for the selection from 'The Visions' from *The Choice Humorous and Satirical Works of Quevedo.*

Charles Scribner's Sons. For the selection from 'The Bonds of Interest' from *Plays*, First Series, by Jacinto Benavente, translated and copyright 1917, 1945 by John Garrett Underhill; for the selection from 'The Sheep Well' from *Four Plays by Lope de Vega*, translated and copyright 1936 by John Garrett Underhill.

Sheed and Ward, Inc., New York, and Sheed and Ward, Ltd., London. For 'I Die Because I Do Not Die' from *The Complete Works of Saint Teresa of Jesus*, Volume III, and 'The Life of the Holy Mother Teresa of Jesus' from *The Complete Works of Saint Teresa of Jesus*, Volume I, in the translation of E. Allison Peers, from the critical edition of P. Silverio de Santa Teresa, C.D.

University of California Press. For the selection 'The Poem of the Cid' from *The Lay of the Cid*; and for 'Green' and 'I Would That All My Verses' by Juan Ramón Jimenez from his *Fifty Spanish Poems* with English translations by J. B. Trend.

Wellesley College. For the selection 'Concerning Lawyers' by López de Ayala, in *Estudios Hispánicos*: Homenaje a Archer M. Huntington.

To

LIL and PAUL

PREFACE

With the exception of Cervantes' *Don Quixote*, Spanish literature is almost unknown to the average English-speaking reader. Yet this rich and varied literature has produced so many original genres and character types, and has inspired the work of so many authors in other countries that it deserves to be explored at first hand—and enjoyed—by all students of world literature. Unhappily, most readers in England and the United States are blocked by the language barrier at the very threshold of this literary treasure-house.

It should not be thought that the literature of Spain has gone entirely unnoticed by Englishmen and Americans. It has had a special appeal for some of our finest writers, and we are indebted to them for many excellent translations. Among the romantic poets of the early nineteenth century, for example, Robert Southey translated the *Chronicle of the Cid*, Lord Byron gave us a touching version of the doleful ballad 'Woe is me, Alhama,' and Shelley rendered into English several selections of Calderón. Later in the century, Edward FitzGerald, also attracted to Calderón, translated freely eight of his dramas. Among American translators of this period, the most noteworthy are Henry Wadsworth Longfellow and William Cullen Bryant. American Hispanists are especially grateful to Longfellow for his skilful presentation of Spanish verse in his *Poets and Poetry of Europe* (1845).

During the past century several collections of Spanish poetry and short stories in English translation have appeared, as well as a good number of novels and plays. Until now, however, there has never been a complete anthology of Spanish prose, verse and drama in English. The purpose of this book is to give the English-speaking reader an over-all picture of Spanish literature, with representative selections of all genres from the medieval to the contemporary period.

The editors have examined all available translations, and after careful comparison have chosen what in their opinion is the best translation of each work. Accuracy, it goes without saying, was a prime consideration. But beyond that obvious standard, our criteria included fidelity to the spirit of the original—the ability of the translator to impart those nuances of expression and style which mark each individual author. In certain cases we have made some

revisions or abridgments, and in several other instances have
prepared our own translations. With few exceptions, all passages
are complete units in themselves that even the most casual reader
may enjoy. Translators' names are listed after the selections.

This anthology omits Spanish-American literature, not because
it is less worthy than the literature of the mother country, but rather
because it merits an extensive treatment of its own. We have
included, however, a short bibliography of Spanish-American
literature for the English-speaking reader on page 605.

The Introduction offers a basic outline of Spanish poetry, prose
and drama, and the selections themselves are preceded by brief
introductory remarks about the authors. For a more detailed background the reader is advised to consult one of the histories of
literature listed in the Bibliography.

S.R.
J.P.

CONTENTS

EIGHTEENTH CENTURY

NINETEENTH CENTURY

INTRODUCTION

Poetry

As is generally the case in the development of a national literature, epic poetry was the first genre to make its appearance in Spain. The *Poema del Cid* (*ca.* 1140) is the foremost of the early epics, most of which have not come down to us. This poetry of the people, known as *mester de juglaría*, was related originally by wandering minstrels. By the thirteenth century certain Spanish poets, writing in a set verse form, had begun to cultivate the type of poetry called *mester de clerecía*, often based on religious themes and frequently in imitation of Latin and French models. Gonzalo de Berceo is the best representative of this school. Of significance also are the four hundred religious poems, in varying metres, composed by Alfonso X. The latter were written in Galician-Portuguese, the language then considered more appropriate to lyric poetry than Castilian.

Spanish lyric poetry seems to begin with the thirteenth-century love poem *Razón de Amor* ('Song of Love'). Expansion of metres and themes continued in the fourteenth century, culminating in one of the greatest works of Spanish literature, the *Libro de Buen Amor* ('Book of Good Love') by the Archpriest of Hita, which brilliantly encompasses narrative, religious, amatory and satirical verse. Satire also marks López de Ayala's *Rimado de Palacio* ('Palace Rhymes') of the latter part of the fourteenth century.

Lyric poetry flourished in the court of Juan II during the first half of the fifteenth century. The *cancioneros* (collections of poems) of this period are filled mainly with love and topical poetry. Outstanding poets were Santillana, with his *serranillas* (mountain songs) and sonnets, and Juan de Mena, author of a long allegorical poem. Later in the century, Jorge Manrique's inspired stanzas on the death of his father overshadowed all other poetic works.

At the same time that this learned and often artificial verse was in vogue, there was developing a truly popular poetry which is one of the glories of Spanish literature—the *romances* (ballads), transmitted orally at first, later recorded and often imitated.

Through the influence of the renaissance in the sixteenth century, Spanish poetry underwent a major change. Garcilaso de la Vega, one of the most delicate of all Spanish poets, introduced certain

Italian metres which have been employed ever since. The *Siglo de Oro* (Golden Age, *ca.* 1550–1650) produced the greatest Spanish authors in all fields. Lyric poetry engaged the talents of the prolific Lope de Vega, the versatile Quevedo, and the enigmatic Góngora, to mention only three of a host of outstanding poets. In this period too, Spanish mysticism reached its highest peak, with the ethereal poems of Fray Luis de León, Santa Teresa de Jesús, San Juan de la Cruz and others. It must also be mentioned that the great dramas of this age were all in verse; Calderón and many other dramatists wrote lyric poetry of surpassing beauty.

The period of decadence which followed the Golden Age did not entirely stifle Spain's poetic genius. Its two leading writers of fables, Iriarte and Samaniego, lived during the second half of the eighteenth century. Meléndez Valdés wrote the best neo-classic poetry of the period, and Ramón de la Cruz composed his numerous *sainetes* (humorous skits) in verse. At the turn of the century, the moving heroic poems of Quintana and Gallego appeared.

The death of the tyrant Fernando VII in 1833 allowed hitherto-banished Spanish intellectuals to return to their homeland. They had, while in exile, come under the influence of British and French romanticism, and they brought its spirit to both the drama and poetry of Spain. The Duque de Rivas, Espronceda and Zorrilla were the three principal poets of Spanish romanticism. During the second half of the 1800s, the outstanding poets of Spain were the semi-philosophical Campoamor, the social-conscious Núñez de Arce, and the melancholy, love-sick Bécquer.

During the twentieth century, modernism, initiated by the Nicaraguan Rubén Darío, was adopted by many Spanish poets. Others developed styles of their own. Outstanding among the twentieth-century poets are Antonio and Manuel Machado, Juan Ramón Jiménez, Pedro Salinas and the short-lived Federico García Lorca. Among other noteworthy poets of the contemporary period we may mention Jorge Guillén, Gerardo Diego, Rafael Alberti, Emilio Prados, Vicente Aleixandre, Luis Cernuda and Manuel Altolaguirre.

Prose

In the thirteenth century, King Alfonso X, called the Wise, helped standardize the Castilian language as a result of the voluminous prose works compiled at his direction. His nephew, Juan Manuel, was Spain's first great fiction writer with his fifty tales of *El Conde Lucanor*. In the fourteenth and fifteenth centuries, alert observers recorded the noteworthy events of their day in chronicles important for their literary as well as historical value. Among the most interesting are the chronicles by López de Ayala and Hernando del Pulgar.

The best prose of the early 1400s is found is *El Corbacho* ('The Scourge'), by the Archpriest of Talavera, a satirical and realistic diatribe against women. During this century, however, books of chivalry, narrating fantastic adventures of ideal knights, became the most popular reading matter. The prototype of chivalric novels, *Amadís de Gaula*, appeared in 1508, although written about one hundred years earlier. Cervantes originally intended his *Don Quixote* (1605 and 1615) as a parody of the chivalric novel, designed both to ridicule and do away with this genre once and for all. He succeeded in creating not only the world's most celebrated novel but also its most perfect book of chivalry.

One of the greatest works in Spanish literature, important for its influence as well as its intrinsic worth, was published in 1499 : the dialogue novel, *La Celestina*. Several other prose genres appeared at the end of the fifteenth and during the sixteenth century. Two—the sentimental novel and the pastoral novel—trace their roots to Italy. The principal sentimental novel was Diego de San Pedro's *Cárcel de Amor* ('Castle of Love') (1492). The first Spanish pastoral novel was Jorge de Montemayor's *Diana* (1559), and other novels of pastoral setting were written by Cervantes (*La Galatea*, 1585) and Lope de Vega (*Arcadia*, 1598). A third type of work found favour, though to a lesser degree, during this period : the *novela morisca* or Moorish novel. The Moorish theme appears most strikingly in the anonymous short story *El Abencerraje* (1565), and in the slightly fictionalized historical account, *Guerras Civiles de Granada* ('Civil Wars of Granada') (1595 and 1604), by Ginés Pérez de Hita.

A literary genre of native Spanish origin also developed in the sixteenth century—the picaresque novel. *Lazarillo de Tormes* (1554) is the first and one of the best of these roguish autobiographies. Other notable picaresque novels are Mateo Alemán's *Guzmán de Alfarache* (1599 and 1604), Quevedo's *La Vida del Buscón* (1608) and Vicente Espinel's *Marcos de Obregón* (1618).

In addition, the prose of the Golden Age includes the elegant, euphuistic essays of Antonio de Guevara, the mystic writings of Fray Luis de Granada, Fray Luis de León, Santa Teresa and others, and the historical works of Hurtado de Mendoza and Father Mariana. At the end of the period we have the brilliant commentaries of the philosopher Baltasar Gracián.

The eighteenth century, while weak in original creations, did produce a number of scholarly works, notably Feijóo's encyclopedia. Father Isla's satiric portrayal of a pompous preacher, *Fray Gerundio de Campazas*, is considered the best novel of the century. Cadalso's *Cartas Marruecas* ('Moroccan Letters') are also noteworthy for their interesting descriptions and criticism of Spain.

The 1830s saw the revival of Spanish prose, first in the form of *artículos de costumbres* (essays on foibles of the day) by Larra and Mesonero Romanos. This was also the period of numerous historical novels in imitation of Walter Scott. In the middle of the century, Fernán Caballero began to write her realistic novels of regional background, which proved to be forerunners of the excellent realistic novels of the late nineteenth century. Pereda, Alarcón, Valera, Galdós, Pardo Bazán, Alas and Valdés are outstanding among the many novelists of the late 1800s.

Vicente Blasco Ibáñez, Pío Baroja, Ramón del Valle-Inclán and Ramón Pérez de Ayala are all leading novelists of the twentieth century. The essay, too, was extensively cultivated by the young authors of the early 1900s, called the Generation of '98. Miguel de Unamuno, philosopher, educator, novelist and poet, 'Azorín,' literary critic and careful stylist, and José Ortega y Gasset, philosopher and teacher, are probably the most noteworthy essayists of the contemporary period.

Drama

The earliest manifestation of the drama in medieval Spain was of a religious nature. The only recorded work of this period which has come down to us is a 150-line fragment of the thirteenth century, *Auto de los Reyes Magos* ('Play of the Three Magi'). Juan del Encina, whose first *églogas* (eclogues) appeared in 1496, is credited with secularizing the Spanish drama. He was followed in the early sixteenth century by Torres Naharro, the Portuguese writer Gil Vicente, and Lope de Rueda, whose short humorous skits called *pasos* attained enormous popular success.

The Golden Age ushered in the greatest period of the national drama. The incomparably prolific Lope de Vega with his two thousand plays practically by himself established the national Spanish drama. Tirso de Molina's *Burlador de Sevilla* ('The Scoffer of Seville') created the striking characterization of Don Juan, often imitated in European literature. Mexican-born Juan Ruiz de Alarcón was the most moral and technically correct dramatist of the period. Pedro Calderón de la Barca, the culmination of the Golden Age drama, is best known abroad for his philosophic *La vida es sueño* ('Life is a Dream'). Lope, Tirso, Alarcón and Calderón are only four among many first-rate dramatists who flourished in the seventeenth century.

The *entremés*, developed from Rueda's *pasos*, is represented in this anthology by Cervantes' *El juez de los divorcios* ('The Judge of the Divorce Court'). In the eighteenth century, Ramón de la Cruz continued this genre in his *sainetes*. Except for the latter, the eighteenth-century theatre consisted mainly of neo-classic imitations of French plays or of Golden Age dramas. Moratín's *El sí de las niñas* ('When A Girl Says "Yes" ') is considered the best work of the neo-classic school.

The brief period of the romantic triumph in Spain witnessed many successful plays. Among these were Martínez de la Rosa's *La conjuración de Venecia* ('The Conspiracy of Venice') (1834), Larra's *Macías* (1834), the Duque de Rivas' overwhelming *Don Alvaro* (1835), Garcí Gutiérrez's *El trovador* ('The Troubadour') (1836), Hartzenbusch's *Los amantes de Teruel* ('The Lovers of Teruel') (1837) and Zorrilla's *Don Juan Tenorio* (1844).

During the mid-nineteenth century, Bretón de los Herreros poured out hundreds of light comedies in the style of Moratín. The finest dramatist of this period was Tamayo y Baus, author of *Un drama nuevo* ('A New Drama'). In the last quarter of the century, Echegaray's neo-romantic melodramas dominated the Spanish theatre.

During the twentieth century, the great novelist Galdós composed many excellent plays, usually dealing with social problems. The most renowned dramatist of the contemporary period is the prolific Jacinto Benavente, whose masterpiece is *Los intereses creados* ('The Bonds of Interest'). Noteworthy also are the Quintero brothers, who collaborated on numerous comedies with an Andalusian background, Eduardo Marquina, who cultivated the historical drama, and Gregorio Martínez Sierra, author of a number of delicate and charming plays.

Jacinto Grau, Eduardo Casona and Federico García Lorca are among the best playwrights of recent years.

THE MEDIEVAL PERIOD
[1140–1400]

THE POEM OF THE CID

[c. 1140]

*Spain's national hero in the history of its wars with the Moors is Rodrigo
Díaz de Vivar (1040?–1099). A nobleman of the court of Alfonso VI of
Castile, he was given the sobriquet* El Cid *(the lord, master) because of his
numerous victories and his intrepid courage. After the Cid's death, tales of
his exploits—somewhat fictionalized and idealized—circulated among the
people, until he became the subject of ballads, chronicles, and the great epic
of early Spanish literature, the* Poema del Cid *(also called* Cantar de
Mio Cid*). Composed about 1140, it has been preserved in a copy made in
1307 by one Pedro Abad. Its 3,730 verses relate some of the adventures of
the Cid in his maturity, and it is divided into three major sections or cantos.
The first (from which the selections presented here are taken) deals with the
exile of the Cid from Castile after falling into the King's disfavour. In
the second canto, King Alfonso is reconciled with the Cid and arranges the
marriage of the Cid's two daughters to the Infantes (Princes) of Aragón.
The final division describes the shameful behaviour of the Infantes towards
their wives and the Cid's revenge upon them.*

The Poema del Cid *does not contain fantastic or superhuman adventures,
so common to the early epics of other nations. Rather it is notable for its
realism and humanity—the stirring story of a flesh-and-blood hero.*

THE POEM OF THE CID

He turned and looked upon them, and he wept very sore
As he saw the yawning gateway and the hasps wrenched off the
    door,
And the pegs whereon no mantle nor coat of vair there hung.
There perched no moulting goshawk, and there no falcon swung.
My lord the Cid sighed deeply such grief was in his heart
And he spake well and wisely: 'Oh Thou, in Heaven that art
Our Father and our Master, now I give thanks to Thee.
Of their wickedness my foemen have done this thing to me.'

Then they shook out the bridle rein further to ride afar.
They had the crow on their right hand as they issued from Bivar;
And as they entered Burgos upon their left it sped.
And the Cid shrugged his shoulders, and the Cid shook his head:
'Good tidings Alvar Fañez! We are banished from our weal,
But on a day with honour shall we come unto Castile.'

Roy Diaz entered Burgos with sixty pennons strong,
And forth to look upon him did the men and women throng.
And with their wives the townsmen at the windows stood hard by,
And they wept in lamentation, their grief was risen so high.
As with one mouth, together they spake with one accord:
'God, what a noble vassal, an he had a worthy lord.'

Fain had they made him welcome, but none dared do the thing
For fear of Don Alfonso, and the fury of the King.
His mandate unto Burgos came ere the evening fell.
With utmost care they brought it, and it was sealèd well:
'That no man to Roy Diaz give shelter now, take heed.
And if one give him shelter, let him know in very deed
He shall lose his whole possession, nay! the eyes within his head
Nor shall his soul and body be found in better stead.'

Great sorrow had the Christians, and from his face they hid.
Was none dared aught to utter unto my lord the Cid.

Then the Campeador departed unto his lodging straight.
But when he was come thither, they had locked and barred the
    gate.
In their fear of King Alfonso had they done even so.
And the Cid forced not his entrance, neither for weal nor woe
Durst they open it unto him. Loudly his men did call.
Nothing thereto in answer said the folk within the hall.
My lord the Cid spurred onward, to the doorway did he go.
He drew his foot from the stirrup, he smote the door one blow.
Yet the door would not open, for they had barred it fast.
But a maiden of nine summers came unto him at last :

'Campeador in happy hour thou girdest on the sword.
'Tis the King's will. Yestereven came the mandate of our lord.
With utmost care they brought it, and it was sealed with care :
None to ope to you or greet you for any cause shall dare.
And if we do, we forfeit houses and lands instead.
Nay we shall lose morever, the eyes within the head.
And, Cid, with our misfortune, naught whatever dost thou gain.
But may God with all His power support thee in thy pain.'

So spake the child and turned away. Unto her home went she.
That he lacked the King's favour now well the Cid might see.
He left the door; forth onward he spurred through Burgos town.
When he had reached Saint Mary's, then he got swiftly down.
He fell upon his knee and prayed with a true heart indeed :
And when the prayer was over, he mounted on the steed.
Forth from the gate and over the Arlanzon he went.
There in the sand by Burgos, the Cid let pitch his tent.
Roy Diaz who in happy hour had girded on the brand,
Since none at home would greet him, encamped there on the sand
With a good squadron, camping as if within the wood.
They will not let him in Burgos buy any kind of food.
Provender for a single day they dared not to him sell.

THE CID'S FAREWELL TO HIS WIFE

And it was night to morning, and the cocks full oft they crew,
When at last my lord the Campeador unto San Pedro came.
God's Christian was the Abbot. Don Sancho was his name;
And he was saying matins at the breaking of the day.
With her five good dames in waiting Ximena there did pray.
They prayed unto Saint Peter and God they did implore :
'O thou who guidest all mankind, succour the Campeador.'

One knocked at the doorway, and they heard the tidings then.
God wot the Abbot Sancho was the happiest of men.
With the lights and with the candles to the court they ran
    forthright,
And him who in good hour was born they welcomed in delight.

'My lord Cid,' quoth the Abbot, 'Now God be praised of grace!
Do thou accept my welcome, since I see thee in this place.'
And the Cid who in good hour was born, thereunto answered he:

'My thanks to thee, don Sancho, I am content with thee.
For myself and for my vassals provision will I make.
Since I depart to exile, these fifty marks now take.
If I may live my life-span, they shall be doubled you.
To the Abbey not a groatsworth of damage will I do.
For my lady do I give you an hundred marks again.
Herself, her dames and daughters for this year do you maintain.
I leave two daughters with you, but little girls they be.
In thine arms keep them kindly. I commend them here to thee.
Don Sancho do thou guard them, and of my wife take care.
If thou wantest yet and lackest for anything whate'er,
Look well to their provision, thee I conjure once more,
And for one mark that thou spendest the Abbey shall have four.'
And with glad heart the Abbot his full assent made plain.
And lo! the Dame Ximena came with her daughters twain.
Each had her dame-in-waiting who the little maiden bore.
And Dame Ximena bent the knee before the Campeador.
And fain she was to kiss his hand, and, oh, she wept forlorn!

'A boon! A boon! my Campeador. In a good hour wast thou
    born.
And because of wicked slanderers art thou banished from the land.

'Oh Campeador fair-bearded a favour at thy hand!
Behold I kneel before thee, and thy daughters are here with me,
That have seen of days not many, for children yet they be,
And these who are my ladies to serve my need that know.
Now well do I behold it, thou art about to go.
Now from thee our lives a season must sunder and remove,
But unto us give succour for sweet Saint Mary's love.'

The Cid, the nobly bearded, reached down unto the twain,
And in his arms his daughters has lifted up again,
And to his heart he pressed them, so great his love was grown,
And his tears fell fast and bitter, and sorely did he moan:

'Ximena as mine own spirit I loved thee, gentle wife;
But o'er well dost thou behold it, we must sunder in our life.
I must flee and thou behind me here in the land must stay.
Please God and sweet Saint Mary that yet upon a day
I shall give my girls in marriage with mine own hand rich and well,
And thereafter in good fortune be suffered yet to dwell,
May they grant me, wife, much honoured, to serve thee then
    once more.'

THE CID AND THE COUNT OF BARCELONA

By the victory there much honour unto his beard he did.
And then the Count to his own tent was taken by the Cid.
He bade his squires guard him. From the tent he hastened then.
From every side together about him came his men.
The Cid was glad, so mighty were the spoils of that defeat.
For the lord Cid don Rodrigo they prepared great stock of meat.
But namely the Count don Remond, thereby he set no store.
To him they brought the viands, and placed them him before.
He would not eat, and at them all he mocked with might and
    main :

'I will not eat a mouthful for all the wealth in Spain;
Rather will I lose my body and forsake my soul forby,
Since beaten in the battle by such tattered louts was I.'

My lord the Cid Roy Diaz you shall hearken what he said :
'Drink of the wine I prithee, Count, eat also of the bread.
If this thou dost, no longer shalt thou be a captive then;
If not, then shalt thou never see Christendom again.'

'Do thou eat, don Rodrigo, and prepare to slumber sweet.
For myself I will let perish, and nothing will I eat.'

And in no way were they able to prevail till the third day,
Nor make him eat a mouthful while they portioned the great prey.

'Ho! Count, do thou eat somewhat,' even so my lord Cid spoke,
'If thou dost not eat, thou shalt not look again on Christian folk;
If in such guise thou eatest that my will is satisfied,
Thyself, Count, and, moreover, two noblemen beside
Will I make free of your persons and set at liberty.'

And when the Count had heard it exceeding glad was he.
'Cid, if thou shalt perform it, this promise thou dost give,
Thereat I much shall marvel as long as I shall live.'

2—SA

'Eat then, oh Count; when fairly thy dinner thou hast ta'en
I will then set at liberty thee and the other twain.
But what in open battle thou didst lose and I did earn,
Know that not one poor farthing's worth to thee will I return,
For I need it for these henchmen who hapless follow me.
They shall be paid with what I win from others as from thee.
With the Holy Father's favour we shall live after this wise,
Like banished men who have not any grace in the King's eyes.'

Glad was the Count. For water he asked his hands to lave.
And that they brought before him, and quickly to him gave.
The Count of Barcelona began to eat his fill
With the men the Cid had given him, and God! with what a will!
He who in happy hour was born unto the Count sate near :

'Ha! Count, if now thou dinest not with excellent good cheer,
And to my satisfaction, here we shall still delay,
And we twain in no manner shall go forth hence away.'
Then said the Count : 'Right gladly and according to my mind!'
With his two knights at that season in mighty haste he dined.
My lord the Cid was well content that all his eating eyed,
For the Count don Remond his hands exceeding nimbly plied.

'If thou art pleased, my lord the Cid, in guise to go are we.
Bid them bring to us our horses; we will mount speedily.
Since I was first Count, never have I dined with will so glad,
Nor shall it be forgotten what joy therein I had.'

They gave to them three palfreys. Each had a noble selle.
Good robes of fur they gave them, and mantles fair as well.
Count don Remond rode onward with a knight on either side.
To the camp's end the Castilian along with them did ride.

'Ha! Count, forth thou departest to freedom fair and frank;
For what thou hast left with me I have thee now to thank.
If desire to avenge it is present to thy mind,
Send unto me beforehand when thou comest me to find.
Either that thou wilt leave thy goods or part of mine wilt seize.'

'Ha! my lord Cid, thou art secure, be wholly at thine ease.
Enough have I paid to thee till all this year be gone.
As for coming out to find thee, I will not think thereon.'

The Count of Barcelona spurred forth. Good speed he made.
Turning his head he looked at them, for he was much afraid

Lest my lord the Cid repent him; the which the gallant Cid
Would not have done for all the world. Base deed he never did.
The Count is gone. He of Bivar has turned him back again;
He began to be right merry, and he mingled with his train.
Most great and wondrous was the spoil that they had won in war,
So rich were his companions that they knew not what they bore.

R. SELDEN ROSE and LEONARD BACON

GONZALO DE BERCEO
[1180?–1250?]

*The first Spanish author known to us by name is Gonzalo de Berceo, who
lived during the first half of the thirteenth century. A lay brother attached to
the Benedictine monastery of San Millán de la Cogolla, Berceo is one of
the most important representatives of the 'learned' school of poetry called*
mester de clerecía; *except for one brief passage, he does not deviate from
the school's characteristic* cuaderna vía *(stanzas of four fourteen-syllable
lines with a single rhyme). His works, all of a religious nature, consist of
ten rather lengthy poems totalling about ten thousand lines. Of these, the best
known is the* Milagros de Nuestra Señora, *which relates twenty-five
stories, in each of which a miracle is performed through the intercession
of the Virgin Mary.*

From THE MIRACLES OF OUR LADY

I, Gonzalo de Berceo, in the gentle summertide,
Wending upon a pilgrimage, came to a meadow's side;
All green was it and beautiful, with flowers far and wide,—
A pleasant spot, I ween, wherein the traveller might abide.

Flowers with the sweetest odours filled all the sunny air,
And not alone refreshed the sense, but stole the mind from care;
On every side a fountain gushed, whose waters pure and fair,
Ice-cold beneath the summer sun, but warm in winter were.

There on the thick and shadowy trees, amid the foliage green,
Were the fig and the pomegranate, the pear and apple seen;
And other fruits of various kinds, the tufted leaves between,
None were unpleasant to the taste and none decayed, I ween.

The verdure of the meadow green, the odour of the flowers
The grateful shadows of the trees, tempered with fragrant showers,
Refreshed me in the burning heat of the sultry noontide hours;
Oh, one might live upon the balm and fragrance of those bowers!

Ne'er had I found on earth a spot that had such power to please,
Such shadows from the summer sun, such odours on the breeze;
I threw my mantle on the ground, that I might rest at ease,
And stretched upon the greensward lay in the shadow of the trees.

There soft reclining in the shade, all cares beside me flung,
I heard the soft and mellow notes that through the woodland rung;
Ear never listened to a strain, for instrument or tongue,
So mellow and harmonious as the songs above me sung.

HENRY WADSWORTH LONGFELLOW

From LIFE OF SAN MILLAN

He walked those mountains wild, and lived within that nook
For forty years and more, nor ever comfort took
Of offer'd food or alms, or human speech a look;
No other saint in Spain did such a penance brook.

For many a painful year he pass'd the seasons there,
And many a night consumed in penitence and prayer—
In solitude and cold, with want and evil fare,
His thoughts to God resigned, and free from human care.

Oh! sacred is the place, the fountain and the hill,
The rocks where he reposed, in meditation still,
The solitary shades through which he roved at will :
His presence all that place with sanctity did fill.

JOHN HOOKHAM FRERE

ALFONSO X
[1221?-1284]

The cultural and literary life of thirteenth-century Castile centred in Toledo, in the court of King Alfonso X, called The Wise. Alfonso ascended to the throne in 1252, and his reign, unfortunate from a political point of view, lasted until his death in 1284. He achieved glory, however, in the field of letters, both as patron and participant. A man of unusual intelligence and catholic interests, Alfonso gathered about him the outstanding scholars of his day, Christian, Arab and Jewish. With their collaboration, he set about the task of compiling an encyclopaedic series of works embracing all human and scientific knowledge. Included are studies on such a variety of topics as law, astronomy, hunting, precious stones and chess.

Alfonso was responsible for the codification of the laws of Spain in the monumental Siete partidas. *The latter is one of the most important works prepared under his direction. The real beginnings of Spanish prose, however, are more clearly evident in the* Primera crónica general, *which treats of the history of Spain. A universal history was also undertaken, resulting in the* Grande y general historia.

In spite of the fact that he is regarded as 'the father of Spanish prose', Alfonso deserted that language in the field of poetry. He wrote his lyric poems—some four hundred Cantigas de Santa María—*in Galician, considered at the time a more elegant tongue.*

LAS SIETE PARTIDAS

PARTIDA II, TITLE I, LAW X

What the Word Tyrant Means, and How a Tyrant Makes Use of His Power in a Kingdom, After He Has Obtained Possession of It.

A tyrant means a lord who has obtained possession of some kingdom, or country, by force, fraud, or treason. Persons of this kind are of such a character, that after they have obtained thorough control of a country, they prefer to act for their own advantage, although it may result in injury to the country, rather than for the common benefit of all, because they always live in the expectation of losing it. And, in order that they might execute their desires more freely, the ancient sages declared that they always employed their power against the people, by means of three kinds of artifice. The first is, that persons of this kind always exert themselves to keep those under their dominion ignorant and timid, because, when they are such, they will not dare to rise up against them, or oppose their wishes. The second is, that they promote disaffection among the people so that they do not trust one another, for while they live in such discord, they will not dare to utter any speech against the king, fearing that neither faith nor secrecy will be kept among them. The third is, that they endeavour to make them poor, and employ them in such great labours that they can never finish them; for the reason that they may always have so much to consider in their own misfortunes, that they will never have the heart to think of committing any act against the government of the tyrant.

In addition to all this, tyrants always endeavour to despoil the powerful, and put the wise to death; always forbid brotherhoods and associations in their dominions; and constantly manage to be informed of what is said or done in the country, trusting more for counsel and protection to strangers, because they serve them voluntarily, than to natives who have to perform service through compulsion. We also decree that although a person may have obtained the sovereignty of a kingdom by any of the methods mentioned in the preceding law, if he should make a bad use of his power in any of the ways above stated in this law, people can denounce him as a tyrant, and his government, which was lawful, will become wrongful; as Aristotle stated in the book which treats of the government of cities and kingdoms.

PARTIDA II, TITLE VII, LAW V

What Should Be Taught the Sons of Kings, in Order That They May Be Elegant and Cleanly.

There were certain wise men who described how tutors should bring up the sons of kings, and who prescribed many ways in which they should be taught how to eat and drink properly and in a well-bred manner. And, for the reason that it seems to us that these are things which should be known, and by means of which tutors can the better rear those entrusted to their charge so that they cannot commit faults through want of knowledge, we order them to be written here. They declared the first thing that tutors should teach boys is how to eat and drink in a cleanly and polite manner; for, although this is something that no creature can avoid, nevertheless, men should not do it in a coarse or awkward way : and especially does this apply to the sons of kings, on account of the race from which they spring, and the place which they will have to occupy, and from the fact that others will have to follow their example. They gave three reasons for this : first, in order that they might receive benefit from eating and drinking; second, to enable them to avoid the injury which might result to them from eating or drinking to excess; third, in order to accustom them to be cleanly and graceful, which is something that is very becoming to them. Children who eat and drink when they have need of it, become, for this reason healthier and more vigorous;

and if they eat too much they will become, on that account, weaker and ill, and the food and the drink which should give them life and health, will bring upon them sickness and death. They declared that they should teach them to eat and drink in a well-bred manner, not putting a second morsel into their mouths until the first has been swallowed : for, leaving out of consideration the ill-breeding which will result from this, there is a great danger that they will be suddenly suffocated : and that they should not permit them to grasp the morsel with all five fingers of their hand, for fear they will make it too large. Also that they should not permit them to eat inordinately with the entire mouth, but with a part of it : for, by doing so, they show themselves to be gluttons, which is rather a characteristic of beasts, than of men : and he who does this, cannot easily prevent what he is eating from dropping out of his mouth, if he should desire to speak. Moreover, they declared that they should teach them to eat slowly, and not in haste, because whoever adopts the other way, cannot thoroughly chew what he eats; and therefore it cannot be well ground up, and necessarily must cause injury, and produce bad humours, from which sickness arises. And they should compel them to wash their hands before eating, that they may be clean and free from what they have handled, for the cleaner food is when it is eaten, the more beneficial it becomes. After eating, they should also cause them to wash them in order that they may be free to handle the face and the eyes, and that they may be clean and neat they should wipe them on towels and on nothing else; for they should not wipe them on their clothes, like some people do who do not know anything about cleanliness or politeness.

They declared, moreover, that they should not talk much while they ate, because where they do so, they must necessarily suffer loss in their food, and be deficient as well with regard to what they discussed. Nor should they sing while they eat, as it is not the proper place for this, and it would appear that they did so, rather through excitement of wine, than for any other reason. They also declared that their tutors should not permit them to bend down over the porringer while they were eating : first, because it is a mark of great ill-breeding; second, since it would appear that he who acts in this way wanted all the food for himself, and desired that no one else should have any share of it.

PARTIDA II, TITLE XXXI, LAW I

What a School Is, How Many Kinds There Are, and By Whose Command It Should Be Established.

A school is a union of masters and scholars, established in some locality with the will and design of teaching the sciences. There are two kinds of these; first, a general school, where there are masters of arts, as, for instance, the grammar, logic, rhetoric, arithmetic, geometry, and astrology, and also where there are masters of ordinances, and lords of laws. This school should be established by order of the pope, the emperor, or the king. The second kind is called a special school, which means one in which a master gives instruction to a few scholars in some town apart, and a school of this kind can be established by the order of a prelate, or the council of any locality.

LAW II

In What Place a School Should be Established, and How the Masters and Pupils Should Be Secure.

The town where it is desired to establish a school should have pure air and beautiful environs, in order that the masters who teach the sciences and the pupils who learn them, may live there in health, and rest and take pleasure in the evening, when their eyes have become weary with study. It should, moreover, be well provided with bread and wine, and good lodging houses, in which the pupils can live and pass their time without great expense. We declare that the citizens of the town where a school is situated, should carefully protect its masters and pupils and everything belonging to them, and that no one should arrest or hinder the messengers who come to them from their homes, on account of any debt that their parents, or any others of the countries where they are natives, may owe. We also declare that no wrong, dishonour, or violence should be shown them on account of any enmity or grudge which any man may entertain against the said pupils or their parents. For which reason we order that the masters and pupils, and their messengers, and all their property, be secure and free from molestation, while going to the schools, while there, and while returning to their homes, and we grant them this security in all the towns of our dominions.

Whoever violates this law, by taking their property by force, or by robbing them shall pay four times the value of what is stolen, and where anyone wounds, dishonours, or kills any of them, he shall be punished without mercy, as a man who violates our truce, and the security which we have granted. And if the judges before whom a complaint of this kind is made are negligent in rendering the parties justice, as above stated, they shall pay the amount aforesaid out of their own property, and be dismissed from office as infamous persons. Where they act in a malicious manner towards the pupils, refusing to punish those who dishonoured, wounded, or killed them, then the officers who acted in this manner shall themselves be punished according to the will of the king.

LAW III

How Many Masters There Should Be in a General School, and at What Times Their Salaries Should Be Paid.

For a general school to be complete, there should be as many masters to teach them as there are sciences, so that each may have at least one teacher. Where, however, there cannot be teachers for all the sciences, it will be sufficient if there is one to teach grammar, one for logic, one for rhetoric, and one for laws and ordinances. The salaries of the teachers should be fixed by the king, through his designating exactly what each one shall have, dependent upon the science he teaches, and in proportion to his knowledge of it. The salary to which each of them is entitled should be paid at three different periods : one-third when the pupils begin their studies; one-third at Easter; and one-third on the festival day of St. John the Baptist.

LAW IV

In What Way Masters Should Teach Pupils the Sciences.

Masters should teach pupils the sciences well and faithfully, by reading books on them, and explaining them to the best of their ability; and after they begin to read them, they should continue until they have finished the books that they have commenced. So long as they are well they should not appoint others to read in their stead, except where some of them may direct another to read at a certain time, in order to show him honour, but not to avoid the trouble of reading. If any teacher should happen to fall ill, after study has begun, and his sickness proves to be so serious and so long that he cannot teach at all, we decree that his salary should be paid him, just as if he had done so; where he dies of his illness, his heirs are entitled to his salary just as if he had taught for the entire year.

SAMUEL PARSONS SCOTT

THE GENERAL CHRONICLE

OF THE GOOD THINGS OF SPAIN

More than all other lands of the earth, Spain has an overflowing abundance of every good thing. It is shut in on all sides; at one end by the mountains of the Pyrenees which sink down to the sea, on another side by the great Ocean, and on a third by the Tyrrhenian Sea. . . .

Spain is like God's paradise, for it is watered by five abundant rivers which are: the Ebro, Duero, Tagus, Guadalquivir, Guadiana; and these have between them great mountains and lands and the plains are great and wide, and by reason of the fertility of the soil and the moisture from the rivers there are many fruits in great abundance. The greater part of Spain is watered by streams and fountains, and there are never lacking wells in all parts where they are needed.

Spain is fruitful in crops, delicious with fruits, abounding in fish, rich in milk and in all things which are made from it, plenteous in deer and all kinds of game, well stocked with horses and mules, securely protected by castles, made glad by good wines, rejoicing in an abundance of bread, with great wealth of minerals, tin and mercury, iron and copper, silver and gold, precious stones and all kinds of marble, salt from land and sea and rock, and many other minerals; lapis lazuli, ochre, clay, alum, and all kinds that are found in other lands; abounding in silk and all things made from it, sweet with honey and sugar, lighted with wax, seasoned with oil, and gay with saffron.

ANONYMOUS

And Spain above all other things is skilled in war, feared and very bold in battle; light of heart, loyal to her lord, diligent in learning, courtly in speech, accomplished in all good things. Nor is there a land in the world that may be accounted like her in abundance, nor may any equal her in strength, and few there be in the world so great. And above all doth Spain abound in magnificence, and more than all is she famous for her loyalty. O Spain! there is no man can tell of all thy worthiness!

GEORGE TICKNOR

THE JEWESS OF TOLEDO

After King Alfonso VIII had undergone all of these difficulties in the beginning of his reign, and he was married, he went with his wife Doña Leonor to Toledo; and while there, he became enamoured of a Jewess, by name Fermosa [Beautiful], and he forgot his wife, and secluded himself with the Jewess and would for no reason leave her, nor did he ever so love any thing; and he remained in seclusion with her for almost seven years, during which time he did not think of himself, nor his kingdom, nor anything else. Then the good men of the kingdom held a meeting to determine how they might put an end to that wicked and unseemly situation; and they decided that they should kill her, and thus they would regain their master, whom they considered lost, and with this determination they went forth and called upon the king saying they wished to speak with him; and while some spoke with the king, others entered the magnificent drawing room where waited the Jewess, and there they beheaded her.

SEYMOUR RESNICK

JUAN MANUEL
[1282–1349?]

Nephew of Alfonso X, the Prince Don Juan Manuel played an important rôle in Spanish affairs during the first half of the fourteenth century. When not entangled in the web of court intrigue, he was out fighting the wars which peppered his age. And when not engaged in these pursuits, he wrote— poetry, history, didactic works, even a book on the art of hunting.

Although his literary production was, like his uncle's, encyclopaedic in nature, his masterpiece is El Conde Lucanor *(also called* El libro de los ejemplos *and* El libro de Patronio*). A collection of fifty tales largely from oriental sources, it is the first great work of Spanish prose fiction. In each story the young noble, Count Lucanor, presents a problem to his adviser, Patronio. In each case Patronio solves the problem by recounting an* ejemplo *(exemplary tale).*

El Conde Lucanor, which anticipates Boccaccio's Decameron by some fifteen years, provided a rich mine of plot sources for later writers in other European countries as well as in Spain.

Of the stories included here, Ejemplo X *is repeated by Calderón in Act I of* La vida es sueño; *Ejemplo* XXXV *contains the plot of Shakespeare's* The Taming of the Shrew.

COUNT LUCANOR

EJEMPLO II

*What Happened to a Good Man and His Son, Leading a
Beast to Market.*

On another occasion, when Count Lucanor was conversing with
Patronio, his adviser, he informed him that he felt much embar-
rassed as to the method of carrying out an object which he had
in view, for he felt that in whatever way he acted many people
would criticise and blame him, some with reason and some without.

'How shall I act?' said the Count. 'I pray you to inform me
what you would advise under the circumstances.'

'Count Lucanor,' said Patronio, 'I know that you can find many
men more able to advise you than I am; besides, God has blessed
you with a good understanding, making my advice but of little
service to you; but, since it is your desire that I should give you
my opinion how to act, I shall have much pleasure in being permitted to recount what once happened, under similar circumstances,
to a man and his son.'

The Count expressing his desire to be informed what that was,
Patronio related as follows :

'A good man had a son, who, although young, had so excellent
an understanding that the father was induced to consult him in
all his projects. The son, however, had no decision or perseverance
in his character; and whatever the father proposed, so many
doubts and objections were raised by the son that each project
was abandoned and it ended by nothing being done.

'It is well known that, although the young may not be deficient
in understanding and spirit, yet they may commit many errors :
having a mind to see the right thing to be done, but, wanting
perseverance and a good guide, never complete anything. And so
this young man, though he had a naturally good understanding,
yet, wanting the resolution to complete anything, caused his
father much trouble in many of his undertakings.

'For a long time the father submitted to this state of things,
suffering much injury from being interfered with in his projects,
and annoyance from many things which his son said to him. At
length he determined to punish his son, and give him an example
by showing him how he managed his own affairs when not
interfered with, as we are told by eye-witnesses.

'The good man and his son were farmers, living in the neighbourhood of a town. One market-day he told him they should

both go there to buy some things which were wanted. They agreed to take a beast to bring back the goods; and accordingly went to market, leading the beast. On their way they met some men returning from the town. After saluting, these latter remarked how strange it was that they should lead the beast and walk. The good man asked his son what he thought of the remarks made by the men. The son replied that what they said was just, for the animal being unladen it was silly for them to be walking. The good man then told his son to mount, and so journeying they met other men, who commenced saying, "How is it that the old man, who appears fatigued, should be walking while the young man is riding?" Again the good man asked his son what he thought of this remark; again he replied that he thought they were right. The father then told his son to dismount, and mounted in his stead. A little way further they met some people who observed how unjust it appeared that the old man, who was accustomed to hardships, should be riding like a gentleman, while he allowed his son, who was young and delicate, to walk. Again the good man inquired of his son what he now thought; he replied that he agreed with them. On this the good man desired his son to mount also, so that neither should walk. Again they met others, who remarked to them that they were committing a great error in both riding on a beast so thin and apparently so ill able to bear them. Again the good man demanded of his son what he thought of these last remarks. The youth replied, it certainly appeared to him that what they said was true.

'Then the father answered his son, saying, "Son, remember when we left home we led the beast unladen, which you thought was best. After meeting some men on the road, who made remarks on our walking, I ordered you to mount, you then agreed with them. We met, afterwards, other men, who said that was not right, in which you also agreed. I then ordered you to dismount, and mounted in your stead; and, forsooth, because others remarked on my riding and your walking, I ordered you to mount with me; and this also you thought was the best. And now, because others said we were both wrong in riding, you concur with them. Such being the case, I beg of you to tell me what it is possible to do that will not admit of being criticised. We were both walking, and they said we were wrong; I walked and you rode, again we erred; then I rode on the beast and you walked, this was judged wrong. Hence, you see, it is not possible, do what you will, to avoid criticism. And this I give you as an example, so certain am I that no action, however worthy, will be thought well of by all. If the action is good, the ill-disposed will find some fault with it; and if it is an evil action, the good must certainly condemn it. So while you endeavour conscientiously to do your best, still many will speak of you and judge your actions according to their own views."

'And now, Count Lucanor, what is it you desire to do and yet fear what the people may say, whether you do it or do it not? Since you command me to advise you, my counsel is this, before commencing the undertaking, look at the good and evil which may follow, taking care that your own inclinations do not mislead you; and seek the advice of those who are of sound understanding and well informed. If such an adviser is not to be met with, take care that you proceed carefully and justly, allowing a day and a night to pass before carrying out your determination, that is, if time permits, carefully avoiding being influenced by the feeling of what people might say of you.'

The Count found Patronio's advice good; and acting accordingly, all ended well.

And Don Juan, approving of this example, ordered it to be written in this book, and composed the following lines, which are an abbreviation of the whole moral; and the lines are :

In thy chosen life's adventure, steadfastly pursue the cause,
Neither moved by critic's censure, nor the multitude's applause.

EJEMPLO X

Of What Happened to a Man Who Through Poverty and Lack of Other Food, Was Reduced to Eating Some Peas.

Count Lucanor, speaking one day to Patronio, said, 'God has been very bountiful to me, in granting me much more than I can individually enjoy; yet it sometimes happens that I am so pressed for money, that my life is a burden to me. I beg of you to direct me in this trouble.'

'My lord,' said Patronio, 'in order that you may better understand how to act under such circumstances, I will, with your permission, illustrate your position by relating what happened to two rich men.'

The Count begged he would do so.

'My lord,' said Patronio, 'it is said that one of these two men became so destitute that he could not even procure bread to eat. After begging from door to door, until wearied out, all he could procure was a handful of dried peas, very hard and bitter. Remembering his former opulence, and seeing himself now reduced through hunger to eat these peas, he began to cry bitterly. As he ate he threw away the pods, when he perceived another man behind him eating them. And this is the point to which I wish to draw your attention. When he saw the man eating the pods, he asked him why he did so. "Because," said this latter, "though I was once richer than you ever were, yet I am now reduced to so great a state of poverty and hunger that I am glad to eat the pods which you are throwing away."

'When the former man saw this, he found there was yet another more destitute than himself, and less deserving to be so. Seeing this, he directed his heart to God and prayed that he might be shown how to escape from so much poverty. His prayers were heard, and he prospered ever after.

'And you, my lord, should know such is the world, and it is ordained that no condition admits of unalloyed happiness. If at any time, as it appears, you are distressed for money, do not let discontent enter your heart; but reflect how many men there are at the same moment, who have been both richer and more honoured than yourself, who would be only too glad to occupy what you consider an unfortunate position.'

The Count was much pleased with what Patronio told him, exerted himself, and God helped him well out of his difficulties.

And Don Juan, liking the example, had it written in this book, and wrote the following lines :

> Let not poverty dismay your mind,
> Since others poorer than yourself you find.

EJEMPLO XXXV

Of What Happened to a Young Man on His Wedding Day.

One day Count Lucanor was talking to Patronio his counsellor, and said to him, 'Patronio, one of my dependants tells me he can make a very advantageous marriage with a woman much richer and more honourable than himself; but there is one difficulty in the way, which is this, he tells me he has been informed that she is of a very violent and impetuous temper. Now I beg you to counsel me whether I should allow him to marry this woman, knowing such to be her disposition, or whether I should forbid it.'

'Count Lucanor,' replied Patronio, 'if the man is like the son of a good man, a Moor, advise the marriage by all means; but if such be not the case, forbid it.'

The Count begged of him to relate the narrative.

'There lived in a city,' said Patronio, 'a Moor who was much respected, and who had a son, the most promising youth in the world; but, not being rich enough to accomplish the great deeds which he felt in his heart equal to, he was greatly troubled, having the will and not the power.

'Now in the same town there lived another Moor, who held a higher position, and was very much richer than his father, and who had an only daughter, the very reverse in character and appearance of the young man, she being of so very violent a temper that no one could be found willing to marry such a virago.

'One day the young man came to his father, and said, "You know that your means will not allow you to put me in a position to live honourably" adding that, as he desired to live an easy and quiet life, he thought it better to seek to enrich himself by an advantageous marriage, or to leave that part of the country.

'The father told him that he would be very happy if he could succeed in such a union. On this, the son proposed, if it were agreeable to his father, to seek the daughter of their neighbour in marriage. Hearing this, the father was much astonished, and asked how he could think of such a thing, when he knew that no man, however poor, could be induced to marry her.

'Nevertheless, the son insisted; and, although the father thought it a strange whim, in the end he gave his consent. The good man then visited his neighbour, telling him the wish of his son.

'When the good man heard what his friend said, he answered, "By heaven, my friend, were I to do such a thing I should prove myself a very false friend, for you have a worthy son, and it would be base in me to consent to his injury or death; and I know for certain that, were he to live with my daughter, he would soon die, or death, at least, would be preferable to life. Do not think I say this from any objection to your alliance, for I should only be too grateful to any man who would take her out of my house."

'The young man's father was much pleased at this, as his son was so intent on the marriage. All being ultimately arranged, they were in the end married, and the bride taken home, according to the Moorish fashion, to the house of her husband, and left to supper; the friends and relations returning to their respective homes, waiting anxiously for the following day, when they feared to find the bridegroom either dead or seriously injured.

'Now, being left alone, the young couple sat down to supper, when the bridegroom, looking behind him, saw his mastiff and said to him, "Bring me water wherewith to wash my hands." The dog, naturally taking no notice of this command, the young man became irritated, and ordered the animal more angrily to bring him water for his hands, which the latter not heeding, the young man arose in a great rage, and, drawing his sword, commenced a savage attack on the dog, who, to avoid him ran away; but, finding no retreat, jumped on the table, then to the fireplace, his master still pursuing him, who, having caught him, first cut off his head, then his paws, hewing him to pieces, covering everything with blood. Thus furious and bloodstained, he returned to the table, and, looking round, saw a cat. "Bring me water for my hands," said he to him. The animal not noticing the command, the master cried out, "How, false traitor, did you not see how I treated the mastiff for disobeying me? If you do not as I tell you this instant you shall share his fate." The poor little harmless cat continuing motionless, the master seized him by the paws and dashed him to pieces against the wall. His fury increasing, he again placed himself at the table, looking about on all sides as if for something to attack next. His wife, seeing this, and supposing he had lost his senses, held her peace. At length he espied his horse, the only one he had, and called to him fiercely to bring him water to wash his hands. The animal not obeying, he cried out in a rage, "How is this? Think you that because you are the only horse I have that you dare thus to disobey my orders? Know then that your fate shall be the same as the others, and that anyone living who dares to disobey me shall not escape my vengeance." Saying this, he seized the horse, cut off his head, and hacked him to pieces.

'And when the wife saw this, and knowing he had no other horse, felt that he was really in earnest, she became dreadfully alarmed.

'He again sat down to table, raging and all bloody as he was, swearing he would kill a thousand horses, or even men or women, if they dared to disobey him. Holding at the same time his bloody sword in his hand, he looked around with glaring eyes until, fixing them on his wife, he ordered her to bring him water to wash his hands.

'The wife, expecting no other fate than to be cut to pieces, if she demurred, immediately arose and brought him the water.

' "Ha! thank God you have done so," said he, "otherwise I am so irritated by these senseless brutes that I should have done by you as by them." He afterwards commanded her to help him to meat. She complied; but he told her, in a fearful tone of voice, to beware, as he felt as if he was going mad.

'Thus passed the night; she not daring to speak, but strictly obeying all his orders. After letting her sleep for a short time, he said to her, "Get up, I have been so annoyed that I cannot sleep; take care that nothing disturbs me, and in the meanwhile prepare me a good and substantial meal."

'While it was yet early the following morning, the fathers, mothers, and other relatives came stealthily to the door of the young people, and, hearing no movement, feared the bridegroom was either dead or wounded; and, seeing the bride approach the door alone, were still more alarmed.

'She, seeing them, went cautiously and tremblingly towards them, and exclaimed: "Traitors, what are you doing? How dare you approach this gate? Speak not—be silent, or all of us, you as well as I, are dead."

'When they heard this they were much astonished, and on learning what had taken place the night previous, they esteemed the young man very much who had made so good a commencement in the management of his household; and from that day forward his wife became tractable and complaisant, so that they led a very happy life.

'A few days later, his father-in-law, wishing to follow the example of his son, likewise killed a horse in order to intimidate his wife, but she said to him, "My friend, it is too late to begin now; it would not avail you to kill a hundred horses; we know each other too well."

'And you, Count Lucanor, if your dependant wishes to marry such a woman, if he be like this young man, advise him that he may do it with safety, for he will know how to rule his house : but if he be not likely to act with resolute determination at the beginning, and to sustain his position in his household, advise him to have nothing to do with her. As also I would counsel you in all cases where you have dealings with men to act with that decision which will leave them no room to think that you can be imposed upon.'

The Count thought this a very good example, and Don Juan had it written in this book, and made these lines, saying :

> Who would not for life be a henpeck'd fool
> Must show, from the first, that he means to rule.

JAMES YORK

ARCHPRIEST OF HITA
[1283?–1350?]

The literary masterpiece of fourteenth-century Spain—indeed, one of the greatest works of all Spanish literature—is the rollicking Libro de buen amor by Juan Ruiz, Archpriest of Hita. What few facts we have of this author's life are largely gathered from references in the poem itself. Juan Ruiz was probably born in Alcalá de Henares, and lived in Guadalajara and Toledo. He became Archpriest of Hita, and was, for reasons now unknown, imprisoned for thirteen years by the Archbishop of Toledo. Apparently while still in jail, Hita completed his only work, the Libro de buen amor—in 1330 according to one manuscript, in 1343 according to another.

Its seven thousand-odd verses vary greatly both in metrical form and subject-matter. Though he primarily gives a picaresque account of his own amorous adventures (so that, he piously states, others may learn the ways of mundane love and thus avoid its pitfalls), the Archpriest also includes numerous digressions—fables, serious religious poems, love poems, advice on courting, an allegory on Lent, etc. The entire work presents a rich view of fourteenth-century society, seen through the merry, if satirical, eyes of a man who truly loved life.

THE BOOK OF GOOD LOVE

THE ARCHPRIEST'S PRAYER

God the Father, God the Son, and God the Holy Ghost,
May He who was of Virgin born inspire us through His Host
That we in song and spoken word may praise His being most,
And may the mantle of His grace become our bravest boast.

May He who formed the sweeping heavens, made the land and sea,
Upon me concentrate His grace and shine His light on me
'Til I compose a book of songs that will so joyous be
All men who hear them will forget their present misery.

Thou gracious God who first set man upon his earthly march,
Inspire and aid this priest of Thine whom thou createdst arch
For I a book on love divine would write for souls that parch
And I would stiffen up their smocks with love's old-fashioned starch.

So, gentlemen, if you would hear a hearty, merry tale,
Come all who heavy laden are and I'll your ears regale,
I shall not tell you silly lies nor spin some romance stale
But sing of things just as they are, of men and women hale.

And that I may the best secure the whole of your attention
I'll trick the story out in rhymes of my supreme invention—
While in its pretty style you'll find no word unfit to mention.
No, you will find my broadest jokes conform to strict convention.

Don't think this is a foolish book replete with giddy verse,
Nor hold the jests therein contained as something even worse;
For oft, as goodly money lies within a filthy purse,
A messy book may likewise hold much wisdom sound and terse.

The fennel seed is kettle-black, as black as poison bane,
But inside all its meat is white as is the marmot's mane.
And whitest flour is wont to lie within the darkest grain,
While sugar sweet and white resides within an ugly cane.

There grows upon the crabbèd thorn the rose's noble bloom,
And parchments writ in strangest script great learning oft entomb.
Full many an honest tippler wears a shoddy cape and plume,
And I to sorry covers cheap this Book of Good Love doom.

Yet since the root and principle of every good that is
Lies in the Virgin Mary's grace, I therefore, Juan Ruiz,
Archpriest of Hita, have a song to please the lady. 'Tis
One where in verse I shall rehearse her seven pleasures, viz:

ELISHA K. KANE

THE JOYS OF THE VIRGIN MARY

Oh blessed ray
Of brightest day,
Dear Mother, pray
Guide me for aye.

Oh bless me, Virgin, with Thy grace
And pray Thy Son to send apace
His comfort to a sinner base
That I may sing alway

The joys our Father sent to Thee
That day beside the holy sea
When angels came to Galilee
From heaven-land to say

'All hail, oh Mary, blessed queen
For Thou by God hast chosen been
To bear his Son a Nazarene
Divine in human clay.'

And when this message Thou receivedst,
Full straight the words Thou then believedst
And, while a Virgin still, conceivedst
    With joy supreme that day.

A second joy of greatest worth
Befell the hour Thou gavest birth
Unto that Sovereign of the earth
    To whom all Christians pray.

Another joy the Gospels name
When Magian kings before Thee came
To worship Him without all blame
    Who in a manger lay.

There Melchior's gifts of incense were,
There Gaspar brought Him precious myrrh
And Balthasar the gold of Ur
    As bright as morning's ray.

The fourth delight next came to Thee
That Sabbath after Calvary
When Magdalen did Jesus see,
    New risen, on her way.

Thy fifth ecstasy took place
When Thou Thyself beheldst His face
Enthroned on high by God's own grace
    In radiant display.

The sixth, oh Holy Saint, I name
When on the blest disciples came
God's spirit like a living flame
    With Thee and them to stay.

Then came the seventh joy of thine
As Thou, to leave the church a sign,
Wast caught up to that realm divine
    Where angels Thee obey.

Thou reignest now, Exalted One,
In heaven with Thy loved Son.
Oh save us when our years have run
    Forever and for aye.

ELISHA K. KANE

Herein Is Related How All Men Should Disport Themselves
Amid Their Cares, and Also Herein Is Related the Disputa-
tion Which the Greeks and the Romans Had With One
Another

These are the words which Cato spoke—they well become a sage—
He holds that man amid his cares should now and then engage
In such delightful pleasures as may well his woes assuage
Since work and worry unalloyed bring premature old age.

Still, since no grave, important wight all by himself will giggle,
Among my sermons, here and there, I've caused a jest to wriggle,
So surely, when you come to them, you'll have no cause to niggle
Save in their style which, I confess, does somewhat jolt and jiggle.

But comb the meaning from my words as you would card out fleece.
Take warning from what happened to the learned man of Greece
Who with a Roman rounder once debated for a piece
That time the Romans tried to get Greek culture on a lease.

It seems that in the Roman land no manners did abound
Wherefore they begged them from the Greeks who were for such
    renowned.
But mightily their supplication did the Greeks astound
Because they viewed the Roman minds as barren, fallow ground.

However, just to be polite and make their stand seem fair,
They said that first of all before they would their wisdom share
They'd have to quiz Rome's wisest man, and from their showing
    there
The Greeks could see if Roman wits were fit for culture rare.

The Romans fell into the trap nor saw the Greek designs
But pledged themselves one day to speak by every oath that binds.
However, since they knew no Greek, nor yet could read Greek
    minds,
They begged the Greeks to suffer them to argue all in signs.

The Greeks agreed. A day was set to hold the disputation.
Then, sudden witting what it meant, a frightful consternation
Took hold upon the Romans for they found in all their nation
No man who even claimed to have a college education.

Now in that hour when Roman hopes seemed just about to flounder
A sharp old Roman, who one time had been a pulpit pounder,
Told them to choose as candidate some lewd, ungodly rounder
And let God send him arguments, if he had nothing sounder.

Thereat they chose a rounder fit to personate Priapus,
Loud-mouthed, obscene, and bold. They said, 'The Greeks intend
    to trap us;
It's up to you to win the bout—beware lest aught mishap us.
But if you win, man, name your price—there is no sum can
    strap us.'

They capped and gowned him like a Doctor of Philosophy
With all the costly, flowing robes of that grave faculty.
Then in the lecture hall he strode, as pompous as could be.
'Bring on your Greeks!' the rounder bawled, 'we'll see what we
    will see!'

Forthwith into the lecture hall there crept a learned coot,
A Greek professor, wondrous wise, with ten degrees to boot,
While both the Greek and Roman nations crowded in to root
And watch their champions, all by signs, engage in fierce dispute.

Full confident the Greek uprose and with unruffled calm
Showed but a single finger, slim, extended from his palm;
That done he took his seat again without the slightest qualm.
The rounder rose like one who would his enemy embalm.

He thrust three fingers, tensely stretched, out toward his adversary,
The thumb, forefinger, and the next, like some rude harpoon, hairy;
He shook them in an attitude belligerent yet wary
And then sat down to wait the sign of repartee contrary.

At this the Greek uprose and showed his empty open hand
And once more smiling, bowed to all, and sat down, ever bland.
The rounder jumped up from his bench—'twas more than he
    could stand—
He clenched his fist and shook it like a furious command.

Before that vast concourse the Greek exclaimed in accents quiet,
'The Romans well deserve our culture, friends, I certify it.'
So every one was satisfied and left without a riot.
The case was won by Rome because they got a boor to try it.

They asked the Greek what were the signs he showed the Roman
    hun,
And how on either side the case did back and forwards run;
Quoth he : 'I said, "There is one God," he answered, "Three in
    one,"
And made a sign to show it thus, and there of course he won.

'I signified with open palm "No power God's purpose blocks";
He said with earnest doubled fist "God's will the world unlocks,"
From which I judge the Romans all in faith are orthodox
And well we may entail them all our intellectual stocks.'

They quizzed the rake to see if aught this version might belie,
Said he, 'He held one finger up to mean he'd gouge me eye,
And, gents, to think a runt like that would have the crust to try
To dim me lamp made me so mad I showed the little guy

'Three fingers, meaning two of them would gouge his goggles out
While with me thumb I'd bust his teeth, but after that the lout
Held up his palm to let me know he'd give me ears a clout
And set me head to buzzin' till I lost this monkey bout.

'I showed him then how with me fist I'd sock him such a crack
The longest day he ever lived he couldn't pay me back
And you can see he realized his chances was too black
Because he quit just like a Greek and all that lousy pack.'

This brings to mind the old bawd's saw—its truth has ne'er been
      shaken—
'No word is wicked in itself unless it's wrongly taken.'
Thus anything that's taken right should ne'er a qualm awaken.
This book will teach success to one whom women have forsaken.

Don't hold my mockery as dull or heavy or forlorn
For if you read between the lines you'll find no cause for scorn;
Not one among a thousand poets in this world is born
Who can with merry, subtle words a tragic thing adorn.

No eye can fail to see a heron flying through the air
But where that bird has hid her nest few hunters can declare;
Don't let the 'prentice tell the tailor how he should repair;
Don't think my Book of Love holds naught but smut beyond
      compare.

My book lies open to the world, it is both grave and jolly;
The wise will in their wisdom plumb its grimmest melancholy;
The fool will only laugh and drink its shallow scum of folly;
The best in it the good alone will ever fathom wholly.

To grasp my book's true, hidden wealth, few persons I allow,
For men must sharply pan its ore ere they discover how;
But should you hap on precious gold and wash away the slough,
No more you'll hold this Book of Love as vain as you do now.

Beware, for when my words sound false, there truth the loudest
   cries,
And when I paint reality my deepest truths are lies.
How shall you judge what's good or bad? What standards shall
   you prize
When fictions live in art, while truth, if it be actual, dies?

This book is like an instrument, to every tune it's true;
Your heart it is which makes the song seem merry, sweet, or blue.
You can't interpret from my book save what resides in you,
And if you'd guess what tune I'd play, you'd have to learn me too.

ELISHA K. KANE

Certain Examples of the Power Which Sir Money Possesses

Much power, indeed, Sir Money has and much for him we dabble,
He makes the dolt a man of worth and sets him o'er the rabble,
He makes the lame leap up and run, he makes the deaf-mute
   babble;
Why those who have no hands at all will after money scrabble!

Suppose a man's an utter fool, a farmer or a boor,
With money he becomes a sage, a knight with prestige sure,
In fact the greater grows his wealth the greater his allure,
While he not even owns himself who is in money poor.

If you have money you can get the blessed consolation
Of worldly bliss, or from the Pope can gain a lofty station,
Or purchase seats in Paradise and buy yourself salvation—
Where wealth is great, there lies the state of beatification.

I noticed over there in Rome where sanctities abound
That every one to Money bowed and humbly kissed the ground,
And paid him many honours with solemnities profound,
Yes, homaged him upon their knees, as slaves a king surround.

. . . . . .

Sir Money causes sentences and unjust dooms at court,
He urges shysters for his sake to sue on false report
With all the sundry other frauds to which they will resort,
In short, for money, one condemned can cut his penance short.

Sir Money breaks those mortal bonds that chain a man for life,
He empties stocks and prisons grim with noisome vermin rife,
But one who has no gold to give must wear the iron wife;
All up and down throughout the world Sir Money causes strife.

Myself have seen real miracles occur through Money's power
As when a man condemned to die is freed within an hour
Or when those innocent the gallows presently devour
Or when a soul is prayed to heaven or damned in Hell to cower.

Sir Money often confiscates a poor man's goods and lands,
His vines, his furniture, and all the things his toil commands.
The world has got the itch and scab of money on its hands;
When Money winks his golden eye, there justice stock-still stands.

Sir Money makes a knight presumptuous from a village clown,
And out of peasant farmers chooses coronet and crown;
With Money anyone can strut in gilt and broidered gown
While all his neighbours kiss his hands and bow their bodies down.

. . . . . .

ELISHA K. KANE

THE SONG OF THE MOUNTAIN GIRL

Tablada I was near
When, passing mountains sheer,
I met Aldea, dear,
As dawn was breaking drear.

Upon that pass I thought
I'd die, for I was caught
In snow and bitter cold
Since numbing mist uprolled
That season of the year.

Yet on my long descent
I ran like one Hell-bent
And met a mountain girl
With whom a god would curl,
She was so pink and clear.

Said I unto the jade,
'I doff my hat, fair maid.'
Said she, 'Since you can hop,
Don't think with me to stop,
But take yourself from here.'

I answered, 'I've a chill,
And for that reason will
Entreat you, pretty one,
So that God's will be done,
To lodge and give me cheer.'

Thereat the buxom slut
Said, 'Kinsman, I've a hut
That's empty, since my man
Away but lately ran.
 But pay me from your gear.'

I countered, 'I'd be glad
But I'm a married lad
Just from Herreros come.
But I will give you some
 Fair payment, never fear.'

Said she, 'All right, come on.'
So quickly we were gone
And she prepared the fire
Which customs there require
 Of every mountaineer.

She gave me bread of rye,
All grimy, dark, and dry;
She gave me watered wine
And meat besoaked in brine
 So that it tasted queer.

She gave me cheese of goat
And said, 'Sir, let your throat
In this brown bread delight
And in this crust of white
 Which I have hoarded here.

'Eat well,' said she, 'my guest,
And drink and take your rest;
Get warm and then be gay,
No harm can come your way
 Till your return career.

'The man who isn't daunted
In giving what I've wanted,
May share my bed with me
And have a wondrous spree
 Which will not cost him dear.'

I answered, 'While you talk,
Do not in begging balk
To ask a certain thing.'

'What,' quoth she, 'will you bring
    The goods in faith sincere?

'Well, give me then a belt
Of full-dyed scarlet pelt
And after that a waist
Exactly to my taste
    With pendant collar sheer.

'Give me a string of beads
Of tin, and more than needs
Give me some precious gems
As good as diadems
    And furs without a peer.

'Give me besides a hood
With ample ribbons good,
And give me next some shoes,
High topped, in scarlet hues,
    And carved like checked veneer.

'With all those presents then,
I tell you once again,
That you shall welcome be
To live as spouse with me
    While I as bride adhere.'

Said I, 'My lady peasant,
So many a costly present
I do not bring with me,
But I'll leave surety
    Until I can appear.'

At that replied the wench,
'No bargain can we clench
Unless some money shows—
Without it nothing goes
    And faces look severe.

'No good was e'er the trade
That moneyless was made.
I do, myself, detest
An empty handed pest
    And will not lodge him here.

'Politeness never will
Get credit on a bill
But one with money can
Have all that's loved by man,
    A truth which all revere.'

ELISHA K. KANE

PRAISE OF LITTLE WOMEN

I wish to make my sermon brief,—to shorten my oration,—
For a never-ending sermon is my utter detestation :
I like short women,—suits at law without procrastination,—
And am always most delighted with things of short duration.

A babbler is a laughing-stock; he's a fool who's always grinning;
But little women love so much, one falls in love with sinning.
There are women who are very tall, and yet not worth the winning,
And in the change of short for long repentance finds beginning.

To praise the little women Love besought me in my musing;
To tell their noble qualities is quite beyond refusing :
So I'll praise the little women, and you'll find the thing amusing;
They are, I know, as cold as snow, whilst flames around diffusing.

They're cold without, whilst warm within the flame of Love is
    raging;
They're gay and pleasant in the street,—soft, cheerful, and
    engaging;
They're thrifty and discreet at home,—the cares of life assuaging :
All this and more;—try, and you'll find how true is my presaging.

In a little precious stone what splendour meets the eyes !
In a little lump of sugar how much of sweetness lies !
So in a little woman love grows and multiplies :
You recollect the proverb says,—*A word unto the wise*.

A pepper-corn is very small, but seasons every dinner
More than all other condiments, although 't is sprinkled thinner :
Just so a little woman is, if Love will let you win her,—
There's not a joy in all the world you will not find within her.

And as within the little rose you find the richest dyes,
And in a little grain of gold much price and value lies,
As from a little balsam much odour doth arise,
So in a little woman there's a taste of paradise.

Even as the little ruby its secret worth betrays,
Colour, and price, and virtue, in the clearness of its rays,—
Just so a little woman much excellence displays,
Beauty, and grace, and love, and fidelity always.

The skylark and the nightingale, though small and light of wing,
Yet warble sweeter in the grove than all the birds that sing :
And so a little woman, though a very little thing,
Is sweeter far than sugar, and flowers that bloom in spring.

The magpie and the golden thrush have many a thrilling note,
Each as a gay musician doth strain his little throat,—
A merry little songster in his green and yellow coat :
And such a little woman is, when Love doth make her dote.

There's naught can be compared to her, throughout the wide
        creation;
She is a paradise on earth,—our greatest consolation,—
So cheerful, gay, and happy, so free from all vexation :
In fine, she's better in the proof than in anticipation.

If as her size increases are woman's charms decreased,
Then surely it is good to be from all the great released.
Now of two evils choose the less,—said a wise man of the East :
By consequence, of woman-kind be sure to choose the least.

                    HENRY WADSWORTH LONGFELLOW

HYMN TO THE VIRGIN

Thou Flower of Flowers ! I'll follow thee,
    And sing thy praise unweariedly :
Best of the best ! O, may I ne'er
    From thy pure service flee !

Lady ! to thee I turn my eyes,
    On thee my trusting hope relies;
O, let thy spirit, smiling here,
    Chase my anxieties !

Most Holy Virgin ! tired and faint,
    I pour my melancholy plaint;
Yet lift a tremulous thought to thee,
    Even 'midst mortal taint.

Thou Ocean-Star! Thou Port of Joy!
From pain, and sadness, and annoy,
O, rescue me! O, comfort me,
    Bright Lady of the Sky!

Thy mercy is a boundless mine;
Freedom from care, and life are thine:
He recks not, faints not, fears not, who
    Trusts in thy power divine.

I am the slave of woe and wrong,
Despair and darkness guide my song;
Do thou avail me, Virgin! thou
    Waft my weak bark along!

HENRY WADSWORTH LONGFELLOW

PERO LÓPEZ DE AYALA
[1332-1407]

Pero López de Ayala was one of the most important figures in Spain during the reigns of Pedro I, Enrique II, Juan I and Enrique III. Diplomat, military leader, scholar and writer, he held many high posts, including that of chancellor of Castile in 1398. He recorded his keen observations of contemporary events in his Chronicles, models of vivid historiography.

For his best-known work—a bitingly satirical poem of over 1,600 stanzas called Rimado de palacio—*López de Ayala also drew upon his many years of experience at the court. He paints an unsympathetic picture of medieval Spanish life, devoting a large section of the poem to court intrigue and corruption. With sincere indignation he satirizes the avarice and immorality of all classes of society, from the churchmen and doctors to the lawyers and merchants of his day.*

PALACE RHYMES

CONCERNING LAWYERS

Now will you please observe our doctors of the law:
In spite of their vast knowledge they have many a flaw.
Their first love is money, for it they wag the jaw;
Their souls they have forgotten, and they worry not a straw.

If you wish to consult them on some legal case,
They will pull their eyebrows down and draw a solemn face.
Say they : 'This suit's a tough one, it will mean a lengthy
    chase,
And labour of the hardest sort, for it covers the whole place.

'I think that I might prove a considerable aid
By studying like mad in all the lawbooks made;
But in order to concentrate on your case, I'm afraid
I should need to lay aside other important trade.'

So he has his tomes laid out before the wretch's eyes,
Enormous volumes of decrees and legal summaries.
Quoth he : 'Twenty chapters here my long experience spies
Damaging to your cause, only one that justifies.

'Believe me, friend,' he says, 'your suit looks pretty black.
It's a nice point of law, a tough nut to crack;
But if I take the case I shall make up the lack.
With me you may feel sure of a stout wall at your back.

'Don't lose your temper if your suit drags on a while;
The long road of the law can't be shortened by a mile.
First we must see what sort of a complaint they file,
For we shall have to dance according to their style.

'In civil and in canon law I'm a graduate bachelor;
You shall not find within this realm such a solicitor.
With many a pain and headache I memorised my lore,
Many *reals* and doubloons in school I paid therefor.

'I sold my entire patrimony in my drive
To keep up my studies, at learning to arrive.
Of real and personal property myself I did deprive,
And with this dear-bought knowledge I must keep myself
    alive.

'Now with a friend like you I will not fix a fee.
After you hear my speeches you can start paying me;
But one of my best books is pawned, and so, you see,
You may bring me twenty *doblas* or good security.'

'Señor,' the unhappy client says, 'a chance to compromise
They offer me, and a little money prize.
I asked my wife, and she says that's what she would advise.
The priest who confesses me thinks acceptance would be wise.'

'That would be a fearful shame,' quoth the bachelor to him,
'When you might for quite some time defend yourself with
    vim,
That without so much as testing your rights, which are not
    slim,
You should give up for beat by yielding to a whim.

'All suits begin in some such way, don't let that trouble you;
A person thinks he has no chance when he begins to sue,
And then he finds in his support some famous doctor's view;
And so, with time, the affair takes on a different hue.

'To save my reputation, since you brought me into this,
I'd rather that the other side did not see you dismiss
My services; cheer up, my friend; text and analysis
Of Blackstone will help you out, if I am not remiss.'

To the tune of such talk the law-suit is begun.
Trusting his advocate, our fellow thinks it good as won;
Of compromise or settlement he wishes to have none;
And so the lawyer fires his learned opening gun.

To be sure, he had his clutches on the sum he first was paid;
So an enormous dossier of arguments he made.
With filing of caveats decision was delayed;
It looked at first as though his client really would make the
    grade.

A year that law-suit lasted, more it could hardly last;
The savings of the victim were dwindling all too fast.
Each month 'More money!' cries the law, each month more
    cash is passed;
Clothing and furniture are sold, the poor man stands aghast.

The time is up, the suit has staggered to its end;
Our fellow finds himself done in, they tell him he's
    condemned.
Says Mr. Lawyer: 'I was wrong, as I now apprehend;
I should have compromised at first, and not tried to contend.

'But pluck up heart, my boy, and quit your whimpering.
There's still a recourse : you can yet appeal to the king.
Give me your mule out there, the pampered idle thing,
In twenty days, I guarantee, a reversal I shall bring.

'You risked your goods before, it should not trouble you
To spend for the same end your remaining revenue;

3—SA

We'll see about those lawyers, who were so sure they knew
The last word of the law; I'll teach them how to sue.'

The wretched man had lost all heart, he had no word to stay;
So that the appeal might lie, he gave his mule away.
Spoke then the bachelor once more : 'Lend me your cloak, I
    pray;
I might die of a chill, for it's very cold today.

'Besides, you'd best hunt up a thousand *reals* for me;
On getting them depends your hope of victory.
God and His Saints defending us, you shall see
That no laws or commentators can do us injury.'

The fool is left in poverty, the lawyer's going still;
He's not so dumb that he will lose the payment of his bill.
Thus it happens, woe to us all, always has and always will.
Who believes what I tell him may save himself a spill.

By such avarice today evil is infinite;
For lack of charity the whole world is full of spite.
Not alone that wicked lawyer is tainted with this blight :
Each one of us is guilty, be he commoner or knight.

S. GRISWOLD MORLEY

THE RENAISSANCE
[1400–1550]

ARCHPRIEST OF TALAVERA
[1398?–1470?]

Alfonso Martínez de Toledo, Archpriest of Talavera, is the author of one of the best prose works of the fifteenth century. Written in 1438, El Corbacho (a title borrowed from Boccaccio) contains a lively satirical description of the customs of the time, with special emphasis on the habits of women—and their faults.

EL CORBACHO

Of How the Talkative Woman Always Speaks of That Which Does Not Concern Her

For a woman to be very talkative is the general rule : for there is no woman who does not like to talk endlessly and be heard. And it is not her wont to give another woman a chance to speak in her presence; and even if each day lasted a year, she would never tire of talking and she would not be displeased day or night. And for that reason you will see many women who, from habit of talking continuously, talk to themselves when they have no one else to talk to. Therefore you will see a woman who is a good talker stop the mouths of ten men and overwhelm them in talking and cursing.

When logic is not on her side she begins to wrangle, and when that happens she cannot keep any secrets. I warn you that as you would guard yourself from fire, so should you beware of having words with a woman who knows some secret of yours : for know, as I have said above, that a woman speaking in anger does not watch what she says. And whether the secret be a matter of life and death or a trivial thing, it cries and gnaws within her to be told and broadcast. Thus you will find women in nooks, on street corners, in secluded spots, talking of their neighbours and friends and of their deeds, and generally of what does not concern them. They are always talking, meddling in other people's affairs : how so and so lives, what she owns, how she behaves, how she married and how her husband does not love her (and for good reason), how in church one heard such-and-such, and the other one answers thus-and-so. And in this way women spend their time, wasting it on nonsense and frivolous things, which it would be impossible to list here. Wherefore it is a general rule that wherever there are women there is a lot of news.

43

The little darlings throng together—some, matrons, and others, of varying ages—and they start and never finish, talking about other people's daughters, about other women. In winter by the fire, in summer out-of-doors, they go on for two or three hours, without saying more than : 'this one, the wife of that one, the daughter of the other one, upon my word, who looks at her? Who does not know her? Pity the poor lamb who trusts her !' etc. Then another answers : 'And if you only knew what an evil tongue she has ! By the Good Lord, my dear, you would blush to hear her, and who even pays attention to her, the little fool !' etc. All day they speak ill of others.

And if you seek news from women, go to the ovens, to a wedding, to church, for there you will find them always whispering in each other's ear, and one making fun of another, and joining those who wish evil to the rest. And they vie with one another in painting and decorating themselves, even if they have to sell their bodies to own jewels, so long as they can be better-dressed than the others, saying : 'May the devil take me if next Sunday you put a better foot forward than I.' The beauties of one neighbourhood join forces against the lovelies of another district : 'Well, let us see now at whom men will look the most, and who will be most discussed and admired. Do you think we are not good enough to appear in public? Better than they, whether they like it or not. Oh, my dear, do you see how angrily they're looking at us? Why do we not put them to shame and ridicule? Let us laugh among ourselves and whisper into each other's ear, looking in their direction, and you will see how they will run away; or before they get up, let us pass quickly in front of them, because the men who are looking at them will have to bow to us first when we go by, and we shall throw it in their teeth about our being first.'

And these and an infinity of other things, too lengthy to relate, women study and plot, for wherever they go and gather they never do anything but talk and gossip and meddle in other people's affairs. Wherefore we may say that woman is very talkative and a very poor keeper of secrets. Therefore he who puts no trust in them does not know what security he has, and he who keeps away from their dealings and most disregards them will live in greatest tranquillity, of this I assure you.

SEYMOUR RESNICK

MARQUÉS DE SANTILLANA
[1398–1458]

Iñigo López de Mendoza, Marquis of Santillana, was not only one of the most powerful noblemen of his day but also an extraordinarily cultured man and writer of uncommon artistry.

He left a number of didactic works in prose and verse. But the greatest fame of the Marquis of Santillana stems from his short and delicately beautiful lyric poems. His serranillas *(mountain songs) are especially delightful, and the* Serranilla de la Finojosa *given here has always been a popular favourite. He also wrote forty-two sonnets in the Italian manner, which are thought to be the first of that type in the Spanish language, and was the author of Spain's first document of literary criticism—the* Proemio e carta al Condestable de Portugal.

SERRANILLA VI

(De la Finojosa)

I ne'er on the border
    Saw girl fair as Rosa,
The charming milk-maiden
    Of Sweet Finojosa.

Once making a journey
    To Santa Maria
Of Calatraveño,
    From weary desire
Of sleep, down a valley
    I strayed, where young Rosa
I saw, the milk-maiden
    Of lone Finojosa.

In a pleasant green meadow,
    'Midst roses and grasses,
Her herd she was tending,
    With other fair lasses;
So lovely her aspect,
    I could not suppose her
A simple milk-maiden
    Of rude Finojosa.

I think not primroses
    Have half her smile's sweetness,
Or mild, modest beauty—
    I speak with discreetness.
O, had I beforehand
    But known of this Rosa,
The handsome milk-maiden
    Of far Finojosa,—

Her very great beauty
    Had not so subdued,
Because it had left me
    To do as I would!
I have said more, O fair one,
    By learning 'twas Rosa,
The charming milk-maiden
    Of sweet Finojosa.

                    JEREMIAH HOLMES WIFFEN

SERRANILLA VIII

Early once in Robledillo
    Hunting venison I came,
But ere long at Colladillo,
    There did front me nobler game;

For at yonder mountain's base,
    That for name Berçosa hath,
Lo, a maiden, fair of face,
    Guarding cattle crossed my path.
If my heart hath not belied me,
    Never sweeter maid was found,
Yet, if one I know should chide me,
    Let her swain her praises sound!

                    IDA FARNELL

CANCIÓN

Whether you love me
I cannot tell.
But that I love you,
This I know well.

You and none other
Hold I so dear.
This shall be always,
Year upon year.

When first I saw you,
So it befell.
I gave you all things—
This I know well.

Myself I gave you
Ever in fee.
Doubt then of all things
But doubt not me.

Since first I saw you,
Under your spell,
All my wits wander,
This I know well.

Still have I loved you,
Still shall I love,
Love you and serve you
All things above.

Her I have chosen
None doth excel.
Trust me, I feign not,
This I know well.

JOHN PIERREPONT RICE

SONNET XVIII

Afar from you and very near to care,
In joy too poor but over-rich in pain,
Deprived of rest yet well endowed again
With mortal woe, I rage and anguish bear;
Though stripped of hope, an ample robe I wear
Of bitter grief, a garment harsh and plain;
My life now flees nor asks if I be fain,
And death so close pursuing will not spare.
Nor will there yet suffice me to assuage
The burning thirst of this my great desire

The Tagus at this hour, nor any wave
Of futile Guadiana; this my gage,
Guadalquivir alone has power entire
To heal me, and that flood alone I crave.

BEATRICE GILMAN PROSKE

JUAN DE MENA
[1411–1456]

*A man dedicated to the art of poetry, Juan de Mena was a leading figure
in the literary court of Juan II in the first half of the fifteenth century. A
Cordovan, he is best known as the author of* Laberinto de fortuna, *an
allegorical-historical vision poem which is also called* Las trescientas *(for
its almost three hundred stanzas).*

*The work describes how the poet is transported in a vision to the palace of
Fortune. There, in a myriad of circles which form the fortune-wheels of past
and present, he sees heroes both historical and mythological. The influence of
Dante's* Divine Comedy *is evident.*

Laberinto de fortuna *is characterized by obscurity in word and thought.
The poem had some effect, however, on succeeding writers, for Juan de Mena
consciously attempted to dignify the subjects and language of Spanish poetry.*

*The selection here presented deals with Macías, the prototype of medieval
lovers, in the circle of Venus.*

LABYRINTH OF FORTUNE
MACÍAS IN THE CIRCLE OF VENUS

We in this radiant circle looked so long
That we found out Macías; in a bower
Of cypress was he weeping still the hour
That ended his dark life and love in wrong.
Nearer I drew for sympathy was strong
In me, when I perceived he was from Spain;
And there I heard him sing the saddest strain
That e'er was tuned in elegiac song.
'Love crowned me with his myrtle crown; my name
Will be pronounced by many, but, alas,
When his pangs caused me bliss, not slighter woe
The mournful suffering that consumed my frame!
His sweet snares conquer the lorn mind they tame,
But do not always then continue sweet;
And since they cause me ruin so complete,
Turn, lovers, turn, and disesteem his fame;

Dangers so passionate be glad to miss;
Learn to be gay; flee from sorrow's touch;
Learn to disserve him you have served so much,
Your devoirs pay at any shrine but his :
If the short joy that in his service is,
Were but proportioned to the long, long pain,
Neither would he that once has loved complain,
Nor he that ne'er has loved despair of bliss.
But even as some assassin or night-rover,
Seeing his fellow wound upon the wheel,
Awed by the agony resolves with zeal
His life to 'mend, and character recover;
But when the fearful spectacle is over,
Reacts his crimes with easy unconcern;
So my amours on my despair return,
That I should die, as I have lived, a lover !'

JEREMIAH HOLMES WIFFEN

JORGE MANRIQUE
[1440?–1479]

Jorge Manrique, a young man of illustrious lineage who died fighting for Queen Isabel, achieved immortality in Spanish literature for his Coplas por la muerte de su padre. This beautiful elegy—worthy of being printed in letters of gold, according to Lope de Vega—was composed upon the death of Manrique's valiant father, Don Rodrigo, in 1476. The entire forty stanzas were rendered into English by Henry Wadsworth Longfellow, and the translation, from which the following excerpts are taken, is itself a work of art.

ODE ON THE DEATH OF HIS FATHER

O, Let the soul her slumbers break !
Let thought be quickened, and awake,—
    Awake to see
How soon this life is past and gone,
And death comes softly stealing on,
    How silently !
Swiftly our pleasures glide away :
Our hearts recall the distant day
    With many sighs;

The moments that are speeding fast
We heed not; but the past—the past—
  More highly prize.

Onward its course the present keeps,
Onward the constant current sweeps,
  Till life is done;
And did we judge of time aright,
The past and future in their flight
  Would be as one.
Let no one fondly dream again
That Hope and all her shadowy train
  Will not decay;
Fleeting as were the dreams of old,
Remembered like a tale that's told,
  They pass away.

Our lives are rivers, gliding free
To that unfathomed, boundless sea,
  The silent grave :
Thither all earthly pomp and boast
Roll, to be swallowed up and lost
  In one dark wave.
Thither the mighty torrents stray,
Thither the brook pursues its way,
  And tinkling rill.
There all are equal. Side by side,
The poor man and the son of pride
  Lie calm and still.

       .   .

This world is but the rugged road
Which leads us to the bright abode
  Of peace above;
So let us choose that narrow way
Which leads no traveller's foot astray
  From realms of love.
Our cradle is the starting-place;
In life we run the onward race,
  And reach the goal;
When, in the mansions of the blest,
Death leaves to its eternal rest
  The weary soul.

       .   .

Behold of what delusive worth
The bubbles we pursue on earth,
    The shapes we chase,
Amid a world of treachery!
They vanish ere death shuts the eye,
    And leave no trace.
Time steals them from us—chances strange,
Disastrous accidents, and change,
    That come to all :
Even in the most exalted state,
Relentless sweeps the stroke of fate;
    The strongest fall.

Tell me—the charms that lovers seek
In the clear eye and blushing cheek,—
    The hues that play
O'er rosy lip and brow of snow,—
When hoary age approaches slow,
    Ah, where are they?
The cunning skill, the curious arts,
The glorious strength that youth imparts
    In life's first stage,—
These shall become a heavy weight,
When Time swings wide his outward gate
    To weary age.

                    .   .   .

Wealth and the high estate of pride
With what untimely speed they glide,
    How soon depart?
Bid not the shadowy phantoms stay,—
The vassals of a mistress they,
    Of fickle heart.
These gifts in Fortune's hands are found;
Her swift-revolving wheel turns round,
    And they are gone!
No rest the inconstant goddess knows,
But changing, and without repose,
    Still hurries on.

Even could the hand of avarice save
Its gilded bawbles, till the grave
    Reclaimed its prey,

Let none on such poor hopes rely,
Life, like an empty dream, flits by,
    And where are they?
Earthly desires and sensual lust
Are passions springing from the dust,—
    They fade and die;
But, in the life beyond the tomb,
They seal the immortal spirit's doom
    Eternally!

The pleasures and delights which mask
In treacherous smiles life's serious task,
    What are they all,
But the fleet coursers of the chase,—
And death an ambush in the race,
    Wherein we fall?
No foe, no dangerous pass, we heed,
Brook no delay,—but onward speed,
    With loosened rein;
And when the fatal snare is near,
We strive to check our mad career,
    But strive in vain.

              .   .   .

Monarchs, the powerful and the strong,
Famous in history and in song
    Of olden time,
Saw, by the stern decrees of fate,
Their kingdoms lost, and desolate
    Their race sublime.
Who is the champion? who the strong?
Pontiff and priest, and sceptred throng?
    On these shall fall
As heavily the hand of Death,
As when it stays the shepherd's breath
    Beside his stall.

I speak not of the Trojan name,—
Neither its glory nor its shame
    Has met our eyes;
Nor of Rome's great and glorious dead,—
Though we have heard so oft, and read,
    Their histories.

Little avails it now to know
Of ages past so long ago,
  Nor how they rolled;
Our theme shall be of yesterday.
Which to oblivion sweeps away,
  Like days of old.

Where is the king, Don Juan? where
Each royal prince and noble heir
  Of Aragon?
Where are the courtly gallantries?
The deeds of love and high emprise,
  In battle done?
Tourney and joust, that charmed the eye,
And scarf, and gorgeous panoply,
  And nodding plume,—
What were they but a pageant scene?
What, but the garlands, gay and green,
  That deck the tomb?

Where are the high-born dames, and where
Their gay attire, and jewelled hair,
  And odours sweet?
Where are the gentle knights, that came
To kneel, and breathe love's ardent flame,
  Low at their feet?
Where is the song of Troubadour?
Where are the lute and gay tambour
  They loved of yore?
Where is the mazy dance of old,—
The flowing robes, inwrought with gold,
  The dancers wore?

                *   *   *

The countless gifts,—the stately walls,
The royal palaces, and halls
  All filled with gold;
Plate with armorial bearings wrought,
Chambers with ample treasures fraught
  Of wealth untold;
The noble steeds, and harness bright,
And gallant lord, and stalwart knight,
  In rich array;—

Where shall we seek them now? Alas!
Like the bright dew-drops on the grass,
  They passed away.

.   .   .

Spain's haughty Constable,—the true
And gallant Master,—whom we knew
  Most loved of all,—
Breathe not a whisper of his pride;
He on the gloomy scaffold died,—
  Ignoble fall!
The countless treasures of his care,
His hamlets green and cities fair,
  His mighty power,—
What were they all but grief and shame,
Tears and a broken heart, when came
  The parting hour?

.   .   .

So many a duke of royal name,
Marquis and count of spotless fame,
  And baron brave,
That might the sword of empire wield,—
All these, O Death, hast thou concealed
  In the dark grave!
Their deeds of mercy and of arms,
In peaceful days, or war's alarms,
  When thou dost show,
O Death, thy stern and angry face,
One stroke of thy all-powerful mace
  Can overthrow!

Unnumbered hosts, that threaten nigh,—
Pennon and standard flaunting high,
  And flag displayed,—
High battlements intrenched around,
Bastion, and moated wall, and mound,
  And palisade,
And covered trench, secure and deep,—
All these cannot one victim keep,
  O Death, from thee,
When thou dost battle in thy wrath,
And thy strong shafts pursue their path
  Unerringly!

.   .   .

And he, the good man's shield and shade,
To whom all hearts their homage paid,
   As Virtue's son,—
Roderick Manrique,—he whose name
Is written on the scroll of Fame,
   Spain's champion;
His signal deeds and prowess high
Demand no pompous eulogy,—
   Ye saw his deeds!
Why should their praise in verse be sung?
The name that dwells on every tongue
   No minstrel needs.

To friends a friend;—how kind to all
The vassals of this ancient hall
   And feudal fief!
To foes how stern a foe was he!
And to the valiant and the free
   How brave a chief!
What prudence with the old and wise!
What grace in youthful gayeties!
   In all how sage!
Benignant to the serf and slave,
He showed the base and falsely brave
   A lion's rage.

      .   .   .

He left no well filled treasury,
He heaped no pile of riches high,
   Nor massive plate;
He fought the Moors,—and, in their fall,
City and tower and castled wall
   Were his estate.
Upon the hard-fought battle-ground
Brave steeds and gallant riders found
   A common grave;
And there the warrior's hand did gain
The rents, and the long vassal train,
That conquest gave.

      .   .   .

And when so oft, for weal or woe,
His life upon the fatal throw
   Had been cast down,—

When he had served, with patriot zeal,
Beneath the banner of Castile,
    His sovereign's crown,—
And done such deeds of valour strong,
That neither history nor song
    Can count them all;
Then, on Ocaña's castled rock,
Death at his portal came to knock,
    With sudden call,—

Saying, 'Good Cavalier, prepare
To leave this world of toil and care
    With joyful mien;
Let thy strong heart of steel this day
Put on its armour for the fray,—
    The closing scene.
Since thou hast been, in battle-strife,
So prodigal of health and life,
    For earthly fame,
Let virtue nerve thy heart again;
Loud on the last stern battle-plain
    They call thy name.

'Think not the struggle that draws near
Too terrible for man, nor fear
    To meet the foe;
Nor let thy noble spirit grieve,
Its life of glorious fame to leave
    On earth below.
A life of honour and of worth
Has no eternity on earth,—
    'Tis but a name;
And yet its glory far exceeds
That base and sensual life which leads
    To want and shame.

    ·   ·   ·

And thou, brave knight, whose hand has poured
The life-blood of the pagan horde
    O'er all the land,
In heaven shalt thou receive, at length,
The guerdon of thine earthly strength
    And dauntless hand.

Cheered onward by this promise sure,
Strong in the faith entire and pure
  Thou dost profess,
Depart, thy hope is certainty;—
The third—the better life on high
  Shalt thou possess.'

'O Death, no more, no more delay!
My spirit longs to flee away
  And be at rest :—
The will of Heaven my will shall be,—
I bow to the divine decree,
  To God's behest.
My soul is ready to depart,—
No thought rebels,—the obedient heart
  Breathes forth no sigh;
The wish on earth to linger still
Were vain, when 'tis God's sovereign will
  That we shall die.'

      .   .   .

And thus the dying warrior prayed,
Without one gathering mist or shade
  Upon his mind,—
Encircled by his family,
Watched by affection's gentle eye,
  So soft and kind,—
His soul to Him who gave it rose.
God lead it to its long repose,
  Its glorious rest!
And, though the warrior's sun has set,
Its light shall linger round us yet,
  Bright, radiant, blest.

HENRY WADSWORTH LONGFELLOW

GÓMEZ MANRIQUE
[1412?–1490?]

Nephew of the Marquis of Santillana and thus a member of one of Spain's most noble families, Gómez Manrique is represented by more than one hundred poems in the fifteenth-century cancioneros. While he is one of the best poets of the time, his literary fame has been overshadowed by that of his own more celebrated nephew, Jorge Manrique.

TO A LADY GOING VEILED

The very heart went out of me
  When first I saw your face,
And soon it did appear to me
  Your eyes in mine would trace.

I could no more than scarcely breathe
  When you drew on your veil
And hid yourself so well beneath
  Your dark cloak's heavy trail.

But under it your gentle grace
  And simple air were seen;
The very masque its charm would trace
  And show, instead of screen;
So very great became my care
  And trouble that I knew
My heart was swift entangled there
  With my enraptured view.

THOMAS WALSH

RODRIGO COTA
[*c.* 1490]

Rodrigo Cota wrote some delightful lyric poetry. His famous Diálogo *entre el amor y un viejo ('Dialogue between Love and an old man') is one of the most graceful works of the period.*

LOVE

Clouded vision, light obscure,
Moody glory, living death,
Fortune that cannot endure,
Fickle weeping, joy a breath,
Bitter-sweet and sweet unsure,
Peace and anger, sudden crossed,
Such is love, its trappings sure
Decked with glory for its cost.

THOMAS WALSH

JUAN ESCRIVÁ
[c. 1490]

The Comendador Escrivá was the author of some refreshingly melodious lyric poems. Beyond this, little is known of the man or his life. His Ven, muerte, tan escondida, given here, has been translated many times and has been quoted by Cervantes, Calderón and Edgar Allan Poe, among others.

WELCOME DEATH

Come, gentle death! come silently,—
   And sound no knell, no warning give,
Lest the sweet bliss of welcoming thee
   Should rouse my wearied soul to live.

Come like the rapid lightning's ray,
   That wounds, but while it wounds is still;
It passes, voiceless, on its way,
   And flings its mortal barb at will.
Thus soft, thus calm, thy coming be,
   Else, death! this warning now I give,
That the sweet bliss of welcoming thee
   Will rouse my weary soul to live.

JOHN BOWRING

ANONYMOUS POEMS

Poetry flourished during the first half of the fifteenth century in the court of the poet-king Juan II. Thousands of verse compositions—almost all lyric love poems written in an artificial, affected tone, and often employing intricate metrical forms —are preserved in several cancioneros dating from this era. Two of the most important collections are the Cancionero de Baena (c. 1445) and the Cancionero general (1511). While the quality of the works contained in these collections has not been highly valued by critics in general, we include some of the better anonymous poems of the period.

THE KISS

Since for kissing thee, Minguillo,
   Mother's ever scolding me,
Give me swiftly back, thou dear one!
   Give the kiss I gave to thee.

Give me back the kiss—that one now,
　　Let my mother scold no more;
　　Let us tell her all is o'er :
What was done is all undone now.
Yes! it will be wise, Minguillo,
　　My fond kiss to give to me,—
Give me swiftly back, thou dear one!
　　Give the kiss I gave to thee.
Give me back the kiss, for mother
　　Is impatient—prithee do!
　　For that one thou shalt have two;
Give me that, and take another.
Help me—let them be contented,
　　Let them not complain of me;
Give me swiftly back, thou dear one!
　　Give the kiss I gave to thee.

JOHN BOWRING

AXA, FÁTIMA, AND MARIÉN

Three Moorish girls I loved
In Jaén,
Axa and Fátima and Marién.

Three Moorish girls so gay
Went olive-plucking there,
And found them plucked away
In Jaén,
Axa and Fátima and Marién.

And found them plucked away
And turned back in dismay,
And pale and sad were they
In Jaén,
Axa and Fátima and Marién.

Three Moorish girls so fair,
Three Moorish girls so fair
Went apple-plucking there
In Jaén,
Axa and Fátima and Marién.

JEAN ROGERS LONGLAND

GLOVE OF BLACK IN WHITE HAND BARE

Glove of black in white hand bare,
And about her forehead pale
Wound a thin, transparent veil,
That doth not conceal her hair;
Sovereign attitude and air,
Cheek and neck alike displayed,
With coquettish charms arrayed,
Laughing eyes and fugitive;—
This is killing men that live,
'Tis not mourning for the dead.

HENRY WADSWORTH LONGFELLOW

THE SIESTA

Airs! that wander and murmur round,
    Bearing delight where'er ye blow,—
Make in the elms a lulling sound,
    While my lady sleeps in the shade below.

Lighten and lengthen her noonday rest,
    Till the heat of the noonday sun is o'er:
Sweet be her slumbers,—though in my breast
    The pain she has waked may slumber no more!
Breathing soft from the blue profound,
    Bearing delight where'er ye blow,
Make in the elms a lulling sound,
    While my lady sleeps in the shade below.

Airs! that over the bending boughs,
    And under the shadows of the leaves,
Murmur soft, like my timid vows,
    Or the secret sighs my bosom heaves,—
Gently sweeping the grassy ground,
    Bearing delight where'er ye blow,
Make in the elms a lulling sound,
    While my lady sleeps in the shade below.

WILLIAM CULLEN BRYANT

LOVE AND DEATH

Death and Cupid chanced to meet,
On a day when they were roaming,
At a wayside country inn,
After sunset in the gloaming.
Cupid he was bound for Seville,
Death was marching on Madrid,
Both with knapsacks on their shoulders,
Where their wicked wares were hid.

Seemed to me that they were fleeing
From the clutches of the law,
For the couple gained a living
Dealing death on all they saw.
Cupid slyly glanced at Death,
As they sat around the board,
Marvelled at her ugly visage,
Shook his merry sides and roared.

'Madam,' quoth he, ''tis so rude
To behave in such a way;
But, in sooth, so fair a fright
I've not seen for many a day.'
Death, whose cheeks grew red and fiery,
Put an arrow in her bow;
Cupid put in his another,
And to combat they would go.

Quick the landlord slipped between them,
As they scowled on one another,
Made them swear eternal friendship,
Bade them sit and sup together.
In the kitchen, by the ingle,
They were fain to lay them down,
For no bed was in the tavern,
And the landlord he had none.

They their arrows, bows and quivers,
Gave into Marina's care,
She a buxom wench who waited
On the guests that harboured there;
On the morrow at the dawning,
Cupid started from the floor,
Bade the landlord fetch his arms,
Broke his fast and paid his score.

'Twas the arms of Death the landlord
In his haste to Cupid brought,
Cupid flung them on his shoulder,
Took the road and gave no thought.
Death rose up a little after,
Sour, and limp, and woe-begone,
Took at once the arms of Cupid,
Shouldered them, and wandered on.

From that very day to this,
Cupid's shafts no more revive;
Youths who feel his fatal arrows
Pass not over twenty-five.
And, 'tis stranger still, the old ones,
Whom Death's arrows used to slay,
When they feel the shafts of Cupid,
Gain a new life and a gay.

What a world, so topsy-turvy !
What a change in people's lives !
Cupid giving life destroys,
Death destroying life revives !

JAMES YOUNG GIBSON

THE DANCE OF DEATH

The theme of the 'Dance of Death', relatively common in medieval European literature and art, did not manifest itself in Spain until the beginning of the fifteenth century. The anonymous Danza de la muerte *(or* Danza general), *probably an imitation of an earlier French model, is composed of seventy-nine* coplas de arte mayor *(twelve-syllable octaves) in dramatic form. The figure of Death summons representatives of many classes of society—emperor, cardinal, duke, archbishop, abbot and a host of lesser clerics and laymen—to appear in turn before him. Each protests or makes a plea for forgiveness. But Death, pointing out their faults and vices, unswervingly condemns them all to join in the funereal dance.*

From THE DANCE OF DEATH

Here begins the general dance, in which it is shown how Death gives advice to all, that they should take due account of the brevity of life, and not to value it more highly than it deserves; and this he orders and requires, that they see and hear attentively what wise

preachers tell them and warn them from day to day, giving them
good and wholesome counsel that they labour in doing good works
to obtain pardon of their sins; and showing them by experience
what he says, calls and requires from all classes, whether they come
willingly or unwillingly; and thus beginning:

Lo! I am Death! With aim as sure as steady,
   All beings that are and shall be I draw near me.
I call thee,—I require thee, man, be ready!
   Why build upon this fragile life?—Now hear me!
   Where is the power that does not own me, fear me?
Who can escape me, when I bend my bow?
I pull the string,—thou liest in dust below,
   Smitten by the barb my ministering angels bear me.

       .   .   .

Come to the dance of Death! Come hither, even
   The last, the lowliest,—of all rank and station!
Who will not come shall be by scourges driven:
   I hold no parley with disinclination.
   List to yon friar who preaches of salvation,
And hie ye to your penitential post!
For who delays,—who lingers,—he is lost,
   And handed o'er to hopeless reprobation.

       .   .   .

I to my dance—my mortal dance—have brought
   Two nymphs, all bright in beauty and in bloom.
They listened, fear-struck, to my songs, methought;
   And, truly, songs like mine are tinged with gloom.
   But neither roseate hues nor flowers' perfume
Will now avail them,—nor the thousand charms
Of worldly vanity;—they fill my arms,—
   They are my brides,—their bridal bed the tomb.

       .   .   .

And since 'tis certain, then, that we must die,—
   No hope, no chance, no prospect of redress,—
Be it our constant aim unswervingly
   To tread God's narrow path of holiness:
   For he is first, last, midst. O, let us press
Onwards! and when Death's monitory glance
Shall summon us to join his mortal dance,
   Even then shall hope and joy our footsteps bless.

ANONYMOUS

BALLADS

Of particular renown in Spanish literature is its extensive collection of popular poetry—the romances. *Colourful, spirited, intensely rhythmic, these ballads enchant the reader as they sing of life and love, hero and traitor, Moor and Christian, adventure and misadventure, history and legend.*

The old romances *were anonymous poems, transmitted orally for many years. Their structure is based on sixteen-syllable lines with assonance (rhyme of the vowel). The question of the actual origin of the* romances, *however, is one of the most puzzling in Spanish literature. Some scholars maintain that they are as old as the early epics, and indeed might be fragments of epics, while others assert that the first were not composed much before the fifteenth century.*

In any case, the Spanish ballads were a literary mine for later authors of all nationalities. The German philosopher Hegel termed them 'a string of pearls'.

COUNT ARNALDOS

Oh, who could have such fortune
   On the sea so far away
As once had Count Arnaldos
   On the morn of St. John's Day.
He was hunting on that morning,
   With a falcon on his hand;
When he saw a small ship coming,
   Coming to the land.
Its sails they were all silken,
   And its rigging lace, but strong,
And the captain on the foredeck
   Was singing such a song
That it made the sea all quiet,
   And it lulled the wind to sleep,
And it lured the silver fishes
   To swim up from the deep.
It drew the birds from Heaven
   To rest upon the mast.
Then up spoke Count Arnaldos,
   Then up he spoke at last:
'For God's sweet sake, oh, Captain,
   A boon I crave of thee;
For I never heard such singing
   On land or on the sea,

Oh, teach me that strange chantey!'
Then the Captain said, said he:
'I do not sing that chantey
Save to him who goes with me.'

NICHOLSON B. ADAMS

THE PRISONER

Oh 'tis May, the month of May,
when the season's heat is high,
and the larks above are singing
and the nightingales reply,
and all lovers are a-running
on love's errands far and nigh;
all but me, afflicted, wretched,
that in prison-house do lie;
neither know I when day cometh,
nor when night is passing by,
were it not for one wee birdie,
singing when the dawn is nigh:
but an archer slew my birdie—
may he earn God's curse thereby!

WILLIAM J. ENTWISTLE

THE FRENCH PRINCESS

Towards France a maiden went,
Towards France her course she bent,
Unto Paris,—there to find
Her father and her mother kind.

Far from any known abode
She had wandered from the road,
And rested on a blasted fir,
Waiting for some passenger.

Towards her came a cavalier,
He to Paris, too, did steer;
When he met the maiden's eyes,
She address'd him in this guise:

'Wilt thou guide me, cavalier,
If to Paris thou dost steer?'
'Will I guide thee, maiden fair?
Yes, by all my hopes I swear.'

In the middle of the way,
He spoke to her of love and play;
The maid, when she his suit had heard,
Cool'd him with a single word:

'Hush thee, hush thee, gentle knight!
Tho' I look so fair and bright,
Diseas'd I am,—diseas'd I came
From a tainted sire and dame,

'The mortal who with me shall lie
Will waste away until he die!'
The cavalier grew pale to see,
But not a sentence answer'd he.

The maid, when Paris was in sight,
Smil'd until she laughed outright.
'What makes thee smile?' the warrior said;
'What make thee laugh, my pretty maid?'

'I laugh at the weak cavalier;
I hold in scorn the dastard's fear,
Who led me thro' the desert plains
And yet got nothing for his pains.'

The warrior's face with shame was dy'd;
He stammer'd and at length replied:
'We must return the way we've crost,
For a something I have lost.'

'No,' answer'd she, 'I'll not turn back,
To cross with thee yon desert track;
And even tho' we did return
Yet would treat thy love with scorn.

'Daughter of France's royal line,
I boast my birth from Constantine:
The man that makes me shed a tear
I reckon it will cost him dear.'

GEORGE BORROW

THE LOVELY INFANTA

Beneath the shade of an olive tree the young infanta fair
With a golden comb held in her hands was combing out her hair.

She raised her eyes to heaven and she searched the western skies,
Then up the Guadalquivir there sailed a fleet before her eyes.

The Admiral of Castile, Alfonso Ramos, she saw there.
'Alfonso Ramos, welcome! Now, what tidings do you bear?

'Of my fleet so brave and well equipped what news do you
    bring me?'
'Madam, an I tell you, will my life the forfeit be?'

'Nay speak, Alfonso Ramos, for you have my promise leal.'
'The Barbary Moors have landed and are ravaging Castile.'

'Your head, but for my promise, would avenge the conquering
    Moors.'
'The price of my head, Madam, would have been the loss of yours.'

ALICE JANE M^CVAN

FOUNT OF FRESHNESS

Fount of freshness! fount of freshness!
    Fount of freshness and of love!
Where the little birds of spring-time
    Seek for comfort, as they rove;
All except the widowed turtle,—
    Widowed, sorrowing turtle-dove.

There the nightingale—the traitor!—
    Lingered on his giddy way;
And these words of hidden treachery
    To the dove I heard him say :
'I will be thy servant, lady!
    I will ne'er thy love betray.'

'Off! false-hearted, vile deceiver!
    Leave me, nor insult me so :
Dwell I, then, midst gaudy flowerets?
    Perch I on the verdant bough?
Even the waters of the fountain
    Drink I dark and troubled now.
Never will I think of marriage,—
    Never break the widow-vow.

'Had I children, they would grieve me,
   They would wean me from my woe :
Leave me, false one ! thoughtless traitor !
   Base one ! vain one ! sad one ! go !
I can never, never love thee,—
   I will never wed thee,—no !'

JOHN BOWRING

ROSE, FRESH AND FAIR

'Rose, fresh and fair, Rose, fresh and fair,
   That with love so bright dost glow,
When within my arms I held thee,
   I could never serve thee, no !
And now that I would gladly serve thee,
   I no more can see thee, no !'

'The fault, my friend, the fault was thine,—
   Thy fault alone, and not mine, no !
A message came,—the words you sent,—
   Your servant brought it, well you know.
And naught of love, or loving bands,
   But other words, indeed, he said :
That you, my friend, in Leon's lands
   A noble dame had long since wed,—
A lady fair, as fair could be;
   Her children bright as flowers to see.'

'Who told that tale, who spoke those words,
   No truth he spoke, my lady, no !
For Castile's lands I never saw,
   Of Leon's mountains nothing know,
Save as a little child, I ween,
   Too young to know what love should mean.'

GEORGE TICKNOR

THE LAMENTATION OF DON RODERICK

The hosts of Don Rodrigo were scattered in dismay,
When lost was the eighth battle, nor heart nor hope had they—
He, when he saw that field was lost, and all his hope was flown,
He turned him from his flying host, and took his way alone.

His horse was bleeding, blind, and lame—he could no farther go;
Dismounted, without path or aim, the King stepped to and fro;
It was a sight of pity to look on Roderick;
For, sore athirst and hungry, he staggered faint and sick.

All stained and strewed with dust and blood, like to some
    smouldering brand
Plucked from the flame Rodrigo shewed—his sword was in his
    hand,
But it was hacked into a saw of dark and purple tint;
His jewelled mail had many a flaw, his helmet many a dint.

He climbed unto a hill top, the highest he could see,
Thence all about of that wide route his last long look took he;
He saw his royal banners, where they lay drenched and torn,
He heard the cry of victory, the Arab's shout of scorn.

He looked for the brave captains that had led the hosts of Spain,
But all were fled except the dead, and who could count the slain!
Where'er his eye could wander, all bloody was the plain,
And while thus he said, the tears he shed run down his cheeks
    like rain :—

'Last night I was the King of Spain—today no king am I;
Last night fair castles held my train, tonight where shall I lie?
Last night a hundred pages did serve me on the knee;
Tonight not one I call mine own :—not one pertains to me.

'O luckless, luckless was the hour, and cursed was the day,
When I was born to have the power of this great signiory!
Unhappy me, that I should see the sun go down tonight!
O Death, why now so slow art thou, why fearest thou to smite?'

JOHN GIBSON LOCKHART

BERNARDO'S MARCH TO RONCESVALLES

The peasant leaves his plough afield,
    The reaper leaves his hook,
And from his hand the shepherd-boy
    Lets fall the pastoral crook.

The young set up a shout of joy,
    The old forget their years,
The feeble man grows stout of heart,
    No more the craven fears.

All rush to Bernardo's standard,
   And on liberty they call;
They cannot brook to wear the yoke,
   When threatened by the Gaul.

'Free were we born,' 'tis thus they cry,
   'And willingly pay we
The duty that we owe our king,
   By the divine decree.

'But God forbid that we obey
   The laws of foreign knaves,
Tarnish the glory of our sires,
   And make our children slaves.

'Our hearts have not so craven grown,
   So bloodless all our veins,
So vigourless our brawny arms,
   As to submit to chains.

'Has the audacious Frank, forsooth,
   Subdued these seas and lands?
Shall he a bloodless victory have?
   No, not while we have hands.

'He shall learn that the gallant Leonese
   Can bravely fight and fall,
But that they know not how to yield;
   They are Castilians all.

'Was it for this the Roman power
   Of old was made to yield
Unto Numantia's valiant hosts
   On many a bloody field?

'Shall the bold lions that have bathed
   Their paws in Libyan gore,
Crouch basely to a feebler foe,
   And dare the strife no more?

'Let the false king sell town and tower,
   But not his vassals free;
For to subdue the free-born soul
   No royal power hath he!'

HENRY WADSWORTH LONGFELLOW

KING DON SANCHO

King don Sancho, King don Sancho,
    I warn thee, warn thee well,
That from Zamora's city
    Hath come a traitor fell.
His name Vellido Dolfos
    Dolfos Vellido's son.
Ere now he wrought four treasons
    With this five will be done.
If traitor was the father
    The son is traitor more.
In don Sancho's camp they're crying
    Don Sancho's wounded sore.
Vellido Dolfos killed him,
    Great treason hath he done.
And after this foul murder
    Through a postern gate he's run.
And through the streets of Zamora
    He shouted as he stepped :
It was high time, Urraca,
    That promises be kept.

                      NICHOLSON B. ADAMS

THE CID AND THE FIVE MOORISH KINGS

With fire and desolation the Moors are in Castile,
Five Moorish kings together, and all their vassals leal;
They've passed in front of Burgos, through the Oca-Hills they've
    run,
They've plundered Belforado, San Domingo's harm is done.

In Najara and Logrono there's waste and disarray :—
And now with Christian captives, a very heavy prey,
With many men and woman, and boys and girls beside,
In joy and exultation to their own realms they ride.

For neither king nor noble would dare their path to cross,
Until the good Rodrigo heard of this skaith and loss;
In old Bivar the castle he heard the tidings told
(He was as yet a stripling, not twenty summers old).

He mounted Bavieca, his friends he with him took,
He raised the country round him, no more such scorn to brook;
He rode to the hills of Oca, where then the Moormen lay,
He conquered all the Moormen, and took from them their prey.

To every man had mounted he gave his part of gain,
Dispersing the much treasure the Saracens had ta'en;
The kings were all the booty himself had from the war,
Then led he to his castle, his stronghold of Bivar.

He brought them to his mother, proud dame that day was she—
They owned him for their Signior, and then he set them free;
Home went they, much commending Rodrigo of Bivar,
And sent him lordly tribute, from their Moorish realms afar.

JOHN GIBSON LOCKHART

BAVIECA

The king looked on him kindly, as on a vassal true;
Then to the king Ruy Diaz spake, after reverence due :
'O king, the thing is shameful, that any man, beside
The liege lord of Castile himself, should Bavieca ride :

'For neither Spain nor Araby could another charger bring
So good as he; and, certes, the best befits my king.
But that you may behold him, and know him to the core,
I'll make him go as he was wont when his nostrils smelt the Moor.'

With that, the Cid, clad as he was in mantle furred and wide,
On Bavieca vaulting, put the rowel in his side;
And up and down, and round and round, so fierce was his career,
Streamed like a pennon on the wind Ruy Diaz' minivere.

And all that saw them praised them,—they lauded man and horse,
As matched well, and rivalless for gallantry and force;
Ne'er had they looked on horseman might to this knight come near,
Nor on other charger worthy of such a cavalier.

Thus to and fro a-rushing, the fierce and furious steed,
He snapped in twain his hither rein :—'God pity now the Cid !
God pity Diaz !' cried the lords;—but when they looked again,
They saw Ruy Diaz ruling him with the fragment of his rein;
They saw him proudly ruling with gesture firm and calm,
Like a true lord commanding,—and obeyed as by a lamb.

And so he led him foaming and panting to the king :—
But 'No !' said Don Alfonso, 'it were a shameful thing
That peerless Bavieca should ever be bestrid
By any mortal but Bivar;—mount, mount again, my Cid !'

JOHN GIBSON LOCKHART

THE DEATH OF DON PEDRO

Henry and King Pedro clasping,
   Hold in straining arms each other;
Tugging hard, and closely grasping,
   Brother proves his strength with brother.

Harmless pastime, sport fraternal,
   Blends not thus their limbs in strife;
Either aims, with rage infernal,
   Naked dagger, sharpened knife.

Close Don Henry grapples Pedro,
   Pedro holds Don Henry strait,—
Breathing, this, triumphant fury,
   That, despair and mortal hate.

Sole spectator of the struggle,
   Stands Don Henry's page afar,
In the chase who bore his bugle,
   And who bore his sword in war.

Down they go in deadly wrestle,
   Down upon the earth they go;
Fierce King Pedro has the vantage,
   Stout Don Henry falls below.

Marking then the fatal crisis,
   Up the page of Henry ran,
By the waist he caught Don Pedro,
   Aiding thus the fallen man.

'King to place, or to depose him,
   Dwelleth not in my desire;
But the duty which he owes him
   To his master pays the squire.'

Now Don Henry has the upmost,
   Now King Pedro lies beneath;
In his heart his brother's poniard
   Instant finds its bloody sheath.

Thus with mortal gasp and quiver,
   While the blood in bubbles welled,
Fled the fiercest soul that ever
   In a Christian bosom dwelled.

JOHN GIBSON LOCKHART

MORAIMA

I was the Moorish maid, Moraima,
   I was that maiden dark and fair,—
A Christian came, he seemed in sorrow,
   Full of falsehood came he there.
Moorish he spoke,—he spoke it well,—
   'Open the door, thou Moorish maid,
So shalt thou be by Allah blessed,
   So shall I save my forfeit head.'
   'But how can I, alone and weak,
   Unbar, and know not who is there?'
   'But I'm the Moor, the Moor Mazote,
   The brother of thy mother dear.
A Christian fell beneath my hand,
   The Alcalde comes, he comes apace,
And if thou open not thy door,
   I perish here before thy face.'
I rose in haste, I rose in fear,
   I seized my cloak, I missed my vest,
And, rushing to the fatal door,
   I threw it wide at his behest.

GEORGE TICKNOR

ABENAMAR, ABENAMAR

O thou Moor of *Morería*,
There were mighty signs and aspects
On the day when thou wert born,
Calm and lovely was the ocean,
Bright and full the moon above.
Moor, the child of such an aspect
Never ought to answer falsely.
Then replied the Moorish captive,
(You shall hear the Moor's reply):

Nor will I untruly answer,
Though I died for saying truth.
I am son of Moorish sire.
My mother was a Christian slave.
In my childhood, in my boyhood,
Often would my mother bid me
Never know the liar's shame.
Ask thou, therefore, King, thy question.
Truly will I answer thee.

Thank thee, thank thee, Abenamar,
For thy gentle answer, thanks.
What are yonder lofty castles,
Those that shine so bright on high?

That, O King, is the Alhambra,
Yonder is the Mosque of God.
There you see the Alixares,
Works of skill and wonder they;
Ten times ten doubloons the builder
Daily for his hire received;
If an idle day he wasted
Ten times ten doubloons he paid.
Farther is the Generalife,
Peerless are its garden groves.
Those are the Vermilion Towers,
Far and wide their fame is known.

Then spake up the King Don Juan
(You shall hear the Monarch's speech):

Wouldst thou marry me, Granada,
Gladly would I for thy dowry
Cordoba and Seville give.

I am married, King Don Juan.
King, I am not yet a widow.
Well I love my noble husband.
Well my wedded lord loves me.

                                  ROBERT SOUTHEY

AY DE MI ALHAMA

The Moorish King rides up and down,
Through Granada's royal town;
From Elvira's gates to those
Of Bivarambla on he goes.
              Woe is me, Alhama!

Letters to the monarch tell
How Alhama's city fell;
In the fire the scroll he threw,
And the messenger he slew.
              Woe is me, Alhama!

He quits his mule and mounts his horse,
And through the streets directs his course;
Through the street of Zacatín
To the Alhambra spurring in.
    Woe is me, Alhama!

When the Alhambra's walls he gained
On the moment he ordained
That the trumpet straight should sound
With the silver clarion round.
    Woe is me, Alhama!

And when the hollow drums of war
Beat the loud alarm afar,
That the Moors of town and plain
Might answer to the martial strain,
    Woe is me, Alhama!

Then the Moors, by this aware,
That bloody Mars recalled them there,
One by one, and two by two,
To a mighty squadron grew.
    Woe is me, Alhama!

Out then spoke an agèd Moor
In these words the King before,
'Wherefore call on us, O King?
What may mean this gathering?'
    Woe is me, Alhama!

'Friends, ye have, alas, to know
Of a most disastrous blow;
That the Christians, stern and bold,
Have obtained Alhama's hold.'
    Woe is me, Alhama!

Out then spake old Alfaquì,
With his beard so white to see,
'Good King! thou art justly served!
Good King! this thou hast deserved.
    Woe is me, Alhama!

'By thee were slain, in evil hour,
The Abencerrage, Granada's flower;
And strangers were received by thee
Of Cordova the chivalry.
    Woe is me, Alhama!

'And for this, O King, is sent
On thee a double chastisement;
Thee and thine, thy crown and realm,
One last wreck shall overwhelm.
        Woe is me, Alhama!

'He who holds no laws in awe,
He must perish by the law;
And Granada must be won,
And thyself with her undone.'
        Woe is me, Alhama!

Fire flashed from out the old Moor's eyes,
The Monarch's wrath began to rise,
Because he answered, and because
He spoke exceeding well of laws,
        Woe is me, Alhama!

'There is no law to say such things
As may disgust the ear of Kings';—
Thus, snorting with his choler, said
The Moorish King, and doomed him dead.
        Woe is me, Alhama!

Moor Alfaquì! Moor Alfaquì!
Though thy beard so hoary be,
The King hath sent to have thee seized
For Alhama's loss displeased.
        Woe is me, Alhama!

And to fix thy head upon
High Alhambra's loftiest stone;
That this for thee should be the law
And others tremble when they saw.
        Woe is me, Alhama!

'Cavalier and man of worth!
Let these words of mine go forth!
Let the Moorish monarch know
That to him I nothing owe.
        Woe is me, Alhama!

'But on my soul Alhama weighs
And on my inmost spirit preys;
And if the King his land hath lost
Yet others may have lost the most.
        Woe is me, Alhama!

'Sires have lost their children, wives
Their lords, and valiant men their lives!
One what best his love might claim
Hath lost, another, wealth and fame.
          Woe is me, Alhama!

'I lost a damsel in that hour,
Of all the land the loveliest flower;
Doubloons a hundred I would pay
And think her ransom cheap that day.'
          Woe is me, Alhama!

And as these things the old Moor said,
They severed from the trunk his head;
And to the Alhambra's walls with speed
'Twas carried as the King decreed.
          Woe is me, Alhama!

And men and infants therein weep
Their loss so heavy and so deep;
Granada's ladies, all she rears
Within her walls, burst into tears.
          Woe is me, Alhama!

And from the windows o'er the walls
The sable web of mourning falls;
The King weeps as a woman o'er
His loss, for it is much and sore.
          Woe is me, Alhama!

                  LORD BYRON

FLIGHT FROM GRANADA

There was crying in Granada when the sun was going down,—
Some calling on the Trinity—some calling on Mahoun!
Here passed away the Koran,—there, in the Cross was borne,—
And here was heard the Christian bell,—and there the Moorish
    horn.

Te Deum Laudamus! was up the Alcala sung;
Down from the Alhambra's minarets were all the crescents flung;
The arms thereon of Aragon they with Castile's display;
One king comes in in triumph,—one weeping goes away.

Thus cried the weeper, while his hands his old white beard did tear,
'Farewell, farewell, Granada! thou city without peer!

Woe, woe, thou pride of Heathendom! seven hundred years and
　　more
Have gone since first the faithful thy royal sceptre bore!

'Thou wert the happy mother of an high renownèd race;
Within thee dwelt a haughty line that now go from their place;
Within thee fearless knights did dwell, who fought with mickle glee
The enemies of proud Castile—the bane of Christientie!

'The mother of fair dames wert thou, of truth and beauty rare,
Into whose arms did courteous knights for solace sweet repair;
For whose dear sakes the gallants of Afric made display
Of might in joust and battle on many a bloody day.

'Here gallants held it little thing for ladies' sake to die,
Or for the Prophet's honour and pride of Soldanry;—
For here did valour flourish and deeds of warlike might
Ennobled lordly palaces, in which was our delight.

'The gardens of thy Vega, its fields and blooming bowers,—
Woe, woe! I see their beauty gone, and scattered all their flowers!
No reverence can he claim, the King that such a land hath lost,—
On charger never can he ride, nor be heard among the host;

'But in some dark and dismal place, where none his face may see,
There weeping and lamenting, alone that King should be.'—

Thus spoke Granada's King as he was riding to the sea,
About to cross Gibraltar's Strait away to Barbary;
Thus he in heaviness of soul unto his Queen did cry
(He had stopped and ta'en her in his arms, for together they did fly).

'Unhappy King! whose craven soul can brook' (she made reply)
'To leave behind Granada—who hast not the heart to die!
Now for the love I bore thy youth, thee gladly could I slay!
For what is life to leave when such a crown is cast away?'

JOHN GIBSON LOCKHART

MY ORNAMENTS ARE ARMS

My ornaments are arms,
　　My bed the flinty stone,
My rest is war's alarms,
　　My sleep to watch alone.
Through gloomy paths unknown,
　　Paths which untrodden be,

From rock to rock I go
Along the dashing sea,
And seek from busy woe
With hurrying steps to flee;
But know, fair lady! know,
All this I bear for thee!

JOHN BOWRING

HERNANDO DEL PULGAR
[1435?–1493?]

Hernando del Pulgar was secretary and official chronicler of the Catholic Monarchs, Ferdinand and Isabel, as well as Ambassador to France for a brief period. His works include Letras *(a collection of thirty-two letters),* Claros varones de Castilla *(twenty-four short biographical sketches of contemporary noblemen) and the* Crónica de los Reyes Católicos.

THE CHRONICLE OF THE CATHOLIC MONARCHS

DON FERNANDO THE CATHOLIC

This king was a man of average height, well-proportioned, with regular features, smiling eyes, smooth black hair, and good colour. His speech was even, neither too fast nor too slow. He was of good judgment and very temperate in his eating and drinking, and in the movements of his body; for neither anger nor pleasure caused any change in him. He rode very well both on ordinary and combat saddle, he jousted easily and with such skill that no one in all of his Kingdoms did it better. He was a great bird hunter, and a man of good courage, and a hard worker in wars.

He was by nature inclined to do justice, and he was also merciful, and took pity on the unfortunates whom he observed in some affliction. And he had an unusual charm, so that anyone who spoke with him at once loved him and desired to serve him, for he had a friendly manner. His counsel was also sought, especially by the Queen his wife, because she knew his great ability.

From childhood he was brought up in wars, where he underwent many hardships and personal dangers. And since he spent all his income on affairs of war, and was in continual need, we cannot say that he was generous. He was a man of truth, notwithstanding that the great straits into which the wars put him occasionally caused him to equivocate. He enjoyed playing all games, ball and chess and checkers, and he indulged in these somewhat more than he should have; and notwithstanding that he loved very much the Queen his wife, he also gave himself to other women. He was a very cordial person with everyone, especially his personal yeomen. This king conquered and won the kingdom of Granada, as will be seen later in this his Chronicle.

QUEEN ISABEL THE CATHOLIC

This Queen was of average height, of good appearance and well-proportioned, and very fair; her eyes a greenish-blue, her gaze pleasant and demure, the features of her countenance well-placed, and her face very beautiful and cheerful; she was circumspect in her modesty and demeanour; she did not drink wine; she was a very good woman, and was pleased to have about her elderly women who were good and of noble lineage.

She reared ladies of high station in her palace, daughters of the Nobles of her Kingdoms; we do not read in a Chronicle that any other Queen did as much. With great diligence she supervised them and the other women of her palace; she gave them magnificent dowries, and did them great kindnesses to marry them well; she detested evil women. She was very courteous in speech. She possessed such control of her countenance that even at the time of her deliveries she concealed her feelings, and forced herself not to reveal or recite the pain which at that hour women feel and show. She loved the King her husband dearly and watched over him exceedingly. She was a very intelligent and discreet woman, which qualities we rarely see combined in one person; she spoke very well and had such an excellent mind that, though busy with such arduous duties as she bore in the governing of her Kingdoms, she undertook the labour of learning Latin; and in the space of one year she succeeded in learning it so well, that she understood anything spoken or written in Latin.

She was a devout Catholic; she gave secret alms in worthy places; she honoured houses of prayer; she visited with pleasure monasteries and religious abodes, especially those where she knew they led a pure life; she endowed them magnificently. She abhorred violently sorcery and fortune-tellers, and all persons of like artifices and falsehoods. She enjoyed the conversation of religious persons of a pure life, with whom she often held special consultations; and while she listened to the opinions of those people and of other learned folk who were near her, nevertheless in general she made her own decisions. She seemed well-favoured by fortune in matters that she undertook. She was disposed to doing justice, so much so that it was imputed that she followed the stern path rather than that of mercy, and this helped to remedy the great criminal corruption which she found in the kingdom when she ascended to the throne. She desired her pronouncements to be fulfilled diligently. . . .

This Queen is the one who extirpated and eliminated the heresy that existed in the Kingdoms of Castile and Aragon, where some Christians of Jewish lineage were returning to Jewish customs and made them live like good Christians. . . .

Through the solicitude of this Queen there was begun, and through her diligence continued, the war against the Moors, until the entire Kingdom of Granada was won. And we swear that we learned of and knew certain great lords and captains of her kingdoms, who wearying lost all hope of being able to win, considering the great difficulty of continuing the struggle, and through the great perseverance of this Queen, and through her work and diligence which she continually made in the provisions, and through the other efforts which she made with great expense of energy, she brought to a conclusion this conquest, which by divine will she seemed to have undertaken, as will be seen later in this her Chronicle.

SEYMOUR RESNICK

DIEGO DE SAN PEDRO
[c. 1490]

The foremost of the early sentimental novels, Cárcel de amor, appeared in 1492. Its author, Diego de San Pedro, held a minor court position, but little else is known of his life. Widely popular in the sixteenth century—both in Spanish and in translations—Cárcel de amor was rendered into English by Lord Berners in 1533 as 'Castle of Love'.

CASTLE OF LOVE

THE DEATH OF LEREANO

The weeping that Lereano's mother made increased the pain of all them that were present, and always Lereano had Laureola in his remembrance. Of that was passed he had but small memory, and considering that he should toy but a short space with the sight of the two letters that Laureola had sent him, he wist not how to order them; when he thought to break them he thought he should offend thereby Laureola, in casting away such words of so worthy price as was written in them, and when he thought to put into any of his servants' hands, he feared lest they should be seen, whereby peril might follow. Then in all these doubts he took the surest way. He called for a cup of water, and then brake the letters into small pieces, and so sat up in his bed, and drank up the water with the pieces of the letters. And so he satisfied thereby his will. And therewith gave up his life in witness of his true faith.

Then what sorrow I felt and what I did is lightly judged, the weepings that was there made of his death, are of such esteem, that methink it cruelty to write it. Then his obsequies and burials were done most honourably, according to the desserts of his virtues. And as for myself, with a better will I would have departed this life than to have tarried on the earth alive. So with sighs I went my way, and departed with weeping and with lamentation. . . .

JOHN BOURCHIER, LORD BERNERS

FERNANDO DE ROJAS
[1465?–1541?]

Next to Don Quixote, *the greatest work in all Spanish literature is the extraordinary dramatized novel by Fernando de Rojas,* La Celestina. *The work first appeared in 1499 as the* Comedia de Calisto y Melibea, *in sixteen acts. Later editions bore the title* Tragicomedia de Calisto y Melibea *and contained twenty-one acts. It is universally known, however, by the name of the principal character, Celestina, the cynical and avaricious 'go-between'.*

Beyond the fact that he was a converted Jewish lawyer, there exists almost no biographical data on Rojas himself. Indeed, many scholars have questioned his authorship of the tragicomedy, although an acrostic in the work names him as the author, and he was further identified as such in the records of an Inquisition trial of the period. Critics now generally agree, however, that Fernando de Rojas wrote most—if not all—of La Celestina.

In any case, its popularity and influence were immense; the work inspired a flood of imitations, adaptations and translations.

The argumento *relates briefly the simple plot: an illicit love affair between two young people of aristocratic background, Calisto and Melibea, which is brought to consummation and tragedy by the wiles of Celestina. The greatness of the book lies in the masterly delineation of its characters both major and minor; its vivid and powerful style; and most of all in the brilliant interplay between two spheres—that of the noble and idealistic lovers with the vulgar, realistic world of Celestina and her cohorts.*

LA CELESTINA

THE ARGUMENT

Calisto, who was of lineage noble, of wit singular, of disposition gentle, of behaviour sweet, with many graceful qualities richly endowed, and of a competent estate, fell in love with *Melibea*, of years young, of blood noble, of estate great, and only daughter and heir to her father *Pleberio* and to her mother *Alisa*, of both exceedingly beloved. Whose chaste purpose conquered by the hot pursuit of amorous *Calisto*, *Celestina* interposing herself in the business, a wicked and crafty woman, and together with her two deluded servants of subdued *Calisto*, and by her wrought to be disloyal, their fidelity being taken with the hook of covetousness and pleasure,—those lovers came, and those that served them, to a wretched and unfortunate end. For entrance whereunto, adverse fortune afforded a fit and opportune place, where, to the presence of *Calisto*, the desired *Melibea* presented herself.

... **ACT I**

CALISTO. Sempronio?

SEMPRONIO. Sir.

CALISTO. Reach me that lute.

SEMPRONIO. Sir, here it is.

CALISTO. Tell me what grief so great can be
    As to equal my misery.

SEMPRONIO. This lute, sir, is out of tune.

CALISTO. How shall he tune it, who himself is out of tune? Or how canst thou hear harmony from him who is at such discord with himself? Or how can he do anything well, whose will is not obedient to reason? Who harbours in his breast needles, peace, war, truce, love, hate, injuries and suspicions; and all these at once and from one and the same cause. Do thou therefore take this lute unto thee, and sing me the most doleful ditty thou canst devise.

SEMPRONIO. Nero from Tarpey doth behold
    How Rome doth burn all on a flame;
    He hears the cries of young and old,
    Yet is not grieved at the same.

CALISTO. My fire is far greater and less her pity, whom now I speak of.

SEMPRONIO. I was not deceived when I said my master had lost his wits.

CALISTO. What's that, Sempronio, thou mutterest to thyself?

SEMPRONIO. Nothing, sir, not I.

CALISTO. Tell me what thou saidst : be not afraid.

SEMPRONIO. Marry I said, how can that fire be greater which but tormenteth one living man than that which burnt such a city as that was and such a multitude of men?

CALISTO. How? I shall tell thee. Greater is that flame which lasteth fourscore years than that which endureth but one day, and greater that fire which burneth one soul than that which burneth an hundred thousand bodies. See what difference there is betwixt apparencies and existencies, betwixt painted shadows and lively substances, betwixt that which is counterfeit and that which is real; so great a difference is there betwixt that fire which thou speakest of and that which burneth me.

SEMPRONIO. I see, I did not mistake my bias, which, for aught I perceive, runs worse and worse. Is it not enough to shew thyself a fool, but thou must also speak profanely?

CALISTO. Did not I tell thee, when thou speakest, that thou shouldest speak aloud? Tell me what's that thou mumblest to thyself.

SEMPRONIO. Only I doubted of what religion your lovers are.

CALISTO. I am a Melibean, I adore Melibea, I believe in Melibea, and I love Melibea.

SEMPRONIO. My master is all Melibea : who now but Melibea? whose heart not able to contain her, like a boiling vessel venting its heat, goes bubbling her name in his mouth. Well, I have now as much as I desire : I know on which foot you halt, I shall now heal you.

CALISTO. Thou speakest of matters beyond the moon. It is impossible.

SEMPRONIO. O, sir, exceeding easy; for the first recovery of sickness is the discovery of the disease.

CALISTO. What counsel can order that which in itself hath neither counsel nor order?

SEMPRONIO. Ha, ha, ha, Calisto's fire! these, his intolerable pains! as if love had bent his bow, shot all his arrows only against him. Oh Cupid, how high and unsearchable are thy mysteries! What reward hast thou ordained for love, since that so necessary a tribulation attends on lovers? Thou hast set his bounds as marks for men to wonder at : lovers ever deeming, that they only are cast behind, and that others still outstrip them, that all men break through but themselves, like your light-footed bulls, which being let loose in the place, and galled with darts, take over the bars as soon as they feel themselves pricked.

CALISTO. Sempronio.

SEMPRONIO. Sir.

CALISTO. Do not you go away.

SEMPRONIO. This pipe sounds in another tune.

CALISTO. What dost thou think of my malady?

SEMPRONIO. That you love Melibea.

CALISTO. And nothing else?

SEMPRONIO. It is misery enough to have a man's will captivated and chained to one place only.

CALISTO. Thou wot'st not what constancy is.

SEMPRONIO. Perseverance in ill is not constancy, but obstinacy or pertinacy, so they call it in my country; however it please you philosophers of Cupid to phrase it.

CALISTO. It is a foul fault for a man to belie that which he preacheth to others : for thou thyself takest pleasure in praising thy Elicia.

SEMPRONIO. Do you that good which I say, but not that ill which I do.

CALISTO. Why dost thou reprove me?

SEMPRONIO. Because thou dost subject the dignity and worthiness of a man to the imperfection and weakness of a frail woman.

CALISTO. A woman? O thou blockhead, she's a goddess.

SEMPRONIO. Are you in earnest, or do you but jest?

CALISTO. Jest? I verily believe she is a goddess.

SEMPRONIO. As goddesses were of old, that is to fall below mortality, and then you would hope to have a share in her deity.

CALISTO. A pox on thee for a fool, thou makest me laugh, which I thought not to do today.

SEMPRONIO. What, would you weep all the days of your life?

CALISTO. Yes.

SEMPRONIO. And why?

CALISTO. Because I love her, before whom I find myself so unworthy, that I have no hope to obtain her.

. . .

SEMPRONIO. . . . Do not you despair; myself will take this business in hand, not doubting but to accomplish your desire.

CALISTO. Jove grant thou mayest : howsoever, I am proud to hear thee, though hopeless of ever obtaining it.

SEMPRONIO. Nay, I will assure it you.

CALISTO. Heav'n be thy good speed; my cloth of gold doublet, which I wore yesterday, it is thine, Sempronio. Take it to thee.

SEMPRONIO. I thank you for this, and for many more which you shall give me. My jesting hath turn'd to my good. I hitherto have the better of it. And if my master clap such spurs to my sides, and give me such good encouragements, I doubt not but I shall bring her to his bed. This which my master hath given me is a good wheel to bring the business about : for without reward it is impossible to go well through with anything.

CALISTO. See you be not negligent now.

SEMPRONIO. Nay, be not you negligent; for it is impossible that a careless master should make a diligent servant.

CALISTO. But tell me, how dost thou think to purchase her pity?

SEMPRONIO. I shall tell you. It is now a good while ago, since at the lower end of this street I fell acquainted with an old bearded woman called Celestina, a witch, subtle as the devil, and well practised in all the rogueries and villainies that the world can afford, one who in my conscience hath marred and made up again a hundred thousand maidenheads in this city : such a power and such authority she hath, what by her persuasions and other her cunning devices, that none can escape her : she will move hard rocks, if she list, and at her pleasure provoke them to luxury.

CALISTO. O that I might but speak with her !

SEMPRONIO. I will bring her hither unto you; and therefore prepare yourself for it, and when she comes, in any case use her kindly, be frank and liberal with her; and whilst I go my ways, do you study and devise with yourself, to express your pains as well as, I know, she is able to give you remedy.

CALISTO. O but thou stayest too long.

SEMPRONIO. I am gone, sir.

CALISTO. A good luck with thee ! You happy powers that predominate human actions, assist and be propitious to my desires, second my intentions, prosper Sempronio's proceedings and his success, in bringing me such an advocatrix as shall, according to his promise, not only negotiate, but absolutely compass and bring to a wished period the preconceived hopes of an incomparable pleasure.

. . .

ACT IV

CELESTINA. Now that I am all alone, I will, as I walk by myself, weigh and consider that which Sempronio feared concerning my travail in this business. For those things which are not well weighed and considered, though sometimes they take good effect, yet commonly fall out ill, so that much speculation brings forth much good fruit. For, although I dissembled with him and did set a good face on the matter, it may be that, if my drift and intent should chance to be found out by Melibea's father, it would cost me little less than my life : or at least, if they should not kill me, I should rest much impaired in my credit, either by their tossing me in a blanket, or by causing me to be cruelly whipped, so that my sweet meats shall have sour sauce, and my hundred crowns in gold be purchased at too dear a rate. Ay, wretched me ! into what a labyrinth have I put myself? What a trap am I like to fall into through mine own folly? For that I might shew myself solicitous and resolute, I have put myself upon the hazard of the dice. Woe is me ! What shall I do? To go back is not for my profit, and to go on stands not with my safety. Shall I persist; Or shall I desist? In what a strait am I? In what a doubtful and strange perplexity? I know not which I were best to choose. On my daringness dependeth manifest danger, on my cowardice shameful damage. Which way shall the ox go, but he must needs plough? Every way, go which way I will, discovers to my eyes deep and dangerous furrows, desperate downfalls; if I be taken in the mainour, if the theft be found about me, I shall be either killed, or carted with a paper crown set upon my head, having my fault written in great text-letters. But in case I should not go, what will Sempronio then say? 'Is this all thou canst do? Thy power, thy wisdom, thy stoutness, thy courage, thy large promises, thy fair offers, thy tricks, thy subtleties, and the great care forsooth thou wouldest take; what? are they all come to this?' And his master Calisto, what will he say? What will he do? Or what will he think? Save only this, that there is much deceit in my steps, and that I have discovered this plot to Pleberio, like a prevaricating sophistress or cunning ambidexter, playing the traitor on both sides, that I might gain by both? And if he do not entertain so hateful a thought, he will rail upon me like a madman; he will upbraid me to my face with most reproachful terms; he will propose a thousand inconveniences, which my hasty deliberation was the cause of, saying, 'Out, you old whore; why didst thou increase my passions with thy promises? False bawd as thou art, for all the world besides thy feet can walk, for me only thy tongue; others can have works, I only words. Others can have remedy at thy hands; I only the man that must endure torment. To all others thy force can extend itself; and to me is it only wanting. To all others thou art light, to me darkness. Out, thou old treacherous, disloyal wretch; why didst

thou offer thyself and service unto me? For it was thy offer that
did put me in hope : and that hope did delay my death, prolonged
my life, and did put upon me the title of a glad man. Now, for
that thy promises have not proved effectual, neither shalt thou
want punishment, nor I woeful despair.' So that, look I on which
side I will (miserable woman that I am), it is ill here, and it is ill
there; pain and grief on either hand : but when extremes shall
want their mean, and no means to avoid either the one or the
other, of two evils it is the wiser course to incline to the lesser. And
therefore I had rather offend Pleberio than displease Calisto. Well
then, I will go. For greater will my shame be, to be condemned
for a coward, than my punishment, in daring to accomplish what
I promised. Besides Fortune still friendeth those that are bold and
valiant. Lo, yonder's the gate; I have seen myself in greater danger
than this in my days. Coraggio, coraggio, Celestina; be of good
cheer; be not dismayed : for there are never suitors wanting for
the mitigating and allaying of punishment. All divinations are in
my favour and shew themselves propitious in my proceedings;
or else I am nobody in this my art, a mere bungler, an idiot, an
ass. Of four men that I met by the way three of them were
Johns; whereof two were cuckolds. The first word that I heard
passing along the street, was a love complaint. I have not stumbled
since I came forth, as at other times I used to do. Methinks the
very stones of the street did sunder themselves one from another
to give me way as I passed. Nor did the skirts of my clothes rumple
up in troublesome folds to hinder my feet. Nor do I feel any faintness or weariness in my legs. Every one saluteth me. Not a dog
that hath once barked at me; I have neither seen any bird of a
black feather, neither thrush nor crow, nor any other of the like
unlucky nature; and, which is a better sign of good luck than all
these, yonder do I see Lucrecia standing at Melibea's gate, which
is kinswoman to Elicia; it cannot but go well with us; it is
impossible we should miss of our purpose; all is cock-sure.
. . .

MELIBEA. . . . Tell, me, mother, art thou not Celestina, that dwelt
in Tanners' Row near the river?
CELESTINA. Even the very same.
MELIBEA. By my fay, you are an old woman. Well, I see it is a
true saying that days go not away in vain. Now (never trust me)
I did not know you; neither should I, had it not been for
that slash over your face; then were you fair, now wonderfully
altered.
LUCRECIA. She changed? Hi, hi, hi! the devil she is : she was fair

when she met with him (saving your reverence) that scotched her over the nose.

MELIBEA. What sayest thou, fool? Speak, what is't thou sayest? What laughest thou at?

LUCRECIA. As though I did not know Mother Celestina!

CELESTINA. Madame, take you hold on time, that it slip not from you. As for my complexion, that will never change : have you not read what they say, the day will come, when thou shalt not know thyself in a glass? Though I am now grown grey before my time, and seem double the years I am of, of four daughters which my mother had, myself was the youngest. And, therefore, I am sure, I am not so old as you take me to be.

MELIBEA. Friend Celestina, I am very glad both to see and know thee; and I have taken great pleasure in thy discourse. Here, take your money and farewell; for thou lookest, poor soul, as if thou hadst eaten nothing all this day.

CELESTINA. O more than mortal image! O precious pearl! How truly have you guessed! Oh! with what a grace do thy words come from thee! I am ravished hearing thee speak. But yet it is not only eating, that maintaineth a man or woman, especially me, who used to be fasting a whole, nay, two days together, in soliciting other folk's business. For I intend no other thing, my whole life is nothing else, but to do good offices for the good, and if occasion serve, to die for them. And it was evermore my fashion rather to seek trouble to myself by serving of others, than to please and content myself. Wherefore, if you will give me leave, I will tell you the necessitated cause of my coming, which is another manner of matter than any you have yet heard; and such as we were all undone, if I should return in vain, and you not know it.

MELIBEA. Acquaint me, mother, with all your necessities and wants, and if I can help you in them or do you any good, I shall willingly do it, as well out of our old acquaintance as out of neighbourhood, which in good and honest minds is a sufficient bond to tie them thereunto.

CELESTINA. My wants, madame? My necessities do you mean? Nay, others', as I told you, not mine. For mine own, I pass at home with myself in mine own house without letting the whole country to know them; eating when I may, and drinking when I can get it. For, for all my poverty, I never wanted a penny to buy me bread, nor a *quart*, that is the eighth part of sixpence, to send for wine, no not in all this time of my widowhood. For before, I never took thought for any, but had always a good vessel still in my house. And when one was empty another was full. I never went to bed, but I did first eat a toast well steeped in wine, and two dozen of draughts, sipping still the wine after every sop, for fear of the mother, wherewith I was then wont to be troubled. But now that I husband all things myself and am at mine own finding, I am fain to fetch my wine in a little poor jar, which will scarce hold a pottle. And sometimes in punishment of my sins (which cross I am willing to bear) I am forced to go six times a day with these my silver hairs about my shoulders, to fill and fetch my wine myself at the tavern. Nor would I by my goodwill die, till I see myself have a good rundlet or tierce of mine own within mine own doors. For, on my life, there is no provision in the world like unto it. For, as the saying is, it is bread and wine, not the young man that is spruce and fine, that makes us rid the way, and travel with mettle; yet let me tell you that, where the good man is missing, all other good is wanting. For ill does the spindle move, when the beard does not wag above. And this I thought good to tell you by the way upon those speeches, which I used concerning others', and not mine own necessities.

MELIBEA. Ask what thou wilt, be it either for thyself or anybody else, whom it pleaseth thee.

CELESTINA. My most gracious and courteous lady, descended of high and noble parentage, your sweet words and cheerful gesture, accompanied with that kind and free proffer, gives boldness to my tongue, to speak what my heart even longeth to utter. I come lately from one, whom I left sick to the death, who only with one word, which should come from your noble mouth, and entrusted in this my bosom to carry it hence with me—I verily assure myself it will save his life, so great is the devotion which he bears to your gentle disposition, and the comfort he would receive by this so great a kindness.

MELIBEA. Good woman, I understand thee not, unless thou deliver thy mind unto me in plain terms. On the one side thou dost anger me and provoke me to displeasure; on the other thou dost move and stir me to compassion. Neither know I how to return thee a convenient answer, because I have not fully comprehended thy meaning; I should think myself happy, if my words might carry that force, as to save the life of any man, though never so mean. For to do good is to be like unto the Deity. Besides he that doth a benefit, receives it, when it is done to a person that desires it. And he that can cure one that is sick, not doing it is guilty of his death; and therefore give not over thy petition, but proceed and fear nothing.

CELESTINA. All fear fled, fair lady, in beholding your beauty. For

I cannot be persuaded that Nature did paint in vain one face fairer than another, more enriched with grace and favour, more fashionable and more beautiful than another, were it not to make them magazines of virtue, mansions of mercy, houses of compassion and pity, ministers of her blessings, and dispensers of those good gifts and graces, which in her bounty she hath bestowed upon them, and upon yourself in a more plentiful manner. Besides, sithence we are all mortal and born to die, as also, that it is most certain that he cannot be said truly to be born, who is only born for himself—for then should men be like unto brute beasts, if not worse, amongst which there are some, that are very pitiful : as your unicorn of whom it is reported that he will humble and prostrate himself at the feet of a virgin; and your dog, for all his fierceness and cruelness of nature, when he comes to bite another, if he throw himself down at his feet, he will let him alone and do him no harm; and this is all out of pity. Again, to come to your birds and fowls of the air, your cock eateth not anything, but he first calleth his hens about him and gives them part of his feeding. The pelican with her beak breaketh up her own breast, that she may give her very bowels and entrails to her young ones to eat. The storks maintain their aged parents as long in the nest, as they did give them food, when they were young and unable to help themselves. Now, if God and Nature gave such knowledge unto beasts and birds, why should we that are men, be more cruel one to another? Why give we not part of our graces and of our persons to our neighbours? Especially when they are involved and afflicted with secret infirmities, and those such that, where the medicine is, thence was the cause of the malady?

MELIBEA. For God's love, without any more dilating tell me who is this sick man, who feeling such great perplexity, hath both his sickness and his cure, flowing from one and the selfsame fountain.

CELESTINA. You cannot choose, lady, but know a young gentleman in this city, nobly descended, whose name is Calisto.

MELIBEA. Enough, enough! no more, good old woman! not a word, not a word more, I would advise you! Is this the sick patient, for whom thou hast made so many prefaces to come to thy purpose? For what or whom camest thou hither? Camest thou to seek thy death? Knowest thou for whom, thou bearded impudent, thou hast trodden these dangerous steps? What ails this wicked one, that thou pleadest for him with such passion? He is fool-sick, is he not? Is he in his wits, I trow? What wouldst thou have thought, if thou shouldst have found me without some suspicion and jealousy of this fool? What a windlass hast thou fetched, with what words hast thou come upon me? I see it is not said in vain that the most hurtful member in a man or woman is the tongue. I will have thee burned, thou false witch, thou enemy to honesty, thou causeress of secret errors; fie upon thee, filth! Lucrecia, out of my sight with her, send her packing; away with her, I pray, she makes me ready to swoon; ay me, I faint, I die; she hath not left me one drop of blood in my body! But I well deserve this and more, for giving ear to such a paltry housewife as she is. Believe me, were it not that I regarded mine honour, and that I am unwilling to publish to the world his presumptuous audaciousness and boldness, I would so handle thee, thou accursed hag, that thy discourse and thy life should have ended both together.

CELESTINA. In an ill hour came I hither, if my spells and conjuration fail me. Go to, go to; I wot well enough to whom I speak. This poor gentleman, this your brother is at the point of death and ready to die.

MELIBEA. Darest thou yet speak before me and mutter words between thy teeth, for to augment my anger and double thy punishment? Wouldst thou have me soil mine honour, for to give life to a fool, to a madman? Shall I make myself sad to make him merry? Wouldst thou thrive by my loss? And reap profit by my perdition? And receive remuneration by my error? Wouldst thou have me overthrow and ruin my father's house and honour, for to raise that of such an old rotten bawd as thou art? Dost thou think I do not perceive thy drift? That I do not track thee step by step? Or that I understand not thy damnable errand? But I assure thee, the reward that thou shalt get thereby, shall be no other, save, that I may take from thee all occasion of farther offending heaven, to give an end to thy evil days. Tell me, traitor as thou art, how didst thou dare to proceed so far with me?

CELESTINA. My fear of you, madame, doth interrupt my excuse; but my innocency puts new courage into me : your presence again disheartens me, in seeing you so angry. But that which grieves and troubles me most, is that I receive displeasure without any reason, and am hardly thought on without a cause. Give me leave, good lady, to make an end of my speech, and then will you neither blame it nor condemn me : then will you see that I rather seek to do good service, than endeavour any dishonest course; and that I do it more to add health to the patient, than to detract anything from the fame and worth of the physician. And had I thought that your ladyship would so easily have made this bad construction out of your late noxious suspicion, your licence should not have been sufficient warrant to have emboldened me to speak anything, that might concern Calisto, or any other man living.

MELIBEA. Let me hear no more of this madman, name not this fool unto me; this leaper over walls; this hobgoblin; this night-walker; this fantastical spirit; long-shanked, like a stork; in shape and proportion, like a picture in arras, that is ill-wrought; or an ill-favoured fellow in an old suit of hangings; say no more of him, unless you would have me to fall down dead where I stand! This is he who saw me the other day, and began to court me with I know not what extravagant phrases, as if he had not been well in his wits, professing himself to be a great gallant. Tell him, good old woman, if he think that I was wholly his and that he had won the field, because it pleased me rather to consent to his folly than correct his fault, and yield to his errand than chastise his error, that I was willing rather to let him go like a fool as he came than to publish this his presumptuous enterprise. Moreover, advise him that the next way to have his sickness leave him is to leave off his loving, and wholly to relinquish his purpose, if he purpose to impart health to himself; which if he refuse to do, tell him from me, that he never bought words all the days of his life at a dearer rate. Besides, I would have him know that no man is overcome, but he that thinks himself so to be. So shall I live secure, and be contented. But it is evermore the nature of fools, to think others like themselves. Return thou with this very answer unto him; for other answer of me shall he none, nor never hope for any : for it is but in vain to entreat mercy of him, of whom thou canst not have mercy. And for thine own part, thou mayest thank God, that thou scapest hence scot-free; I have heard enough of you heretofore and of all your good qualities, though it was not my hap to know you.

CELESTINA. Troy stood out more stoutly, and held out longer. And many fiercer dames have I tamed in my days. Tush! No storm lasteth long.

MELIBEA. You mine enemy, what say you? Speak out, I pray, that I may hear you. Hast thou anything to say in thy excuse, whereby thou mayest satisfy my anger, and clear thyself of this thy error and bold attempt?

CELESTINA. Whilst your choler lives, my cause must needs die. And the longer your anger lasteth, the less shall my excuse be heard. But I wonder not that you should be thus rigorous with me : for a little heat will serve to set young blood a-boiling.

MELIBEA. Little heat, say you? Indeed thou mayest well say little; because thyself yet lives, whilst I with grief endure thy great

presumption. What words canst thou demand of me for such a one
as he is, that may stand with my good? Answer to my demand,
because thou sayest thou hast not yet concluded. And perhaps
thou mayest pacify me for that which is past.

CELESTINA. Marry, a certain charm, madame, which as he is informed by many of his good friends, your ladyship hath, which
cureth the toothache; as also that same admirable girdle of yours,
which is reported to have been found and brought from Cumae
the cave there, and was worn, 'tis thought, by the Sibylla or
prophetess of that place; which girdle, they say, hath such a
singular and peculiar property and power, with the very touch to
abate and ease any ache or anguish whatsoever. Now this gentleman I told you of, is exceedingly pained with the toothache, and
even at death's door with it. And this was the true cause of my
coming : but since it was my ill hap to receive so harsh and un-
pleasing an answer, let him still for me continue in his pain, as a
punishment due unto him for sending so unfortunate a messenger.
For since in that muchness of your virtue I have found much of
your pity wanting, I fear me he would also want water, should he
send me to the sea to fetch it. And you know, sweet lady, that the
delight of vengeance and pleasure of revenge endureth but a
moment, but that of pity and compassion continueth for ever and
ever.

MELIBEA. If this be that thou wouldst have, why didst thou not
tell me of it sooner? Why wentest thou about the bush with me?
What needed all those circumstances? Or why didst thou not
deliver it in other words?

CELESTINA. Because my plain and simple meaning made me
believe that, though I should have proposed it in any other words
whatsoever, had they been worse than they were, yet would you
not have suspected any evil in them. For, if I were failing in the
fitness of my preface and did not use so due and convenient a
preamble as I should have done, it was because truth needeth no
colours. The very compassion that I had of his pain, and the confidence of your magnificency did choke in my mouth, when I first
began to speak, the expression of the cause. And for that you
know, lady, that sorrow works turbation, and turbation doth disorder and alter the tongue, which ought always to be tied to the
brain, for heaven's love, lay not the fault on me; and if he hath
committed an error, let not that redound to my hurt; for I am no
farther blameable of any fault, than as I am the messenger of the
faulty. Break not the rope where it is weakest. Be not like the cobweb, which never shows its force but on poor little flies. No human

law condemns the father for the son's offence, nor the son for the father's : nor indeed, lady, is it any reason, that his presumption should occasion my perdition; though considering his desert, I should not greatly care that he should be the delinquent and myself be condemned, since that I have no other trade to live by, save to serve such as he is; this is my occupation, this I make my happiness. Yet withal, madame, I would have you to conceive, that it was never in my desire to hurt one, to help another, though behind my back your ladyship hath perhaps been otherwise informed of me. But the best is, it is not the vain breath of the vulgar that can blast the truth; assuredly I mean nothing in this, but only plain and honest dealing. I do little harm to any; I have as few enemies in this city, as a woman can have : I keep my word with all men; and what I undertake, I perform as faithfully as if I had twenty feet and so many hands.

MELIBEA. I now wonder not that your ancients were wont to say that one only teacher of vice was sufficient to mar a great city. For I have heard such and so many tales of thy false and cunning tricks, that I know not whether I may believe thy errand was for this charm.

CELESTINA. Never let me pray, or if I pray, let me never be heard, if you can draw any other thing from me, though I were to be put to a thousand torments !

MELIBEA. My former late anger will not give me leave to laugh at thy excuse. For I wot very well that neither oath nor torment shall make thee to speak the truth. For it is not in thy power to do it.

CELESTINA. You are my good lady and mistress, you may say what you list, and it is my duty to hold my peace; you must command, and I must obey, but your rough language, I hope, will cost your ladyship an old petticoat.

MELIBEA. And well hast thou deserved it.

CELESTINA. If I have not gained it with my tongue, I hope I have not lost it with my intention.

MELIBEA. Thou dost so confidently plead thy ignorance, that thou makest me almost ready to believe thee; yet will I in this thy so doubtful an excuse hold my sentence in suspense, and will not dispose of thy demand upon the relish of so light an interpretation. Neither for all this would I have thee to think much of it, nor make it any such wonder that I was so exceedingly moved; for two things did concur in thy discourse, the least of which was sufficient to make me run out of my wits. First, in naming this gentleman unto me, who thus presumed to talk with me : then, that thou shouldst entreat me for him, without any further cause given; which could not but engender a strong suspicion of hurt to my honour. But since all is well meant and no harm intended, I pardon all that is past; for my heart is now somewhat lightened, sithence it is a pious and a holy work to cure the sick and help the distressed.

CELESTINA. Ay, and so sick, madame, and so distressed, that, did you know it as well as I, you would not judge him the man, which in your anger you have censured him to be. By my fay, the poor gentleman hath no gall at all, no ill meaning in his heart. He is endued with thousands of graces; for bounty he is an Alexander; for strength an Hector; he has the presence of a prince; he is fair in his carriage, sweet in his behaviour, and pleasant in his conversation; there is no melancholy or other bad humour, that reigneth in him; nobly descended, as yourself well knows; a great tilter; and to see him in his armour, it becomes him so well, that you would take him to be another Saint George. Hercules had not that force and courage as he hath; his deportment, his person, his feature, his disposition, his agility and activeness of body, had need of another manner of tongue to express it than mine. Take him all together and for all in all, you shall not find such another; and for admired form, a miracle : and I am verily persuaded that that fair and gentle Narcissus, who was enamoured with his own proper beauty, when, as in a glass, he viewed himself in the water, was nothing so fair as he, whom now one poor tooth with the extremity of its pain doth so torment, that he doth nothing but complain.

MELIBEA. The age, I pray, how long hath he had it?

CELESTINA. His age, madame? Marry, I think he is about some three and twenty. For here stands she, who saw him born, and took him up from his mother's feet.

MELIBEA. This is not that which I ask thee; nor do I care to know his age. I ask thee how long he hath been troubled with his toothache?

CELESTINA. Some eight days, madame, but you would think he had had it a year, he is grown so weak with it, and the greatest ease and best remedy he hath, is to take his viol, whereto he sings so many songs, and in such doleful notes, that I verily believe they did far exceed those which that great emperor and musician Hadrian composed concerning the soul's departure from the body, the better to endure without dismayment his approaching death. For, though I have but little skill in music, methinks he makes the viol, when he plays thereon, to speak; and when he sings thereunto, the birds with a better will listen unto him than to that musician of old, which made the trees and stones to move. Had he been born then, Orpheus had lost his prey. Weigh then with yourself, sweet lady, if such a poor old woman as I am, have not cause to count myself happy, if I may give life unto him, to whom the heavens have given so many graces? Not a woman that sees him, but praiseth Nature's workmanship, whose hand did draw so perfect a piece; and, if it be their hap to talk with him, they are no more mistresses of themselves, but are wholly at his disposing; and of commanders, desire to be commanded by him. Wherefore, seeing I have so great reason to do for him, conceive, good lady, my purpose to be fair and honest, my courses commendable and free from suspicion and jealousy.

MELIBEA. O how I am fallen out with mine own impatience! How angry with myself that, he being ignorant and thou innocent of any intended ill, thou hast endured the distemperature of my enraged tongue! But the great reason I had for it, frees me from any fault of offence, urged thereunto by thy suspicious speeches : but in requital of thy sufferance, I will forthwith fulfil thy request and likewise give thee my girdle. And, because I have not the leisure to write the charm, till my mother comes home, if this will not serve the turn, come secretly for it tomorrow morning.

LUCRECIA. Now, now, is my mistress quite undone. All the world cannot save her; she will have Celestina come secretly tomorrow. I smell a rat; there is a pad in the straw; I like not this *como secretly tomorrow*; I fear me she will part with something more than words. . . .

JAMES MABBE

AMADÍS DE GAULA
[1508]

The most famous of all the old Spanish novels of chivalry, Amadís de Gaula, was published in 1508, but was probably written more than a century earlier. Its heroic, fantastic and supernatural adventures so fascinated sixteenth-century readers that the success of Amadís gave rise to countless imitations, far inferior to the original. In chapter 6 of Don Quixote, Cervantes consigns almost all books of chivalry to the flames, but spares Amadís as the first and best of its kind.

The following selection is taken from the Robert Southey version of the book. While not a literal translation—Southey greatly condensed and simplified—it does impart some of the 'blood and thunder' flavour of the original Amadís de Gaula.

AMADIS OF GAUL

THE TRIALS OF AMADIS IN DEFENCE OF A DAMSEL

Such speed made Amadis, that, having overthrown the Knight who would have known whither he went, he overtook him who misused the Damsel, and cried to him, Sir Knight, you have been committing great wrong : I pray you do so no more—What wrong? —The shamefullest that could be devised, in striking that Damsel. —And you are come to chastise me?—Not so : but to counsel you for your own good. It will be more for your's to turn back as you came, said the Knight. Thereat was Amadis angered : and he went to the Squire and said, let go the Damsel, or thou diest! and the Squire in fear put her down. Sir Knight, you shall dearly abide this, quoth his master. Amadis answered, we shall see! and ran his career and drove him from his saddle, and was about to ride over him, but he cried for mercy!—Swear then never to wrong Dame or Damsel! And, as he approached to receive the oath, the traitor stabbed his horse. Amadis recovered from the fall, and with one blow paid him for the treason.

The Damsel then besought him to compleat his courtesy by accompanying her to a castle whither she was going. He took the horse of the slain, and they went on together. . . . About midnight they came to a river-side, and, because the Damsel would fain sleep, they stopt. Amadis spread Gandalin's cloak for her bed, and he laid his head upon his helmet, and they all slept. There came up a Knight as they were sleeping, and he seeing the Damsel, gently wakened her with the end of his lance. She seeing an armed Knight, thought it was Amadis, and said, do you wish us to depart? He answered, it is time! In God's name then, quoth she; and, being still drowsy, she suffered the stranger to place her before him; but then recollecting, what is this? she cried : the Squire should have carried me. And when she saw it was a stranger, she shrieked out and called to Amadis, let not a stranger carry me off! But the Knight clapt spurs to his horse, and galloped away. Amadis awoke at her voice, and called to Gandalin for his horse, and pursued full speed till he entered a thicket and lost the track. Then albeit he were the mildest Knight in the world; he was sorely wroth against himself. The Damsel may well report, thought he, that I have done her as much wrong as succour; for, if I saved her from one ravisher, I have suffered her to be stolen by another. So he rode about, wearying his horse, till at length he heard a horn, and followed the sound, and came to a strong Castle set upon a hill, walled high, and with strong towers, and the gate was shut. The watchman saw him, and called out to know what man was there at such an hour, and what he sought. A Knight, quoth Amadis, who hath stolen a Damsel from me.—We have seen none such. Then Amadis went round the Castle, and in another part he found an open postern, and saw the Knight on foot, and his men unsaddling the horse, who could not else pass through. Stop, Sir Knight, quoth Amadis, and tell me if you have taken my Damsel?—You took no care to keep her.—You stole her from me in a way neither courteous nor knightly. Friend! quoth the Knight, she came with me by her own will; I offered her no force, and here I have her. Shew me the Damsel, said Amadis, and, if she says the same, I will rest contented.—To-morrow you shall see her, here within, if you will enter upon the custom of the Castle.— What is the custom?—I will not now tell you, for it is night: if you wait till morning you may know. And he then shut the postern. So Amadis passed the remainder of the night under the trees.

When the sun was up he saw the gate open, and riding up to it saw an armed Knight in the gateway, and the porter with him, who asked Amadis if he would enter? Why have I tarried here else? answered Amadis. First then, said the Porter, you must hear our custom that you may not complain of it hereafter: if you enter here, you must do combat with this Knight, and if he get the victory you must swear to obey the command of the Lady of this Castle, otherwise you will be cast into a miserable prison; if the victory be yours, you will find two other Knights at the next gate, and farther in three more; with all these you must fight under the same condition; but, if you bear away the honour in these attempts, not only will it be great renown of prowess, but right shall be done in whatsoever you demand. Dear terms! cried Amadis: but I must see the Damsel. The first champion en- countered him to his cost. Amadis held his lance to him as he lay on the ground, yield or die! The Knight cried, mercy! and shewed a broken arm: then he of Gaul rode on. The two who kept the next pass ran at him; the one missed his blow, the other he drove down, all stunned, breaking his lance in his shield; then, with the truncheon of the lance, he smote the one who was on horseback, so that the helmet came off: both drew their swords. Knight, quoth Amadis, it is folly to continue the combat bareheaded! Look to thine own head! was the answer; but Amadis staggered him with one stroke, then with the side of the sword struck his head as he was reeling. Knight, it had been gone, if I had laid on with the edge! And after this victory he past on.

There within he saw Dames and Damsels on the wall, and heard them say, if this Knight pass the bridge in despite of the three, he will have done a most rare feat of chivalry. Presently there came out three Knights, well armed on goodly coursers; yield, said they, or swear to perform our Lady's will. I am not yet won, quoth Amadis; and for the Lady's will, I know not what it may be. With that there began a fierce battle, for the three of the Castle were hardy Knights, practised in arms, and he whom they encountered was not one that would leave off with shame. Amadis so displayed himself, that his antagonists, no longer able for many wounds and great loss of blood to sustain him, took to flight. The one he overtook and made him yield, the other twain he followed into the hall; there stood at the door thereof about twenty Dames and Damsels, and the fairest of them all said to him, hold, Sir Knight, you have done enough. Lady, let them own themselves vanquished.—Wherefore? how have they wronged you?—I was told to slay or conquer them before I could obtain my demand.— They told you if you could penetrate here by force you should obtain it: say then what you would have.—A Damsel, whom a Knight stole from me while I slept, and has brought hither. I pray you, Sir, replied the Lady, rest while I send for the Knight to answer you. . . .

While they were thus devising there came in another Knight, large limbed and strong, compleatly armed, except his head and hands. Sir Knight, quoth he to Amadis, they tell me you claim a Damsel whom I brought here: I did not force her from you; she chose to come with me, rather than remain with you, therefore it is no reason that I should resign her.—Shew me then the Damsel.—It is no reason that I should; if you say otherwise, I am ready to do battle. Now the name of this Knight was Gasinan, Uncle to Grovenesa, the Lady of the Castle; and she, who loved him the best of all his kin, and was altogether governed by his counsel, for he was the best knight of his race, said to him, I pray you, Uncle, forbear this difference. . . . Niece, quoth Gasinan, . . . so help me God, as I will not give up the Damsel! They gave spurs to their horses and met; their spears brake, their shields and breasts encountered, and Gasinan fell: yet he arose quickly, and drawing his sword stood by a strong pillar in the midst of the court, thinking Amadis could little endamage him, while he was on horseback, and as Amadis drew nigh, he struck at the head of his horse; but he of Gaul, moved to anger thereby, made a blow at him with his sword, which fell upon the pillar, and cut away a fragment thereof, though the stone was very hard, but the sword brake in three pieces. Seeing in what danger he was, he leaped from his horse; and Gasinan came at him, saying, confess the Damsel to be mine, or thou art but dead! That, quoth Amadis, shall I never do, till she tell me it be with her good will. And with his shield he warily received the blows that fell full fast upon him, and at times smote at Gasinan with his broken sword, so that he twisted the helmet on his head, and made him often give back. The battle lasted long, to the great peril of Amadis, for his shield was cut away and his harness laid open in sundry places; he, knowing his danger, ran suddenly upon Gasinan and grappled with him, and dashed him against the pillar, so as for a moment to stun him and make him drop his sword, which Amadis quickly seized, and cut the laces of his helmet, saying, Sir Knight, you have handled me hardly and wrongfully, now will I be revenged! and he lifted his sword as if to slay him. Seeing that, Grovenesa cried aloud, mercy, good Knight! and she ran towards him; but he seeing her fear, made the more semblance of anger, saying, he hath so wronged me that I must have his head. For God's sake, quoth she, ask any thing else that he may live! Give me my Damsel, then, said he, and swear that you will go to the first court which King Lisuarte shall hold, and there grant me what I shall ask. Swear it, niece! cried Gasinan, who had now recovered speech : and suffer me not to be slain! and upon that Grovenesa made the oath. . . . Then was the Damsel sent for, and she kneeling to Amadis, said, truly, Sir, great pains have you taken for my sake; and Gasinan, though he stole me, must love me well, since he preferred to fight rather than deliver me. As God shall help me, fair Damsel, cried Gasinan, if you think so you think rightly : I beseech you to stay with me. That will I do, willingly, she answered, if it please this good Knight. Amadis replied, Certes, you have chosen one of the best Knights in the world; but if this be not with your free will, speak now, that I may not be blamed hereafter. She answered, I thank you truly that you let me remain. In God's name, quoth he. Then albeit he was greatly intreated to abide there that night, he would depart to rejoin Galaor; and mounting horse, he bade Gandalin take with him the pieces of his sword. Hearing that, Gasinan besought him to accept his weapon; which, having thankfully accepted, and a lance also from Grovenesa, he rode away.

ROBERT SOUTHEY

JUAN DEL ENCINA
[1468?–1529?]

Juan del Encina secularized the Spanish drama by writing, primarily on non-religious themes, plays to be presented at the palaces of nobles. (Encina himself was for some time a musician-poet in the household of the Duke of Alba.) His églogas, as the plays are called, are simple verse dialogues. Generally the characters are shepherds. While these eclogues—despite their comic lyricism—do not rank as outstanding works of literature, their importance in the development of the Spanish theatre is such that Encina is called 'father of the Spanish drama'.

MINGO

But look ye, Gil, at morning dawn,
How fresh and fragrant are the fields;
And then what savoury coolness yields
The cabin's shade upon the lawn.

And he that knows what 'tis to rest
Amidst his flocks the livelong night,
Sure he can never find delight
In courts, by courtly ways oppressed.
O, what a pleasure 'tis to hear
The cricket's cheerful, piercing cry!
And who can tell the melody
His pipe affords the shepherd's ear!

Thou know'st what luxury 'tis to drink,
As shepherds do, when worn with heat,
From the still fount, its waters sweet,
With lips that gently touch their brink;
Or else, where, hurrying on, they rush
And frolic down their pebbly bed,
O, what delight to stoop the head,
And drink from out their merry gush!

GEORGE TICKNOR

GIL VICENTE
[1470?–1539?]

Gil Vicente, Portuguese poet and dramatist, is one of the glories of the literature of that country and the founder of Portugal's national drama. He also stands high, however, in Spanish literature, for he wrote eleven of his jorty-three plays in Spanish. Indeed he frequently introduced some Spanish even into his Portuguese plays. Almost all of Gil Vicente's works are based on popular themes, and his poetry is noteworthy for its lyric charm and richness of language.

GRACE AND BEAUTY HAS THE MAID

Grace and beauty has the maid;
Could anything more lovely be?

Sailor, you who live on ships,
Did you ever see
Any ship or sail or star
As beautiful as she?

Knight of war, in armour clad,
Did you ever see
Horse or arms or battle-field
As beautiful as she?

Shepherd, you who guard your flock,
Did you ever see
Cattle, vale, or mountain range
As beautiful as she?

ALICE JANE McVAN

CASSANDRA'S SONG OF CELIBACY

They say, "'Tis time, go, marry! go!'
But I'll no husband! Not I! no!
For I would live all carelessly,
Amidst these hills, a maiden free,
And never ask, nor anxious be,
    Of wedded weal or woe.
Yet still they say, 'Go, marry! go!'
But I'll no husband! not I! no!

So, mother, think not I shall wed,
And through a tiresome life be led,
Or use, in folly's ways instead,
    What grace the heavens bestow.
Yet still they say, 'Go, marry! go!'
But I'll no husband! not I! no!

The man has not been born, I ween,
Who as my husband shall be seen;
And since what frequent tricks have been
    Undoubtedly I know,
In vain they say, 'Go, marry! go!'
For I'll no husband! not I! no!

GEORGE TICKNOR

GARCILASO DE LA VEGA
[1503?–1536]

To Garcilaso and his friend Juan Boscán, Spanish poetry owes the introduction of certain Italian metres, notably the eleven-syllable line and the sonnet. Boscán is important only as an innovator, but Garcilaso was, in addition, the finest poet of the first half of the sixteenth century. His total literary production is slight, but highly polished, and his poetry was held in the highest esteem by the writers of the Golden Age. In contrast to his turbulent life as courtier and soldier (he died on the battlefield), Garcilaso's verse deals only with the theme of love.

ECLOGUE I

The sweet lament of two Castilian swains,
Salicio's love and Nemoroso's tears,
In sympathy I sing, to whose loved strains
Their flocks, of food forgetful, crowding round,
Were most attentive. . . .

.   .   .

The sun, from rosy billows risen, had rayed
With gold the mountain tops, when at the foot
Of a tall beech romantic, whose green shade
Fell on a brook, that, sweet-voiced as a lute,
Through lively pastures wound its sparkling way,
Sad on the daisied turf Salicio lay;
And with a voice in concord to the sound
Of all the many winds, and waters round,
As o'er the mossy stones they swiftly stole,
Poured forth in melancholy song his soul
Of sorrow with a fall
So sweet, and aye so mildly musical,

None could have thought that she whose seeming guile
Had caused his anguish, absent was the while,
But that in very deed the unhappy youth
Did, face to face, upbraid her questioned truth.

Salicio

More hard than marble to my mild complaints,
And to the lively flame with which I glow,
Cold, Galatea, cold as winter snow!
I feel that I must die, my spirit faints,
And dreads continuing life; for, alienate
From thee, life sinks into a weary weight,
To be shook off with pleasure; from all eyes
I shrink, ev'n from myself despised I turn,
And left by her for whom alone I yearn,
My cheek is tinged with crimson; heart of ice!
Dost thou the worshipped mistress scorn to be
Of one whose cherished guest thou ever art;
Not being able for an hour to free
Thine image from my heart?
This dost thou scorn? in gentleness of woe
Flow forth, my tears, 'tis meet that ye should flow!

.   .   .

Through thee the silence of the shaded glen,
Through thee the horror of the lonely mountain
Pleased me no less than the resort of men;
The breeze, the summer wood, and lucid fountain,
The purple rose, white lily of the lake,
Were sweet for thy sweet sake;
For thee the fragrant primrose, dropt with dew,
Was wished when first it blew!
Of how completely was I in all this
Myself deceiving! oh the different part
That thou wert acting, covering with a kiss
Of seeming love, the traitor in thy heart!
This is my severe misfortune, long ago,
Did the soothsaying raven, sailing by
On the black storm, with hoarse sinister cry,
Clearly presage; in gentleness of woe,
Flow forth, my tears, 'tis meet that ye should flow.

.   .   .

In the charmed ear of what beloved youth
Sounds thy sweet voice? on whom revolvest thou
Thy beautiful blue eyes? on whose proved truth
Anchors thy broken faith? who presses now
Thy laughing lip, and hopes thy heaven of charms,
Locked in the embraces of thy two white arms?
Say thou, for whom hast thou so rudely left
My love, or stolen, who triumphs in the theft?
I have not yet a bosom so untrue
To feeling, nor a heart of stone, to view
My darling ivy, torn from me, take root
Against another wall or prosperous pine,
To see my virgin vine
Around another elm in marriage hang
Its curling tendrils and empurpled fruit,
Without the torture of a jealous pang,
Ev'n to the loss of life; in gentle woe,
Flow forth, my tears, 'tis meet that ye should flow!

Over my griefs the mossy stones relent
Their natural durity, and break; the trees
Bend down their weeping boughs without a breeze,
And full of tenderness, the listening birds,
Warbling in different notes, with me lament,
And warbling prophesy my death; the herds
That in the green meads hang their heads at eve,
Wearied, and worn, and faint,
The necessary sweets of slumber leave,
And low, and listen to my wild complaint.
Thou only steel'st thy bosom to my cries,
Not ev'n once rolling thine angelic eyes
On him thy harshness kills; in gentle woe,
Flow forth, my tears, 'tis meet that ye should flow!

But though thou wilt not come for my sad sake,
Leave not the landscape thou hast held so dear;
Thou may'st come freely now, without the fear
Of meeting me, for though my heart should break,
Where late forsaken I will now forsake.
Come then, if this alone detains thee, here
Are meadows full of verdure, myrtles, bays,
Woodlands, and lawns, and running waters clear,
Beloved in other days,

To which, bedewed with many a bitter tear,
I sing my last of lays.
These scenes perhaps, when I am far removed,
At ease thou wilt frequent
With him who rifled me of all I loved;
Enough! my strength is spent;
And leaving thee in his desired embrace,
It is not much to leave him this sweet place.

Nemoroso

Smooth sliding waters, pure and crystalline!
Trees, that reflect your image in their breast!
Green pastures, full of fountains and fresh shades!
Birds, that here scatter your sweet serenades!
Mosses, and reverend ivies serpentine,
That wreathe your verdurous arms round beech and pine,
And, climbing, crown their crest!
Can I forget, ere grief my spirit changed,
With what delicious ease and pure content
Your peace I wooed, your solicitudes I ranged,
Enchanted and refreshed where'er I went!
How many blissful noons I here have spent
In luxury of slumber, couched on flowers,
And with my own fond fancies, from a boy,
Discoursed away the hours,
Discovering nought in your delightful bowers,
But golden dreams and memories fraught with joy!

And in this very valley where I now
Grow sad, and droop, and languish, have I lain
At ease, with happy heart and placid brow;
Oh pleasure fragile, fugitive, and vain!
Here, I remember, waking once at noon,
I saw Eliza standing at my side;
Oh cruel fate! of finespun web, too soon
By Death's sharp scissors clipt! sweet, suffering bride,
In womanhood's most interesting prime,
Cut off, before thy time!
How much more suited had his surly stroke
Been to the strong thread of my weary life!
Stronger than steel, since in the parting strife
From thee, it has not broke.

Who would have said, my love, when late through this
Romantic valley, we from bower to bower
Went gathering violets and primroses,
That I should see the melancholy hour
So soon arrive that was to end my bliss,
And of my love destroy both fruit and flower?
Heaven on my head has laid a heavy hand;
Sentencing, without hope, without appeal,
To loneliness and ever-during tears
The joyless remnant of my future years;
But that which most I feel,
Is to behold myself obliged to bear
This condemnation to a life of care;
Lone, blind, forsaken, under sorrow's spell,
A gloomy captive in a gloomy cell.

.   .   .

Divine Eliza! since the sapphire sky
Thou measurest now on angel-wings, and feet
Sandalled with immortality, oh why
Of me forgetful? Wherefore not entreat
To hurry on the time when I shall see
The veil of mortal being rent in twain,
And smile that I am free?
In the third circle of that happy land,
Shall we not seek together, hand in hand,
Another lovelier landscape, a new plain,
Other romantic streams and mountains blue,
Fresh flowery vales, and a new shady shore,
Where I may rest, and ever in my view
Keep thee, without the terror and surprise
Of being sundered more!

Ne'er had the shepherds ceased these songs, to which
The hills alone gave ear, had they not seen
The sun in clouds of gold and crimson rich
Descend, and twilight sadden o'er the green;
But noting now, how rapidly the night
Rushed from the hills, admonishing to rest,
The sad musicians, by the blushful light
Of lingering Hesperus, themselves addressed
To fold their flocks, and step by step withdrew,
Through bowery lawns and pastures wet with dew.

JEREMIAH HOLMES WIFFEN

SONNET X

O precious locket, found by luckless me,
Precious and pleasing when the Lord hath willed;
Thou art made one with mine own memory,
And with my death thou too shalt be stilled.

Who could foresee in the so recent past,
When thou wert a source of true joy to me,
That our delightful bliss would not long last,
But would turn to heartache and misery?

For in one sole hour thou didst remove
All the joy and good thou didst ever bring;
Take too the grief left by thee with me.

If not, I shall think thou didst falsely love,
And didst leave me a victim to Remorse's sting
That I might die with thy sad memory.

SEYMOUR RESNICK

CRISTÓBAL DE CASTILLEJO
[1490?–1550]

*Cristóbal de Castillejo, a monk whose interests tended more towards the
secular than the spiritual, led the opposition to the Italian forms in poetry
introduced by Boscán and Garcilaso. Of his own works—written, needless
to say, in the old Castilian metres—his light, satirical poems are the most
popular.*

SOME DAY, SOME DAY

Some day, some day
O troubled breast,
Shalt thou find rest.
If Love in thee
To grief give birth,
Six feet of earth
Can more than he;
There calm and free
And unoppressed
Shalt thou find rest.

The unattained
In life at last,
When life is passed
Shall all be gained;
And no more pained,
No more distressed,
Shalt thou find rest.

HENRY WADSWORTH LONGFELLOW

KISSES

Give me, Love, kisses unnumbered,
As many as hairs on my head,
And hundreds and hundreds beyond that,
Then reckon by thousands instead.
After
Those thousands, but three—
Now swiftly, lest anyone see,
We'll cross off the sum, and then
Count from there backwards again.

JEANNE PASMANTIER

GUTIERRE DE CETINA
[1518?–1554?]

The author of many charming poems, Gutierre de Cetina was born in Seville of well-to-do parents. He spent much of his brief life as a military man and courtier, finally going in 1546 to the New World. There, in Mexico, he died—the story goes—as the result of wounds inflicted by the jealous friend of a woman to whom Cetina paid court. If true, this was a sad but appropriate end, for Cetina has been called the 'poet of love'.

His exquisite madrigal Ojos claros, serenos *is one of the most frequently quoted poems in the Spanish language.*

MADRIGAL

Clear eyes, sweet and serene,
If for your gentle looks you are so praised,
Why, seeing me, are you in anger raised?
Since for their pitying glance

They lovelier seem to him on whom they gaze,
   Dispel their angry haze
Lest beauty's eyes thus look at you askance,
   Oh, rage and torture keen!
   Clear eyes, sweet and serene,
E'en though your look be harsh, by you let me be seen.

NICHOLSON B. ADAMS

ANACREON

Cupid has woven the tresses
Of thy bright, golden hair
Into a murderous bowstring,
Ungrateful Doris, fair.

'Now laugh,' he smilingly told me,
'At the potence of my dart';
And drawing one from his quiver,
He aimed it straight at my heart.

In answer, I said, 'Oh Cupid,
Take back thy arrow and bow;
For against such subtle weapons
No shield or defence I know.'

PAUL T. MANCHESTER

THE GOLDEN AGE
[1550–1650]

ANTONIO DE GUEVARA
[1480?–1545]

Though little read today, Bishop Antonio de Guevara was one of the most popular didactic writers of the sixteenth century, both in Spain and abroad. He wrote in a highly polished, rhetorical style and was early translated into English and other languages. Guevara no doubt had an influence on the development of culteranismo *and* conceptismo *in the seventeenth century, and some critics consider him a forerunner of Euphuism in English literature.*

In Menosprecio de corte y alabanza de aldea, *his own favourite book and perhaps his best, Guevara praises country life as opposed to city living. Our excerpts, however, come from his most famous work,* Reloj de príncipes y libro áureo de Marco Aurelio, *first translated by Lord Berners in 1534 and again by Sir Thomas North in 1557. Its aim was to advise the would be courtier on how to conduct himself at all times.*

THE DIAL OF PRINCES

Of the good countenance and modesty the courtier should have in behaving himself at the prince or noble man's table in the time of his meal.

Those that are abiding still in princes' courts, must in any case go seldom, or not at all, abroad to others' tables, but always to keep their own. For that courtier that runneth from table to table, to eat of others' cost, to have his meat free, is not so sparing of his purse, as he is too prodigal and lavish in his good reputation. . . .

But if the courtier will determine to visit noble men's boards, he must be very ware that in coming to a noble man's table, he do not so much commend his fare and ordinary, that he complain of other men's tables where he hath fed. For it is a kind of treason to defame and slander those whose houses they are wont to visit oft. And when he is set at the table, the courtier must behave himself modestly, he must eat temperately and finely, he must delay his wine with water, and speak but little : so that those that are present can not but praise him for his temperancy and sober diet, but also for his wisdom and moderate speech. To feed mannerly is to be understood, not to blow his nose in his napkin, nor to lean his arms upon the table, not to eat to leave nothing in the dish, not to find faults with the cooks, saying the meat is not enough, or not well dressed. For it were a great shame for the courtier to be noted of the waiters, to be a belly gut and to be counted a gross feeder.

There are some also that make themselves so familiar and homely in the house, that they are not contented with that is served them in the dish, but shamefully they pluck that to them that is left in other dishes, so that they are esteemed for jesters, no less saucy and malapert in their order, than insatiable in their beastly eating. The good courtier must also take heed he lay not his arms too far on the table, nor that he make any noise with his teeth or tongue, nor smack with his mouth when he eateth, and that he drink not with both his hands on the cup, nor cast his eyes too much upon the best dishes, that he gnaw nor tear his bread with his teeth, that he lick not his fingers, nor have done eating before others, nor to have too greedy an appetite to the meat or sauce he eats, and that in drinking he gulp not with his throat. For such manner of feeding rather becometh an ale house than a noble man's table.

And although the courtier cannot go over all the dishes that come to the board, yet at least let him prove a little of every one, and then he must praise the good cookery and fine dressing of them all. For commonly the noble men and gentlemen that invite any to their board take it uncourteously, and are ashamed if the invited praise not their meat and drink they give them, and not only the noble men are ashamed of it, but also the other officers that have the charge to see it well dressed, and in good order. Always he that eateth at another man's table, to do as he ought, should praise the worthiness of him that had him (yea though perhaps he made a lie) and commend the great care and diligence of his officers in furnishing his table with so good meats, and in setting it forth in so good order. . . .

Now therefore continuing our begun purpose, the courtier that eateth at other men's tables, must see he drink little, and that his wine be well delayed with water. For wine tempered with water bringeth two commodities : the one, it makes him sober that drinks it, and shall not be overseen : the other, he shall not distemper himself that the waiters have any occasion to laugh at him. If it should happen sometimes that he found the wine well watered before, that it had stood appalling long, or that it were somewhat sharp or sour, or that the water were too hot : the good courtier should not therefore immediately complain and find fault at the table, for so he should shame the servants, and make them angry with him, and also displease their master.

Truly it is a grief to suffer it, to see that he that hath nothing at home in his own house, either to eat or to drink, will yet look to be well used at another man's house, and is never satisfied. I speak it for certain indiscreet courtiers, and wanting judgment, that being at any man's board (without any shame) dare dispraise the cooks, and speak ill of them, if perhaps the taste of their porridge and meat mislike them, and that it be not good, and according to their appetite : and of the butlers, if the wine be not cold and fresh : of those that wait above, if everything they call for be not done at a beck and quickly : of the stewards of the house, if they be not served immediately : and of the boys and pages, if they give them not drink suddenly : of the carvers, if they carve them not to their liking : and also with the clerks of the kitchen, if they see them not served with meat enough, that there be enough left upon the table. So that the noble men's officers (for the more part) have more trouble and displeasure, by the discontentation of those that come to their master's table, than they have by the evil words their masters speak to them. And for this respect, therefore, no man ought to be so bold as once to open his lips to complain of any want in another man's house, as if they serve him with claret wine rather than with white : or with white than claret. For a right and perfect courtier should not set his appetite in the taste or variety of wines or meats in another's house. . . .

And when he is at the table, he should not enter in argument or dispute with any, neither should he be obstinate in opinion, and much less use filthy or uncomely talk : and he must also bridle nature much that he cry not out in laughing as some do. For like as it soundeth to his reproach, to be noted a glutton and drunkard, it is in like case far worse, to be accounted a fool, and a jester. Also it prevaileth little that a courtier be moderate and honest in eating, if he be dishonest and insolent in his talk. For many times it happeneth at noble men's boards, that they take more pleasure in some than in other some : not to see them eat and drink well, but to hear them tell lies, and to be pleasant at the board.

Therefore, as we have said, the wise courtier should praise and commend all that he seeth served at another man's table, and it is not lawful for him to dislike or dispraise it. And further, because he is fed at another man's charge, he must of necessity take all in worth that is given him, and set before him, and not to look to have that that he desireth. And when there is any question moved at the table of the best and most delicate dishes, and of the finest cooks and of the new kinds of broths and sauces, and from whence the fattest capons come, it shall not be fit for the wise courtier to

say in that all that he knoweth and understandeth. For how much
honour it is for him to be able to talk in martial feats, or chivalry :
so much more dishonour and reproach it is to him, to be skilful in
dressing of meats, and all to fill the belly. I remember that being
one day at a bishop's board, I heard a knight make great boast
and vaunt, that he could make seven manner of fricassees, four
kinds of pies, twelve sorts of sauces, and ten of fruit tarts, and
twelve divers ways to dress eggs : but to hear him tell all these
things was not to be accounted of so much as the gestures and
countenance he made in telling them. For he did lively shew with
his hands the present making of them, the eating of them, and the
right tasting of them with his tongue.

And because it happeneth many times that in some noble man's
house there is not like fare and entertainment that another hath,
the civil courtier should not be so dishonest, as to make report he
leaveth the noble man's table, to go to another's that is better
served. For the worthy courtier should not haunt that table where
he fareth best, but where he findeth himself best welcome and
esteemed. . . .

SIR THOMAS NORTH

(Revised by K. N. Colvile)

LAZARILLO DE TORMES
[1554]

*Perhaps the most characteristic of literary genres in Spain is its own native
product, the picaresque novel. Although the ancestry of the* pícaro *or rogue
may be traced back to characters in folklore, and to* La Celestina *in Spanish
literature, the birth of the first important picaresque novel took place in 1554
with the publication—in three different editions—of* Lazarillo de Tormes.

*In contrast to the types of novels then prevalent—the chivalrous, pastoral
and sentimental—the picaresque novel is marked by a down-to-earth, highly
satirical portrayal of real life, and most generally the life of the lower classes.
Its structure is uncomplicated. The* pícaro *recounts, in autobiographical
form, his experiences with a variety of masters, and his tricks, both harrowing
and amusing, in the struggle to survive.*

Lazarillo de Tormes *itself was enormously popular, inspiring many
translations and imitations throughout Europe. The author is unknown,
although for many years the book was attributed to the noted poet and historian
Don Diego Hurtado de Mendoza (1503–1575). There is negative evidence
however, plus the fact that Hurtado de Mendoza was of noble family*

*Critics now generally believe that to have written so intimately of the picaresque
life, the author must have been himself, at one time or another, a penniless
rogue.*

LAZARILLO DE TORMES

Treatise First

WITH A BLIND MAN

Then know Your Worship, before anything else that my name
is Lazaro of Tormes, son of Thome Gonçales and Antona Perez,
natives of Tejares, a hamlet near Salamanca. My birth took place
in the river Tormes, for which reason I had the surname, and it
was in this manner. My father (whom God forgive) had the job of
overseeing the grinding of a water-mill, which is by the bank of
that river, wherein he was miller more than fifteen years; and my
mother being one night in the water-mill, big with me, her pains
took her and she delivered me there; so that I can truthfully say
I was born in the river. Well, when I was a child of eight, they
imputed to my father certain awkward bleedings in the sacks of
those who came there to grind, for which he was taken, and he
confessed, and denied not, and suffered persecution for justice' sake.
I trust in God that he is in glory, for the Gospel calls them
blessed. At this time there was an expedition made against the
Moors, in the which went my father, who had been banished for
the misfortune abovesaid, serving as muleteer to a knight; and
with his lord, like a loyal servant, he ended his life.

My widow mother when she found herself without husband or
support determined to get among worthy people and be one of
them, and betook herself to live in the city, and hired a little
house, and undertook to do the cooking for some students, and
washed clothes for certain stable-boys . . . [later] she went into
service with those who were then living at the inn of La Solana;
and there suffering a thousand annoyances, she managed to bring
up my small brother to the point where he knew how to walk,
and me to where I was a good-sized little fellow, who fetched
wine and candles for the guests, or whatever else they bade me.

At this time there came a blind man to lodge at the inn; and as
it seemed to him that I would be suitable for leading him, he
begged me of my mother, and she turned me over to him, telling
him how I was the son of a good man, who had died to exalt the
faith in the affair of Los Gelves, and that she had trust in God I
should not turn out a worse man than my father, and she begged

him to treat me well and look after me, for I was an orphan. He answered that he would do so, and that he was receiving me not as his boy but as his son. And so I began to serve and to lead my new old master.

After we had remained in Salamanca several days and it appeared to my master that the profits were not to his satisfaction, he determined to leave there; and when we were about to depart I went to see my mother, and both weeping she gave me her blessing and said : 'Son, now I know that I shall never see thee more; try to be good, and God guide thee; I have reared thee and placed thee with a good master, take care of thyself.' And so I went along to my master who was waiting for me.

We went out of Salamanca, and as you approach the bridge there is a stone animal at the entrance, almost in the shape of a bull, and the blind man bade me go close to the animal, and when I was there, said to me : 'Lazaro, put thine ear close to this bull and shalt hear a great noise inside.' Naïvely I went, believing this to be so; and when he perceived that I had my head close to the stone, he swung out his hand hard and gave my head a great blow against the devil of a bull, so that for three days the pain of the butting remained, and said to me : 'Silly fool, learn that the blind man's boy has to know one point more than the devil,' and laughed a great deal at the joke. It seemed to me that in that instant I awoke from the childish simplicity in which I had always been asleep. I said to myself : 'This man says the truth, for it behooves me to open mine eyes and look about, since I am alone, and to consider how to take care of myself.'

We began our journey, and in a very few days he taught me thieves' jargon, and when he saw me to be of a good wit, was well pleased, and used to say : 'Gold or silver I cannot give thee, but I will show thee many pointers about life.' And it was so; for after God this man gave me my life, and although blind lighted and guided me in the career of living. I enjoy relating these puerilities to Your Worship in order to show how much virtue there is in men's knowing how to rise when they are low, and in their letting themselves lower when they are high, how much vice! To return to my good blind man and his affairs, Your Worship must know that since God created the world, He never formed any one more astute or sagacious. In his trade he was an eagle; he knew a hundred and odd prayers by heart; had a bass voice, tranquil and very sonorous, which made the church where he prayed resound, a humble and devout countenance which he put on with very good effect when he prayed, without making faces or grimaces with his mouth or eyes, as others wont to do. Besides, he had a thousand other modes and fashions for getting money : he said he knew prayers to many and divers effects : for women that did not bear, for those that were in travail, for those badly married to make their husbands love them; he cast prognostications for the pregnant whether they were carrying son or daughter. Then in regard to medicine, he used to say that Galen didn't know the half of what he knew about grinders, swoons, the vapours; in a word, nobody could tell him that he was suffering any illness, but straightway he would reply : 'Do this, you will do that, pluck such an herb, take such a root.' Accordingly he had all the world marching after him, especially the women, for they believed whatever he told them; from them he extracted large profits by the arts I tell you of, and used to gain more in a month than a hundred blind men in a year.

But also I wish Your Worship to know, that with all he acquired and possessed, never did I see so miserly or mean a man, to such a point that he was killing me with hunger, and didn't share even the necessaries with me. I am telling the truth : if I had not known how to cure myself by my slyness and good devices, many times I should have died of hunger; but with all his experience and vigilance I worked against him in such fashion, that the biggest and best part, always or more generally, fell to me. To this end I played him devilish tricks, some of which I shall relate, though not all to my advantage.

He used to carry bread and everything else in a linen sack which closed at the mouth with an iron ring and a padlock and key, and when he put things in and took them out, it was with so much attention, so well counted, that the whole world wouldn't have been equal to making it a crumb less. But I would take what stingy bit he gave me, and finish it in less than two mouthfuls. After he had fastened the lock and stopped worrying about it, thinking me to be engaged in other things, by a little seam, which I unsewed and sewed up again many times in the side of the sack, I used to bleed the miserly sack, taking out bread,—not measured quantities but good pieces,—and slices of bacon and sausage; and thus would seek a convenient time to make good the devilish state of want which the wicked blind man left me in.

All I could filch and steal I carried in half-farthings; and when they bade him pray and gave him a farthing, it was no sooner proffered than I had it popped into my mouth and a half-farthing ready, so that however soon he held out his hand, his remuneration was already reduced by my money-changing to half its real

value. The wicked blind man used to complain to me, for he at
once perceived by the feeling that it was not a whole farthing, and
would say : 'Why the devil is it that since thou art with me they
don't give me but half-farthings, and before, they paid me a farthing and oftentimes a maravedi? This bad luck must come through
thee.' He used also to shorten his prayers and not half finish them,
having ordered me that when the person went away who had
ordered him to pray, I should pluck him by the end of his hood.
And so I used to do; and at once he began again to lift his voice,
saying : 'Who would like to have me say a prayer?' as the custom
is.

When we ate he used to put a little jug of wine near him. I
would quickly seize it and give it a couple of silent kisses and
return it to its place; but this plan didn't work long, for he noticed
the deficiency in his draughts, and in order to keep his wine safe,
he never after let go the jug, but kept hold of the handle. But
there is no lode-stone that draws things to it so strongly as I with
a long rye straw, which I had prepared for that purpose, and
placing which in the mouth of the jug, I would suck up the wine to
a fare-ye-well. But the villain was so clever that I think he heard
me; and from then on he changed procedure and set his jug between his legs and covered it with his hand, and thus drank secure.
Now that I had grown accustomed to wine, I was dying for it; and
seeing that the straw-cure was no longer helping me, I decided to
make a tiny hole in the bottom of the jug for a little drain, and to
bung it neatly with a very thin cake of wax, and at dinner-time,
pretending to be cold, I got between the wretched blind man's legs
to warm me at the miserable fire we had, in whose heat the wax
being soon melted, for there was very little, the streamlet began to
drain into my mouth, which I held in such a way that devil a
drop was lost. When the poor creature went to drink, he found
nothing : he was astounded, damned himself, and sent the jug and
the wine to the devil, not knowing what it all could mean. 'You
won't say, uncle, that I drank it for you,' said I, 'for you haven't
let it out of your hand.' He turned and felt the jug so much, that
he found the outlet and fell on to the trick; but made as though
he had not perceived it. And the next day, when I had my jug
leaking as before, and was not dreaming of the injury in store for
me, or that the wicked blind man heard me, I sat as before, in the
act of receiving those sweet draughts, my faced turned toward
heaven, my eyes partly closed, the better to enjoy the delicious
liquid, when the desperate blind man perceived that now was his
time to take vengeance of me, and with all his might, raising that

sweet and bitter jug with both hands, he let it fall upon my mouth, making use (as I say) of all his strength, so that poor Lazaro, who was expecting none of this, but, as at other times, was careless and joyful, verily it seemed to me that the heavens, with all that in them is, had fallen on top of me. Such was the gentle tap he gave me that it stupefied and knocked me senseless, and the blow so hard that the pieces of the jug stuck in my face, breaking it in many places, and cracked off my teeth which I remain without until this very day. From that hour forth I hated the wicked blind man; and although he liked and caressed me and cared for me, well I saw that the cruel chastisement had diverted him. He washed with wine the wounds he had made me with the pieces of the jug, and smiling, said: 'How seems it to thee, Lazaro? That which made thee sick cures thee and gives thee health,' and other pleasantries which to my taste were none.

Once I was half well of my horrid bumps and bruises, considering that with a few such blows the cruel blind man would be rid of me, I was anxious to be rid of him; but I did not manage it too quickly, in order to do it with more safety and profit. Even though I should have been willing to soften my heart and forgive him the blow with the jug, the ill-treatment the wicked blind man gave me from this point on, left no chance for that; for he abused me without cause or reason, beating me over the head and pulling my hair. And if anybody asked him why he treated me so badly, he at once retailed the story of the jug, saying: 'Would you take this boy of mine for an innocent? Then listen, whether the devil himself could teach another such exploit.' Those that listened would say, making the sign of the cross: 'Well, now, who would expect such badness from a lad so small!' and would laugh heartily at the trick, and say to him: 'Chastise him, chastise him, for you'll get your reward from God,' and on that he never did anything else.

And meantime I always led him by the worst roads, and purposely, to do him harm and damage; if there were stones, through them, if mud, through the deepest; for although I didn't go through the dryest part, it pleased me to put out one of my own eyes in order to put out two for him, who had none. Therefore he used always to keep the upper end of his staff against the back of my head, which was continually full of bumps, and the hair pulled out by his hands; and although I swore I didn't do it of malice, but because I found no better road, that didn't help me, nor did he believe me any more for that; such was the perspicacity and the vast intelligence of the traitor.

And that Your Worship may see how far the cleverness of this astute blind man extended, I will relate one instance of many that befel me with him, wherein it seems to me he made his great astuteness very manifest. When we left Salamanca his intention was to go to the region around Toledo, because he said the people were richer, although not very charitable; he pinned his faith to the proverb : The hard give more than the poor. And we came along that route through the best places : where he found good welcome and profit, we would stop, where not, on the third day, we would move away. It happened that on arriving at a place called Almorox at the time when the grapes are gathered, a vintager gave him a bunch for alms. And as the paniers generally get hard treatment, and the grapes at that time are very ripe, the bunch fell apart in his hand : if put into the sack, it would turn to must, and so he decided on this : he resolved to have a banquet, as much because we could not carry it, as to comfort me, for that day he had given me many kicks and blows. We sat down on a wall and he said : 'Now I wish to be generous with thee : we will both eat this bunch of grapes, and thou shalt have as big a share as I; we will divide in this way : thou shalt pick once and I once; provided thou promise me not to take more than one grape each time. I shall do the same until we finish, and in this way there will be no cheating.' The agreement thus made, we began; but directly at the second turn the traitor changed his mind and began to take two at a time, supposing that I must be doing likewise. As I saw he was breaking the agreement, I was not content to keep even with him, but went still farther : I ate them two at a time, three at a time, and as I could. The bunch finished, he waited awhile with the stem in his hand and shaking his head said : 'Lazaro, thou hast cheated : I will swear to God that thou hast eaten the grapes by threes.' 'I have not,' said I; 'but why do you suspect that?' The clever blind man replied : 'Knowest how I see that thou wast eating them by threes? Because I ate by twos and thou saidst nothing.' . . . I laughed inwardly, and although only a lad noted well the blind man's just reasoning.

But not to be prolix, I omit an account of many things, as funny as they are worthy of note, which befel me with this my first master, but I wish to tell our leave-taking and with that to finish. We were at Escalona, town of the Duke of that ilk, in an inn, and he gave me a piece of sausage to roast. When he had basted the sausage and eaten the bastings, he took a maravedi from his purse and bade me fetch wine from the tavern. The devil put the occasion before my eyes, which, as the saying is, makes the thief; and it was this : there lay by the fire a small turnip, rather long and bad, and which must have been thrown there because it was not fit for the stew. And as nobody was there at the time but him and me alone, as I had an appetite whetted by having got the toothsome odour of the sausage inside me (the only part, as I knew, that I had to enjoy myself with), not considering what might follow, all fear set aside in order to comply with desire,—while the blind man was taking the money out of his purse, I took the sausage, and quickly put the above-mentioned turnip on the spit, which my master grasped, when he had given me the money for the wine, and began to turn before the fire, trying to roast what through its demerit had escaped being boiled. I went for the wine, and on the way did not delay in despatching the sausage, and when I came back I found the sinner of a blind man holding the turnip ready between two slices of bread, for he had not yet recognized it, because he had not tried it with his hand. When he took the slices of bread and bit into them, thinking to get part of the sausage too, he found himself chilled by the chilly turnip; he grew angry and said : 'What is this, Lazarillo?' 'Poor Lazaro,' said I, 'if you want to blame me for anything. Haven't I just come back with the wine? Somebody was here, and must have done this for a joke.' 'No, no,' said he, 'for I've not let the spit out of my hand. It's not possible.' I again swore and forswore that I was innocent of the exchange, but little did it avail me, for nothing was hid from the sharpness of the confounded blind man. He got up and seized me by the head and came close up to smell me; and since he must have caught the scent like a good hound, the better to satisfy himself of the truth in the great agony he was suffering, he seized me with his hands, opened my mouth wider than it ought to go, and unconsideringly thrust in his nose,—which was long and sharp, and at that crisis a palm longer from rage,—with the point of which he reached my gorge; what with this and with the great fright I was in, and the short time the black sausage had had to get settled in my stomach, and most of all, with the tickling of his huge nose nearly half-choking me,—all these things conjointly were the cause that my misconduct and gluttony were made evident, and his own returned to my master; for before the wicked blind man withdrew his bugle from my mouth, my stomach was so upset that it abandoned its stolen goods, and thus his nose and the wretched, half-masticated sausage went out of my mouth at the same time. O great God, that I had been buried at that hour ! for dead I already was. Such was the depraved blind man's fury, that if they had not come to my assistance at the noise, I think he had not left me alive. They dragged me from out his hands, leaving them full of what few hairs I had, my face scratched and my neck and throat clawed; and well my throat deserved this, for such abuse befel me through its viciousness. The wicked blind man related my disgraceful actions to all that approached, and gave them the history once and again, both of the wine-jug and of the bunch of grapes, and now of the actual trouble. Everybody laughed so much that all the passers-by came in to see the fun; for the blind man related my doings with so much wit and sprightliness that although I was thus abused and weeping, it seemed to me that I was doing him injustice not to laugh. And while this was going on, I remembered a piece of cowardly weakness I had been guilty of, and I cursed myself for it; and that was my leaving him with a nose, when I had such a good chance, half the distance being gone, for by only clinching my teeth it would have remained in my house, and because it belonged to that villain, perhaps my stomach would have retained it better than the sausage. . . .

In view of this and the evil tricks the blind man played me, I decided to leave him once and for all, and as I had everything thought out and in my mind, on his playing me this last game I determined on it more fully. And so it was that the next day we went out about time to beg alms, and it had rained a great deal the night before; and as it was still raining that day he walked in prayer under some arcades which there were in that town, where we didn't get wet; but as night was coming on and the rain didn't stop, the blind man said to me: 'Lazaro, this water is very persistent, and the more night shuts down, the heavier it is: let us get back to the inn in time.' To go there we had to cross a gutter which was running full because of all the water; I said to him: 'Uncle, the gutter runs very wide; but if you wish, I see where we can get over more quickly without wetting us, for there it becomes much narrower, and by jumping we can cross with dry feet.' This seemed good advice to him, and he said: 'Thou art clever, I like thee for that. Bring me to the place where the gutter contracts, for it is winter now and water is disagreeable, and going with wet feet still more so.' Seeing the scheme unfolding as I desired, I led him out from the arcades and brought him in front of a pillar or stone post which was in the square, and upon which and others like it projections of the houses rested, and said to him: 'Uncle, this is the narrowest crossing there is in the gutter.' As it was raining hard, and the poor creature was getting wet, and what with the haste we made to get out of the water that was falling on us, and most of all because God blinded his intelligence in that hour,—it was to give me revenge on him,—he trusted me, and said: 'Place me quite straight, and do thou jump the gutter.' I placed him quite straight in front of the pillar, and gave a jump, and put myself behind the post like one who awaits the charge of a bull, and said to him : 'Hey, jump all you can, so as to get to this side of the water.' Scarcely had I finished saying it, when the poor blind man charged like a goat and with all his might came on, taking a step back before he ran, for to make a bigger jump, and struck the post with his head, which sounded as loud as if he had struck it with a big gourd, and fell straight down backwards half dead and with his head split open. 'What, thou smeltest the sausage and not the post? Smell, smell !' said I, and left him in charge of many folk who had come to help him, and took the town-gate on foot in a trot, and before night had struck into Torrijos. I knew no more of what God did with him, nor cared to know.

Treatise Third

WITH AN ESQUIRE

Thus was I obliged to extract strength from weakness; and little by little, with assistance from good people, got myself to this famous city of Toledo, where by God's mercy, my wound closed a fortnight later. And while I was ill, people would always give me alms; but after I was well they would all say to me : 'Thou ! a rogue and vagabond art thou. Go, seek a master to work for.' 'And where shall he be found,' I would say to myself, 'unless God create him fresh, as he created the world ?'

I was wandering thus aimlessly from door to door, with mighty little alleviation,—because Charity had already mounted to heaven, —when God threw me in with an esquire who was walking along the street, with pretty good clothes, well-kempt, his gait and bearing orderly. He looked at me and I at him, and he said to me : 'Boy, seekest a master?' I told him : 'Yes, sir.' 'Then come along behind me,' he answered, 'for God has shown thee a mercy in throwing thee in with me. Thou hast said some good prayer today.' And I followed him, thanking God for what I heard, and also because he seemed to me, from his dress and air, to be the person I was in need of.

It was in the morning when I fell in with this my third master; and he led me behind him through a large part of the city. We passed by the squares where bread and other provisions were selling : I was thinking and wishing that he would want to load me there with what was selling, because this was just the time when it is usual to lay in what is necessary : but he passed by these things at a very lively gait. 'Perhaps he sees nothing to his taste here,' said I, 'and wishes to try in another quarter.' In this way we rambled about until it struck eleven : then he entered the principal church, and I behind him; and I saw him very devoutly hear mass and the other divine offices, until everything was ended and the people gone : then we left the church. At a good round pace we began to go down a street; I walked along the happiest in the world because we had not occupied ourselves in laying in provisions : I considered it certain that my new master must be a man who provided in bulk, and that dinner would be ready, and such as I desired and even was in need of.

At this time the clock struck one after noon, and we reached a house in front of which my master halted, and I with him, and, throwing back the end of his cape on the left, he drew out a key from his sleeve, and opened the door, and we entered the house; whose entrance was so dark and dismal that it seemed to cause dread to those that entered, although inside there was a small court and fairly good rooms. After we had entered, he took off his cape, and having asked whether I had clean hands, we shook and folded it, and when he had very neatly blown the dust off a stone bench that was there, he placed it upon it. This done he sat down beside it, and asked me in great detail whence I was and how I had come to that city. I gave him a longer account than I liked, because it seemed to me a more fitting time for bidding the table be set and the stew dished, than for his questions : nevertheless, I satisfied him about me the best I knew how to lie, telling him my good points and keeping silent about the rest, which did not seem to me to be appropriate. This done, he remained as he was for a while, and I immediately saw a bad sign, for it was now nearly two and I didn't see him show any more keenness for his dinner than a dead man. Thereupon I considered his keeping the door locked, and my not hearing, above or below, the footsteps of a living soul in the house : all I had seen was walls without a chair between them, or a meat-block, or bench, or table, or even a big chest like that of other days. In a word, it seemed like an enchanted house. With this, he said to me : 'Thou, boy, hast eaten?' 'No, sir,' said I, 'for it hadn't yet struck eight when I met Your Worship.' 'Well, although it was early, I had breakfasted; and when I eat something that way, I tell thee I go on the same way until night. Therefore, manage as thou canst, for afterwards we will sup.'—Your Worship may believe, that when I heard this, I was within a little of falling in my tracks, not so much from hunger as from knowing now absolutely that fortune was against me. Then my troubles presented themselves anew to me, and I began again to weep over my misfortunes; then there came into my memory the reasoning I followed when I was thinking of quitting the priest, telling myself that although he was miserable and mean, perhaps I should fall in with another worse. In a word, I then wept over my unhappy life past and my death near to come. And with it all, dissembling the best I could, I told him: 'Sir, I am a lad who don't bother myself much about eating, blessed be God! Therefore I can boast myself the most abstemious among all my contemporaries; and thus I have been praised for it until today by the masters I have had.' 'That is a virtue,' said he, 'and on that account I shall like thee better: because stuffing is for pigs, and eating moderately is for gentlemen.' 'I understand thee well,' said I to myself; 'confound such medicine and virtue as these masters I get find in hunger!'

I put myself at one end of the arcade, and took out some pieces of bread from my bosom, which remained of those I had got in God's name. He, on seeing this, said to me: 'Come here, boy, what eatest?' I approached and showed him the bread. He took one piece, the best and biggest of the three there were, and said: 'By my life, but this looks like good bread.' 'Why, indeed,' said I, 'it is good, sir.' 'Yes, in faith,' said he; 'where didst thou get it? Was it kneaded by clean hands?' 'I don't know that,' I told him, 'but for my part the taste of it doesn't nauseate me.' 'May it so please God,' said my poor master; and lifting it to his mouth, began to take as fierce bites as I of the other piece. 'Most delicious bread it is,' said he, 'by Jove.' And when I perceived on what foot he limped, I made haste, for I saw he was disposed, if he finished first, to be civil enough to help with what remained; and thus we finished almost together. With his hands he began to brush off some crumbs, and very small ones, which had remained on his breast; and went into a little room there, and brought out a mouth-less jug, not very new, and after he had drunk offered it to me. I, to play the abstemious, said: 'Sir, I don't drink wine.' 'It is water,' he answered; 'thou mayst drink all right.' So I took the jug and drank; not much, for thirst was not my affliction.

So there we were until night, talking about things he asked me, to which I answered the best I knew how: during this time he took me into the room where the jug we drank from was, and said: 'Boy, get over there, and thou shalt see how we make this bed, that thou may know how to do it from now on.' I got on one side and he on the other, and we made the wretched bed. There was not much to make, for it had a reed framework upon

some benches, on which were spread the bed-clothes over a dirty
mattress, which, from not being very constantly washed, did not
appear a mattress, although it served for one, with a great deal
less wool than was necessary. We spread it out, trying to soften
it, which was impossible, because what is hard can ill be made soft.
The miserable saddlepad had devil a thing inside, and when it was
placed on the reed framework all the reeds showed, and looked
exactly like the spine of a most skinny pig; and over that starved
mattress a cover of the same stamp, whose colour I could not
decide. The bed made and night come, he said to me : 'Lazaro,
it's already late, and from here to the square is a big stretch :
besides, many robbers wander about in this city at night and
snatch people's capes. Let us get through as we can, and tomorrow,
when day is come, God will be merciful. Being alone, I am not
provided, but have been eating outside these days. But now we
shall have to do otherwise.' 'Sir, about me,' said I, 'let your
Worship not worry, for I well know how to pass one night, and
even more, if necessary, without eating.' 'Thou wilt live longer and
more healthily,' he answered, 'because, as we were saying today,
there's no such thing in the world for living long, as eating little.'
'If that is the road,' said I to myself, 'I shall never die, for I have
always observed that rule perforce, and even expect, with my bad
luck, to keep it all my life.' And he went to bed, putting his hose
and his pourpoint for a pillow, and bade me stretch at his feet,
which I did. But devil a wink I slept, for the reeds and my pro-
truding bones didn't leave off quarrelling and fighting the whole
night, for with my hardships, woes, and hunger, I think I hadn't
a pound of flesh on my body; and besides, as I had eaten almost
nothing that day, I was raging with hunger, which has no friendship with sleep. A thousand times I cursed myself (God forgive
me for it) and my wretched luck, most of the night from then
on; and worse yet, not daring to turn over lest I awaken him, I
many times begged death of God.

When morning came we got up, and he began to clean and
shake his hose and pourpoint, coat and cape, and with me serving
as an idle assistant, dressed himself slowly to his great pleasure. I
poured water on his hands, he combed his hair, and put his sword
into his baldric, and while he was putting it in, said to me : 'Oh,
if thou knewest, boy, what a piece this is ! There is not a mark
of gold in the world I would give it for; the more so, because of
all those that Antonio made, he didn't manage to get the edges of
any so keen as this one;' and he drew it from the scabbard and
tried it with his fingers, saying : 'Dost see it? I engage to sever a

puff of wool with it.' And I said to myself : 'And I with my teeth, although they are not steel, a four-pound loaf.' He put it in again, and girded it and a string of fat beads in his baldric. And with an easy step and body erect, making very genteel movements with it and his head, throwing the end of his cape over his shoulder and at times under his arm, and placing his right hand on his hip, he issued out the door, saying : 'Lazaro, see for the house while I go hear mass; and make the bed, and go for a pitcher of water to the river, which is here below; and lock the door so that they won't steal anything from us, and put the key here over the door, so that if I come back in the meanwhile I can get in.' And he went down the street with so genteel visage and carriage, that any one who didn't know him would have thought he was a very near kinsman to the Count of Arcos, or at least the chamberlain who handed him his clothes. 'Blessed be thou, Lord,' I remained behind saying, 'who causest the sickness and appliest the cure ! Who that might meet this master of mine but would think, judging by his air of self-content, that he had supped well last night and slept in a good bed, and though now it is early morning, would not suppose he had breakfasted well? Great secrets, Lord, are those that thou makest and people are ignorant of ! Who will not be deceived by that fair appearance and decent cape and coat? And who will imagine that genteel man passed the whole of yesterday on a morsel of bread, which his servant Lazaro had carried a day and a night in the cupboard of his bosom, where much cleanness cannot have clung to it, and that today, when he washed his hands and face, he used the skirt of his coat for lack of a towel? Surely nobody would suspect it. O Lord, how many such thou must have, scattered through the world, who suffer for the jade they call honour that which they would not suffer for thee !' . . .

I set to thinking what I should do, and it seemed well to me to await my master until the day should be half over, if perhaps he should come and bring something to eat; but my experiment was in vain. After I saw that it was two, and he came not, and hunger was distressing me, I closed the door and put the key where he bade me, and returned to my trade : with low and feeble voice, and my hands crossed on my breast, God set before my eyes, his name on my tongue, I began to beg bread at the doors and houses that seemed the greatest to me; but as I had sucked this mystery in my milk,—I mean to say I learned it with the grand master the blind man,—I came out so expert a disciple, that although there was no charity in this town, nor had it been a very abundant year, I was so crafty that before the clock struck four, I already had that many pounds of bread in my body, and over two more stowed away in my sleeves and my bosom. I returned to our lodging, and in passing by the tripery, begged from one of those women there, who gave me a piece of cow's-heel and some little bits of boiled tripe.

When I reached the house, my good master was already in, his cape folded and laid on the stone bench, and he taking a walk about the court. As I entered, he came toward me : I thought he wanted to reprove my tardiness, but God made it better. He asked me whence I came; I told him : 'Sir, I stayed here until it struck two, and when I saw that Your Worship was not coming, I went out about the city to commend myself to the worthy people, and they have given me what you see.' I showed him the bread and the tripe which I carried in one end of my skirt, at which he put on a good face, and said : 'Well, I awaited thee for dinner, and when I saw that thou didst not come, I dined. But thou doest like a man of honour in this, for it is better to beg in God's name than to steal. And may God bless me as much as this seems right to me, and I only charge thee that they do not know thou livest with me, because it touches on my honour; although I well believe that it will remain secret, seeing how little I am known in this town; I ought never to have come to it !' 'Have no care about that sir,' I told him, 'for nobody cares a hang about asking me this question, or I about answering.' 'Now, eat them, sinner, for if it please God, we shall soon see ourselves out of necessity; though I tell thee, since I entered this house nothing has gone well with me; it must be an evil location, for there are unlucky and ill-placed houses, which communicate bad luck to those that live in them; this must doubtless be one of them, but I promise thee, and that when the month is once ended, I don't remain in it, even if they gave it to me for my own.'

I sat down on the end of the bench, and that he might not take me for a glutton, I said nothing about my lunch, and began my supper, biting into my bread and tripe, and kept looking askance at my unfortunate master, who did not take his eyes from my lap, which at that time was serving for a plate. May God have as much pity for me as I had for him, for I felt what he was feeling, and had passed through it many times, and was passing through it every day. I was thinking whether it would be well to be so polite as to invite him; but since he had told me he had dined, I feared he would not accept the invitation. In a word, I was wishing that the poor wretch would help out his trouble by the fruits of mine, and would break his fast as he had the day before, since there was better wherewithal, through the victuals being better and my hunger less. God willed to fulfil my desire, and I even think his too, because as I began to eat, and he was wandering about taking a walk, he approached me and said : 'I tell thee, Lazaro, thou hast the best grace in eating that I ever saw a man have in my life, and nobody could see thee eat without thy giving him an appetite, even though he had none.' 'The very good one thou hast,' said I to myself, 'makes mine appear beautiful to thee.' However, I thought I would aid him, since he was aiding himself and opening me a way for it, and I said to him : 'Sir, good tools make a good workman; this bread is most delicious, and this cow's-heel so well boiled and seasoned, that there could be nobody it would not invite by its savour.' 'Cow's-heel, is it?' 'Yes, sir.' 'I tell thee it is the best morsel in the world, and there is no pheasant tastes so good to me.' 'Then try it, sir, and you shall see how good it is.' I put the heel into his hand, and also three or four pieces of bread, of the whitest; he sat down by my side, and began to eat like a person with an appetite, gnawing each knuckle of it better than one of his grey-hounds would do. 'With garlic sauce,' said he, 'this is excellent feeding.' 'Thou art eating it with a better sauce,' I answered, apart. 'By'r Lady, but it tasted as good to me, as if I had not eaten a mouthful today.' 'May happy years come to me as surely as that!' said I to myself. He asked me for the water-pitcher, and I gave it him just as I had fetched it : a sign, since there was not water missing, that my master's dinner had not been excessive; we drank and well content went to sleep as the night before. And to avoid prolixity, we went on eight or ten days in this way, the sinner going out in the morning with that satisfied manner and affected gait of his to swallow the air in the streets, having in poor Lazaro a wolf's head.

Many times I reflected on my misfortune, how escaping from the wretched masters I had had and seeking an improvement, I had happened to run across one who not only didn't maintain me, but whom I had to maintain. However, I liked him well, for I saw that he had nothing more and could do nothing more, and I rather had pity for him than enmity; and often, because of carrying home what he might live on, I lived poorly. Because one morning, the unhappy man getting up in his shirt, went up to the top of the house for a certain necessity; and meanwhile in order to be free from doubt, I unrolled his pourpoint and his hose which he left at the head of the bed, and found a satin-velvet purse, folded a hundred times, and with devil a farthing in it, or sign that it had held one for a long time. 'This master,' said I, 'is poor, and nobody

6—SA

gives which he has not; but the miserly blind man and the cursed
mean priest, who, although God had provided for them both, one
through his hand-kissing and the other through a glib tongue, used
to kill me with hunger, them it is right to abhor, and this one to
be sorry for.' God is my witness that even today, when I run across
any of his kind with that gait and pomposity, I pity him, wondering whether he suffers what I saw that one suffer, whom, with all
his poverty, I was more glad to serve than the others, for the
reason I have given. Only I was a little bit discontented with him;
for I could have wished that he had not so much vanity, but
would diminish his ideas a little with the great increase of his
necessity; but, as it appears to me, it is a rule still regarded and
kept among such folk : although they have not a copper of change,
their caps must be well cocked. The Lord help them, for they will
go to their graves having this infirmity.

Well, then, I being in such a condition, leading the life I say,
my bad luck would have it,—for it had not had enough of pursuing me,—that I should not keep on in that laborious and shameful
mode of life. And it was this way; as that year the region was short
of bread, the town council agreed that all stranger paupers should
leave the city, making a proclamation that any they came across
from that time on should be punished by whipping. And so,
enforcing the law, four days after the proclamation was made, I
saw them conduct a procession of paupers, whipping them through
the Quatro Calles; the which caused me so much terror that I
never dared take upon me to beg again. Hence, whoever could see
it, might see the abstinence of our house and the sadness and silence
of its inmates; to such an extent, that we would happen to be two
or three days without eating a mouthful or speaking a word. Some
wenches, cotton-spinners, who made caps and lived near us, kept
me alive, for I was on terms of neighbours and acquaintances with
them; out of the pittance they earned, they used to give me some
little bit, with which I barely managed to bear up. And I had not
so much pity for myself as for my pitiful master, for during eight
days devil a mouthful did he eat; at least at the house we certainly
passed them without eating; I know not how or where he went, or
what he ate. And to see him come down the street at midday, with
stiff body, longer than a greyhound of good breed; and with regard
to what touched his wretched honour, as they call it, he would take
a straw, of which even there were not enough in the house, and
go out the door picking those that had nothing in them, complaining still of that evil location, saying : 'It is bad to see how the bad
luck of this dwelling brings evil. As thou seest, it is dismal, sad,

dark. While we remain here we shall suffer; I wish this month
were ended so we could get out.'

Well, while we were in this distressed and hungry affliction, one
day, I know not by what luck or chance, into the poor control of
my master there entered one bit, with which he came home as
satisfied as if he had had the treasure of Venice, and with a very
joyous and smiling face, he gave it to me saying: 'Take it, Lazaro,
for now God is opening his hand. Go to the square and buy bread
and wine and meat. Let us put out the devil's eye. And moreover,
I'll let thee know, that thou may rejoice, that I have rented another
house, and we have not to be in this disastrous one longer than
until the month is ended; may it be damned, and he who put the
first tile on it, for in an evil day I entered it. By our Lord, so long
as I have lived here, drop of wine or mouthful of bread have I not
eaten, nor have I had any rest, such a look it has and such darkness and sadness. Go, and come quickly, and today let us dine like
counts.' I took the bit and the pitcher, and giving wings to my feet,
I began to mount the street directing my steps toward the square,
very contented and joyful. But what does it profit me, if it is
written in my sad fate that no pleasure come to me without
anguish? And so it was now, because while going up the street
casting up how I should lay out my bit that it might be best and
most profitably spent, giving infinite thanks to God who had made
my master have some money, in an evil hour there came toward
me a dead man, whom many priests and people were carrying
down the street on a bier. I flattened myself against the wall to
give them room, and after the body had passed, there came, just
behind the litter, one that must have been the wife of the defunct,
loaded with mourning, and with her many other women; she
walked along weeping in a loud voice and saying: 'My husband
and lord, whither are they taking you from me? To the sad and
unhappy house, to the dismal and dark house, to the house where
they never eat or drink!' When I heard this, the heaven joined
with the earth, and I said: 'O unhappy me! They are taking this
dead man to my house.' I changed my course and pushed through
the middle of the folk, and returned down the street as fast as I
could run toward home; and entering, I closed in great haste,
invoking the aid and support of my master, clinging to him, that
he would come to assist me and to defend the entrance. He, somewhat disturbed, thinking it to be something else, said: 'What is this,
boy? What art thou crying about? What's the matter with thee?
Why art thou closing the door with such fury?' 'O sir,' said I,
'help me, for they are bringing us a dead man hither.' 'How so?'

he replied. 'I met him up there, and his wife walked along, saying, "My husband and lord, whither are they taking you? To the dismal and dark house, to the sad and unhappy house, to the house where they never eat or drink!" Hither to us, sir, they are bringing him.' And certainly when my master heard this, although he had no reason to be very cheerful, he laughed so much that he was a very great while without being able to speak. During this time I still had the bar dropped across the door, and my shoulder placed against it for more security. The people passed with their dead, and I still feared that they were going to put him into our house; and after my good master was fuller with laughing than with eating, he said to me : 'True it is, Lazaro, judging from what the widow is saying, thou wast right in thinking what thou didst think; but since God has made it better and they are passing on, open, open, and go for something to eat.' 'Let them, sir, finish passing through the street,' said I. At last my master came to the door, and opened it, reassuring me, which was right necessary because of my fear and disturbance, and I went again on my way. But although we dined well that day, devil a bit of pleasure I took in it, nor in the next three days did my colour return; and my master very laughing every time he remembered that supposition of mine.

In this manner I continued with my third master, this esquire, for some days, always wishing to know the purpose of his coming and remaining in that region; for from the first day I was in service with him, I knew him to be a stranger, from the slight acquaintance and intercourse he had with the natives there. At last my wish was fulfilled and I knew what I desired; for one day when we had dined reasonably well and he was rather contented, he gave me an account of his affairs, and told me he was from Old Castile, and that he had left his country for nothing more than to avoid taking off his hat to a knight, his neighbour. 'Sir,' said I, 'if he was what you say and richer than you, you did not err in taking it off to him first, since you say that he used also to take his off to you.' 'He is what I say, and was richer, and he also did take his off to me; but, as often as I took mine off first, it would not have been ill of him to be civil sometimes and anticipate me.' 'It appears to me, sir,' I said, 'that I should not have considered that, particularly with my betters and people who have more.' 'Thou art a lad,' he replied, 'and dost not understand questions of honour, wherein consists today the whole capital of gentlemen; but I'll let thee know that I, as thou seest, am esquire; but I swear to God, if I run across the count in the street and he does not take off his hat to me, quite entirely off, the next time he comes, it may suit me better to enter

a house, pretending some business there, or to turn down another
street, if there be one, before he gets near me, in order not to take
mine off to him. For a gentleman owes nothing to anybody but
God and the king, nor is it fit, being a man of worth, to omit a
single point in having a high opinion of one's own self.' . . .

'Especially,' he said, 'since I am not so poor but that I have in
my own country a place for building houses, and if these houses
were up and fine ones, sixteen leagues away from where I was born,
on that slope of Valladolid, they would be worth over two hundred
thousand maravedis, so big and good they might be made; and I
have a dove-cote, which were it not fallen down as it is, would give
every year over two hundred young doves; and other things that I
don't mention, which I left because of my honour's sake. And I
came to this city, thinking that I should find a good situation, but
it has not turned out for me as I thought. Canons and lords of the
church I find a-plenty, but it is a folk so frugal, that the whole
world will not draw them out of their gait. Knights of middling
rank also seek me; but to serve these is a great labour, because you
have to be changed from a man to a manille; or it not, "God go
with thee," they will tell you; and most often the wages are at
long intervals, and the most likely is, food for service; and when
they wish to still their consciences and recompense your sweats, you
are paid off in the wardrobe with a sweated doublet or worn-out
cape or coat. Now when a man takes service with a gentleman of
title, then his indigence passes. For is it not peradventure in my
ability to serve and satisfy these? By the Lord, if I fell in with
one, I think I should be his prime favourite, and that I should do
him a thousand services, because I should know how to lie to him
as well as another, and how to be most marvellously agreeable to
him : to laugh hard at his pleasantries and ways, although they
were not the best in the world; never to tell him anything that
might weigh upon him, although it might be very important to
him; to be very diligent about his person, in word and deed; not
to kill myself over doing things well which he would not see; and
to set myself to quarrelling with the serving-people, when he would
hear it, so that I should appear to be very careful of what concerned him; if he should quarrel with any of his servants, to tell
some trifles to fire his wrath, and which should appear to be in
favour of the culprit; to tell him good about what seemed good to
him, and about the contrary, to be malicious, a mocker; to slander
those of the house and those outside; to search out and try to know
the lives of others to relate to him; and many other amusing things
of this sort, which are customary nowadays in palaces, and seem

good to the lords there. And they don't wish to have virtuous men
in their houses : but abhor them and hold them of little account,
and call them asses, and that they are not men of affairs or with
whom the lord can be at ease; and the clever nowadays behave
with such lords in the way, as I say, that I should behave. But my
fate does not will me to find one.' In this manner my master de-
plored his adverse fortune, giving me an account of his worthy self.

Well, while we were thus occupied, a man and an old woman
came in at the door. The man asked him for the rent of the house,
and the old woman for that of the bed : they cast the account, and
for two months they made it what he wouldn't make in a year; I
think it was twelve or thirteen bits. And he gave them a very good
reply : that he would go out to the square to change a doubloon,
and they should return later in the evening; but his going-out was
without return. By this token, that later in the evening they returned, but it was too late; I told them that he was not yet come.
The night being come and he not, I was afraid to stay in the
house alone, and betook myself to the neighbour-women and told
them the situation, and slept there. The morning being come, the
creditors return and ask for the neighbour, but 'Try next door!'
The women reply : 'Here you have his boy and the door-key.'
They asked me about him, and I told them that I didn't know
where he was, and that he had not returned home again after he
went out to change the piece of money, and that I thought he had
gone away with the change from me as well as from them. When
they hear this, they go for a constable and a notary; and behold!
they soon return with them, and take the key, and call me, and
call witnesses, and open the door, and go in to attach my master's
effects until they should be paid their debt. They went over the
whole house and found it unfurnished, as I have related, and said
to me : 'How about thy master's effects, his chests and wall-hang-
ings, and furnishings?' 'I don't know,' I answered. 'No doubt,' they
say, 'they must have removed it all last night and taken it somewhere. Mr. Constable, arrest this lad, for he knows where it is.'
On this came the constable and laid his hand on the collar of my
doublet, saying : 'Boy, thou art arrested, unless thou disclose the
goods of this master of thine.' I, never having seen myself in
another such situation,—because I had been seized by the collar,
yes, many times; but it was gently, by the blind man, so that I
might show the road to him who saw not,—I was greatly scared,
and weeping, promised to tell what they asked me. 'That is good,'
they say; 'then tell what thou knowest and be not afraid.' The
notary sat down on a stone bench to write the inventory, asking

me what there was. 'Sirs,' said I, 'what this master of mine has, according to what he told me, is a very good place for building houses and a fallen-down dove-cote.' 'That is good,' they say; 'little as that may be worth, there is enough to settle us this debt. And in what part of town has he that?' they asked me. 'In his own country,' I replied. 'By'r Lady, but this is a good business,' said they. 'And where is his country?' 'In Old Castile he told me it was,' I told them. The constable and the notary laughed a great deal, saying : 'This is information enough to cover your debt, even were it better.' The neighbour-women, who were present, said : 'Sirs, this is an innocent child, and it is only a few days he has been with this esquire, and he knows no more of him than Your Worships. Besides, the poor little sinner comes here to our house, and we give him what we can to eat for the love of God, and at nights he went back to sleep with him.' My innocence being seen, they let me go, liberating me. And the constable and the notary asked their fees of the man and of the women; upon which they had a grand dispute and uproar, because they maintained they were not obliged to pay, since there was not wherewithal and the attachment was not made : the others said they had given up going to other business which was more important to them, to come to this. Finally, after much talking, at the end they loaded a bailiff with the old woman's old bedding, but he wasn't very heavy laden. All five went away disputing. I don't know how it came out : I believe the poor wretched bedding paid for everything; and it served it right, for at the time when it ought to have reposed and rested from its former labours, it was going about for rent. Thus, as I have related, my poor third master left me; wherein I fully realized my wretched luck, for behaving as outrageously as possible toward me, it did my business so contrariwise, that whereas masters are wont to be left by their boys, in my case it was not so, but my master left me and ran away from me.

LOUIS HOW

JORGE DE MONTEMAYOR
[1520?–1561]

One of the most widely read books in sixteenth-century Spain was the pastoral novel La Diana *(1559?), by Jorge de Montemayor, a Portuguese-born court musician who spent most of his life in Spain. The setting is a perfumed paradise of flowers, music and enchantment, with a few sheep thrown in for background. Noblemen and ladies, in the guise of shepherds and shepherdesses, people this unreal love world, pursuing their amours with high flown delicacy.*

Despite its artificiality (indeed, perhaps because of it) the pastoral novel enjoyed immense popularity, and Montemayor's Diana—*the first and best of this genre in Spain—had many imitations and continuations. In England it influenced Sir Philip Sidney's* Arcadia *and Shakespeare's* Two Gentlemen of Verona.

Bartholomew Young's translation, from which the following excerpt is taken, appeared in 1598.

DIANA

THE SHEPHERDESS FELISMENA

. . . And because there is not anything which I am not forced to tell you, fair ladies, as well for the great virtue and deserts which your excellent beauties do testify, as also for that my mind doth give me that you shall be no small part and means of my comfort; know, that as I was in my grandmother's house and almost seventeen years old, a certain young gentleman fell in love with me who dwelt no farther from our house than the length of a garden terrace, so that he might see me every summer's night when I walked in the garden.

Whenas, therefore, ungrateful Felix had beheld in that place the unfortunate Felismena (for this is the name of the woful woman that tells you her mishaps), he was extremely enamoured of me, or did else cunningly dissemble it; I not knowing then whether of these two I might believe, but am now assured, that whosoever believes least or nothing at all in these affairs, shall be most at ease. Many days Don Felix spent in endeavouring to make me know the pains which he suffered for me, and many more did I spend in making the matter strange, and that he did not suffer them for my sake. And I know not why love delayed the time so long by forcing me to love him, but only that (when he came indeed) he might enter into my heart at once, and with greater force and violence. When he had therefore by sundry signs, as by music and tourneys, and by prancing up and down upon his proud jennet before my windows, made it manifest that he was in love with me (for at the first I made as if I did not so well perceive it), he determined in the end to write a letter unto me. And having spoken divers times with a maid of mine, and at length with many gifts and fair promises gotten her good will and furtherance, he gave her the letter to deliver to me. But to see the means that Rosina made unto me (for so was she called), the dutiful services and unwonted circumstances before she did deliver it, the oaths that she sware unto me and the subtle words and serious protestations that she used, it was a pleasant thing and worthy the noting.

To whom (nevertheless) with an angry countenance I turned again saying :

'If I had not regard of mine own estate and what hereafter might be said, I would make this shameless face of thine be known ever after for a mark of an impudent and bold minion. But because it is the first time, let this suffice that I have said, and give thee warning to take heed of the second.'

Methinks I see now the crafty wench : how she held her peace, dissembling very cunningly the sorrow that she conceived by my angry answer. For she feigned a counterfeit smiling, saying :

'Jesus, mistress! I gave it you because you might laugh at it, and not to move your patience with it in this sort. For if I had any thought that it would have provoked you to anger, I pray God he may show his wrath as great towards me as ever he did to the daughter of any mother.'

And with this she added many words more (as she could do well enough) to pacify the feigned anger and ill opinion that I conceived of her, and taking her letter with her she departed from me.

This having passed thus, I began to imagine what might ensue thereof, and love (methought) did put a certain desire into my mind to see the letter, though modesty and shame forbade me to ask it of my maid, especially for the words that had passed between us, as you have heard. And so I continued all that day until night, in variety of many thoughts. But when Rosina came to help me to bed, God knows how desirous I was to have her entreat me again to take the letter; but she would never speak unto me about it, nor (as it seemed) did so much as once think thereof. Yet to try, if by giving her some occasion I might prevail, I said unto her :

'And is it so, Rosina, that Don Felix without any regard to mine honour dares write unto me?'

'These are things, mistress,' said she demurely to me again, 'that are commonly incident to love. Wherefore I beseech you pardon me, for if I had thought to have angered you with it, I would have first pulled out the balls of mine eyes.'

How cold my heart was at that blow, God knows; yet did I

dissemble the matter, and suffer myself to remain that night only with my desire and with occasion of little sleep. And so it was indeed; for that (methought) was the longest and most painful night that ever I passed. But when with a slower pace than I desired the wished day was come, the discreet and subtle Rosina came into my chamber to help me to make me ready; in doing whereof, of purpose she let the letter closely fall.

Which, when I perceived, 'What is that that fell down?' said I. 'Let me see it.'

'It is nothing, mistress,' said she.

'Come, come; let me see it!' said I. 'What! Move me not, or else tell me what it is.'

'Good Lord, mistress,' said she, 'why will you see it? It is the letter I would have given you yesterday.'

'Nay, that it is not,' said I. 'Wherefore show it me, that I may see if you lie or no.'

I had no sooner said so than she put it into my hands, saying: 'God never give me good, if it be any other thing.'

And although I knew it well indeed, yet I said: 'What! This is not the same, for I know that well enough; but it is one of thy lover's letters. I will read it, to see in what need he standeth of thy favour.'

And opening it, I found it contained this that followeth:

I ever imagined (dear Mistress) that your discretion and wisdom would have taken away the fear I had to write unto you, the same knowing well enough (without any letter at all) how much I love you; but the very same hath so cunningly dissembled, that wherein I hoped the only remedy of my griefs had been, therein consisted my greatest harm. If according to your wisdom you censure my boldness, I shall not then (I know) enjoy one hour of life; but if you do consider of it according to love's accustomed effects, then will I not exchange my hope for it.

Be not offended I beseech you (good lady) with my letter, and blame me not for writing unto you, until you see by experience whether I can leave off to write. And take me besides into the possession of that which is yours, since all that is mine doth wholly consist in your hands, the which with all reverence and dutiful affection a thousand times I kiss.

When I had now seen my Don Felix his letter, whether it was for reading it at such a time when by the same he showed that he loved me more than himself, or whether he had disposition and regiment over part of this wearied soul to imprint that love in it whereof he wrote unto me, I began to love him too well; and (alas for my harm), since he was the cause of so much sorrow as I have passed for his sake. Whereupon asking Rosina forgiveness of what was past (as a thing needful for that which was to come) and committing the secrecy of my love to her fidelity, I read the letter once again, pausing a little at every word, (and a very little indeed it was), because I concluded so soon with myself to do that I did, although in very truth it lay not otherwise in my power to do.

Wherefore calling for paper and ink, I answered the letter thus :

Esteem not so slightly of mine honour, Don Felix, as with feigned words to think to enveigle it. I know well enough what manner of man thou art, and how great thy desert and presumption is; from whence thy boldness doth arise, and not from the force (which thing thou wouldst fain persuade me) of thy fervent love.

And if it be so (as my suspicion suggesteth), thy labour is as vain as thy imagination presumptuous, by thinking to make me do anything contrary to that which I owe unto mine honour. Consider (I beseech thee) how seldom things commenced under subtlety and dissimulation have good success; and that it is not the part of a gentleman, to mean them one way and speak them another.

Thou prayest me (amongst other things) to admit thee into possession of that that is mine. But I am of so ill an humour in matters of this quality, that I trust not things experienced; how much less, then, thy bare words. Yet nevertheless, I make no small account of that, which thou hast manifested to me in thy letter; for it is enough that I am incredulous, though not unthankful.

This letter did I send, contrary to that I should have done, because it was the occasion of all my harms and griefs. For after this, he began to wax more bold by unfolding his thoughts, and seeking out the means to have a parley with me. In the end, a few days being spent in his demands and my answers, false love did work in me after his wonted fashions, every hour seizing more strongly upon my unfortunate soul.

The tourneys were now renewed, the music by night did never cease, amorous letters and verses were recontinued on both sides; and thus passed away almost a whole year, at the end whereof I felt myself so far in his love that I had no power to retire, or stay myself from disclosing my thoughts unto him, the thing which he desired more than his own life. But my adverse fortune afterwards would that of these our mutual loves (whenas now they were most assured) his father had some intelligence; and whosoever revealed them first, persuaded him so cunningly that his father (fearing lest he would have married me out of hand) sent him to the great princess Augusta Cesarina's court, telling him it was not meet that a young gentleman, and of so noble a house as he was, should spend his youth idly at home where nothing could be learned but examples of vice, whereof the very same idleness (he said) was the only mistress. He went away so pensive, that his great grief would not suffer him to acquaint me with his departure; which when I knew, how sorrowful I remained she may imagine that hath been at any time tormented with like passion.

To tell you now the life that I led in his absence, my sadness, sighs and tears, which every day I poured out of these wearied eyes, my tongue is far unable; if then my pains were such that I cannot now express them, how could I then suffer them? But being in the midst of my mishaps, and in the depth of those woes which the absence of Don Felix caused me to feel, it seemed to me that my grief was without remedy if he were once seen or known of the ladies in that court, more beautiful and gracious than myself. By occasion whereof, as also by absence (a capital enemy to love) I might easily be forgotten, I determined to adventure that which I think never any woman imagined : which was to apparel myself in the habit of a man and to hie me to the court to see him, in whose sight all my hope and content remained. Which determination I no sooner thought of than I put in practice, love blinding my eyes and mind to an inconsiderate regard of mine own estate and condition. To the execution of which attempt I wanted no industry; for being furnished with the help of one of my approved friends and treasuress of my secrets, who bought me such apparel as I willed her, and a good horse for my journey, I went not only out of my country but out of my dear reputation (which, I think, I shall never recover again), and so trotted directly to the court. . . .

BARTHOLOMEW YOUNG
(Revised by J. B. Trend)

EL ABENCERRAJE
[1565]

Though lesser in popularity and influence, the 'Moorish' novel stands with the picaresque as a native Spanish genre. This type of semi-historical work— called the novela morisca—*is set against the struggle of Christian Spain against the Moors. One of the best examples is the charming novelette,* Historia del Abencerraje y la hermosa Jarifa, *written by an unknown author. The story recounts the chivalrous behaviour of a Christian captain, Rodrigo de Narváez, towards a noble Moorish captive, and his aid in bringing Abindarráez's and Jarifa's love to a happy conclusion.*

From EL ABENCERRAJE

. . . The Governor as he rode did continually cast an eye upon the Moor whom he thought with himself a goodly man of person and gracious of visage, remembering therewithall how stoutly he had defended himself; but thought his sadness too great for so brave a mind as he carried. And because he intermixed his sorrow with sighs which were tokens of greater grief than could be imagined in so brave a man, and also desirous to know more of the matter, he said unto him :

'Behold, Sir Knight, how the prisoner that loseth his heart and magnanimity for fear of imprisonment, doth hazard the law of his liberty; for in martial affairs, adversity must be entertained with as merry a countenance, as by this greatness of mind it may deserve to enjoy prosperity again. And these sighs are not (methinks) beseeming that valour and courage which thou hast showed by trial of thy person; neither are thy wounds so mortal that thy life is in hazard, whereof besides thou hast showed not to make so much account, but that thou wouldest willingly have left it for thine honour's sake. If there be then any other occasion of thy heaviness, tell it me; for by the faith of a gentleman, I swear unto thee that I will use as much courtesy and friendship towards thee as thou shalt not have occasion to repent thee that thou hast told me it.'

The Moor, hearing the Governor's gentle speech, whereby he argued in him a brave and noble mind, and his courteous and friendly offer to help him, thought it no point of wisdom to conceal the cause of his grief from him; because of his mild words and gracious countenance he had such great hope of help and favour, that lifting up his face which with the weight of sorrow he went carrying in his bosom, he said unto him :

'How art thou called, Sir Knight, that dost thus comfort me in my sadness, whereof thou seemest to have some feeling and the which thou dost enforce me to tell thee?'

'My name is Rodrigo of Narvaez, and Governor I am of Álora and Antequera, of both which towns of garrison the King of Aragon my lord and master hath appointed me chieftain.'

When the Moor heard this, with a merrier countenance than before, he said :

'I am glad that my misfortune hath been so fortunate to make me fall into thy hands, of whose force and manhood I have been long since informed. The trial whereof though it had cost me dearer, could not have greatly grieved me, since it doth so greatly content me to see myself his prisoner whose virtues, valour, and dexterity in arms doth importune every one's ears so much. And because the subduing of my person doth oblige me to esteem thee the more, and that thou mayst not think it is any kind of pusillanimity or fear in me (without some other great occasion which lies not in my power to forsake) that makes me so sad and pensive, I pray thee, gentle knight, by what thou art, to command thy gentlemen to ride on before, because thou mayst know that neither the pain of my green wounds nor the grief of my present captivity is cause of my heavy thoughts.'

The Governor hearing these words made greater reckoning of the Moor, and because he was very desirous to be thoroughly resolved what he was, he willed his gentlemen to ride on before. And they two coming on fair and softly behind, the Moor fetching a profound sigh from his soul, began thus to say :

'If time and trial of thy great virtues (most valiant Governor) and that golden fame wherewith they are spread in every place, had not penetrated my heart with desire of knowing them and now put them manifestly before mine eyes, these words which thy will doth enforce me to relate should be now excused; and the discourse which I mean to tell thee of a life continually environed with disquiets and suspects, the least whereof being (as thou wilt judge no less) worse than a thousand deaths, remain untold. But as I am on the one side assured of that I speak, and that (on the other) thou art a worthy knight and noble gentleman, and hast either heard or else thyself passed the like passion to mine, know that my name is Abindarraez the younger, in difference to an uncle of mine, my father's brother, who is also called so. Descended I am from the noble house of the Abencerrajes in Granada, by whose unlucky destinies I did learn to be unfortunate. And because thou mayst know what theirs was, and mayst by them the better conjecture what may be expected of mine, thou shalt understand that in Granada was a noble lineage of lords and knights called Abencerrajes whose valiant deeds and grave persons, as well in martial adventures as in peaceable and wise government of our commonwealth, were the mirrors of the kingdom. The old men were of the King's counsel; the young gentlemen exercised their minds and bodies in feats of arms in the service of ladies and gentlewomen, and by showing in every point their valour and gentility. And as they were honoured of the popular sort and well-beloved among the principal (for in all those good parts that a gentleman should have, they far excelled others) so were they very well thought of with the King. They never did anything in war abroad nor in counsel at home, that their experience was not correspondent to their expectation; their valour, bounty, and humanity was so highly commended that for a common example it was ever alleged that there was never Abencerraje coward, niggard, or ill-disposed person. In the city they were the masters of brave inventions for apparel; in the court, of masks, dances, and triumphs, and in the court and city in the service and courting of dames passing gracious. For never did Abencerraje love and serve any lady of whom he was not favoured, nor any lady (were she never so fair and amiable) think herself worthy of the name and title of an Abencerraje his mistress. They living therefore in as great prosperity, honour, and reputation as might be, came fortune (an enemy to the rest and contentment of happy men) to cast them down from that joyful estate, to the most unfortunate and grievous condition of disgrace that might be. The beginning whereof was, that the King having done a certain injury to the Abencerrajes, they made an insurrection, wherein, with ten gentlemen more of their kindred, they conspired to kill the King, and to divide the kingdom amongst themselves, and so to be revenged of the unworthy disgrace received by him. This conspiracy (whether it was true or false) was discovered before it could be put in practice, and they, apprehended and condemned to die, before the citizens had intelligence thereof; who, without all doubt for the great love they bare them, would have risen, not consenting that justice should have been done upon them. For carrying them to execution, it was the strangest spectacle in the world to see the lamentations that some made; the privy murmuring of one to another, and the bootless excuses that for compassion of these gentlemen were generally made in all the city. They ran all to the King, and offered to buy his mercy with great sums of gold and silver; but such was his severity, that

it expelled all motions of pity and clemency. Which when the
people beheld, they began to weep and lament again; the lords,
knights, and gentlemen did weep and mourn, with whom they
were wont to keep company; the tender ladies and damsels of the
Court wept, for the great honour and authority that such noble
citizens gave them. The lamentations and outcries were so many
and so loud, as if the earth had sunk or the world been drowned
anew. But the King, who to all these tears, lamentations, and
pitiful outcries did stop his ears, commanded that this definitive
sentence should be presently executed; so that of all that house
and lineage there remained not one man alive that was not
beheaded that day, except my father and mine uncle who were
not found complices in that conspiracy. These ills resulted to them
(besides this miserable chance), that their houses were ruined,
they proclaimed traitors to the King, their goods, lands, and
possessions confiscated; and that no Abencerraje should live any
longer in Granada, except my father and mine uncle; and they
but with this condition : that if they had any issue, they should
send the men-children (as soon as they were born) to be brought
up out of the city, never to return to it again; and if they were
women, and marriageable, to be married out of the realm.'

When the Governor heard the strange discourse of Abindarraez
and the terms wherewith he complained of his misfortune, he
could not stop his tears, but did show by them the sensible grief
which of such a disastrous accident could not but be felt. And
therefore, turning himself to the Moor, he said unto him :

'Thou hast good cause, Abindarraez, to be sorry for the fall
of thy noble house and kindred, whose heads, I think, could never
hatch so great treason. And were it for no other proof but that so
worthy a gentleman as thyself came out of it, this only were
sufficient to make me believe that they never pretended such
wickedness.'

'This gentle opinion which thou hast of me,' said the Moor,
'may Allah requite thee; for he is witness of that which is generally
held concerning the goodness of my ancestors in this respect. But
now, when I was born into the world with the inheritance of
the self-same mishap of my kindred, they sent me (because they
would not infringe the King's edict) to be nursed and brought up
in a certain fort belonging sometimes to the Christians, called
Cártama, committing the charge and care of me to the Governor
thereof, with whom my father had ancient familiarity and
acquaintance : a man of great account in the kingdom, upright in
the manner of his life and very rich, but chiefly in a daughter

which he hath, which is the greatest felicity which I account in this life, the which, may Allah take her from me, if in anything (but only her) I ever took content and pleasure. With her I was brought up from my childhood (for she was born but three years after me), and as we were generally thought of to be brother and sister (for like such was our education), so did we also think ourselves to be. The love that I did bear Sharifa (for thus is the lady called that is mistress of my liberty) were but little if I could tell it; let it suffice that time hath so confirmed the same, that I would give a thousand lives (if I had them) but to enjoy one momentary sight of her fair face. Every day increased our age, but every hour augmented our love, and so much, that now (methought) I was made of another kind of metal than consanguinity. I remember that Sharifa, being on a day in the orchard of the Jasmines dressing her fair head, by chance I espied her, amazed at her singular beauty, and how (methought) it grieved me that she was my sister. And by the extreme passion of my love, driven out of my musing, I went to her, who as soon as she saw me with open arms came to receive me. And sitting upon the fountain by her, she said unto me :

' "Why hast thou, good brother, left me so long alone?"

' "It is, sweet lady," said I again, "a good while since I, having sought thee in every place, and found not any that could tell me what was become of thee, my heart at last conjectured where thou wert. But tell me now, I pray thee, what certainty hast thou that we are brother and sister?"

' "No other," said she, "than of the great love I bear thee, and to see how every one doth call us so, and that my father doth bring us up like his son and daughter."

' "And if we were not brother and sister," said I, "wouldest thou then love me so much as thou dost?"

' "Oh, seest thou not," said she, "that we should not be suffered to go so continually together and all alone, if we were not."

' "But if we were deprived of this joy, that which I feel in myself is a great deal more."

'At which words her fair face being tainted with a vermilion blush, she said unto me :

' "What couldest thou lose by it, if we were brother and sister?"

' "Myself and thee too," said I.

' "I understand thee not," said she, "but methinks, being brother and sister, it binds us to love one another naturally."

' "Thy only beauty," said I, "doth oblige me to this brotherhood, which rather qualifieth my love and sometimes distempers my thoughts."

'At which words blushing for too much boldness, casting down mine eyes, I saw her divine figure in the crystalline fountain so lively represented as if it had been she herself, and in such sort, that wheresoever she turned her head, I still beheld her image and goodly counterfeit truly translated into my very heart.

'Then said I softly to myself : "O, if I were now drowned in this fountain where with pride I behold my sweet lady, how more fortunate should I die than Narcissus ! And if she loved me as I do her, how happy should I be ! And if fortune would let us live ever together, what a happy life should I then lead !"

'These words I spake to myself, and it would have grieved me that another had heard them. But having spoken this, I rose up, and reaching up my hand to certain jasmines that grew round about that fountain, I made of them, and some orange flowers, a fair and redolent garland, and putting it upon my head, I sat down again crowned, and conquered.

'Then did she cast her eyes upon me to my thinking more sweetly than before, and taking it from my head did put it upon her own, seeming then more fair than Venus. And looking upon me, she said :

' "How dost thou like me now, Abindarraez?"

' "That in beauty," said I, "and sweet perfections thou over-comest all the world, and that crowned queen and lady of it."

'At which words, rising out of her place, she took me by the hand and said unto me :

' "If it were so indeed, brother, thou shouldest lose nothing by it."

'And so without answering her again, I followed her out of the garden.

'But now from that time certain days after, wherein cruel Love thought he was too long from discoursing unto me the deceit that I had of myself, and time meaning then to lay open hidden and secret things, we came to perfect knowledge that the kindred between us was as much as nothing; whereupon our firm affections were confirmed more strongly in their former and true places. All my delight was in her, and my soul cut out so just to the proportion of hers, that all that was not in her face seemed to mine eyes foul, frivolous, and unprofitable in the whole world.

'And now were our pastimes far different from our first, and I beheld her with a certain kind of fear, and suspect to be perceived of any; and now had I also a certain envy and jealousy of the sun that did touch her. For though she looked on me again with the very same desire and intent wherewith she had beheld me before, yet I thought it was not so, because one's own distrust is the most assured and certain thing in an enamoured heart.

'It fell out afterwards, that she being on a day at the clear fountain of the Jasmines, I came by chance thither; and beginning to talk with her, her speech (methought) and countenance was not like to her former looks and communication. She prayed me to sing, for she was greatly delighted with songs and music; and I was then so trustless and misconceiving of myself that I thought she bade me sing, not for any pleasure that she took by hearing me, but to pass away the time, and only to entertain my company with such a request, so that I then wanted to tell her the whole sum of my grief. But I who employed my mind in nothing else, but to do whatsoever my lady Sharifa commanded me, in the Arabic tongue began to sing a song; whereby I gave her to understand the cruelty that I suspected of her. . . .

'The words were of such force that, being helped by the love of her in whose praise they were sung, I saw her shed certain tears, that I cannot tell you now (noble Governor) how much they moved my heart, nor whether the content that I had by seeing so true a testimony of my mistress' love, or the grief (myself being the occasion of her tears) was greater.

'Calling me to her, she made me sit down by her, and thus began to say unto me :

' "If the love, Abindarraez, whereunto I am obliged (after I was fully assured of thy thoughts) is but small, or such that cannot but with extinction of life be ended, my words (I hope) before we leave this only place shall make thee sufficiently know. And blame thee I will not for thy mistrust which hath made thee conceive amiss; for I know it is so sure a thing to have it, as there is nothing more proper and incident to love. For remedy whereof, and of the sorrow that I must needs have by seeing myself at any time separated from thy sweet company, from this day forth forever thou mayst hold and esteem thyself lord and master of my liberty; as thou shalt be indeed, if thou art willing to combine thyself in sacred bonds of marriage with me, the refusal whereof is (before every other thing) no small impediment to both our contents, a prejudice to mine honour, and the sole obstacle of enjoying the great love which I bear thee."

'When I heard these words (love working my thoughts to things clean contrary) I conceived such great joy, that had it not been but by only bowing down my knees to the ground and kissing her fair hands, I was not able to do any other thing. With the hope of these words I lived certain days in the greatest joy in the world, whilst mutable Fortune (envying my prosperity and joyful life) bereaved us both of this sweet contentment. For not long after, the King of Granada, minding to prefer the Governor of Cártama to some higher charge, by his letters commanded him forthwith to yield up the charge of that fort, which lies upon the frontiers, and go to Coïn, where his pleasure was he should be captain and Governor; and also to leave me in Cártama under the charge of him that came to be Governor in his place. When I heard these unlucky news for my mistress and myself, judge you, noble gentleman (if at any time you have been a lover), what a world of grief we conceived. We went both into a secret place, to weep and lament our misfortunes, and the departure and loss of each other's company. There did I call her my sovereign mistress, mine only joy, my hope, and other names that Love did put into my mouth. With weeping I said unto her :

' "When the view of thy rare beauty shall be taken from mine eyes, wilt thou then, Sharifa, sometimes remember me?"

'Here did my tears and sighs cut off my words, and enforcing myself to speak more (being troubled in mind), I uttered I know not what foolish words unto her; for the apprehended absence of my dear mistress in my thoughts did utterly carry away my wits, senses, and memory with it. But who can tell what sorrow my dear lady felt for this departure, and what bitter potions of grief her tears (which for this cross of fortune she poured forth) made me sup up?

'She did then speak such words unto me, the least of which was enough to have made the hardest heart think of them all its life long; which (valiant Governor) I will omit to tell thee, because thou wilt think them (if thy breast was never possessed with love) impossible. And if it hath been for fear, left by hearing some of them, thou couldest not, but with hazard of life, stay out to hear the rest.

'Let it suffice that the end of them was by telling me that, having any fit occasion by her father's sickness or by his absence, she would send for me, that that might have effect which was betrothed and agreed upon between us both. With this promise my heart was somewhat lightened, and for this infinite courtesy (which she did promise me when time and occasion served) I kissed her dainty hands. The next day after, they went away, and I tarried still behind like one that (wandering upon craggy and wild mountains, and having lost the comfortable light of the sun) remained in hideous darkness. With great grief I began to feel her absence, and sought all the false remedies I could against it; for sometimes I did cast mine eyes up to the windows where she was wont to look out, sometimes upon the bed where her tender body was accustomed to take rest, and went sometimes into the garden where daily she used to disport herself, and in the heat of the day to the crystalline fountain where she bathed and refreshed herself under the shade of lemon and pomegranate trees : I walked and went to all her stations, and in every one of them I found a certain representation of my sorrowful thoughts. Truth it is, that the hope that she gave me (to send for me) eased my pains a little, and with it I dissembled some part of my woes. But forasmuch as the continual thought of my desire so long deferred did increase my pain the more, methought sometimes I would have been glad if I had been left altogether without hope; for desperation doth but trouble one until it be certainly known, but hope until the desire be accomplished.

'But my good fortune did so much favour me, that this morning my lady stood to her word, by sending for me by a gentlewoman of hers (a trusty secretary of her thoughts); for the Governor, her father, was gone to Granada, and being sent for thither by the King was to return home in a short time again. Awaked out of my heavy slumber and melancholic cares with these inopinate and happy news, I prepared myself to go with winged speed unto her; yet staying for night, and because I might the better escape unknown, I did put on this habit, as thou seest, and the bravest I could devise, to make the better show to my lady of my proud and joyful heart. In which journey (truly) I would not have thought, that two of the best knights at arms had been sufficient to abide me the field, because I carried my mistress with me.

'Wherefore, Rodrigo, if thou hast overcome me, it was not by pure strength, which was impossible; but it was either my hard fortune or the determination of the heavens, that would prevent me of such a supreme good. Wherefore consider now in the end of my true tale, and of the good that I have lost, and the ill which I possess : I came from Cártama to go to Coïn, but a short journey, although the desire of the proudest Abencerraje that ever lived made it a great deal longer. I went, sent for by my lady, to see my lady, to enjoy my lady. But now I see myself wounded, captive, and in subjection to him who will do I know not what with me. And that which grieves me most is that the time and enjoying of my desire endeth with this present night. O suffer me then,

Christian, to comfort myself at the least with my secret lamentations; let me evacuate out of my sorrowful breast my choking and smothering sighs, and water mine eyes with burning tears. All which impute not any to imbecility or fear of mind, though it were a great deal better for me that I had a heart that could bear and suffer this hard and sinister chance of Fortune, than to do that which I now do.'

The discourse of the enamoured Moor pierced deeply into the valiant Narvaez his soul, who was not a little amazed at the strange course of his love. And thinking with himself, that for the better dispatch of his affairs nothing might hinder them more than his long staying, he said unto him :

'I am minded, Abindarraez, to make thee know how much my virtue surmounteth thy ill fortune; for if thou wilt but promise me to return to my prison within three days, I will set thee at liberty, because thou mayst not leave off thy amorous enterprise. For it would grieve me to cut off so good, and so honest an endeavour.'

The Abencerraje hearing this, in token of thanks would have fallen down at his feet, and said unto him :

'If thou dost me this unexpected favour, noble Governor of Alora, thou shalt restore me again to life, and show the greatest gentility of mind that ever any conqueror did. Take what security thou wilt of me, for whatsoever thou dost demand, I will not fail to accomplish.'

Then Rodrigo of Narvaez called his gentlemen unto him, and said :

'Gentlemen, trust me for this prisoner, for whose ransom myself will be a pledge.'

They answered him again that he might dispose of him at his own pleasure, for whatsoever he did, they would be well content withal.

Then the Governor, taking the Abencerraje by his right hand, said unto him :

'Dost thou promise me as thou art a gentleman to come to my castle of Alora, there to yield thyself my prisoner within three days?'

'I do,' said he, 'and with solemn oath bind it.'

'Then go,' said the Governor, 'and good fortune with thee; and if thou standest in need of mine own person to accompany thee, or of any other thing for the way, speak, and thou shalt have it.'

The Moor thanked him very much, but took no more but a horse which the Governor gave him; for his own was hurt in the late encounter between them and went very heavy, being also wearied and faint with much blood which he lost by the way. And so, turning the reins, he rode as fast as he could towards Coïn. . . .

BARTHOLOMEW YOUNG
(Revised by J. B. Trend)

GINÉS PÉREZ DE HITA
[1544?–1619?]

Blending fact with fiction, Ginés Pérez de Hita wrote a fascinating account of the last years of the Moors in Granada in Part I (1595) of his Guerras civiles de Granada. *Along with vivid descriptions of the customs and splendid court of the Moors, he depicts the internal strife and intrigue which led to the fall of Granada in 1492. Part II (1604) is an historical review of the uprising of the* moriscos *in the second half of the sixteenth century.*

THE CIVIL WARS OF GRANADA

The Combination of the Zegries against the Abencerrages and the Queen of Granada

The king, greatly fatigued with his expedition, retired to a palace, called the Alijares, to recruit his spirits, attended only by the Zegries and Gomeles, not one Abencerrage or Gazul being in his suite, the major part of them having accompanied Muza, on a fresh alarm of the incursion of some Christians, who had newly entered the Vega. The king being one day diverting himself in his retirement at the palace, the discourse, after dinner, turned on the battle of Jaen, and the spoils which the Abencerrages and the Alabeces had taken from the enemy, when a Zegri, to whom the charge of opening the treason against the queen and the Abencerrages was committed, replied, 'If they are brave, the Cavaliers of Jaen are still braver, for they retook a great part of the spoils, and by dint of arms compelled us to retire.'

'It may be as you say,' replied the king, 'but had it not been for the valour and resistance of the Abencerrages and Alabeces, we should have been totally routed, while it was by the signal bravery with which they maintained the fight, that we were enabled to carry away the cattle, and the captives, in defiance of the Christian force.'

'O how kind is your majesty!' exclaimed the Zegri, 'how affectionate to overlook these traitors to your royal crown! But it proceeds from your abundant goodness, and the confidence you place in this lineage, unacquainted with the wicked treason which they plot against you. Many Cavaliers have desired to make known their daring projects, but they were deterred by the well known interest which your majesty takes in their favour; although it is with pain I must wound your royal bosom by unfolding a scene of wickedness unparalleled, yet I should ill perform the duty of a loyal subject, to conceal the falsehood and dishonour practised against the king, my lord and master, and it is therefore I am impelled to entreat your majesty not to put your confidence in the Abencerrages, if you desire to preserve your kingdom, and not to die, which Alla forbid! by the hand of violence.'

'Tell me,' cried the king, 'what it is you know! You alarm me strangely by your insinuations; speak plainly, and I will reward your loyalty.' 'Your majesty shall be obeyed, and I will undertake to prove, beyond contradiction, the notoriety of the facts I allude to, the unbridled length to which the parties have proceeded, the contempt the Abencerrages have for your royal person, the security with which they walk in the commitment of the foulest treason, and how confident in the favours your majesty is daily granting them, they deem themselves above the reach of justice : that your majesty may be satisfied, I am not induced to make the discovery which has hitherto been concealed from your royal ear, either from the motives of personal hatred or malice, or the meaner passion, envy; and that it is the honour of my king alone which compels me to declare my knowledge, let Mahandin Gomel, and my two nephews, Mahomet and Ali Hamet, who can attest the truth of what I assert, and four cousins also of Mahandin Gomel, of the same lineage, be summoned into your royal presence, and before them I will relate the story.'

The king commanded the persons who had been named by the Zegri to be immediately sent for, and when they arrived, the other Cavaliers arose and left the saloon, leaving only the accuser and his false witnesses with the king. The Zegri expressing, outwardly, signs of the deepest concern, thus began his narrative :

'Your majesty must know then that these Abencerrages have conspired to deprive you of your kingdom and your life, and this the better to carry on the wanton and adulterous criminality of their chief Albin Hamet, the most powerful and the richest of all the nobles of Granada, (oh! heavens, how shall I name it? Grief overwhelms me) with the queen my royal mistress. What shall I state to convince your majesty? Is it necessary that I should add that the Abencerrages spend their fortunes to win the affections of the people, and in seeking popularity, and that, by the exercise of the continual deceptions which they practise, they stand well with the gentlemen and the plebeian, and both rich and poor esteem this lineage. Your majesty must well recollect the day on which the Zambra was danced in Generalife, when the Master of Calatrava gave the general challenge, which fell to Muza's lot to answer? On that day I was walking with this Gomele gentleman in one of the myrtle groves in the royal garden, when I observed beneath a rose-tree the queen and the adulterous Albin Hamet, in the act of foul dishonesty, and so lost were they in the enjoyment of their lustful passion, that we remained unnoticed, notwithstanding we stood close by them. I was the first to point them out to Mahandin Gomel; when, confounded at their shameless audacity, we withdrew aside to observe their further conduct. In a short time the queen rose from the place, and walked towards the fountain of laurels, where she joined the ladies of the court. Albin Hamet soon after came from the grove, gathering as he walked white and red roses, which he formed into a garland, and put on his head; not seeming to have noticed what had passed, we approached Albin Hamet and accosted him, enquiring how he was amusing himself? In viewing, he replied, the beauties of this charming garden : it contains every thing that can delight the eye, or feast the senses; and saying this, he presented each of us with a rose which he had plucked, and presently after we joined the gentlemen with your majesty, and should at the time have mentioned the offensive conduct of the parties, but we feared to raise a tumult in the court, when your majesty had so recently ascended the throne. . . . Look therefore, dread sire, to your royal person, let the adulterer die, and the dishonest queen, for having rebelled against your royal throne.'

The king was thunderstruck at the relation of the false and abominable Zegri, and giving credit to his story, fell lifeless on the ground, and remained a considerable time before he could be brought to himself again : at length recovering he breathed forth a lamentable sigh, 'O Mahomet,' cried he, 'how have I offended you? Is this the reward of all my services, the mosques I have built, and the incense I have burnt on your altars? O traitors! traitors! As Alla lives every Abencerrage shall die, and the adultress queen shall be consumed alive with fire! Let us hasten to the city; I will order her to be confined, and made such an example that the whole world shall be astonished, and applaud the justice of the sentence.'

One of the traitors, a Gomele, replied, 'It might be hazardous, and endanger the royal person, to condemn the queen to punishment without the form of a trial, it might raise the city in a flame, and Albin Hamet and his faction would gladly make the defence of the queen a pretence for flying to arms, and under the delusion draw in the Alabeces, Vanegas, and Gazules (who are so partial to the race) to support them in effecting their evil purposes. A surer mode of revenge, in my opinion, presents itself, by not appearing to be acquainted with what has passed, and by alluring the Abencerrages one by one to the palace, and to appoint twenty Cavaliers, in whom confidence may be placed, to attend and see them immediately beheaded; when the adoption of such resolute measures come to the knowledge of their friends, not one of them will dare to raise his hand against your majesty; should any be found sufficiently hardy, the Zegries, Gomeles, and Mazas will fight in your defence; by this means your majesty will be free from danger; the queen may then be thrown into confinement, accused of adultery, and brought to trial.'

'The counsel is good,' exclaimed the king. 'Let us hasten then to the city, and I will give the orders which my honour seems to require.'

O unfortunate city! About to be overthrown by fierce contentions, and intestine rebellion! Ill-advised king! To listen to Sirens who enchant your ears with such wicked calumnies!

The king returned to Granada, attended by the false accusers, and entered the Alhambra, where he was received by the queen and the ladies of the court with the accustomed ceremonies; but his majesty passed on without deigning to notice them; the queen was greatly chagrined at the king's disrespect, and in confusion retired to her apartment, unacquainted with the cause of the disdain she had never before experienced. The king spent the remainder of the day with the Zegries, and after supper, feigning himself indisposed, retired to a separate chamber, and the gentlemen to their houses.

The mind of the unfortunate monarch was bewildered the whole night in a maze of thought; amidst the chaos of imagination he could get no repose, woefully uttering to himself, 'O wretched monarch! How nigh art thou and thy kingdom to perdition! If you destroy this race what calamities are in store for you; if you chastise them not, death is better. Destroy them! Yes, because their audacity in committing adultery with the queen is unparalleled, and their plots to slay me and obtain the kingdom must be punished. Yet, yet consider how worthy, and how modest a wife thou hast; thou art not ignorant neither of the goodness and loyalty of the noble Abencerrages, and that the Zegries are their mortal enemies. This way perhaps they seek to annihilate that virtuous lineage; therefore if you propose revenge, first verify the case; yet what can exceed that which the eye has witnessed? The Zegries would not dare to bear this testimony, and to maintain it too in battle, if it was not true.'

Thus did the king spend the night; early in the morning he rose, and found many of the Zegries, Gomeles, and Mazas in waiting: at this moment a messenger arrived, and informed him that Muza was returned from the skirmish with the Christians, in which he had gained two standards, and had brought in more than thirty heads; this intelligence gave the king a temporary relief from the anxiety of his mind; but calling the Zegri apart, he commanded him to provide thirty Cavaliers well armed, and an executioner, for the business they had agreed on, and to await him in the court of the lions.

The treacherous Zegri, leaving the palace, soon put the king's command into execution, and sent his majesty word that all was prepared: the king immediately withdrew and went to the court of the lions, where he found the Zegri, and thirty other Zegries and Gomeles assembled, with the executioner.

A page was now dispatched for an Abencerrage, the Alguazil Major of the city, who being informed that the king desired to see him, hastened to the palace: the moment he entered the saloon he was seized, before he could make the least resistance, and his head was instantly struck off. The next Abencerrage who was sent for was Albin Hamet, whom they accused of the commitment of adultery with the queen, and he was beheaded in the same way as the Alguazil Major; in this secret manner six and thirty of the principal Abencerrages of the city were also destroyed, without its having come to the knowledge of any of their friends or partisans, and the whole race had certainly perished if the hand of Providence had not interfered in their innocent cause, and defeated the wicked projects of their enemies. The good works of the Abencerrages merited not indeed this vile return, for they were highly charitable, and great friends both to the poor and to the Christians, and some of the Cavaliers who saw them beheaded, afterwards affirmed they called upon Christ crucified to succour them in their great distress, that they might not be put to death, and that they died in the Christian faith.

The great ruler of the universe was at length pleased so to order it, to preserve this virtuous race from entire destruction, that a page of one of the Abencerrages should follow his master into the court, where seeing him beheaded immediately on his entry, and observing the rest of the gentlemen, who were slaughtered before, lying dead on the floor, every one of whom were known to him, he could with difficulty restrain his sorrow, and in silent terror gently crept to the door, and the moment it was opened to admit another Abencerrage, trembling he fled the court. Weeping for his master's fate, he sallied from the Alhambra; and near the fountain which jets its water in the front of the fortress, he met Malique Alabez, Abenamar, and Sarracino, who were on their way to attend the summons of the king. When he beheld them, trembling and weeping, with broken accents, he exclaimed, 'Ah! Signors, for the love of Alla pass not that way, unless you desire to die a cruel death.' 'How?' cried Alabez. 'Oh! Sirs, in the court of the lions a great many Cavaliers lie beheaded, all Abencerrages, and my poor slaughtered master is of the number; I saw his head struck off with my own eyes, having followed him into the apartment. Would to heaven we had never gone there! I saw every thing they did, remaining myself unperceived, for so Alla permitted it, and the instant they opened the private door I stole out, leaving my poor dead master behind, and almost myself stupefied with horror at the dreadful spectacle I had witnessed. For the love of Mahomet, gentlemen, put a stop to these wicked doings!'

The three knights looked with amazement at each other, not knowing how to credit the story of the page. 'If this be true,' said Abenamar, 'there is great treason indeed now perpetrating; but how shall we be able to ascertain the truth of what he says?' 'I will tell you,' replied Alabez, 'remain you here, and if you observe an Abencerrage, or any other gentleman going to the Alhambra, stop him, while I will go to the palace, and discover what is passing therein, and speedily return to you.' 'Alla guard you,' cried Abenamar, 'we will remain here as you desire.'

Malique then went to the Alhambra, and at the gate he saw a page, who was going in haste from the king, and enquired of him whither he was going. The page replied, 'In search of an Abencerrage.' 'And who,' cried Alabez, 'commands you to seek him?' 'The king,' answered the page, 'and if you would perform a good office, descend to the city, and persuade all the Abencerrages instantly to quit Granada, unless they desire to be the principal victims of the dreadful tragedy now performing in the court of the lions. May heaven, Signor, preserve you in peace!'

Certified the truth of what the first page had related, Alabez returned to the place where he had left Abenamar and Sarracino. 'Friends,' he cried, 'what the page has declared is the truth; there

is dreadful treason acting, and a great slaughter among the
Abencerrages; one of the king's pages has confirmed the statement, and requested I would warn the Abencerrages to leave the
city.'

'As Alla lives,' exclaimed Sarracino, 'the Zegries must be the
authors of this horrid plot! Let us hasten to the city, and seek
immediate redress for our wrongs.' 'Away then,' said Abenamar,
'there is no time to lose.' Making all possible dispatch they soon
reached the street of the Gomeles, where they found Muza and
more than twenty Abencerrages, who had returned from the sally
against the Christians on the Vega, and were going to the king
to give him an account of their success; to these Alabez exclaimed,
'Cavaliers, to your defence! If you wish not to die by treachery;
the king has already slain more than thirty of your race.'

'The astonished Abencerrages made no answer, but Muza
replied, 'By the faith of knighthood, if there is treachery the Zegries
and Gomeles are the authors of it; not one of them sallied out on
the alarm, nor is there one to be seen throughout the city; they
are doubtless with the king in the Alhambra, and are guilty of
the death of these innocent and noble gentlemen. Follow me,
friends, I will put a speedy termination to their crimes.'

They followed Muza to the New-Square, where, as Captain-
General, he ordered a trumpet to sound an alarm; a multitude of
people, both horse and foot, immediately assembled and joined
them, but not one of the Zegries, Gomeles, or Mazas appeared
among the many families of the first distinction who were present,
which plainly proved to the party who were the authors of the
mischief. When Alabez saw so many citizens assembled, he thought
it a fit opportunity to acquaint them with the horrid cruelty that
was practised against the guiltless Abencerrages, and taking his
station in the centre, he thus addressed them :

'Friends, and fellow citizens, and all who hear me, learn that
there is a dreadful treason now perpetrating. King Boabdil has
caused many of the Abencerrages to be beheaded, and had it
not been discovered by the will of heaven, the whole race would
have perished in the same manner.' Scarce had Alabez made an
end of speaking, when the multitude gave a loud shout, calling
'To arms, to arms!' and crying, 'Treason! Perish the king that has
slain the Abencerrages! We will have no traitor for our king!'
Ungovernable fury now possessed them; seizing the first weapons
that came to hand, the multitude began to ascend to the
Alhambra; in a short time more than forty thousand men had
assembled, and above two hundred Abencerrages who still

remained, with numbers of Gazules, Vanegas, Almoradies, Almo-hadies, and Azarques, and others of the Granadine nobility, crying, 'If this is suffered with impunity, another day will end another race.'

The shouts of the men, and shrieks of the women and children were so great, and there was such a tumult in the city, that it seemed desolated by war, and drowned in tears. The clamour soon reached the Alhambra, when the king, apprehending the cause of the tumult, ordered the gates to be barred, dreading he had been too hasty in following evil counsels, and not conceiving how the matter could have so soon gone abroad. At length the people reached the summit of the hill, shouting, 'Perish the king! Let him die!' Finding the gates secured within, they called for fire to consume them, and fire was immediately applied in many places at the same time, and which had already begun to burn with great fury.

King Muley-hascem, father of Boabdil, hearing the dreadful tumult, and being made acquainted with the cause of it, was highly enraged at the wickedness of his son, and desiring he should be punished for his crimes, ordered a postern gate of the Alhambra to be opened, pretending he meant only to pacify the people; no sooner was the gate opened, than a thousand men were ready to rush in; and when they saw the old king, they lifted him on their shoulders, exclaiming, 'This is our king, we will have no other. Long live king Muley-hascem!' And leaving a strong guard to protect his person, many of the Abencerrages, Alabeces, and Gazules, and more than an hundred foot soldiers pressed forward. Muley-hascem now gave orders for the postern to be shut, that no damage might be done to the Alhambra, but it was too late, as sufficient numbers were already within it to destroy an hundred Alhambras; flying through the streets and avenues they shouted, 'Perish the king and the traitors!' At length they came to the royal palace, where they found the queen and the ladies of the court half dead with fear, not knowing the occasion of so strange a tumult. Enquiring for the king, they were informed he was in the court of the lions. Thither they flew without delay, and found the doors fastened with strong bars, but this afforded no security to those within, for they were in an instant burst open, in spite of the defence made by the Zegries. The Abencerrages, Alabeces, and Gazules, on entering it, saw the heaps of their friends in that accursed charnel-house, slaughtered by the king's command, and such was their frantic fury at the sight that had they been able to find him and his wicked advisers, they would have deceived the

justness of the law of retaliation, and considering beheading too
mild a punishment, they would have inflicted a thousand tortures
in putting them to death, as some small consolation in their heavy
affliction. Breathing vengeance they attacked with their swords
and poniards more than five hundred Zegries, Gomeles, and
Mazas, who were present, crying, 'Kill the villains who have given
the king these wicked counsels!' The Zegries defended themselves
resolutely, but notwithstanding they were armed for the event, they
were soon hewed to pieces, and in less than an hour, more than
two hundred of those three races were slain; they still however
continued to fight, and the Abencerrages and their friends made
such a dreadful slaughter among them, that not one of those who
were in the court escaped with life.

The unhappy king secreted himself, and was no where to be
found. The bodies of the dead Abencerrages were now laid on
black cloth, and carried to the New-Square, that all the citizens
might behold them, and, moved at the sight of so dreadful a
spectacle, compassionate their wrongs. The people hurried up and
down the Alhambra enquiring for the king, and so great was the
confusion that the towers and houses resounded with the noise,
which was re-echoed by the neighbouring mountains. The city,
like the Alhambra, was also involved in the general distress, and
the slaughtered Abencerrages were publicly mourned by all the
citizens, while the friends of the Zegries, Gomeles, and Mazas,
and the others of their partisans who fell in the conflict, dared only
to lament their deaths in private. The following ballad records
the event:

> Through the tow'rs of the Alhambra
>   Shouts and fearful shrieks resound,
> And the city of Granada
>   Is in tears of sorrow drown'd.
>
> Because the cruel king beheaded,
>   All in one disastrous day,
> Thirty-six Abencerrages,
>   Whom he did in treachery slay.
>
> Zegries vile and base Gomeles,
>   Falsely did these knights accuse;
> Sad Granada, deeply grieving,
>   Weeps her noblest sons to lose.
>
> Men and women, little children,
>   Cry as if their hearts would break,

For these bold and generous barons,
   For their friends and parents sake.

Every house is full of mourning,
   Mourning's seen in every street,
Not a gentleman or lady,
   But in dismal black you meet.

Zegries only and Gomeles,
   These no signs of mourning shew,
These whose wicked wiles prevailing,
   Caus'd such cruel scenes of woe.

If they mourn 'tis for their kindred,
   Those indeed were not a few,
Whom Gazuls and Alabeces,
   To revenge their falsehood slew.

In th' apartment of the lions
   Where they triumph'd, there they fell;
Had they found the king, he had not
   Liv'd the horrid tale to tell.

THOMAS RODD

JUAN DE MARIANA
[1535–1624]

The erudite Jesuit Juan de Mariana is one of Spain's greatest historians. His monumental Historia de España *appeared first in Latin (1592) and then in Spanish (1601). Its thirty volumes cover the entire history of Spain through the reign of Ferdinand and Isabel. Written in a classic style and embellished with national legends, Mariana's history is reminiscent of Livy and Tacitus.*

GENERAL HISTORY OF SPAIN

DESCRIPTION OF SPAIN

The country of Spain is no way inferior to any of the best in the world, either in regard of the climate, or of the plenty of all things necessary for life, which it abundantly produces; or of the great quantity of gold and silver, and other metals, and precious stones, which are found in it. It is not scorched with the violent heat of the sun as Africa, nor so subject to stormy winds, frost, and damps as France, but being seated between both enjoys a greater temperature than either, so that the heat of the summer and winter frosts and rain, render it so fruitful, that it not only abundantly supplies the natives, but also furnishes other countries; its product being whatever is necessary for the support of human life, and satisfaction of man's pride and ambition. The fruit is most delicious to the taste, the vines exuberant, and the wines generous. The plenty of corn, honey, oil, cattle, sugar and silk, is extraordinary; but the quantity of wool is beyond measure. There are mines of gold and silver, and veins of iron; transparent stones like looking-glasses, as also many quarries of rich marble of several colours. . . . The soil in several places varies, some produces woods, some corn, and some is bare; for the most there are but few rivers and springs, but the ground is of that goodness it commonly yields twenty or thirty for one increase, some good years eighty for one; yet this is but very rare. In many parts of Spain, there are barren mountains, and some bare and stony hills, which have something of deformity. This is mostly in the northern parts, for the southern are fruitful and pleasant. Along the seacoast there is plenty of fish, which is very scarce in the inland, by reason there are but few rivers, and fewer lakes. Nevertheless there is no part of the country that is wholly fruitless.

KING RODERICK, LAST KING OF THE GOTHS

Spain being in this condition, Roderick excluding the sons of Witiza, ascended the throne of the Goths, by choice, as is believed of the nobles. The kingdom was full of distractions, by reason of the several interests, the people were grown effeminate, giving themselves up to feasting, drink, and lewdness; the military discipline was quite lost, and the kingdom of the Goths was now running headlong to destruction. The new king had good natural parts, and seemed to be well inclined. He was hardy, resolute, bountiful, and had excellent ways of gaining of men. Such he was before his accession to the crown, but no sooner put into possession of it, than he sullied all these virtues with no less vices. Above all, he was implacable when offended, wholly given up to lust, and had no discretion in his undertakings; and in fine, was more like to Witiza, than to his father, or grandfather. There are pieces of money of his to be seen, with his name, and effigies armed, and with a stern countenance, on the reverse, these words, *Igeditania Pius,* a motto he merited not; but was given to flatter him. King

7—SA

Roderick enlarged, and beautified the palace built by his father near Cordova, which the Moors afterwards, called Roderick's palace. He called home his cousin Pelayus, and made him Captain of the Guards, the greatest trust at court. Witiza's sons he treated so ill, that they, for fear of worse consequences, fled into that part of Barbary that was subject to the Goths, called Mauritania Tingitana. At that time, Count Requila governed that province as lieutenant, I believe, to Count Julian, a man in such power, that besides it, he had the government of that part of Spain about the Straight of Gibraltar, whence, is a short cut into Africa. Besides all this, he held a great estate of his own, about Consuegra, inferior to none in the kingdom. Hence sprung all the mischiefs that ensued, for Witiza's sons before they went over into Africa, had sowed the seeds of a rebellion, and were assisted by Oppas the Bishop, who was of the blood royal, and very powerful. These beginnings, which ought to have been suppressed, were heightened by another accident. It was the custom of Spain, for the sons of the nobility to bred up at Court, and attend upon the King, and their daughters upon the Queen. Among the latter, was a daughter of Count Julian, called Cava, of singular beauty. As she played with her equals, it fell out she discovered some part of her body, which the King from a window perceiving, was so taken with her, he could think of nothing else. The continual sight of her, blew the coals, and having used all possible means to gain her consent, without any success, at last he ravished her; and by that act, cast himself, and his kingdom, headlong into destruction, as a dissolute man, and one wholly abandoned by God. Count Julian was at that time in Africa, his daughter in a rage, wrote to him, lamenting her misfortune, and stirring him up to revenge. The Count having received this news, resolved to hasten the execution of the treason he had till then been hatching. Therefore putting an end to his affairs in Africa, he came over into Spain, being well skilled in the art of dissimulation. Being come to Court, both in regard of his good service, and for the sake of his daughter, he was highly honoured and intrusted. The better to carry on his design, he persuaded the King, since Spain was at peace, to send all the forces he had towards the frontiers, to oppose the Moors and French, who committed some hostilities on the borders, by this means to leave the kingdom naked and defenceless. This done, he gave the King to understand, that his wife being sick in Africa, nothing could be so great a comfort to her as the sight of her dear daughter. The request was so reasonable, and he urged it so, that the King could not deny it. At Malaga there is a gate

called De la Cava, at which, there is a tradition, she went out to
take shipping for Africa. At the same time, the King is said to
have committed another great error, which was, that he caused
to be broke open an old castle at Toledo, said to be enchanted,
locked up with many locks and bolts, it being a received opinion,
that whensoever it was opened the ruin of Spain was at hand.
This the King imagined, was only a report spread abroad, to
conceal some treasures hid there, but being within found none,
only a chest, and in it a picture, on which were drawn men of
strange faces and habit, with a Latin inscription to this effect, *By
these people Spain shall soon be destroyed*. The countenances and
habit were like the Moors, whence it was inferred all the mischief
would come from Africa. The King too late repented his rashness.
Some look upon this as a mere fiction, I will give no judgment
upon it, the reader has his liberty to believe, or disbelieve. I would
not totally omit it, because grave authors relate it, tho' not all in
the same manner.

JOHN STEVENS

LUIS DE GRANADA
[1504–1588]

*The most learned and eloquent preacher of sixteenth-century Spain was
Fray Luis de Granada of the Dominican order. The son of poverty-stricken
Galician parents—his mother worked as a washerwoman in a Dominican
convent—Fray Luis reached high eminence in ecclesiastical circles, and
international fame both for his moving sermons and his religious writings.*

*Guía de pecadores (1567) reflects his homiletic ability. This powerful
and persuasive exhortation to sinners has been translated into English several
times.*

THE SINNER'S GUIDE

OF THOSE WHO REFUSE TO PRACTISE VIRTUE BECAUSE
THEY LOVE THE WORLD

If we examine the hearts of those who refuse to practise virtue
we shall frequently find a delusive love for the world to be one of
the chief causes of their faint-heartedness. I call it a delusive love
because it is founded on that imaginary good which men suppose
they will find in the things of this world. Let them examine with
closer attention these objects of their affection, and they will soon

recognize that they have been pursuing shadows. If we study the happiness of the world, even under its most favourable aspects, we shall find that it is ever accompanied by six drawbacks, which tend very much to lessen its sweetness. No one will question the truth of this; for who can deny that the happiness of this life is brief, that it is exposed to changes, that it leads to danger or blindness, and that it frequently ends in sin and deceit?

As to the first of these, who will say that that is enduring which at best must end with the brief career of man on earth? Ah! we all know the shortness of human life, for how few attain even a hundred years? There have been popes who reigned but a month; bishops who have survived their consecration but little longer; and married persons whose funerals have followed their weddings in still less time. These are not remarkable occurrences of the past only; they are witnessed in every age. Let us suppose, however, that your life will be one of the longest. 'What,' asks St. Chrysostom, 'are one hundred, two hundred, four hundred years spent in the pleasures of this world compared to eternity?' For 'if a man live many years, and have rejoiced in them all, he must remember the darksome time, and the many days; which when they shall come, the things passed shall be accused of vanity.' All happiness, however great, is but vanity when compared to eternity. Sinners themselves acknowledge this : 'Being born, forthwith we ceased to be; we are consumed in our wickedness.' How short, then, will this life seem to the wicked! It will appear as if they had been hurried immediately from the cradle to the grave. All the pleasures and satisfactions of this world will then seem to them but a dream. Isaias admirably expressed this when he said : 'As he that is hungry dreameth and eateth, but when he is awake his soul is empty; and as he that is thirsty dreameth and drinketh, and after he is awake is yet faint with thirst, and his soul is empty, so shall be the multitude that fought against Mount Sion.' Their prosperity will be so brief that it will seem like a fleeting dream. What more, in fact, remains of the glory of monarchs and of princes? 'Where,' asks the prophet, 'are the princes of the nations, and they that rule over the beasts that are upon the earth? They that take their diversion with the birds of the air; that hoard up silver and gold wherein men trust, and there is no end of their getting; that work in silver and are solicitous, and their works are unsearchable? They are cut off and are gone down to hell, and others are risen up in their place.' What has become of the wise men, the scholars, the searchers into the secrets of nature? Where is the famous Alexander? Where is the mighty

Assuerus? Where are the Caesars and the other kings of the earth? What does it now avail them that they lived in pomp and glory, that they had legions of soldiers, and servants, and flatterers almost without number? All have vanished like a shadow or a dream. In one moment all that constitutes human happiness fades away as the mist before the morning sun. Behold, then, dear Christian, how brief it is.

Consider also the innumerable changes to which human happiness is exposed in this valley of tears, this land of exile, this tempestuous sea which we call the world. The days of man on earth scarcely suffice to number his sorrows, for almost every hour brings new cares, new anxieties, or new miseries. Who can fitly describe these? Who can count all the infirmities of the body, all the passions of the soul, all the disasters which come upon us not only from our enemies, but even from our friends and from ourselves? One disputes your inheritance; another attempts your life. You are pursued by hatred, calumny, envy, revenge, and by a lying tongue, the most dangerous of all. Add to these miseries the innumerable accidents which daily befall us. One man loses an eye; another an arm; a third one is thrown from a horse or falls from a window; while still another loses all he possesses through succouring a friend. If you would know more of these miseries ask worldlings to tell you the sum of their sorrows and their joys. If balanced in the scales of truth you will find that their disappointments far outweigh their pleasures. Since, then, human life is so short, and so constantly beset with miseries, what possibility is there of knowing real happiness in this world? The vicissitudes of which we have been speaking are common to the good and the wicked, for both sail on the same sea and are exposed to the same storms. There are other miseries, however, which, as the fruits of iniquity, are the portion of the wicked. 'We wearied ourselves in the way of iniquity and destruction,' they tell us by the Wise Man, 'and have walked through hard ways, but the way of the Lord we have not known.' Thus, while the just pass from a paradise in this life to Heaven in the next, from the peace of virtue to the rest of their eternal reward, the wicked pass from a hell in this life to an eternal hell in the next, from the torments of an evil conscience to the unspeakable tortures of the undying worm.

Different causes multiply the miseries of the sinner. God, Who is a just Judge, sends them suffering, that crime may not remain unavenged; for though the punishment of sin is generally reserved for the next world, it sometimes begins in this. The government of Divine Providence equally embraces nations and individuals. Thus we see that sin, when it has become general, brings upon the world universal scourges, such as famines, wars, floods, pestilences, and heresies. . . .

Other misfortunes, such as imprisonment, banishment, loss of fortune, come upon the wicked through God's representatives upon earth, the ministers of justice. Dearly bought, then, is the pleasures of sin, for which they pay a hundred-fold even in this life.

Man's irregular appetites and passions are another and inexhaustible source of afflictions. What, in fact, can you expect from immoderate affections, inordinate sorrow, groundless fears, uncertain hopes, unreasonable solicitude, but violent shocks and continual anxieties which take from man all freedom and peace of heart? Living in the midst of tumult, he scarcely ever prays, he knows not the sweets of repose. From man himself, from his uncontrolled appetites, spring all these miseries. Judge, then, what happiness is possible under such conditions. . . .

The blindness and darkness which prevail in the world render these snares still more dangerous. This blindness of worldlings is represented by the Egyptian darkness, which was so thick it could be felt, and which, during the three days it lasted, prevented every one from leaving the place in which he was or beholding the face of his neighbour. The darkness which reigns in the world is even more palpable. For could there be greater blindness than to believe what we believe and yet live as we are living? Is it not a blindness equal to madness to pay so much attention to men and to be so wholly regardless of God? to be so careful in the observance of human laws and so indifferent in the observance of God's laws? to labour so earnestly for the body, which is but dust, and to neglect the soul, which is the image of the Divine Majesty? to amass treasure upon treasure for this life, which may end to-morrow, and to lay up nothing for the life to come, which will endure for all eternity? to live as if we were never to die, wholly forgetful of the irrevocable sentence which immediately follows death? If his life were never to end the sinner could scarcely act with more unbridled licence. Is it not absolute blindness to sacrifice an eternal kingdom for the momentary gratification of a sinful appetite? to be so careful of one's estate and so careless of one's conscience? to desire that all we possess should be good except our own life? The world is so full of such blindness that men seem bewitched. They have eyes, and see not; they have ears, and hear not. They have eyes as keen as those of the eagle in discerning the things of this world; but they are as blind as beetles to the things of eternity. Like St. Paul, who could see nothing, though his eyes were open, when he was thrown to the ground on his way to Damascus, their eyes are open to this life, but utterly blind to the life to come.

In the midst of such darkness and so many snares what can worldlings expect but to stumble and fall? This is one of the greatest miseries of life, one that should inspire us with strong aversion for the world. St. Cyprian, desiring to excite in a friend contempt for the world, makes use of this argument only. He goes with him in spirit to a high mountain, whence he points out to him lands, seas, courts of justice, palaces and public places, all defiled with the abominations of sin. At the same time he shows his friend, from this spectacle, how justly such a world merits his contempt, and how great should be his gratitude to God for having rescued him from all these evils. Imitate this saint, and, rising in spirit above the world, gaze on the scene laid before you. You will be overwhelmed by the sight of so much falsehood, treachery, perjury, fraud, calumny, envy, hatred, vanity, and iniquities of every kind, but particularly the total forgetfulness of God which prevails in the world. You will see the majority of men living like beasts, following the blind impulse of brutal passions, and living as regardless of justice or reason as if they were pagans, ignorant of the existence of God, and knowing no other object than to live and die. You will see the innocent oppressed, the guilty acquitted, the just despised, the wicked honoured and exalted, and interest always more powerful than virtue. You will see justice bribed, truth disfigured, modesty unknown, arts ruined, power abused, public places corrupted. You will see knaves, worthy of rigorous punishment, who, having become rich through fraud and rapine, are universally feared and honoured. You will see creatures like these, having little more than the appearance of men, filling high places and holding honourable offices. You will see money worshipped instead of God, and its corrupting influence causing the violation of all laws, both human and divine. Finally, you will behold in the greater part of the world justice existing only in name. . . .

What, then, is human glory but the son of the siren which lures men to destruction, a sweet but poisoned cup, a viper of brilliant colours breathing only venom? It attracts us only to deceive us; it elevates us only to crush us. Consider, moreover, what a return it exacts for all that it gives. Grief at the loss of a child far exceeds the pleasure of health. An insult wounds us more than honour flatters us; for nature dispenses joys and sorrows so unequally that

the latter affect us much more powerfully than the former.
These reflections manifestly prove the delusiveness of worldly
happiness.

You have here, dear Christian, a true picture of the world,
however contrary it is to what the world appears to be. Judge,
therefore, of its happiness, so brief, so uncertain, so dangerous,
and so delusive. What is this world, then, but a land of toil, as a
philosopher has wisely said, a school of vanity, an asylum of
illusions, a labyrinth of errors, a prison of darkness, a highway
of thieves, a stream of infected water, an ocean of perpetual
storms? It is a barren soil, a stony field, a thorny wood, a meadow
whose flowers conceal serpents, a garden full of blossoms but
yielding no fruit, a river of tears, a fountain of cares, a deceptive
poison, a perfect fiction, a pleasing frenzy. Its good is false,
unfounded, its fears groundless, its labour profitless, its tears
fruitless, its hope vain, its joy false, its grief real. . . .

REMEDIES AGAINST ENVY

Envy consists in grieving at another's good or repining at another's happiness. The envious man looks with hatred upon his
superiors who excel him, upon his equals who compete with him,
upon his inferiors who strive to equal him. Saul's envy of David
and the Pharisees' envy of Christ could only be satisfied by death;
for it is the character of this cruel vice to stop at nothing until it
has compassed its end. Of its nature it is a mortal sin, because, like
hatred, it is directly opposed to charity. However, in this, as in
other sins, there are degrees which do not constitute a mortal sin,
as, for example, when hatred or envy is not grave, or when the
will does not fully consent.

Envy is a most powerful, a most injurious vice. It is spread
all over the world, but predominates particularly in the courts
of kings and in the society of the rich and powerful. Who, then,
can be free from its attacks? Who is so fortunate as to be neither
the slave nor the object of envy? From the beginning of the world
history abounds with examples of this fatal vice. It was the cause
of the first fratricide which stained the earth, when Cain killed
Abel. It existed between the brothers Romulus and Remus, the
founders of Rome, and the latter fell a victim to the envy of the
former. Behold its effects in the brothers of Joseph, who sold him
as a slave; in Aaron and Mary, the brother and sister of Moses.
Even the disciples of our Lord, before the coming of the Holy
Ghost, were not wholly free from it. Ah! when we see such

examples, what must we expect to find among worldlings, who are far from possessing such sanctity, and who are seldom bound to one another by any ties? Nothing can give us an idea of the power of this vice or the ravages it effects. Good men are its natural prey, for it attacks with its poisoned dart all virtue and all talent. Hence Solomon says that all the labours and industries of men are exposed to the envy of their neighbours.

Therefore, you must diligently arm yourself against the attacks of such an enemy, and unceasingly ask God to deliver you from it. Let your efforts against it be firm and constant. If it persevere in its attacks, continue to oppose an obstinate resistance, and make little account of the unworthy sentiments it suggests. If your neighbours enjoy a prosperity which is denied you, thank God for it, persuaded that you have not merited it or that it would not be salutary for you. Remember, moreover, that envying the prosperity of others does not alleviate your own misery but rather increases it.

To strengthen your aversion to this vice make use of the following reflections: Consider, first, what a resemblance the envious man bears to the devils, who look with rage upon our good works and the heavenly reward we are to receive for them. They have no hope of the happiness of which they would deprive us, for they know that they have irretrievably lost it; but they are unwilling that beings created out of dust should enjoy honours of which they have been dispossessed. For this reason St. Augustine says: 'May God preserve from this vice not only the hearts of all Christians, but of all men, for it is the special vice of devils, and one which causes them the most hopeless suffering.' The crime of Satan is not theft or impurity, but enviously seeking, after his fall, to make man imitate his rebellion. This is truly the feeling which actuates the envious. Oftentimes the prosperity of others is no prejudice to them; they could not profit by what they strive to take from their neighbour; but they would have all equally miserable with themselves. If, then, the possessions which you envy in another could not be yours were he dispossessed of them, why should they be a cause of grief to you? When you envy the virtue of another you are your own greatest enemy; for if you continue in a state of grace, united to your neighbour through charity, you have a share in all his good works, and the more he merits the richer you become. So far, therefore, from envying his virtue, you should find it a source of consolation. Alas! because your neighbour is advancing will you fall back? Ah! if you would love in him the virtues which you do not find in yourself, you would share in them through charity; the profit of his labours would also become yours.

Consider, moreover, how envy corrodes the heart, weakens the understanding, destroys all peace of soul, and condemns us to a melancholy and intolerable existence. Like the worm which eats the wood in which it is engendered, it preys upon the heart in which it was given birth. Its ravages extend even to the countenance, whose paleness testifies to the passion which rages within. This vice is itself the severest judge against its victim, for the envious man is subjected to its severest tortures. Hence certain authors have termed it a *just* vice, not meaning that it is good, for it is a most heinous sin, but meaning that it is its own greatest punishment.

Consider, again, how opposed is the sin of envy to charity, which is God, and to the common good, which every one should promote to the best of his ability; for when we envy another's good, when we hate those to whom God unceasingly manifests His love, when we persecute those whom He created and redeemed, do we not, at least in desire, strive to undo the work of God?

But a more efficacious remedy against this vice is to love humility and abhor pride, which is the father of envy. A proud man, who cannot brook a superior or an equal, naturally envies all who appear to excel him, persuading himself that he descends in proportion as another rises. Hence the Apostle says : 'Let us not be desirous of vain-glory, provoking one another, envying one another.' In other words, let us destroy the root of envy, which is vain-glory. Let us wean our hearts from worldly honours and possessions, and seek only spiritual riches, for such treasures are not diminished when enjoyed by numbers, but, on the contrary, are increased. It is otherwise with the goods of the earth, which must decrease in proportion to the numbers who share them. For this reason envy finds easy access to the soul which covets the riches of this life, where one necessarily loses what another gains.

Do not be satisfied with feeling no grief at the prosperity of your neighbour, but endeavour to benefit him all you can, and the good you cannot give him ask God to grant him. Hate no man. Love your friends in God, and your enemies for God. He so loved you while you were still His enemy that He shed the last drop of His Blood to save you from the tyranny of your sins. Your neighbour may be wicked, but that is no reason for hating him. In such a case imitate the example of a wise physician, who loves his patient, but hates his disease. We must abhor sin, which is the work of man, but we must always love our neighbour, who is the work

of God. Never say in your heart : 'What is my neighbour to me?
I owe him nothing. We are bound by no ties of blood or interest.
He has never done me a favour, but has probably injured me.'
Reflect rather on the benefits which God unceasingly bestows
upon you, and remember that all He asks in return is that you be
charitable and generous, not to Him, for He has no need of you
or your possessions, but to your neighbour, whom He has
recommended to your love.

ANONYMOUS

LUIS DE LEÓN
[1528?–1591]

*The question—Who is the greatest of all Spanish lyric poets?—is as
highly debatable in that country as in any nation which has produced a like
treasure of fine poetry. Many critics place at the top of the list an Augustinian
professor at the University of Salamanca—Fray Luis de León. A provoking
and erudite teacher, known throughout Spain during his lifetime for his
translations and prose writings, Fray Luis himself gave little importance
to his original poems. They are relatively few in number. But each is distinguished for the polished, classic style in which Fray Luis phrases his
yearning towards peace both celestial and earthly, and for the lyric beauty
of his language and sentiment.*

Fray Luis also left two valuable prose works, De los nombres de Cristo,
a theological treatise on the names of Christ, and La perfecta casada, *a
guide to the Christian wife. His Spanish translation of the* Song of Solomon
*was a factor cited by jealous associates who denounced him to the Inquisition.
Fray Luis thereupon spent almost five years in prison until his acquittal in
1576. It is said that when he returned to the University, amid tumultuous
acclaim, he began his first lecture with the simple statement 'We were saying
yesterday . . .'*

ODE TO RETIREMENT

O, happy, happy he, who flies
    Far from the noisy world away,—
Who, with the worthy and the wise,
    Hath chosen the narrow way,—
The silence of the secret road
That leads the soul to virtue and to God !

No passions in his breast arise;
   Calm in his own unaltered state,
He smiles superior, as he eyes
   The splendour of the great;
And his undazzled gaze is proof
Against the glittering hall and the gilded roof.

He heeds not, though the trump of fame
   Pour forth the loudest of its strains,
To spread the glory of his name;
   And his high soul disdains
That flattery's voice should varnish o'er
The deed that truth or virtue would abhor.

Such lot be mine : what boots to me
   The cumbrous pageantry of power;
To court the gaze of crowds, and be
   The idol of the hour;
To chase an empty shape of air,
That leaves me weak with toil and worn with care?

O streams, and shades, and hills on high,
   Unto the stillness of your breast
My wounded spirit longs to fly,—
   To fly, and be at rest !
Thus from the world's tempestuous sea,
O gentle Nature, do I turn to thee !

Be mine the holy calm of night,
   Soft sleep and dreams serenely gay,
The freshness of the morning light,
   The fulness of the day;
Far from the sternly frowning eye
That pride and riches turn on poverty.

The warbling birds shall bid me wake
   With their untutored melodies;
No fearful dream my sleep shall break,
   No wakeful cares arise,
Like the sad shapes that hover still
Round him that hangs upon another's will.

Be mine my hopes to Heaven to give,
   To taste the bliss that Heaven bestows,

Alone and for myself to live,
    And 'scape the many woes
That human hearts are doomed to bear,—
The pangs of love, and hate, and hope, and fear.

A garden by the mountain-side
    Is mine, whose flowery blossoming
Shows, even in spring's luxuriant pride,
    What autumn's sun shall bring:
And from the mountain's lofty crown
A clear and sparkling rill comes trembling down;

Then pausing in its downward force
    The venerable trees among,
It gurgles on its winding course;
    And, as it glides along,
Gives freshness to the day, and pranks
With ever changing flowers its mossy banks.

The whisper of the balmy breeze
    Scatters a thousand sweets around,
And sweeps in music through the trees,
    With an enchanting sound,
That laps the soul in calm delight,
Where crowns and kingdoms are forgotten quite.

Theirs let the dear-bought treasure be,
    Who in a treacherous bark confide;
I stand aloof, and changeless see
    The changes of the tide,
Nor fear the wail of those that weep,
When angry winds are warring with the deep:

Day turns to night; the timbers rend;
    More fierce the ruthless tempest blows;
Confused the varying cries ascend,
    As the sad merchant throws
His hoards, to join the stores that lie
In the deep sea's uncounted treasury.

Mine be the peaceful board of old,
    From want as from profusion free:
His let the massy cup of gold,
    And glittering bawbles be,
Who builds his baseless hope of gain
Upon a brittle bark and stormy main.

While others, thoughtless of pain
   Of hope delayed and long suspense,
Still struggle on to guard or gain
   A sad pre-eminence,
May I, in woody covert laid,
Be gayly chanting in the secret shade,—

At ease within the shade reclined,
   With laurel and with ivy crowned,
And my attentive ear inclined
   To catch the heavenly sound
Of harp or lyre, when o'er the strings
Some master-hand its practised finger flings.

ANONYMOUS

ODE TO FRANCISCO SALINAS

The air grows pure and clear,
Steeped in unearthly loveliness and light,
When we, Salinas, hear
Thy music take its flight,
Pressed from the keys by hands of magic might;

And, at that wondrous sound,
My soul, that long in apathy had lain,
New wisdom now hath found;
And taught by thee would fain
Of her high origin take thought again.

.   .   .

So, journeying through the air,
Till in the highest sphere in joy immersed,
She hears that music rare
Stilling the Spirit's thirst,
That music, of all harmonies the first;

And with enraptured gaze
She sees the Master, Who o'er all hath reign;
He His great cithern plays,
Striking those chords amain,
Whereby He doth the universe sustain.

.   .   .

Here in this sea of sound
Floats the tired soul in endless ecstasy,
Till, therein wholly drowned
She's lost to things that be.
From all that fetters her, divinely free.

O thou most blessed swoon!
O death that givest life, O gentle peace!
Would that thy gracious boon
Of joy might never cease,
And from low earth-born cares bestow release!

Let then the glorious stream
Of thy grand music, my Salinas, flow,
That to the Good Supreme
My senses wake, and so
Remain for ever dead to things below.

IDA FARNELL

THE LIFE OF THE BLESSED

Region of life and life!
Land of the good whose earthly toils are o'er!
Nor frost nor heat may blight
Thy vernal beauty, fertile shore,
Yielding thy blessed fruits for evermore!

There, without crook or sling,
Walks the Good Shepherd; blossoms white and red
Round his meek temples cling;
And, to sweet pastures led,
His own loved flock beneath his eye is fed.

He guides, and near him they
Follow delighted; for he makes them go
Where dwells eternal May,
And heavenly roses blow,
Deathless, and gathered but again to grow.

He leads them to the height
Named of the infinite and long-sought Good,
And fountains of delight;
And where his feet have stood,
Springs up, along the way, their tender food.

And when, in the mid skies,
The climbing sun has reached his highest bound,
    Reposing as he lies,
    With all his flock around,
He witches the still air with numerous sound.

    From his sweet lute flow forth
Immortal harmonies, of power to still
    All passions born of earth,
    And draw the ardent will
Its destiny of goodness to fulfil.

    Might but a little part,
A wandering breath, of that high melody
    Descend into my heart,
    And change it till it be
Transformed and swallowed up, O love! in thee:

    Ah! then my soul should know,
Beloved! where thou liest at noon of day;
    And from this place of woe
    Released, should take its way
To mingle with thy flock, and never stray.

                    WILLIAM CULLEN BRYANT

HYMN ON THE ASCENSION

And dost thou, holy Shepherd, leave
    Thine unprotected flock alone,
Here, in this darksome vale, to grieve,
    While thou ascend'st thy glorious throne?

O, where can they their hopes now turn,
    Who never lived but on thy love?
Where rest the hearts for thee that burn,
    When thou art lost in light above?

How shall those eyes now find repose
    That turn, in vain, thy smile to see?
What can they hear save mortal woes,
    Who lose thy voice's melody?

And who shall lay his tranquil hand
    Upon the troubled ocean's might?
Who hush the winds by his command?
    Who guide us through this starless night?

For thou art gone!—that cloud so bright,
That bears thee from our love away,
Springs upward through the dazzling light,
And leaves us here to weep and pray!

GEORGE TICKNOR

THE ASSUMPTION OF THE VIRGIN

Lady! thine upward flight
The opening heavens receive with joyous song;
Blest, who thy garments bright
May seize, amid the throng,
And to the sacred mount float peacefully along.

Bright angels are around thee,
They that have served thee from thy birth are here:
Their hands with return have crowned thee;
Thou,—peerless Queen of air,
As sandals to thy feet the silver moon dost wear.

Celestial dove! so meek
And mild and fair! oh, let thy peaceful eye
This thorny valley seek,
Where such sweet blossoms lie,
But where the sons of Eve in pain and sorrow sigh.

For if the imprisoned soul
Could catch the brightness of that heavenly way,
'Twould own its sweet control
And gently pass away,
Drawn by the magnet power to an eternal day.

HENRY WADSWORTH LONGFELLOW

ON LEAVING PRISON

Falsehood and hatred here
Held me in this prison pent:
Happy whose life is spent
In learning's humble sphere,
Far from the world malevolent;

He, with poor house and fare,
Communing with God alone,
Doth in the country fair
Dwell solitary, there
By none envied, envying none.

AUBREY F. G. BELL

THE NAMES OF CHRIST

THE PRINCE OF PEACE

Even if reason should not prove it, and even if we could in no other way understand how gracious a thing is peace, yet would this fair show of the heavens over our heads and this harmony in all their manifold fires sufficiently bear witness to it. For what is it but peace, or, indeed, a perfect image of peace, that we now behold, and that fills us with such deep joy? Since if peace is, as Saint Augustine, with the brevity of truth, declares it to be, a quiet order, or the maintenance of a well-regulated tranquillity in whatever order demands,—then what we now witness is surely its true and faithful image. For while these hosts of stars, arranged and divided into their several bands, shine with such surpassing splendour, and while each one of their multitude inviolably maintains its separate station, neither pressing into the place of that next to it, nor disturbing the movements of any other, not forgetting its own; none breaking the eternal and holy law God has imposed on it; but all rather bound in one brotherhood, ministering one to another, and reflecting their light one to another,—they do surely show forth a mutual love, and, as it were, a mutual reverence, tempering each other's brightness and strength into a peaceful unity and power, whereby all their different influences are combined into one holy and mighty harmony, universal and everlasting. And therefore may it be most truly said, not only that they do all form a fair and perfect model of peace, but that they all set forth and announce, in clear and gracious words, what excellent things peace contains within herself and carries abroad whithersoever her power extends.

GEORGE TICKNOR

SANTA TERESA DE JESÚS
[1515–1582]

Few men have won the eminence in religious and literary spheres which was achieved almost unwillingly by Teresa de Cepeda y Ahumada, the renowned Santa Teresa de Jesús. This extraordinary woman, founder against enormous odds of the Spanish Order of Discalced Carmelites, composed most of her works reluctantly. Indeed, she wrote at the express order of her superiors, for she declared that she had 'neither health nor head' for writing. Santa Teresa became nevertheless one of Spain's greatest mystic authors in prose and verse.

The ecstasy of the divine visions which she experienced permeate her prose works, although some also include very down-to-earth details of her life and duties. The style is spontaneous and unaffected, reflecting both the vivacious personality and brilliant mind for which she was famous. Religious intensity also marks her verse.

Santa Teresa's finest prose is found in El castillo interior, *a mystic description of the prayerful means by which the soul reaches its divine essence. The selection presented here, however—chosen for its interest to the contemporary reader—is taken from Santa Teresa's spiritual biography, which she entitled* El libro de las misericordias de Dios.

I DIE BECAUSE I DO NOT DIE

I live, yet no true life I know,
And, living thus expectantly,
I die because I do not die.

Since this new death-in-life I've known,
Estrang'd from self my life has been,
For now I live a life unseen :
The Lord has claim'd me as His own.
My heart I gave Him for His throne,
Whereon He wrote indelibly :
'*I die because I do not die.*'

Within this prison-house divine,
Prison of love whereby I live,
My God Himself to me doth give,
And liberate this heart of mine.
And, as with love I yearn and pine,
With God my prisoner, I sigh :
'*I die because I do not die.*'

How tedious is this life below,
This exile, with its griefs and pains,
This dungeon and these cruel chains
In which the soul is forced to go!
Straining to leave this life of woe,
With anguish sharp and deep I cry:
'*I die because I do not die.*'

How bitter our existence ere
We come at last the Lord to meet!
For, though the soul finds loving sweet,
The waiting-time is hard to bear.
Oh, from this leaden weight of care,
My God, relieve me speedily,
Who die because I do not die.

I only live because I know
That death's approach is very sure,
And hope is all the more secure
Since death and life together go.
O death, thou life-creator, lo!
I wait upon thee, come thou nigh:
I die because I do not die.

Consider, life, love's potency,
And cease to cause me grief and pain.
Reflect, I beg, that, thee to gain,
I first must lose thee utterly.
Then, death, come pleasantly to me.
Come softly: undismay'd am I
Who die because I do not die.

That life, with life beyond recall,
Is truly life for evermore:
Until this present life be o'er
We cannot savour life at all.
So, death, retreat not at my call,
For life through death I can descry
Who die because I do not die.

O life, what service can I pay
Unto my God Who lives in me
Save if I first abandon thee

That I may merit thee for aye?
I'd win thee dying day by day,
Such yearning for my Spouse have I,
Dying because I do not die.

E. ALLISON PEERS

IF, LORD, THY LOVE FOR ME IS STRONG

If, Lord, Thy love for me is strong
As this which binds me unto Thee,
What holds me from Thee, Lord, so long,
What holds Thee, Lord, so long from me?

O soul, what then desirest thou?
—Lord, I would see Thee, who thus choose Thee.
What fears can yet assail thee now?
—All that I fear is but to lose Thee.

Love's whole possession I entreat,
Lord, make my soul Thine own abode,
And I will build a nest so sweet
It may not be too poor for God.

O soul in God hidden from sin,
What more desires for thee remain,
Save but to love, and love again,
And, all on flame with love within,
Love on, and turn to love again?

ARTHUR SYMONS

LET NOTHING DISTURB THEE

Let nothing disturb thee,
Nothing affright thee;
All things are passing;
God never changeth;
Patient endurance
Attaineth to all things;
Who God possesseth
In nothing is wanting;
Alone God sufficeth.

HENRY WADSWORTH LONGFELLOW

THE LIFE OF THE HOLY MOTHER TERESA OF JESUS

CHAPTER I

Describes how the Lord began to awaken her soul in childhood to a love of virtue and what a help it is in this respect to have good parents.

If I had not been so wicked it would have been a help to me that I had parents who were virtuous and feared God, and also that the Lord granted me His favour to make me good. My father was fond of reading good books and had some in Spanish so that his children might read them too. These books, together with the care which my mother took to make us say our prayers and to lead us to be devoted to Our Lady and to certain saints, began to awaken good desires in me when I was, I suppose, about six or seven years old. It was a help to me that I never saw my parents inclined to anything but virtue. They themselves had many virtues. My father was a man of great charity toward the poor, who was good to the sick and also to his servants—so much so that he could never be brought to keep slaves, because of his compassion for them. On one occasion, when he had a slave of a brother of his in the house, he was as good to her as to his own children. He used to say that it caused him intolerable distress that she was not free. He was strictly truthful : nobody ever heard him swear or speak evil. He was a man of the most rigid chastity.

My mother, too, was a very virtuous woman, who endured a life of great infirmity : she was also particularly chaste. Though extremely beautiful, she was never known to give any reason for supposing that she made the slightest account of her beauty; and, though she died at thirty-three, her dress was already that of a person advanced in years. She was a very tranquil woman, of great intelligence. Throughout her life she endured great trials and her death was most Christian.

We were three sisters and nine brothers : all of them, by the goodness of God, resembled their parents in virtue, except myself, though I was my father's favourite. And, before I began to offend God, I think there was some reason for this, for it grieves me whenever I remember what good inclinations the Lord had given me and how little I profited by them. My brothers and sisters never hindered me from serving God in any way.

I had one brother almost of my own age. It was he whom I most loved, though I had a great affection for them all, as had they for me. We used to read the lives of saints together; and, when I read of the martyrdoms suffered by saintly women for God's sake, I used to think they had purchased the fruition of God very cheaply; and I had a keen desire to die as they had done, not out of any love for God of which I was conscious, but in order to attain as quickly as possible to the fruition of the great blessings which, as I read, were laid up in Heaven. I used to discuss with this brother of mine how we could become martyrs. We agreed to go off to the country of the Moors, begging our bread for the love of God, so that they might behead us there; and, even at so tender an age, I believe the Lord had given us sufficient courage for this, if we could have found a way to do it; but our greatest hindrance seemed to be that we had a father and mother. It used to cause us great astonishment when we were told that both pain and glory would last for ever. We would spend long periods talking about this and we liked to repeat again and again, 'For ever—ever— ever!' Through our frequent repetition of these words, it pleased the Lord that in my earliest years I should receive a lasting impression of the way of truth.

When I saw that it was impossible for me to go to any place where they would put me to death for God's sake, we decided to become hermits, and we used to build hermitages, as well as we could, in an orchard which we had at home. We would make heaps of small stones, but they at once fell down again, so we found no way of accomplishing our desires. But even now it gives me a feeling of devotion to remember how early God granted me what I lost by my own fault.

I gave alms as I could, which was but little. I tried to be alone when I said my prayers, and there were many such, in particular the rosary, to which my mother had a great devotion, and this made us devoted to them too. Whenever I played with other little girls, I used to love building convents and pretending that we were nuns; and I think I wanted to be a nun, though not so much as the other things I have described.

I remember that, when my mother died, I was twelve years of age or a little less. When I began to realize what I had lost, I went in my distress to an image of Our Lady and with many tears besought her to be a mother to me. Though I did this in my simplicity, I believe it was of some avail to me; for whenever I have commended myself to this Sovereign Virgin I have been conscious of her aid; and eventually she has brought me back to herself. It grieves me now when I observe and reflect how I did not keep sincerely to the good desires which I had begun.

O my Lord, since it seems Thou art determined on my salvation—and may it please Thy Majesty to save me!—and on granting me all the graces Thou hast bestowed on me already, why has it not seemed well to Thee, not for my advantage but for Thy honour, that this habitation wherein Thou hast had continually to dwell should not have become so greatly defiled? It grieves me, Lord, even to say this, since I know that the fault has been mine alone, for I believe that there is nothing more Thou couldst have done, even from this early age, to make me wholly Thine. Nor, if I should feel inclined to complain of my parents, could I do so, for I saw nothing in them but every kind of good and anxiety for my welfare. . . .

E. ALLISON PEERS

SAN JUAN DE LA CRUZ
[1542–1591]

Santa Teresa's disciple and assistant, San Juan de la Cruz, wrote only about one thousand lines of poetry. But in them, and their accompanying prose commentaries, he achieves the highest expression of Spanish mysticism. Indeed he is considered by many the greatest poet Spain has produced. The eminent Spanish critic Menéndez y Pelayo calls his poetry 'angelic, celestial and divine', and E. Allison Peers refers to it as 'the sweetest music in the Spanish language'.

San Juan's most famous poems are the Noche oscura, Llama de amor viva *and the* Cántico espiritual. *The anonymous sonnet* A Cristo crucificado, *sometimes attributed to San Juan de la Cruz, follows his other selections.*

SONGS OF THE SOUL

Songs of the soul that rejoices at having reached the high estate of perfection, which is union with God, by the road of spiritual negation.

Upon a darksome night,
Kindling with love in flame of yearning keen
—O moment of delight!—
I went, by all unseen,
New-hush'd to rest the house where I had been.

Safe sped I through that night,
By the secret stair, disguisèd and unseen
—O moment of delight!—
Wrapt in that night serene,
New-hush'd to rest the house where I had been.

O happy night and blest!
Secretly speeding, screen'd from mortal gaze,
Unseeing, on I prest,
Lit by no earthly rays,
Nay, only by heart's inmost fire ablaze.

'Twas that light guided me,
More surely than the noonday's brightest glare,
To the place where none would be
Save one that waited there—
Well knew I whom or ere I forth did fare.

O night that led'st me thus!
O night more winsome than the rising sun!
O night that madest us,
Lover and lov'd, as one,
Lover transform'd in lov'd, love's journey done!

Upon my flowering breast,
His only, as no man but he might prove,
There, slumbering, did he rest,
'Neath my caressing love,
Fann'd by the cedars swaying high above.

When from the turret's height,
Scattering his locks, the breezes play'd around,
With touch serene and light
He dealt me love's sweet wound,
And with the joyful pain thereof I swoon'd.

Forgetful, rapt, I lay,
My face reclining on my lov'd one fair.
All things for me that day
Ceas'd, as I slumber'd there,
Amid the lilies drowning all my care.

E. ALLISON PEERS

O FLAME OF LIVING LOVE

O flame of living love,
That dost eternally
Pierce through my soul with so consuming heat,
Since there's no help above,
Make thou an end of me,
And break the bond of this encounter sweet.

O burn that burns to heal!
O more than pleasant wound!
And O soft hand, O touch most delicate,
That dost new life reveal,
That dost in grace abound,
And, slaying, dost from death to life translate!

O lamps of fire that shined
With so intense a light
That those deep caverns where the senses live,
Which were obscure and blind,
Now with strange glories bright,
Both heat and light to His belovèd give!

With how benign intent
Rememberest thou my breast,
Where thou alone abidest secretly;
And in thy sweet ascent,
With glory and good possessed,
How delicately thou teachest love to me!

ARTHUR SYMONS

VERSES WRITTEN AFTER AN ECSTASY
OF HIGH EXALTATION

I entered in, I know not where,
And I remained, though knowing naught,
Transcending knowledge with my thought.

Of when I entered I know naught,
But when I saw that I was there
(Though where it was I did not care)
Strange things I learned with greatness fraught.
Yet what I heard I'll not declare.
But there I stayed, though knowing naught,
Transcending knowledge with my thought.

Of peace and piety interwound
This perfect science had been wrought,
Within the solitude profound
A straight and narrow path it taught,
Such secret wisdom there I found
That there I stammered, saying naught,
But topped all knowledge with my thought.

So borne aloft, so drunken-reeling,
So rapt was I, so swept away,
Within the scope of sense or feeling
My sense or feeling could not stay.
And in my soul I felt, revealing,
A sense that, though its sense was naught,
Transcended knowledge with my thought.

The man who truly there has come
Of his own self must shed the guise;
Of all he knew before the sum
Seems far beneath that wondrous prize :
And in this lore he grows so wise
That he remains, though knowing naught,
Transcending knowledge with his thought.

The farther that I climbed the height
The less I seemed to understand
The cloud so tenebrous and grand
That there illuminates the night
For he who understands that sight
Remains for aye, though knowing naught,
Transcending knowledge with his thought.

This wisdom without understanding
Is of so absolute a force
No wise man of whatever standing
Can ever stand against its course,
Unless they tap its wondrous source,
To know so much, though knowing naught,
They pass all knowledge with their thought.

This summit all so steeply towers
And is of excellence so high
No human faculties or powers
Can ever to the top come nigh.
Whoever with its steep could vie,
Though knowing nothing, would transcend
All thought, forever, without end.

If you would ask, what is its essence—
This summit of all sense and knowing :
It comes from the Divinest Presence—
The sudden sense of Him outflowing,

In His great clemency bestowing
The gift that leaves men knowing naught,
Yet passing knowledge with their thought.

ROY CAMPBELL

TO CHRIST CRUCIFIED

I am not moved, my God, to love Thee so,
By that fair heaven which Thou hast promised me;
Nor am I moved to fear offending Thee,
By terror of that dreaded hell below;

Thou movest me, my God; my heart doth glow
To see Thee nailed upon that shameful tree,
To see Thy body wounded piteously,
To see Thee die, with agonizing throe;

Thy love, in sooth, doth move me in such wise,
That if there were no heaven, my love would burn,
And if there were no hell, my will would bow;

I love Thee not for hopes beyond the skies,
For did my every hope to nothing turn,
I'd love Thee still, as I do love Thee now.

JAMES YOUNG GIBSON

FERNANDO DE HERRERA
[1534–1597]

Fernando de Herrera, called el divino, *is the foremost representative of the Sevillian school of poetry, which flourished during the sixteenth century and in product is characterized by rich sonority of phrase. He wrote some highly polished sonnets and love lyrics, but is most celebrated for his majestic and eloquent patriotic odes,* Canción por la victoria de Lepanto *and* Canción por la pérdida del rey don Sebastián.

ODE ON THE DEATH OF DON SEBASTIAN

With sorrowing voice begin the strain,
With fearful breath and sounds of woe,—
Sad prelude to the mournful lay
For Lusitania's fallen sway,
Spurned by the faithless foe!

And let the tale of horror sound
From Libyan Atlas and the burning plain
E'en to the Red Sea's distant bound;
And where, beyond that foaming tide,
The vanquished East, with blushing pride,
And all her nations fierce and brave,
Have seen the Christian banners wave.

O Libya! through thy deserts wide,
With many a steed, and chariot boldly driven,
Thou saw'st Sebastian's warriors sweep the shore :
On rushed they, fierce in martial power,
Nor raised their thoughts to Heaven;
Self-confident, and flushed with pride,—
Their boastful hearts on plunder bent,—
Triumphant o'er the hostile land,
In gorgeous trim the stiff-necked people went.
But the Lord opened his upholding hand,
And left them; down the abyss, with strange uproar,
Horseman and horse amain, and crashing chariots, pour.

Loaded with wrath and terror came
The day, the cruel day,
Which gave the widowed realm to shame,
To solitude, and deep dismay.
Dark lowered the heavens; in garb of woe,
The sun, astonished, ceased to glow.
Jehovah visited the guilty land,
And passed in anger, with his red right-hand
Humbling her pride : he made the force
Of weak barbarians steady in its course;
He made their bosoms firm and bold,
And bade them spurn at baneful gold,
Their ruthless way through yielding legions mow,
Fulfil his vengeful word, and trample on the foe.

O'er thy fair limbs, so long by valour saved,
Sad Lusitania, child of woe!
O'er all that rich and gallant show,
With impious hate the heathen's fearless arm
His flaming falchion waved :
His fury marred thine ancient fame,
And scattered o'er thy squadrons wild alarm,
Fell slaughter, and eternal shame.

A tide of blood o'erflowed the plain;
Like mountains stood the heaps of slain :
Alike, on that ill-fated day,
War's headlong torrent swept away
The trembling voice of fear, the coward breath,
And the high soul of valour, proud in death.

Are those the warriors once renowned;
For deeds of glory justly crowned;
Whose thunder shook the world,
Whene'er their banners were unfurled;
Who many a barbarous tribe subdued,
And many an empire stretching wide and far;
Who sacked each state that proudly stood;
Whose arms laid waste in savage war
What realms lie circled by the Indian tide?
Where now their ancient pride?
Where is that courage, once in fight secure?
How in one moment is the boast
Of that heroic valour lost !
Without the holy rites of sepulture,
Far from their homes and native land,
Fallen, O, fallen on the desert sand !

Once were they like the cedar fair
Of mighty Lebanon, whose glorious head
With leaves and boughs immeasurably spread.
The rains of heaven bade it grow
Stately and loftiest on the mountain's brow;
And still its branches rose to view
In form and beauty ever new.
High nestled on its head the fowls of air,
And many a forest beast
Beneath its ample boughs increased,
And man found shelter in its goodly shade.
With beauteous limbs unrivalled did it rise,
Lord of the mountain, towering to the skies.

Its verdant head presumptuously grew,
Trusting to wondrous bulk alone,
And vain of its excelling height :
But from the root its trunk the Lord o'erthrew,
To barbarous despite
And foreign hate a hopeless prey.

Now, by the mountain torrent strown,
Its leafless honours naked lie;
And far aloof the frighted wanderers fly,
Whom once it shielded from the burning day :
In the sad ruin of its branches bare
Dwell the wild forest beasts and screaming birds of air.

Thou, hateful Libya, on whose arid sand
Proud Lusitania's glory fell,
And all her boast of wide command,—
Let not thine heart with triumph swell,
Though to thy timid hand by angry Heaven
A praiseless victory was given !
For when the voice of grief shall call
The sons of Spain to venge her fall,
Torn by the lance, thy vitals shall repay
The fatal outrage of that bitter day,
And Luco's flood, impurpled by the slain,
Its mournful tribute roll affrighted to the main.

W. HERBERT

SONNET

Hard is yon rock, around whose head,
Unfelt, the rudest tempests blow;
And chilling cold the silver snow
On nature's ample bosom spread.
But harder is that heart of thine,
And colder all its frozen streams,
Where passion ne'er inscribed a line,
And love's warm sunshine never gleams.

Deaf are the surges of the sea
To the loud plaint of misery,
Though less than thou unkind and rude:
Dark is the evening's dying fall,—
But what are these,—or aught, or all,
To a tired spirit's solitude?

JOHN BOWRING

BALTASAR DEL ALCÁZAR
[1530–1606]

Baltasar del Alcázar, a Sevillian-born soldier and sometime administrator, was a master of epigrammatic, festive verse. La cena jocosa *is his best-known poem.*

THE JOLLY SUPPER

In Jaën where I'm abiding
Don Lope de Sosa dwells,
And my story, Ines, tells
Wonders past your mind's providing.
On this gentleman attended
A young squire from Portugal—
But to supper let us fall
So my hunger may be ended.
For the table is awaiting
Where together we may sup;
Forth are set the steaming cup
And the glass,—no more debating,—
Cut the bread, ah, what a savour!—
This *hors d'œuvre* is Paradise!
From the *salpicón* arise
Odours of a heavenly flavour.
Pour the wine into the glasses
And invoke a blessing now;
Every time I drink I vow
And bless each ruby drop that passes.
That was sure a healthy portion,
Ines, pass the bottle here;
Every mouthful would appear
Worth a florin,—no extortion.
In what tavern do you buy it?
From the place by the ravine;
Ten and six a measure, clean,
Fresh and good and cheap to try it.
By the Lord, it is a treasure
That Alcocer tavern wine;
Certainly, I think it's fine
To have at hand so just a measure.
Whether old or new invention,
On my faith, I do not know,
But this I see that here below
The tavern came with good intention.

For 'tis there I go a-thirsting,
Order up the newest brew,
Mixing it they serve to you,
You pay and drink yourself to bursting.
This, my Ines, is its merit,—
There's no need to sing its praise—
The one objection that I raise,
The fleeting joy that we inherit.
Now, the lighter dishes over,
Tell me what is coming now?
The meat-pie!—O blesséd brow,
Worthy of such noble cover!
What a dish it is, how hollow!—
What meat and luscious fat it holds!—
It seems, Ines, that it unfolds
Its depths for you and me to swallow.
But onward, onward, without question,
For straight and narrow is the road;
No more water,—let the load
Of wine, Ines, invite digestion.
Pour out the three-year vintage freely,
'Twill aid your stomach in its work.
How good to see you do not shirk
But take a grown man's portion, really!
Now tell me, is it not delightful
To have a dish so fine and rare,
With all its biting flavours there,
And all its spices fresh and spiteful?
Pine-nuts in its luscious dressing
Make the brave dame's meat-pie sweet;
And roasted by her there's a treat
In suckling pig that is a blessing.
As true as heaven 'tis fit to honour
The very table of the King;
A pork, Ines,—the sweetest thing
With her delicious tripe upon her!
My very heart is filled with rapture;
I don't know how it is with you,
But taking now and then a view,
You seem contentment here to capture.
Great heavens! I am full of liquor;
But I would make a sage remark;

You brought one lamp to light the dark,
Now two before me seem to flicker.
But these are really drunken notions;
I know of course it had to be,
That with this heavy drink I'd see
The lights increasing with the potions.
Now let us try the tankard's juices,
Celestial beverage refined,
Superior to what we bind
In casks, it livelier joy produces.
What smoothness and what glassy clearness!
What taste and odour rarefied!
What touch! What colour there beside
And all that makes for luscious dearness!
But now there come the cheese and berry
To take their place upon the board;
And both it seems would claim award
Of cup and tankard passing merry.
Try the cheese,—the choice from many,—
Quite as good as Pinto's best;
And the olives—for the rest
They can hold their own with any.
Now then, Ines, if you're able
Take six mouthfuls from the flask—
There is nothing more to ask;
Clear the covers from the table.
And as we have supped and rested
To our very hearts' content
It would seem the moment meant
For the story I suggested.
'Tis a tale, Ines, to win you—
For the Portuguese fell ill—
Eleven striking?—Wait until
To-morrow, I'll the tale continue—

THOMAS WALSH

SLEEP

Sleep is no servant of the will,—
    It has caprices of its own :
    When most pursued, 'tis swiftly gone;
When courted least, it lingers still.

With its vagaries long perplexed,
   I turned and turned my restless sconce,
   Till, one bright night, I thought at once
I'd master it;—so hear my text!

When sleep will tarry, I begin
   My long and my accustomed prayer;
   And in a twinkling sleep is there,
Through my bed-curtains peeping in :
When sleep hangs heavy on my eyes,
   I think of debts I fain would pay;
   And then, as flies night's shade from day,
Sleep from my heavy eyelids flies.

And thus controlled, the winged one bends
   E'en his fantastic will to me;
   And, strange yet true, both I and he
Are friends,—the very best of friends :
We are a happy wedded pair,
   And I the lord and he the dame;
   Our bed, our board, our hours the same;
And we're united everywhere.

I'll tell you where I learned to school
   This wayward sleep :—a whispered word
   From a church-going hag I heard,—
And tried it,—for I was no fool.
So from that very hour I knew,
   That having ready prayers to pray,
   And having many debts to pay,
Will serve for sleep and waking too.

                        JOHN BOWRING

LOPE DE RUEDA
[1510–1565]

   In the introduction to his Ocho comedias, *Cervantes speaks admiringly of Lope de Rueda, one of the forerunners of the Spanish drama. Director and principal actor of a comic troupe, Lope de Rueda was the author—among other dramatic pieces—of delightful one-act farces called* pasos. *These developed into the* entremeses *of the Golden Age, and the* sainetes *of the eighteenth century.*

   The paso *presented here is his famous* Las aceitunas.

THE OLIVES

TORUVIO .... an old man
AGUEDA DE TORUÉGANO ... his wife
MENCIGÜELA ...... their daughter
ALOJA .... a neighbour

Scene: Outside the door of Toruvio's house. It has been raining, but has cleared.

(*Enter* Toruvio, *dripping wet, and carrying firewood.*)

TOR. Good Heavens, what a storm raged through the ravines of that wooded hill out yonder. Every minute I expected the sky to fall and the clouds to come down on top of me. And am I hungry? I wonder what my wife has ready to eat. (*He tries the door and finds it locked. He throws down his load.*) Plague take her! Wife! Where's that daughter of mine, Mencigüela? Is everybody fast asleep! Agueda de Toruégano! Wife!

(Mencigüela *comes to the door.*)

MEN. For goodness' sake, father, are you going to break down the door?
TOR. What a chatterbox! What a regular magpie! And where is your mother, young lady?
MEN. She's next door at the neighbour's, for she's gone to help her wind some skeins.
TOR. May evil skeins carry her away, and you, too! Go and call her.

(*Enter* Agueda, *his wife.*)

AGUE. Well, well, here's the frequenter of witches' revels just come back from hauling a little bit of wood, and so grouchy that nobody can get along with him.
TOR. Maybe you think it's only a little bit of wood, but I swear to heaven that I and your godchild were both hauling it, and it was all we could handle.
AGUE. But, bad luck to you, husband, how wet you are!
TOR. Indeed I'm wet as sop. Wife, as you value your life, get me something to eat.
AGUE. And what the devil am I to give you, if I haven't anything?
MEN. Dear me, father, how wet the wood is!
TOR. Yes, your mother will be saying next 'Fiddlesticks!'
AGUE. Hurry, daughter. Cook a couple of eggs for your father to eat and then make up the bed. (Mencigüela *goes into the house.*)

I'm sure, husband, that it never once entered your head to plant that olive sapling as I asked you to.

TOR. Well, what made me so late, if it wasn't planting it as you wanted?

AGUE. Really, husband? And where did you plant it?

TOR. Out there near the early fig tree where, if you remember, I once gave you a kiss.

(Mencigüela *opens the door.*)

MEN. Dad, come in and eat now, for everything is ready.

AGUE. Husband, you don't know what I'm thinking, do you? That in six or seven years that olive tree you planted today will bear four or five bushels of olives, and that setting out trees here and there, twenty or thirty years from now you'll have a really and truly olive grove.

TOR. That's true, wife, and won't that be fine!

AGUE. See here, husband, do you know what I've thought? That I'll pick the olives and you'll take them in the donkey cart and Menciguela will sell them in the main square. And look here, child, I tell you not to bring me back less than two Castilian reales a peck!

TOR. What do you mean, two reales? Why, my conscience will trouble me, and besides, the clerk of the market who regulates prices will fine us every day. A third of that is plenty to ask for a peck.

AGUE. Nonsense, husband, for they are the very best quality, as good as the horses of Cordoba.

TOR. Well, even if they are better than the best that Cordoba can show, you sell them for what I say, because that's plenty.

AGUE. Go away and don't bother me. See here, daughter, I order you not to sell a peck for less than two Castilian reales.

TOR. What are you talking about with your two reales? Come here, child. How much are you going to ask? (*He tugs at her.*)

MEN. Whatever you want, father.

TOR. Seven or eight maravedis.

MEN. Yes, sir, that's what I'll do.

AGUE. What do you mean: 'That's what I'll do'? Come here, girl. How much are you going to ask? (*She pulls Mencigüela away.*)

MEN. Whatever you tell me, mother.

AGUE. Two Castilian reales.

TOR. Two reales, bosh! I promise you that if you don't do as I tell you, I'm going to give you more than two hundred lashes. Now, how much are you going to sell a peck for?

MEN. Just what you say, father.

TOR. Eight maravedis.

MEN. That's what I'll do.

AGUE. There you go again with your : 'That's what I'll do.' Take that and that (*beating her*) and do what I tell you.

TOR. Let that girl alone. (*He pulls* Mencigüela *and tries to push* Agueda *away.*)

MEN. Ouch, mother! Oh, father, you're pulling me apart.

(*Enter* Aloja, *a neighbour.*)

ALO. What's the matter, neighbours? Why are you maltreating the girl that way?

AGUE. Oh, sir, this bad man wants to sell things for less than they're worth, and wants to ruin us all. And olives as big as walnuts!

TOR. I vow by the bones of my ancestors that they're not even as big as hickory nuts.

AGUE. They are, too!

TOR. They are not!

ALO. Now, good madame, my neighbour, be kind enough to go in there and I'll find out everything.

AGUE. Find out, or let everything go to smash. (Agueda *goes into the house.*)

ALO. Now, sir, what's all this about olives? Bring them out for me. Even if there are twenty bushels, I'll buy them.

TOR. You can't, because things aren't the way you think. The olives aren't here in the house. They're out on the farm.

ALO. Well, go fetch them, then, because I'll buy all of them at what will be a just price.

MEN. At two reales a peck, my mother wants to sell them.

ALO. That's pretty expensive.

TOR. Yes, don't you think so?

MEN. And my father at a third of that.

ALO. May I have a sample of them?

TOR. Bless us, sir! You don't try to understand me. Today I planted an olive shoot, and my wife says that six or seven years from now it will bear four or five bushels of olives and that she'll pick them, and for me to cart them and the girl to sell them, and that by all rights she ought to ask two reales a peck. I say 'no' and she says 'yes', and that's what the argument has been about.

ALO. Oh, what a funny argument! Who ever heard of anything like that before! The olives aren't even planted, and has the girl got to be brought to task for them?

MEN. Yes, isn't that awful?

TOR. Don't cry, girl! That child, sir, is as good as gold. Now go, dear, and set the table for me, and I promise to get you a pretty frock from the first olives that are sold. (Mencigüela *goes into the house.*)

ALO. Go on, sir. Go in and make peace with your wife.

TOR. Goodbye, neighbour. (Toruvio *goes into the house.*)

ALO. Well, I swear, life is full of surprises. The olives aren't planted and yet we see them quarrelled over. But I guess I've done my job in settling things.

WILLIS KNAPP JONES

MIGUEL DE CERVANTES SAAVEDRA
[1547–1616]

Beyond his pre-eminence as Spain's foremost writer, Miguel de Cervantes Saavedra ranks among the true giants of world literature. His magnificent work Don Quixote *is considered one of the greatest literary creations ever produced by a single human mind. It is certainly the world's finest novel.*

Cervantes was born in Alcalá de Henares in 1547. During the famous naval battle of Lepanto in 1571 he was maimed in the left hand, 'for the greater glory of the right'. On his way back to Spain in 1575, Cervantes was captured by pirates, and held prisoner in Algiers until freed by ransom in 1580.

*Between 1582 and 1587, Cervantes claims to have composed some twenty or thirty dramas, of which group only two—*El trato de Argel *and* La Numancia—*have come down to us. In 1585 he wrote the pastoral novel* La Galatea, *which remained his favourite work; throughout his life, Cervantes promised to write a second part but never did so.*

For many years he worked as a Government tax agent, and was several times imprisoned for irregularities caused by his financial ineptitude and dishonest associates.

In 1605 the first part of the immortal Don Quixote *appeared. It met with overwhelming success. The* Novelas ejemplares, *twelve charming novelettes, were published in 1613. The following year marked the publication of* Viaje del Parnaso, *a long verse work whose theme is poets and poetry. (Cervantes had always liked to write poetry, although aware of his limitations.)*

He was working at a leisurely pace on a second part of Don Quixote *when one Alonso Fernández de Avellaneda published an apocryphal continuation in 1614. Cervantes then hastened to finish his own second part, and it appeared in 1615*

During the same year his Ocho comedias y ocho entremeses *were published. The all-verse comedias, however, cannot be compared with the plays of the outstanding Golden Age dramatists. In contrast, his entremeses (interludes), written mostly in prose, are clever, fast-moving farces which may still be staged or read with pleasure.*

Cervantes did not live to see the publication of his last work, Los trabajos de Persiles y Sigismunda, *a dream-like novel of fantastic adventures and wanderings. Indeed, recognizing that his days were numbered by illness, he had rushed to complete its final chapters. He wrote the prologue only a few days before his death in 1616.*

The Quixote, *his masterpiece, inspired countless volumes of comment and interpretation. Some critics see in it a study of all humanity; others believe Cervantes' expressed intention—that he wanted to write a parody ridiculing books of chivalry, and thus provide entertainment for his readers. It seems most likely that Cervantes started to write a novelette—another* novela ejemplar—*about a mad knight, but finding that he had not exhausted his subject, expanded its scope.*

In the first part, Don Quixote and his squire Sancho Panza are caricatured types, one representing illogical idealism—'quixotism'—the other, hard-headed materialism. The adventures of the poor knight are mainly farcical, intended simply to provoke laughter. Part II is superior in its organization, style, universality and character development. Don Quixote's madness is less obvious, and Sancho becomes more idealistic. By the end of the novel the two characters are almost entirely blended.

Don Quixote has become the most widely published of all books with the exception of the Bible. Editions and translations in all languages are innumerable. The first English translation, by Thomas Shelton, appeared in 1612 (Part I) and 1620 (Part II). Of the many subsequent English translations, the three best are by John Ormsby, London, 1885; Samuel Putnam, New York, 1948; and J. M. Cohen, London, 1950.

THE JUDGE OF THE DIVORCE COURT

CHARACTERS

The Judge	*A Soldier*
The Clerk	*Doña Guiomar,* his wife
The Prosecuting Attorney	*A Surgeon*
An Old Man	*Aldonza de Minjaca,* his wife
Mariana, his wife	*Two Musicians*
A Labourer	

Enter the Judge, and with him two other men, namely the Clerk and the Prosecuting Attorney. The Judge takes a seat. Enter a comic figure of an old man and his wife Mariana.

MARIANA. At last, there's the honourable Judge of the Divorce Court ready to hear my case. This time I must know where I stand; once and for all I must be set free as a hawk of taxes and levies.

OLD MAN. Please, please, Mariana, don't yell out your affairs so loud. Speak softly, by the passion of Christ. You have deafened the whole neighbourhood with your shouts. Now the Judge is right in front of you and you can tell him your claims with less screaming.

JUDGE. What is your dispute, good people?

MARIANA. Your Honour, divorce, divorce and more divorce, a thousand times divorce!

JUDGE. From whom, or for what cause, señora?

MARIANA. From whom? From this oldster here.

JUDGE. On what grounds?

MARIANA. Because I can't put up with his pestering, and I can't always be attending to his innumerable ailments. My parents didn't bring me up to be a nurse or run a hospital. I brought a fat dowry to this bag of bones, who has worn out the days of my life. When I came into his power my face shone like a mirror, and now it is as rough as old burlap. Unmarry me, Your Highness, unless you wish me to hang myself. Look, look how my cheeks are furrowed by the tears I shed daily for being married to this skinny freak!

JUDGE. Don't cry, madam. Lower your voice and wipe away your tears, for I shall see that you receive justice.

MARIANA. Let me cry, it relieves my feelings. In well-governed kingdoms and republics, marriages should have a time limit, and every three years they should either be dissolved or confirmed anew, like a rent contract; they ought not to last a lifetime, with perpetual grief to both parties.

JUDGE. If that idea of yours could or should be put in practice, and money would do it, it would have happened long since. But please be more specific, señora, as to the reasons that lead you to seek a divorce.

MARIANA. My husband's winter and the springtime of my age. I lose sleep getting up at midnight to heat cloths and bran sacks to lay on the small of his back; I put a truss on him first in one place and then in another—I hope to see him trussed to a stake, and serve him right! I have to prop up his pillow nights, and mix cough syrups to relieve his asthma; and I have to stand his foul breath that you can smell a mile away.

CLERK. It's no doubt due to some decayed molar.

OLD MAN. That can't be so; I haven't a damned molar or tooth
in my head!

PROSECUTING ATTORNEY. There is in fact a law, as I have heard,
that bad breath is a sufficient cause of divorce either in husband
or wife.

OLD MAN. The truth is, gentleman, that the bad breath which
she says I have does not come from my decayed teeth (for I don't
own any), much less from my stomach, for my digestion is perfect,
but from her vile disposition. You gentlemen don't know this lady;
if you did, believe me, you wouldn't touch her with a ten-foot
pole, or you'd lambaste her with it. For twenty-two years I have
lived a martyr's life with her, without ever breathing a word of
her insolence, her screeching, and her caprices; for the last two
years she has never missed a day of poking and shoving me toward
the grave. I am half deaf from her shouts, and wholly mad from
her scoldings. If she does nurse me, as she says, she does it crossly,
though the hand and temper of a physician should be gentle. In
short, gentlemen, I am the one who is done for under her power,
while she lives on me, for she is the mistress with plenary power
over my property.

MARIANA. *Your* property? What property do you have that does
not come from profits made off the dowry I brought you? And
half of the estate earned since our marriage is mine, whether you
like it or not; and of my half of it and of my dowry, if I should die
today, I would not leave you a red cent, that's how much I love you.

JUDGE. Tell me, sir. When you came into the power of your wife,
were you not lively, healthy and physically able?

OLD MAN. As I said, twenty-two years ago I came into her power
as does a galley slave sentenced to row under the orders of a cruel
Calabrian slave-driver; and I was then so healthy that I could
match all her bids.

MARIANA. A new broom, worn out in three days!

JUDGE. Be still, be still, confound you, woman, and be on your way,
for I find no sufficient cause to unmarry you. You enjoyed his
prime, put up with his old age; no husband is under obligation to
stay the swift course of time from rushing past his threshold and
carrying away his days. Discount the hardships he now causes you
in consideration of the good times he gave you when he could.
And don't answer me back.

OLD MAN. If it were possible, I should be greatly obliged to you if
you would do me the favour of putting an end to my misery, by
releasing me from this jail; for if you leave me in this state, after
we have had this open break, you are only handing me over to the

torture of an executioner. If you cannot release me, let us compromise : shut her up in one monastery, and me in another. We will divide the estate, and in this way we can pass our remaining years in peace and the service of God.

MARIANA. What the devil! Do you think I enjoy being shut up? Tell that to some young novice, perhaps she likes screens and revolving wickets and gratings and sentinels. Shut yourself up, for you can stand it; you have neither eyes to see, nor ears to hear, nor feet to walk with, nor fingers to feel with. But I'm healthy and my five senses are sound and keen, and I want to use them in open freedom, and not by guesswork, fumbling in the dark.

CLERK. This woman has a fresh tongue!

PROSECUTING ATTORNEY. The husband is sensible; but he won't get anywhere.

JUDGE. I cannot grant this divorce, *quia nullam inuenio causam.*

(*Enter a well-dressed soldier and his wife, doña Guiomar.*)

DOÑA GUIOMAR. Thank the Lord, at last my wish is granted to come before Your Honour. I beg you with all the strength of my soul please to unmarry me from this.

JUDGE. 'From this'? Hasn't he a name? You might at least say 'from this man'.

DOÑA GUIOMAR. If he were a man, I should not try to be quit of the marriage.

JUDGE. What is he then?

DOÑA GUIOMAR. A stick of wood.

SOLDIER. (By Heavens, I have to be a stick of wood to suffer in silence! Perhaps, if I do not defend myself and do not contradict this woman, the judge may be inclined to condemn me, and, thinking he is inflicting punishment, he will ransom me from captivity, as though by some miracle a captive were freed from the dungeons of Tetuan.)

PROSECUTING ATTORNEY. Speak more civilly, woman, and tell us your business without insulting your husband; for the Judge of the Divorce Court, here present, will deal out evenhanded justice.

DOÑA GUIOMAR. Do you expect me not to call him a stick? This dummy has no more action than a plank.

MARIANA. This woman and I are certainly complaining of a similar offence.

DOÑA GUIOMAR. I tell you, Your Honour, that I was married to this man, since you want me to call him one; but this is not the man I married.

JUDGE. What's that? I don't understand you.

Doña Guiomar. I mean, I thought I was marrying a man in good running order, and in a few days I discovered that I had married a block, as I told you; for he doesn't know his right hand from his left, and he won't hustle about to earn two bits to help support his house and family. In the morning he goes to Mass and then to the Guadalajara gate to gossip, swap the news and tell and listen to lies; in the afternoon, and some mornings too, he circulates from one gambling den to another, where he only swells the number of idle gawks; and they tell me that the gamblers despise and detest all such *kibitzers*. At two o'clock in the afternoon he comes to lunch, without having received a single tip, for tipping the gapers is no longer in fashion. Then he goes off again, and returns at midnight, sups if he finds anything to eat, and if not, crosses himself, yawns and goes to bed. All night long he flops about, not quiet a minute. I ask him what's the matter; he answers that he is composing a sonnet in his mind for a friend who asked him for one; for he persists in being a poet, as though it were not the most impecunious profession in the whole world.

Soldier. My lady doña Guiomar has been absolutely right in everything she has said; and if I were not as right in my course of action as she is in her speech, I would long ago have managed to curry favour here and there, and like lots of other shrewd and bustling little chaps, I would have found myself holding a wand of authority, riding some little, lanky mean hired mule, with no mule-boy to accompany me (for you can rent such mules only with all their defects and when no one wants them); so I would have some saddle-bags slung behind me, in one of them a collar and a shirt, in the other, half a cheese and a loaf and a wineskin; and all the change I would make from house-clothes to travelling costume would be to put on some gaiters and a single spur; and with a commission, likewise an itch, in my bosom, I would go pricking over the Toledo bridge, in spite of the bad acting of the sluggish mule; and after a few days I'd send home some hams and some yards of unbleached linen, such items as can be picked up cheap in the villages of the district under my commission, for that is the way a poor devil supports his house as best he can. But I, having neither profession nor benefice, I don't know what to do with myself. No gentleman wishes to employ me because I am married; so I shall be compelled to beg Your Honour to separate and part us, as my wife likewise desires. Hidalgos are bad enough because of their poverty.

Doña Guiomar. And there's more to it, Your Honour; when I see my husband so shiftless and in want, I am dying to help him out;

but I can't, because after all I am an honest woman, and some things I mustn't do.

SOLDIER. For that quality alone this woman would merit a man's love; but this sense of honour of hers covers up the nastiest disposition on earth. She throws a jealous fit without cause, she screams without motive, she is vain without property, and since she knows I am poor, she has no more regard for me than for a strawman. And the worst of it is, Your Honour, that in exchange for her fidelity she expects me to put up with all sorts of rudeness and impertinence.

DOÑA GUIOMAR. Well, why not? And why shouldn't you honour and respect me, since I am chaste?

SOLDIER. Listen, doña Guiomar. Here in the presence of these gentlemen I want to tell you something : why do you boast to me that you are chaste, when it is your ordinary duty to be, because you are of good family, because you are a Christian, and because you owe it to yourself? It is all very fine for women to wish their husbands to respect them because they are chaste and decent, as if their perfection of character lay in that and in nothing else, and they do not notice the leaks that siphon off the cream of a thousand other virtues that they lack. What do I care that you are chaste in your own person, when I care a lot that you neglect to insist on it in your serving-maid, and that you always go about the house scowling, grouchy, jealous, moody, wasteful, lie-abed, lazy, quarrelsome, grumbling, with other vices of the sort, enough to wear out the lives of two hundred husbands? But of course, Your Honour, I don't mean to say that doña Guiomar acts in any such way. I confess that I am the stick of wood, the incompetent, the slovenly and the lazy; and that by ordinary common sense, if for no other reason, Your Honour is obliged to separate us : for I tell you at once that I can allege nothing against what my wife has said, that I consider the case closed, and I shall be happy to be found guilty.

DOÑA GUIOMAR. What can you allege against my statement? You don't even feed me and my maid; and I don't have a lot of them, only one, and she a puny creature who doesn't eat as much as a cricket.

CLERK. Be quiet, for more complainants are arriving.

(Enter a man dressed as a doctor, but in reality a mere bone-setter, and his wife Aldonza de Minjaca.)

DOCTOR. For four good and sufficient causes I come to beg Your Honour to grant a divorce to me and my lady doña Aldonza de Minjaca, here present.

JUDGE. You know your own mind! State the four causes.

DOCTOR. First, because I can't bear the sight of her more than of all the devils in hell; second, for a reason she knows; third, for one that I don't care to tell; fourth, because I hope demons may fly away with me when I die, if I will remain in her company for the rest of my life.

PROSECUTING ATTORNEY. He has proved his case to the utmost efficiency!

MINJACA. Your Honour, please listen to me, and consider that if my husband seeks a divorce for four reasons, I seek it for four hundred. First, because every time I look at him I think he is Lucifer himself; second, because I was deceived when I married him, for he said he was a bona fide doctor, and he turned out to be only a barber-surgeon, a man who sets bones and treats slight illnesses, which means that he is nothing like a regular doctor; third, because he is jealous of the sun's rays when they touch me; fourth, I can't endure the sight of him, and I want to get two million leagues away from him. . . .

CLERK. Who can ever make these two clocks keep time together, when their wheels are so out of gear?

MINJACA. Fifth . . .

JUDGE. Hold on, woman, if you are going to enumerate all four hundred causes, I am in no mood to listen to them, nor is there time to do so. Your case will be taken under advisement, so farewell. There is other business to attend to.

DOCTOR. What more testimony do you want, besides the fact that I do not wish to die with her, and she does not wish to live with me? JUDGE. If that sufficed to part married couples, an infinite number would shake from their shoulders the yoke of matrimony.

(Enter a man in the garb of a day labourer, with a four-cornered hood to his cape.)

LABOURER. Your Honour, I'm only a street-porter, I admit, but I am a Christian of pure blood, and a straight and honourable man; and if it weren't for my taking a drop of wine now and then (or its taking me, which is nearer the truth), I would have been manager of the Charcoal-Carriers Union. However, leaving that aside, for it would be a long story, I would have Your Honour know that once when I was under the influence I promised to marry a woman of the street. When I came to, I recovered my reason and kept my promise and married this woman whom I took from a life of vice; I set her up as a market-vendor; she has turned out so arrogant and ill-tempered that she quarrels with everyone who approaches her stand, either over short weight or because somebody touches the fruit, and in a second she picks up a weight and whacks them on the head or wherever she happens to hit; and she insults their ancestry back to the fourth generation, and never has an hour's peace with any of her neighbours and partners. And I have to keep my sword all day in motion like a slide trombone to defend her; and we don't earn enough to pay the fines for selling underweight and the mulcts for fighting. I should like, if Your Honour would be so kind, either to have you remove me from her, or at least to change her hasty temper into one more controlled and gentle; and I promise Your Honour to unload free all the charcoal you buy this summer, for I have some credit with the brothers who traffic in their backs.

DOCTOR. I am acquainted with this good man's wife, and she is as mean as my Aldonza : I can't make it any stronger.

JUDGE. Look, my good people; although some of you who are here have adduced reasons sufficient for divorce, none the less it must all be set down in writing and witnesses must testify; so I will take all your cases under advisement. But what is this? Music and guitars in my courtroom? This is a novelty !

(Enter two musicians.)

MUSICIANS. Your Honour, that discordant couple that you harmonized, subdued and pacified the other day are awaiting you in their home with a grand celebration; and they have sent us to ask you to be kind enough to honour it with your presence.

JUDGE. I shall do that most gladly; and I wish that all those present might make up in the same manner.

PROSECUTING ATTORNEY. If they did, we clerks and lawyers of this precinct would starve. No, no; let everybody sue for divorce : for in the long run most of them remain as they were, and we have profited by their quarrels and follies.

MUSICIANS. Well, from this point on we will enliven the show.

The musicians sing
    A man and wife may disagree
    but decent folk, of course,
    know reconcilement, even the worst,
    is better than the best divorce.
    Unless the two are blind indeed,
    foolish and insincere,
    quarrels that fall on St. John's Day
    mean peace the rest of the year.

Spat and make up : so love, once dead,
and honour take new force;
for reconcilement, even the worst,
is better than the best divorce.
The keenest pains and stings of love
from jealousy arise,
yet when a pretty woman's jealous
that is a paradise.
Cupid, the most expert of judges,
will certainly endorse
that reconcilement, even the worst,
is better than the best divorce.

S. GRISWOLD MORLEY

DON QUIXOTE

PART I

Chapter I. Which treats of the quality and way of life of the famous knight Don Quixote de la Mancha.

In a certain village in La Mancha, which I do not wish to name, there lived not long ago a gentleman—one of those who have always a lance in the rack, an ancient shield, a lean hack and a greyhound for coursing. His habitual diet consisted of a stew, more beef than mutton, of hash most nights, boiled bones on Saturdays, lentils on Fridays, and a young pigeon as a Sunday treat; and on this he spent three-quarters of his income. The rest of it went on a fine cloth doublet, velvet breeches and slippers for holidays, and a homespun suit of the best in which he decked himself on weekdays. His household consisted of a housekeeper of rather more than forty, a niece not yet twenty, and a lad for the field and market, who saddled his horse and wielded the pruning-hook.

Our gentleman was verging on fifty, of tough constitution, lean-bodied, thin-faced, a great early riser and a lover of hunting. They say that his surname was Quixada or Quesada—for there is some difference of opinion amongst authors on this point. However, by very reasonable conjecture we may take it that he was called Quexana. But this does not much concern our story; enough that we do not depart by so much as an inch from the truth in the telling of it.

The reader must know, then, that this gentleman, in the times when he had nothing to do—as was the case for most of the year—gave himself up to the reading of books of knight errantry; which he loved and enjoyed so much that he almost entirely forgot his hunting, and even the care of his estate. So odd and foolish, indeed, did he grow on this subject that he sold many acres of cornland to buy these books of chivalry to read, and in this way brought home every one he could get. And of them all he considered none so good as the works of the famous Feliciano de Silva. For his brilliant style and those complicated sentences seemed to him very pearls, especially when he came upon those love-passages and challenges frequently written in the manner of : 'The reason for the unreason with which you treat my reason, so weakens my reason that with reason I complain of your beauty'; and also when he read : 'The high heavens that with their stars divinely fortify you in your divinity and make you deserving of the desert that your greatness deserves.'

These writings drove the poor knight out of his wits; and he passed sleepless nights trying to understand them and disentangle their meaning, though Aristotle himself would never have unravelled or understood them, even if he had been resurrected for that sole purpose. He did not much like the wounds that Sir Belianis gave and received, for he imagined that his face and his whole body must have been covered with scars and marks, however skilful the surgeons who tended him. But, for all that, he admired the author for ending his book with the promise to continue with that interminable adventure, and often the desire seized him to take up the pen himself and write the promised sequel for him. No doubt he would have done so, and perhaps successfully, if other greater and more persistent preoccupations had not prevented him.

Often he had arguments with the priest of his village, who was a scholar and a graduate of Siguenza, as to which was the better knight—Palmerin of England or Amadis of Gaul. But Master Nicholas, the barber of that village, said that no one could compare with the Knight of the Sun. Though if anyone could, it was Sir Galaor, brother of Amadis of Gaul. For he had a very accommodating nature, and was not so affected nor such a sniveller as his brother, though he was not a bit behind him in the matter of bravery.

In short, he so buried himself in his books that he spent the nights reading from twilight till daybreak and the days from dawn till dark; and so from little sleep and much reading, his brain dried up and he lost his wits. He filled his mind with all that he read in them, with enchantments, quarrels, battles, challenges, wounds, wooings, loves, torments and other impossible nonsense; and so deeply did he steep his imagination in the belief that all the fanciful stuff he read was true, that to his mind no history in the world was more authentic. He used to say that the Cid Ruy Diaz must have been a very good knight, but that he could not be compared to the Knight of the Burning Sword, who with a single backstroke had cleft a pair of fierce and monstrous giants in two. And he had an even better opinion of Bernardo del Carpio for slaying the enchanted Roland at Roncesvalles, by making use of Hercules' trick when he throttled the Titan Antaeus in his arms.

He spoke very well of the giant Morgante; for, though one of that giant brood who are all proud and insolent, he alone was affable and well-mannered. But he admired most of all Reynald of Montalban, particularly when he saw him sally forth from his castle and rob everyone he met, and when in heathen lands overseas he stole that idol of Mahomet, which history says was of pure gold. But he would have given his housekeeper and his niece into the bargain, to deal the traitor Galaon a good kicking.

In fact, now that he had utterly wrecked his reason he fell into the strangest fancy that ever a madman had in the whole world. He thought it fit and proper, both in order to increase his renown and to serve the state, to turn knight errant and travel through the world with horse and armour in search of adventures, following in every way the practice of the knights errant he had read of, redressing all manner of wrongs, and exposing himself to chances and dangers, by the overcoming of which he might win eternal honour and renown. Already the poor man fancied himself crowned by the valour of his arm, at least with the empire of Trebizond; and so, carried away by the strange pleasure he derived from these agreeable thoughts, he hastened to translate his desires into action.

The first thing that he did was to clean some armour which had belonged to his ancestors, and had lain for ages forgotten in a corner, eaten with rust and covered with mould. But when he had cleaned and repaired it as best he could, he found that there was one great defect: the helmet was a simple head-piece without a visor. So he ingeniously made good this deficiency by fashioning out of pieces of pasteboard a kind of half-visor which, fitted to the helmet, gave the appearance of a complete head-piece. However, to see if it was strong enough to stand up to the risk of a sword-cut, he took out his sword and gave it two strokes, the first of which demolished in a moment what had taken him a week to make. He was not too pleased at the ease with which he had destroyed it, and to safeguard himself against this danger, reconstructed the visor, putting some strips of iron inside, in such a way as to satisfy himself of his protection; and, not caring to make another trial of it, he accepted it as a fine jointed head-piece and put it into commission.

Next he went to inspect his hack, but though, through leanness, he had more quarters than there are pence in a groat, and more blemishes than Gonella's horse, which was nothing but skin and bone, he appeared to our knight more than the equal of Alexander's Bucephalus and the Cid's Babieca. He spent four days pondering what name to give him; for, he reflected, it would be wrong for the horse of so famous a knight, a horse so good in himself, to be without a famous name. Therefore he tried to fit him with one that would signify what he had been before his master turned knight errant, and what he now was; for it was only right that as his master changed his profession, the horse should change his name for a sublime and high-sounding one, befitting the new order and the new calling he professed. So, after many names invented, struck out and rejected, amended, cancelled and remade in his fanciful mind, he finally decided to call him Rocinante, a name which seemed to him grand and sonorous, and to express the common horse he had been before arriving at his present state : the first and foremost of all hacks in the world.

Having found so pleasing a name for his horse, he next decided to do the same for himself, and spent another eight days thinking about it. Finally he resolved to call himself Don Quixote. And that is no doubt why the authors of this true history, as we have said, assumed that his name must have been Quixada and not Quesada, as other authorities would have it. Yet he remembered that the valorous Amadis had not been content with his bare name, but had added the name of his kingdom and native country in order to make it famous, and styled himself Amadis of Gaul. So, like a good knight, he decided to add the name of his country to his own and call himself Don Quixote de la Mancha. Thus, he thought, he very clearly proclaimed his parentage and native land and honoured it by taking his surname from it.

Now that his armour was clean, his helmet made into a complete head-piece, a name found for his horse, and he confirmed in his new title, it struck him that there was only one more thing to do : to find a lady to be enamoured of. For a knight errant without a lady is like a tree without leaves or fruit and a body without a soul. He said to himself again and again : 'If I for my sins or by good luck were to meet with some giant hereabouts, as generally happens to knights errant, and if I were to overthrow him in the encounter, or cut him down the middle or, in short, conquer him and make him surrender, would it not be well to have someone to whom I could send him as a present, so that he could enter and kneel down before my sweet lady and say in tones of humble sub-mission : "Lady, I am the giant Caraculiambro, lord of the island of Malindrania, whom the never-sufficiently-to-be-praised knight, Don Quixote de la Mancha, conquered in single combat and ordered to appear before your Grace, so that your Highness might dispose of me according to your will"?' Oh, how pleased our knight was when he had made up this speech, and even gladder when he found someone whom he could call his lady. It happened, it is believed, in this way : in a village near his there was a very good-looking farm girl, whom he had been taken with at one time, although she is supposed not to have known it or had proof of it. Her name was Aldonza Lorenzo, and she it was he thought fit to call the lady of his fancies; and, casting around for a name which should not be too far away from her own, yet suggest and imply a princess and great lady, he resolved to call her Dulcinea del Toboso —for she was a native of El Toboso—a name which seemed to him as musical, strange and significant as those others that he had devised for himself and his possessions.

Chapter II. Which treats of the First Expedition which the ingenious Don Quixote made from his village.

Once these preparations were completed, he was anxious to wait no longer before putting his ideas into effect, impelled to this by the thought of the loss the world suffered by his delay, seeing the grievances there were to redress, the wrongs to right, the injuries to amend, the abuses to correct, and the debts to discharge. So, telling nobody of his intention, and quite unobserved, one morning before dawn—it was on one of those sweltering July days—he armed himself completely, mounted Rocinante, put on his badly-mended head-piece, slung on his shield, seized his lance and went out into the plain through the back gate of his yard, pleased and delighted to see with what ease he had started on his fair design. But scarcely was he in open country when he was assailed by a thought so terrible that it almost made him abandon the enterprise he had just begun. For he suddenly remembered that he had never received the honour of knighthood, and so, according to the laws of chivalry, he neither could nor should take arms against any knight, and even if he had been knighted he was bound, as a novice, to wear plain armour without a device on his shield until he should gain one by his prowess. These reflections made him waver in his resolve, but as his madness outweighed any other argument, he made up his mind to have himself knighted by the first man he met, in imitation of many who had done the same, as he had read in the books which had so influenced him. As to plain armour, he decided to clean his own, when he had time, till it was whiter than ermine. With this he quieted his mind and went on his way, taking whatever road his horse chose, in the belief that in this lay the essence of adventure.

As our brand-new adventurer journeyed along, he talked to himself, saying: 'Who can doubt that in ages to come, when the authentic story of my famous deeds comes to light, the sage who writes of them will say, when he comes to tell of my first expedition so early in the morning: "Scarce had the ruddy Apollo spread the golden threads of his lovely hair over the broad and spacious face of the earth, and scarcely had the forked tongues of the little painted birds greeted with mellifluous harmony the coming of the rosy Aurora who, leaving the soft bed of her jealous husband, showed herself at the doors and balconies of the Manchegan horizon, when the famous knight, Don Quixote de la Mancha, quitting the slothful down, mounted his famous steed Rocinante and began to journey across the ancient and celebrated plain of Montiel"?' That was, in fact, the road that our knight actually took, as he went on: 'Fortunate the age and fortunate the times in which my famous deeds shall come to light, deeds worthy to be engraved in bronze, carved in marble and painted on wood, as a memorial for posterity. And you, sage enchanter, whoever you may be, to whose lot it falls to be the chronicler of this strange history, I beg you not to forget my good Rocinante, my constant companion on all my rides and journeys!' And presently he cried again, as if he had really been in love: 'O Princess Dulcinea, mistress of this captive heart! You did me great injury in dismissing me and inflicting on me the cruel rigour of your command not to appear in your beauteous presence. Deign, lady, to be mindful of your captive heart, which suffers such griefs for love of you.'

He went on stringing other nonsense on to this, all after the fashion he had learnt in his reading, and imitating the language of his books at best he could. And all the while he rode so slowly and the sun's heat increased so fast that it would have been enough to turn his brain, if he had had any. Almost all that day he rode without encountering anything of note, which reduced him to despair, for he longed to meet straightway someone against whom he could try the strength of his strong arm.

There are authors who say that the first adventure he met was that of the pass of Lapice. Others say it was the windmills. But what I have been able to discover of the matter and what I have found written in the annals of La Mancha, is that he rode all that day, and that at nightfall his horse and he were weary and dying of hunger. Looking in all directions to see if he could discover any castle or shepherd's hut where he could take shelter and supply his urgent needs, he saw, not far from the road he was travelling on, an inn, which seemed to him like a star to guide him to the gates, if not to the palace, of his redemption. So he hurried on, and reached it just as night was falling. Now there chanced to be standing at the inn door two young women *of easy virtue,* as they are called, who were on the way to Seville with some carriers who happened to have taken up their quarters at the inn that evening. As everything that our adventurer thought, saw or imagined seemed to follow the fashion of his reading, as soon as he saw the inn he convinced himself that it was a fortress with its four towers and pinnacles of shining silver, complete with a drawbridge, a deep moat and all those appurtenances with which such castles are painted. So he approached the inn, which to his mind was a castle, and when still a short distance away reined Rocinante in, expecting some dwarf to mount the battlements and sound a trumpet to announce that a knight was approaching the fortress. But when he saw that there was some delay, and that Rocinante was in a hurry to get to the stable, he went up to the inn door and, seeing the two young women standing there, took them for two beauteous maidens or graceful ladies taking the air at the castle gate. Now at that very moment, as chance would have it, a swineherd was collecting from the stubble a drove of hogs—pardon me for naming them—and blew his horn to call them together. But Don Quixote immediately interpreted this in his own way, as some dwarf giving notice of his approach. So with rare pleasure he rode up, whereupon those ladies, thoroughly frightened at seeing a man come towards them dressed in armour with lance and shield, turned to go back into the inn. But Don Quixote, gathering from their flight that they were afraid, raised his pasteboard visor, partly revealing his lean and dusty face, and addressed them with a charming expression and in a calm voice : 'I beg you, ladies, not to fly, nor to fear any outrage; for it ill fits or suits the order of chivalry which I profess to injure any-one, least of all maidens of such rank as your appearance proclaims you to be.'

The girls stared at him, trying to get a look at his face, which was almost covered by the badly made visor. But when they heard

themselves called maidens—a title ill-suited to their profession—
they could not help laughing, which stung Don Quixote into
replying : 'Civility befits the fair; and laughter arising from trivial
causes, is, moreover, great folly. I do not say this to offend you nor
to incur your displeasure, for I have no other wish than to serve
you.'

His language, which was unintelligible to them, and the uncouth
figure our knight cut, made the ladies laugh the more. Whereat he
flew into a rage, and things would have gone much farther, had not
the innkeeper, a very fat man and therefore very peaceable,
emerged at this moment. Now when he saw this grotesque figure in
his equipment of lance, shield and coat of armour, which sorted so
ill with his manner of riding, he was on the point of joining the
young women in their demonstrations of amusement. But, fearing
such a collection of armaments, he decided to speak politely, and
addressed him thus : 'If your worship is looking for lodging, Sir
Knight, except for a bed—we have none in this inn—you will find
plenty of everything.'

And Don Quixote replied, seeing the humility of the warden of
the fortress—for such he took the innkeeper to be : 'For me, Sir
Castellan, whatever you have is enough. My ornaments are arms,
my rest the bloody fray.'

The host thought that he had called him castellan because he
took him for a safe man from Castile, though he was an Andalusian
from the Strand of San Lucar, as thievish as Cacus and as tricky as
a student or a page. So he replied : 'At that rate, your bed shall be
the cruel rock, your sleep to watch till day, and that being so, you
can safely dismount here in the certainty that you will find in this
house ample reason for lying awake not only for one night but for
a whole year.'

As he spoke he went to take Don Quixote's stirrup, and our
knight dismounted with great labour and difficulty, as he had
fasted all day. He then bade the host take good care of his steed,
saying that no better piece of horseflesh munched oats in all the
world. The innkeeper stared at the beast, which did not seem as
good as Don Quixote said, not by a half. However, he put him up
in the stable and, when he came back for his guest's orders, he
found that the maidens had made it up with him and were taking
off his armour. But although they had got off his breast-plate and
back-piece, they had no idea how to get him out of his gorget, nor
how to take off his counterfeit head-piece, which was tied with
green ribbons that would have to be cut, as they could not undo
the knot. But to this he would on no account agree, and so he

stayed all that night with his helmet on, cutting the strangest and most ridiculous figure imaginable. And whilst he was being disarmed, imagining that these draggled and loose creatures were illustrious ladies and the mistresses of that castle, he addressed them most gracefully :

> 'Never was there knight
> By ladies so attended
> As was Don Quixote
> When he left his village.
> Maidens waited on him,
> On his horse, princesses—

or Rocinante, which, dear ladies, is the name of my horse, and Don Quixote de la Mancha is mine. For, although I did not wish to reveal myself till deeds done in your service and for your benefit do so for me, the need to adapt this old ballad of Lancelot to the present occasion has betrayed my name to you before the due season. But the time will come when your ladyships may command me and I shall obey; and the valour of my arms will then disclose the desire I have to serve you.'

The girls, who were not used to hearing such high-flown language, did not say a word in reply, but only asked whether he would like anything to eat.

'I would gladly take some food,' replied Don Quixote, 'for I think there is nothing that would come more opportunely.'

That day happened to be a Friday, and there was no food in the inn except some portions of a fish that is called pollack in Castile and cod in Andalusia, in some parts ling and in others troutlet. They asked whether his worship would like some troutlet, as there was no other fish to eat.

'So long as there are plenty of troutlet they may serve me for one trout,' replied Don Quixote, 'for I had just as soon be paid eight separate *reals* as an eight *real* piece. What is more, these troutlet may be like veal, which is better than beef, or kid, which is better than goats' meat. But, however that may be, let me have it now, for the toil and weight of arms cannot be borne without due care for the belly.'

They set the table for him at the inn door for coolness' sake, and the host brought him a portion of badly soaked and worse cooked salt cod with some bread as black and grimy as his armour. It made them laugh a great deal to see him eat because, as he kept his helmet on and his visor up, he could get nothing into his mouth with his own hands, and required someone's assistance to put it in;

and so one of those ladies performed this task for him. But to give him anything to drink would have been impossible if the innkeeper had not bored a reed, put one end into his mouth and poured the wine into the other. All this he bore with patience rather than break the ribbons of his helmet.

While they were thus occupied there happened to come to the inn a sow-gelder, and as he arrived he blew his reed whistle four or five times; which finally convinced Don Quixote that he was at some famous castle, that they were entertaining him with music, that the pollack was trout, the black bread of the whitest flour, the whores ladies and the innkeeper warden of the castle. This made him feel that his resolution and his expedition had been to good purpose, but what distressed him most deeply was that he was not yet knighted, for he believed that he could not rightfully embark on any adventure without first receiving the order of knighthood.

Chapter III. Which tells of the pleasant method by which Don Quixote chose to be knighted.

So, troubled by these thoughts, he cut short his scanty pothouse supper, and when he was done called the host. Then, shutting the stable door on them both, he fell on his knees before him and said : 'Never will I arise from where I am, valiant knight, till you grant me of your courtesy the boon I am going to beg of you; it is one which will redound to your praise and to the benefit of the human race.'

Seeing his guest at his feet and hearing such language, the innkeeper stared in confusion, not knowing what to do or say, and pressed him to get up; but in vain, for the knight refused to rise until his host had promised to grant him the boon he begged.

'I expected no less from your great magnificence, dear sir,' replied Don Quixote. 'So I will tell you that the boon I begged of you, and you in your generosity granted, is that you will knight me on the morning of tomorrow. This night I will watch my arms in the chapel of this castle of yours, and tomorrow, as I said, my dearest wish will be fulfilled, and I shall have the right to ride through all quarters of the world in search of adventures, for the benefit of the distressed, according to the obligations of knight-hood and of knights errant like myself, whose minds are given to such exploits.'

The innkeeper, who, as we have said, was pretty crafty and had already a suspicion that his guest was wrong in the head, was confirmed in his belief when he heard this speech, and, to make

some sport for that night, decided to fall in with his humour. So he
told him that he was doing a very proper thing in craving the boon
he did, and that such a proposal was right and natural in a knight
as illustrious as he seemed and his gallant demeanour showed him
to be. He added that he, too, in the day of his youth had devoted
himself to that honourable profession and travelled in divers parts
of the world in search of adventures, not omitting to visit the Fish
Market of Malaga, the Isles of Riaran, the Compass of Seville, the
Little Market Place at Segovia, the Olive Grove at Valencia, the
Circle of Granada, the Strand of San Lucar, the Colt-fountain of
Cordova, the Taverns of Toledo and sundry other places, where he
had exercised the agility of his heels and the lightness of his fingers,
doing many wrongs, wooing many widows, ruining sundry maidens
and cheating a few minors—in fact, making himself well known in
almost all the police-courts and law-courts in Spain. Finally he
had retired to this castle, where he lived on his own estate and
other people's, welcoming all knights errant of whatever quality
and condition, only for the great love he bore them—and to take
a share of their possessions in payment for his kindness.

He added that there was no chapel in the castle where he could
watch his arms, for it had been pulled down to be rebuilt. But he
knew that a vigil might be kept in any place whatever in case of
need. So that night he might watch his arms in a courtyard of the
castle, and in the morning, God willing, the due ceremonies might
be performed, and he emerge a full knight, as much a knight as
any in the whole world. He asked him if he had any money with
him, and Don Quixote replied that he had not a penny, since he
had never read in histories concerning knights errant of any knight
that had. At this the innkeeper said that he was wrong : for,
granted that it was not mentioned in the histories, because their
authors could see no need of mentioning anything so obvious and
necessary to take with one as money and clean shirts, that was no
reason for supposing that knights did not carry them. In fact, he
might take it for an established fact that all knights errant, of
whom so many histories were stuffed full, carried purses well lined
against all eventualities, and also took with them clean shirts and a
little box full of ointments to cure the wounds they got. For on the
plains and deserts where they fought and got their wounds they
had not always someone at hand to cure them, unless of course
they had some magician for a friend. A sorcerer, of course, might
relieve them at once by bearing through the air on a cloud some
maiden or dwarf with a flask of water of such virtue that after
tasting a single drop they were immediately cured of their sores

and wounds, and it was as if they had never had any injuries. However, in default of this, the knights of old made certain that their squires were provided with money and other necessaries, such as lint and ointment, to dress their wounds. But when such knights chanced to have no squires—there were only a few rare instances—they carried it all themselves on the cruppers of their horses in bags so very thin that they hardly showed, as though they contained something of even more importance. For, except for such purposes, the carrying of bags was not tolerated among knights errant. So he advised Don Quixote—though as his godson, which he was so soon to be, he might even command him—not to travel in future without money and the other requisites he had mentioned, and he would see how useful they would prove when he least expected it.

Don Quixote promised to do exactly as he recommended, and promptly received his instructions as to keeping watch over his armour in a great yard which lay on one side of the inn. He gathered all the pieces together and laid them on a stone trough, which stood beside a well. Then, buckling on his shield, he seized his lance and began to pace jauntily up and down before the trough. And just as he began his watch, night began to fall.

The innkeeper told everyone staying in the inn of his guest's craziness, of the watching of the armour, and of the knighting he was expecting; and, wondering at this strange form of madness, they came out to observe him from a distance, and watched him, sometimes pacing up and down with a peaceful look and sometimes leaning on his lance and gazing on his armour, without taking his eyes off it for a considerable time. Night had now fallen, but the moon was so bright that she might have rivalled the orb that lent her his light; so that whatever the novice knight did was clearly visible to all. Just then it occurred to one of the carriers who was staying at the inn to go and water his mules, and to do this he found it necessary to remove Don Quixote's armour, which lay on the trough. But the knight, seeing him draw near, addressed him in a loud voice: 'You, whoever you are, rash knight, who come to touch the armour of the most valorous errant that ever girt on a sword, take heed what you do. Do not touch it unless you wish to lose your life in payment for your temerity.'

The carrier paid no attention to this speech—it would have been better if he had regarded it, for he would have been regarding his own safety—but, laying hold of the straps, threw the armour some distance from him. At this sight Don Quixote raised his eyes to heaven, and addressing his thoughts, as it seemed, to his lady Dulcinea, cried: 'Assist me, lady, in the first affront offered to this enraptured heart! Let not your favour and protection fail me in this first trial!'

And, uttering these words and others like them, he loosened his shield and, raising his lance in both hands, dealt his adversary a mighty blow on the head with it, which threw him to the ground so injured that, if it had been followed by a second, the carrier would have had no use for a surgeon to cure him. This done, Don Quixote gathered his arms together again and paced up and down once more with the same composure as before.

A little later a second carrier, not knowing what had happened since the first man still lay stunned, came out with the same intention of watering his mules. But, just as he was going to clear the armour from the trough, Don Quixote, without uttering word or begging anyone's favour, loosened his shield again, once more raised his lance and made more than three pieces of the second carrier's head—for he opened it in four places—without damage to his weapon. At the noise all the people in the inn rushed out, among them the innkeeper. Whereupon Don Quixote buckled on his shield and, putting his hand to his sword, cried: 'O beauteous lady, strength and vigour of this enfeebled heart! Now is the time to turn your illustrious eyes on this your captive knight, who is awaiting so great an adventure.'

With this it seemed to him that he gained so much courage that if all the carriers in the world had attacked him he would not have yielded a foot. When the fellows of the wounded men saw them in that plight they began to shower stones on Don Quixote from some way off. He protected himself from them as best he could with his shield, but dared not leave the trough, for fear of abandoning his armour. And the innkeeper shouted to them to leave him alone, for he had already told them that he was a madman and, being mad, would go scot-free, even though he killed them all.

Don Quixote shouted also, even louder, calling them cowards and traitors, and swearing that the lord of the castle must be a despicable and base-born knight for allowing knights errant to be so treated, and that if he had received the order of knighthood he would have made him sensible of his perfidy.

'But of you, base and vile rabble, I take no account,' he cried. 'Throw stones! Come on, attack! Assail me as hard as you can, and you will see what penalty you have to pay for your insolent folly!'

He spoke with such spirit and boldness that he struck a lively terror into all who heard him; and for that reason, as much as for the innkeeper's persuasions, they stopped pelting him. Then Don

Quixote allowed them to remove the wounded, and returned to watch his arms with the same quiet assurance as before.

Now the innkeeper had begun to dislike his guest's pranks, and decided to cut the matter short and give him his wretched order of knighthood immediately, before anything else could go wrong. So he apologized for the insolence with which those low fellows had behaved without his knowledge, adding, however, that they had been soundly punished for their audacity. And seeing, as he had said before, that there was no chapel in that castle, there was no need, he declared, for the rest of the ceremony; for, according to his knowledge of the ceremonial of the order, the whole point of conferring knighthood lay in the blow on the neck and the stroke on the shoulder, and that could be performed in the middle of a field. And Don Quixote had already more than fulfilled the duty of the watching of arms, for he had been more than four hours on vigil, whereas all that was required was a two hours' watch.

Don Quixote believed all this, and said he was ready to obey him. He begged him to conclude the matter as briefly as possible; for if he were again attacked, once knighted, he was resolved to leave no one alive in the castle, except such as he might spare at the castellan's bidding, and out of regard for him.

Forewarned and apprehensive, the castellan then brought out the book in which he used to enter the carriers' accounts for straw and barley. Then, followed by a boy carrying a candle-end and by the two maidens already mentioned, he went up to Don Quixote and ordered him to kneel. Next, reading out of his manual, as if he were reciting some devout prayer, in the middle of his reading he raised his hand and dealt the knight a sound blow on the neck, followed by a handsome stroke on the back with the Don's own sword, all the while muttering in his teeth as if in prayer. When this was over he bade one of the ladies gird on Don Quixote's sword, which she did with great agility and some discretion, no small amount of which was necessary to avoid bursting with laughter at each stage of the ceremony. But what they had already seen of the new knight's prowess kept their mirth within bounds. And as she girt on his sword the good lady said: 'God make your worship a fortunate knight and give you good luck in your battles.'

Don Quixote asked her to tell him her name, as he wished to know in future days to whom he owed the favour received, for he meant to confer on her some part of the honour he was to win by the strength of his arm. She replied very humbly that her name was La Tolosa, and that she was the daughter of a cobbler in

Toledo who lived among the stalls of Sancho Bienaya, adding
that, wherever she might be, she was at his service and he should
be her master. Don Quixote begged her, in reply, as a favour to
him, henceforth to take the title of lady and call herself Doña
Tolosa, which she promised to do. The other lady then put on
his spurs, and his conversation with her was almost the same as
with the lady of the sword. He asked her her name, and she replied
that she was called La Molinera, and that she was the daughter
of an honest miller in Antequera. The Don requested her also
to take the title of lady and call herself Doña Molinera, renewing
his offers of service and favours.

Now that these unprecedented ceremonies had been hurried
through post-haste and at top speed, Don Quixote was impatient
to be on horseback and to ride out in search of adventures. So,
saddling Rocinante at once, he mounted; then, embracing his host,
he thanked him for the favour of knighting him in such extravagant terms that it is impossible to write them down faithfully. The
innkeeper, once he saw him safely out of the inn, replied to his
speech rather more briefly but in no less high-flown terms and,
without even asking him to pay the cost of his lodging, was heartily
glad to see him go.

*Chapter VIII. Of the valorous Don Quixote's success in the
dreadful and never before imagined Adventure of the Windmills,
with other events worthy of happy record.*

At that moment they caught sight of some thirty or forty windmills, which stand on that plain, and as soon as Don Quixote saw
them he said to his squire : 'Fortune is guiding our affairs better
than we could have wished. Look over there, friend Sancho Panza,
where more than thirty monstrous giants appear. I intend to do
battle with them and take all their lives. With their spoils we will
begin to get rich, for this is a fair war, and it is a great service to
God to wipe such a wicked brood from the face of the earth.'

'What giants?' asked Sancho Panza.

'Those you see there,' replied his master, 'with their long arms.
Some giants have them about six miles long.'

'Take care, your worship,' said Sancho; 'those things over there
are not giants but windmills, and what seem to be their arms are
the sails, which are whirled round in the wind and make the
millstone turn.'

'It is quite clear,' replied Don Quixote, 'that you are not experienced in this matter of adventures. They are giants, and if you are

afraid, go away and say your prayers, whilst I advance and engage them in fierce and unequal battle.'

As he spoke, he dug his spurs into his steed Rocinante, paying no attention to his squire's shouted warning that beyond all doubt they were windmills and no giants he was advancing to attack. But he went on, so positive that they were giants that he neither listened to Sancho's cries nor noticed what they were, even when he got near them. Instead he went on shouting in a loud voice : 'Do not fly, cowards, vile creatures, for it is one knight alone who assails you.'

At that moment a slight wind arose, and the great sails began to move. At the sight of which Don Quixote shouted : 'Though you wield more arms than the giant Briareus, you shall pay for it!' Saying this, he commended himself with all his soul to his Lady Dulcinea, beseeching her aid in his great peril. Then, covering himself with his shield and putting his lance in the rest, he urged Rocinante forward at a full gallop and attacked the nearest windmill, thrusting his lance into the sail. But the wind turned it with such violence that it shivered his weapon in pieces, dragging the horse and his rider with it, and sent the knight rolling badly injured across the plain. Sancho Panza rushed to his assistance as fast as his ass could trot, but when he came up he found that the knight could not stir. Such a shock had Rocinante given him in their fall.

'O my goodness!' cried Sancho, 'Didn't I tell your worship to look what you were doing, for they were only windmills? Nobody could mistake them, unless he had windmills on the brain.'

'Silence, friend Sancho,' replied Don Quixote. 'Matters of war are more subject than most to continual change. What is more, I think—and that is the truth—that the same sage Friston who robbed me of my room and my books has turned those giants into windmills, to cheat me of the glory of conquering them. Such is the enmity he bears me; but in the very end his black arts shall avail him little against the goodness of my sword.'

'God send it as He will,' replied Sancho Panza, helping the knight to get up and remount Rocinante, whose shoulders were half dislocated.

As they discussed this last adventure they followed the road to the pass of Lapice where, Don Quixote said, they could not fail to find many and various adventures, as many travellers passed that way. He was much concerned, however, at the loss of his lance, and, speaking of it to his squire, remarked : 'I remember reading that a certain Spanish knight called Diego Perez de Vargas, having broken his sword in battle, tore a great bough or limb from an oak, and performed such deeds with it that day, and pounded so many Moors, that he earned the surname of the Pounder, and thus he and his descendants from that day onwards have been called Vargas y Machuca. I mention this because I propose to tear down just such a limb from the first oak we meet, as big and as good as his; and I intend to do such deeds with it that you may consider yourself most fortunate to have won the right to see them. For you will witness things which will scarcely be credited.'

'With God's help,' replied Sancho, 'and I believe it all as your worship says. But sit a bit more upright, sir, for you seem to be riding lop-sided. It must be from the bruises you got when you fell.'

'That is the truth,' replied Don Quixote. 'And if I do not complain of the pain, it is because a knight errant is not allowed to complain of any wounds, even though his entrails may be dropping out through them.'

'If that's so, I have nothing more to say,' said Sancho, 'but God knows I should be glad if your worship would complain if anything hurt you. I must say, for my part, that I have to cry out at the slightest twinge, unless this business of not complaining extends to knights errant's squires as well.'

Don Quixote could not help smiling at his squire's simplicity, and told him that he could certainly complain how and when he pleased, whether he had any cause or no, for up to that time he had never read anything to the contrary in the law of chivalry.

Sancho reminded him that it was time for dinner, but his master replied that he had need of none, but that his squire might eat whenever he pleased. With this permission Sancho settled himself as comfortably as he could on his ass and, taking out what he had put into the saddle-bags, jogged very leisurely along behind his master, eating all the while; and from time to time he raised the bottle with such relish that the best-fed publican in Malaga might have envied him. Now, as he went along like this, taking repeated gulps, he entirely forgot the promise his master had made him, and reckoned that going in search of adventures, however dangerous, was more like pleasure than hard work.

They passed that night under some trees, from one of which our knight tore down a dead branch to serve him as some sort of lance, and stuck into it the iron head of the one that had been broken. And all night Don Quixote did not sleep but thought about his Lady Dulcinea, to conform to what he had read in his books about knights errant spending many sleepless nights in woodland and desert dwelling on the memory of their ladies. Not so Sancho

Panza; for, as his stomach was full, and not of chicory water, he slept right through till morning. And, if his master had not called him, neither the sunbeams, which struck him full on the face, nor the song of the birds, who in great number and very joyfully greeted the dawn of the new day, would have been enough to wake him. As he got up he made a trial of his bottle, and found it rather limper than the night before; whereat his heart sank, for he did not think they were taking the right road to remedy this defect very quickly. Don Quixote wanted no breakfast for, as we have said, he was determined to subsist on savoury memories. . . .

PART II

Chapter X. In which is related the device Sancho adopted to enchant the Lady Dulcinea, and other incidents as comical as they are true.

When the author of this great history comes to recount the contents of this chapter, he says that he would have liked to pass it over in silence, through fear of disbelief. For Don Quixote's delusions here reach the greatest imaginable bounds and limits, and even exceed them, great as they are, by two bow-shots. But finally he wrote the deeds down, although with fear and misgivings, just as our knight performed them, without adding or subtracting one atom of truth from the history, or taking into account any accusations of lying that might be laid against him. And he was right, for truth, though it may run thin, never breaks, and always flows over the lie like oil over water. So, continuing his history, he says that as soon as Don Quixote had hidden himself in the thicket, or oak wood, or forest, beside great El Toboso, he ordered Sancho to go back to the city, and not return to his presence without first speaking to his lady on his behalf, and begging her to be so good as to allow herself to be seen by her captive knight, and to deign to bestow her blessing on him, so that he might hope thereby to meet with the highest success in all his encounters and arduous enterprises. Sancho undertook to do as he was commanded, and to bring his master as favourable a reply as he had brought the first time.

'Go, my son,' said Don Quixote, 'and do not be confused when you find yourself before the light of the sun of beauty you are going to seek. How much more fortunate you are than all other squires in the world! Bear in your mind, and let it not escape you, the manner of your reception; whether she changes colour whilst you

9—SA

are delivering her my message; whether she is stirred or troubled on hearing my name; whether she shifts from her cushion, should you, by chance, find her seated on the rich dais of her authority. If she is standing, watch whether she rests first on one foot and then on the other; whether she repeats her reply to you two or three times; whether she changes from mild to harsh, from cruel to amorous; whether she raises her hand to her hair to smooth it, although it is not untidy. In fact, my son, watch all her actions and movements; because, if you relate them to me as they were, I shall deduce what she keeps concealed in the secret places of her heart as far as concerns the matter of my love. For you must know, Sancho, if you do not know already, that between lovers the outward actions and movements they reveal when their loves are under discussion are most certain messengers, bearing news of what is going on in their innermost souls. Go, friend, and may better fortune than mine guide you, and send you better success than I expect, waiting between fear and hope in this bitter solitude where you leave me.'

'I'll go, and come back quickly,' said Sancho. 'Cheer up that little heart of yours, dear master, for it must be no bigger now than a hazel nut. Remember the saying that a stout heart breaks bad luck; and where there are no flitches there are no hooks; and they say, too, where you least expect it, out jumps the hare. This I say because now that it's day I hope to find my lady's palaces or castles where I least expect them, even though we didn't find them last night : and once found, leave me to deal with her alone.'

'Indeed, Sancho,' said Don Quixote, 'you always bring in your proverbs very much to the purpose of our business. May God give me as good luck in my ventures as you have in your sayings.'

At these words Sancho turned away and gave Dapple the stick; and Don Quixote stayed on horseback, resting in his stirrups and leaning on his lance, full of sad and troubled fancies, with which we will leave him and go with Sancho Panza, who parted from his master no less troubled and thoughtful than he. So much so that scarcely had he come out of the wood than he turned round and, seeing that Don Quixote was out of sight, dismounted from his ass. Then, sitting down at the foot of a tree, he began to commune with himself to this effect :

'Now, let us learn, brother Sancho, where your worship is going. Are you going after some ass you have lost? No, certainly not. Then what are you going to look for? I am going to look, as you might say, for nothing, for a Princess, and in her the sun of beauty and all heaven besides. And where do you expect to find this thing you speak of, Sancho? Where? In the great city of El Toboso. Very well, and on whose behalf are you going to seek her? On behalf of the famous knight Don Quixote de la Mancha, who rights wrongs, gives meat to the thirsty, and drink to the hungry. All this is right enough. Now, do you know her house? My master says it will be some royal palace or proud castle. And have you by any chance ever seen her? No, neither I nor my master have ever seen her. And, if the people of El Toboso knew that you are here for the purpose of enticing away their Princesses and disturb- ing their ladies, do you think it would be right and proper for them to come and give you such a basting as would grind your ribs to powder and not leave you a whole bone in your body? Yes, they would be absolutely in the right, if they did not consider that I am under orders, and that

> You are a messenger, my friend
> And so deserve no blame.

'Don't rely on that, Sancho, for the Manchegans are honest people and very hot-tempered, and they won't stand tickling from anyone. God's truth, if they smell you, you're in for bad luck. Chuck it up, you son of a bitch, and let someone else catch it. No, you won't find me searching for a cat with three legs for someone else's pleasure. What's more, looking for Dulcinea up and down El Toboso will be like looking for little Maria in Ravenna, or the Bachelor in Salamanca. It's the Devil, the Devil himself who has put me into this business. The Devil and no other!'

This colloquy Sancho held with himself, and it led him to the following conclusion : 'Well, now, there's a remedy for everything except death, beneath whose yoke we must all pass, willy-nilly, at the end of our lives. I have seen from countless signs that this master of mine is a raving lunatic who ought to be tied up—and me, I can't be much better, for since I follow him and serve him, I'm more of a fool than he—if the proverb is true that says : tell me what company you keep and I will tell you what you are; and that other one too : not with whom you are born but with whom you feed. Well, he's mad—that he is—and it's the kind of mad- ness that generally mistakes one thing for another, and thinks white black and black white, as was clear when he said that the windmills were giants and the friars' mules dromedaries, and the flocks of sheep hostile armies, and many other things to this tune. So it won't be very difficult to make him believe that the first peasant girl I run across about here is the lady Dulcinea. If he doesn't believe it I'll swear, and if he swears I'll outswear him, and if he sticks to it I shall stick to it harder, so that, come what may, my word shall always stand up to his. Perhaps if I hold out I shall put an end to his sending me on any more of these errands, seeing what poor answers I bring back. Or perhaps he'll think, as I fancy he will, that one of those wicked enchanters who, he says, have a grudge against him, has changed her shape to vex and spite him.'

With these thoughts Sancho quieted his conscience, reckoning the business as good as settled. And there he waited till afternoon, to convince Don Quixote that he had had time to go to El Toboso and back. And so well did everything turn out that when he got up to mount Dapple he saw three peasant girls coming in his direction, riding on three young asses or fillies—our author does not tell us which—though it is more credible that they were she-asses, as these are the ordinary mounts of village women; but as nothing much hangs on it, there is no reason to stop and clear up the point. To continue—as soon as Sancho saw the girls, he went back at a canter to look for his master and found him, sighing and uttering countless amorous lamentations. But as soon as Don Quixote saw him, he cried: 'What luck, Sancho? Shall I mark this day with a white stone or with a black?'

'It'll be better,' replied Sancho, 'for your worship to mark it in red chalk, like college lists, to be plainly seen by all who look.'

'At that rate,' said Don Quixote, 'you bring good news.'

'So good,' answered Sancho, 'that your worship has nothing more to do than to spur Rocinante and go out into the open to see the lady Dulcinea del Toboso, who is coming to meet your worship with two of her damsels.'

'Holy Father! What is that you say, Sancho my friend?' cried Don Quixote. 'See that you do not deceive me, or seek to cheer my real sadness with false joys.'

'What could I gain by deceiving your worship?' replied Sancho. 'Especially as you are so near to discovering the truth of my report. Spur on, sir, come, and you'll see the Princess, our mistress, coming dressed and adorned—to be brief, as befits her. Her maidens and she are one blaze of gold, all ropes of pearls, all diamonds, all rubies, all brocade of more than ten gold strands; their hair loose on their shoulders, like so many sunrays sporting in the wind and, what's more, they are riding on three piebald nackneys, the finest to be seen.'

'Hackneys you mean, Sancho.'

'There is very little difference,' replied Sancho, 'between nackneys and hackneys. But let them come on whatever they may, they are the bravest ladies you could wish for, especially the Princess Dulcinea, my lady, who dazzles the senses.'

'Let us go, Sancho my son,' replied Don Quixote, 'and as a reward for this news, as unexpected as it is welcome, I grant you the best spoil I shall gain in the first adventure that befalls me; and, if that does not content you, I grant you the fillies that my three mares will bear me this year, for you know that I left them to foal on our village common.'

'The fillies for me,' cried Sancho, 'for it's not too certain that the spoils of the first adventure will be good ones.'

At this point they came out of the wood and discovered the three village girls close at hand. Don Quixote cast his eye all along the El Toboso road, and seeing nothing but the three peasant girls, asked Sancho in great perplexity whether he had left the ladies outside the city.

'How outside the city?' he answered. 'Can it be that your worship's eyes are in the back of your head that you don't see that these are they, coming along shining like the very sun at noon?'

'I can see nothing, Sancho,' said Don Quixote, 'but three village girls on three donkeys.'

'Now God deliver me from the Devil,' replied Sancho. 'Is it possible that three hackneys, or whatever they're called, as white as driven snow, look to your worship like asses? Good Lord, if that's the truth, may my beard be plucked out.'

'But I tell you, Sancho my friend,' said Don Quixote, 'that it is as true that they are asses, or she-asses, as that I am Don Quixote and you Sancho Panza. At least, they look so to me.'

'Hush, sir!' said Sancho. 'Don't say such a thing, but wipe those eyes of yours, and come and do homage to the mistress of your thoughts, who is drawing near.'

As he spoke he rode forward to receive the three village girls, and dismounting from Dapple, took one of the girls' asses by the bridle and sank on both knees to the ground, saying: 'Queen and Princess and Duchess of beauty, may your Highness and Mightiness deign to receive into your grace and good liking your captive knight, who stands here, turned to marble stone, all troubled and unnerved at finding himself in your magnificent presence. I am Sancho Panza, his squire, and he is the travel-weary knight, Don Quixote de la Mancha, called also by the name of the Knight of the Sad Countenance.'

By this time Don Quixote had fallen on his knees beside Sancho, and was staring, with his eyes starting out of his head and a puzzled look on his face, at the person whom Sancho called

Queen and Lady. And as he could see nothing in her but a country girl, and not a very handsome one at that, she being round-faced and flat-nosed, he was bewildered and amazed, and did not dare to open his lips. The village girls were equally astonished at seeing these two men, so different in appearance, down on their knees and preventing their companion from going forward. But the girl they had stopped broke the silence by crying roughly and angrily : 'Get out of the way, confound you, and let us pass. We're in a hurry.'

To which Sancho replied : 'O Princess and world-famous Lady of El Toboso! How is it that your magnanimous heart is not softened when you see the column and prop of knight errantry kneeling before your sublimated presence?'

On hearing this, one of the two others exclaimed : 'Wait till I get my hands on you, you great ass! See how these petty gentry come and make fun of us village girls, as if we couldn't give them as good as they bring! Get on your way, and let us get on ours. You had better!'

'Rise, Sancho,' said Don Quixote at this; 'for I see that Fortune, unsatisfied with the ill already done me, has closed all roads by which any comfort may come to this wretched soul I bear in my body. And you, O perfection of all desire! Pinnacle of human gentleness! Sole remedy of this afflicted heart, that adores you! Now that the malignant enchanter persecutes me, and has put clouds and cataracts into my eyes, and for them alone, and for no others, has changed and transformed the peerless beauty of your countenance into the semblance of a poor peasant girl, if he has not at the same time turned mine into the appearance of some spectre to make it abominable to your sight, do not refuse to look at me softly and amorously, perceiving in this submission and prostration, which I make before your deformed beauty, the humility with which my soul adores you.'

'Tell that to my grandmother!' replied the girl. 'Do you think I want to listen to that nonsense? Get out of the way and let us go on, and we'll thank you.'

Sancho moved off and let her pass, delighted at having got well out of his fix. And no sooner did the girl who had played the part of Dulcinea find herself free than she prodded her nackney with the point of a stick she carried, and set off at a trot across the field. But when the she-ass felt the point of the stick, which pained her more than usual, she began to plunge so wildly that my lady Dulcinea came off upon the ground. When Don Quixote saw this accident he rushed to pick her up, and Sancho to adjust and strap on the pack-saddle, which had slipped under the ass's belly. But when the saddle was adjusted and Don Quixote was about to lift his enchanted mistress in his arms and place her on her ass, the lady picked herself up from the ground and spared him the trouble. For, stepping back a little, she took a short run, and resting both her hands on the ass's rump, swung her body into the saddle, lighter than a hawk, and sat astride like a man.

At which Sancho exclaimed : 'By St. Roque, the lady, our mistress, is lighter than a falcon, and she could train the nimblest Cordovan or Mexican to mount like a jockey. She was over the crupper of the saddle in one jump, and now without spurs she's making that hackney gallop like a zebra. And her maidens are not much behind her. They're all going like the wind.'

And so they were, for once Dulcinea was mounted, they all spurred after her and dashed away at full speed, without once looking behind them till they had gone almost two miles. Don Quixote followed them with his eyes, and, when he saw that they had disappeared, turned to Sancho and said :

Do you see now what a spite the enchanters have against me, Sancho? See to what extremes the malice and hatred they bear me extend, for they have sought to deprive me of the happiness I should have enjoyed in seeing my mistress in her true person. In truth, I was born a very pattern for the unfortunate, and to be a target and mark for the arrows of adversity. You must observe also, Sancho, that these traitors were not satisfied with changing and transforming my Dulcinea, but transformed her and changed her into a figure as low and ugly as that peasant girl's. And they have deprived her too of something most proper to great ladies, which is the sweet smell they have from always moving among ambergris and flowers. For I must tell you, Sancho, that when I went to help my Dulcinea on to her hackney—as you say it was, though it seemed a she-ass to me—I got such a whiff of raw garlic as stank me out and poisoned me to the heart.'

'Oh, the curs !' cried Sancho at this. 'Oh, wretched and spiteful enchanters ! I should like to see you strung up by the gills like pilchards on a reed. Wise you are and powerful—and much evil you do ! It should be enough for you, ruffians, to have changed the pearls of my lady's eyes into corktree galls, and her hair of purest gold into red ox tail bristles, and all her features, in fact, from good to bad, without meddling with her smell. For from that at least we have gathered what lay concealed beneath that ugly crust. Though, to tell you the truth, I never saw her ugliness, but only her beauty, which was enhanced and perfected by a mole she had on her right lip, like a moustache, with seven or eight red hairs like threads of gold more than nine inches long.'

'To judge from that mole,' said Don Quixote, 'by the correspondence there is between those on the face and those on the body, Dulcinea must have another on the fleshy part of her thigh, on the same side as the one on her face. But hairs of the length you indicate are very long for moles.'

'But I can assure your worship,' replied Sancho, 'that there they were, as if they had been born with her.'

'I believe it, friend,' said Don Quixote, 'for nature has put nothing on Dulcinea which is not perfect and well-finished. And so, if she had a hundred moles like the one you speak of on her, they would not be moles, but moons and shining stars. But tell me, Sancho, that which appeared to me to be a pack-saddle and which you set straight—was it a plain saddle or a side-saddle?'

'It was just a lady's saddle,' replied Sancho, 'with an outdoor-covering so rich that it was worth half a kingdom.'

'And to think that I did not see all this, Sancho!' cried Don Quixote. 'Now I say once more—and I will repeat it a thousand times—I am the most unfortunate of men.'

And that rascal Sancho had all he could do to hide his amusement on hearing this crazy talk from his master, whom he had so beautifully deceived. In the end, after much further conversation between the pair, they mounted their beasts once more, and followed the road to Saragossa, where they expected to arrive in time to be present at a solemn festival which is held every year in that illustrious city. . . .

Chapter XLII. Of Don Quixote's advice to Sancho Panza before he went to govern his Isle, and other grave matters.

. . . At this moment Don Quixote came up, and when he learned what was happening and how soon Sancho was to leave for his governorship, by the Duke's permission he took his squire by the hand and led him to his apartment to give him advice as to his behaviour in office. Then, having entered, he shut the door after him and, almost forcing Sancho to sit down beside him, addressed him with great deliberation :

'I give infinite thanks to Heaven, Sancho my friend, that first and foremost, before I strike any good luck myself, prosperity has come out to meet and receive you. I who had staked the payment for your services on my own success find myself at the beginning of my advancement; while you find yourself rewarded with your heart's desire before your time and contrary to all reasonable expectations. Some bribe, importune, solicit, rise early, entreat, pester, and yet fail to achieve their aims; then there comes another, and without knowing how or why he finds himself with the place and office which many others have sought for. Here the proverb comes in pat, that there is good and bad luck in petitionings. You are, in my opinion, most certainly a dullard. Yet without rising early or working late or putting yourself to great pains, with only the breath of knight errantry which has touched you, you find yourself without more ado governor of an isle, as if that were nothing. I say all this, Sancho, so that you shall not attribute this favour to your own merits, but shall give thanks to God, who disposes things so kindly, and afterwards to the greatness implicit in the profession of knight errantry.

'With your heart disposed to believe my words, be attentive, my son, to this your Cato, who will advise you and be the pole-star and guide to direct you and bring you to a safe port, out of this stormy sea in which you are likely to drown. For offices and great places are nothing but a deep gulf of confusion.

'Firstly, my son, you must fear God; for in fearing Him is wisdom and, being wise, you can make no mistake.

'Secondly, you must consider what you are, seeking to know yourself, which is the most difficult task conceivable. From self-knowledge you will learn not to puff yourself up, like the frog who wanted to be as big as an ox. If you achieve this, the memory that you kept hogs in your own country will come to be like the peacock's ugly feet to the tail of your folly.'

'True enough,' answered Sancho, 'but that was when I was a boy. Afterwards, when I was more of a man, it was geese I kept, not hogs. But this doesn't seem to me to the point, for not all governors come from royal stock.'

'True,' replied Don Quixote, 'and therefore those who are not of noble origin must accompany the gravity of the office they exercise with a mild suavity which, guided by prudence, may save them from malicious slanderers, from whom no station is free.

'Rejoice, Sancho, in the humbleness of your lineage, and do not think it a disgrace to say you come of peasants; for, seeing that you are not ashamed, no one will attempt to shame you. Consider it more meritorious to be virtuous and poor than noble and a sinner. Innumerable men there are, born of low stock, who have mounted to the highest dignities, pontifical and imperial; and of this truth I could weary you with examples.

'Remember, Sancho, that if you take virtue for your means, and pride yourself on performing virtuous deeds, you will have no reason to envy those who were born princes and lords. For blood is inherited but virtue acquired, and virtue has an intrinsic worth, which blood has not.

'This being so, if any of your relations should chance to come and visit you when you are in your isle, do not reject them or insult them. On the contrary, you must receive them, make much of them and entertain them. In that way you will please God, who would have no one disdain His creation; and what is more, you will be complying with your duty to the order of nature.

'If you should take your wife with you—for it is not right that those engaged in government should be for long without wives of their own—instruct her, indoctrinate her and pare her of her native rudeness; for often everything a wise governor gains is lost and wasted by an ill-mannered and foolish wife.

'If you should chance to be widowed—a thing which may happen—and wish to make a better match to suit your office, do not choose a wife to serve you as a bait and a fishing-rod and take bribes in her hood; for I tell you truly that whatever a judge's wife receives her husband will have to account for at the Last Judgment, where he will have to pay fourfold in death for the statutes of which he has taken no account in his lifetime.

'Never be guided by arbitrary law, which has generally great influence with the ignorant who set up to be clever.

'Let the poor man's tears find more compassion in you, but not more justice, than the pleadings of the rich.

'Try to discover the truth behind the rich man's promises and gifts, as well as behind the poor man's sobbings and importunities.

'Where equity may justly temper the rigour of the law do not pile the whole force of it on to the delinquent; for the rigorous judge has no higher reputation than the merciful.

'If you should chance to bend the rod of justice, do not let it be with the weight of a bribe, but with that of pity.

'When you happen to judge the case of some enemy of yours, turn your mind away from your injury and apply it to the truth of the case.

'Do not let personal passion blind you in another's case, for most of the errors you make will be irremediable, and if you should find a remedy it will cost you your reputation, or even your fortune.

'If a beautiful woman comes to beg you for justice, turn your eyes from her tears and your ears from her groans, and consider the substance of her plea at leisure, if you do not want your reason to be drowned in her sobs and your honour in her sighs.

'Do not revile with words the man you must punish with deeds, since the pain of the punishment is sufficient for the wretch without adding ill-language.

'Consider the culprit who comes before you for judgment as a wretched man, subject to the conditions of our depraved nature, and so far as in you lies without injury to the contrary party, show yourself pitiful and lenient; for although all godlike attributes are equal, mercy is more precious and resplendent in our sight than justice.

'If you follow these precepts and rules, Sancho, your days will be long, your fame eternal, your rewards abundant, your happiness indescribable. You will marry your children as you wish to; they and your grandchildren will have titles; you will live in peace and good-will among men, and in your life's last stages you will arrive at the hour of death in a mild and ripe old age, and the tender and delicate hands of your great-grandchildren will close your eyes.

'The instructions I have so far given you are for the embellishment of your soul. Listen now to some which will serve you for the adornment of your body.'

Chapter XLIII. Of Don Quixote's further Advice to Sancho Panza.

Could anyone hear this last discourse of Don Quixote's and not take him for a person of singular intelligence and excellent intentions? For as has often been said in the course of this great history, he went astray only in the matter of chivalry, but in the rest of his talk showed a clear and unbiased understanding, so that his acts discredited his judgment and his judgment his acts at every step. But in this matter of the second set of precepts which he gave Sancho, he showed himself possessed of a very nice humour and displayed both his sense and his madness to an exalted degree. Most attentively did Sancho listen to him and endeavour to commit his counsels to memory, resolved to observe them and thereby to bring the pregnancy of his government to a happy delivery. Don Quixote then went on to say :

'So far as concerns the government of your person and your house, Sancho, my first charge to you is to be clean, and to pare your nails and not let them grow as do some, who are ignorantly persuaded that long nails beautify the hands; as if that excrescence and appendage which they omit to cut were merely nail, whereas it is like the claws of a lizard-catching kestrel—a foul and unsightly object.

'Do not go unbelted and loose; for disorderly clothes are the indication of a careless mind, unless this disorderliness and negligence falls under the head of cunning, as it was judged to do in the case of Julius Caesar.

'Discreetly take the measure of your office's value; and if it will allow you to give your servants liveries, let them be modest and useful, not gaudy and grand, and divide them between your servants and the poor—I mean that if you have six pages to dress, dress three of them and three poor men. Then you will have pages both for heaven and earth. Your vainglorious have not attained to this new fashion of giving liveries.

'Do not eat garlic or onions; for their smell will reveal that you are a peasant.

'Walk leisurely and speak with deliberation; but not so as to seem to be listening to yourself, for all affectation is bad.

'Eat little at dinner and less at supper, for the health of the whole body is forged in the stomach's smithy.

'Be temperate in drinking, remembering that excess of wine keeps neither a secret nor a promise.

'Take care, Sancho, not to chew on both sides of your mouth nor to eruct in anyone's presence.'

'This about *eruct* I don't understand,' said Sancho.

'Eruct, Sancho,' said Don Quixote, 'means belch, and that is one of the coarsest words in the Castilian language, though it is very expressive; and so refined people have resorted to Latin, and instead of *belch* say *eruct* and for *belches eructations*; and if some people do not understand these terms it is of little consequence, for they will come into use in time, and then they will be generally understood; for that is the way to enrich the language, which depends upon custom and the common people.'

'Indeed, sir,' said Sancho, 'I shall bear your counsel about belching in mind, for I generally do it very often.'

'*Eructing*, Sancho, not *belching*,' said Don Quixote.

'Eruct I shall say from now on,' replied Sancho, 'and I swear I won't forget.'

'Also, Sancho, you must not interlard your conversation with the great number of proverbs you usually do; for though proverbs are maxims in brief, you often drag them in by the hair, and they seem more like nonsense.'

'Let God look after that,' answered Sancho, 'for I know more proverbs than a book, and so many of them come all together into my mouth when I speak that they fight one another to get out; and the tongue seizes hold of the first it meets with, even though it mayn't be just to the point. But from now on I'll take care to bring in only those that suit the gravity of my office. For in a well-stocked house the supper is soon cooked; and a good bargain doesn't hold up the business; and the man who sounds the alarm is safe; and giving and taking need some sense.'

'Go on, Sancho,' said Don Quixote. 'Cram them in, thread and string your proverbs together; no one will stop you. My mother scolds me and I whip the top. I tell you to refrain from proverbs, and in one moment you have brought out a whole litany of them which have as much to do with what we are discussing as have the hills of Ubeda. Look you, Sancho, I do not find fault with a proverb aptly introduced, but to load and string on proverbs higgledy-piggledy makes your speech mean and vulgar.

'When you are riding horseback do not throw your body all on the crupper, nor carry your legs stiffly stuck out from the horse's belly; and do not go so slackly either, and look as if you were riding Dapple; for horse-riding makes horsemen of some and stable boys of others.

'Be moderate in your sleeping, for he that does not rise with the sun does not enjoy the day; and remember, Sancho, that industry is the mother of good fortune, and slothfulness, its opposite, never yet succeeded in carrying out an honest purpose.

'This final precept I am going to give you does not concern the adornment of the body, but I would have you keep it carefully in your memory, for I believe that it will be of no less service to you than those I have just given you. It is never to engage in disputes about lineage, or at least never to compare one family with another; for one of the two must necessarily be the better, and you will be hated by the one you set lower and get no sort of reward from the one you place higher.

'Let your clothing be full breeches, a long coat and a cloak a little longer; on no account tight-fitting breeches, for they do not suit either gentlemen or governors.

'This, Sancho, is all the advice that occurs to me for the present. In the course of time my instructions will suit occasions as they arise, if you take care to inform me of your circumstances.'

'Sir,' replied Sancho, 'I can see very well that all you have told me is good, godly and profitable. But of what use will it be to me if I remember none of it? True enough, that about not letting my nails grow, and about marrying a second time if I have a chance, I shan't easily forget. But as for your other bits and pieces, they're already gone out of my head as clean as last year's clouds. So I shall have to have them in writing; for though I can't read or write I can give them to my confessor, and he'll ram them in and refresh my memory in time of need.'

'Oh, sinner that I am!' said Don Quixote. 'How wrong it is for a governor not to be able to read and write! For you must know, Sancho, that for a man to be illiterate or left-handed argues one of two things : either he is the son of exceedingly poor and base parents, or so perverse and wicked himself that neither good example nor good teaching have been able to penetrate him. It is a great defect in you, and so I should like you to learn at least to sign your name.'

'I can sign my name very well,' replied Sancho. 'For when I was warden of a brotherhood in my village I learnt to make some letters, like they put on bales of goods, and they said they spelt my name. But I'll tell you what, I'll pretend that my right hand is paralysed, and have someone else sign for me. For there's a remedy for everything except death, and as I wield the power and the staff I'll do as I like; the more so because he that has the mayor for his father. . . . And I being a governor, which is higher than a mayor, let them come on and play at bo-peep with me. Let them flout me and slander me; let them come for wool and they'll go away shorn; and whom God loves, his house knows it; and the rich man's foolishness passes for wisdom in the world; and since I shall be rich, and a governor and liberal as well, which I intend to be, no one will see a fault in me. Make yourself honey and the flies will suck you; you're worth as much as you've got, as my old grandmother used to say; and there's no getting revenge on a well-rooted man.'

'Confound you, Sancho!' interrupted Don Quixote. 'Sixty thousand devils take you and your proverbs! You have been stringing them together for a whole hour and giving me the pangs of torture with each one. Mark my words, those proverbs of yours will bring you to the gallows one day. Your vassals will take away your government for them, or break into revolts. Tell me, nit-wit, where do you find them? And how do you apply them, stupid? For to utter one and apply it well makes me sweat and labour as if I were digging.'

'Goodness me, my dear master,' answered Sancho, 'you complain about very small matters. Why the devil do you fret yourself because I make use of my wealth? For I have no other. My only fortune is proverbs and still more proverbs. Why, four of them occur to me now, that come in slick to the point or like pears in a basket. But I won't say them, for Sage Silence is Sancho's name.'

'You are not that Sancho,' said Don Quixote. 'You are not Sage Silence, but wicked chatter and perverse obstinacy. But all the same I should like to know what four proverbs come to your mind just now so slick to the point; for I have been racking mine —and it is a good one—and I cannot think of one.'

'What better,' said Sancho, 'than—don't put your thumbs between two back teeth, and—"Get out of my house, what do you want with my wife?" admits of no answer—and whether the pot strikes the stone or vice versa, it's a bad look-out for the pot— every one of which fits to a hair. For no one should meddle with his governor nor with those in authority, for he will come off second best, like the man who puts his finger between the back teeth—and whether they're back teeth or not doesn't matter so long as they're molars. And there's no answering the governor any more than there's a reply to "Get out of my house! What do you want with my wife?" As to the one about the stone and the pot, a blind man can see that. So he who sees the mote in the other man's eye must see the beam in his own, so that it shan't be said of him that the dead woman was frightened by the one with her throat cut. And your worship's well aware that the fool knows more in his own house than the wise man in another's.'

'No, no, Sancho,' replied Don Quixote, 'the fool knows nothing in his own house nor in anyone else's, since no edifice of wisdom can rest on a foundation of folly. But let us leave the matter here, Sancho, for if you govern badly the fault will be yours, and the shame mine. But it consoles me that I have done my duty in advising you as truly and wisely as I can. For that absolves me of my obligation and my promise. God guide you, Sancho, and govern you in your government, and deliver me from my suspicion that you will turn your whole isle upside down, a thing which I could prevent by informing the Duke of your character, and telling him that all that fat little body of yours is nothing but a sackful of proverbs and mischief.'

'Sir,' answered Sancho, 'if I don't seem to your worship worthy of this governorship, I give it up from this moment. For I love a single black nail's breadth of my soul more than my whole body, and plain Sancho can live just as well on bread and onions as Governor Sancho on partridges and capons. What's more we're all equal while we're asleep, great and small, poor and rich alike; and if your worship reflects, you'll see that it was only you who put this business of governing into my head, for I know no more of

governing isles than a vulture; and if anyone thinks that the Devil
will get me for being a governor, I had rather go to Heaven plain
Sancho than to Hell a governor.'

'By God, Sancho,' said Don Quixote, 'if only for those last words
of yours, I consider you worthy to be governor of a thousand isles.
You have a good instinct, without which all knowledge is of no
avail. Commend yourself to God and try not go astray in your
main resolution. I mean that you must always maintain your
unshaken purpose and design to do right in whatever business
occurs, for Heaven always favours honest intentions. Now let us go
to dinner, for I think that my Lord and Lady are waiting for us.'

*Chapter XLV. Of how the great Sancho Panza took possession of
his Isle and of the fashion in which he began to govern.*

O perpetual discoverer of the Antipodes! Torch of the world!
Eye of Heaven! Sweet stirrer of wine coolers! Here Thymbrius,
there Phoebus, now archer, now physician! Father of Poetry,
inventor of Music, you who always rise and—though you seem to
—never set! On you I call, sun, by whose aid man engenders man.
On you I call to favour me and to light the darkness of my
mind, that I may be scrupulous in the narration of the great
Sancho Panza's government; for without you I feel myself timid,
faint-hearted and confused.

I must tell you then that Sancho Panza with all his escort
arrived at a village of about a thousand inhabitants, which was
one of the best in the Duke's dominions. They gave him to understand that this was called the Isle Barataria, either because the
town's name was *Baratario,* or because of the '*barato,*' or low price,
at which he had got the government. When they reached the gates
of the place, which was walled, the town-council came out to
receive him. They rang the bells, and all the inhabitants demonstrated their general rejoicing and conducted him in great pomp
to the principal church to give thanks to God. Then with some
comical ceremonies they delivered him the keys of the town, and
admitted him as perpetual governor of the Isle Barataria. The new
governor's apparel, his beard, his fatness and his smallness surprised everyone who was not in the secret, and even those many
who were. Next they bore him from the church to the judge's
throne and seated him upon it, where the Duke's steward thus
addressed him :

'It is an ancient custom in this famous isle, Lord Governor, that
everyone who comes to take possession of it is obliged to reply to a

question, and this must be a rather intricate and difficult one. By this reply the town touches and feels the pulse of its new governor's understanding and, accordingly, is either glad or grieved at his coming.'

Whilst the steward was thus addressing him, Sancho was gazing at a number of large letters inscribed on the wall facing his seat. Now, as he could not read, he asked what those paintings were on that wall, and the answer came : 'Sir, yonder is written and recorded the day on which your Lordship took possession of this isle, and the inscription says : "*This day, such a date of such a month in such a year, there took possession of the isle the Lord Don Sancho Panza; may he enjoy it for many years.*" '

'Who are they calling Don Sancho Panza?' asked Sancho.

'Your Lordship,' answered the steward, 'for no other Panza has entered this isle but the one seated on that seat.'

'Then take notice, brother,' said Sancho, 'that I'm no Don, and there has never been a Don in my whole family. Plain Sancho Panza's my name, and Sancho my father was called, and Sancho my grandfather, and they were all Panzas without the addition of Dons or Doñas. I fancy there are more Dons than stones in this isle. But enough. God knows my meaning, and perhaps if my government lasts four days I may weed out these Dons, for judging by their numbers they must be as tiresome as gnats. Go on with your question, Master Steward, for I'll reply as best I can, whether the town be sorry or rejoice.'

At this moment two men came into the judgment-hall, one dressed as a labourer and the other as a tailor with scissors in his hand, the latter crying :

'My lord Governor, here's why I and this countryman have come before your worship. That fellow came to my shop yesterday —I, saving your presence, am a licensed tailor, God be praised !— and put a piece of cloth into my hands, and asked me : "Would there be enough here, sir, to make a cap?" I measured the stuff and answered him yes. I suppose he must have suspected that I intended to rob him of part of the cloth, basing his belief on his own roguery and the bad reputation of tailors. And he was quite right. Then he asked me to examine it again and see if there was enough for two. I guessed his drift, and said yes. Then, persisting in his damned idea, he went on adding caps, and I added more yeses till we came to five. And he has just come this very moment for his caps, and I've offered them to him. And he won't pay me for the making, but demands that I shall pay him instead or return him his cloth.'

'Is all this true, brother?' asked Sancho.

'Yes, sir,' answered the fellow, 'but make him show you the five caps he has made me, your worship.'

'With pleasure,' said the tailor.

And taking his hand suddenly from under his cloak, he displayed five caps, one on the tip of each finger, and said : 'Here are the five caps this good man ordered and, by God and my conscience, there wasn't a scrap of cloth over, and I'll submit the work to be examined by the inspectors of the trade.'

Everyone present laughed at the number of caps and the novel nature of the case. But Sancho set himself to consider a little and said : 'There seems to me no need for long delays in this suit; it can be decided on the spot by a wise man's judgment. My sentence, therefore, is that the tailor shall lose his making and the countryman his cloth, the caps to be given to the prisoners in the jail, and let that be an end to the matter.'

This judgment moved the audience to laughter, but the Governor's orders were carried out.

Next there came before him two old men, one of them carrying a cane for a walking-stick. 'Sir,' said the one without the stick, 'some time ago I lent this fellow ten crowns in gold, as a favour and a service to him, on condition that he should repay me on demand. I didn't ask him for them for a long time, so as not to put him into greater difficulties through repaying than he was in when I lent him them. But as he didn't seem to me to be troubling about his debt, I asked him for them, not once but many times. Now not only does he not repay me but he denies the debt, saying that I never lent him these ten crowns, or that if I did he has returned them. I have no witnesses of the loan—nor he of the repayment, for he never made it. So I want your worship to put him under oath, and if he swears that he has repaid me I will let him off the debt here, before God.'

'What do you say to this, you fellow with the stick?' asked Sancho.

'I confess that he lent them to me, sir,' answered the old man. 'Hold down your wand of justice, your worship, and since he leaves it to my oath, I'll swear that I really and truly returned them to him.'

The Governor lowered his wand, and at the same time this old man gave his stick, as if it were very much in his way, to the other old man to hold whilst he took his oath. Then he put his hand on the cross of the wand and declared that he had truly borrowed the ten crowns demanded of him, but that he had returned them into the plaintiff's own hands, and that it was only the other man's forgetfulness that made him continually demand them back.

At this the great Governor asked the creditor what answer he had to give to his adversary. For beyond all doubt the debtor must be speaking the truth since, in his opinion, he was an honest man and a good Christian. It must, in fact, have been the plaintiff who had forgotten how and when the money had been returned, and thenceforward he must never ask for repayment again. The debtor took back his stick, bowed and went out of the court. Now when Sancho saw the defendant depart without more ado and also observed the plaintiff's resignation, he bowed his head on his breast and, placing the first finger of his right hand over his brows and his nose, remained as if in thought for a short while. Then he raised his head and ordered the old man with the stick, who had already left the building, to be recalled; and when he was brought back into his presence, Sancho said: 'Give me that stick, my fellow. I've need of it.'

'With great pleasure,' replied the old man, putting it into Sancho's hand. 'Here it is, sir.' Sancho then took it and, handing it to the other old man, said to him: 'Go, in God's name. You're repaid now.'

'What, sir?' replied the old man. 'Is this stick worth ten gold crowns then?'

'Yes,' said the Governor. 'If it isn't I'm the greatest dolt in the world. And now you'll see whether I haven't the gumption to govern a whole kingdom.'

Then he ordered the cane to be broken open in the presence of everyone; and when this was done they found ten gold crowns inside. Whereupon everyone expressed astonishment, and hailed the governor as a new Solomon. And when asked how he had deduced that the ten crowns were inside the cane, he answered that he had watched the defendant give the stick to the plaintiff whilst he took his oath that he had really and truly returned the money; and when the fellow had completed his oath and asked for the stick back, it had occurred to him that the sum in dispute must be inside. From this, he added, they might see that sometimes God directs the judgments of governors, even if some of them are fools. Besides, he had heard the priest of his village tell of a similar case, and he had so good a memory that, if it weren't that he forgot everything he wanted to remember, there would not be a better in the whole isle. Finally they departed, one abashed and the other satisfied. The audience was flabbergasted, and the secretary who noted down Sancho's words, acts and gestures was unable to decide whether to write him down a wise man or a fool.

But no sooner was this case over than a woman came into the court, stoutly clinging to a man dressed like a rich herdsman, and crying out loudly as she came : 'Justice, Lord Governor ! Justice ! If I don't find it on earth, I'll go and seek it in Heaven ! Sweet governor, this wicked man sprang on me in the middle of a field, and abused my body like a dirty dish-rag and, poor wretch that I am, he robbed me of a treasure I've kept for more than twenty-three years, and defended from Moors and Christians, natives and foreigners. I've always been as resistant as a cork-tree and preserved myself as pure as the salamander in the fire, or as wool on the briars, for this fellow now to come and handle me with his clean hands !'

'We have still to discover whether this fine fellow has clean hands or not,' said Sancho.

Then, turning to the man, he asked him what answer he had to offer to the woman's complaint. And the man replied in great confusion : 'Sirs, I am a poor herdsman with a herd of swine, and this morning I left this place to sell—saving your presence—four pigs, and what with dues and exactions they took from me very nearly their full value. Now as I was coming back to my village I met this good woman on the way, and the Devil, the author of all mischief, made us couple together. I paid her sufficient, but she wasn't content and caught hold of me and wouldn't let me go until she had dragged me to this place. She says I forced her, and that's a lie, as I'll swear on oath; and that's the whole truth, to the last crumb.'

Then the Governor asked him if he had any silver money on him, and he replied he had about twenty ducats inside his shirt in a leather purse. This the governor ordered him to take out and hand over to the plaintiff just as it was. He obeyed trembling, and the woman took it, making a thousand curtseys to the company, and praying God for the life and health of the good governor, who thus looked after needy orphans and maidens. With this she left the court, grasping the purse tightly with both hands, although she looked first to see if the money in it was really silver. Then, no sooner was she gone than Sancho said to the herdsman, who was on the point of tears, for his eyes and his heart yearned after his purse, 'Run after that woman, my good fellow, and take the purse away from her, whether she likes it or not. Then come back here with her.'

It was not a fool or a deaf man he spoke to, for the man dashed out at once like lightning and ran to obey. All the audience were in suspense as they awaited the outcome of the case. Then shortly afterwards the man and woman came back, more close entwined and locked together than before, she with her skirt tucked up and the purse in the fold, and the man struggling to get it away from her. But it was impossible, so stoutly did she defend it, crying out loudly : 'Justice, in God's name ! Justice ! See, Lord worshipful Governor, the shamelessness of this bold, godless fellow. In the middle of the town, in the middle of the street, he's been trying to rob me of the purse your worship made him give me.'

'And did he rob you?' asked the Governor.

'How rob me?' replied the woman. 'I had rather lose my life than this purse. A pretty babe I should be ! You must set other cats at my chin than this miserable, filthy fellow. Pincers and hammers, mallets and chisels, won't be enough to get it out of my clutches, nor lion's claws either. They shall sooner have my soul from the very heart of my body !'

'She's right,' said the man. 'I'm beaten, I admit, and tired out. I confess I haven't the strength to take it from her. I give up.'

Then the Governor said to the woman : 'Show me that purse, honest and valiant woman.'

She gave it to him at once, and the Governor returned it to the man, saying to the forcible but unforced woman : 'Sister, if you'd shown the same valorous spirit you've displayed in defending that purse, or even half as much, in defending your body, the strength of Hercules couldn't have forced you. Get out, confound you, and ill luck go with you. Don't stay anywhere in this isle, nor within twenty miles of it, under pain of two hundred lashes. Get out at once, I say, you loose-tongued, shameless swindler.'

The woman was thrown into confusion, and went off hanging her head, in high dudgeon, and the Governor said to the man : 'Good fellow, go back home, in God's name, with your money, and in future, if you don't want to lose it, try not to get a fancy for coupling with anyone.'

The man thanked him with the worst possible grace and departed, and the audience were once more astonished at their new governor's judicious decisions. All this, duly recorded by his chronicler, was straightway written down for the Duke, who was most eagerly waiting for news. But here let good Sancho rest.

J. M. COHEN

MATEO ALEMÁN
[1547–1614?]

In 1599 there appeared the first part of Guzmán de Alfarache, *the most famous picaresque novel after* Lazarillo de Tormes. *It is, unlike* Lazarillo, *a lengthy work with much moralizing and a number of interpolated stories. A heavier tone pervades* Guzmán; *for all its comic surface, it is rooted in anger and disillusionment. The novel was nevertheless extremely popular, and its author, Mateo Alemán, published a second part in 1604— spurred to do so by the appearance of a false continuation.*

His literary success, however, did little to alleviate Alemán's personal difficulties. An adventurous Sevillian who had studied medicine but never practised it, he engaged for the most part in small business ventures which provided but a scant living. Twice he tasted the bitterness of a debtors' prison, the second time during the same period and in the same jail in which languished Miguel de Cervantes. At sixty, poverty-stricken, he gathered up his family and emigrated to the New World. He died in Mexico.

Guzmán de Alfarache *was translated into English by James Mabbe in 1623 under the title* The Rogue.

GUZMÁN DE ALFARACHE

How Guzmán Excited the Compassion of a Cardinal, and What Followed

I was stirring one morning betimes, according as I had formerly been accustomed, and trudged along with my sore leg, with which I sat me down to beg at one of the Cardinal's gates. And he coming forth for to go to the Palace, stayed to hear me, in how loud a voice and extravagant a tune I besought his pity; not using those plainer notes of eight, but saying: Give me somewhat (noble Christian; friend of Jesus Christ), take pity of this sore afflicted sinner, maimed and pained in his members; look upon these wretched limbs; consider my unfortunate years, and take some compassion of this miserable creature! O my most reverend Father, my most noble Lord, show some sense of sorrow, have some little feeling, I beseech your most illustrious Lordship, of this poor young wretched youth, and pour forth your fatherly compassion upon such a pitiful piece of misery and wretchedness as you see here before you. I beg it at your noble and charitable hands, in that glorious name of the blessed (though most painful) passion of our dear Master and Redeemer Jesus Christ.

My Lord Cardinal (after that he had heard me with a great deal of attention) was extremely moved therewith, and conceived an extraordinary pity towards me, insomuch that I did not seem unto him to be a man, but that I represented unto him even God himself. Thereupon he forthwith gave orders to his servants that they should take me up in their arms and carry me into the house, and that stripping me of those old and rotten rags, they should lay me in his own bed, and in another chamber adjoining thereunto, they should make his. All which was done in a moment.

O the great goodness of God! O the largeness of His noble condition! They stripped me naked, for to clothe me; they would not let me beg, but were ready to give me; and to make me likewise able to give unto others. God never takes any thing away from us, but when He means to bestow greater blessings upon us. When God will give thee anything, He will first ask something of thee. He comes weary about noon to the fountain, sits Him down, asks thee a little water whereof the beasts of the field do drink. Thou givest it Him; in exchange whereof, He gives thee the water of the well of life, the drink of angels, whereof he that drinketh shall never thirst any more. This holy man made Him his pattern, who sending presently for two skilful surgeons, and promising to see them well rewarded, committed my cure to their charge and that they should do their best to make me a sound man. This care being taken, leaving me in the hands of these two hangmen, and in the power of my enemies, he gets him away to the Palace.

Although we used many and sundry counterfeitings of sores, yet that which I had then made me was rubbed over with a certain herb, which caused it to look so ill and so vile, that whosoever had seen it would have thought the sore incurable and that great remedies must be used, as to a thing that was shrewdly festered and grown to a canker; yet if the use of this roguish herb be but left off for three whole days, nature itself, without any other help, will reduce the flesh to that perfection and soundness that it was in before. To these two surgeons, it seemed at the first sight a thing of much moment. They threw off their cloaks, they called for a pan of coals, fresh butter and other things; and when they had all that they would in a readiness, they unswathed me and unbound the clouts that were about my leg, which they performed very neatly and handsomely. That done, they asked me how long I had had this sore, if I could guess whence it should come; if I did use to drink wine, what meats I did most usually feed on, and such other questions as these. Which those that are skilful in that art, are wont to do on the like occasions.

All these I answered with silence, lying all along as if I had been dead, for I was not almost myself, nor was I indeed for a pretty while, seeing such a deal of preparation to cut, to cauterize and the like; and in case I should escape all this, I was at my wits end, to think that my malady would be found out, and so my roguery be discovered. That which I suffered in Gaeta, seemed but a flea-biting unto me. But now I lived in fear that the Cardinal would inflict some notable punishment upon me, for this cheating trick that I had put upon him. I knew not how to help myself, nor what to do, nor whom to make use of in this my extremity. For, neither in all the Litany, nor in *Flos Sanctorum*, could I find any saint that was a defender and protector of villains, or that would seek to excuse me.

By this time they had viewed me again and again, a hundred times, and turned me to and fro, this way and that way, that I thought they would never make an end; when at last I brake forth and said; I am undone, I am undone; yet there is some life left in me : I die if you ask me any more questions or if you meddle with me any more. Two hours of trouble have I already endured under their hands; if they do not bury me now in Tiber (thought I), I will pass over the rest as well as I can. And say they should agree to cut off my leg, the condition were better and the gain more certain, so as I did not die in the doing of it. But suppose also that this should befall me I should then be beforehand with Death, and I shall not be put to endure that brunt another time. What can I do more? (unfortunate man that I am) I was born into the world, here I must suffer, patience must be my best comfort, shuffle the cards therefore anew, and see whether we shall have any better luck. For my rest is up, and the care is already taken.

While I was thus doubtful what would become of me, the covetousness of these surgeons and their greediness of gain opened the door to my remedy. The one of them (who was better experienced than the other), came to know at last that this sore was a counterfeit sore, and that by the signs and symptoms of it, it proceeded from the effects of that very selfsame herb which I had used. But this he kept close to himself, telling his fellow : This flesh is cankered all over, and therefore it is necessary that to hinder it from spreading any farther, and that other new flesh may come up in its place, to cut it all away to the quick, and then there was no doubt of the well curing of it.

The other said unto him : This cure will ask a great deal of time; all this filthy matter must be taken away till we come to the very belly, as it were, wherein the very pith and core of it lies, before

we can well tell what to say of it. Howsoever, we have here a fair
occasion offered to show our skill, and to pick out something of it
for the better passing over of this hard year. He that was the more
expert man of the two, took the other by the hand, and led him
forth aside into a withdrawing room, that joined close to the
chamber. I, when I saw them thus go forth together (suspecting
some secret consultation) I stole me out of my bed after them, that
I might listen to their talk, and it was my hap at last to hear the
one of them say to the other: Master Doctor, I do think (be it
spoken under correction) that Your Worship doth not rightly and
truly understand this young man's malady; for you shall seldom
meet with the like kind of cures, and there is scarce one of a hundred, when they do meet with them, that doth know them, or can
tell what to make of them, yet shall I acquaint you with what I
know: we are partners in this business, and therefore I will hide
nothing from you; but it is a great secret that I have to communicate unto you. What (for God's sake) said the other? I shall tell
you, sir; and with that he said: This beggar is a notable dissembling rogue, a subtle villain; these sores that you see are feigned
ware, counterfeit stuff. What shall we do in this case? Let me be
advised by you. If we leave him off thus, the bird will escape our
hands, and so we shall lose both the credit and profit of this cure.
If we take upon us to cure him, we have no cure to work upon,
and then this rascal will befool us, and laugh at our ignorance;
and if we cannot one way or other come off fairly to our best
advantage, the best course will be (in my opinion) to acquaint the
Cardinal how the case standeth, and what a counterfeit knave we
have under our hands.

No, sir (said the other) I hold not that so fit. Let us hold the bird
fast while we have him; it is a less evil that upon this young fellow
(that is no better than a *Picaro*, and an errant rogue) we should
gain us a little reputation, and come off with some good opinion,
than to let slip so fine and so fair an occasion. Let us therefore take
no notice of his counterfeit sores, but rather lay some plasters thereunto, that may entertain and delay the time; and if need be, we
shall afterwards apply some corrosives that shall eat into the sound
flesh, in the cure whereof we will spend some few days. Nay
then (quoth the other) the best way will be, sir (as I take it),
to begin first with fire, cauterizing that part which appears thus
infected.

Now which of these two remedies they should first begin withal,
as also how they were to share the gains between them, a great
quarrel there was, they could not agree upon the point; for he that

first found out the nature of my sore would have the greater share, or else he would acquaint the Cardinal with the whole business.

When I saw upon what they stuck, and that it was a matter of little or no moment, and that upon their difference, which was occasioned by my miserable poverty, I might run the hazard of my utter ruin, I rushed in between them, and throwing myself down at their feet, I said thus unto them : Gentlemen, on your hands and tongues depends my life or death : my remedy or my ruin. From my hurt no good can come to you; but from my good, you may reap assured both profit and credit.

I know you are not ignorant of the necessity and want which the poor suffer, and the hardness of rich men's hearts, insomuch, that to move them to the more compassion, and the easier to get an alms from them, we are enforced to wound our flesh with these kind of sores and martyrdoms, enduring much trouble and suffering much pain, yet neither these, nor greater miseries that we abide, are of power to prevail with them. It were a great misfortune in others to endure that out of necessity, which we willingly suffer, for that poor and miserable maintenance which we draw from thence. I beseech you (for God's sake) to take pity on me, seeing that you are men that run through the troublesome street of this world, and are made of flesh and blood, as well as myself; and that, which hath driven me to this hard exigent, may likewise light upon yourselves.

Do not (I beseech you) betray me, work your will upon me, and wherein I may serve and help you, I will not be wanting to do as you will have me, and in all things to be so ruled by you that you may gain much by this your cure. You may be confident of me and trust me as you would your own lives; for if there were no other means to make me sure upon you, the fear of mine own punishment is sufficient of itself to bind me to be secret. Nor let not the respect of gain restrain your kindness; for it is better to get than to lose. We are three of us, let us all play booty, and join together to cozen the Cardinal; for he is rich, and something is better than nothing.

These entreaties, seasoned with a few tears, and uttered with that earnestness as I delivered them unto them, were sufficient to make them approve of my counsel; and so much the rather, for that they saw that I had hit the nail right on the head. Wherewith they were so well pleased that they were ready for joy to take me up upon their shoulders, to carry me to my bed. And so they and myself grew fully agreed to play every man his part as well as he could.

Whilst this business was in debating, they were so long before

they could agree upon the matter, that I was scarce put into my
bed and the clothes cast upon me but that my Lord Cardinal was
come to the chamber door; who, when he was entered, one of the
surgeons said unto him :

This young man's malady (may it please your Lordship) is a very
grievous one, and we must necessarily apply great remedies thereunto. For the flesh is festered and cankered in many places, and it
hath taken such deep root, that it is impossible for the plasters that
we are to apply to work any good effect, without some long tract
of time; but I am very confident, and dare be bold to assure your
Lordship, that (by the help of God) we shall make him as sound a
man as ever he was in his life.

Then said the other, If this youth had not thus luckily fallen
into your Lordship's pitiful and charitable hands, within a few
days these his sores would have been so putrified, and have so corrupted the whole body, that all the world could not have saved his
life, but he must have perished and died. But we shall so stop this
canker from spreading itself any farther, and use such good means
for his recovery, that I make no question but within six months, if
not sooner, his flesh shall come to be as whole and as fair as mine.

The good Cardinal (whom charity had only moved hereunto)
told them : Be it in six or in ten, let me have it thoroughly healed
and cured as it ought to be cured, and I shall take order that you
be provided of all things necessary for it; you shall want nothing.
With this, he left them, and withdrew himself into another room.
This did put new life into me; and as if they had drawn my heart
out of the one side, and had thrust it in on the other into my
body again, so did I feel myself. For even till that very instant, I
did not rest assured of these two traitorous surgeons. I still feared
they would have wheeled about another way, and have been the
cause of my undoing. But by that which I had heard in my
presence, I was somewhat cheered, and began to be of good
comfort.

But the custom of swearing, gaming, and begging, are things that
are hard to be left off. It could not choose but grieve me very
much that I was hindered in my course, mewed up, debarred my
liberty, and made unable to enjoy those good and plentiful alms
which I gained by begging. Which loss notwithstanding did seem
the less, in regard of that curious entertainment, choice diet, and
good lodging that I had, that man's desire could not have wished
it to have been better. For I was waited on like a prince, and
cured with that care as if I had been the Cardinal himself. And so
had he given commandment to the servants of his house; besides

his daily coming in his own proper person to visit me. And sometimes he would sit down and make some stay with me, talking of
such things, wherein he took pleasure to hear me.

At length, being healed of this infirmity (when the surgeons saw
their time), they were dismissed, and receiving a great deal of pay
for a little pains. And I was commanded to be new clothed, and to
be listed in the roll of the pages; that as one of them, from that
time forward, I might attend and wait upon his Lordship.

JAMES MABBE

FRANCISCO GÓMEZ DE QUEVEDO
[1580–1645]

*One of the outstanding men of Spain's Golden Age was the prolific and
energetic Francisco de Quevedo. Born in Madrid of a family which enjoyed
marked royal favour, Quevedo reached eminence both in court and literary
circles before he was twenty-five. He engaged actively and often unhappily
in the politics of early seventeenth-century Spain, seesawing from high posts
to exile in the turbulent intrigues of the day. Towards the end of his life his
alleged criticism of King Philip IV's favourite, the* Conde-duque *of
Olivares, netted him four years' imprisonment, much of which time he passed
in the dank horror of a subterranean cell.*

*A writer of keen perception and enormous skill, Quevedo cultivated almost
all genres of literature. His prose works include serious treatises on philosophy,
religion, politics, history and literary criticism. They all reveal encyclopaedic
erudition. His forte, however, is wit and satire, and he is at his best in his
picaresque novel* La vida del Buscón (*written 1608, published 1626*),
and in his masterpiece, Los sueños. *In the latter work, under the guise of
recording his dreams, Quevedo presents a trenchant, bitter satire of the
corruption and degeneracy of seventeenth-century Spain.*

*Quevedo is also one of the country's finest poets. He explored all forms of
verse with remarkable facility, but, as in his prose works, he excelled in
witty satire. His* Poderoso caballero es Don Dinero *is one of the most
popular poems in the Spanish language.*

*In both prose and verse Quevedo is a master of language, dazzling the
reader with verbal pirouettes and a seemingly inexhaustible vocabulary. His
style helped fashion the school of writing called* conceptismo, *in contrast to
the elegantly obscure* culteranismo *developed by Góngora. Ironically,*
conceptismo *became almost as involved as the* culteranismo *which Quevedo
despised, and it had a deleterious effect on Spanish letters of the second half
of the seventeenth century.*

PAUL, THE SPANISH SHARPER

How I went to a boarding school to wait on Don Diego Coronel

Don Alonzo determined to send his son to a boarding school, both to wean him from his tender treatment at home, and also to ease himself of that care. He was informed there was a master of arts in Segovia, whose name was Cabra, and who made it his business to educate *gentlemen's* sons; thither accordingly he sent his, and me to wait upon him. It was the first Sunday after Lent we were brought into the house of famine, for it is impossible to convey a just idea of the penury of such a place.

The master was himself a skeleton, a mere shotten herring, or like a long cane with a little head upon it. He was red-haired, and no more need be said to those who know the proverb, 'that neither cat nor dog of that colour are good'; his eyes almost sunk into his head, as if he had looked through a perspective glass, or the deep windows in a linen-draper's shop; his nose turned up and was somewhat flat, the bridge being almost carried away by an inundation of cold rheum, for he never incurred any worse disorder because it would cost money. His beard had lost its colour from fear of his mouth, which being so near, seemed to threaten to eat it out of mere hunger; his teeth had many of them deserted him from want of employment; his neck was as long as a crane's, with the gullet sticking out so far that it seemed as if compelled by necessity to start out for sustenance; his arms withered; his hands like a bundle of twigs, each of them, hanging downwards, looking like a pair of compasses, with long slender legs. His voice was weak and hollow; his beard shaggy, for he never shaved in order to save soap and razor; besides, it was odious, he said, to feel the barber's hands all over his face, and he would rather die than endure it; but he let one of the boys cut his hair.

In fair weather he wore a threadbare cap, an inch thick in grease and dirt, made of a thing that was once cloth, and lined with scurf and dandruff. His cassock, some said, was really miraculous, for no man knew what colour it was of; some, seeing no hair on it, concluded it was made of frogs' skins; others that it was a mere shadow; near at hand it looked somewhat black, and at a distance bluish. He wore no girdle, cuffs, or band, so that his long hair and scanty short cassock made him look like the messenger of death. Each shoe might have served for an ordinary coffin. As for his chamber, there was not so much as a cobweb in it, the spiders being all starved to death. He put spells upon the mice, for fear they should gnaw some scraps of bread he treasured up. His bed was on the floor, and he always lay upon one side, from fear of wearing out the sheets; in short, he was the superlative degree of the word avarice, and the very *ne plus ultra* of want.

Into this prodigy's hands I fell, and lived under him along with Don Diego. On the night we came he showed us our room, and made us a short speech,—not longer out of sheer love of economy of words. He told us how we were to behave. The next morning we were engaged till dinner time; we went to it; the masters dined first and the servants waited. The dining-room was as big as a half-peck; five gentlemen ate in it at one table; I looked about for the cat, and seeing none, asked a servant, an old stager, who in his leanness bore the mark of a boarding-school, how it came they had none? The tears stood in his eyes, and he said :

'Why do you talk of cats? Pray who told you that cats loved penance and mortification? Ah, your fat sides show you are a new comer.'

This to me was an augury of sorrow, but I was worse scared when I observed that all those who were before us in the house looked like so many pictures of death on the white horse. Master Cabra said grace, then sat down, and they ate a meal which had neither beginning nor end. They brought the broth in wooden dishes, but it was so clear that a man might have seen to the bottom had it been ten fathoms deep. I observed how eagerly they all dived down after a single pea that was in every dish. Every sip he gave, Cabra cried :

'By my troth, there is no dainty like the *olla*, or boiled meat and broth. Let the world say what it will, all the rest is mere gluttony and extravagancy; this is good for the health, while it sharpens the wits.'

'A curse on thee and thy wit,' thought I, and at the same time I saw a servant, like a walking ghost, bring in a dish of meat, which looked as if he had picked it off his own bones. Among it was one poor stray turnip, at sight of which the master exclaimed :

'What, have we turnips today; no partridge is in my opinion to compare with them. Eat heartily, for I love to see you eat.'

He gave every one such a wretched bit of mutton that it stuck to their nails and in their teeth so that not a shred of it could reach their stomachs. Cabra looked on, and repeated :

'Eat heartily, for it is a pleasure to me to see what good stomachs you have.'

Now just think what comfort this was for them that were pining with hunger. When dinner was over, there remained some scraps of bread on the table, and a few bits of skin and bone, and the master said :

'Let this be left for the servants; they must dine as well as we.'

'Perdition seize thee, ruthless wretch,' thought I, 'and may what thou hast eaten stick in thy gizzard for evermore! What a consternation you have thrown my stomach into!'

He next returned thanks, saying, 'Come, let us make way for the servants, and you go and exercise until two o'clock, lest your dinner should be too heavy for you.'

I could no longer forbear laughing aloud for my life, on which he grew very angry, and bade me conduct myself like a modest youth, quoting two or three mouldy old proverbs, and then took himself off. We sat down to this mournful spectacle, and hearing my great guns roar for provender, and as a new comer having more strength than the rest, I seized by force upon two scraps of bread, and bolted them down along with one piece of skin. The others began to mutter, for they were too weak to speak aloud; on which in came Cabra once more, observing :

'Come, come, eat quietly together, since God provides for you, be thankful; there is enough for all.'

Now, I declare it solemnly, there was one of these servants, a Biscayan, named Surre, who had so completely forgotten the way to his mouth, that he put a small bit of crust that was given him into his eye, as if happy that he was thus saved the trouble of swallowing. I asked for drink; the rest who had hardly broken fast never thought of it, and they gave a dish with some water, which I no sooner put to my lips, before the sharp-set lad I spoke of snatched it away, as if I had been Tantalus, and that the flitting river he stands in up to the chin. I got up from table with a sigh, perceiving for truth that I was in a house where they drank to a good appetite, but would not permit it to pledge. It is impossible to express my trouble and concern; and considering how little was likely to go into my belly, I was actually afraid, though hard pressed, of feeling the process of digestion going on.

Thus we passed on till night. Don Diego asked me how he should do to persuade himself that he had dined, for his stomach could not be made to submit, and only grumbled when he alluded to the subject. The house, in short, was a hospital of dizzy heads, proceeding from empty insides,—a different kind of dizziness to that incurred by surfeits.

Supper time came, for afternoon meals were never dreamed of. It was still shorter than the dinner, and consisted of a little roasted

goat instead of mutton. Surely the devil could never have contrived
a worse little beast. Our starving master Cabra said : 'It is very
wholesome and beneficial to eat light suppers, that the stomach
may not be overwhelmed'; and then he quoted some cursed
physician who has been long in hell. He extolled spare diet, alleg-
ing that it prevented uneasy dreams, though he knew that in his
house it was impossible to dream of anything but eating. Our
master and we supped, but in reality we had none of us supped.
On going to bed, neither Diego nor I could sleep a wink, for he
lay contriving how to complain to his father, that he might remove
him, and I advising him so to do. . . .

Having spent the whole night in this discourse, we got a little
nap towards morning, till it was time to rise; six o'clock struck,
Cabra called, and we all went to school, but when I went to dress
me, my doublet was two handfuls too big, and my breeches,
which before were close, now hung as loose as if they had been
none of my own. In fact, when I was ordered to decline some
nouns, such was my hunger that I ate half of my words, for want
of more substantial diet. . . .

In this misery we continued till the next Lent, at the beginning
of which one of our companions fell sick; Cabra, to save charges,
delayed sending for a physician till the patient was just giving up
the ghost, and desired to prepare for another world; then he called
a young quack, who felt his pulse, and said hunger had been
beforehand with him, and prevented his killing that man. These
were his last words; the poor lad died, and was buried meanly,
because he was a stranger. This struck a terror into all that lived
in the house; the dismal story flew all about the town, and came
at last to Don Alonzo Coronel's ears, who having no other son,
began to be convinced of Cabra's inhumanity, and to give credit
to the words of two mere shadows, for we were no better at that
time. He came to take us from the boarding-school, and asked for
us, though we stood before him; till at length, seeing us with some
difficulty, and in so deplorable a condition, he gave our master
some hard words. We were carried away in two chairs, taking
leave of our famished companions, who followed us with their eyes
and wishes, lamenting like those who remain slaves at Algiers,
when their other associates are ransomed.

JOHN STEVENS
(Revised by Thomas Roscoe)

THE VISIONS

PLUTO'S LAIRS, OR HELL

I, who in the first *Vision* saw so many things, and in the *Catch-pole Caught* heard much that I hadn't seen (and being aware that dreams are mostly tricks of the imagination and spirit; and that Evil never spoke truth because she counts not those things that are hidden from us) was guided by my fancy, and, by a stroke of fate that made me fear for my own peace, saw what follows :

Being one autumn at a friend's house in the country (which was indeed a most delicious retreat) I took a walk one moonlight night into the park. At length the humour took me to leave the path, and go further into the wood : what impulse carried me to this, I know not. Whether I was moved by my good angel, or some higher power, but so it was that in half a quarter of an hour, I found myself a great way from home, and in a place where 'twas no longer night; with the pleasantest prospect round about me that ever I saw since I was born. The air was calm and temperate; and it was no small advantage to the beauty of the place, that it was both innocent and silent. On the one hand I was entertained with the murmurs of crystal rivulets; on the other, with the whispering of the trees; the birds singing all the while either in emulation, or requital of the other harmonies. And now to show the instability of our affections and desires, I was grown weary even of tranquillity itself, and in this most agreeable solitude began to long for company.

When in the very instant (to my great wonder) I discovered two paths, issuing from one and the same beginning but dividing themselves forward, more and more, by degrees, as if they liked not one another's company. That on the right hand was narrow, almost beyond imagination; and being very little frequented, it was so overgrown with thorns and brambles, and so stony withal, that a man had all the trouble in the world to get into it. One might see, however, the print and marks of several passengers that had rubbed through, though with exceeding difficulty; for they had left pieces of heads, arms, legs, feet, and many of them their whole skins behind them. Some we saw yet upon the way, pressing forward, without ever so much as looking back; and these were all of them pale-faced, lean, thin, and miserably mortified. There was no passing for horsemen; and I was told that St. Paul himself left his horse, when he went into it. And indeed, there was not the footing of any beast to be seen. Neither horse nor mule, nor the track of any coach or chariot. Nor could I learn that any had passed that way in the memory of man. While I was bethinking myself of what I had seen, I spied at length a beggar that was resting himself a little to take breath; and I asked him what inns or lodgings they had upon the road. His answer was that there was no stopping there, till they came to their journey's end. 'For this,' said he, 'is the way to Paradise, and what should they do with inns or taverns, where there are so few passengers? Do not you know that in the course of nature, to die is to be born, to live is to travel; and the world is but a great inn, after which it is but one stage either to pain or glory?' And with these words he marched forward, and bade me Godspeed, telling me withal that it was time lost to linger in the way of virtue, and not safe to entertain such dialogues as tend rather to curiosity than instruction. And so he pursued his journey, stumbling, tearing his flesh, sighing and groaning at every step; and weeping as if he thought to soften the stones with his tears. This is no way for me, thought I to myself; and no company either; for they are a sort of beggarly, morose people, and will never agree with my humour. So I drew back and struck off into the left-hand way.

And there, I found company enough and room for more. What a world of brave cavaliers! Gilt coaches, rich liveries, and handsome, lively lasses, as glorious as the sun! Some were singing and laughing, others tickling one another and toying; some again, at their cheese-cakes and China oranges, or appointing a set at cards; so that taking altogether, I durst have sworn I had been in the park. This minded me of the old saying, 'Tell me thy company, and I'll tell thee thy manners,' and to save the credit of my education, I put myself into the noble mode, and jogged on. And there was I at the first dash up to the ears, in balls, plays, masquerades, collations, dalliances, amours, and as full of joy as my heart could hold.

It was not here, as upon t'other road, where folks went barefoot and naked, for want of shoemakers and tailors, for here were enow and to spare; beside mercers, drapers, jewellers, bodice-makers, peruke-makers, milliners, and a French ordinary at every other door. You cannot imagine the pleasure I took in my new acquaintance; and yet there was now and then some jostling and disorder upon the way, chiefly between the physicians upon their mules, and the infantry of the lawyers, that marched in great bodies before the judges, and contested for place. But the physicians carried it in favour of their charter, which gives them privilege to study, practise, and teach the art of poisoning, and to read lectures of it in the universities. While this point of honour was in dispute, I perceived divers crossing from one way to the other, and changing of parties. Some of them stumbled and recovered; others fell downright. But the pleasantest gambol of all was that of the vintners. A whole litter of them tumbled into a pit together, one over another, but finding they were out of their element, they got up again as fast they could. . . .

. . . I heard a cry behind me, 'Make way there; make way for the 'pothecaries.' Bless me, thought I, if they be here, we are certainly going to the devil. And so it proved, for we were just then come to a little door, that was made like a mouse-trap; where 'twas easy to get in, but there was no getting out again.

It was a strange thing, that scarce anybody so much as dreamt of hell, all the way we went; and yet everybody knew where they were, as soon as they came there; and cried out with one voice, 'Miserable creatures! we are damned, we are damned.' That word made my heart ache; and is it come to that? said I. Then did I begin with tears in my eyes to reflect upon what I had left in the world, as my relations, friends, ladies, mistresses, and in fine, all my old acquaintances: when with a heavy sigh, looking behind me, I saw the greater part of them posting after me. It gave me, methought, some comfort, that I should have so good company; vainly imagining that even hell itself might be capable of some relief.

Going farther on I was gotten into a crowd of tailors, that stood up sneaking in a corner, for fear of the devils. At the first door, there were seven devils, taking the names of those that came in; and they asked me mine, and my quality, and so they let me pass. But, examining the tailors, 'These fellows,' cried one of the devils, 'come in such shoals, as if hell were made only for tailors.' 'How many are they?' says another. Answer was made, 'About a hundred.' 'About a hundred? They must be more than a hundred,' says t'other, 'if they be tailors; for they never come under a thousand, or twelve hundred strong. And we have so many here already, I do not know where we shall stow them. Say the word, my masters, shall we let them in or not?' The poor pricklice were damnedly startled at that, for fear they should not get in: but in the end, they had the favour to be admitted. 'Certainly,' said I, 'these folks are but in an ill condition, when 'tis a menace for the devils themselves to refuse to receive them.' Thereupon a huge, overgrown, club-footed, crump-shouldered devil, threw them all into a deep hole. Seeing such a monster of a devil, I asked him how he came to be so deformed. And he told me, he had spoiled his back with carrying of tailors, 'For,' said he, 'I have been formerly made use of as a sumpter to fetch them; but now of late

they save me that labour, and come so fast themselves, that it's
one devil's work to dispose of them.' While the word was yet
speaking there came another glut of them, and I was fain to make
way that the devil might have room to work in, who piled them
up, and told me they made the best fuel in hell.

I passed forward then into a little dark alley, where it made me
start to hear one call me by my name, and with much ado I perceived a fellow there all wrapt up in smoke and flame. 'Alas! sir,'
says he, 'have you forgotten your old bookseller?' 'I cry thee
mercy, good man,' quoth I. 'What? art thou here?' 'Yes, sir,' says
he, ''tis e'en too true I never dreamt it would have come to this.'
He thought I must needs pity him : but truly I reflected upon the
justice of his punishment. For in a word, his shop was the very
mint of heresy, schism, and sedition. I put on a face of compassion, however, to give him a little ease, which he took hold of,
and vented his complaint. 'Well, sir,' says he, 'I would my father
had made me a hangman, when he made me a stationer; for we
are called to account for other men's works, as well as for our own.
And one thing that's cast in our dish, is the selling of translations,
so dog cheap, that every sot knows now as much as would formerly
have made a passable doctor, and every nasty groom and roguey
lackey is grown familiar with the classics.' He would have talked
on, if a devil had not stopped his mouth with a whiff from a roll
of his own papers, and choked him with the smoke on't. The pesti-
lent fume would have despatched me too, if I had not got presently
out of the reach on't. But I went my way, saying this to myself,
if the bookseller be thus criminal, what will become of the author!
. . . and so I struck off, upon the left hand, where I saw a
number of old men beating their breasts and tearing their faces,
with bitter groans and lamentations. It made my heart ache to
see them, and I asked what they were : answer was made, that I
was now in the quarter of the fathers that damned themselves to
raise their posterity; which were called by some, the unadvised.
'Wretch that I am!' cried one of them, 'the greatest penitent that
ever lived, never suffered the mortifications I have endured, I have
watched, I have fasted, I have scarce had any clothes to my back;
my whole life has been a restless course of torment, both of body
and mind : and all this, to get money for my children; that I
might see them well married; buy them places at court, or procure
them some other preferment in the world : starving myself in the
conclusion, rather than I would lessen the provision I had made
for my posterity. And yet, notwithstanding this my fatherly care,
I was scarce sooner dead than forgotten; and my next heir buried

me without tears, or mourning; and indeed without so much as paying the legacies, or praying for my soul : as if they had already received certain intelligence of my damnation. And to aggravate my sorrows the prodigals are now squandering and consuming that estate in gaming, whoring, and debauches, which I had scraped together by so much industry, vexation and oppression, and for which I suffer at this instant such insupportable torments.' 'This should have been thought on before,' cried a devil, 'for sure you have heard of the old saying, "Happy is the child whose father goes to the devil".' At which word, the old misers broke out into fresh rage and lamentation, tearing their flesh, with tooth and nail, in so rueful a manner that I was no longer able to endure the spectacle.

A little farther there was a dark, hideous prison, where I heard the clattering of chains, the crackling of flames, the slapping of whips, and a confused outcry of complaints. I asked what quarter this was; and they told me it was the quarter of the 'Oh that I had's!' 'What are those?' said I. Answer was made that they were a company of brutish sots, so absolutely delivered up to vice that they were damned insensibly, and in hell before they were aware. They are now reflecting upon their miscarriages and omissions, and perpetually crying out, 'Oh that I had examined my conscience!' 'Oh that I had frequented the Sacraments!' 'Oh that I had served God as I ought!' 'Oh that I had visited the sick, and relieved the poor!' 'Oh that I had set a watch before the door of my lips!'

My next encounter was a number of people making their moan that they had been taken away by sudden death. 'That's an impudent lie,' cried a devil, '(saving this gentleman's presence) for no man dies suddenly. Death surprises no man, but gives all men sufficient warning and notice.' I was much taken with the devil's civility and discourse; which he pursued after this manner. 'Do ye complain,' says he, 'of sudden death? that have carried death about ye, ever since you were born; that have been entertained with daily spectacles of carcasses and funerals; that have heard so many sermons upon the subject; and read so many good books upon the frailty of life and the certainty of death. Do ye not know that every moment ye live brings ye nearer to your end? Your clothes wear out, your woods and your houses decay, and yet ye look that your bodies should be immortal. What are the common accidents and diseases of life, but so many warnings to provide yourself for a remove? Ye have death at the table, in your daily food and nourishment; for your life is maintained by the death of other creatures. And you have the lively picture of it, every night for your bedfellow. With what face then can you charge your misfortunes upon sudden death? that have spent your whole life, both at bed, and at board, among so many remembrances of your mortality. No, no; change your style, and hereafter confess yourselves to have been careless and incredulous. You die, thinking you are not to die yet; and forgetting that death grows upon you, and goes along with ye from one end of your life to the other, without distinguishing persons or ages, sex or quality; and whether it finds ye well or ill-doing. "As the tree falls, so it lies".'

. . . to my great wonder, I found myself in the park again, where I begun my story : not without an odd medley of passions, partly reflecting upon what others endured, and in part upon my own condition of ease and happiness, that had deserved, perhaps, the contrary as well as they. This thought put me upon a resolution of leading such a course of life, for the future, that I might not come to feel these torments in reality which I had now only seen in vision.

And I must here entreat the reader to follow my example, without making any further experiment; and likewise not to cast an ill construction upon a fair meaning. My design is to discredit and discountenance the works of darkness, without scandalizing of persons; and since I speak only of damned, I'm sure no honest man alive will reckon this discourse a satire.

ROGER L'ESTRANGE
(Revised by Charles Duff)

THE LORD OF DOLLARS

Over kings and priests and scholars
Rules the mighty Lord of Dollars.

Mother, unto gold I yield me,
   He and I are ardent lovers;
   Pure affection now discovers
How his sunny rays shall shield me !
   For a trifle more or less
   All his power will confess,—
Over kings and priests and scholars
Rules the mighty Lord of Dollars.

In the Indies did they nurse him,
   While the world stood round admiring;
   And in Spain was his expiring;

And in Genoa did they hearse him;
  And the ugliest at his side
  Shines with all of beauty's pride;
Over kings and priests and scholars
Rules the mighty Lord of Dollars.

He's a gallant, he's a winner,
  Black or white be his complexion;
  He is brave without correction
As a Moor or Christian sinner.
  He makes cross and medal bright,
  And he smashes laws of right,—
Over kings and priests and scholars
Rules the mighty Lord of Dollars.

Noble are his proud ancestors
  For his blood-veins are patrician;
  Royalties make the position
Of his Orient investors;
  So they find themselves preferred
  To the duke or country herd,—
Over kings and priests and scholars,
Rules to mighty Lord of Dollars.

Of his standing who can question
  When there yields unto his rank, a
  Hight-Castillian Doña Blanca,
If you follow the suggestion?—
  He that crowns the lowest stool,
  And to hero turns the fool,—
Over kings and priests and scholars,
Rules the mighty Lord of Dollars.

On his shields are noble bearings;
  His emblazonments unfurling
  Show his arms of royal sterling
All his high pretensions airing;
  And the credit of his miner
  Stands behind the proud refiner,—
Over kings and priests and scholars
Rules the mighty Lord of Dollars.

Contracts, bonds, and bills to render,
  Like his counsels most excelling,
  Are esteemed within the dwelling
Of the banker and the lender.

So is prudence overthrown,
And the judge complaisant grown,—
Over kings and priests and scholars
Rules the mighty Lord of Dollars.

Such indeed his sovereign standing
  (With some discount in the order),
  Spite the tax, the cash-recorder
Still his value fixed is branding.
  He keeps rank significant
  To the prince or man in want,—
Over kings and priests and scholars
Rules the mighty Lord of Dollars.

Never meets he dames ungracious
  To his smiles or his attention,
  How they glow but at the mention
Of his promises capacious!
  And how bare-faced they become
  To the coin beneath his thumb!—
Over kings and priests and scholars
Rules the mighty Lord of Dollars.

Mightier in peaceful season
  (And in this his wisdom showeth)
  Are his standards, than when bloweth
War his haughty blasts and breeze on;
  In all foreign lands at home,
  Equal e'en in pauper's loam,—
Over kings and priests and scholars
Rules the mighty Lord of Dollars.

THOMAS WALSH

MY FORTUNE

Since, then, my planet has looked on
  With such a dark and scowling eye,
My fortune, if my ink were gone,
  Might lend my pen as black a dye.

No lucky or unlucky turn
  Did fortune ever seem to play,
But, ere I'd time to laugh or mourn,
  'Twas sure to turn the other way.

Ye childless great, who want an heir,
  Leave all your vast domains to me,
And Heaven will bless you with a fair,
  Alas ! and numerous progeny.

They bear my effigy about
  The village, as a charm of power;
If clothed, to bring the sunshine out,—
  If naked, to call down the shower.

When friends request my company,
  No feasts and banquets meet my eye;
To holy mass they carry me,
  And ask me alms, and bid good-bye.

Should bravos chance to lie *perdu,*
  To break some happy lover's head,
I am their man, while he in view
  His beauty serenades in bed.

A loosened tile is sure to fall
  In contact with my head below,
Just as I doff my hat;—'mong all
  The crowd, a stone still lays me low.

The doctor's remedies alone
  Ne'er reach the cause for which they're given.
And if I ask my friends a loan,
  They wish the poet's soul in heaven.

So far from granting aught, 'tis I
  Who lend my patience to their spleen.
Mine is each fool's loquacity,
  Each ancient dame will be my queen.

The poor man's eye, amidst the crowd,
  Still turns its asking looks on mine;
Jostled by all the rich and proud,
  No path is clear, whate'er my line.

Where'er I go, I miss my way;
  I lose, still lose, at every game;
No friend I ever had would stay,
  No foe but still remained the same.

I get no water out at sea,
  Nothing but water at my inn;

My pleasures, like my wine, must be
Still mixed with what should *not* be in.

THOMAS ROSCOE

TO A NOSE

There was a man well fastened to a nose—
A nose superlative did he escort;
An executioner or scribe, in short,
A sword well barbed and sharp against its foes.
It was a sundial badly out of pose,
It was a musing alchemist's retort,
An elephant with trunk upraised in sport,
More nose than Roman Ovid did expose,
It was a fighting galley's pointed beak,
It was a pyramid on Egypt's pate,
Twelve tribes of noses in one nose sublime,
An infinite nose of noses, so to speak,
Very much of a nose it was, a nose so great
That in the face of Annas 'twere a crime.

JEAN WILLARD BURNHAM

ROME IN HER RUINS

Amidst these scenes, O Pilgrim, seek'st thou Rome!
Vain is thy search—the pomp of Rome is fled;
Her silent Aventine is glory's tomb;
Her walls, her shrines, but relics of the dead.

That hill, where Caesars dwelt in other days,
Forsaken mourns where once it towered sublime;
Each mouldering medal now far less displays
The triumphs won by Latium, than by Time.

Tiber alone survives—the passing wave
That bathed her towers now murmurs by her grave,
Wailing with plaintive sound her fallen fanes.
Rome! of thine ancient grandeur all is past
That seemed for years eternal framed to last,
Nought but the wave, a fugitive—remains.

FELICIA D. HEMANS

DEATH WARNINGS

I saw the ramparts of my native land
  One time so strong, now dropping in decay,
  Their strength destroyed by this new age's way
That has worn out and rotted what was grand.
  I went into the fields; there I could see
  The sun drink up the waters newly thawed;
  And on the hills the moaning cattle pawed,
Their miseries robbed the light of day for me.

  I went into my house; I saw how spotted,
  Decaying things made that old home their prize;
  My withered walking-staff had come to bend.
  I felt the age had won; my sword was rotted;
  And there was nothing on which to set my eyes
  That was not a reminder of the end.

JOHN MASEFIELD

LUIS DE GÓNGORA Y ARGOTE
[1561–1627]

A Cordovan priest who attained the post of royal chaplain, Luis de Góngora began his poetic career in a traditional, popular vein. He wrote many charming lyrics, ballads, sonnets and other verse. Góngora became, however, one of the most controversial figures in Spanish literature. In an attempt to refine his poetry he developed an obscure style characterized by loose syntax and an abundance of foreign words, metaphors and mythological references. This rhetorical exuberance—called 'cultism' and 'Gongorism'.— has been termed 'poetic nihilism' by Menéndez y Pelayo, and earned for Góngora the dubious title, 'Angel of Darkness'.

A host of outstanding writers of the Golden Age, including Lope de Vega and Quevedo, attacked culteranismo *with scornful passion. It was widely adopted by numerous mediocre imitators of Góngora, who hastened the decay of Spanish letters in the second half of the seventeenth century.*

Many critics today, however, consider Góngora a rare poetic genius, and he is greatly esteemed by modernist writers.

Góngora's two longest works, Polifemo y Galatea *and the* Soledades, *best exemplify—to his detractors—the involved artificiality of* culteranismo. *To his partisans, they represent the highest expression of a polished and brilliant artist.*

LET ME GO WARM

Let me go warm and merry still;
And let the world laugh, an' it will.

Let others muse on earthly things,—
The fall of thrones, the fate of kings,
　　And those whose fame the world doth fill;
Whilst muffins sit enthroned in trays,
And orange-punch in winter sways
The merry sceptre of my days;—
　　And let the world laugh, an' it will.

He that the royal purple wears,
From golden plate a thousand cares
　　Doth swallow as a gilded pill;
On feasts like these I turn my back,
Whilst puddings in my roasting-jack
Beside the chimney hiss and crack;—
　　And let the world laugh, an' it will.

And when the wintry tempest blows,
And January's sleets and snows
　　Are spread o'er every vale and hill,
With one to tell a merry tale
O'er roasted nuts and humming ale,
I sit, and care not for the gale;—
　　And let the world laugh, an' it will.

Let merchants traverse seas and lands
For silver mines and golden sands;
　　Whilst I beside some shadowy rill
Just where its bubbling fountain swells
Do sit and gather stones and shells,
And hear the tale the blackbird tells;—
　　And let the world laugh, an' it will.

For Hero's sake the Grecian lover
The stormy Hellespont swam over;
　　I cross without the fear of ill
The wooden bridge that slow bestrides
The Madrigal's enchanting sides,
Or barefoot wade through Yepes's tides;—
　　And let the world laugh, an' it will.

But since the Fates so cruel prove,
That Pyramus should die of love,
   And love should gentle Thisbe kill;
My Thisbe be an apple-tart,
The sword I plunge into her heart
The tooth that bites the crust apart,—
   And let the world laugh, an' it will.

HENRY WADSWORTH LONGFELLOW

THAT'S A LIE!

Riches will serve for titles, too,
   That's true—that's true!
And they love most who oftenest sigh,
   That's a lie—that's a lie!

That crowns give virtue—power gives wit,
That follies well on proud ones sit;
That poor men's slips deserve a halter;
While honours crown the great defaulter;
That 'nointed kings no wrong can do,
No right, such worms as I and you—
That's true—that's true!

To say a dull and sleepy warden
Can guard a many-portal'd garden;
That woes which darken many a day
One moment's smile can charm away;
To say you think that Celia's eye
Speaks aught but trick and treachery,
That's a lie—that's a lie!

That wisdom's bought and virtue sold;
And that you can provide with gold
For court a garter or a star,
And valour fit for peace or war;
And purchase knowledge at the U-
Niversity for P. or Q.—
That's true—that's true!

They must be gagged who go to court,
And bless, beside, the gagger for 't;
That rankless must be scourged, and thank
The scourgers when they're men of rank;

The humble, poor man's form and hue
Deserve both shame and suffering too—
That's true—that's true!

But wondrous favours to be done,
And glorious prizes to be won;
And downy pillows for our head,
And thornless roses for our bed;
From monarch's words—you'll trust and try,
And risk your honour on the die—
That's a lie—that's a lie!

That he who in the courts of law
Defends his person or estate,
Should have a privilege to draw
Upon the mighty River Plate;
And spite of all that he can do,
He will be plucked and laughed at too—
That's true, that's true!

To sow of pure and honest seeds,
And gather nought but waste and weeds;
And to pretend our care and toil
Had well prepared the ungrateful soil;
And then on righteous heaven to cry,
As 'twere unjust—and ask it why?—
That's a lie, that's a lie!

JOHN BOWRING

THE LOVELIEST GIRL

The loveliest girl in all our country-side,
Today forsaken, yesterday a bride,
Seeing her love ride forth to join the wars,
With breaking heart and trembling lips implores :
'My hope is dead, my tears are blinding me,
Oh let me walk alone where breaks the sea !'

'You told me, Mother, what too well I know,
How grief is long, and joy is quick to go,
But you have given him my heart that he
Might hold it captive with love's bitter key,—
My hope is dead, my tears are blinding me.

'My eyes are dim, that once were full of grace,
And ever bright with gazing on his face,
But now the tears come hot and never cease,
Since he is gone in whom my heart found peace,
My hope is dead, my tears are blinding me.

'Then do not seek to stay my grief, nor yet
To blame a sin my heart must needs forget;
For though blame were spoken in good part,
Yet speak it not, lest you should break my heart.
My hope is dead, my tears are blinding me.

'Sweet Mother mine, who would not weep to see
The glad years of my youth so quickly flee,
Although his heart were flint, his breast a stone?
Yet here I stand, forsaken and alone,
My hope is dead, my tears are blinding me.

'And still may night avoid my lonely bed,
Now that my eyes are dull, my soul is dead.
Since he is gone for whom they vigil keep,
Too long is night, I have no heart for sleep.
My hope is dead, my tears are blinding me,
Oh let me walk alone where breaks the sea!'

JOHN PIERREPONT RICE

THE ROSEMARY SPRAY

The flowers upon the rosemary spray,
Young Maid, may school thy sorrow;
The blue-eyed flower, that blooms today,
To honey turns tomorrow.

A tumult stirs thy tender breast.
With jealous pain true-hearted,
That he, whom thy first love hath bless'd
From thee hath coldly parted.

Ungracious boy, who slights thy love,
And overbold, disdaining
To ask forgiveness, and remove
The cause of thy complaining.

Hope, come and drive those tears away!
For lovers' jealous sorrow,
Like dewy blue-eyed flower on spray
To honey turns tomorrow.

By thine own joy thou wast undone:
A bliss thou couldst not measure,
Like star at dawn too near the sun,
Eclipsed thee by its pleasure.

Walk forth with eyes serene and fair;
The pearls, that deck the morning,
Are wasted in the day's fierce glare;
With calmness tame his scorning.

Disperse those clouds that but dismay;
Distrust that jealous sorrow;
The blue-eyed flower, that blooms today,
To honey turns tomorrow.

EDWARD CHURTON

COME, WANDERING SHEEP, O COME!

Come, wandering sheep, O come!
    I'll bind thee to my breast,
I'll bear thee to thy home,
    And lay thee down to rest.

I saw thee stray forlorn,
    And heard thee faintly cry,
And on the tree of scorn,
    For thee I deign'd to die—
    What greater proof could I
Give,—than to seek the tomb?
Come, wandering sheep, O come!

I shield thee from alarms,
    And wilt thou not be blest?
I bear thee in my arms,
    Thou bear me in thy breast!
    O this is love—come, rest—
This is blissful doom.
Come, wandering sheep, O come!

JOHN BOWRING

SONNET

Circean cup, and Epicurus' sty;
   Vast broods of harpies fattening on our purse;
   Empty pretensions that can only nurse
Vexation; spies who swear the air will lie;
Processions, lackeys, footmen mounted high,
   Coaching the way; new fashions always worse,
   A thousand modes,—with unflesh'd swords, the curse
Of citizens, not foes;—loquacity
Of female tongues; impostures of all kind,
   From courts to cabarets; lies made for sale,
Lawyers, priests riding mules, less obstinate;
Snares, miry ways, heroes lame, halting, blind;
   Titles, and flatteries, shifting with each gale :
Such is Madrid, this hell of worldly state.

                                    THOMAS ROSCOE

From POLYPHEMUS AND GALATEA

Cyclops—terrific son of Ocean's God !
   Like a vast mountain rose his living frame;
His single eye cast like a flame abroad
   Its glances, glittering as the morning beam;
A mighty pine supported where he trod
   His giant steps, a trembling twig for him,
Which sometimes served to walk with, or to drive
His sheep to pasture, where the sea-nymphs live.

His jet-black hair in wavy darkness hung,
   Dark as the tides of the Lethean deep,
Loose to the winds, and shaggy masses clung
   To his dread face; like a wild torrent's sweep,
His beard far down his rugged bosom flung
   A savage veil; while scarce the massy heap
Of ropy ringlets his vast hands divide,
That floated like the briny waters wide.

Not mountainous Trinacria ever gave
   Such fierce and unform'd savage to the day;
Swift as the winds his feet, to chase or brave
   The forest hordes, whose battle is his play,

Whose spoils he bears; o'er his vast shoulders wave
   Their variegated skins, wont to dismay
The shepherds and their flocks. And now he came
Driving his herds to fold 'neath the still twilight beam.

With hempen cords and wild bees' wax he bound
   A hundred reeds, whose music wild and shrill,
Repeated by the mountain echoes round,
   Shook every trembling grove, and stream, and hill.
The ocean heaves, the Triton's shells resound
   No more; the frighted vessel's streamers fill
With the shook air, and bear in haste away;
Such was the giant's sweetest harmony.

THOMAS ROSCOE

From SOLITUDES

'Twas now the blooming season of the year,
And in disguise Europa's ravisher
(His brow arm'd with a crescent, with such beams
Encompast as the sun unclouded streams
The sparkling glory of the zodiac!) led
His numerous herd along the azure mead.

   When he, whose right to beauty might remove
The youth of Ida from the cup of Jove,
Shipwreck't, repuls'd, and absent, did complain
Of his hard fate and mistress's disdain;
With such sad sweetness that the winds, and sea,
In sighs and murmurs kept him company. . . .

By this time night begun t'ungild the skies,
Hills from the sea, seas from the hills arise,
Confusedly unequal; when once more
The unhappy youth invested in the poor
Remains of his late shipwreck, through sharp briars
And dusky shades up the high rock aspires.
The steep ascent scarce to be reach'd by aid
Of wings he climbs, less weary than afraid.

   At last he gains the top; so strong and high
As scaling dreaded not, nor battery,

An equal judge the difference to decide
'Twixt the mute load and ever-sounding tide.
His steps now move secur'd; a glimmering light
(The Pharos of some cottage) takes his sight.

                                        THOMAS STANLEY

VICENTE ESPINEL
[1550–1624]

Writer-musician Vicente Espinel led, during his youth, a life of wild
adventure which culminated in capture by Algerian pirates. Rescued from
slavery, he eventually took sacred orders, though he proved to be somewhat
less than a model priest.

His picaresque novel, La vida de Marcos de Obregón, greatly
influenced the famed French work in this genre, Le Sage's Gil Blas de
Santillana. Espinel was also responsible for innovations in both music (the
addition of a fifth string to the guitar) and poetry (the ten-line stanza called
décima or espinela).

IF SHE FROWN MY HEART WOULD BREAK

A thousand, thousand times I seek
My lovely maid;
But I am silent, still, afraid
That if I speak
The maid might frown, and then my heart would break.

I've oft resolved to tell her all,
But dare not—what a woe 'twould be
From doubtful favour's smiles to fall
To the harsh frown of certainty.
Her grace—her music cheers me now;
The dimpled roses on her cheek,
But fear restrains my tongue, for how,
How should I speak,
When, if she frowned, my troubled heart would break?

No! rather I'll conceal my story
In my full heart's most secret cell;
For though I feel a doubtful glory
I 'scape the certainty of hell.

I lose, 'tis true, the bliss of heaven—
I own my courage is but weak;
That weakness may be well forgiven,
For should she speak
In words ungentle, O my heart would break.

JOHN BOWRING

FAINT HEART NEVER WON FAIR LADY

He who is both brave and bold
    Wins the lady that he would;
But the courageless and cold
    Never did and never could.

Modesty, in women's game,
    Is a wide and shielding veil :
    They are tutored to conceal
Passion's fiercely burning flame.
He who serves them brave and bold,
    He alone is understood;
But the courageless and cold
    Ne'er could win, and never should.

If you love a lady bright,
    Seek, and you shall find a way
    All that love would say to say,—
If you watch the occasion right.
Cupid's ranks are brave and bold,
    Every soldier firm and good;
But the courageless and cold
    Ne'er have conquered,—never could.

JOHN BOWRING

RODRIGO CARO
[1573–1647]

*Rodrigo Caro was a noted archaeologist and writer. A las ruinas de
Itálica—inspired, as the title implies, by the ruins of a once great city—is
his most famous poem.*

THE RUINS OF ITÁLICA

Fabius, this region desolate and drear,
These solitary fields, this shapeless mound
Were once Itálica, the far-renowned;
For Scipio the mighty planted here
His conquering colony, and now, o'erthrown,
Lie its once-dreaded walls of massive stone,
Sad relics, sad and vain
Of those invincible men
Who held the region then.
Funereal memories alone remain
Where forms of high example walked of yore.
Here lay the forum, there arose the fane—
The eye beholds their places, and no more.
Their proud gymnasium and their sumptuous baths,
Resolved to dust and cinders, strew the paths;
Their towers that looked defiance at the sky,
Fallen by their own vast weight, in fragments lie.

This broken circus, where the rock-weeds climb,
Flaunting with yellow blossoms, and defy
The gods to whom its walls were piled so high,
Is now a tragic theatre, where Time
Acts his great fable, spreads a stage that shows
Past grandeur's story and its dreary close.
Why, round this desert pit,
Shout not the applauding rows
Where the great people sit?
Wild beasts are here, but where the combatants?
With his bare arms, the strong athlete where?
All have departed from this once gay haunt
Of noisy crowds, and silence holds the air.
Yet on this spot, Time gives us to behold
A spectacle as stern as those of old.
As dreamily I gaze, there seem to rise,
From all the mighty ruin, wailing cries.

The terrible in war, the pride of Spain
Trajan, his country's father, here was born;
Good, fortunate, triumphant, to whose reign
Submitted the far regions, where the morn
Rose from her cradle, and the shore whose steeps
O'erlooked the conquered Gaditanian deeps.

Of mighty Adrian here,
Of Theodosius, saint,
Of Silius, Virgil's peer,
Were rocked the cradles, rich in gold and quaint
With ivory carvings, here were laurel-boughs
And sprays of jasmine gathered for their brows
From gardens now a marshy, thorny waste.
Where rose the palace, reared for Caesar, yawn
Foul rifts to which the scudding lizards haste.
Palaces, gardens, Caesars, all are gone,
And even the stones their names were graven on.

Fabius, if tears prevent thee not, survey
The long-dismantled streets, so thronged of old,
The broken marbles, arches in decay,
Proud statues, toppled from their place and rolled
In dust when Nemesis, the avenger, came,
And buried in forgetfulness profound,
The owners and their fame.
Thus Troy, I deem must be,
With many a mouldering mound;
And thou, whose name alone belongs to thee,
Rome, of old gods and kings the native ground;
And thou, sage Athens, built by Pallas, whom
Just laws redeemed not from the appointed doom—
The envy of earth's cities once wert thou—
A weary solitude and ashes now!
For Fate and Death respect ye not; they strike
The mighty city and the wise alike.

But why goes forth the wandering thought to frame
New themes of sorrow, sought in distant lands?
Enough the example that before me stands;
For here are smoke wreaths seen, and glimmering flame,
And hoarse lamentings on the breezes die;
So doth the mighty ruin cast its spell
On those who near it dwell.
And under night's still sky,
As awe-struck peasants tell,
A melancholy voice is heard to cry:
'Itálica is fallen!' the echoes then
Mournfully shout 'Itálica' again.

The leafy alleys of the forest round
Murmur 'Itálica,' and all around
A troop of mighty shadows at the sound
Of that illustrious name, repeat the call
'Itálica' from ruined tower and wall.

WILLIAM CULLEN BRYANT

FRANCISCO DE RIOJA
[1583–1659]

*Francisco de Rioja, the Sevillian-born 'poet of the flowers', is best known
for his delicate silva called A la rosa.*

TO THE ROSE

Thou pure and glowing rose,
Bright as the sunshine, hail !
Born at the dawn of day
How comst thou into life so glad and gay,
When well thou knowst that Heaven hath given thee light
But for the moment of a swift bird's flight?
Nor may the sweet buds of thy stem avail,
Nor all thy beauty's dower
To stay but one brief hour
The feet of Fate that all too swiftly mows.
The orb that e'en doth send
From Heaven his beams shall know
At last, I fear, an end,
And Death shall rob him of his ruddy glow.
To form those leaves that close around thy heart
Love from his wings the softest feathers gave,
And gold from his bright locks to deck thy brow,
O faithful image of his beauty rare !
Then bathed thee in the blood of that most fair
And lovely goddess, born of the foamy wave;
And yet, O purple flower, can thy sweet face
Not move the scorching ray to show thee grace?
Behold, his fiery dart
Of thy bright beauty all too soon bereaves thee,
And pale and faded leaves thee;
With flaming wings no sooner wouldst thou fly
Than to the earth they drooping sink and die;

Alas! So soon is done
The life but just begun,
I needs must doubt if Dawn with dewy breath
And weeping eyes laments thy birth or death.

IDA FARNELL

LOPE DE VEGA
[1562–1635]

Lope Félix de Vega Carpio astonished his own contemporaries by his productivity—Cervantes called him the 'prodigy of nature'—and his accomplishments evoke no less amazement in our own day. An impassioned genius, Lope cultivated every literary genre with phenomenal ease. His works include a dramatic novel, a pastoral novel, long narrative poems, innumerable lyric poems, some four hundred religious autos and the formidable total of over 1,800 plays.

With all this, Lope found time not only to live, but to live in such a fashion as to inspire scandalized tongue-wagging and venomous jibes from his enemies. He plunged into love as naturally and deeply as his pen into ink; his years were crowded with a succession of mistresses and children in addition to his two marriages. Lope was not, however, a man of casual affections. Intense sincerity marked each romantic attachment, and the happiness and tragedy which often accompanied them inspired some of his finest poetry.

Lope's multitudinous dramatic works cover all themes—the classics, religion, mythology, history, comedy, intrigue, adventure. Written entirely in verse, they contain a plot and sub-plot, and are divided into three acts. Except for action, Lope disregarded the classical unities. He frankly wrote to please his audiences. And to the vast and enthusiastic public which jammed the theatres of his day, Lope was an idol. His plays, however, had more than transitory success; their structure set the pattern for the Spanish national drama which had so many excellent exponents in the seventeenth century.

The moving excerpt presented here is from Act III of one of Lope's best plays, Fuenteovejuna, in which the people of that town take the law into their own hands against the persecution of a local tyrant.

FUENTEOVEJUNA

A room in the Town Hall at Fuenteovejuna. Esteban, Alonso, and Barrildo enter.

ESTEBAN. Is the Town Board assembled?
BARRILDO. Not a person can be seen.

ESTEBAN. Bravely we face danger!

BARRILDO. All the farms had warning.

ESTEBAN. Frondoso is a prisoner in the tower and my daughter Laurencia in such plight that she is lost save for the direct interposition of heaven.

(Juan Rojo *enters with the* Second Regidor.)

JUAN ROJO. Who complains aloud when silence is salvation? Peace, in God's name, peace!

ESTEBAN. I will shout to the clouds till they re-echo my complaints while men marvel at my silence.

(*Enter* Mengo *and* peasants.)

MENGO. We came to attend the meeting.

ESTEBAN. Farmers of this village, an old man whose grey beard is bathed in tears, inquires what rites, what obsequies we poor peasants, assembled here, shall prepare for our ravished homes, bereft of honour? And if life be honour, how shall we fare since there breathes not one among us whom this savage has not offended? Speak? Who but has been wounded deeply, poisoned in respect? Lament now, yes, cry out! Well? If all be ill, how then say well? Well, there is work for men to do.

JUAN ROJO. The direst that can be. Since by report it is published that Castile is subject now to a King, who shall presently make his entrance into Cordoba, let us despatch two Regidors to that city to cast themselves at his feet and demand remedy.

BARRILDO. King Ferdinand is occupied with the overthrow of his enemies, who are not few, so that his commitments are warlike entirely. It were best to seek other succour.

REGIDOR. If my voice have any weight, I declare the independence of the village.

JUAN ROJO. How can that be?

MENGO. On my soul, my back tells me the Town Board will be informed as to that directly.

REGIDOR. The tree of our patience has been cut down, the ship of our joy rides storm-tossed, emptied of its treasure. They have rept the daughter from one who is Alcalde of this town in which we dwell, breaking his staff over his aged head. Could a slave be scorned more basely?

JUAN ROJO. What would you have the people do?

REGIDOR. Die or rain death on tyrants! We are many while they are few.

BARRILDO. Lift our hands against our Lord and Master?

ESTEBAN. Only the King is our master, save for God, never these devouring beasts. If God be with us, what have we to fear?

MENGO. Gentlemen, I advise caution in the beginning and ever after. Although I represent only the very simplest labourers, who bear the most, believe me we find the bearing most unpleasant.

JUAN ROJO. If our wrongs are so great, we lose nothing with our lives. An end, then! Our homes and vineyards burn. Vengeance on the tyrants!

(*Enter* Laurencia, *her hair dishevelled.*)

LAURENCIA. Open, for I have need of the support of men! Deeds, or I cry out to heaven! Do you know me?

ESTEBAN. Martyr of God, my daughter?

JUAN ROJO. This is Laurencia.

LAURENCIA. Yes, and so changed that, gazing, you doubt still!

ESTEBAN. My daughter!

LAURENCIA. No, no more! Not yours.

ESTEBAN. Why, light of my eyes, why, pride of the valley?

LAURENCIA. Ask not, reckon not,
> Here be it known
> Tyrants reign o'er us,
> We are ruled by traitors,
> Justice is there none.
> I was not Frondoso's,
> Yours to avenge me,
> Father, till the night
> I was yours
> Though he was my husband,
> You the defender
> Guarding the bride.

As well might the noble pay for the jewel lost in the merchant's hand!
> I was lost to Fernán Gómez,
> Haled to his keep,
> Abandoned to wolves.
> A dagger at my breast
> Pointed his threats,
> His flatteries, insults, lies,
> To overcome my chastity
> Before his fierce desires.

My face is bruised and bloody in this court of honest men. Some of you are fathers, some have daughters. Do your hearts sink within you, supine and cowardly crew? You are sheep, sheep! Oh, well-named, Village of Fuenteovejuna, the Sheep Well! Sheep, sheep, sheep! Give me iron, for senseless stones can wield none, nor images, nor pillars—jasper though they be—nor dumb living things that lack the tiger's heart that follows him who steals its young, rending the hunter limb from limb upon the very margin of the raging sea, seeking the pity of the angry waves.

> But you are rabbits, farmers,
> Infidels in Spain,
> Your wives strut before you
> With the cock upon their train!
> Tuck your knitting in your belts,
> Strip off your manly swords,
> For, God living, I swear
> That your women dare
> Pluck these fearsome despots,
> Beard the traitors there!
> No spinning for our girls;
> Heave stones and do not blench.
> Can you smile, men?
> Will you fight?
> Caps we'll set upon you,
> The shelter of a skirt,
> Be heirs, boys, to our ribbons,
> The gift of the maidenry,

For now the Commander will hang Frondoso from a merlon of the tower, without let or trial, as presently he will string you all, you race of half-men, for the women will leave this village, nor one remain behind! Today the age of amazons returns, we lift our arms and strike against this villainy, and the crash of our blows shall amaze the world!

ESTEBAN. Daughter, I am no man to bear names calmly, opprobrious and vile. I will go and beard this despot, though the united spheres revolve against me.

JUAN ROJO. So will I, for all his pride and knavery.

REGIDOR. Let him be surrounded and cut off.

BARRILDO. Hang a cloth from a pike as our banner and cry 'Death to Monsters!'

JUAN ROJO. What course shall we choose?

MENGO. To be at them, of course. Raise an uproar and with it the village, for every man will take an oath and be with you that to the last traitor the oppressors shall die.

ESTEBAN. Seize swords and spears, cross-bows, pikes and clubs.
MENGO. Long live the King and Queen!
ALL. Live our lords and masters!
MENGO. Death to cruel tyrants!
ALL. To cruel tyrants, death!

JOHN GARRETT UNDERHILL

COUNTRY LIFE

Let the vain courtier waste his days,
Lured by the charms that wealth displays,
The couch of down, the board of costly fare;
Be his to kiss the ungrateful hand
That waves the sceptre of command,
And rear full many a palace in the air :
Whilst I enjoy, all unconfined,
The glowing sun, the genial wind,
And tranquil hours, to rustic toil assigned;
And prize far more, in peace and health,
Contented indigence, than joyless wealth.
Not mine in Fortune's face to bend,
At Grandeur's altar to attend,
Reflect his smile, and tremble at his frown;
Nor mine a fond aspiring thought,
A wish, a sigh, a vision, fraught
With Fame's bright phantom, Glory's deathless crown!
Nectareous draughts and viands pure
Luxuriant nature will insure;
These the clear fount and fertile field
Still to the wearied shepherd yield;
And when repose and visions reign
Then we are equals all, the monarch and the swain.

FELICIA D. HEMANS

LULLABY OF THE VIRGIN

Holy angels and blest,
Through these palms as ye sweep,
Hold their branches at rest,
For my babe is asleep.

And ye Bethlehem palm-trees,
        As stormy winds rush
In tempest and fury,
        Your angry noise hush;—
Move gently, move gently,
        Restrain your wild sweep;
Hold your branches at rest,—
        My babe is asleep.

My babe all divine,
        With earth's sorrows oppressed,
Seeks in slumber an instant
        His grievings to rest;
He slumbers,—he slumbers,—
        O, hush, then, and keep
Your branches all still,—
        My babe is asleep!

Cold blasts wheel about him—
        A rigorous storm,—
And ye see how, in vain,
        I would shelter his form;—
Holy angels and blest,
        As above me ye sweep,
Hold these branches at rest,—
        My babe is asleep!

                            GEORGE TICKNOR

TOMORROW

Lord, what am I, that with unceasing care
        Thou did'st seek after me, that Thou did'st wait
        Wet with unhealthy dews before my gate,
And pass the gloomy nights of winter there?

Oh, strange delusion, that I did not greet
        Thy blest approach, and oh, to heaven how lost
        If my ingratitude's unkindly frost
Has chilled the bleeding wounds upon Thy feet.

How oft my guardian angel gently cried,
        'Soul, from thy casement look, and thou shalt see
        How he persists to knock and wait for thee!'

And oh, how often to that Voice of sorrow,
'Tomorrow we will open,' I replied,
And when the morrow came I answered still 'Tomorrow'.

HENRY WADSWORTH LONGFELLOW

VARIED EFFECTS OF LOVE

To swoon, to dare, to anger yield,
Harsh, tender, ever-bold, yet shy,
In health, yet dead, alive to die,
Brave knight behind a coward's shield,

And not to find a peaceful field
Apart from love; now sad, with pride
Thy mood oft times at whim will fly,
Offended, haughty, glad, annealed.

Forgetting gain, to court defeat,
To shun the truth that breaks the spell,
To quaff the hemlock as nectar sweet :

To think that heaven fits in hell,
To give up life and soul to clear deceit :
This is love. Who tastes it knows it well.

MARGUERITE GAMBLE

SONNET ON A SONNET

To write a sonnet doth Juana press me,
  I've never found me in such stress and pain;
  A sonnet numbers fourteen lines 'tis plain,
And three are gone ere I can say, God bless me!

I thought that spinning rhymes might sore oppress me,
  Yet here I'm midway in the last quatrain;
  And, if the foremost tercet I can gain,
The quatrains need not any more distress me.

To the first tercet I have got at last,
  And travel through it with such right good-will,
  That with this line I've finished it, I ween.

I'm in the second now, and see how fast
  The thirteenth line comes tripping from my quill—
Hurrah, 'tis done! Count if there be fourteen!

JAMES YOUNG GIBSON

THE NEW ART OF MAKING PLAYS

Who writes by rule must please himself alone,
Be damn'd without remorse, and die unknown.
Such force has habit—for the untaught fools,
Trusting their own, despise the ancient rules.
Yet true it is, I too have written plays.
The wiser few, who judge with skill, might praise;
But when I see how show (and nonsense) draws
The crowds and—more than all—the fair's applause,
Who still are forward with indulgent rage
To sanction every master of the stage,
I, doom'd to write, the public taste to hit,
Resume the barbarous taste 'twas vain to quit :
I lock up every rule before I write,
Plautus and Terence drive from out my sight, . . .
To vulgar standards then I square my play,
Writing at ease; for, since the public pay,
'Tis just, methinks, we by their compass steer,
And write the nonsense that they love to hear.

LORD HOLLAND

SOR MARCELA DE CARPIO DE SAN FÉLIX
[1605–1688]

Few of Lope de Vega's many children survived childhood. But one of them, Marcela, who entered a convent at the age of seventeen, earned her own place in Spanish literature. Sor Marcela wrote mystic poetry; the following is a fine example.

AMOR MYSTICUS

Let them say to my Lover
That here I lie!
The thing of His pleasure,—
His slave am I.

Say that I seek Him
Only for love,
And welcome are tortures
My passion to prove.

Love giving gifts
Is suspicious and cold;
I have all, my Belovéd
When Thee I hold.

Hope and devotion
The good may gain;
I am but worthy
Of passion and pain.

So noble a Lord
None serves in vain,
For the pay of my love
Is my love's sweet pain.

I love Thee, to love Thee,—
No more I desire;
By faith is nourished
My love's strong fire.

I kiss Thy hands
When I feel their blows;
In the place of caresses
Thou givest me woes.

But in Thy chastising
Is joy and peace.
O Master and Love,
Let Thy blows not cease.

Thy beauty, Belovéd,
With scorn is rife,
But I know that Thou lovest me
Better than life.

And because Thou lovest me,
Lover of mine,
Death can but make me
Utterly Thine.

I die with longing
Thy face to see;
Oh! sweet is the anguish
Of death to me!

                                        JOHN HAY

TIRSO DE MOLINA
[1584–1648]

Fray Gabriel Téllez, who wrote under the pseudonym of Tirso de Molina, was a most enthusiastic follower of Lope de Vega. Like his master, Tirso produced numerous dramas (about four hundred) of many types—historical, religious, Biblical, 'cloak and sword'. His character-analysis, however, especially his portrayal of women, is superior to Lope's.

Tirso is best known for his creation of the dramatic character of the libertine Don Juan in El burlador de Sevilla. *Don Juan has become a universal type and has inspired hundreds of imitations. Among the outstanding authors and composers indebted to Tirso de Molina are Molière, Goldoni, Mozart, Byron, Pushkin and Shaw. In Spanish literature, the most famous imitation is the romantic melodrama* Don Juan Tenorio *(1844), by José Zorrilla, in which Don Juan attains salvation through last-minute repentance.*

The selections here presented come from the lively 'transmutation' by Harry Kemp.

THE LOVE-ROGUE

Act I

SCENE I

Court of the King of Naples—inner room of the palace. It is dark. Enter Don Juan *and the* Duchess Isabela.

ISABELA. Since I have given all a woman can
   I hope you'll prove as generous a man :
   Only your faith fulfilled can keep me pure. . . .
   Octavio, here's the way that's most secure !
DON JUAN. Don't doubt me, I will keep my promise, dear.
ISABELA. I should have been a trifle more severe. . . .
   Wait till I bring a light !
DON JUAN. A light ! . . . what for?
ISABELA. Humour my fond mood for a little space;
   I would look deeper, dear, into your face.
DON JUAN. I have put out the only light you bore.
ISABELA. 'The only light I bore' ! . . . what man are you?
DON JUAN. A man without a name. . . .
ISABELA. Not the Duke !
DON JUAN. No !
ISABELA. You mean that you—are not—Octavio? . . .
   I'll rouse the King and all his serving men !

11—SA

Don Juan. Wait, Duchess! Let me have your hand again,—
Keep silence, if but for your honour's sake!
Isabela. Don't touch me, villain! Everybody, wake,—
King! Courtiers! . . .

SCENE II

Enter, rapidly, the King of Naples, *with a candle.*

King. What's wrong?
Isabela. I am undone!
King. Who is it? Tell me, woman, who's the one
That dares?
Don Juan. Why take the trouble to enquire?
It's nothing but a man and woman, sire!
King. The rogue's adroit. . . . (*Apart.*)
Ho, guards, arrest this man!
Isabela. I've given to him all a woman can,
I've lost my honour, and I am undone. (*Goes out.*)

SCENE III

Enter, Don Pedro, *with guard.*

Don Pedro. In your apartments I heard voices, sire,
That cried for help,
Breaking the sacred silence of the night. . . .
I come to seek the cause.
King. Don Pedro Tenorio,
I render up this man into your charge:
Be brief: move quickly . . . find out who they were,
These two; and hold enquiry secretly,
For that which I suspect I must not see,
Lest I must needs delve deeper into it
And to an ill deed, equal judgment fit. (*Goes out.*)

SCENE IV

Don Pedro. Take him!
Don Juan. Let the man who dares
Come on and try,—a life the more or less
Is nothing to me, and I must confess
If any would take mine, they'll have to lay
A dearer price to it than they might care to pay.
Don Pedro. Then slay him and have done.
Don Juan. Don't play with death!
I am resolved to fight to the last breath;

Then you can take my corpse when I am slain—
Because I am a Spanish nobleman
Attending the Ambassador from Spain!
So, sir, I would explain to you alone.

DON PEDRO. (*To the guards.*) Go where the woman went. . . .
(*To* Don Juan) We'll walk apart. . . .

SCENE V

DON PEDRO Now we're but two, alone,—show if your heart
Is equal to your boasting.

DON JUAN. Uncle, do
Put up your sword . . . why should I fight with you?

DON PEDRO. Why, who are you?

DON JUAN. I've said it . . . I'm your nephew.

DON PEDRO. Good God! What fresh betrayal must I fear? (*Apart.*)
Tell me, my nephew, yet my enemy,
Quickly, what evil thing has taken place,
What unheard outrage, or what new disgrace
Born of this madness burning in your brain? . . .
Come, speak, what have you done?

DON JUAN. My uncle and my elder,
I was a boy and I am still a boy :
In making love, you know, I find most joy. . . .
Let making love, then, be my sole defence. . . .
Descending from romance to common sense,
And pleading but my passion and my youth,
Listen, and I will tell the brief, sweet truth :
While all the palace slept, I have employed
An hour to happier purpose; I've enjoyed
The Duchess Isabela, deceiving her—

DON PEDRO. Hold your mouth! Keep a still tongue in your
          head!
So . . . you deceived her . . . was that what . . . you said? . . .
Tell me just how you did it, quietly, so. . . .

DON JUAN. Pretending I was Duke Octavio—

DON PEDRO. Stop! Say no more! If the King hears of this
You are a dead man . . . all my wit and strength
I'll have to strain for such a dangerous business.
It was for a like crime, my precious nephew,
You father sent you hither from Castile
And gave you to these bright Italian shores;
And you return its hospitality
And stab sharp to its very heart of honour

11*—SA

By cozening a woman of its first
Nobility—but, come, while we stand talking
Each minute darkens danger over you . . .
Tell me, my boy, what you propose to do?
DON JUAN. The thing I've done is ugly to the sight;
I do not seek to paint its blackness white;
Uncle, shed all my blood to cleanse my guilt :
Here, take my sword and plunge it to the hilt!
I kneel down, I surrender at your feet.
DON PEDRO. Your humbleness plays on my heart; arise,
And show again as great a bravery—
Dare you leap over from this balcony,
Far down below, where yon green garden lies?
DON JUAN. To win once more your favour that I lack
I would grow angel's wings upon my back.
DON PEDRO. I'll help you . . . that's the way to talk . . . leap
down. . . .
Make all speed to Sicilia or Milan,
And hide yourself away a little while,
Till this blows over
DON JUAN. I will go straightway.
DON PEDRO. From day to day
I'll send you letters and keep you informed
Of this sad case.
DON JUAN. To me so great a pleasure
That still my heart flows on with quicker measure. . . .(Apart.)
Alas, sir, I confess my sinfulness.
DON PEDRO. We've all beguiled our women, more or less,
And youth's a time of snares, and hours misspent. . . .
Leap down . . . the garden mould is soft with rain . . .
DON JUAN. (Apart.) In just this way I had to flee from Spain,
Rejoicing in my cause of banishment. (He leaps.)

SCENE XIV

The Coast of Tarragon, as before. Don Juan *and* Catalinón
come in.

DON JUAN. Get the two mares; have them ready to gallop away.
CATALINON. Yes, as I'm Catalinón and a true man,
I'll see to it that there's exactly two
So that they shan't fall on me with their clubs
And pay me doubly for the lack of you.

Don Juan. While the fishers dance and play
  Take two mares whose flying feet
  Will whisk us off at break of day
  And add the sauce to my deceit.
Catalinon. And so you hold your purpose still
  To cozen Tisbea to your will?
Don Juan. To turn this trick with women has become
  A habit of my very blood,—you know
  My nature, then why ask me foolish questions?
Catalinon. Yes, yes, I know by now
  You are a scourge for women.
Don Juan. Ah, I die
  For Tisbea . . . she'll make a dainty morsel.
Catalinon. Fine payment for their hospitality,
  I must say.
Don Juan. You ninny, I've a classic precedent
  In what Aeneas did to royal Dido.
Catalinon. Some day you'll find your death in fooling women.
Don Juan. You're generous, I must say,
  In your prognostications, and, thereby,
  You live up to your name
  Of Catalinón, 'the cautious one'.
Catalinon. Unless you twist that edge of irony
  Against yourself, and also grow more cautious
  At your grand game of cozening and deceit,
  You'll surely pay with some most monstrous ill.
Don Juan. You've talked enough . . . go, get the two mares ready.
Catalinon. Poor little woman, you'll be well rewarded!

  (*He goes out.* Tisbea *enters.*)

SCENE XV

Tisbea. When I am not with you time is a sick thing.
Don Juan. Don't speak that way—because—I don't believe you.
Tisbea. You don't—believe me?
Don Juan. If it is true you love me
  You'd fill my empty heart with more than words.
Tisbea. I am all yours. What more can you require?
Don Juan. Then why withhold the love we both desire?
Tisbea. Because that same love tears my life apart!
Don Juan. Accept the full devotion of my heart. . . .
  I lay my life in service at your feet . . .
  Now give me all, and make your gift complete.
  Then—we'll get married!

TISBEA. No, my place in life
    Is low, as yours is high . . . that could not be!
DON JUAN. Rank clad in silk and beauty clad in wool
    Are equal in love's kingdom . . . beautiful
    Are you!
TISBEA. I almost make myself believe
    That what you say is true—yet—men deceive!
DON JUAN. Oh, can't you see I love as I declare . . .
    Look deep into my eyes . . . my soul waits there
    That you could trammel with a single hair. . . .
TISBEA. Give me your solemn word, your hand, that you
    Will wed me, then, as you—you promise to!
DON JUAN. I swear by your sweet eyes that madden me
    Marriage shall seal our stolen ecstasy.
TISBEA. Remember, if you lie, there's God and Death.
DON JUAN. I swear again that while God gives me breath
    I'll be the servant of your least command;
    Here is my solemn word, and here's my hand.
    You can put your utmost faith in me.
TISBEA. Then take me; do with me as you desire.
DON JUAN. Only the uttermost can quench this fire.
TISBEA. Come then, my little fisher hut will be
    Our bridal bower . . . stay hidden in these reeds
    Until the hour of opportunity.
DON JUAN. What way shall I get in?
TISBEA. I'll come and show you.
DON JUAN. You have laid bare heaven's brightness for me.
TISBEA. The very way I give myself should bind you :
    If it does not, then God revenge your crime.
DON JUAN. I'll keep my faith until the end of time.

                                   (They go out.)

SCENE XVIII

Tisbea *comes in.*

TISBEA. Fire! Fire! my world is overturning,
    My little hut of straw is burning
    Of a flame that never ends!
    Ring all the bells! help, help, my friends!
    The Fire that once I pleased to flout
    All my tears cannot put out;
    The sudden, climbing flames destroy
    My cottage, like another Troy.

How could I hope that love's great power
That beats down citadels, would spare
My virgin frailty an hour
Beyond the time he found it fair?
Help, help, my friends! the flames roar past control.
Have mercy, love, you burn my very soul!
My little cottage built of straw,
How sweet you were till you became
A vile, abandoned cave of thieves
That bound and made me slave to shame!
Poor, silly girl! . . . The burning stars
Of passion shot their streams of fire
And caught those tresses that you combed
In vanity and light desire!
False guest! you came up from the waves
And swooped upon me like a cloud
Heavy with night and falling fire
And black woes raining in a crowd,—
To leave, when it had served your mood,
My frail, dishonoured womanhood!
Help, help, my friends! the flames roar past control!
Have mercy, love, you burn my very soul!
Alas, I've made a jest of men
And I am served right fittingly
If, ravaging my virgin pride,
A man should make a jest of me.
The gentleman, beneath his word of honour
And his sworn faith, has reaped my flower of honour.
Promising me that he would marry me
He has defiled my honesty and bed,
And I'm deceived, deceived! . . . and worse, alas,
I alone gave his cruelty wings to fly
In my two mares that my own hands have reared—
For he pretended we should fly on them,
But with them he has mocked me and escaped. . . .
Pursue him, every one! . . .
But it does not matter
Which way he goes, for I'll go to the King
And on my naked knees with cries and tears
Implore his sacred Majesty for vengeance! . . .
Help, help, my friends, the flames roar past control!
Have mercy, love! you burn my very soul!

(Tisbea *goes out*.)

ACT III

SCENE XI

Near the sepulchre of Don Gonzalo de Ulloa, *outskirts of the City of Seville.* Catalinón *and* Don Juan.

DON JUAN. Whose sepulchre is this?
CATALINON. Here Don Gonzalo
Lies buried.
DON JUAN. It was I who made him a dead man.
What a stately monument they've reared him!
CATALINON. They reared it up, stone upon weighty stone,
At the King's order—what have they lettered upon it?
DON JUAN. It says—
'Here lies a nobleman, who, foully murdered,
Waits to be revenged upon the traitor
Who slew him.' This inscription shakes me deep
With laughter. . . .
Grey lad, though you have a beard
All stone, I'll pluck it to your further insult.
CATALINON. Don't pluck it, sir,—there is an ancient proverb
That says there's power and danger in plucked beards.
DON JUAN. Old bully, listen to my invitation—
If you have hearing in those ears of stone;
Come to my inn tonight and dine with me.
I hurl defiance in your marble visage;
If vengeance seem so sweet, come take it then;
Although I think you'll have a harder task
Than ever, fighting with a sword of stone.
CATALINON. Master, it's getting darker every instant;
Let's go . . . this place is not much to my liking.
DON JUAN. The vengeance you would execute on me,
Old dotard, stretches to eternity,
And I shall draw full many a jolly breath
Before we meet, the other side of death.
There is no man, alive, on earth, I dread,—
And I have yet to fear a man that's dead.
So, if you care to come tonight and dine,
I'll serve you with cold meat and boiling wine,
As I have heard men wine and dine in hell!
CATALINON. Master, you speak as if you wove a spell.

(*They go out.*)

SCENE XXI

At the sepulchre of Don Gonzalo de Ulloa.

DON JUAN. Who comes?

DON GONZALO. It is I!

CATALINON. Oh, I am dead already—here comes our Dead Man!

DON GONZALO. Yes, I am dead. It is my natural state now;
No man could live with such a wound as this.
I hardly thought that you would keep your word
Since your one pleasure is deception, sir!

DON JUAN. Surely you did not think I am a coward?

DON GONZALO. I did. . . because you ran away that night
On which you put my age to death.

DON JUAN. I fled to escape being known
And not for any fear : tonight you'll find me
Ready for any danger . . . tell me swiftly
Your will.

DON GONZALO. Merely that I've invited you to dine.

CATALINON. Excuse us from your table, sir, tonight.
Your food is cold, and I observe no kitchen
To heat it in.

DON JUAN. Be quiet! Then let us dine!

DON GONZALO. To dine, we'll have to lift this burial slab.

DON JUAN. I'll tear the tombstones up for seats, if need be.

DON GONZALO. You are no coward; you are brave indeed!

DON JUAN. It is not that I'm more than other men,
But that I rule my flesh with resolution.

CATALINON. Pst! Master, see, the table's made of gold!

DON GONZALO. Be seated, guests!

DON JUAN. I find no chairs to sit on.

CATALINON. Here come his two black footmen, bearing chairs.

(*Two black-shrouded figures, bearing chairs, come in.*)

DON GONZALO. Sit down!

CATALINON. I, sir—lunched quite late, sir.

DON GONZALO. Don't answer back!

CATALINON. Yes, I won't answer back, sir.
(*Aside.*) Now may God bring me from this place alive;
I see it isn't pleasant, being dead.
What dish is this, sir?

DON GONZALO. A dish of scorpions.

CATALINON. What a dainty dish!

DON GONZALO. This is the favourite food we dead men eat—
   Why don't you eat?
DON JUAN. I'll eat your food
   If you serve all the asps that hell contains.
DON GONZALO. And now I'll have them sing a song for you.
CATALINON. What kind of wine do dead men drink?
DON GONZALO. Taste and see.
CATALINON. —A bitter drink of gall and vinegar.
DON GONZALO. It is the only wine our presses give.

Song; without.

Behold the souls whom God has judged
   Beyond the crimes of men :
They'll see no rest until they've paid
   Again and yet again.

CATALINON. I find an evil meaning in that song.
   It's sung at us.
DON JUAN. A living fire from hell
   Clutches my breast.

Song; continued.

Though Man walk big about the earth
   It is not fitting he should say
'I have a long time yet to live,'
   Because the living die each day.

DON JUAN. Now that we've dined, let's put the burial slab
   Back where we found it.
DON GONZALO. Give me your hand, you do not fear to give me
   Your hand?
DON JUAN. Why must you always ask me if I fear?
   You burn me ! Do not burn me with your fire !
DON GONZALO. This is a foretaste of the fire you'll know.
   The miracles of God are manifest
   And are past finding out as they are many.
   Witness it, that you pay now for your crimes
   At a slain man's hands—the man you murdered;
   The Living Dead that pays you in this fashion
   Beyond the knowledge of recorded time.
   There is no stranger thing than God's revenge.
   For your strange sins you pay in a strange way !
DON JUAN. Alas, a searing fire flows through my body.
   From you—your hand crushes my aching fingers
   Until the blood streams from their bursting ends.

You monstrous hell-thing,
Take this in the wound I gave you!
It only wounds the unwounded air with blows.
No more, good God! No more!
I swear I did not touch your daughter, sir—
You came before I played the game quite through!
DON GONZALO. That will not save you, in your soul you did.
DON JUAN. Let me go but a little while. . . .
    I will come back . . . my word, you know, is good. . . .
    I am Don Juan Tenorio. . . .
    A gentleman of the King's court. . . .
    I will come back. . . .
    As you're a Christian, let me die confessed.
DON GONZALO. Upon the threshold of eternity
    It is too late now for a good resolve.
DON JUAN. God, how I burn! God, how the flames melt through
    me!
    They pour like water, yet they spread like fire!
    I die. (Falls dead.)

                                        HARRY KEMP

PEDRO CALDERÓN DE LA BARCA
[1600 1681]

The writing career of Pedro Calderón de la Barca spanned a period of sixty years. Before he was twenty-five he had gained some fame as an author of plays and poetry; when he died at eighty-one he was well established as the greatest Spanish dramatist of the end of the Golden Age, as well as one of its finest poets.

Calderón left some two hundred dramatic works on all themes. In particular he was the master of the auto, *or short religious play. While his full-length plays are often less spontaneous and lively than Lope de Vega's, they generally have a more universal appeal.*

Of his works for the theatre, El alcalde de Zalamea, *dealing with the* pundonor *(point of honour) is considered one of the most perfect dramas in the Spanish language; his philosophical drama* La vida es sueño *is probably the most universally known of Spanish plays.* El mágico prodigioso, *the Calderón treatment of the Faust theme, also achieved international acclaim. Excerpts from the latter were translated into English by Percy Bysshe Shelley. (Indeed, the romantic authors of the early nineteenth century especially exalted Calderón.) During the Victorian Age, Edward FitzGerald, of* Rubáiyát *fame, wrote free translations of eight of Calderón's plays.*

LIFE IS A DREAM

ACT THE FIRST

At one side a craggy mountain, at the other a tower, the lower part of which serves as the prison of Sigismund. The door facing the spectators is half open. The action commences at nightfall.

SCENE II

Sigismund, *in the tower.* Rosaura, Clarin.

SIGISMUND (*within*). Alas! Ah, wretched me! Ah, wretched me!
ROSAURA. Oh what a mournful wail!
 Again my pains, again my fears prevail.
CLARIN. Again with fear I die.
ROSAURA. Clarin!
CLARIN.   My lady!
ROSAURA.   Let us turn and fly
 The risks of this enchanted tower.
CLARIN.   For one,
 I scarce have strength to stand, much less to run.
ROSAURA. Is not that glimmer there afar—
 That dying exhalation—that pale star—
 A tiny taper, which, with trembling blaze
 Flickering 'twixt struggling flames and dying rays,
 With ineffectual spark
 Makes the dark dwelling place appear more dark?
 Yes, for its distant light,
 Reflected dimly, brings before my sight
 A dungeon's awful gloom,
 Say rather of a living corse, a living tomb;
 And to increase my terror and surprise,
 Drest in the skins of beasts a man there lies:
 A piteous sight,
 Chained, and his sole companion this poor light.
 Since then we cannot fly,
 Let us attentive to his words draw nigh,
 Whatever they may be.

(*The doors of the tower open wide, and* Sigismund *is discovered in chains and clad in the skins of beasts. The light in the tower increases.*)

SIGISMUND. Alas! Ah, wretched me! Ah, wretched me!
  Heaven, here lying all forlorn,
  I desire from thee to know,
  Since thou thus dost treat me so,
  Why have I provoked thy scorn
  By the crime of being born?—
  Though for being born I feel
  Heaven with me must harshly deal,
  Since man's greatest crime on earth
  Is the fatal fact of birth—
  Sin supreme without appeal.
  This alone I ponder o'er,
  My strange mystery to pierce through;
  Leaving wholly out of view
  Germs my hapless birthday bore,
  How have I offended more,
  That the more you punish me?
  Must not other creatures be
  Born? If born, what privilege
  Can they over me allege
  Of which I should not be free?
  Birds are born, the bird that sings,
  Richly robed by Nature's dower,
  Scarcely floats—a feathered flower
  Or a bunch of blooms with wings—
  When to heaven's high halls it springs,
  Cuts the blue air fast and free,
  And no longer bound will be
  By the nest's secure control :—
  And with so much more of soul,
  Must I have less liberty?
  Beasts are born, the beast whose skin
  Dappled o'er with beauteous spots,
  As when the great pencil dots
  Heaven with stars, doth scarce begin
  From its impulses within—
  Nature's stern necessity,
  To be schooled in cruelty,—
  Monster, waging ruthless war :—
  And with instincts better far
  Must I have less liberty?
  Fish are born, the spawn that breeds
  Where the oozy sea-weeds float,

Scarce perceives itself a boat,
Scaled and plated for its needs,
When from wave to wave it speeds,
Measuring all the mighty sea,
Testing its profundity
To its depths so dark and chill :—
And with so much freer will,
Must I have less liberty?
Streams are born, a coiled-up snake
When its path the streamlet finds,
Scarce a silver serpent winds
'Mong the flowers it must forsake,
But a song of praise doth wake,
Mournful though its music be,
To the plain that courteously
Opes a path through which it flies :—
And with life that never dies,
Must I have less liberty?
And when I think of this I start,
Aetna-like in wild unrest
I would pluck from out my breast
Bit by bit my burning heart :—
For what law can so depart
From all right, as to deny
One lone man that liberty—
That sweet gift which God bestows
On the crystal stream that flows,
Bird and fish that float or fly?

ROSAURA. Fear and deepest sympathy
Do I feel at every word.

SIGISMUND. Who my sad lament has heard?
What ! Clotaldo !

CLARIN (aside to his mistress). Say 'tis he.

ROSAURA. No, 'tis but a wretch (ah, me !)
Who in these dark caves and cold
Hears the tale your lips unfold.

SIGISMUND. Then you'll die for listening so,
That you may not know I know
That you know the tale I told.
Yes, you'll die for loitering near :
In these strong arms gaunt and grim
I will tear you limb from limb.

CLARIN. I am deaf and couldn't hear :—
    No!
ROSAURA. If human heart you bear,
    'Tis enough that I prostrate me.
    At thy feet, to liberate me!
SIGISMUND. Strange thy voice can so unbend me,
    Strange thy sight can so suspend me,
    And respect so penetrate me!
    Who art thou? for though I see
    Little from this lonely room,
    This, my candle and my tomb,
    Being all the world to me,
    And if birthday it could be,
    Since my birthday I have known
    But this desert wild and lone,
    Where throughout my life's sad course
    I have lived, a breathing corse,
    I have moved, a skeleton;
    And though I address or see
    Never but one man alone,
    Who my sorrows all hath known,
    And through whom have come to me
    Notions of earth, sky, and sea;
    And though harrowing thee again,
    Since thou'lt call me in this den,
    Monster fit for bestial feasts,
    I'm a man among wild beasts,
    And a wild beast amongst men.
    But though round me has been wrought
    All this woe, from beasts I've learned
    Polity, the same discerned
    Heeding what the birds had taught,
    And have measured in my thought
    The fair orbits of the spheres;
    You alone, 'midst doubts and fears,
    Wake my wonder and surprise—
    Give amazement to my eyes,
    Admiration to my ears.
    Every time your face I see
    You produce a new amaze :
    After the most steadfast gaze,
    I again would gazer be.
    I believe some hydropsy

Must affect my sight, I think
Death must hover on the brink
Of those wells of light, your eyes,
For I look with fresh surprise,
And though death result, I drink.
Let me see and die : forgive me;
For I do not know, in faith,
If to see you gives me death,
What to see you not would give me;
Something worse than death would grieve me,
Anger, rage, corroding care,
Death, but double death it were,
Death with tenfold terrors rife,
Since what gives the wretched life,
Gives the happy death, despair !

ROSAURA. Thee to see wakes such dismay,
Thee to hear I so admire,
That I'm powerless to inquire
That I know not what to say :
Only this, that I today,
Guided by a wiser will,
Have here come to cure my ill,
Here consoled my grief to see,
If a wretch consoled can be
Seeing one more wretched still.
Of a sage, who roamed dejected,
Poor and wretched, it is said,
That one day, his wants being fed
By the herbs which he collected,
'Is there one' (he thus reflected)
'Poorer than I am today?'
Turning round him to survey,
He his answer got, detecting
A still poorer sage collecting
Even the leaves he threw away.
Thus complaining to excess,
Mourning fate, my life I led,
And when thoughtlessly I said
To myself, 'Does earth possess
One more steeped in wretchedness?'
I in thee the answer find.
Since revolving in my mind,
I perceive that all my pains

To become thy joyful gains
Thou hast gathered and entwined.
And if haply some slight solace
By these pains may be imparted,
Hear attentively the story
Of my life's supreme disasters,
I am . . .

SCENE III

Clotaldo, *Soldiers,* Sigismund, Rosaura, Clarin.

CLOTALDO (*within*). Warders of this tower,
Who, or sleeping or faint-hearted,
Give an entrance to two persons
Who herein have burst a passage. . . .

ROSAURA. New confusion now I suffer.

SIGISMUND. 'Tis Clotaldo, who here guards me;
Are not yet my miseries ended?

CLOTALDO (*within*). Hasten hither, quick! be active!
And before they can defend them,
Kill them on the spot or capture!
(*Voices within*) Treason!

CLARIN.   Watchguards of this tower,
Who politely let us pass here,
Since you have the choice of killing
Or of capturing, choose the latter.

(*Enter* Clotaldo *and Soldiers; he with a pistol, and all with
faces covered.*)

CLOTALDO (*aside to the Soldiers*). Keep your faces all well covered,
For it is a vital matter
That we should be known by no one,
While I question these two stragglers.

CLARIN. Are there masqueraders here?

CLOTALDO. Ye who in your ignorant rashness
Have passed through the bounds and limits
Of this interdicted valley,
'Gainst the edict of the King,
Who has publicly commanded
None should dare descry the wonder
That among these rocks is guarded,
Yield at once your arms and lives,
Or this pistol, this cold aspic
Formed of steel, the penetrating

Poison of two balls will scatter,
The report and fire of which
Will the air astound and startle.
SIGISMUND. Ere you wound them, ere you hurt them,
Will my life, O tyrant master,
Be the miserable victim
Of these wretched chains that clasp me;
Since in them, I vow to God,
I will tear myself to fragments
With my hands, and with my teeth,
In these rocks here, in these caverns,
Ere I yield to their misfortunes,
Or lament their sad disaster.
CLOTALDO. If you know that your misfortunes,
Sigismund, are unexampled,
Since before being born you died
By Heaven's mystical enactment;
If you know these fetters are
Of your furies oft so rampant
But the bridle that detains them,
But the circle that contracts them.
Why these idle boasts? The door (*To the Soldiers.*)
Of this narrow prison fasten;
Leave him there secured.
SIGISMUND.   Ah, heavens,
It is wise of you to snatch me
Thus from freedom! since my rage
'Gainst you had become Titanic,
Since to break the glass and crystal
Gold-gates of the sun, my anger
On the firm-fixed rocks' foundations
Would have mountains piled of marble.
CLOTALDO. 'Tis that you should not so pile them
That perhaps these ills have happened.

(*Some of the Soldiers lead* Sigismund *into his prison, the doors
of which are closed upon him.*)

SCENE VI

*A hall in the Royal Palace.
The King* Basilius *with his retinue.*

BASILIUS. . . . Clorilene, my wife, a son
Bore me, so by fate afflicted

That on his unhappy birthday
All Heaven's prodigies assisted.
Nay, ere yet to life's sweet light
Gave him forth her womb, that living
Sepulchre (for death and life
Have like ending and beginning),
Many a time his mother saw
In her dreams' delirious dimness
From her side a monster break,
Fashioned like a man, but sprinkled
With her blood, who gave her death,
By that human viper bitten.
Round his birthday came at last,
All its auguries fulfilling
(For the presages of evil
Seldom fail or even linger):
Came with such a horoscope,
That the sun rushed blood-red tinted
Into a terrific combat
With the dark moon that resisted;
Earth its mighty lists outspread
As with lessening lights diminished
Strove the twin-lamps of the sky.
'Twas of all the sun's eclipses
The most dreadful that it suffered
Since the hour its bloody visage
Wept the awful death of Christ.
For o'erwhelmed in glowing cinders
The great orb appeared to suffer
Nature's final paroxysm.
Gloom the glowing noontide darkened,
Earthquake shook the mightiest buildings,
Stones the angry clouds rained down,
And with blood ran red the rivers.
In this frenzy of the sun,
In its madness and delirium,
Sigismund was born, thus early
Giving proofs of his condition,
Since his birth his mother slew,
Just as if these words had killed her,
'I am a man, since good with evil
I repay here from the beginning,'—
I, applying to my studies,

Saw in them as 'twere forewritten
This, that Sigismund would be
The most cruel of all princes,
Of all men the most audacious,
Of all monarchs the most wicked;
That his kingdom through his means
Would be broken and partitioned,
The academy of the vices,
And the high school of sedition;
And that he himself, borne onward
By his crimes' wild course resistless,
Would even place his feet on me :
For I saw myself down-stricken,
Lying on the ground before him
(To say this what shame it gives me !)
While his feet on my white hairs
As a carpet were imprinted.
Who discredits threatened ill,
Specially an ill previsioned
By one's study, when self-love
Makes it his peculiar business?—
Thus then crediting the fates
Which far off my science witnessed,
All these fatal auguries
Seen though dimly in the distance,
I resolved to chain the monster
That unhappily life was given to,
To find out if yet the stars
Owned the wise man's weird dominion.
It was publicly proclaimed
That the sad ill-omened infant
Was stillborn. I then a tower
Caused by forethought to be builded
'Mid the rocks of these wild mountains
Where the sunlight scarce can gild it,
Its glad entrance being barred
By these rude shafts obeliscal.
All the laws of which you know,
All the edicts that prohibit
Anyone on pain of death
That secluded part to visit
Of the mountain, were occasioned
By this cause, so long well hidden.

There still lives Prince Sigismund,
Miserable, poor, in prison.
Him alone Clotaldo sees,
Only tends to and speaks with him;
He the sciences has taught him,
He the Catholic religion
Has imparted to him, being
Of his miseries the sole witness.
Here there are three things : the first
I rate highest, since my wishes
Are, O Poland, thee to save
From the oppression, the affliction
Of a tyrant King, because
Of his country and his kingdom
He were no benignant father
Who to such a risk could give it.
Secondly, the thought occurs
That to take from mine own issue
The plain right that every law
Human and divine hath given him
Is not Christian charity;
For by no law am I bidden
To prevent another proving,
Say, a tyrant, or a villain,
To be one myself : supposing
Even my son should be so guilty,
That he should not crimes commit
I myself should first commit them.
Then the third and last point is,
That perhaps I erred in giving
Too implicit a belief
To the facts foreseen so dimly;
For although his inclination
Well might find its precipices,
He might possibly escape them :
For the fate the most fastidious,
For the impulse the most powerful.
Even the planets most malicious
Only make free will incline,
But can force not human wishes.
And thus 'twixt these different causes
Vacillating and unfixed,
I a remedy have thought of

Which will with new wonder fill you.
I tomorrow morning purpose,
Without letting it be hinted
That he is my son, and therefore
Your true King, at once to fix him
As King Sigismund (for the name
Still he bears that first was given him)
'Neath my canopy, on my throne,
And in fine in my position,
There to govern and command you,
Where in dutiful submission
You will swear to him allegiance.
My resources thus are triple,
As the causes of disquiet
Were which I revealed this instant.
The first is; that he being prudent,
Careful, cautious, and benignant,
Falsifying the wild actions
That of him had been predicted,
You'll enjoy your natural prince,
He who has so long been living
Holding court amid these mountains,
With the wild beasts for his circle.
Then my next resource is this :
If he, daring, wild, and wicked,
Proudly runs with loosened rein
O'er the broad plain of the vicious,
I will have fulfilled the duty
Of my natural love and pity;
Then his righteous deposition
Will but prove my royal firmness,
Chastisement and not revenge
Leading him once more to prison.
My third course is this : the Prince
Being what my words have pictured,
From the love I owe you, vassals,
I will give you other princes
Worthier of the crown and sceptre;
Namely, my two sisters' children
Who their separate pretensions
Having happily commingled
By the holy bonds of marriage,
Will then fill their fit position.

This is what a king commands you,
This is is what a father bids you,
This is what a sage entreats you,
This is what an old man wishes;
And as Seneca, the Spaniard,
Says, a king for all his riches
Is but slave of his Republic,
This is what a slave petitions.

ASTOLFO. If on me devolves the answer,
As being in this weighty business
The most interested party,
I, of all, express the opinion :—
Let Prince Sigismund appear;
He's thy son, that's all-sufficient.

ALL. Give to us our natural prince,
We proclaim him king this instant !

BASILIUS. Vassals, from my heart I thank you
For this deference to my wishes :—
Go, conduct to their apartments
These two columns of my kingdom,
On tomorrow you shall see him.

ALL. Live, long live great King Basilius ! . . .

ACT THE SECOND

A Hall in the Royal Palace.

SCENE I

Basilius *and* Clotaldo.

CLOTALDO. Everything has been effected
As you ordered.

BASILIUS. How all happened
Let me know, my good Clotaldo.

CLOTALDO. It was done, sire, in this manner.
With the tranquillising draught,
Which was made, as you commanded,
Of confections duly mixed
With some herbs, whose juice extracted
Has a strange tyrannic power,
Has some secret force imparted,
Which all human sense and speech
Robs, deprives, and counteracteth,
And as 'twere a living corpse

Leaves the man whose lips have quaffed it
So asleep that all his senses,
All his powers are overmastered. . . .
—No need have we to discuss
That this fact can really happen,
Since, my lord, experience gives us
Many a clear and proved example;
Certain 'tis that Nature's secrets
May by medicine be extracted,
And that not an animal,
Not a stone, or herb that's planted,
But some special quality
Doth possess : for if the malice
Of man's heart, a thousand poisons
That give death, hath power to examine,
Is it then so great a wonder
That, their venom being abstracted,
If, as death by some is given,
Sleep by others is imparted?
Putting, then, aside the doubt
That 'tis possible this should happen,
A thing proved beyond all question
Both by reason and example. . . .
—With the sleeping draught, in fine,
Made of opium superadded
To the poppy and the henbane,
I to Sigismund's apartment—
Cell, in fact—went down, and with him
Spoke awhile upon the grammar
Of the sciences, those first studies
Which mute Nature's gentle masters,
Silent skies and hills, had taught him;
In which school divine and ample,
The bird's song, the wild beast's roar,
Were a lesson and a language.
Then to raise his spirit more
To the high design you planned here,
I discoursed on, as my theme,
The swift flight, the stare undazzled
Of a pride-plumed eagle bold,
Which with back-averted talons,
Scorning the tame fields of air,
Seeks the sphere of fire, and passes

Through its flame a flash of feathers,
Or a comet's hair untangled.
I extolled its soaring flight,
Saying, 'Thou at last art master
Of thy house, thou'rt king of birds,
It is right thou should'st surpass them.'
He who needed nothing more
Than to touch upon the matter
Of high royalty, with a bearing
As became him, boldly answered;
For in truth his princely blood
Moves, excites, inflames his ardour
To attempt great things : he said,
'In the restless realm of atoms
Given to birds, that even one
Should swear fealty as a vassal !
I, reflecting upon this,
Am consoled by my disasters,
For, at least, if I obey,
I obey through force; untrammelled,
Free to act, I ne'er will own
Any man on earth my master.'—
This, his usual theme of grief,
Having roused him nigh to madness,
I occasion took to proffer
The drugged draught : he drank, but hardly
Had the liquor from the vessel
Passed into his breast, when fastest
Sleep his senses seized, a sweat,
Cold as ice, the life-blood hardened,
In his veins, his limbs grew stiff,
So that, knew I not 'twas acted,
Death was there, feigned death, his life
I could doubt not had departed.
Then those, to whose care you trust
This experiment, in a carriage
Brought him here, where all things fitting
The high majesty and the grandeur
Of his person are provided.
In the bed of your state chamber
They have placed him, where the stupor
Having spent its force and vanished,
They, as 'twere yourself, my lord,

Him will serve as you commanded :
And if my obedient service
Seems to merit some slight largess,
I would ask but this alone
(My presumption you will pardon),
That you tell me, with what object
Have you, in this secret manner,
To your palace brought him here?

BASILIUS. Good Clotaldo, what you ask me
Is so just, to you alone
I would give full satisfaction.
Sigismund, my son, the hard
Influence of his hostile planet
(As you know) doth threat a thousand
Dreadful tragedies and disasters;
I desire to test if Heaven
(An impossible thing to happen)
Could have lied—if having given us
Proofs unnumbered, countless samples
Of his evil disposition,
He might prove more mild, more guarded
At the least, and self-subdued
By his prudence and true valour
Change his character; for 'tis man
That alone controls the planets.
This it is I wish to test,
Having brought him to this palace,
Where he'll learn he is my son,
And display his natural talents.
If he nobly hath subdued him,
He will reign; but if his manners
Show him tyrannous and cruel,
Then his chains once more shall clasp him.
But for this experiment,
Now you probably will ask me
Of what moment was't to bring him
Thus asleep and in this manner?
And I wish to satisfy you,
Giving all your doubts an answer.
If today he learns that he
Is my son, and some hours after
Finds himself once more restored
To his misery and his shackles,

Certain 'tis that from his temper
Blank despair may end in madness—
But once knowing who he is,
Can he be consoled thereafter?
Yes, and thus I wish to leave
One door open, one free passage,
By declaring all he saw
Was a dream. With this advantage
We attain two ends. The first
Is to put beyond all cavil
His condition, for on waking
He will show his thoughts, his fancies:
To console him is the second;
Since, although obeyed and flattered,
He beholds himself awhile,
And then back in prison shackled
Finds him, he will think he dreamed.
And he rightly so may fancy,
For, Clotaldo, in this world
All who live but dream they act here.

CLOTALDO. Reasons fail me not to show
That the experiment may not answer;
But there is no remedy now,
For a sign from the apartment
Tells me that he hath awoken
And even hitherward advances.

BASILIUS. It is best that I retire;
But do you, so long his master,
Near him stand; the wild confusions
That his waking sense may darken
Dissipate by simple truth.

CLOTALDO. Then your licence you have granted
That I may declare it?

BASILIUS.   Yes;
For it possibly may happen
That admonished of his danger
He may conquer his worst passions.

SCENE VI

Basilius, Sigismund, and Clarin.

BASILIUS. What's all this?
SIGISMUND.   A trifling thing:

One who teased and thwarted me
I have just thrown into the sea.
CLARIN (*to* Sigismund). Know, my lord, it is the King.
BASILIUS. Ere the first day's sun hath set,
    Has thy coming cost a life?
SIGISMUND. Why he dared me to the strife,
    And I only won the bet.
BASILIUS. Prince, my grief, indeed is great,
    Coming here when I had thought
    That admonished thou wert taught
    To o'ercome the stars and fate,
    Still to see such rage abide
    In the heart I hoped was free,
    That thy first sad act should be
    A most fearful homicide.
    How could I by love conducted,
    Trust me to thine arms' embracing,
    When their haughty interlacing,
    Has already been instructed
    How to kill? For who could see,
    Say, some dagger bare and bloody,
    By some wretch's heart made ruddy,
    But would fear it? Who is he,
    Who may happen to behold
    On the ground the gory stain
    Where another man was slain
    But must shudder? The most bold
    Yields at once to Nature's laws;
    Thus I, seeing in your arms
    The dread weapon that alarms,
    And the stain, must fain withdraw;
    And though in embraces dear
    I would press you to my heart,
    I without them must depart,
    For alas! your arms I fear.
SIGISMUND. Well, without them I must stay,
    As I've staid for many a year,
    For a father so severe,
    Who could treat me in this way,
    Whose unfeeling heart could tear me
    From his side even when a child,
    Who, a denizen of the wild,
    As a monster there could rear me,

And by many an artful plan
Sought my death, it cannot grieve me
Much his arms will not receive me
Who has scarcely left me man.

BASILIUS. Would to God it had not been
Act of mine that name conferred,
Then thy voice I ne'er had heard,
Then thy boldness ne'er had seen.

SIGISMUND. Did you manhood's right retain,
I would then have nought to say,
But to give and take away
Gives me reason to complain;
For although to give with grace
Is the noblest act 'mongst men,
To take back the gift again
Is the basest of the base.

BASILIUS. This then is thy grateful mood
For my changing thy sad lot
Is a prince's!

SIGISMUND. And for what
Should I show my gratitude!
Tyrant of my will o'erthrown,
If thou hoary art and grey,
Dying, what do'st give me? Say,
Do'st thou give what's not mine own?
Thou'rt my father and my King,
Then the pomp these walls present
Comes to me by due descent
As a simple, natural thing.
Yes, this sunshine pleaseth me,
But 'tis not through thee I bask;
Nay, a reckoning I might ask
For the life, love, liberty
That through thee I've lost so long:
Thine 'tis rather to thank me,
That I do not claim from thee
Compensation for my wrong.

BASILIUS. Still untamed and uncontrolled:—
Heaven fulfils its word I feel,
I to that same court appeal
'Gainst thy taunts, thou vain and bold,
But although the truth thou'st heard,
And now know'st thy name and race,

And do'st see thee in this place,
Where to all thou art preferred,
Yet be warned, and on thee take
Ways more mild and more beseeming,
For perhaps thou art but dreaming,
When it seems that thou'rt awake.   (*Exit.*)
SIGISMUND. Is this, then, a phantom scene?—
    Do I wake in seeming show?—
    No, I dream not, since I know
    What I am and what I've been.
    And although thou should'st repent thee,
    Remedy is now too late.
    Who I am I know, and fate,
    Howsoe'er thou shouldst lament thee,
    Cannot take from me my right
    Of being born this kingdom's heir.
    If I saw myself erewhile
    Prisoned, bound, kept out of sight,
    'Twas that never on my mind
    Dawned the truth; but now I know
    Who I am—a mingled show
    Of the man and beast combined.

                    SCENE XVII

        Prison of the Prince in the Tower.
Sigismund, *as at the commencement, clothed in skins, chained,
and lying on the ground;* Basilius, *disguised, and* Clotaldo.

BASILIUS. Hark, Clotaldo!
CLOTALDO.   My lord here?
    Thus disguised, your majesty?
BASILIUS. Foolish curiosity
    Leads me in this lowly gear
    To find out, ah me! with fear,
    How the sudden change he bore.
CLOTALDO. There behold him as before
    In his miserable state.
BASILIUS. Wretched Prince! unhappy fate!
    Birth by baneful stars watched o'er!—
    Go and wake him cautiously,
    Now that strength and force lie chained
    By the opiate he hath drained.

CLOTALDO. Muttering something restlessly,
  See he lies.
BASILIUS. Let's listen; he
  May some few clear words repeat.
SIGISMUND. (*Speaking in his sleep*)
  Perfect Prince is he whose heat
  Smites the tyrant where he stands,
  Yes, Clotaldo dies by my hands,
  Yes, my sire shall kiss my feet.
CLOTALDO. Death he threatens in his rage.
BASILIUS. Outrage vile he doth intend.
CLOTALDO. He my life has sworn to end.
BASILIUS. He has vowed to insult my age.
SIGISMUND. (*Still sleeping*) On the mighty world's great stage,
  'Mid the admiring nations' cheer,
  Valour mine, that has no peer,
  Enter thou : the slave so shunned
  Now shall reign Prince Sigismund,
  And his sire his wrath shall fear.   (*He awakes.*)
  But, ah me ! Where am I ? Oh—
BASILIUS. Me I must not let him see. (*To Clotaldo.*)
  Listening I close by will be,
  What you have to do you know.
SIGISMUND. Can it possibly be so?
  Is the truth not what it seemed?
  Am I chained and unredeemed?
  Art not thou my lifelong tomb,
  Dark old tower? Yes ! What a doom !
  God ! what wondrous things I've dreamed !
CLOTALDO. Now in this delusive play
  Must my special part be taken :—
  Is it not full time to waken?
SIGISMUND. Yes, to waken well it may.
CLOTALDO. Wilt thou sleep the livelong day?—
  Since we gazing from below
  Saw the eagle sailing slow,
  Soaring through the azure sphere,
  All the time thou waited here,
  Didst thou never waken?
SIGISMUND.   No,
  Nor even now am I awake,
  Since such thoughts my memory fill,
  That it seems I'm dreaming still :

Nor is this a great mistake;
Since if dreams could phantoms make
Things of actual substance seen,
I things seen may phantoms deem.
Thus a double harvest reaping,
I can see when I am sleeping,
And when waking I can dream.

CLOTALDO. What you may have dreamed of, say.

SIGISMUND. If I thought it only seemed,
I would tell not what I dreamed,
But what I beheld, I may.
I awoke, and lo! I lay
(Cruel and delusive thing!)
In a bed whose covering,
Bright with blooms from rosy bowers,
Seemed a tapestry of flowers
Woven by the hand of Spring.
Then a crowd of nobles came,
Who addressed me by the name
Of their prince, presenting me
Gems and robes, on bended knee.
Calm soon left me, and my frame
Thrilled with joy to hear thee tell
Of the fate that me befell,
For though now in this dark den,
I was Prince of Poland then.

CLOTALDO. Doubtless you repaid me well?

SIGISMUND. No, not well : for, calling thee
Traitor vile, in furious strife
Twice I strove to take thy life.

CLOTALDO. But why all this rage 'gainst me?

SIGISMUND. I was master, and would be
Well revenged on foe and friend.
Love one woman could defend. . . .
That, at least, for truth I deem,
All else ended like a dream,
That alone can never end. (*The King withdraws.*)

CLOTALDO (*aside*). From his place the King hath gone,
Touched by his pathetic words :—   (*Aloud.*)
Speaking of the king of birds
Soaring to ascend his throne,
Thou didst fancy one thine own;
But in dreams, however bright,

Thou shouldst still have kept in sight
How for years I tended thee,
For 'twere well, whoe'er we be,
Even in dreams to do what's right.   (*Exit.*)

SCENE XVIII

SIGISMUND. That is true : then let's restrain
This wild rage, this fierce condition
Of the mind, this proud ambition,
Should we ever dream again :
And we'll do so, since 'tis plain,
In this world's uncertain gleam,
That to live is but to dream :
Man dreams what he is, and wakes
Only when upon him breaks
Death's mysterious morning beam.
The king dreams he is a king,
And in this delusive way
Lives and rules with sovereign sway;
All the cheers that round him ring,
Born of air, on air take wing.
And in ashes (mournful fate !)
Death dissolves his pride and state :
Who would wish a crown to take,
Seeing that he must awake
In the dream beyond death's gate?
And the rich man dreams of gold,
Gilding cares it scarce conceals,
And the poor man dreams he feels
Want and misery and cold.
Dreams he too who rank would hold,
Dreams who bears toil's rough-ribbed hands,
Dreams who wrong for wrong demands,
And in fine, throughout the earth,
All men dream, whate'er their birth,
And yet no one understands.
'Tis a dream that I in sadness
Here am bound, the scorn of fate;
'Twas a dream that once a state
I enjoyed of light and gladness.
What is life? 'Tis but a madness.
What is life? A thing that seems,

A mirage that falsely gleams,
Phantom joy, delusive rest,
Since is life a dream at best,
And even dreams themselves are dreams.

DENIS FLORENCE MACCARTHY

BALTASAR GRACIÁN
[1601–1658]

Spain's foremost Golden Age philosopher was the Jesuit priest Baltasar Gracián. A concise and emotionless writer, a master of language and the perfect phrase, Gracián has been greatly admired by German philosophers, especially Schopenhauer and Nietzsche.

Of his works, El héroe *and* El político *deal with political philosophy.* El discreto *describes the ideal man of the world. The* Agudeza y arte de ingenio *is a book of literary criticism which defends cultism and conceptism.*

Gracián's masterpiece is the brilliant allegorical novel, El criticón. *But, outside of Spain, his best-known work is probably the* Oráculo manual, *a compilation of three hundred maxims, which has been translated into many languages and was a source for La Rochefoucauld and La Bruyère.*

THE ART OF WORLDLY WISDOM

i *Everything is at its Acme;*

especially the art of making one's way in the world. There is more required nowadays to make a single wise man than formerly to make Seven Sages, and more is needed nowadays to deal with a single person than was required with a whole people in former times.

xi *Cultivate those who can teach you.*

Let friendly intercourse be a school of knowledge, and culture be taught through conversation : thus you make your friends your teachers and mingle the pleasures of conversation with the advantages of instruction. Sensible persons thus enjoy alternating pleasures : they reap applause for what they say, and gain instruction from what they hear. We are always attracted to others by our own interest, but in this case it is of a higher kind. Wise men frequent the houses of great noblemen not because they are temples of vanity, but as theatres of good breeding. There be gentlemen who have the credit of worldly wisdom, because they are not only themselves oracles of all nobleness by their example and their behaviour, but those who surround them form a well-bred academy of worldly wisdom of the best and noblest kind.

xxviii *Common in Nothing.*

First, not in taste. O great and wise, to be ill at ease when your deeds please the mob! The excesses of popular applause never satisfy the sensible. Some there are such chameleons of popularity that they find enjoyment not in the sweet savours of Apollo but in the breath of the mob. Secondly, not in intelligence. Take no pleasure in the wonder of the mob, for ignorance never gets beyond wonder. While vulgar folly wonders wisdom watches for the trick.

xxxviii *Leave your Luck while Winning*

All the best players do it. A fine retreat is as good as a gallant attack. Bring your exploits under cover when there are enough, or even when there are many of them. Luck long lasting was ever suspicious; interrupted seems safer, and is even sweeter to the taste for a little infusion of bitter-sweet. The higher the heap of luck, the greater the risk of a slip, and down comes all. Fortune pays you sometimes for the intensity of her favours by the shortness of their duration. She soon tires of carrying any one long on her shoulders.

lviii *Adapt Yourself to your Company.*

There is no need to show your ability before everyone. Employ no more force than is necessary. Let there be no unnecessary expenditure either of knowledge or of power. The skilful falconer only flies enough birds to serve for the chase. If there is too much display today there will be nothing to show tomorrow. Always have some novelty wherewith to dazzle. To show something fresh each day keeps expectation alive and conceals the limits of capacity.

lxxvi *Do not always be Jesting.*

Wisdom is shown in serious matters, and is more appreciated than mere wit. He that is always ready for jests is never ready for serious things. They resemble liars in that men never believe either, always expecting a lie in one, a joke in the other. One never knows when you speak with judgment, which is the same as if you had none. A continual jest soon loses all zest. Many get the repute of being witty, but thereby lose the credit of being sensible. Jest has its little hour, seriousness should have all the rest.

lxxvii *Be all Things to all Men*

--a discreet Proteus, learned with the learned, saintly with the sainted. It is the great art to gain every one's suffrages; their goodwill gains general agreement. Notice men's moods and adapt yourself to each, genial or serious as the case may be. Follow their lead, glossing over the changes as cunningly as possible. This is an indispensable art for dependent persons. But this *savoir faire* calls for great cleverness. He only will find no difficulty who has a universal genius in his knowledge and universal ingenuity in his wit.

lxxxii *Drain Nothing to the Dregs, neither Good nor Ill*

A sage once reduced all virtue to the golden mean. Push right to the extreme and it becomes wrong : press all the juice from an orange and it becomes bitter. Even in enjoyment never go to extremes. Thought too subtle is dull. If you milk a cow too much you draw blood, not milk.

clii *Never have a Companion who casts you in the Shade.*

The more he does so, the less desirable a companion he is. The more he excels in quality the more in repute : he will always play first fiddle and you second. If you get any consideration, it is only his leavings. The moon shines bright alone among the stars : when the sun rises she becomes either invisible or imperceptible. Never join one that eclipses you, but rather one who sets you in a brighter light. By this means the cunning Fabula in Martial was able to appear beautiful and brilliant, owing to the ugliness and disorder of her companions. But one should as little imperil oneself by an evil companion as pay honour to another at the cost of one's own credit. When you are on the way to fortune associate with the eminent; when arrived, with the mediocre.

ccli. *Use human Means as if there were no divine ones, and divine as if there were no human ones.*

A masterly rule : it needs no comment.

JOSEPH JACOBS

EIGHTEENTH CENTURY

BENITO JERÓNIMO FEIJÓO Y MONTENEGRO
[1676–1764]

The erudite Benedictine monk, Benito Jerónimo Feijóo y Montenegro, published two voluminous collections of his essays entitled Teatro crítico universal *and* Cartas eruditas y curiosas. *While his writing is sometimes undistinguished, Feijóo, fighting against injustice, ignorance and superstition, was for Spain far in advance of his time.*

TEATRO CRÍTICO UNIVERSAL
A DEFENCE OF WOMEN

Father Malebranche argues in another manner, and denies women to be equal in understanding to men by reason of the fibres of their brain being more soft and impressible. I, for my part, know not whether there be any thing in this supposed softness or not. I have read two anatomical treatises which say not a word about it. The female brain having been supposed moister, it has been inferred to be likewise softer; yet, this is no absolute consequence. Ice is moist, and far from being soft; metal in fusion is soft, but cannot be said to be moist. Woman, as of the more soft and pliant temper, has likewise been conjectured to be more soft in the material part of her composition : for some men of superficial knowledge form their ideas, by such analogies; and afterwards, not being duly digested, such reveries spread even among persons of sense.

But be it so, what analogy is there between the softness of the brain, and the dubility of reason? Or rather, the brain being thus more impressible by the spirits, one would conceive it better adapted to mental operations, and this argument receives an additional force from our author's doctrine, for in another part, he says that the vestiges, left in the brain by the motion of the animal spirits, being the lines with which the imaginative faculty delineates in it the effigies of objects; the more strongly marked and more distinct those vestiges and impressions are, the more clearly and sensibly will the understanding perceive the very objects themselves.

Now it is clear, that the brain being softer and its fibres more flexible, the spirits will more easily impress it, and the vestiges be more strongly marked and distinct. The resistance of the substance being less and the more distinct, as the fibres in males,

being something rigid, make, by their power of elasticity, some
effort to recover their former position; and thus, in some measure,
efface the path made by the motion of the spirits, whereas the fibres
of female brains, being more flexible, will form those images larger
and distinct, and women of course, will have better perceptions of
the objects.

Let it not be thought, that on this account, I am for giving
more understanding to women than to men. I only take the liberty
of animadverting on Father Malebranche and indicating that
such an advantage may be inferred from his doctrine, contrary to
what he himself asserts in another part of his work; but what I
affirm is, that by these philosophical ratiocinations, any thing may
be proved, and nothing is really proved. Every one philosophises
according to his fancy; and did I write from adulation, humour,
or to display my wit, I could easily, by deducting a chain of
consequences from received principles, shew that man's understanding, weighed in the balance with female capacity, would be
found so light as to kick the beam. But I am far from any such
thoughts, all I intend, is to declare my mind, and I therefore aver,
that neither Father Malebranche, nor any other writer hitherto,
knew the precise mode or specific mechanism, by which the organs
of the head assist the faculties of the soul. We know not yet, how
fire burns, or water freezes though objects of sense and within
the verge of the sight and touch; yet would Father Malebranche,
with the other Carthesians persuade us, that they have clearly
seen into all that passes in the most secret recesses of the rational
soul. . . .

But this greater softness of the brain, in reality, neither implys
the one nor the other, neither a superiority nor an inferiority in the
female intellects, as the impressions of the spirits, cannot from it
be inferred to be larger; and from this largeness, it is that both
the contrarieties are deduced. The reason is, the movement or
impulse of the spirits may be proportioned to the impressibility
of the substance, and thus make no greater impression than that
of more rapid spirits on a brain of a stronger texture, as by
moderating the action of the hand as superficial a line may be
traced on wax, as those which a greater force of the hand would
make in lead. After all, what I think of this whole system of female
brains is that bodily motions may be less vigorous and forcible
in them than men, as the nerves which have their origin in the
fibres of the brain, and the spinal marrow must of course be less
strong or moved by fainter impulses; but not that the mental
operations of women are more or less perfect. . . .

I shall conclude this discourse with an exception, which may be raised against the whole tenor of it; which is, to promote a persuasion, that both sexes are equal in intellectual qualities, is so far from being of any public advantage, that it may rather occasion many mischiefs, as fomenting the pride and presumption of women.

This difficulty may be removed only by saying, that in every thing, which comes under the cognizance of reason, it is of use to display truth, and explode error. A true knowledge of things is valuable in itself, without regard to any other end. Truth has an intrinsical worth, and of such coin the whole treasure of understanding consists. Some pieces indeed are more valuable than others, but not one is useless. Neither can the truth which we have proved, of itself elevate women to vanity and presumption. If they be really our equals in mental faculties and in virtue, there is not the least harm in their knowing it and thinking so. St. Thomas, speaking of vain glory says: *Quod autem aliquis bonum suum cognoscat, et approbet, non est peccatum*, 'that for any one to know and feel a complacency in any good or perfection of which he is possessed, is no sin'. And in another part, speaking of presumption, he says, that this fault always arises from some error in the understanding; therefore, as women's knowing what they are does not lead them to entertain any overweaning conceits of their accomplishments, it cannot puff them up with vain glory or presumption; or rather, the rectitude of mind, which it is the scope of this discourse to establish by removing a vulgar error, adds no presumption to women, and abates it in men.

But I claim a still greater merit; the maxim which we have corroborated, so far from tending to any moral evil, may bring about much good. Let it be considered how many men this imaginary superiority of talents has prompted to undertake criminal conquests on the other sex. In all disputes, a confidence or diffidence in one's own strength, greatly contributes to the gain or loss of the battle. Man relying on his superiority in reasoning, speaks boldly; and woman, thinking herself inferior in argument, hears with deference and timidity. Who can deny but that here is a great presage that he will compass his ends, and she fall the victim?

Let women therefore be intimately convinced, cherish a strong persuasion that they are not inferior in sagacity to men, then will they confidently encounter their sophisms, and confound their seducers, however artful in disguising their injurious fallacies with the pigments of argumentation. If woman be brought to a persuasion that man, in respect to her, is an oracle, she will listen to the basest proposal, and acquiesce in the most notorious falsity, as a truth which she is not to question. It is well known to what shocking infamies those heretics called Molinists have inveigled many women, who, before, were not only irreproachable in their lives, but of shining characters; and whence arose this sad seduction, but from entertaining strange notions of man's superior intellects, and an extreme mistrust of their own understanding, when those poisonous doctrines were urged to them?

Another very interesting consideration is, that any woman yields the more easily to the man whom she fancies to be greatly her superior. A man finds little reluctancy to serve another of higher birth, but where that circumstance is equal, servitude goes sorely against the grain. It is the very same in our case. If a woman is so far mistaken as to think man of a much more noble sex, and that as for herself, she is but an imperfect animal, a kind of inferior being, she will think it no shame to submit to him, and the flattery of compliments and promise of obsequiousness working on her own debasing notion, she may be led to account that honour which is the very worst of infamies. Therefore, according to the energetic St. Leo, *Woman, entertain a due sense of thy dignity. Know that our sex is not in any respect preferable to thine; and therefore to allow man the dominion over thy body, except when authorised by the sacredness of marriage, is servile, infamous and sinful.*

I have not yet displayed all the moral benefit, which would accrue from men and women being cured of their mistake, with regard to the disparity of the sexes. It is my real belief, that this mistake is of infinite prejudice to the marriage bed. Here some may imagine, I am running into a strange paradox, yet, it is an evident truth, as a little attention will shew.

When some months are elapsed after two hearts were united in the bands of marriage, the woman loses that high value, which was before placed on her as a new piece of furniture. The husband passes from fondness to coldness, and coldness often degenerates into a settled and declared contempt. The husband once come to this culpable extremity, begins to play the master, and insult his spouse, building on the imagined superiority of his sex. Having imbibed those common sayings; *that the most knowing woman, knows as much as a raw school boy; that their scull is as empty as a bladder full of soap suds,* and the like elegant apothegms, every thing his poor wife says or does, he sneers at. If she argues, she raves, every word is an absurdity, and every action a blunder. The allurement of beauty, if she has any beauty, is now overlooked.

Fruition has thrown a shade over its brilliancy, and being at the husband's command, it is undervalued. All the husband thinks on, now is, that woman is a defectuous creature; and, when out of humour, the best word he can afford his wife, though ever so neat and cleanly, is, *that she is a foul vessel.*

Whilst the unhappy wife labours under this tyranny, a gallant begins to ogle her; a smiling countenance must naturally please one wearied out of her life with frowns, contemptuous looks, and imperious gestures. This suffices to bring about a conversation, in which, to be sure, every thing is calculated to please her. Before, it was nothing but taunts, threats, and insults; whereas, every word of the gallant is fraught with complaisance, praise, and adoration. Before, she was not treated even like a woman; now, she sees herself exalted to a deity; before, she was bluntly told that she was a fool; now, she hears herself extolled for incomparable wit and sense; to the husband, she was an object of vain ridicule and disgust; the gallant approaches her with the awe of a submissive slave. And though the enamorato, if a husband, may act the same part as the other within his own walls, the wretched wife, unacquainted with this dissimulation, thinks there is as much difference between them, as between an angel and a brute. In the husband, she sees a heart bristled with thorns, and in the gallant, a heart crowned with flowers. On one side, she sees a chain of iron, on the other, a bracelet of gold; here slavery, there despotism; with one a dungeon, the other a throne.

In such a situation, how shall the most discrete, the most resolute woman act? How resist two impulses, directed to one and the same end, one impelling her, the other gently drawing her? Without the powerful support of heaven, fall she must; and if she falls, who can deny, but that it was by the hand of her own husband. Had he not treated her with contempt, all the blandishments of the gallant, would not have prevailed against her. The rigour of the one, enforced the complaisance of the other. Such are the evils which frequently spring from that mean opinion of the other sex, which married men so often harbour and delight in exemplifying. Would these but throw aside such false maxims, their wives would spurn at every temptation to infidelity. God has enjoined affection to them, and that contempt and affection towards the same object can ever dwell in one heart, is utterly irreconcilable, a contradiction; and thus to treat a wife with contempt, is a breach of the divine command, than which, words cannot express any thing more horrible.

ANONYMOUS

JOSÉ FRANCISCO DE ISLA
[1703–1781]

El Padre Isla, a member of the Jesuit order, wrote the best Spanish novel of the eighteenth century, Historia del famoso predicador Fray Gerundio de Campazas. *It is a satire ridiculing the pompous, affected preachers of the time. Isla also made an excellent translation of Le Sage's* Gil Blas de Santillana, *with the assertion that he was restoring this picaresque novel to its original tongue.*

FRAY GERUNDIO DE CAMPAZAS

A POMPOUS PREACHER

He was in the full perfection of his strength, just about thirty-and-three years old; tall, robust, and stout; his limbs well set and well proportioned; manly in gait, inclining to corpulence, with an erect carriage of his head, and the circle of hair round his tonsure studiously and exactly combed and shaven. His clerical dress was always neat, and fell round his person in ample and regular folds. His shoes fitted him with the greatest nicety, and, above all, his silken cap was adorned with much curious embroidery and a fanciful tassel,—the work of certain female devotees who were dying with admiration of their favourite preacher. In short, he had a very youthful, gallant look; and, adding to this a clear, rich voice, a slight fashionable lisp, a peculiar grace in telling a story, a talent at mimicry, an easy action, a taking manner, a high-sounding style, and not a little effrontery, —never forgetting to sprinkle jests, proverbs, and homely phrases along his discourses with a most agreeable aptness,—he won golden opinions in his public discourses, and carried every thing before him in the drawing-rooms he frequented. . . .

It was well known, that he always began his sermons with some proverb, some jest, some pot-house witticism, or some strange fragment, which, taken from its proper connections and relations, would seem, at first blush, to be an inconsequence, a blasphemy, or an impiety; until, at last, having kept his audience waiting a moment in wonder, he finished the clause, or came out with an explanation which reduced the whole to a sort of miserable trifling. Thus, preaching one day on the mystery of the Trinity, he began his sermon by saying, 'I deny that God exists a Unity in essence and a Trinity in person', and then stopped short for an instant. The hearers, of course, looked round on one another, scandalized, or, at least, wondering what would be the end of this heretical blasphemy. At length, when the preacher thought he had fairly caught them, he went on,—'Thus says the Ebionite, the Marcionite, the Arian, the Manichean, the Socinian; but I prove it against them all from the Scriptures, the Councils, and the Fathers.'

In another sermon, which was on the Incarnation, he began by crying out, 'Your health, cavaliers!' and, as the audience burst into a broad laugh at the free manner in which he had said it, he went on :—'This is no joking matter, however; for it was for your health and for mine, and for that of all men, that Christ descended from heaven and became incarnate in the Virgin Mary. It is an article of faith, and I prove it thus : *"Propter nos homines, et propter nostram salutem descendit de cœlis et incarnatus est."* ' —whereat they all remained in delighted astonishment, and such a murmur of applause ran round the church, that it wanted little of breaking out into open acclamation.

GEORGE TICKNOR

JOSÉ CADALSO
[1741–1782]

José Cadalso, a colonel in the Spanish Army, died at forty-one fighting the British in the siege of Gibraltar. He had already achieved fame as a writer and as a literary mentor who exercised great formative influence particularly upon the poet Juan Meléndez Valdés.

His prose works include Noches lúgubres, *an elegy in imitation of Edward Young's* Night Thoughts; Los eruditos a la violeta, *a literary satire on pseudo-knowledge; and* Cartas marruecas. *The latter, inspired by Montesquieu's* Lettres Persanes, *is a criticism of Spanish society, as seen—supposedly—in the letters of two Moors, one of whom is travelling through the country. Cadalso also published a volume of verse called* Ocios de mi juventud.

MOROCCAN LETTERS

LETTER 26—DIVERSITY OF THE PROVINCES OF SPAIN

By your last letter, I see how strange has seemed to you the dissimilarity of the provinces which compose this monarchy. After having visited them, I consider the information which Nuño had given me, regarding this diversity, to be very accurate.

In point of fact, the Cantabrians, understanding by this name all those who speak the Biscayan language, are a simple people, famed for their truthfulness. They were the first mariners of Europe, and they have always maintained their reputation as excellent seamen. Their land, although extremely rugged, has a most numerous population, which does not seem to diminish even with the colonies which it continually sends to America. Even when a Biscayan is away from his fatherland he always feels at home as soon as he meets a fellow-countryman. They have such unity among themselves that the highest qualification which one can have for another is the very fact of being a Biscayan; with no greater difference among several of them, when they seek to attain the favour of a potentate, than the greater or lesser proximity of their respective villages. The seigniory of Biscay, Guipuzcoa, Alava, and the kingdom of Navarre enjoy such solidarity that some call these territories the *United Provinces* of Spain.

The people of Asturias and Montaña place high esteem on their lineage, and on the memory of it having been their country which engendered the Reconquest of Spain with the expulsion of our forefathers. Their population, too great for the poverty and physical limitations of the land, causes a considerable number of them to employ themselves continually in Madrid in liveried positions, which is the inferior class of servants; so that, if I were a native of this territory and were to find myself in the Court, I should examine with much prudence the papers of my coachmen and lackeys, so as not to experience one day the mortification of seeing a cousin of mine throwing barley to my mules, or one of my uncles cleaning my shoes. Regardless of all this, various respectable families of this province maintain themselves with rightful splendour, are meritorious of the highest regard, and continually produce officers of the greatest merit in the army and navy.

The Galicians, notwithstanding the poverty of their land, are vigorous. They scatter themselves throughout all of Spain to undertake the hardest physical occupations, in order to bring a bit of money into their homes at the cost of such laborious industry. Their soldiers, although they lack that outward glitter of other nations, are excellent for the infantry because of their subordination, firmness of body, and their ability to suffer discomforts of hunger, thirst, and fatigue.

The Castilians are, of all the peoples of the world, those who merit first place in the ranks of loyalty. When the army of the first Spanish king from the royal house of France was destroyed in the battle of Zaragoza, the province of Soria alone gave to its sovereign a new and large army with which to take the field, and it was that army which won the victories that resulted in the destruction of the Austrian army and faction. An illustrious historian who relates the revolutions of the beginning of this century—with all the precision and truth which History demands in order to distinguish itself from fiction—extols the faithfulness of these peoples so greatly, that he says it will live eternal in the memory of kings. This province still preserves a certain pride born of its ancient glory, lost today but for the ruins of its cities and the integrity of its inhabitants.

Extremadura produced the conquerors of the New World, and it has continued to be the mother of outstanding warriors. Its people are little inclined to learning, but those among them who have cultivated letters have achieved no less success than their compatriots in the military.

The Andalusians, born and reared in an abundant, delightful, and passionate land, possess the reputation of being somewhat arrogant. But if this defect is real, it should be attributed to their climate, since the influence of the physical over the moral is so well-known. The good things with which nature endowed those provinces make them regard with scorn the poverty of Galicia, the ruggedness of Biscay, and the austerity of Castile. But, be this as it may, among them there have been outstanding men who have bestowed much honour on all Spain, and, in ancient times, the Trajans, Senecas, and others like them, who may well fill with pride the country in which they were born. The gaiety, cunning, and charm of the Andalusian women makes them incomparable : I assure you that just one of them would be enough to throw the Moroccan empire into a tumult, so that we should all kill one another over her.

The Murcians share the character of the Andalusians and Valencians. The latter are considered to be men of excessive slightness, this defect being attributed to the climate and soil : some claiming that even in their very foods there is lacking that pith which is found in those of other countries. My impartiality does not permit me to acquiesce to this prejudice, universal though it may be; rather I should observe that the Valencians of this century are the Spaniards who make the greatest advances in the natural sciences and in the dead languages.

The Catalonians are the most industrious people of Spain; manufacturing, fishing, navigation, commerce, contracts, are matters scarcely known in the other provinces of the Peninsula in comparison with the Catalonians. Not only are they useful in peacetime,

but also they are of the greatest service in war : the casting of
cannon, manufacture of arms, equipment for armies, conveyance
of artillery, munitions, provisions, the formation of light troops of
excellent quality, all this comes from Catalonia. The fields are
cultivated, the population grows, wealth increases, and in sum, that
nation seems to be a thousand leagues away from the Galician,
Andalusian, and Castilian. But they are by temperament rather
unsociable, and are dedicated solely to their own profit and interest,
and therefore some call them the Hollanders of Spain. My friend
Nuño tells me that this province will flourish so long as there are
not introduced into it personal luxury and the mania of
ennobling artisans : two vices which until now are opposed to the
talent which enriched the country.

The Aragonese are men of valour and spirit, honourable, tena-
cious in judgment, lovers of their province and notably prejudiced
in favour of their fellow-countrymen. In other days they cultivated
the sciences with success, and they bore arms with much glory
against the French in Naples and against our forefathers in Spain.
Their land, as all the rest of the Peninsula, was thickly populated
in ancient times, and so much so that there is a familiar tradition
among them that for the wedding of one of their kings there
entered into Zaragoza ten thousand noblemen, each one with a
servant, and the twenty thousand mounted on an equal number
of native horses.

Because of the many centuries that these peoples were divided,
warred with each other, spoke different languages, governed themselves under different laws, wore different costumes, and in sum,
were separate nations, there was nourished among them a certain
hatred, which without doubt has lessened and even come to disappear. But there still continues a certain coolness among those of
distant provinces. And if this can do harm in time of peace, because
it is a considerable obstacle to perfect union, it can be most advantageous in time of war, through mutual rivalry : a regiment made
up entirely of Aragonese will not view with dispassion the glory
acquired by an all-Castilian troop; and a ship manned by Biscayans
will not surrender to the enemy so long as another, manned by
Catalonians, resists.

JEANNE PASMANTIER

SATIRICAL LETRILLA

That much a widowed wife will moan,
When her old husband's dead and gone,
    I may conceive it :
But that she won't be brisk and gay,
If another offer the next day,
    I won't believe it.

That Chloris will repeat to me,
'Of all men, I adore but thee,'
    I may conceive it :
But that she has not often sent
To fifty more the compliment,
    I won't believe it.

That Celia will accept the choice
Elected by her parents' voice,
    I may conceive it :
But that, as soon as all is over,
She won't elect a younger lover,
    I won't believe it.

That, when she sees her marriage gown,
Inez will modestly look down,
    I may conceive it :
But that she does not, from that hour,
Resolve to amplify her power,
    I won't believe it.

That a kind husband to his wife,
Permits each pleasure of this life,
    I may conceive it :
But that the man so blind should be
As not to see what all else see,
    I won't believe it.

That in a mirror young coquettes
Should study all their traps and nets,
    I may conceive it :
But that the mirror, above all,
Should be the object principal,
    I won't believe it.

ANONYMOUS

JOSÉ IGLESIAS
[1748–1791]

José Iglesias de la Casa, a Salamanca-born cleric, wrote some charming lyric and bucolic poetry. But he is best known for the scintillating wit of his satirical letrillas *and epigrammatic verse.*

ALEXIS CALLS ME CRUEL

Alexis calls me cruel;
   The rifted crags that hold
The gathered ice of winter,
   He says are not more cold.

Where even the very blossoms
   Around the fountain's brim,
And forest-walks can witness
   The love I bear to him.

I would that I could utter
   My feelings without shame,
And tell him how I love him
   Nor wrong my virgin fame.

Alas! to seize the moment
   When heart inclines to heart,
And press a suit with passion,
   Is not a woman's part.

If man come not to gather
   The roses where they stand,
They fade among their foliage;
   They cannot seek his hand.

WILLIAM CULLEN BRYANT

TOMÁS DE IRIARTE
[1750–1791]

For all the dedicated scholarship of this Canary Island-born author, Iriarte's dramatic works and serious poetry are now forgotten. His fame rests on the seventy-six Fábulas literarias, in which he ridicules, among other things, the literary vices of his contemporaries. Iriarte skilfully employs a great variety of metrical forms in these fables, many of which have become extremely popular.

THE BEAR, THE MONKEY AND THE HOG

A Bear, with whom a Piedmontese
    A wandering living made,
A dance he had not learn'd with ease,
    On his two feet essay'd :

And, as he highly of it thought,
    He to the Monkey cried,
'How's that?' who, being better taught,
    ' 'Tis very bad,' replied.

'I do believe,' rejoin'd the Bear,
    'You little favour show :
For have I not a graceful air,
    And step with ease to go?'

A Hog, that was beside them set,
    Cried, 'Bravo! good!' said he;
'A better dancer never yet
    I saw, and ne'er shall see.'

On this the Bear, as if he turn'd
    His thoughts within his mind,
With modest gesture seeming learn'd
    A lesson thence to find.

'When blamed the Monkey, it was cause
    Enough for doubting sad;
But when I have the hog's applause,
    It must be very bad!'

As treasured gift, let authors raise
    This moral from my verse :
'Tis bad, when wise ones do not praise;
    But when fools do, 'tis worse.

JAMES KENNEDY

THE ASS AND THE FLUTE

This little fable heard,
   It good or ill may be;
But it has just occurr'd
   Thus accidentally.

Passing my abode,
   Some fields adjoining me
A big ass on his road
   Came accidentally.

And laid upon the spot,
   A Flute he chanced to see,
Some shepherd had forgot
   There accidentally.

The animal in front
   To scan it nigh came he,
And snuffing loud as wont,
   Blew accidentally.

The air it chanced around
   The pipe went passing free
And thus the Flute a sound
   Gave accidentally.

'O then,' exclaimed the Ass,
   'I know to play it fine;
And who for bad shall class
   This music asinine?'

Without the rules of art,
   Even asses, we agree,
May once succeed in part,
   Thus accidentally.

JAMES KENNEDY

THE SWORD AND THE SKEWER

(Against two kinds of poor translators)

On many a gallant battle-field
A sword had served, its fine, well steeled,
Sharp and pridefully polished blade
The best a Toledan smith had made.
Many a day it had saved with grace
Till passing through hands, from place to place
It went by untold circumstance
To more than one auction and by chance
Reached at length (ah, sad to say)
A roadside inn and there it lay,
Unknown, unused, a thickening crust
Obscuring it with shameful rust.

The innkeeper ordered his kitchen maid
(Though he was crack-brained, she obeyed)
To take the sword to the hostel kitchen
And use its blade to cut up a chicken.
The sword once held in honour secure
Became, alas, a common skewer.

While this was taking place, toward
The court there came, to buy a sword,
A late arrived and foreign knight,
Transformed from bumpkin overnight.
The bladesmith, seeing this new lord
For an ornament only wished a sword
And that a fine blade would not count,
The style of the hilt being paramount,
Told the knight to return; he'd fix
A worthy sword; he was up to tricks.
He took a skewer, filed and burnished it,
Then as Tomás de Ayala's furnished it
To the poor and gullible foreign lord.
This bladesmith with his tricked-out sword
Was a knavish villain, a rogue as great
As the innkeeper was a silly pate.

But is it not true we are no better off
And, as a nation, that we cannot scoff?
Are we not afflicted with two evil phases
Of translating gentry with ill-spoken phrases?
Some take our classics and turn them quite badly
From swords into skewers, and others as sadly
Take our worst works and their finished translations
From skewers to swords have wrought transformations.

ALICE JANE M^CVAN

FÉLIX MARÍA DE SAMANIEGO
[1745–1801]

Iriarte's rival as Spain's leading fabulist is Félix María de Samaniego,
author of Fábulas morales. *While he is less original than Iriarte—*
Samaniego often imitated La Fontaine and Phèdre—he is considered by
many critics the better poet of the two.

THE WOLF AND THE DOG

A prowling wolf, whose shaggy skin
(So strict the watch of dogs had been)
Hid little but his bones,
Once met a mastiff dog astray;
A prouder, fatter, sleeker Tray
No human mortal owns.
Sir Wolf in famished plight,
Would fain have made a ration
Upon his fat relation;
But then he first must fight;
And well the dog seemed able
To save from wolfish table
His carcass snug and tight.
So, then in civil conversation,
The wolf expressed his admiration
Of Tray's fine case. Said Tray, politely,
'Yourself, good Sir, may be as sightly:
Quit but the woods, advised by me;
For all your fellows here, I see,

Are shabby wretches, lean, and gaunt,
Belike to die of haggard want;
With such a pack, of course, it follows
One fights for every bit he swallows.
Come, then, with me, and share
On equal terms our princely fare.'
'But what, with you,
Has one to do?'
Inquires the wolf. 'Light work indeed,'
Replies the dog; 'you only need
To bark a little, now and then,
To chase off duns and beggar-men,—
To fawn on friends that come or go forth,
Your master please, and so forth;
For which you have to eat
All sorts of well cooked meat,—
Cold pullets, pigeons, savoury messes,—
Besides unnumbered fond caresses.'—
The Wolf, by force of appetite,
Accepts the terms outright,
Tears glistening in his eyes.
But, faring on, he spies
A galled spot on the mastiff's neck.
'What's that?' he cries. 'O, nothing but a speck.'
'A speck?' 'Ay, ay, 'tis not enough to pain me;
Perhaps the collar's mark by which they chain me.'
'Chain,—chain you? What, run you not, then,
Just where you please, and when?'
'Not always, Sir; but what of that?'
'Enough for me, to spoil your fat!
It ought to be a precious price
Which could to servile chains entice;
For me, I'll shun them, while I've wit.'
So ran Sir Wolf, and runneth yet.

ANONYMOUS

THE YOUNG PHILOSOPHER AND HIS FRIENDS

A gentleman young and carefully reared
By a venerable scholar of learning,
Abandoned the books which he long revered—
For the taste of the world he was yearning.

He found himself soon with light company
In whose manner and charm he delighted.
He joined in their quests for gay revelry
And to dine with them soon was invited.

But when he arrived with his comraderie
To sup at the table's sweet savours,
—Unspeakable horrors ! Brute savagery !—
The table was full of cadavers !

'You eat unashamed these spoils of death ?'
Declaimed the young man with a sigh.
The guests, looking up without catching breath,
Whilst devouring a bird, did reply :

'If you want to live with us happily,
Our manners and customs you'll follow.'
So saying, they passed to him graciously
A bird they implored him to swallow.

'That may be so, what you have just said;
Remorse your reflections instill.
But after all, it's already dead,
And if you don't eat it, we will.'

Looking on those who partook with delight
Of the food in this sumptuous feast,
And breathing the scent of the bird did excite
In the young man a lust for the beast.

'Who could have said that me too they would find
Eating an innocent creature !'
But still he ate on, not seeming to mind
His own philosophic forfeiture.

Once having fallen, he fell once again;
From his early maxims he did stray.
From quail to woodcock he went without strain,
Like a wild beast devouring his prey.

In this way we may see how bad habits creep in,
And our hearts from good ways they sever.
Enslaved we become and continue to sin,
Their whims we must follow forever.

So rash never be in deed or in word—
Take heed and beware : resist the first bird !

LILLIAN RESNICK

JUAN MELÉNDEZ VALDÉS
[1754–1817]

*Juan Meléndez Valdés was the outstanding lyric poet of the eighteenth
century. A teacher, magistrate and high government official under Joseph
Bonaparte, Meléndez Valdés died in exile after the defeat of the French
invaders.*

*The early compositions of this elegant and graceful poet include traditional
eclogues, odes, love poetry and ballads, all distinguished for their technical
perfection. He later cultivated the neo-classic school of poetry, and his works
of this second period bear a strong philosophic tendency.*

SACRED ODE

Lord! in whose sight a thousand years but seem
A fleeting moment,—O Eternal Being!
   Turn towards me thy clemency,
Lest like a shadow vain my brief existence flee!

Thou who dost swell with thine ineffable
Spirit the world,—O Being Infinite!
   Regard me graciously,
Since than an atom more invisible am I !

Thou in whose mighty, all-protecting hand
The firmament of heavens abides,—O Power!
    Since of my soul thou know'st
The fallen and abject state, unveil the virtuous boast!

Thou who dost feed the world's immensity,
O Fount of Life, still inexhaustible!
    Hear my despised breath,
Since before thee my life will seem but wretched death!

Thou who dost see within thy boundless mind
Whatever was or will be!—knowledge vast!—
    Thy light I now implore,
That I in error's shades may wander lost no more!

Thou, who upon the sacred throne of heaven
In glorious light dost sit, Immutable!
    For thine eternal rest,
Exchange, my Lord, the thoughts of this unstable breast!

Thou, whose right hand, if from the abyss withdrawn,
Doth cause the stars to fall,—Omnipotent!
    Since I am nothing, take
Sweet mercy upon me, for thy dear Jesus' sake!

Thou, by whose hand the sparrow is sustained,
Father of all, God of the universe!
    Thy gifts with gracious speed
Scatter upon my head, since I am poor indeed!

Being Eternal, Infinite! Soul! Life!
Father all-knowing! wise, omniscient Power!
    From thine exalted throne,
Since I thy creature am, look down upon thine own!

ANONYMOUS

JUVENILITIES

When I was yet a child,
    A child Dorila too,
To gather there the flowerets wild,
    We roved the forest through.

And gaily garlands then,
    With passing skill display'd
To crown us both, in childish vein,
    Her little fingers made.

And thus our joys to share,
    In such our thoughts and play,
We pass'd along, a happy pair,
    The hours and days away.

But ev'n in sports like these,
    Soon age came hurrying by!
And of our innocence the ease
    Malicious seem'd to fly.

I knew not how it was,
    To see me she would smile;
And but to speak to her would cause
    Me pleasure strange the while.

Then beat my heart the more,
    When flowers to her I brought;
And she, to wreathe them as before,
    Seem'd silent, lost in thought.

One evening after this
    We saw two turtle-doves,
With trembling throat, who, wrapt in bliss,
    Were wooing in their loves.

In manifest delight,
    With wings and feathers bow'd,
Their eyes fix'd on each other bright,
    They languish'd, moaning loud.

The example made us bold,
    And with a pure caress,
The troubles we had felt we told,
    Our pains and happiness.

And at once from our view
    Then, like a shadow, fled
Our childhood and its joys, but new,
    Love gave us his instead.

JAMES KENNEDY

NISÉ

When first a gentle kiss
Upon Nisé I pressed,
Paradise-grain and cassia
Her lovely breath confessed.
And on her smiling lips
Such luscious sweets I found
As never knew the hills
Or bees of Hybla's ground.
To purify its balm
With love's essential dews,
A thousand and a thousand times
Each day her lips I choose;
Until the sum and total
Of all our score amount
To kisses more than Venus
Did from Adonis count.

THOMAS WALSH

RAMÓN DE LA CRUZ
[1731–1794]

The first dramatic efforts of Ramón de la Cruz were translations and adaptations of French, Italian and Spanish classics. But on the basis of his own numerous sainetes—comic one-act plays developed as a genre from the pasos of Lope de Rueda and the Golden Age entremeses—he became the most popular playwright of the eighteenth century.

The sainetes, all in verse, paint in their totality a realistic and historically priceless picture of life in Madrid, with subjects ranging from fiestas and fairs to dandies and dancers. De la Cruz often ridicules a human or social foible, but always with the good humour of a detached, tolerant observer. One of the best sainetes, La presumida burlada, is given here in a slightly abridged version.

PRIDE'S FALL

Characters

Don Carlos
Don Gil Pascual
María Martín, his wife
Old María, her mother
Tonilla, her sister
Colas Morado, a peasant
Perico, Pascual's valet
Lady and Gentlemen visitors

SCENE I

A street in Madrid
From one side Gil enters, from the other, his friend Carlos, military costume.

CARLOS. I saw you the minute I turned on to this street. Did you see how I most ran my head off to say hello to you? How's good old Gil? But what does this mean? Why aren't you still in mourning? Here, I've been away from Madrid barely a month and I come back to find you dressed in your gayest clothes, you who are supposed to be still in mourning for your wife!
GIL. Well, I may not look so, but I'm more in mourning than ever.
CARLOS. I'd never think it to look at you.
GIL. The veil of my fine clothes is hiding the mourning of my heart.
CARLOS. What do you have to mourn for now?

GIL. Because I'm married again. I had to pretend tears when my wife died, but they're real tears now.

CARLOS. What's so sad now?

GIL. Alas, that's a long story, Carlos.

CARLOS. Oh, well, if you won't tell your troubles to an old friend like me, I won't insist. But at least tell me whom you married.

GIL. The devil.

CARLOS. I take it she's not much to look at, so no doubt, you fell in love with her cleverness, since that's where the devil is subtle.

GIL. If she were as discreet as she is good-looking, that would be another story.

CARLOS. But who is she? Do I know her?

GIL. As well as you do me or my first wife, may she rest in peace!

CARLOS. Then tell me who she is.

GIL. Do you remember that servant girl from Cuacos that we hired five or six years ago?

CARLOS. Do you mean the girl called María the Drudge?

GIL. She's the girl, but go easy. Fortune has made her my wife and I insist that she be treated with respect.

CARLOS. I mean no disrespect. That's the only name I knew.

GIL. Well, that's the girl I lost my head over, and thanks to her I've got the brain of a donkey now.

CARLOS. What did she do to you?

GIL. People talk about the fatal hour. She gave me my fatal quarter of an hour. She was such a good servant and knew where everything belonged around the house, so she won the esteem of her mistress and also of her master. A man is so crazy about marrying, you know. Well, after I became a widower, one day while I was walking in the Prado, I had an unfortunate idea, and I returned home thinking it was better to marry and settle down rather than gad about all the time. Just as I was threshing over the problem the girl came into my room to set the table. I don't remember what we talked about at first but I know we got into an argument. Somehow or other I found I'd got engaged to her and a couple of days later we were secretly married.

CARLOS. But everybody knows about it, don't they?

GIL. Of course they do! No sooner had she married me than she put on more airs than a peacock and began to boss not only the servants, but me as well. And the way she treats me! Thinking about it is enough to make me stand on my head, and I swear to you on the word of an honourable man, that I spend more money on her than if I had married the daughter of a marquis.

CARLOS. She makes you hustle, then?

GIL. And you should see her vanity.

CARLOS. Lowborn people are always that way when they get the opportunity.

GIL. It isn't because she's low born, for she tells me that her father came from one of the noblest families in that part of Spain, though he became poor and had to work, afterward; and in Madrid she says she has a lot of relatives in high society.

CARLOS. That's what she says; but I suppose you haven't tried to verify it and don't know them.

GIL. It's too late for that. I believe her and keep quiet; besides, she's proving it by the ambitions she has. As soon as we were married, she made me go and hire the best teachers of music and dancing. And the way she sits at ease in the drawing room and makes people wait on her! She's got a bad disposition, but I must confess, she is a surprising woman.

SCENE II

An elaborate room in the house of Don Gil Pascual
(*Enter* don Carlos.)

CARLOS. Your husband, my best friend, just told me about his marriage. I'm sorry I was so slow in coming with my congratulations.

SEÑORA. Don Carlos, you are very welcome; but tell me, where did you leave my husband?

CARLOS. With some relatives who have just come from the country and will soon be here.

SEÑORA. Coming to my house? That's a pretty note! I'm not fond of guests, and if that man doesn't listen to reason, they'll all be kicked out of the house, he and his relatives both.

FIRST MAN. There's nothing like everybody staying in his own house. You are absolutely right, señora.

SECOND MAN. And especially relatives.

CARLOS (*aside*). How you'll be fooled!

SEÑORA. I've refused even to write to any of mine about my marriage so as to save the expense of sending the letter, and my relatives are a very different sort of people. Why, my mother owns a palace, and after a while she'll be heir to an estate as big as Madrid; and I have an uncle, a curate, with six or seven houses even larger.

CARLOS. Must be a regular kingdom!

SEÑORA. You'd better believe it! Why, my least important relative is a grandee, and the poorest of them has two hundred lackeys.

VALET. The other day I saw a thief with as many as that. (*Exit the valet.*)

CARLOS. I suppose that your esteemed mother is a widow.

SENORA. Yes, I'm sorry to say. Not because she doesn't have an income of twenty thousand ducats, but if I'd had a father, I wouldn't have married anyone under a Count. But now, it can't be helped. The mistake is made, and one just has to put up with it.

FIRST LADY (*aside to second lady*). They tell me she comes from very lowborn people!

SECOND LADY. There's always someone to say bad and good about everyone.

(*Enter the valet.*)

VALET. Señora, there's a woman outside who'd have walked right in and made herself at home if I hadn't stopped her.

SENORA. Who is she?

VALET. She says her name is María Martín.

SENORA (*aside*). Merciful Heavens, my mother! (*To valet.*) Tell her to come back tomorrow when the master isn't here.

VALET (*aside*). What'll you bet she isn't the barber's wife trying to act as go-between in some love affair? (*He goes out.*)

SENORA. It's a poor old woman to whom I sometimes give alms.

(*Re-enter the valet.*)

VALET. She says there's some mistake, because she's your mother and wants to give you a hug, and with her is your sister and Colas Morado.

SENORA. How amusing! Now I know who they are. They are some poor peasants, and I called her mama because she used to look after me when I was a year old.

VALET. Well, I've looked after you, too, but you never called me 'mama'.

SENORA. Have her come back tomorrow, as I tell you; and if she gets obstinate, order her never to come back, for I don't want anything to do with people who put on airs.

(*Enter* don Gil *and the three country people.*)

GIL. Neither do I. And nothing has made me so angry with you as when you, out of vanity, refused to recognize the woman who gave you life.

TONILLA. Marica, darling, how I've wept because I couldn't see you!

COLAS (*seriously*). Well, I'd never have thought it of one who received all that your mother gave you, as I'm a Christian!

VALET. I wonder how much she has left of that twenty thousand ducats a year the mistress said she gets to feed the family and repair the palace.

MARIA. So you don't know me?

SENORA. Yes, mother, with arms and lips I beg your pardon at your feet.

MARIA. I'm not surprised that you're ashamed of us, because everybody looks upon poverty as something dishonourable.

SENORA. I'm sorry only for those who are looking at us, and on account of my husband who thought I was noble.

GIL. I'm glad to learn the truth, and provided you make amends, you'll see how you'll be forgiven.

FIRST LADY. And don't be sorry on our account, because if the relatives of all these here should suddenly appear, there'd be a lot of apologizing to do.

CARLOS. There's no shame in being born humble if one has virtue to make up for it.

GIL. Enough of this conversation; let's go on enjoying ourselves, for I want to be different from the common run of son-in-law.

MARIA. Blessings on my son-in-law. He's gay and very different.

GIL. And blessings on my mother-in-law if she helps make my marriage a success.

MARIA. Because of your kindness we three are slaves rather than relatives.

SENORA. And I'll be, too, of so kind a husband, if I have his permission to give away some of the abundance of this house.

GIL. Of course. From now on the appearance of your family and the care of your mother are in my hands.

ALL. Hurray for don Gil!

VALET. I hope we are going to see miracles in this house.

GIL. Come on, then, have a good time; and what's past is past.

SENORA. Then let's have some music, and let the dance we planned begin.

ALL. And let those who witnessed this play grant us at least your pardon, if you didn't like it well enough to applaud.

WILLIS KNAPP JONES

LEANDRO FERNÁNDEZ DE MORATÍN
[1760–1828]

Leandro Fernández de Moratín, son of the poet and dramatist Nicolás Fernández de Moratín (1737-1780), was the foremost eighteenth-century playwright of the neo-classic school. Of his five plays the best is El sí de las niñas. This skilfully executed comedy criticizes parental choice of a young girl's husband—and the type of education which taught the daughter to obey her elders' edict wordlessly, her own emotions notwithstanding.

WHEN A GIRL SAYS 'YES'

Characters

Don Diego
Don Carlos, his nephew
Doña Francisca, a young lady
Doña Irene, her mother
Rita, a servant

The scene is an inn in Alcalá de Henares.

ACT III

SCENE VIII

Don Diego, Doña Francisca

DON DIEGO. So you didn't sleep last night?
DOÑA FRANCISCA. No, sir. And you?
DON DIEGO. I didn't either.
DOÑA FRANCISCA. It has been very hot, hasn't it?
DON DIEGO. What is bothering you? (*Sits down beside her.*)
DOÑA FRANCISCA. It's nothing. Just a little . . . oh, it really is nothing at all, sir.
DON DIEGO. It must be something for you look so downcast and tearful and distressed. What is the matter, Fanny? You know I love you so much.
DOÑA FRANCISCA. Yes, sir.
DON DIEGO. Then why not have a little more confidence in me? Will you believe me when I say nothing gives me greater joy than to do something to make you happy.
DOÑA FRANCISCA. I know that is true.

DON DIEGO. Why then, knowing that you have a friend, will you not open your heart to him?

DOÑA FRANCISCA. Because that very thing compels me to keep silent.

DON DIEGO. By that you mean that I am the cause of your trouble.

DOÑA FRANCISCA. No, sir, you have in no way offended me. It is not of you that I complain.

DON DIEGO. Of whom then, my dear girl? Look here, Fanny. For once at least, let's talk without evasions or dissimulations. Tell me, isn't it true that you look upon this proposed marriage with something akin to repugnance? If you were left entirely free to choose would you marry me?

DOÑA FRANCISCA. I would marry no one else.

DON DIEGO. Isn't it barely possible that you know someone else more attractive than I, one whom you love and who reciprocates your love as you deserve?

DOÑA FRANCISCA. No, sir; there is none such.

DON DIEGO. Are you very sure of that?

DOÑA FRANCISCA. I tell you there isn't anyone else who loves me.

DON DIEGO. Then must I believe perchance that you have a longing for the convent in which you were brought up, that you prefer its pious atmosphere to a life more . . .

DOÑA FRANCISCA. Not that either, sir. I have never thought of that.

DON DIEGO. I shall not press you further. But there is a serious contradiction in what I have heard. You do not, it seems, feel inclined to the life of a nun. You assure me that you have no complaint to make of me, that you are persuaded how much I love you, have no thought of marrying anyone else, that I ought not to suspect that anyone disputes with me the possession of your hand. If all this is true, why all this weeping? What is the reason for this profound sadness which in a little while has changed your appearance so that I hardly know you? Are these to be taken as signs that you love me exclusively, that you will be glad to marry me in a few days? Is it in such ways that love and happiness announce themselves?

(The theatre becomes light gradually, as if dawning.)

DOÑA FRANCISCA. And what has given you reasons for this lack of trust?

DON DIEGO. What indeed! If I ignore these considerations, if I hasten the preparations for our wedding, if your mother continues her approval and the affair reaches a point . . .

DOÑA FRANCISCA. I will do what my mother commands me, and marry you.

DON DIEGO. And afterward, Fanny?

DONA FRANCISCA. Afterward—while my life lasts I will be a faithful wife.

DON DIEGO. I do not doubt that in the least. But if you consider me the one who must be till death your companion and friend, then tell me, do not these titles merit some confidence on your part? Can't you reveal to me the cause of your grief? I'm not asking this, Fanny, to satisfy an impertinent curiosity, but to give myself wholly to the task of consoling you, of bettering your lot in life, of making you happy—if my efforts and zeal can accomplish as much.

DONA FRANCISCA. Happiness, for me! That is all ended.

DON DIEGO. And why, may I ask?

DONA FRANCISCA. I can never tell you why.

DON DIEGO. But what an obstinate and unwise silence when you might at least have a surmise that I am not ignorant of how matters stand.

DONA FRANCISCA. If you are ignorant, Don Diego, then for God's sake don't pretend that you know. And if you really know, then don't ask any more questions.

DON DIEGO. So be it. If there is no more to be said, if this affliction and these tears signify nothing, then today we reach Madrid and within eight days you shall be my wife.

DONA FRANCISCA. And make my mother happy.

DON DIEGO. And you will be happy, don't you think so?

DONA FRANCISCA. Oh, yes, I too : yes, surely.

DON DIEGO. Here are the fruits of our system of education. This is what we call bringing up a girl right. We teach them to belie and hide their most innocent feelings with a perfidious dissimulation. They are called honourable when they are expert in the arts of silence and lying. We are determined that neither temperament nor age nor disposition shall affect their inclinations in the least; their wills must bend to the caprice of those who govern. Everything is permitted except frankness and sincerity. So long as they do not say what they feel, so long as they are willing to utter when they are commanded to do so a perjured, sacrilegious *yes;* source of so many scandals, we call them well brought up. It is an excellent education which inspires in them the fear and cunning and silence of the slave!

DONA FRANCISCA. That is true. Oh, it is all too true! That is what they demand of us, that is what they teach us in the schools. But the reason for my grief is much greater than that.

DON DIEGO. Let it be what it may, my poor child, you must cheer up. If your mother should see you in this plight what will she say? I think she is already up.

DONA FRANCISCA. Oh, my heavens! What will she say!

DON DIEGO. Yes, Fanny, you must try to control yourself. Don't give way entirely. Have faith in God. Our afflictions are never so great as the imagination paints them. You have wept so long that you tremble all over; but give me your word that you will try to brace up a bit, to face her with as much composure as possible. Can you do that, little lady?

DONA FRANCISCA. And you, sir? You know what a temper my mother has. If you don't defend me to whom shall I turn? Who will have pity on me in my unhappiness?

DON DIEGO. Your staunch friend, Fanny. I, myself. I'm not going to abandon you, depend on that. (*He takes her hands.*)

DONA FRANCISCA. Really? Can I believe that?

DON DIEGO. How little you know my heart!

DONA FRANCISCA. I know it well. (*Tries to kneel to him.*)

DON DIEGO. Girl, what are you trying to do?

DONA FRANCISCA. I hardly know. How little I deserve this kindness after being so ungrateful toward you. . . . No, not ungrateful, just unhappy. Ah, Don Diego, if you only knew how unhappy I am.

DON DIEGO. I do know that you are grateful so far as you are able, for the love I give you. The rest has been—oh, what shall I call it —a blunder on my part, yes, a stupid blunder, nothing else. But it is no fault of yours, and you shall not bear the blame.

DONA FRANCISCA. Let us go. Aren't you coming?

DON DIEGO. Not just now, Fanny. In a little while.

DONA FRANCISCA. Yes, but come soon. (*Goes toward* doña Irene's *room, turns quickly and runs to* Don Diego, *kissing his hands.*)

DON DIEGO. Yes, yes, I'll come soon.

SCENE X

Don Diego, Don Carlos

DON DIEGO. Come here, young man, come here, I say. Where have you been since we met last?

DON CARLOS. In the tavern outside the walls.

DON DIEGO. Never left it all night long, eh?

DON CARLOS. Yes, sir, I entered the city and . . .

DON DIEGO. And what . . . Sit down.

DON CARLOS. It was very necessary that I speak with someone. . . . (*Sits.*)

13—SA

DON DIEGO. Necessary?

DON CARLOS. Yes, sir. I am indebted to this person for many favours and it was not possible to return to Zaragoza without explaining . . .

DON DIEGO. I see. And with so many obligations . . . But to come to see this—this person—at three o'clock in the morning seems to me a bit—blundering, indiscreet as it were. Why didn't you write a note? A little note like this for instance. If you'd sent one like this at an opportune time, you wouldn't have needed to keep the person up all night, nor to bother anybody. (*Giving him the paper that had been thrown at the window.* Don Carlos, *as soon as he recognizes it, returns it, and rises as if to go.*)

DON CARLOS. Very well, since you know all, why did you send for me? Why didn't you let me go my way and escape a dispute which will not add to the happiness of either of us?

DON DIEGO. Your uncle wants to know what is the meaning of all this, and wants you to tell him.

DON CARLOS. Why do you want to know more?

DON DIEGO. Because I wish it, and command it. Hear me!

DON CARLOS. Very well.

DON DIEGO. Sit down here. . . . (Don Carlos *sits down.*) Where did you meet this girl? What love affair is this? Tell me the details. What understanding is there between you? When and where have you seen her?

DON CARLOS. Returning to Zaragoza last year I arrived at Guadalajara without any intention of stopping. But the governor at whose house we alighted, insisted that I stay there all day, it being the birthday of a relative of his. The next day he said he would let me proceed on my way. Among the invited guests there was a Doña Francisca, whom the lady of the house had brought that day out of the convent to amuse herself a bit, and get a little recreation. I don't know what there was in her that aroused in me a constant irresistible desire to look at her, to make myself entertaining and agreeable. The governor said among other things—joking of course —that I was very much in love, and he suggested that I call myself Don Felix of Toledo. I entered into the scheme and conceived the idea of remaining some time in that town and keeping the news from you. I observed that Doña Fanny treated me with a particular courtesy and when we separated that evening I was full of vanity and hope seeing myself the preferred one among many rivals. As a matter of fact . . . but I don't wish to offend you by talking about it.

DON DIEGO. Go on.

DON CARLOS. I found out she was the daughter of a lady in Madrid, a widow and poor, but of a very good family. It was necessary to confide in my friend the love intrigues which obliged me to remain in her company. And he, without approving or disapproving, invented the most ingenious excuses to keep me with him at his country home. As the place was near the city it was easy to go and come by night. There were two or three letters exchanged between Doña Francisca and myself, little brief notes on her part to be sure, but they sufficed to involve me in an ecstasy of passion which will make me unhappy as long as I live.

DON DIEGO. Well, well—go on with your story.

DON CARLOS. My groom, who is as you know a man with an active imagination and knows the world pretty well, contrived in a thousand ways to overcome all obstacles. There was the signal three hand claps responded to by three others from a certain little window looking out on the convent yard. Every night we talked together until a rather unseasonable hour—with a good deal of caution, you may imagine. To her I was always Don Felix of Toledo, an army officer, esteemed by my superiors and a man of honour. I never told her more; I never spoke to her of my relatives nor of my purpose in life; I never mentioned that by marrying me she might gain money and social position. I did not speak to her of you, for I did not want self interest or ambition, but only love, to influence her. Each time I saw her she seemed to me fonder, more beautiful, more worthy to be adored. For almost three months I lingered there; but at last it was necessary that we separate and one sad night I took leave of her, left her forlorn and almost fainting, while I fled whither duty called me. Her letters consoled for some time my exile. Then one day . . . a few days ago there came one which said that her mother had decided she must marry. She assured me that she would rather die than give her hand to any other but me. She reminded me of my promises and begged me to fulfil them. I mounted my horse, I rode in hot haste to Guadalajara. Not finding her there, I came here. You know the rest.

DON DIEGO. And what intention might you have in coming here at this time?

DON CARLOS. To comfort her, to swear to her anew an eternal love; to stop at Madrid to see you, tell you the whole thing and beg of you—not money, not my inheritance, not your protection and patronage—I can get along without all these—only your consent and your benediction upon a longed-for union in which she and I had founded all our hope and joy in life.

DON DIEGO. But Carlos, you surely understand that such a thing is now out of the question.

DON CARLOS. Yes, my lord.

DON DIEGO. If you love her, I love her too. Her mother and all her family approve this marriage. She—whatever may be the promises she has made to you—she herself, not half an hour ago told me she was ready to obey her mother and give me her hand.

DON CARLOS. Her hand—but not her heart! (*Gets up.*)

DON DIEGO. What are you saying?

DON CARLOS. I tell you no. To think that would be an insult to her. You may celebrate your wedding when you please. She will conduct herself always as befits her honour and her virtue. But I was the first and only object of her affection—I was and shall be. You may call yourself her husband; but sometimes or many times, if you come upon her unexpectedly, you will find her beautiful eyes flooded with tears; and they will be shed for me. Never ask her the reason for her sadness. I shall be the cause. Her sighs, which she will try in vain to suppress, will be sighs of love breathed for one absent.

DON DIEGO. What foolhardiness is this? (*Goes angrily toward* Don Carlos.)

DON CARLOS. I have said it and I say it again; though I should have known that it was impossible to speak of her without offending you. So let us end this painful conversation. May you live happy; and do not hate me who never intentionally did anything to displease you. The highest proof I can give you of my obedience and respect is to go away from here at once. But do not deny me the consolation of knowing that you pardon me.

DON DIEGO. So then, you really intend to go?

DON CARLOS. At once, sir. And it will be a long absence this time.

DON DIEGO. Why so?

DON CARLOS. Because in my lifetime it is not fitting that I see her. If the rumours of a coming war are verified then . . .

DON DIEGO. What do you mean by that? (*He seizes* Don Carlos *by the arm and drags him forward.*)

DON CARLOS. Nothing . . . except that I am a soldier, and I love war.

DON DIEGO. Carlos! . . . How horrible! How can you say that to me?

DON CARLOS. Some one is coming. . . . (*Looks uneasily toward Doña Irene's room, breaks from* Don Diego *and makes as if to go through door up stage.* Don Diego *tries to stop him.*) It may be she. Farewell.

DON DIEGO. Where are you going? No, my boy, you must not go away.

DON CARLOS. There is no other way. I cannot see her. If we should meet face to face even for a moment, it might cause you much unhappiness.

DON DIEGO. I have told you it must not be. Go into that room.

DON CARLOS. But if . . .

DON DIEGO. Do as I command you. (Don Carlos *enters Don Diego's room.*)

SCENE XI

Doña Irene, Don Diego

DONA IRENE. So we are ready to start, Don Diego? Good morning. (*Extinguishes light on table.*) Are you saying your prayers?

DON DIEGO. Yes, I'm in the mood for praying!

DONA IRENE. If you wish it the servants will bring up the chocolate and tell the stage driver to have the horses harnessed. . . . But what ails you, sir? . . . Has anything happened?

DON DIEGO. Yes, there's no end of strange happenings, it seems.

DONA IRENE. But what . . . For God's sake, tell me. You don't know how frightened I am; and any little things upset me so. Since my last miscarriage, you know, my nerves are so delicate. It was nineteen years ago, or maybe twenty; but ever since every trifle positively shocks me to death. And neither hot baths nor snake broth, nor tamarind preserves seem to do me any good.

DON DIEGO. Well, let's not talk about miscarriages or preserves now. . . . There is a more important matter to consider. What are the girls doing?

DONA IRENE. Picking up the clothes and packing trunks so that everything may be in ship shape and no delays.

DON DIEGO. Very well. Will you be seated? And don't get frightened nor cry out (*both sit*) at anything I say; please bear that in mind. Don't lose your judgment when we all need it most. Your daughter, Doña Irene, is in love.

DONA IRENE. Well, haven't I already said so a thousand times? Yes, sir, indeed she is; all I had to do was say . . .

DON DIEGO. That confounded habit of interrupting! Let me speak.

DONA IRENE. Well, go on then.

DON DIEGO. She is in love; but not with me.

DONA IRENE. What's that you say?

DON DIEGO. Just what you hear.

DONA IRENE. Who in the world has been telling you these absurdities?

DON DIEGO. No one. I know it. I have seen it. No one has told me. And when I tell it to you, be sure that I know whereof I'm speaking. Well, well, what is this weeping?

DONA IRENE. Oh, poor unhappy me! (*Cries.*)

DON DIEGO. I can see no reason . . .

DONA IRENE. Because I am a widow and alone, and without means, it seems that everybody despises me and conspires against me.

DON DIEGO. But Doña Irene, please . . .

DONA IRENE. Nearing the end of my days and my chronic ailments, to be treated in this manner, cast aside like a rag, like a smutty cinderella, as I might say. . . . Who would have thought it of you! May the Lord help me! If only my three husbands were alive! . . . The last one alone would be enough, with his devil of a temper. . . .

DON DIEGO. Look, madam, I am coming to the end of my patience.

DONA IRENE. If any one answered back he'd get into a perfect fury. One Corpus Christi day, I don't remember what trifling thing occurred, he struck an army officer in the face, and if it hadn't been for the intervention of two priests he would have choked him to death against the portals of Santa Cruz.

DON DIEGO. Is it possible that you won't listen to what I am going to say?

DONA IRENE. Alas, I understand very well, sir. I'm no fool, I want you to know. You don't want the girl and you're trying to find some pretext for throwing her over. My little girl, the darling of my heart!

DON DIEGO. Doña Irene, I ask you again to listen to me, not to interrupt, not to talk nonsense. Then when you know what it is, you may weep and groan and cry out, and say whatever you please. But in the meantime, for heaven's sake don't drive me to distraction.

DONA IRENE. Well, sir, say anything you please.

DON DIEGO. And you'll not rage or cry or . . .

DONA IRENE. No sir, I'm not crying any more. (*Wipes her eyes.*)

DON DIEGO. Listen then: for about a year Doña Fanny has had another lover. They have spoken together often, they have written to each other, they have sworn each other love, faith, constancy. And finally there exists in each of them a passion so intense that obstacles and absence, instead of diminishing its ardour, has increased it. This being granted . . .

DONA IRENE. But don't you know, my dear sir, that all this is merely gossip, the invention of some evil tongue that is trying to injure us?

DON DIEGO. The same thing again! It is not gossip, madam. I repeat anew that I know whereof I am speaking.

DONA IRENE. And I repeat that there is not a trace of truth in it. My daughter, the child of my heart, inclosed in a convent, fasting seven Fridays in succession, watched over all the time by those saintly nuns. She who doesn't know what the world is, who is scarcely out of the shell, as the saying goes. Oh, you don't know what an eagle eye Sister Dolores has, and what a temper! She'd be just the easy going woman to pass over the slightest slip on the part of her niece! Yes, indeed!

DON DIEGO. There is no question here of slips, madam. It is a question of an honourable feeling of love, of which up to now we had had no inkling. Your daughter is a girl of stainless character, no one questions that. What I say is that Sister Dolores and all the rest of the nuns, and you and I, I especially, have committed a colossal blunder. The girl wishes to marry someone else, not me. We've come to our senses rather late. You had forgotten to reckon with the will of your daughter. Just read this letter and you will understand. (*Hands her Don Carlos' letter.* Doña Irene, *without reading it, rises, very agitated, goes to door of her room and calls.* Don Diego *rises and tries to calm her.*)

DONA IRENE. Oh, I know I shall go mad! Francisca, my child! Holy Virgin of the Quagmire! Rita! Francisca!

DON DIEGO. But what is the idea of bringing them here?

DONA IRENE. Yes, sir. I want them to come, so that the poor child can have her eyes opened. I want her to know what sort of a person you are.

DON DIEGO (*aside*). She's upset everything. That's what comes of confiding in a woman.

Rita, Doña Francisca, Doña Irene, Don Diego

RITA. What is it, my lady?

DONA FRANCISCA. You called me, mother?

DONA IRENE. Yes, my daughter, I did, because this fine gentleman, Don Diego, treats us in a way that is not to be endured. What love affairs have you had, my child? Whom have you promised to marry? What entanglements are these, I ask. . . . (*To* Rita.) What do you know about this, hussy? For you must know something. Who has written this letter? What does it say? (*Showing the open letter to* Doña Francisca.)

RITA (*aside to* Doña Francisca.) It's his handwriting.

Dona Francisca. What wickedness! Don Diego, is that the way you keep faith with me?

Don Diego. God knows I am not to blame. Come here. (*Takes her by the hand and brings her to his side.*) Don't be afraid. . . . And you, madam, listen and be silent and don't drive to do what I may wish undone. Give me the letter. (*Takes the letter from* Doña Irene.) Fanny, do you remember the three hand claps of last night?

Dona Francisca. I shall hear them as long as I live.

Don Diego. At that time this note was thrown in through the window. Don't be frightened, I beg of you. (*He reads.*) 'My darling: If I am not able to speak with you personally I will do my best that this letter shall reach you. I had scarcely left you when I met at the inn the man I called my enemy. On seeing him I was struck dumb with sorrow and amazement. He commanded me to leave the city at once and I could do no other than obey him. My name is Carlos, not Felix. Don Diego is my uncle. May you be happy and forget the unfortunate   Carlos de Urbina.'

Dona Irene. So that's how the wind blows!

Dona Francisca. Poor miserable me!

Dona Irene. It's true then what the gentleman said, you great big liar and cheat. I'll give you reason to remember this. (*She goes toward* Doña Francisca *very angrily, as if to strike her.* Rita *and* Don Diego *try to stop her.*)

Dona Francisca. Oh, mother, mother! . . . Forgive me!

Dona Irene. I'll kill her!

Don Diego. What madness is this?

Dona Irene. I'll kill her, I tell you.

SCENE XIII

Don Carlos, Don Diego, Doña Francisca, Doña Irene, Rita

(Don Carlos *rushes out of the room, takes* Doña Francisca *by the arm to the back of the stage; he places himself in front of her to defend her.* Doña Irene *is startled and draws back.*)

Don Carlos. No, you won't, while I'm here. Nobody shall touch her.

Dona Francisca. Carlos!

Don Carlos. (*Approaches* Don Diego.) Forgive my boldness. I saw she was being insulted and I couldn't contain myself.

Dona Irene. What is happening here anyhow? My God! Who are you? What unseemly conduct! What a scandal!

Don Diego. Nothing scandalous about this, madam. This is the man with whom your daughter is in love. To separate them and to kill them amounts to the same thing. Carlos, my boy . . . well, never mind that. . . . Kiss your sweetheart. (*They kiss and kneel before* Don Diego.)

DONA IRENE. So that is your nephew?

DON DIEGO. Yes, madam, my nephew, the fellow who with his hand clapping and his serenading and his love notes has given me the most terrible night I ever spent in my life. . . . What is this, my children, what are you doing?

DONA FRANCISCA. You forgive us then, and make us happy?

DON DIEGO. Yes, treasures of my soul, yes. (*Makes them get up.*)

DONA IRENE. Is it possible that you're going to make this sacrifice?

DON DIEGO. I could separate them forever and claim this lovely girl for myself; but my conscience will not permit it. . . . Carlos! Fanny! It is not without a struggle and much aching of the heart that I do this; for after all I am human. . . .

DON CARLOS. (*Kissing his hands.*) If our love, if our gratitude can console you in your love

DONA IRENE. So Don Carlos is the fine fellow . . .

DON DIEGO. He and your daughter were madly in love with each other, while you and the aunts built castles in the air and filled my old head with illusions, which have disappeared like a dream. . . . This is the result of the abuse of authority and our young people pay the penalty. These are the assurances which parents and tutors give, and this shows how much you can trust a young girl's yes. . . . We learned in time the error of our ways. Woe unto those who learn it too late!

DONA IRENE. Well, may they have a long and happy life. Come here, young man, and let me embrace you. (Doña Irene *and* Don Carlos *embrace;* Doña Francisca *kneels and kisses her hand.*) You've made a good choice, my darling Francisca. . . . My, he's good looking, too. . . . A little dark, but his eyes are captivating.

RITA. Yes, tell her that, for she may not have noticed it. Señorita, a thousand kisses. (Rita *and* Fanny *kiss each other with signs of joy.*)

DONA FRANCISCA. Oh, what great joy! . . . And you, Rita, who love me so much, you will always, always be my friend.

DON DIEGO. Beautiful Francisca (*Embraces* Doña Francisca), receive the first kiss of your new father. I am not afraid now of the terrible loneliness that was threatening my old age. . . . You (*taking* Doña Francisca *and* Don Carlos *by the hand*) will be the delight of my heart; and the first fruit of your love . . . yes, my children . . . he will be for me. And when I caress him in my arms, I shall be able

to say : 'This innocent child owes his existence to me; if his parents
live, if they are happy, I have been the cause.'
DON CARLOS. May you be blessed for all your kindness.
DON DIEGO. Blessed be God for His kindness.

ANNA EMILIA BAGSTAD

(Revised by the editors)

MANUEL JOSÉ QUINTANA
[1772–1857]

*Although he lived well into the nineteenth century, Quintana is classified
as an eighteenth-century author because of his neo-classic style and the fact
that his best poems were written at the turn of the century.*

*A fiery patriot—he is most celebrated for his noble odes in praise of liberty,
progress and love of country—Quintana was secretary of the Junta Central,
which governed unoccupied Spain following the Napoleonic invasion of
1808. He also fought home-grown tyranny, suffering six years of imprisonment for his support of the Constitution during the reign of Fernando VII.
In his final years, Quintana became poet laureate of Spain under Isabel II.*

*His passionate ode A España ranks with Juan Nicasio Gallego's El dos
de mayo as the most famous poetic commemoration of the Spanish resistance
to the French occupation. Quintana's principal prose work is an interesting
collection of biographies, Vidas de españoles célebres.*

ODE TO SPAIN—AFTER THE REVOLUTION OF MARCH

What nation, tell me, in the older day
Proclaimed its destiny across the world,
Through all the climes extending its broad sway
From east to west with golden pomp unfurled?
Where from the sunset the Atlantic swept
Its glorious fortunes—there was mighty Spain !—
America and Asia's confines kept
And Africa's upon its boundary main.
The hardy sail upon its fickle course
In vain would 'scape the reaches of its power;
All earth for mineral riches was its source,
All ocean was its pearls' and corals' bower.

Nor where the tempests raged the most
Met they on any but a Spanish coast.
Now to the depths of shame reduced,
Abandoned to the alien eye of scorn,
Like some poor slave unto the market used
To the vile whip and shackle basely borne !—
What desolation, God !—The plague respires
Its deadly breath of poison on the air
And Hunger scarce with feeble arms aspires
For a poor morsel there !
Thrice did the temple gates of Janus ope
And on Mars' trumpet was a mighty blast !
Thrice, but oh see, where even without a glance of hope
The tutelary gods have passed,
And on the sea and land have left us cast !
Throughout thy spreading realms what hast thou seen,
O Spain?—but bitter mourning spread,
Sorrow and misery between
Thy fruits of slavery full harvested?
Thus the sail rends, the hulk is smashed,
And broken goes the bark upon its way;
With every wave a torment it is lashed;
Its prows no more their garlands old display.
Nor sign of hope nor of content appears;
Its standard floats no more upon the air.
The voyager's song is broken by his tears;
The mariner's voice is hushed by weight of care,
And dread of death comes ever on his heart,
A dread of death in silence; there apart
He drifts where the destroying shoals prepare.
Then the fell moment ! Reaching forth his hand
The Tyrant threatening the west, exclaims :
'Behold, thou now art mine, O Western Land !'
His brow with barbarous lightning flames,
As from the cloud the summer tempest brings
The horror spreading bolt's appalling wings.
His warriors afar
Fill the great winds with pæans of their war;
The anvils groan, the hammers fall,
The forges blaze. O shame, and dost thou dream
To make their swords their toil, and that is all?
See'st thou not where within their fiery gleams
'Tis chains and bars and shackles they prepare

To bind the arms that lie so limp and bare?
Yea, let Spain tremble at the sound,
And let her outraged ire
From the volcano of her bosom bound,
High justice for its fire,
And 'gainst her despots turn,
Where in their dread they hide,
And let the echoes learn
And all the banks of Tagus wide
Hear the great sound of rage outcried,—
'Vengeance !'—Where, sacred river, where
The titans who with pride and wrong
Opposed our weal so long?
Their glories are no more, while ours prepare;
And thou so fierce and proud
Seeing Castile and thy Castilians there
Urgest thy ruddy waves in seaward pour,
Crying aloud :—'The tyrants are no more !'
Triumph ! and glory ! O celestial time !
Would that my tongue might speak our country's name
Unto the very winds sublime !
Gladly would I—but not on harp of gold—
My song acclaim; not in the prison hold
Where the inspired breast
Grows weak and cold,
With breathless lips opprest.
Old Tyrteus' lyre untomb,
In the bright sun and the uplifting wind
Of pineclad, rocky Fuenfría's bloom !
High be my flight consigned
To noble singing that shall rouse the plain
And wake Castilians to the sound again
Of glory and of war combined !
War, awful name and now sublime !
The refuge and the sacred shield in time
To stay the savage Attila's advance
With fiery steed and lance !—
War ! War ! O Spaniards, on the shore
Of Guadalquivir, see arise once more
Thy Ferdinand the Third's imposing brows !
See great Gonzalo o'er Granada rear !
Behold the Cid with sword in mad carouse !
And o'er the Pyrenees the form appear

Of brave Bernardo, old Jimena's son!
See how their stormy wraiths are interspun!
How valour breathes from out their hollow tombs
Where 'War' upon the mighty echoes booms!
And then! Canst thou with face serene
Behold the fertile plains
Where endless greed would glean
Our heritage and gains,
And to destruction cast? Awake,
O hero-race, the moment is at hand
When victory thou must take—
Our glory owning thine more grand,—
Thy name a higher place than ours to take!—
It was no little day they raised
Nor vain—the altar of our fathers grand;
Swear then to keep its praise;
Swear,—'Rather death than tyrants in the land!'—
Yea, I do swear it, Venerable Shades,
And with the vow mine arm is stronger grown.
Give me the lance, tie on my helm and blades,
And to my vengeance bid me swift be gone!
Let him despairing bow his coward head
To dust and shame! Perchance the mighty flood
Of devastation on its course shall spread
And bear me on? What matter? One can shed
But once his mortal blood!
Shall I not go to meet
Our mighty ones upon the field of old?
'Hail, warrior forefathers!' there to greet
Their mighty 'Hail.' Where hero-Spain
Amid the horror and the carnage cold
Lifts up her bleeding head again,
And turns anew from her unhappy reign,
A Victress, her reconquered lands to sign
With golden sceptre and device divine!

                                          THOMAS WALSH

GASPAR MELCHOR DE JOVELLANOS
[1744–1811]

One of the noblest figures of eighteenth-century Spain, Gaspar Melchor de Jovellanos was a statesman of high integrity and devotion to his country who held many important government posts. After the Napoleonic invasion he helped organize the Junta *of Spanish patriots, and died while being hounded by the French in 1811. A year before his death he wrote the famous* Memoria en defensa de la Junta Central. *An excerpt is presented here.*

In addition to his prose works—including brilliant treatises on economics, education, government, agriculture and other topics—Jovellanos wrote poetry and several dramas.

IN DEFENCE OF THE CENTRAL JUNTA

. . . And now that I am about to lay down my pen, I feel a secret trouble at my heart, which will disturb the rest of my life. It has been impossible for me to defend myself without offending others; and I fear, that, for the first time, I shall begin to feel I have enemies whom I have myself made such. But, wounded in that honour which is my life, and asking in vain for an authority that would protect and rescue me, I have been compelled to attempt my own defence by my own pen; the only weapon left in my hands. To use it with absolute moderation, when I was driven on by an anguish so sharp, was a hard task. One more dexterous in such contests might, by the cunning of his art, have oftener inflicted wounds, and received them more rarely; but, feeling myself to be fiercely attacked, and coming to the contest unskilled and alone, I threw my unprotected person into it, and, in order to free myself from the more imminent danger before me, took no thought of any that might follow. Indeed, such was the impulse by which I was driven on, that I lost sight, at once, of considerations which, at another time, might well have prevailed with me. Veneration for public authority, respect for official station, the private affections of friendship and personal attachment,—every thing within me yielded to the love of justice, and to the earnest desire that truth and innocence should triumph over calumny and falsehood. And can I, after this, be pardoned, either by those who have assailed me, or by those who have refused me their protection? Surely it matters little. The time has come in which all disapprobation, except that of honourable men and the friends of justice must be indifferent to me. For now that I find myself fast approaching the final limits of human life, now that I am alone and in poverty, without a home or a shelter, what remains for me to ask, beyond the glory and liberty of my country, but leave to die with the good name I have laboured to earn in its service?

GEORGE TICKNOR

NINETEENTH CENTURY

MARIANO JOSÉ DE LARRA
[1809–1837]

The precocious Mariano José de Larra, journalist, novelist, poet, dramatist, critic and costumbrista, *committed suicide at the age of twenty-eight over an unhappy love affair. Had he lived, there is little doubt that he would have become one of the greatest of all Spanish writers. For sharp critical insight and descriptive skill, Larra had no competitors in his own time and few in the entire history of Spanish literature.*

His romantic drama Macías *and his fine historical novel* El doncel de Don Enrique el Doliente *(both 1834) deal with the ill-starred loves of the fourteenth-century troubadour Macías. But it is as a writer of articles satirizing the customs of his day that Larra is most famous. His style is characterized by choice vocabulary, purity of expression, subtle irony and humour. Larra often used the pseudonym* Fígaro, *as he does in* El castellano viejo, *given here.*

THE OLD CASTILIAN

Since I have grown older I very seldom care to change the order of my way of living, which has now been settled a long time, and I base this repugnance upon the fact that I have never for a single day abandoned my Lares to break my system without being overtaken by a most sincere repentance as the aftermath of my deluded hopes. Nevertheless a remnant of the old-fashioned courtesy adopted by our forefathers in their intercourse obliges me at times to accept certain invitations, which to refuse would be rudeness, or at least a ridiculous affectation of delicacy.

Some days ago I was walking through the streets in search of material for my articles. Buried in my thoughts, I surprised myself several times, laughing like a poor wretch at my own fancies, and mechanically moving my lips. A stumble or so reminded me now and again that to walk on the pavements of Madrid it is not the best of circumstances to be either poet or philosopher; more than one malicious smile, more than one look of wonder from the passers-by, made me reflect that soliloquies should not be made in public; and when turning corners not a few collisions with those who turned them as heedlessly as I made me recognize that the absent-minded are not among the number of elastic bodies, much less among glorious and insensible beings. Such being my frame of mind, imagine my sensations upon receiving a horrible smack which a huge hand attached (it seemed to me) to a brawny arm administered to one of my shoulders, which unfortunately bear not the slightest resemblance to those of Atlas!

Not wishing to make it understood that I would not recognize this energetic way of announcing oneself, nor to rebuff the good-will, which doubtless wished to show itself to be more than mediocre by leaving me crooked for the rest of the day, I was merely about to turn round to see who was so much my friend as to treat me so badly. But my Old Castilian is a man who, when he is joking, does not stop half-way. What?—my reader will ask—he gave further proofs of his intimacy and affection? He clasped his hands tightly over my eyes from behind, crying out, 'Who am I?' bubbling with delight at the success of his pretty trick. 'Who you are? A brute,' I was about to reply; but I suddenly remembered who it might be, and substituted the words, 'It's Braulio.' Upon hearing me he loosened his hands, held his sides for laughter, disturbing the whole street, and making us both very conspicuous.

'Good, good! How did you recognize me?'

'Who could it be but you? . . .'

'Well, so you've come from your dear Biscay?'

'No, Braulio, I have not come.'

'Always the same merry humour. What does it matter? It's a way we have of talking in Spain. . . . Do you know it's my birthday tomorrow?'

'I wish you many happy returns of the day.'

'Oh, no formalities between us; you know I'm a plain fellow and an Old Castilian, and call a spade a spade; consequently I require no compliments from you, but consider yourself invited——'

'To what?'

'To dine with me.'

'Impossible.'

'You must.'

'I cannot,' I insist, trembling.

'You can't?'

'Very many thanks——'

'Thanks? Very well, my dear friend; as I'm not the Duke of F., or Count P., of course——'

Who can resist an attack of this kind? Who cares to appear proud? 'It is not that, but——'

'Well, if it's not that,' he breaks in, 'I shall expect you at two. We dine early at my house—Spanish style. I expect a lot of people;

there will be the famous improvisor X.; T. will sing after dinner in his usual first-rate style; and in the evening J. will play and sing some trifles.'

This consoled me somewhat, and I had to give way. 'Everybody,' said I to myself, 'has an evil day sometimes. In this world, if one wishes to preserve friends, one must endure their civilities.'

'You won't fail, unless you want to quarrel with me?'

'I shall not fail,' I said in a lifeless voice and low spirits, like a fox vainly revolving in the trap in which it has allowed itself to be caught.

'Then good-bye till tomorrow,' and he gave me a parting slap.

I watched him as the farmer watches the cloud go away from his newly sown field, and remained wondering how one could explain such adverse and fatal friendships.

.   .   .

Two o'clock arrived. As I knew my friend Braulio, I did not think it advisable to make myself too fine for his party; that, I am sure, would have annoyed him; nevertheless I could not dispense with a light frock-coat and a white pocket-handkerchief as essential for such birthday festivities. Above all, I dressed myself as slowly as possible, like the wretched criminal confessing at the foot of the gallows, who would like to have committed a hundred more sins the which to confess in order to gain more time. I was invited for two, and I entered the parlour at half-past two.

I shall not dwell on the ceremonious calls made before dinner-time by an infinite number of visitors, among which were not least all the officials of his department with their spouses and children, their cloaks, umbrellas, galoshes, and house-dogs; I shall be silent as to the foolish compliments paid to the head of the family on his birthday, nor describe the monstrous circle which was formed in the parlour by the assembly of so many hetero-geneous people, discoursing upon how the weather was about to change, and how the winter is generally colder than the summer. Let us come to the point : four o'clock struck, and we, the invited guests, found ourselves alone. Unluckily for me, Senor X., who was to have entertained us, being a connoisseur of this class of invita-tion, had had the good idea to fall sick that morning; the celebrated T. found himself opportunely compromised by another invitation, and the young lady who was to sing and play so well was hoarse to such a degree that she was surprised that a single word she said could be understood, and further she had an infection in one of her fingers. Alas, for my beguiled expectations!

'Since all who are to dine are here,' exclaimed Don Braulio, 'let us go to the table, my dear.'

'Wait a bit,' replied his wife in a loud whisper. 'Such a lot of callers prevented my being in the kitchen, and . . .'

'But, look, it's four o'clock . . .'

'Dinner will be ready in a moment . . .'

It was five o'clock when we sat down.

'Ladies and gentlemen,' said our amphitryon, as we staggered into our respective chairs, 'I insist upon your making yourselves quite at home; we don't stand upon ceremony in my house. Oh, Figaro! I want you to be quite comfortable; you are a poet, and besides, these gentlemen who know how intimate we are will not be offended if I make an exception of you; take off your coat; it won't do to stain it.'

'Why should I stain it?' I replied, biting my lips.

'Oh, that's all right; I'll lend you a loose jacket; I'm sorry I haven't one for everybody.'

'I'd sooner not, thank you.'

'Nonsense! My jacket! Here it is; it will be a little large for you!'

'But, Braulio . . .'

'You must have it—bother etiquette!' and he thereupon pulled off my coat himself, *velis nolis*, and buried me in a great striped jacket, through which only my feet and head protruded, and the sleeves of which would probably not permit me to eat. I thanked him; he thought he was doing me a favour.

The days upon which my friend has no visitors he contents himself with a low table, little more than a cobbler's bench, because he and his wife, as he says, what should they want more? From this little table he carries his food, like water drawn up a well, to his mouth, where it arrives dripping after its long journey; for to imagine that these people keep a proper table and eat comfortably every day in the year is to expect too much. It is easy, therefore, to conceive that the installation of a large table for a dinner-party was an event in that house, so much so that a table at which scarcely eight people could have eaten comfortably had been considered capable of sitting the whole fourteen of us. We had to sit sideways with one shoulder towards the dinner, and the elbows of the guests entered on intimate relationship with each other in the most confiding fashion possible. They put me as in a place of honour between a child five years old, raised on some cushions, which I had to arrange every minute, as the natural restlessness of my youthful neighbour caused them to slip, and one of those men that occupy in this world the room of three, whose corpulency overflowed on all sides the chair upon which he was seated like, so to speak, upon the point of a needle. The table-napkins which we silently unfolded were new, for they were commodities of little daily use, and were pulled by these good gentlemen through a button-hole of their frock-coats to serve as intermediary bodies between the sauces and their broadcloth.

'You will have to take pot luck, gentlemen,' exclaimed our amphitryon as soon as he had sat down.

'What ridiculous affectation if untrue,' said I to myself; 'and if it is true, what folly to invite one's friends to take pot luck.' Unfortunately it was not long before I knew that there was in that expression more truth than my good Braulio imagined. Interminable and of poor taste were the compliments with which, upon passing and receiving each dish, we wearied one another. 'Pray help yourself.' 'Do me the favour.' 'I couldn't think of it.' 'Pass it on to the lady.' 'Ah, that's right.' 'Pardon me.' 'Thank you.'

'No ceremony, gentlemen,' exclaimed Braulio, and was the first to dip his spoon into his plate.

The soup was followed by an *olla*, an assortment of the most savoury impertinences of that most annoying but excellent dish; here was some meat, there some green stuff; here the dried beans, there the ham; the chicken to the right, the bacon in the middle, and the Estremaduran sausage to the left. Then came some larded veal, upon which may the curse of Heaven alight, and after this another dish, and another and another and another, half of which were brought over from a hotel, which will suffice to excuse our praising them, the other half made at home by their own maid and a Biscayan wench, a help hired for this festivity, and the mistress of the house, who on such occasions is supposed to have a hand in everything, and can consequently superintend nothing properly.

'You must be indulgent with this dish,' said the latter of some pigeons, 'they are a little burnt.'

'But, my dear . . .'

'I only left them for a moment, and you know what servants are.'

'What a pity this turkey was not half an hour longer before the fire! It was put in too late. And don't you think that stew is a little smoked?'

'What can you expect? A woman can't be everywhere at once.'

'Oh, they're excellent!' we all exclaimed, leaving the pieces on our plates—'delicious!'

'This fish is bad.'

'Well, they said in the fish market that it had only just arrived; the servant is so stupid!'

'Where does this wine come from?'

'Now there you're wrong, for it's . . .'

'Detestable.'

These short dialogues were accompanied by a number of furtive glances from the husband to acquaint his wife of some negligence, and both tried to give us to understand that they were quite at home in all those formulae which in similar cases are reputed correct, and that all the blunders were the fault of the servants, who can never learn to serve. But these omissions were so numerous, and looks were of such little avail, that the husband had recourse to pinches and kicks, and his wife, who, until the present, had barely succeeded in rising superior to her spouse's persecutions, now became inflamed in the face, and had tears in her eyes.

'Dear madam, do not distress yourself about such trifles,' said her neighbour.

'Ah! I assure you I shall not do this kind of thing in the house again; you don't know what it means; another time, Braulio, we'll dine at the hotel, and then you'll not have . . .'

'You, madam, shall do what I . . .'

'Braulio! Braulio!'

A terrible storm was about to burst; however, all the guests vied with each other in settling these disputes born of the desire to demonstrate the greatest refinement, and of which not the smallest components were Braulio's mania, and the concluding remark which he again directed to the assembly with regard to the inutility of ceremony, by which he understood being properly served and knowing how to eat. Is there anything more ridiculous than those people who wish to pass for refined in the depths of the crassest ignorance of social usage, and who, to favour you, forcibly oblige you to eat and drink, and will not allow you to do what you like? And why are there people who only care to eat with a little more comfort on birthdays?

To add to all this, the child to my left was making olives jump into a dish of ham and tomatoes, and one of them hit one of my eyes, and prevented me from seeing clearly for the rest of the day; the stout gentleman to my right had taken the precaution to heap up on the tablecloth, by the side of my bread, the crumbs of his own and the bones of the birds which he had gnawed; and the guest opposite me, who piqued himself on his carving, had taken upon himself to make the autopsy of a capon, or cock, for nobody knew which, and whether by reason of the advanced age of the victim, or the lack of anatomical science of the executioner, the joints never appeared.

'This bird has no joints!' exclaimed the poor wretch, the drops of perspiration running down his face from his struggles, looking more like a person digging than carving. And then a wonderful occurrence took place! Upon one of the attacks, the fork slipped upon the animal as if it had scales, and the bird, thus violently dispatched, took flight as in its happier days, and then quietly alighted on the tablecloth, as on a roost in the poultry yard.

The fright was general, and the alarm reached its climax when a sauce-boat, impelled by the bird's wild career, upset, splashing my snow-white shirt. At this point the carver rose hastily, with a mind to chase the fugitive fowl, and as he precipitated himself upon it, a bottle to the right, which he knocked with his arm, abandoning its perpendicular position, poured out an abundant stream of Valdepeñas wine over the capon and the cloth. The wine ran; the uproar increased; salt was abundantly sprinkled over the wine to save the cloth; to save the table a napkin was inserted below the cloth, and an eminence arose on the site of so many ruins. A terrified maid, bearing away the capon now reposing in a dish of gravy, tilted it slightly as she lifted it over me, and an accursed shower of grease descended like the dew upon the meadows to leave lasting traces on my pearl-grey trousers. The anguish and confusion of the girl were beyond bounds; she withdrew, unsuccessful in her excuses, and, turning round, collided with the waiter, who was carrying a dozen clean plates and a salver for the dessert wines, and the whole business came to the ground with the most horrible clatter and commotion.

'By St. Peter!' roared Braulio, and a mortal pallor diffused itself over his features, while a fire broke out on his wife's face. 'But no matter; let us continue, friends,' said he calming down.

Oh, honest homes where a modest stew and one more course constitute the daily happiness of a family; flee from the tumult of a birthday dinner-party! The custom of eating well and being well served every day can alone avert similar discomfiture.

Are there any more disasters? Alas, there are for my miserable self! Doña Juana, the lady with the black and yellow teeth, holds out to me from her plate and with her own fork a dainty bit, which I am bound to accept and swallow; the child amuses himself by shooting cherry-stones at the eyes of the assembly; Don Leandro makes me taste the delicious orange liqueur, which I had refused, in his own glass, which preserves the indelible traces of his greasy lips; my fat friend is smoking, and makes me the flue of his chimney; finally, oh last of miseries! the clamour and uproar increase, voices already hoarse demand couplets and stanzas, and Figaro is the only poet present.

'You must. It's for you to say something,' they all shout.

'Start him with the first line; let him compose a couplet for each of us.'

'I'll start him : *To Don Braulio on this day* . . .'

'Gentlemen, for Heaven's sake !'

'There's no getting out of it.'

'I've never improvised in my life.'

'Don't play the bashful.'

'I shall leave.'

'Lock the door. He shan't leave here until he recites something.'

And so I repeat some verses at last, and vomit absurdities, which they praise, and the smoke, the hubbub, and the purgatory increase.

Thank Heavens, I succeed in escaping from that new pandemonium. At last I again breathe the pure air of the street; there are now no more lunatics, no more Old Castilians around me.

'Ye gods, I thank you !' I exclaimed, breathing freely like a stag who has just escaped a dozen dogs and can barely hear their distant barks. 'Henceforward I do not pray for riches, office, or honours. But deliver me from invitations to dinner and birthday parties; deliver me from those houses in which a dinner-party is an event, in which a decent table is only laid for visitors, in which they think they are doing you a good turn while they are doing you a bad one, in which they are over-polite, in which they recite verses, in which there are children, in which there are fat men, in which, finally, there reigns the brutal frankness of the Old Castilians ! If I fall by similar temptations, may I ever lack roast beef, may beefsteaks vanish from this world, may timbales of macaroni be annihilated, may there be no turkeys in Perigueux, nor pies in Perigord, may the wines of Bordeaux dry up, and finally may everybody but myself drink the delicious foam of champagne !'

SUSETTE M. TAYLOR
(Revised by the editors)

RAMÓN DE MESONERO ROMANOS
[1803–1882]

Mesonero Romanos' delightful sketches of life in Madrid are gathered in Escenas matritenses *and other volumes. A business man turned writer, he often chose a foible of Madrid society—or its members—as the object of his good-natured satire. He published some of his works under the pseudonym* El curioso parlante.

THE NEARSIGHTED LOVER

'What!' (some critic will exclaim with surprise upon reading the title of this discourse). 'Even physical shortcomings are not beyond the range of the *Curioso's* potshots? Doesn't this fellow know that it is not proper for him to particularize circumstances which may rob his scenes of general application? And who has told him that it is fair to ridicule a physical shortcoming, unless—at the very least—it is accompanied by some moral.'

——Patience, my friend, and let's understand each other, which is not perhaps difficult. Come, now; when certain physical defects are so common among a people that they help to describe its particular physiognomy, is it wise for a chronicler of customs and habits to ignore them, without profiting from the various vignettes which they ought to provide him? If, for example, there were an entire nation composed of the lame, would it not be interesting to know the manner of march of their armies, their games, their dances, their gymnastic exercises? Well, why can't one describe nearsighted love when there is hardly a lover alive who isn't?

And furthermore, who has told you that this stylish infirmity does not present its own moral aspect? Would it be so difficult to prove its origin in the depravity of customs, the shortcomings of education, or the excesses of youth? Therefore you see, Mr. Critic, that this subject falls naturally under the jurisdiction of my benign lash; therefore you perceive that there is nothing wrong in speaking of it—No?—well, to work.

Examples come to me instantly, and I have but to choose one. Today the lot falls to Maurice R——, and pardon if I use him to unwrinkle the foreheads of my kind readers. And who is this Maurice? This Maurice, my dear ladies, is a young man of twenty-three years, whose expressive countenance and sentimental air reveal at first glance a heart which is tender and inclined to love; it is not, therefore, strange that he should find favour among you. Well, that is what has happened, and a few little flirtations in the

streets and the boulevards made young Maurice aware of his
advantageous circumstances; but, unhappily, the budding young
man has a major defect, and it is—he is nearsighted, *very* nearsighted, a fact which upsets all his plans.

Just a minute, ladies; don't laugh, because my hero does not
regard it as a joke, nor does he know how to take advantage of
this defect, as many others do, in order to be more daring and
demanding, in order to display above his nose shiny gold-rimmed
spectacles, or in order to surprise with his inevitable pince-nez the
furtive glances of the ladies. Far from that, Maurice is sensitive
but very obliging; he would rather deprive himself of comfort than
cause another person displeasure. He might well have wanted to
wear glasses all the time, as some do unnecessarily and just as a
whim; but a pair of eyeglasses bouncing to the quick rhythm of
the mazurka harmonize so poorly! And Maurice, at twenty-three,
could not bring himself to stop dancing the mazurka. A good
remedy, of course, would be a dangling monocle; but aside from
the reluctance with which these were used, how was one to foresee
the scenes which might occur in order to be prepared with it in
hand? If a beautiful damsel quickly turned her lovely eyes to him,
or let her handkerchief fall in order to give him a chance to speak
with her; how was he to foresee it a moment before? If, thinking
he was asking the prettiest girl in the room to dance, he found
that he had offered his arm to an Egyptian mummy, what good
would his monocle be a moment later? Come, it is clear that the
monocle is useless, and Maurice, who realized this, truly despaired.

Love, which for a long time had been satisfied merely to prick
him lightly, came at last to slash his heart in two, and one night
at the ball of the Marquesa of ——, Maurice, who was dancing
with the beautiful Matilda de Lainez, could not refrain from
blurting out a straightforward declaration of love. The young
lady, on whom the charms of Maurice undoubtedly had their
effect, did not reprehend him,

'*Faute d'avoir le temps de se mettre en courroux.*'

And here we have my fine young man in the happiest moment
of love, that of seeing his feelings shared by the adored person.

By now our sweethearts had conversed extensively; three
rigadoons and one galop had done no more than fan the flame of
their passion; but the ball was ending and the conquered Maurice
renewed his protestations and vows; he jotted down exactly the
hour and minute in which Matilda would appear upon her
balcony; the church where she went to hear mass; the boulevards
and gatherings which she frequented; her mother's favourite

operas; in short, all those preliminaries which you, skilled youths, do not overlook in these matters. But the inexpert Maurice at the same time forgot to take a good look at the mother and an older sister of Matilda who were at the ball; he did not observe her father, a colonel of the cavalry, and, lastly, he did not dare to apprise his beloved of the fatal circumstance of his nearsightedness. What happened later led him to realize his mistake.

When, the next day, the appointed hour had barely arrived, he ran to the street where his lady lived, checking carefully the address of the house. Matilda had told him it was Number 12 and that it was on the corner of a certain street, but inasmuch as the house on the other corner, which was Number 72, looked like 12 to the unfortunate lover, *that* was the one which he chose as the object of his siege.

Matilda, who saw him come (feminine eyes, what don't you see when you are in love!), tossed away her embroidery, and rushing out to the balcony, she displayed to her lover all the charms of her pulchritude in a simple gown; but all in vain, for Maurice, six yards away on the other corner, his eyes fixed on the balconies of the opposite house, scarcely noticed the beauty which had appeared on the other verandah.

This unexpected disdain stung Matilda's ego beyond measure; she coughed twice, she pulled out her white handkerchief, all was useless; her heartsick lover glanced at her quickly, and turned his back to her in order to concentrate upon the other object. This scene lasted for an hour or more until, despairing and believing himself abandoned by his lady, the fine young man felt strong temptations to employ the time profitably with the other neighbour who remained so motionless. Finally, not being able to resist the enticement, and seeing that otherwise he was completely wasting the afternoon, he decided at last (although with anguish in his heart) to digress from his love and talk with the graceful neighbour.

No sooner said than done; he crosses the street, he goes determinedly under Matilda's balcony; he raises his head to speak to her; but at the very same moment she tosses in his face the handkerchief that she held in her hand (in which, during her rage, she had made a few knots), and without saying a single word to him, she goes inside and slams the balcony door. Maurice unfolded the handkerchief and recognized embroidered on it the same initials which he had seen on the one Matilda carried the night of the ball. Then he looked at the house and managed to make out *Number 12*. How can one describe his desperation?

Three days and three nights he walked her street in vain; the implacable balcony remained shut, and the entire neighbourhood, except the object of his love, bore faithful witness to his sighs. The third night one of the mother's favourite operas was being presented in the theatre; located in his orchestra seat, with the help of opera glasses Maurice avidly peruses the theatre and sees nothing which might please him; however, in one of the box seats he thinks he sees the mother accompanied by the cause of his torment. He goes upstairs, walks through the corridors, he peeks through the door of the box; there is no doubt—it is they— Maurice wears himself out with signals and grimaces, but he accomplishes nothing; finally the opera ends, he awaits their descent, and in the darkest part of the stairway, he comes up to the girl and says to her :

—Señorita, pardon my blunder. If you come out upon your balcony later I will tell you—in the meantime, here is the handkerchief.

—Sir, what are you saying?—a strange voice answered him at the very moment that a miserable lantern (one of the lanterns which so weakly light our theatre stairways) suddenly revealed to him that he was speaking to another person, although she greatly resembled his idol.

—Madam—

—Why, this handkerchief is my sister's !

—What's this, child?

—Nothing, Mamá; just this gentleman who is giving me Matilda's handkerchief.

—And how is it that this gentleman has Matilda's handker-chief?

—Madam, I—pardon me, the other day, the other night, I mean—at the ball of the Marquesa of—

—That's true, Mamá; this gentleman danced with my sister, and it is not strange that she should have forgotten her handkerchief.

—Yes, that's it, señorita; she forgot it, forgot—

—Truly it is odd; but nevertheless, sir, we thank you.

A thunderbolt fallen at his feet could not have upset poor Maurice more, and what most aggravated him was that in a corner of the handkerchief he had tied a note in which he spoke of his love, of the mistake of the house address, of the protestations at the ball, in short, he detailed the whole exposition of the drama, and he did not know to what fate that paper would come.

Trembling and uncertain, he followed the ladies at a distance, until they entered their house and left him in the street in the most utter abandonment. In vain he cocked his ear to see if he could hear some animated dialogue; the distant voice of the night watchman who was calling midnight, or the sonorous march of the dirty cleaning wagons were the only things which struck his ears and his nostrils; until, tired of waiting fruitlessly, he went home to lie awake and ponder his unhappy love.

In the meanwhile, what was happening inside the other house? Mama, who took the handkerchief in order to scold her daughter, had discovered the note, had read its contents, and after the first moments of wrath, had resolved, on the sister's advice, not to make a scene but quietly to write a short-worded and decisive answer to the young gallant—with the purpose that he should have no desire to return; they did this, and the note was written, signed in a woman's handwriting (they all look alike), sealed with sealing-wax and paste, and as a stronger proof, pricked with a pin. This undertaking completed, they went to bed, certain that the next morning the hapless lover would pass through the street. Actually, this was not asking for much; for it was not even 8 a.m. when he was already at the entrance across the way, not daring to look. As he waits thus, he hears a balcony open—and—o joy! a white hand throws out a small paper; the happy youth runs to catch it and he finds—the balcony has already closed and with it the hope of his heart.

In vain one might attempt to describe the effect which that series of misadventures had upon Maurice; let it suffice to say that he renounced love *forever*; but after all, he was a young man, and at the end of two weeks he thought differently, and out he one of those pleasant July nights which invite one to enjoy the agreeable surroundings beneath the leafy trees and, both comrades seated, they began the usual discussion of their respective love affairs. Maurice, with his accustomed frankness, related his last adventure to his friend, with all the intrigues and sudden changes in fortune which it involved, even unto the bitter farewell to which his hapless blunders had brought him; but upon finishing his tale, he perceived a rapid movement on the next benches, where among other persons he saw seated a military man and a young lady; he moves a little closer, he pulls out his eyeglass (Stupid! why didn't you take it out from the very beginning?) and he learns that the young lady seated at his back listening to his conversation is none other than the beautiful Matilda.

—Ingrate!—was all he was able to say, while the father called a boy to light his cigar.

—I did not write that letter. (This answer he received after a quarter of an hour.)

—Well then, who?

—I don't know. Bring it. At twelve I will be on the balcony.

Hope again poured its healing balm on poor Maurice's heart, and filled with pleasing thoughts he awaited the appointed hour; he runs swiftly to the balcony, and indeed, she is there; now he sees her lovely eyes shining, now he glimpses her white hand, now—But oh, how wisely says Shakespeare that *when sorrows come, they come not single spies, but in battalions*! That night it had occurred to Papa to enjoy some fresh air after dinner, and it was *he* who was stretched out there, feet on the balcony rail, notwithstanding the agitation of Matilda, who begged him to retire and avoid the night dew.

—My darling—said Maurice, in honeyed tones—is it you?

—Daughter, Matilda (said the father in a low voice), is that for you?

—Me, Papa? No sir, I don't have any idea—

—No? Well, these things are either yours or your sister's.

—So that you may see (continues the smitten young gallant) whether I had reason to be angry, there is the letter.

—Let me see it, let me see it, girl, now get away, get away, and bring a light, I'm going to read it!

No sooner said than done; glaring at his daughter with threatening eyes, he enters the parlour, opens the letter, and reads: 'Sir, if the night of the Marquesa's ball I, in my indiscretion, inspired in you wild expectations . . .'

—Heavens! But what do I see—this handwriting is my wife's!

—Oh, father!

—Infamous one! At forty you go about inspiring wild expectations!

—But, Papa—

—Just let me wake her up and let the whole house explode!

And indeed, he did just that, and for an hour the outcries, the sobs, the weepings interested the entire neighbourhood, with no small fright on the part of the Phantom Lover, who from the street came to half-understand the extraordinary *quid pro quo*.

His nobility and punctiliousness did not allow him to permit that all should suffer any longer on his account, and strongly determined, he knocks at the door; the father appears on the balcony:

—Sir, please be so kind as to listen to an explanatory word of my conduct.

The father grabs two pistols and hurriedly descends; he opens the door.

—Choose!—he tells him.

—Calm yourself, answers the young man;—I am a gentleman; my name is ——, and my family is well-known; an unfortunate combination of events has made me disturb the tranquillity of your family, and I cannot permit this without explaining it to you.

At this point he gave a detailed and truthful account of all the happenings, which the mother and the girls successively confirmed, with which the agitation of the jealous colonel was calmed.

The next day the Marquesa formally presented Maurice in the home of Matilda, and the father, informed of the circumstances, did not object.

From here on, the history of these amours followed a more tranquil path; and those who wish to rush things to their conclusion may relax, knowing that Maurice and his beloved were married, in spite of that fact that she, seen at close range in a good light, and through eyeglasses, appeared to him not so beautiful, by reason of smallpox pits and a few other little defects; nevertheless, her moral qualities were very creditable, and Maurice overlooked the physical, for all he had to do in order to forget these was one simple operation, which was—take off his glasses.

JEANNE PASMANTIER

FRANCISCO MARTÍNEZ DE LA ROSA
[1787–1862]

Martínez de la Rosa, distinguished diplomat, dramatist and poet, came into contact with French romanticism while an exile in France. His prose drama, La conjuración de Venecia (*1834*), *was the first great triumph of romanticism on the Spanish stage. He continued, however, to write poetry in his favoured neo-classic style.*

THE ALHAMBRA

Come to my bidding, gentle damsels fair,
    That haunt the banks of Douro and Genil!
Come, crowned with roses in your fragrant hair,
    More fresh and pure than April balms distil!

With long, dark locks adown your shoulders straying;
    With eyes of fire, and lips of honeyed power;
Uncinctured robes, the bosom bare displaying,
    Let songs of love escort me to the bower.

With love resounds the murmur of the stream;
    With love the nightingale awakes the grove;
O'er wood and mountain love inspires the theme,
    And Earth and Heaven repeat the strain of love.

Even there, where, 'midst the Alcazar's Moorish pride,
    Three centuries of ruin sleep profound,
From marble walls, with gold diversified,
    The sullen echoes murmur love around.

Where are its glories now?—the pomps, the charms,
    The triumph, the emprise of proud display,
The song, the dance, the feast, the deeds of arms,
    The gardens, baths, and fountains,—where are they?

Round jasper columns thorns and ivy creep;
    Where roses blossomed, brambles now o'erspread:
The mournful ruins bid the spirit weep;
    The broken fragments stay the passing tread.

Ye nymphs of Douro! to my words give heed;
  Behold how transient pride and glory prove;
Then, while the headlong moments urge their speed,
  Taste happiness, and try the joys of love.

HENRY WADSWORTH LONGFELLOW

ANACREONTIC

Let thunder burst,
  Pour out and drink the wine!
Thou never saw'st a thunderbolt
  Strike the tender vine.

Vesuvius himself
  To Bacchus tribute pays,
And spares the vineyard flourishing
  Where his lava sways.

In Italy in vain
  I hero sought or sage;
Mine eyes but dusty ruins found,
  Mouldering with age.

Of Rome the image scarce
  Remains to be portrayed;
A tomb is Herculaneum,
  Pompeii is a shade.

But I found Falernum,
  His nectar rich remained,
And in memory of Horace
  A bottleful I drained.

JAMES KENNEDY

DUQUE DE RIVAS
[1791–1865]

Though he was later to hold posts as an honoured statesman and diplomat of his country, Angel de Saavedra, Duque de Rivas, spent many years banished from Spain. While an exile in Malta he read the works of the great English romantics, and turned wholeheartedly to that school in his own writings.

Rivas is most famous for his sensational romantic melodrama, Don Alvaro o La fuerza del sino *(1835). Composed in prose and verse, disregarding the unities, combining fantastic, violent and passionate elements,* Don Alvaro *enjoyed overwhelming acclaim. It served as the basis for Verdi's opera* La Forza del Destino.

Besides his success as a dramatist, Rivas was Spain's outstanding romantic poet in the early years of the nineteenth century. His verse legends and historical ballads are among his best works.

ODE TO THE LIGHTHOUSE AT MALTA

The world in dreary darkness sleeps profound;
   The storm-clouds hurry on, by hoarse winds driven;
And night's dull shades and spectral mists confound
    Earth, sea, and heaven!

King of surrounding Chaos! thy dim form
   Rises with fiery crown upon thy brow,
To scatter light and peace amid the storm,
    And life bestow.

In vain the sea with thundering waves may peal
   And burst beneath thy feet in giant sport,
Till the white foam in snowy clouds conceal
    The sheltering port:

Thy flaming tongue proclaims, 'Behold the shore!'
   And voiceless hails the weary pilot back,
Whose watchful eyes, like worshippers, explore
    Thy shining track.

Now silent night a gorgeous mantle wears,—
   By sportive winds the clouds are scattered far,
And lo! with starry train the moon appears
    In circling car:

While the pale mist, that thy tall brow enshrouds,
　　In vain would veil thy diadem from sight,
Whose form colossal seems to touch the clouds
　　　With starlike light.

Ocean's perfidious waves may calmly sleep,
　　Yet hide sharp rocks,—the cliff, false signs display,—
And luring lights, far flashing o'er the deep,
　　　The ship betray.

But thou, whose splendour dims each lesser beam,—
　　Whose firm, unmoved position might declare
Thy throne a monarch's,—like the North Star's gleam,
　　　Reveal'st each snare.

So Reason's steady torch, with light as pure,
　　Dispels the gloom, when stormy passions rise,
Or Fortune's cheating phantoms would obscure
　　　The soul's dim eyes.

Since I am cast by adverse fortunes here,
　　Where thou presidest o'er this scanty soil,
And bounteous Heaven a shelter grants to cheer
　　　My spirit's toil.

Frequent I turn to thee, with homage mute,
　　Ere yet each troubled thought is calmed in sleep,
And still thy gem-like brow my eyes salute
　　　Above the deep.

How many now may gaze on this seashore,
　　Alas! like me, as exiles doomed to roam!
Some who, perchance, would greet a wife once more,
　　　Or children's home!

Wanderers, by poverty or despots driven
　　To seek a refuge, as I do, afar,
Here find, at last, the sign of welcome given,—
　　　A hospitable star!

And still, to guide the bark, it calmly shines,—
　　The bark that from my native land oft bears
Tidings of bitter griefs, and mournful lines
　　　Written with tears.

When first thy vision flashed upon my eyes,
    And all its dazzling glory I beheld,
O, how my heart, long used to miseries,
    With rapture swelled!

Inhospitable Latium's shores were lost,
    And, as amid the threatening waves we steered,
When near to dangerous shoals, by tempests tossed,
    Thy light appeared.

No saints the fickle mariners then praised,
    But vows and prayers forgot they with the night,
While from the silent gloom the cry was raised,
    'Malta in sight!'

And thou wert like a sainted image crowned,
    Whose forehead bears a shower of golden rays,
Which pilgrims, seeking health and peace, surround
    With holy praise.

Never may I forget thee! One alone
    Of cherished objects shall with thee aspire,
King of the Night! to match thy lofty throne
    And friendly fire:

That vision still with sparkling light appears
    In the sun's dazzling beams at matin hour,
And is the golden angel memory rears
    On Córdova's proud tower.

ANONYMOUS

JUAN EUGENIO HARTZENBUSCH
[1806–1880]

Hartzenbusch, Director of the National Library in his later years, was a literary scholar of international eminence. His tragedy Los amantes de Teruel *(1837), based on a well-known legend, ranks as one of the most technically perfect of the romantic dramas.*

THE LOVERS OF TERUEL

Act I

SCENE IV

Marsilla, Zulima.

MARSILLA. My name is Diego Marsilla. I was born
  In Teruel, which, founded but yesterday,
  Is now a mighty city, whose proud walls
  Amid the horrors of atrocious strife
  Were fashioned, and cemented with the blood
  Of her brave citizens. I think when God
  Decreed my birth, His purpose was to form
  A man and woman, patterns of pure love;
  So, to maintain in perfect equipoise
  Their mutual affection, first He shared
  The twin halves of a single radiant soul
  Between them both, and then said 'Live and love'.
  And at the sound of that creative voice
  My Isabel and I came into being :
  Both saw the light the selfsame day and hour.
  Already from our earliest years were we
  Devoted lovers. The very day we met,
  Before we met indeed, we loved each other.
  For love began to inflame our souls when God
  Moulded them from mere nothing, and they felt
  The quickening touch of the Creator's hand.
  And so the miracle of our young love,
  Of love made flesh before we both were born,
  Destined my Isabel and me to love,
  And to love with all our heart, as first
  With all our soul.
ZULIMA.   A passion so well matched
  Presages nought but happiness.

MARSILLA.   I am poor.
    And Isabel is rich.
ZULIMA (*aside*).   I breathe again.
MARSILLA. I had a rival.
ZULIMA.   Yes?
MARSILLA.   A man of wealth.
ZULIMA. What then . . . ?
MARSILLA.   He boasted of his riches . . .
ZULIMA.   Well?
    Did he o'ercome the lady's constancy?
MARSILLA. For one who loves, gold has but little charm.
    Her father, he indeed was dazzled . . .
ZULIMA.   And
    Refused thy suit, and robbed thee of her sight.
MARSILLA. I saw him, told him of my love, and he,
    Moved by my passionate appeal, at length
    Put off their marriage, granting me a space
    Wherein I should with my unaided arm
    Win for myself an honourable fortune.
ZULIMA. And has the time appointed now expired?
MARSILLA. Ah, lady, as thou seest . . . I am still alive.
    Six years, and six days more, were granted me.
    Today the years come to an end; tomorrow
    Ends one of six days only.
ZULIMA.   Tell me more.
MARSILLA. I bade my love farewell, who is the light
    Of my adoring eyes, went to the wars,
    And at Las Navas de Tolosa fought
    Against the Crescent. There by my brave bearing
    I won repute for a most gallant soldier.
    Next I was made a prisoner in France
    By Count de Montfort. I escaped from him.
    Then, in the Holy Land, a refugee
    From the Albigensian wars, whose life I saved
    By Béziers, dying soon, left me his heir.
    But coming back to Spain with great increase
    Of fame and fortune, I fell into the hands
    Of Moorish pirates, and was brought by them
    A captive to Valencia. With my own hands
    I burst the iron bonds that held me fast,
    And for my pains was buried dead-alive,
    Deep in a dungeon, where a mysterious guard,
    Unseen, unheard, in pity or in hate,

Prolonged my wretched life. From that foul den
You rescue me. Fair lady, I can feel
And can be grateful. Tell me, how can I
Repay the debt I owe?

ZULIMA. Bear well in mind
What thou hast rightly offered, and give heed
To this strange story thou shalt hear. One day
A youth from Aragon was brought in chains
To this harem. No need to give his name
And quality. Thou knowest whom I mean.
A woman grieves to see a noble youth
Exposed to insult and indignity.
Zulima set her eyes upon the slave,
And pity soon gave place to ardent passion.
With us, the heart's a mass of flaming fire;
With you, a lump of snow. He tried to escape.
He is caught, and by his master doomed to die.
Zulima, ever heedful for his good,
Blinded by her mad passion, saves him, nay,
She even offers him her heart and hand.
In such a vital issue, she deserves
An answer. So, do thou speak for the slave,
I will speak for Zulima.

MARSILLA. In all my life,
In poverty and in prosperity,
Deceit did never yet defile my lips.
This heart belongs to Isabel de Segura.

ZULIMA. Reflect awhile, and thou wilt grant that Time
Takes tribute from us all. How dost thou know
If she still loves thee? Art thou sure that thou
Wilt ever see her?

MARSILLA. My own constancy
Is my assurance of her steadfast love.
My life I'll gladly give, if so I must.
My soul—our souls once given in exchange—
I keep for one who claims it.

ZULIMA. 'Tis rash indeed.
To mock thy royal mistress, when thou knowest
The blood of Africa runs in her veins,
And makes her prompt alike to love and hate.
And if she knows I offer thee her heart,
And suffer for her sake the bitter pain
Of seeing thee coolly tread it underfoot,

Thou soon wilt find thyself back in thy chains
And in thy gloomy prison. There shall I,
With pleasure that shall deepen thy distress,
Bring thee the news that Isabel is married.

MARSILLA. And in so horrible a den, how long
Shall I remain alive?

ZULIMA.   Ye heavens! The wretch
Brings all my plans to nought. He hides behind
The menace of the tomb, and mocks my rage.
But soon I'll change thy laughter into tears:
They shall bring Isabel from Teruel
A captive here to me.

MARSILLA.   And who art thou
To dare so much?

ZULIMA.   Beware my wrath.

MARSILLA.   Thy wrath
Is all in vain.

ZULIMA.   Thou fool! She whom thou seest
Is not the daughter of Mervàn, she is
Zulima.

MARSILLA. You, the Sultana!

ZULIMA.   I, the Queen.

ACT II

SCENE VI

Doña Margarita, Isabel.

ISABEL (*following her mother*).   O mother,
For heaven's sake, hear me.

MARGARITA.   No : 'tis mad of you
To show this great aversion for a match
That promises such profit for us all.
You are noble, true; but then, remember well
That he who offers you his life and love
Is Don Rodrigo de Azagra, who
Holds higher rank and boasts of greater wealth.
In Aragon his family and friends
Respect him, and he shows, towards you at least,
A friendly disposition.

ISABEL.   To me he seems
Proud and revengeful.

MARGARITA. Your father thinks him fit
  To be your husband. 'Tis not right a maid
  Herself should choose her lover. Her will should be
  No other than her father's. That is how,
  These days, a marriage is arranged. And thus
  We all are wed; and thus was I.
ISABEL. Have you
  No other comfort then for my distress?
MARGARITA. I cannot listen to your stupid talk
  Of childish love. I hold no brief for folly.
  Leave me.
ISABEL.   My hopes were vain.
    (*Sobbing as she goes to withdraw.*)
MARGARITA. What! are you weeping?
ISABEL. You have not yet denied me that relief.
MARGARITA. If I refuse to hear you, Isabel,
  You must not think me cruel. I understand
  your grief, and feel for you indeed. But, child
  For four long years Marsilla has not written.
  If he is dead . . .
ISABEL. No, Mother, he still lives! . . .
  But how? Perchance he toils in chains for me,
  Weeping in Zion, or perchance he groans
  On Libyan sands. He has not wished to grieve me
  With such sad tidings. I often dwell on this,
  And fain would deem it true. I once resolved
  To train myself to banish him from mind,
  Thinking he was unfaithful, and enjoyed
  The raptures of another woman's love.
  I listened to his rival's hateful pleas,
  And steeled myself to fancy even they
  Did not offend my ears. But then, alas,
  When reason was about to rise supreme
  In boastful triumph o'er rebellious passion,
  Fond memory would recall a single sigh
  Of my long-absent lover, and suddenly
  My vaunted stronghold fell, and once again,
  The battle lost and over, Love surged in
  With all the greater force of blood and fire
  Through the defenceless tangle of my senses.
  Then I called virtue a deceitful jade,
  And weeping bitter angry tears, I swore

In my mad passion I would sooner lie
Dead in my grave than yield to this man's will,
This murderer, this my evil genius.

MARGARITA. For heaven's sake, Isabel, restrain yourself.
You little know what torture you inflict
With these wild words on your poor mother.

ISABEL.   What!
You marvel at my boldness? But when the heart
Is so exceeding full of rancour, it needs
Must burst its bounds. Not you, but the dull stone
Of these bare walls, this roof that mutely heard
The cry of my despair, this earth my tears
Might well impress, were it not even as hard
And cold as some that tread it—these, all these
I call to witness my profound distress,
For if they give no comfort, they at least
Take no offence.

MARGARITA (aside). I cannot bear to hear her.—
Oh, grieve no more, come to thy mother's arms,
Rest on this loving bosom. Learn to know me.
Let not my harsh appearance frighten thee :
'Tis a forced mask that grief fixed on my face;
But behind that, to comfort thy distress,
There lies the tender and indulgent love
Of a true mother.

ISABEL.   Mother!   (They embrace.)

MARGARITA.   I hid my love,
My tenderness, from thee . . . because I must. . . .
For fifteen years I have kept hidden here
Such store of bitterness. Oh, I have yearned
For mutual love; yet must I yearn in vain
For love, for happiness, since I put on
Horse-hair and sackcloth.

ISABEL.   Mother!

MARGARITA.   I was afraid—
I feared I might encourage thy young love,
And only to prevent it, showed myself
Severe towards thee; but night after night
Hearing thee lying groaning on thy bed,
Cursing my harshness even in thy despair,
I offered, weeping floods of silent tears,
My life to God to purchase thy repose.

ISABEL. Oh, what a happy revelation ! Heavens !
　　How unjust I have been to you ! How much
　　You must have loved me, mother of my heart !
　　Forgive me. . . . What a thrill of joy I feel,
　　Although you see me weep ! I have not known
　　Such happiness for six long years and more.
　　Consider what my sufferings must have been,
　　When I count it happiness to feel
　　This momentary respite from my pain.
　　Surely you will not let this ray of light,
　　That has illumined my afflicted soul,
　　Fade into blacker darkness than before.
　　Mother, O my dear mother, at your feet
　　A suppliant I kneel, and here I'll yield　　　　(*Kneels.*)
　　My life's last breath, unless you heed my prayers.
MARGARITA. Rise up, dear Isabel; come, dry these tears,
　　And trust me. . . . Yes, so far as in me lies. . . .
ISABEL. You see the allotted time runs to its close.
　　But three days more, three only, and the rest
　　Are nought to me, when every hope is dead.
　　My father to fulfil his solemn pledge,
　　Will at the altar freely offer him
　　The sacrifice of my enforced consent.
　　Your pleading has the power to convey
　　Conviction to his heart, whereas in me
　　Reluctance would be disrespect, a crime.
　　Mother, I see it clearly. He may well
　　Force me to wed, but let him furnish then,
　　Instead of bridal dress and jewels rare,
　　A simple shroud and cross : this is the dress,
　　This is the only jewel I shall need.
MARGARITA. No, Isabel, no, no ! Not one word more !
　　I pledge myself to speak for thee. Azagra
　　Shall never be thy lord and master. I
　　Will urge thy father to withdraw his pledge,
　　And he will heed my voice, and will prevent
　　So great a tragedy. Today I'll be—
　　What I've not been these many years—thy mother.

ACT IV

SCENE VII

Marsilla, Isabel.

MARSILLA. Merciful Heaven!

ISABEL.   Dear God!

MARSILLA.   Is it not she?

ISABEL. 'Tis he!

MARSILLA.   O my belovèd, my adored! . . .

ISABEL. Marsilla!

MARSILLA.   O my glorious love!

ISABEL.   Alas! . . .

How did you dare to set foot in this house?
If they have seen you . . . Oh, why did you come?

MARSILLA. By heaven . . . I had forgot. But, for Marsilla
To fly to Isabel, is it not enough
To wish, to long, to need to see her? Oh,
How beautiful thou seemest in my sight!
I never saw thee so magnificent. . . .
And yet these jewels and this brave attire
Fill me with vague misgiving. Cast them off,
My love; let modest woollen frocks, and flowers
Of purest white, gathered in my own garden,
Once more set off thy maiden charm : my heart
Is troubled at the sight of so much wealth.

ISABEL (aside). Unhappy man! He is beside himself.
I cannot bear his sad bewildered glance.—
Do you not understand this rich attire,
Which you can only view with loathing, means
Our separation?

MARSILLA.   God in heaven! Ah, yes,
The awful truth!

ISABEL.   I am married.

MARSILLA.   Yes, I know.
I came too late. In sight of happiness,
I reached my hand to grasp it. At my touch,
It flew away.

ISABEL.   They lied to me. They thought
That you were dead, unfaithful.

MARSILLA.   Horrible!
Infamous!

ISABEL.   I believed that you were dead.

MARSILLA. Since you were living, and your life and mine
   Are both but one, how could the life that lives
   In me be parted from you, without you?
   Together on our earthly pilgrimage
   He exiled us who with discerning hand
   Apportions joy and grief; when at the end
   Our mortal course is run, it shall be ours
   To win together our celestial home.
ISABEL. Oh, if God heard me . . .
MARSILLA.   Listen, Isabel,
   I come not to complain : 'tis useless now.
   Nor have I come to say that I might well
   Have looked for greater constancy in you,
   Better fulfilment of those tender vows
   Which, calling on the Immaculate Mother's name,
   You swore so lovingly on that last night
   When dawn forced me to leave your balcony.
   'Thy bride', you said between sobs, 'or Christ's.'
   Sweet words, that never failed to comfort me
   In all my sorrows, on the burning plains
   Of Asia, and in my captivity!
   Today, you are not my bride, nor yet the bride
   Of Christ. Tell me—'tis all I ask to know—
   Whence this amazing, this disastrous change?
   There must have been some cause.
ISABEL.   There was indeed.
MARSILLA. Great cause.
ISABEL.   Most powerful, irresistible :
   One who has loved as I have does not wed,
   Unless compelled by the most potent force
   That man can wield.
MARSILLA.   Tell me then what it is;
   Come, tell me, quickly.
ISABEL.   No. Impossible.
   You must not know it.
MARSILLA.   Yes.
ISABEL.   No.
MARSILLA.   Everything.
ISABEL. Nothing. But in my place you would have bent
   Your neck as meekly to the yoke.
MARSILLA.   Not I.
   No, Isabel. Marsilla had the strength
   To scorn a royal hand, defying death,

For one who sells her own, and hides from him
  The cause.
ISABEL (*aside*). O mother, mother!
MARSILLA.   Answer me.
ISABEL (*aside*). What shall I tell him?—Yes, I must confess. . . .
  I am guilty. What else can I do? You see
  I am another's. Forgive me. . . . Punish me (*Weeping*.)
  For being faithless. . . . Kill me, if you will. . . .
  Here on my knees I await the fatal blow.
MARSILLA. My angel, no; rather it is for me
  To kiss the ground thou treadest. Oh, rise up.
  The tears that dim with sadness those bright eyes
  Are not tears of repentance, they are tears
  Of love, full well I know, of constant love,
  Love without guile, love without spot or blemish,
  Ardent, passionate love, matching my own.
  O Isabel, is it not true? Come, tell me
  In all sincerity : my life depends
  Upon thy answer.
ISABEL.   Will you promise then
  To obey your Isabel?
MARSILLA.   Unkind, unkind!
  When did I once rebel against thy pleasure?
  Is not thy will mine too? Speak; I'll obey thee.
ISABEL. Swear it.
MARSILLA.   I swear.
ISABEL.   Well then . . . I love thee.—Go now.
MARSILLA. Ah, cruel! Didst thou fear such happiness
  Would kill me at thy feet, unless the sweet
  Were tempered with the poisoned touch of gall?
  How couldst thou link in this strange brotherhood
  Such enemies as love and banishment?
ISABEL. I am not my own mistress, as thou seest;
  I am wedded to a husband now who leaves
  His honour in my keeping, and I must
  Be faithful to him. Virtue kept our love
  Free from the stain of sin : let us preserve
  Its ermine purity. Here we shall win
  A cross, in heaven a crown of victory.
  Thine is my love, and ever will be thine,
  And in my heart I'll treasure and adore
  Thy most dear likeness. That I promise thee.

I swear it, Oh, but leave me. Go at once,
And save me from the danger of thy presence.
Be generous : save me from myself. . . .

MARSILLA.   No more!
So thou wouldst have me gone. Well then, I'll leave thee.
Courage . . . and we will part. In recompense,
In memory at least of so much pain
Borne gladly for the sake of thy dear love,
Let me, my Isabel, clasp thee this once
Within my arms. . . .

ISABEL.   Oh, let the slave fulfil
Her duty to her lord.

MARSILLA.   The embrace shall be
That of a loving brother and his sister;
Our kiss shall be such as with childlike love
In happy innocence on our mothers' laps
We exchanged so oft.

ISABEL.   Do not recall it.

MARSILLA.   Come . . .

ISABEL. No, never.

MARSILLA.   'Tis vain to oppose me.

ISABEL.   Hold, or I call. . . .

MARSILLA. For whom? For Don Rodrigo? Do not think
He will come forward at your summons. No!
He does not feed his pride in solemn state,
Filling his ears with flattering compliment.
Far from the city walls he bites the dust
Now moistened with his blood.

ISABEL.   Oh, horrible!
You have killed him?

MARSILLA.   Faithless creature! You regret it?
If I thought that, what power on earth could save him?

ISABEL. He lives then?

MARSILLA.   Yes. Thanks to my generous folly,
He lives. We both had scarce crossed swords, ere mine
Had fleshed itself so furiously in him,
That in a moment his o'erweening pride
Sank to the ground. His sword was in my power.
O cursèd skill in arms! Thrice cursèd he
Who scatters virtues that produce a crop
Of nothing but misfortunes! Away with kindness!
Henceforth I must have crimes. Your cruel words
Have goaded me to cruelty, and I

Must practise it on you. You must leave here
At once with me.

ISABEL.   No, no!

MARSILLA.   Yes, Isabel.
I mean to save you. Do you know what he—
This coward you bewail so tearfully—
Said as he fell? 'The victory is yours;
And yet my blood shall cost someone full dear.'

ISABEL. What did he mean? Oh, what . . . ?

MARSILLA.   'I'll be revenged
On Pedro, on his wife, ay, on all three.
The letters still are in my hands.'

ISABEL.   Ah, God!

MARSILLA. What letters did he mean?

ISABEL.   You have ruined me!
Misfortune dogs your steps. Where is my husband?
Tell me at once, that as a faithful wife
I may make haste to help him, and o'ercome
His anger with my prayers.

MARSILLA.   God help me! And,
She said she loved me!

ISABEL.   What! You dare reproach
Azagra's wife, vengeful Azagra's wife,
With her unhappy love? Oh, I hate you!   (*Exit.*)

SCENE VIII

MARSILLA. Good God! From her own lips! In anger too!
I am not deceived. There is no love left here.
The deadly poisonous words she flung at me
Sink in my tortured bosom and consume
My throbbing, bursting heart. With her, through her,
For her sweet sake I lived. . . . Oh, without her,
Without her love, I cannot breathe. To me
Her love became the very breath of life!
She has refused it, she has taken it from me:
I cannot breathe, I cannot live.

VOICES (*within*).   In there!
Surround the house.

SCENE IX

Isabel, *hurrying back in great agitation*. Marsilla.

ISABEL.   Fly, they are coming, fly.

MARSILLA (*quite overcome*). I cannot.

VOICES (*within*). Death to him, death!

ISABEL. Come quick, come quick.

MARSILLA. God help me!

(Isabel *seizes his hand and drags him through the door at the back of the stage.*)

SCENE X

Adel, *pursued by various Gentlemen with drawn swords;* Don Pedro, Doña Margarita. *Servants.* Isabel *and* Marsilla *within.*

GENTLEMEN. Death to him!

Death to him!

PEDRO and MARGARITA. Listen.

ADEL. Men of Aragon,
I slew the Moorish Queen; but know, the King,
Her lord and master, sent me from Valencia
To take and kill her. She, a faithless wife,
A wicked trafficker in love, conspired
Marsilla's death, Isabel's too. . . .

ISABEL (*within*). Ah, woe
Is me!

ADEL. In proof behold this poisoned blade.

(*Showing Zulima's dagger.*)

Marsilla will confirm what I have said:
He must be somewhere here.

(*The door at the back opens, and* Isabel *comes forward and throws herself in her mother's arms.* Marsilla *is seen lying across a couch.*)

ISABEL. My darling mother!

ADEL. Behold him there. . . .

MARGARITA. Ah, God!

PEDRO. Motionless. . . .

ISABEL. Dead!

ADEL. Zulima then has wreaked her cruel vengeance.

ISABEL. No! Not the vengeance of the Moorish Queen
Has killed him. I being there, who would have dared
To touch him? No! My ill-starred love, that was
His very life . . . his own disastrous love . . .
'Twas this that killed him. Beside myself with wrath,
I said to him 'I hate you'. He believed
That sacrilegious word, and died of grief.

MARGARITA. Merciful Heaven!

ISABEL.   Yes, Heaven that parted us
   In life, will re-unite us in the grave.
PEDRO. My daughter!
ISABEL.   See, Marsilla signifies
   My place is by his side.
MARGARITA.   Isabel!
PEDRO.   Isabel!
ISABEL. My love, forgive those fatal angry words.
   I loved thee. I was thine. Thine I remain.
   In quest of thee my loving spirit hies.

   (*Goes towards* Marsilla's *body, but before reaching it, falls
     lifeless, with her arms outstretched towards her lover.*)

HENRY THOMAS

JOSÉ DE ESPRONCEDA
[1808–1842]

The stormy life of José de Espronceda, the greatest lyric poet of the romantic period, in itself exemplified the spirit of romanticism. A tortured soul, ever rebelling, he battled his way through exile from Spain for political activity, the Parisian barricade fighting of 1830, Spanish revolutionary struggles in 1835 and 1836, and a host of other freedom-seeking causes. His brief, trouble-streaked years—he died at thirty-four—held one great love: Teresa Mancha, who deserted husband and family for him. Their frequent separations brought bitterness to both; their raptures inspired some of Espronceda's most gripping poetry.

Himself a social outcast by choice and romantic inclination, he often in his short poems describes others beyond the pale of society: the beggar, the criminal, the executioner, the pirate. His two longest works are El estudiante de Salamanca, *on the Don Juan theme, and* El diablo mundo, *an extraordinary attempt to synthesize the struggle of humanity.*

Espronceda's poetry is generally tinged by rebellion, melancholy and despair. But every line rings with innate rhythm. This musical quality is most evident in his famous Canción del pirata.

PIRATE'S SONG

With cannon ten on port and starboard,
Wind just aft and strong,
Flying the sea, not ploughing through,
A brigantine skims along.
    She is called the *Dreaded* by a host
And feared on every side,
From the eastern to the western coast,
Wherever she may ride.

    Across the sea the moonlight shines,
The wind goes wailing through,
Shrill in the canvas, ruffling waves
Of silver and of blue.
    There on the poop the captain sings
By whom the band is led,
With Asia left and Europe right
And Istambul ahead.

Sail on, swift bark, at my command,
  So brave and bold,
No warship by your foemen manned,
Nor storm, nor calm, nor any force
Shall turn you from your chosen course
Nor daunt your hardy soul.

    A score of ships
    We've seized aright
    And this despite
    The English fleet.
    And I have forced
    A hundred lords
    To lay their swords
    Beneath my feet.

My only treasure a pirate ship,
My god but liberty,
My law, brute force and a hearty wind,
My land, the open sea.

Kings are plunging into war,
  Unseeing fools,
To fight for land, for a trifle more,
While anything that sails the sea
Belongs by my own laws to me,
Unchecked by others' rules.

    There nowhere lies
    A foreign land
    Or distant strand
    That does not feel,
    Whate'er its flag,
    My crushing might,
    Admit my right,
    And to me yield.

My only treasure a pirate ship . . .

The cry, 'A ship !' is a sudden threat.
  Watch them veer.
See how fast, full canvas set,
In desperate fright they try to flee :
I am king of all the sea,
My wrath inspires their fear.

The spoils of war
That raids provide
I then divide
With justice fine,
Unless I claim
Some damsel rare,
Surpassing fair,
And make her mine.

My only treasure a pirate ship . . .

And I have been condemned to die !
  I laugh at that.
Upon good fortune I rely,
And hope to hang him by the neck,
Perhaps from a yardarm on his deck,
Who sentenced me to die.

If I should fall,
If life's the cost?
I'd count well lost
The life I gave.
I knew the risk
Yet with one stroke
Cast off the yoke
That held me slave.

My only treasure a pirate ship . . .

Melodies in the winds abound :
  I love to hear
The cables' splashing, scraping sound,
The roar and bark of the loud Black Sea,
The crash of the cannon's battery,
Delightful to my ear.

Rolls of thunder
Snap and growl
And seawinds howl
Across the deep.
I am calmed
As sounds grow dulled,
And by them lulled
I drift to sleep.

My only treasure a pirate ship,
My god but liberty,
My law, brute force and a hearty wind,
My land, the open sea.

ALICE JANE MᶜVAN

THE CONDEMNED TO DIE

I

His form upon the ground reclined,
    With bitter anguish inward drawn,
Full of the coming day his mind
    That soon will sadly dawn,
The culprit waits, in silence laid,
    The fatal moments hastening now,
In which his last sun's light display'd
    Will shine upon his brow.

O'er crucifix and altar there,
    The chapel cell in mourning hung,
From the dim candle's yellow glare
    A funeral light is flung;
And by the wretched culprit's side,
    His face with hood half cover'd o'er,
The friar, with trembling voice to guide,
    Is heard his prayers implore.

His brow then raises he again,
    And slowly lifts to heaven his eyes;
Perhaps a prayer for mercy fain
    May in his grief arise.
A tear flows : whence had that release?
    Was it from bitterness or fear?
Perhaps his sorrows to increase
    Some thought to memory dear?

So young! and life, that he had dream'd
    Was full of golden days to glide,
Is pass'd, when childhood's tears it seem'd
    As scarcely yet were dried.
Then on him of his childhood burst
    The thought, and of his mother's woe,
That he whom she so fondly nursed
    Was doom'd that death to know.

And while that hopelessly he sees
   His course already death arrest,
He feels his life's best energies
   Beat strongly in his breast;
And sees that friar, who calmly now
   Is laid, with sleep no more to strive,
With age so feebly doom'd to bow,
   Tomorrow will survive.

But hark! what noise that silence breaks
   This hour unseasonably by?
Some one a gay guitar awakes
   And mirthful songs reply;
And shouts are raised, and sounds are heard
   Of bottles rattling, and perchance
Others, remember'd well, concurr'd
   Of lovers in the dance.
And then he hears funereal roll,
   Between each pause in accents high,
'Your alms, for prayers to rest the soul
   Of him condemn'd to die.'

And so combined the drunkard's shout,
   The toast, the strifes, and fancies wild
Of all that Bacchanalian rout,
   With wanton's songs defiled,
And bursts of idle laughter, reach
   Distinct into the gloomy cell,
And seem far off ejected each
   The very sounds of hell.
And then he hears, funereal roll
   Between each pause, those accents high,
'Your alms, for prayers to rest the soul
   Of him condemn'd to die.'
He cursed them all, as one by one
   The impious echoes each express'd;

He cursed the mother as a son
   Who nursed him at her breast:
The whole world round alike he cursed,
   His evil destiny forlorn,
And the dark day and hour when first
   That wretched he was born.

II

The moon serene illumes the skies,
And earth in deepest stillness lies;
No sound is heard, the watchdog's mute,
And even the lover's plaintive lute.

Madrid enveloped lies in sleep;
    Repose o'er all its shade has cast,
And men of him no memory keep
    Who soon will breathe his last.
Or if perchance one thinks to wake
    At early dawn, no thoughts whate'er
Rise for the wretched being's sake,
    Who death is waiting there.
Unmoved by pity's kind control,
    Men hear around the funeral cry,
'Your alms, for prayers to rest the soul
    Of him condemn'd to die.'

Sleeps in his bed the judge in peace;
    And sleeps and dreams of how his store,
The executioner, to increase;
    And pleased he counts it o'er.
Only the city's silence breaks,
    And destined place of death portrays,
The harden'd workman who awakes
    The scaffolding to raise.

III

Confused and mad his heated mind,
With raving feverish dreams combined,
The culprit's soul exhaustion press'd,
His head sunk heavy on his breast.

And in his dreams he life and death
    Confounds, remembers, and forgets;
And fearful struggling every breath,
    And sigh he gives besets.

And in a world of darkness seems
   As now to stray; feels fear and cold,
And in his horrid madness deems
   The cord his neck infold :
And so much more, in desperate fight,
   In anguish to escape his lot,
He strives, with so much more the might
   He binds the fatal knot :
And voices hears, confused the whole,
   Of people round, and then that cry,
'Your alms, for prayers to rest the soul
   Of him condemn'd to die !'

Or fancies now that he is free;
   And breathes the fresh pure air, and hears
Her sigh of love, the maid whom he
   Had loved in happier years :
Beauteous and kind as e'er of old,
   Sweet flower of spring-time's gay resort,
As could for love the meads behold,
   Or gallant April court.

And joyful he to see her flies,
   And seeks to reach her, but in vain;
For as with anxious hands he tries
   His hoped-for bliss to gain,
The illusion suddenly to break,
   He finds the dream deceitful fled !
A cold stiff corpse the shape to take,
   And scaffold in its stead.
And hears the mournful funeral knoll,
   And hollow voice resounding nigh,
'Your alms, for prayers to rest the soul
   Of him condemn'd to die !'

                JAMES KENNEDY

TO HARIFA, IN AN ORGY

Thy hand, Harifa ! bring it me;
   Come near, and place it on my brow;
As on some lava's boiling sea
   I feel my head is burning now.

Come, bring with mine thy lips to meet,
    Though they but madden me astray,
Where yet I find the kisses beat,
    There left thy loves of yesterday.
What is virtue, what is joy,
    Or love, or purity, or truth?
The false illusions of a boy,
    The cherish'd flatteries of my youth.
Then bring me wine; there let me try
    Remembrance drown'd to hold repress'd,
Without a pang from life to fly;
    In frenzy death may give me rest.

O'erspreads my face a burning flood,
    And red and glaring wildly start
My eyes forth out in heated blood,
    And forth leaps restlessly my heart.
Woman! I hate thee; fly thee—go :
    I feel thy hands my hands infold,
And feel them freezing, cold as snow,
    As snow thy kisses are as cold.

Ever the same, try, tempters weak !
    Other endearments to enthral;
Another world, new pleasures seek,
    For such your joys I curse them all.
Your kisses are a lie; a cheat
    Is all the tenderness you feign;
Your beauty ugly in deceit,
    The enjoyment suffering and pain.

I wish for love, ethereal, high,
    For some diviner joy my lot;
For such my heart will imaged sigh,
    For such as in the world is not.
And 'tis that meteor light afar,
    The phantom that deceived my mind,
The treacherous guide, the vapour star,
    That leads me wandering and blind.

Why is my soul for pleasure dead,
    And yet alive to grief and care?
Why doom'd in listless stupor laid
    This arid loathing still to bear?

Why this consuming wild desire,
 This restless passion vague and strange?
That well I know I rave, 'tis fire,
 Yet plunge in its deceitful range.

Why do I dream of love and joy,
 That I am sure a lie will prove?
Why where fantastic charms decoy,
 Will thus my heart delirious move,
If soon it finds for meads and flowers,
 But arid wastes and tangled thorns,
And soon a loathing rage o'erpowers
 The mad or mournful love it scorns?

Flung as a rapid comet wide,
 On ardent fancy's wings I flew,
Where'er my wayward mind espied
 Or joys or triumphs to pursue.
I launch'd myself, in daring flight,
 Beyond the world through heavenward space,
And found but doubt, and all so bright
 That seem'd, illusive proved the chase.

Then on the earth I anxious sought
 For virtue, glory, love sublime;
And my worn spirit found there nought
 But fetid dust and loathsome slime.
Mid clouds with heavenly hues o'ercast
 Women of virgin lustre shone;
I saw, I touch'd them, and they pass'd,
 And smoke and ashes left alone.

I found the illusion fled; but rife,
 Unquench'd desires their longings crave;
I felt the real, I hated life,
 And peace believed but in the grave.
And yet I seek, and anxious seek,
 For pleasures still I ask and sigh,
And hear dread accents answering speak,
 'Unhappy one! despair, and die.

'Die : Life is a torment, joy a cheat,
 Hope not for good on earth for thee,
But fruitless struggles look to meet
 In thy vain longings endlessly!

For so God punishes the soul
      That in its madness dares espy
The unfathom'd secrets of the scroll
      Of truth, denied to mortal eye !'

O ! cease : no more I ask to know,
      No more to see : my soul oppress'd
Is humbly bow'd, and prostrate low,
      Now only asks, and longs for rest.
In me let feeling then lie dead,
      Since died my hopes of happiness,
Nor joys nor griefs be o'er me spread
      My soul returning to depress.

Pass, as in magic optic glass,
      And other youthful hearts deceive,
Bright images of glory ! pass,
      That crowns of gold and laurel weave.
Pass, ye voluptuous fair ones, on !
      With dance and mirthful songs attuned,
Like vaporous visions, pass, begone !
      No more my heart to move or wound.
And let the dance, and festal din,
      O'er my revolted fancy reign,
And fled the night, see morn begin,
      Surprised in senseless stupor's chain.

Harifa, come ! Like me this woe
      Thou too hast borne ! Thou ne'er dost weep !
But, ah ! how wretched 'tis to know
      Feelings so bitter and so deep !
The same our sufferings and care;
      In vain thou hold'st thy tears apart;
Like me thou also hast to bear
      A wounded and an aching heart !

JAMES KENNEDY

JOSÉ ZORRILLA
[1817–1893]

José Zorrilla, Spain's exceedingly popular romantic poet, wrote with an easy and instinctive brilliance; words cascaded from his pen in a stunning melodic flow. His excellent leyendas, *stemming from Spanish traditions and tales, helped earn for him the title 'el poeta nacional'. Zorrilla is equally famous for his religious-romantic drama* Don Juan Tenorio (1844), *based on Tirso de Molina's often-imitated* El burlador de Sevilla (1630). *The success of Zorrilla's play, in which Don Juan attains salvation, has exceeded that of any other Spanish dramatic work. For more than a century it has been unfailingly presented during the first week of November in almost all Spanish theatres.*

BOABDIL

Lady of the dark head-dress,
    And monkish vest of purple hue,
Gladly would Boabdil give
    Granada for a kiss of you.

He would give the best adventure
    Of the bravest horseman tried,
And with all its verdant freshness
    A whole bank of Darro's tide.

He would give rich carpets, perfumes,
    Armours of rare price and force,
And so much he values you,
    A troop, ay, of his favourite horse.

'Because thine eyes are beautiful,
    Because the morning's blushing light
From them arises to the East,
    And gilds the whole world bright.

'From thy lips smiles are flowing,
    From thy tongue gentle peace,
Light and aerial as the course
    Of the purple morning's breeze.

'O! lovely Nazarene, how choice!
   For an Eastern harem's pride,
Those dark locks waving freely
   Thy crystal neck beside.

'Upon a couch of velvet,
   In a cloud of perfumed air,
Wrapp'd in the white and flowing veil
   Of Mahomet's daughters fair.

'O, Lady! come to Cordova,
   There Sultana thou shalt be,
And the Sultan there, Sultana,
   Shall be but a slave for thee.

'Such riches he will give thee,
   And such robes of Tunisine,
That thou wilt judge thy beauty,
   To repay him for them, mean.'

    .   .   .

O! Lady of the dark head-dress!
That him a kiss of thee might bless,
   Resign a realm Boabdil would!
But I for that, fair Christian, fain
Would give of heavens, and think it gain,
   A thousand if I only could.

JAMES KENNEDY

THE CHRISTIAN LADY AND THE MOOR

Hastening to Granada's gates,
   Came o'er the Vega's land,
Some forty Gomel horsemen,
   And the Captain of the band.

He, entering in the city,
   Check'd his white steed's career;
And to a lady on his arm,
   Borne weeping many a tear,

Said, 'Cease your tears, fair Christian,
   That grief afflicting me,
I have a second Eden,
   Sultana, here for thee.

'A palace in Granada,
   With gardens and with flowers,
And a gilded fountain playing
   More than a hundred showers.

'And in the Henil's valley
   I have a fortress grey,
To be among a thousand queen
   Beneath thy beauty's sway.

'For over all yon winding shore
   Extends my wide domain,
Nor Cordova's, nor Seville's lands,
   A park like mine contain.

'There towers the lofty palm-tree,
   The pomegranate's glowing there,
And the leafy fig-tree, spreading
   O'er hill and valley fair.

'There grows the hardy walnut,
   The yellow nopal tall,
And mulberry darkly shading
   Beneath the castle wall;

'And elms I have in my arcades
   That to the skies aspire,
And singing birds in cages
   Of silk, and silver wire.

'And thou shalt my Sultana be,
   My halls alone to cheer;
My harem without other fair,
   Without sweet songs my ear.

'And velvets I will give thee,
   And eastern rich perfumes,
From Greece I'll bring thee choicest veils,
   And shawls for Cashmere's looms :

'And I will give thee feathers white,
   To deck thy beauteous brow,
Whiter than ev'n the ocean foam
   Our eastern waters know.

'And pearls to twine amid thy hair,
    Cool baths when heat's above,
And gold and jewels for thy neck,
    And for thy lips be—love!'

'O! what avail those riches all,'
    Replied the Christian fair,
'If from my father and my friends,
    My ladies, me you tear?

'Restore me, O! restore me, Moor,
    To my father's land, my own;
To me more dear are Leon's towers
    Than thy Granada's throne.'

Smoothing his beard, awhile the Moor
    In silence heard her speak;
Then said as one who deeply thinks,
    With a tear upon his cheek,

'If better seem thy castle there,
    Than here our gardens shine,
And thy flowers are more beautiful,
    Because in Leon thine;

'And thou hast given thy youthful love
    One of thy warriors there,
Houri of Eden! weep no more,
    But to thy knights repair!'

Then giving her his chosen steed,
    And half his lordly train,
The Moorish chieftain turn'd him back
    In silence home again.

                          JAMES KENNEDY

ORIENTAL

Seen in moonlight's silver ray,
    Far away,
Gleams an Arab tower tall,
And the Darro's water clear,
    Flowing near,
Break against its wall.

Elms that murmur o'er the river,
Leaves aquiver,
Restful solace bring.
In the reeds and in the cane,
Soft refrain
Fleeting breezes sing.

Flowers on the yellow sand
Along the strand
Perfumes sweet exhale.
Hovering with plumage rare,
O'er flowers fair
Wings the nightingale.

Dewdrops falling brightly shine,
Crystalline,
Silvery pearls aglimmer.
Mirrored in the drops of dew,
Rainbow hue,
Moorish turrets shimmer.

Jalousies are opened wide
While inside
The fair Sultana sings.
From her fretted tower's height,
Through the night,
Clear the music rings.

Freely through the ambient air,
Everywhere,
Floats her mournful song.
Lost in grasses far below
Strong winds blow
Bearing it along.

And in time to her soft cry,
Lilting high,
A linnet's answer rings
Flitting through the garden's maze,
Where ablaze,
Many a tulip springs.

To the sound of that sweet trill,
Echoing still,
Of beauty, bird, and lyre,

Elm and field and lovely flower,
Lofty tower,
Listening never tire.

To the Moorish maid's lament
The linnet sent
Answering reply.
This the jealous Moor could hear,
Listening near,
Where dark shadows lie.

'A Moorish heart is mine to hold,
Pearls and gold,
Crowns that richly gleam.
Tell me, flower, what I miss
Of loveliness
In this sad hareem.

'Rugs the Caliphs give and shawls;
In these vast halls
Garlands rare are seen.
Tell me, garden, what I miss
Of loveliness
In this sad hareem.

'Festivals and gardens gay,
Where waters play,
In Eden false I dream.
Tell me, river, what I miss
Of loveliness
In this sad hareem.

'Feathers light as foam on sea
They give to me,
Veils that cobwebs seem.
Tell me what I still bewail,
Nightingale,
In this sad hareem.

'Smooth my forehead is from care,
And unaware
My eyes of sorrow's theme.
Tell me, pale moon, what I miss
Of loveliness
In this sad hareem.'

Where the lamplight's fitful glow
Burns most low,
A shadow passes by.
She hears the Sultan softly glide
To her side,
Murmuring reply.

'You have gold and towers bright,
Pearls so white,
Wreaths for your forehead pale.
Say what in this pleasant bourne
You still mourn,
In what gift I fail.

'Dusky garden, flying bird,
River heard
Swiftly flowing on,
What do all of these possess
Of happiness
That I'd not bring at dawn?

'What mad fancies are there still
To fulfil,
What lacks your beauty fair?'
'Alas, my Lord, these nightingales
In flowery vales
Have *liberty and air*.'

ELIZABETH DU GUÉ TRAPIER

MANUEL BRETÓN DE LOS HERREROS
[1796–1873]

Bretón de los Herreros was a facile, light poet and a prolific author of popular comedies of manners. Like his contemporary, Hartzenbusch, he served at one time as Director of the National Library.

SATIRICAL LETRILLA III

Such is, dear girl, my tenderness,
   Naught can its equal be!
If thou a dowry didst possess
The charms to rival of thy face,
   I would marry thee.

Thou wert my bliss, my star, my all!
   So kind and fair to see;
And me thy consort to install,
At once for witness Heaven I call,
   I would marry thee.

Thou dost adore me? yes, and I,
   Thy love so raptures me,
If thou wouldst not so anxious try
To know my pay, and what I buy,
   I would marry thee.

If thou wert not so always coy,
   Ne'er listening to my plea,
But when I, fool! my cash employ
To bring thee sweets, or some fine toy,
   I would marry thee.

If thou must not instructions wait,
   As may mamma agree,
To write or speak to me, or state
When thou wilt meet me at the gate,
   I would marry thee.

If 'twere not when to dine, the most
   Thy meagre soup bouillie
Thou givest, as many airs thou show'st,
As Roderic at the hanging-post
   I would marry thee.

If for my punishment instead
　Of ease and quiet, we
Might not three hungry brothers dread,
And mother too, to keep when wed,
　I would marry thee.

If 'twere not when these plagues combine
　With thy tears flowing free,
The virtues of a heavenly sign
I see must solace me, not thine,
　I would marry thee.

Go, get another in thy chain,
　And Heaven for you decree
A thousand joys, for me 'tis vain;
I know thee cheat, and tell thee plain,
　I will not marry thee.

JAMES KENNEDY

SATIRICAL LETRILLA IV

Whene'er Don Juan has a feast at home
I am forgotten as if at Rome;
But he will for funerals me invite,
To kill me with the annoyance quite;
Well, be it so!

Cœleste, with a thousand coy excuses
Will sing the song that set she chooses,
And all about her that environ,
Though like an owl, call her a siren;
Well, be it so!

A hundred bees, without reposing,
Work their sweet combs, with skill composing;
Alas! for an idle drone they strive,
Who soon will come to destroy the hive;
Well, be it so!

Man to his like moves furious war,
As if he were too numerous far;
Alone the medical squadrons wait
The world itself to depopulate;
Well, be it so!

There are of usurers heaps in Spain,
Of catchpoles, hucksterers, heaps again,
And of vintners too, yet people still
Talk about robbers in the hill;
Well, be it so !

In vain may the poor, O Conde, try
Thy door, for the dog makes sole reply;
And yet to spend thou hast extollers,
Over a ball two thousand dollars;
Well, be it so !

Enough today, my pen, this preaching;
A better time we wait for teaching;
If vices in vain I try to brand,
And find I only write on sand,
Well, be it so !

                                        JAMES KENNEDY

FERNÁN CABALLERO
[1796–1877]

Fernán Caballero is the pseudonym of Cecilia Böhl de Faber, daughter of a famous German Hispanist and a Spanish mother. Though born in Switzerland and educated in Germany, she spent most of her life in Andalusia and made a careful study of its traditions and customs. This background of folklore constitutes one of the chief merits of her many novels and short stories.

She is generally considered to have initiated the revival of the realistic novel in Spain. Her first and finest novel, La Gaviota, *appeared in 1849. The title, which means 'Seagull', was a term applied to the heroine, María, because of her temperamental character.*

LA GAVIOTA

THE DEATH OF PEPE VERA

. . . Maria began to weep.

'Come!' replied Pepe, 'dry your tears, the *refugium peccatorum* of women. You know the proverb which says, "Make a woman weep, and you vanquish her"; but, my beautiful, there is another proverb, "Confide not either in the barking of dogs, or in the tears of women." Keep your tears for the theatre; here we do not play comedy. Look well to yourself. If you deceive me, you make me incur the danger of death; I do not prove my love by the recipes of the apothecary, nor by dollars. I am not satisfied with grimaces, I must have acts. If you do not come this afternoon to the bull-fight you will repent of it.'

And Pepe Vera went away, without even saying *Adios* to his mistress. He was at that moment borne down by two opposite feelings which required iron nerves to conceal them, as he did, under appearances the most tranquil, under a countenance the most calm, and the most perfect indifference.

He had studied the bulls he was about to fight with; never had he seen any so ferocious. One of them strangely preoccupied him; as often happens to men of his profession, who, without caring for the other bulls, believe themselves saved if they can conquer the one which causes their anxiety. Besides, he was jealous. Jealous! he who knew only how to vanquish, and be cheered by bravos. He was told that they mocked him, and in a few hours he went to find himself between life and death, between love and treason. At least he believed so.

When he had quitted Maria, she tore the lace trimmings of her bed, unjustly scolded Marina, and shed abundance of tears. Then she dressed herself, called one of her maids, and went with her to the bull-fight, where she seated herself in the box which Pepe had reserved for her.

The noise and the heat increased her fever. Her cheeks, ordinarily pale, were inflamed, and a feverish ardour shone in her large black eyes. Anger, indignation, jealousy, offended pride, terror, anxiety, physical pain, combined in vain to force a complaint, even a sigh, from that mouth closed like a tomb. Pepe Vera perceived her : he smiled; but his smile in no way moved the Gaviota, who, under her icy countenance, swore to revenge her wounded vanity.

One bull had already bitten the dust, under the blow of another *toreador*. This bull had been *good* : he had been well fought.

The trumpet again sounded. The *toril* opened its narrow and sombre door, and a bull, black as night, dashed into the arena.

'It is *Medianoche* !' cried the crowd.

Medianoche was the *bull of the corrida*; that is to say, the king of the *fête*.

Medianoche was in no way like an ordinary bull, who at once seeks his liberty, his fields, and his deserts. He would, before every thing, show them they were not playing with a contemptible enemy; he would revenge himself, and punish. At the noise made by the cries of the crowd, he stopped suddenly.

There is not the least doubt of the bull being a stupid animal. Nevertheless, whether it be the sharp anger, or intelligence the most rebellious, whether it be that he has the faculty to render clear instincts the most blind; it is the fact that some bulls can divine and baffle the most secret ruses of the course. The *picadores* attracted, at first, the attention of the bull. He charged the one he found nearest to him, and felled him to the earth; he did the same with the second, without leaving the spot, without the lance being able to arrest him, and which inflicted but a slight wound. The third *picador* shared the fate of his comrades.

Medianoche, his horns and front bloody, raised his head towards the seats whence came cries of admiration at such bravery.

The *chulos* conveyed the *picadores* outside the arena. One of them had a broken leg; they took him to the infirmary, and the other two changed their horses.

A new *picador* replaced the wounded, and while the *chulos* occupied the attention of the bull, the three *picadores* resumed their places, their lances in rest.

The bull divided them, and after a combat of two minutes all three were overthrown. One had fainted from having his head cut open; the furious animal attacked the horse, whose lacerated body served as a shield to the unfortunate cavalier.

There was then a moment of profound stupefaction. The *chulos* searched in vain, at the risk of their lives, to turn aside *Media-noche*, who appeared to have a thirst for blood, and quenched his rage upon his victim.

At this terrible moment a *chulo* rushed towards the animal, and covered his head with his cloak. His success was of short duration.

The bull disengaged himself promptly; he made the aggressor fly, and pursued him; but, in his blind fury, he passed him; the *chulo* had thrown himself on the ground. When the animal suddenly turned round, for he was one of those who never abandon their prey, the nimble *chulo* had already risen, and leaped the barrier amid the acclamations of the enthusiastic crowd for so much courage and agility.

All this had passed with the rapidity of light. The heroic devotion with which the *toreros* aid and defend each other, is the only thing really noble and beautiful displayed in these cruel, immoral, inhuman *fêtes*, which are a real anachronism in our times, so much vaunted as an age of light.

The bull, full of the pride of triumph, walked about as master of the arena. A sentiment of terror pervaded all the spectators.

Various opinions were expressed. Some wished that the *cabestro* (the bull who leads the troop . . .) be let into the arena, to lead out the formidable animal, as much to avoid new misfortunes as to preserve the propagation of his valiant race. They sometimes have recourse to this measure; but it frequently happens that the bull withdrawn does not survive the inflammation of blood which had provoked the fight. Others insisted that his tendons be cut, thus killing the bull easily. Unfortunately the greatest number cried out that it would be a crime not to see so beautiful a bull killed according to all the rules of art.

The alcalde did not know which party to side with. To preside over a bull-fight is not an easy thing.

At last, that which happens in all similar cases occurred in this : victory was with those who cried the loudest, and it was decided that the powerful and terrible *Medianoche* should die according to rule, and in possession of all his means of defence.

Pepe Vera then appeared in the arena, armed for the combat. He saluted the authorities, placed himself before Maria, and offered her the *brindo*—the honour of the bull. He was pale.

Maria, her countenance on fire, her eyes darting from their sockets, breathed with difficulty. Her body bent forward, her nails forced into the velvet cushions of her box, she contemplated this young man, so beautiful, so calm before death, and whom she loved. She felt a power in his love which subjugated her, which made her tremble and weep; because that this brutal and tyrannical passion, this exchange of profound affection, impassioned and exclusive, was the love which she felt : as with certain men of a special organization, who require in place of sweet liqueurs and fine wines the powerful excitement of alcoholic drinks.

Everywhere reigned the most profound silence. A gloomy presentiment seemed to agitate every soul. Many arose and left the place.

The bull himself, now in the middle of the arena, appeared valiant; he proudly defied his adversary.

Pepe Vera chose the spot which seemed to him the most favourable, with his habitual calm and self-possessed manner; and designated it to the *chulos*, by pointing with his finger.

'Here !' he said to them.

The *chulos* sprang out like rockets in a display of fireworks; the bull had not for an instant the idea of pursuing them. They disappeared. *Medianoche* found himself face to face with the *matador*.

The situation did not last long. The bull precipitated himself with a rapidity so sudden, that Pepe had not time to put himself on guard. All he could do was to dodge the first attack of his adversary. But the animal, contrary to the habits of those of his species, took a sudden spring, and turning suddenly, he came like a clap of thunder on the *matador*, caught him on his horns, furiously shook his head, and threw at a distance from him the body of Pepe Vera, which fell like an inert mass upon the ground of the arena.

A cry, such as the imagination of Dante alone could conceive, broke forth from a thousand human breasts, a cry profound, mournful, prolonged, and terrific.

The *picadores* rushed towards the bull to prevent his returning to his victim. The *chulos* also surrounded him.

'The *medias lunas* ! the *medias lunas* !' (long partisans by which sometimes the tendons are cut) cried the crowd.

The alcalde repeated the cry of the crowd.

Then were seen to appear these terrible weapons, and soon

Medianoche had his tendons cut; he was red with rage and with pain.

At last he fell under the ignoble poniard of the horse-killer.

The *chulos* raised up the body of Pepe Vera.

'Dead!'

Such was the cry which escaped from the lips of the group of *chulos*; and which, passing from mouth to mouth throughout the vast amphitheatre, brought mourning to all hearts. . . .

J. LEANDER STARR

MANUEL TAMAYO Y BAUS
[1829–1898]

Manuel Tamayo y Baus, one of the best Spanish dramatists of the nineteenth century, wrote many successful plays on a variety of themes—classic, romantic, historical, realistic. His masterpiece is the tragedy Un drama nuevo (1867). This work, in one sense, is of special interest to English-speaking readers since William Shakespeare and his acting troupe are the characters.

A NEW DRAMA

Characters

Yorick, comedian in Shakespeare's company.
Alice, his wife.
Edmund, his foster-son.
Shakespeare.
Walton, tragedian.

The scene is London, 1605

ACT I

A room in Yorick's house.

SCENE II

YORICK. 'It is so easy to cause laughter,' they said to me last night —Walton and the rest. They'll see right soon that when the time comes I can bring tears as well. They'll see it and they'll storm; when I, no more with mirth, but now with tragic passions, compel the public's bravos and applause. (*He takes from the top of the table the manuscript.*) None the less, one must proceed with plentiful caution, because the blessed rôle of Count Octavio is just a trifle difficult, and at the slightest stumbling one might take a fall and destroy himself.

'Tremble, thou faithless spouse ! . . .'

(*Reading in the manuscript.*) Here's where the big scene comes. One Signor Rodolfo or Pandolfo . . . Landolfo, Landolfo is his name,—(*Finding this name in the manuscript*),—a sly knave, delivers to the Count a letter which proves that Manfredo, to whom he has been a father, is the lover of his wife, the enchanting Beatrice. The Count was jealous of every living creature except this fine young squire; and when at last his house of cards comes tumbling about his ears, he is left, poor fellow, as stupefied as if the world were falling on him.

'Tremble, thou faithless spouse ! thou ingrate, tremble !
Destroyer of my honour and my peace !
Vain was thy craft—behold the damning proof !

(*He opens the letter.*)

My blood is freezing.

(*Without daring to look at the letter.*)

Let it flame with wrath !
Woe be to him—the infamous wretch—for whom
Thou blindly dost defile me.
Alas ! what do I see ! A thousand devils !'

(*He fixes his glance on the letter, gives a horrible cry, and falls on a bench as though struck by lightning.*) (*From 'Tremble, thou faithless spouse' up to this point, reading in the manuscript; the stage directions in a tone different from that of the verses.*) Now to see how I manage that yell. (*He takes an affectedly tragic attitude, doubles up the manuscript so that it may serve as a letter, and declaims stupidly with ridiculous intonation.*)

'Woe be to him—the infamous wretch—for whom
Thou blindly dost defile me.
Alas ! what do I see ! . . .'

(*Giving a discordant yell.*) No . . . 'tis true, I do it less than perfectly yet.—'Oh !' (*Giving a yell worse than before.*) Bad, unconscionably bad; 'tis thus one yells when someone treads upon his foot.—'Oh !' (*Yelling again.*) Nay, no human noise that—'tis the croaking of some great bird. Bah ! Later with the heat of the situation . . . Let's see here . . .

'So then, 'tis thou who art the villain. . . .'

Too weak.

'So then, 'tis thou who art the villain. . . .'

Too strong.

    'So then, 'tis thou who art the villain. . . .'

Nay, the villain I, the madman I, at my age to insist on going counter to my nature and old custom.—Perhaps now the fault's not altogether mine. . . . Perhaps the author is somewhat to blame. . . . These poets sometimes write the veriest stuff. . . .

    'So then, 'tis thou who art the villain. . . .'

Beshrew me, how to say't aright! What if William's prophecy be fulfilled, and they hiss me. . . . No, I'll not consider that. I should die of rage and shame. Well, we'll see what happens. Away with fear! Set on! (*Pause, during which he reads in a low tone from the manuscript, making facial expressions and gestures.*) Ay, now I begin to like my rendering. I perceive that in a low tone everything I say sounds wondrous fine. Oh, I'll carry it off triumphantly! Faith, I'll do it to suit the Queen's taste!

SCENE V

Edmund, and shortly afterward Alice.

EDMUND. What must I think? Does Walton know my secret? God forbid! Was he speaking without malice, or with base intent? Always to fear, to tremble at every whisper! How timorous is guilt! Oh, what a life the guilty lead! (*He sits near the table, on which he leans his arms, allowing his head to fall upon them. Alice comes from the door at left and on seeing him in that attitude shudders and runs toward him, terrified.*)

ALICE. Edmund, what's this? What has happened to you? What is the matter?

EDMUND. You too, poor girl, forever trembling, even as I!

ALICE. What can I do but tremble? One struggles not with conscience without fear.

EDMUND. And must we always live thus? Tell me, in pity's name, is this life?

ALICE. You ask me this? It may be one could count the moments of the day; but not the griefs and frights I suffer in the day. If someone looks at me, I say: He knows it. If one draws near my husband, I say: He is about to tell him. In every face methinks I find a threatening look; the innocentest word re-echoes in my bosom like a threat. The light makes me afraid; I fear it will expose my conscience. The darkness frightens me; for in its midst my conscience seems a still more shadowy thing. At times I would take oath that here upon my brow I feel the brand of sin; I want to touch it with my hand, and hardly can I ban the fixed illusion by looking on myself within the glass. Now all my strength's exhausted; my heart no longer wills to go on suffering. Even the hour that's welcomed by the weary brings me new terrors. What torment! Alas, if I sleep, perchance I'll dream of him; perchance his name will escape my lips; perhaps I'll cry aloud that I love him! And if at last I sleep despite myself, then I am still more wretched, for the vague fears of my waking hours take on in sleep the vivid form of dread reality. And again it is day; and the bitterness of yesterday which seemed so limitless is outdone by today's; and the bitterness of today, seeming to crowd upon the infinite, is ever outdone by tomorrow's. To weep, oh, how much I have wept! How sighed! I have no longer tears nor sighs to console me. You come?—what fear! What longing to have you gone! You leave me? What disquietude, what longing for your coming! You come again, and when as now I talk with you alone, it seems my words resound so loud that they can everywhere be heard. The flutter of an insect stops my blood; everywhere, meseems, are ears that hear, eyes that see, and I know not where to turn mine own . . . (*Looking with terror in one direction and another.*) and . . . Oh! (*Cries out.*)

EDMUND. What? Speak! (*With fear and anxiety, looking in the same direction as* Alice.)

ALICE. Nothing! My shadow—my shadow, which seemed to me an accusing witness. And you would ask me if this be life? Edmund, how can it be? It is not life—not life. It is but death on death.

EDMUND. Alice, be calm, and think on this: had you but more of guilt, you would believe yourself less guilty. For sin seems ever horrible when virtue gleams beside it still.

ALICE. Oh, tell me not of virtue. Merely by loving you I trample every duty under foot; I offend earth and heaven. Save me! O save me as a strong man saves a helpless woman.

EDMUND. Oh, yes, we must both be saved! But how? To see my Alice, my heart's idol, and not to speak with her; to speak with her and tell her not I love her; to cease to love her, having loved her once! . . . What folly! what madness! Still every day I cheer myself in forming high resolves with no intention of fulfilling them; thus does one give the devil cause for laughter. I set myself the task that everyone proposes in such straits: to turn love into friendship. And love that strives to abate itself, grows ever greater. Love is not to be turned to friendship; forsooth it may be changed to odium as deep and active as itself. To love you with delirium, or to hate with frenzy, there is no other way. Let us face it. Tell me, how could I come to hate you?

ALICE. Whole days I, too, spend planning means to break this tyrant of my will. If only Edmund loved another woman, I tell myself, 'twould settle all. And at the mere thought of seeing you at the side of another woman, I tremble with anger; nay, compared with that grief there's none which does not in my eyes seem joy. I set myself to asking God that you'll forget me, and presently I find myself imploring Him to make you love me. No longer can I fight this losing battle. I know myself an ingrate to the best of men —I love you. I know my vileness—yet I love you. Save me, I said —when my salvation's only this—to love you not. You can not save me.

EDMUND. Alice! Alice, my darling!

ALICE. Edmund! (*They are about to embrace, and stop, hearing a noise in the background.*) Oh, stay!

SCENE VI

The same and Shakespeare.

Later, Yorick *and* Walton.

SHAKESPEARE. Blessed be God that I find you alone. I was seeking you.

EDMUND. Whom . . . me? (*With suspicion.*)

SHAKESPEARE. You, and her.

ALICE. Both of us?

SHAKESPEARE. Both.

EDMUND. Heavens! (*Aside.*)

ALICE. Dear God! (*Aside.*)

SHAKESPEARE. Can I speak without fear of being overheard?

EDMUND. So secret, then, is what you have to tell us?

SHAKESPEARE. Would I were deaf to it myself!

ALICE. What's to come? (*Aside.*)

EDMUND. Speak, but have a care what 'tis you speak.

SHAKESPEARE. Nay, it is for you to have a care. (*Fixing him with a look.*)

EDMUND. I cannot tolerate . . .

SHAKESPEARE. Silence, and listen. (*Imperiously.*)

EDMUND. Oh! (*Lowering his head, dominated by the tone and attitude of* Shakespeare.)

SHAKESPEARE. I should long since have ventured what today I do from hard compulsion. I was a coward. These curst conventions that turn good men to cowards! I no longer hesitate: I regard nothing. Edmund, you love that woman.

EDMUND. I? . . .

SHAKESPEARE. Alice, you love him.

ALICE. Ah! (*With fright and grief.*)

EDMUND. By what right dare you . . . ?

SHAKESPEARE. By the right that's given me as the friend of your father, the friend of her husband.

EDMUND. And if it is not true—if they've deceived you?

ALICE. They have deceived you, doubt it not.

SHAKESPEARE. Hypocrisy and guilt are twin sisters. Come here. (*Seizing* Alice *by one hand and drawing her near.*) And you. (*Seizing* Edmund, *and placing him opposite her.*) Raise your head, Edmund. You, yours. (*Lifting their heads.*) Look at each other face to face with the calmness of innocence. Look!—Ah! you were pale: why blush you now? Before, the colour of remorse; and now of shame.

ALICE. Pity!

EDMUND. Enough! (*With profound grief.*)

ALICE. So sudden were your words . . .

EDMUND. The charge has fallen on us like a thunderbolt.

ALICE. We were afraid.

EDMUND. I'll tell you all the truth.

ALICE. Ay, it is truth—he loves me, I love him.

EDMUND. You are noble and generous.

ALICE. You will have pity on two unhappy beings.

EDMUND. Nor wish to increase our misery.

ALICE. Nay, so, you will protect us, you will defend us against our very selves.

SHAKESPEARE. Come, my children, be calm.

ALICE. Children he calls us. Do you hear?

EDMUND. We'll throw ourselves at your feet.

ALICE. (*Starting to kneel.*) Yes!

SHAKESPEARE. (*Opening his arms.*) No, better be ye in my arms.

EDMUND. (*Restraining himself with shamefaced diffidence.*) William! . . .

ALICE. (*With joy.*) Is it possible?

SHAKESPEARE. Come.

EDMUND. (*Throwing himself into his arms.*) Save us!

ALICE. (*Throwing herself also into* Shakespeare's *arms.*) Save us, in pity's name!

SHAKESPEARE. Yes, with God's aid I will save you.

(*A pause during which one hears the sobs of* Edmund *and* Alice.)

ALICE. But what's this? You are weeping?

SHAKESPEARE. Seeing tears, what can one do but weep?

ALICE. Edmund, it is a protector that Heaven sends us. And we wanted to deceive him, we wanted to reject him! How blind are the wretched! To have a friend to comfort us, to take upon himself some of our woe—protected by the one who best can cure the ills of the soul because 'tis he who knows them best. . . . Oh, what unexpected joy! Who would have told me a moment ago that happiness was so near? Once more I begin to breathe. Ah, Edmund, this is life indeed!

SHAKESPEARE. There is no time to lose. Speak. I must know everything. (*Pause.*)

EDMUND. Two years ago, Alice joined your company. 'Twas then I met her. Would I never had!

ALICE. Would I had ne'er met him!

EDMUND. I saw her from a distance; a mysterious force drew me toward her. I reached her side. My vision was enrapt—'twas no mere look I gave her. I spoke, but no one heard my words. I trembled: I loved her!

ALICE. And I loved him!

EDMUND. Love, even rightful, inclines to live hidden in the depths of the heart. Days passed . . . I resolved at last to declare myself. . . . Impossible!

ALICE. Yorick had already told me of his affection.

EDMUND. My rival was the man to whom I owed everything.

ALICE. My mother fell dangerously sick; we lacked resources. To our eyes, Yorick seemed as one sent by the Infinite Pity.

EDMUND. Could I prevent my benefactor's doing good to others?

ALICE. And one day, 'Alice,' saith my mother, 'thou wilt be left abandoned; marry Yorick—he loves thee so, and is so worthy.'

EDMUND. Yorick had picked me up, naked and starving, from the gutter, to give me shelter and love and happiness and a place in the world.

ALICE. 'Twas Yorick cheered the last days of my mother's life with all manner of comforts.

EDMUND. For me to destroy his happiness would have been the depth of meanness.

ALICE. My mother on her death-bed begged me . . .

EDMUND. I did but pay the tribute that gratitude demands.

ALICE. And I but gave the answer that one gives a dying mother.

EDMUND. I swore to forget her.

ALICE. And I, in striving to love him less, but loved him more.

EDMUND. Vain resistance!

ALICE. Yes, thought I, Edmund is his son.

EDMUND. Yorick is my father, so I told myself.

ALICE. And when I marry Yorick, 'twill end the love that Edmund has inspired.

EDMUND. The instant Yorick's bound to her in wedlock, my love for her is ended.

ALICE. To love my husband's son? How horrible—Nay, impossible!

EDMUND. So I—to love my father's wife? What madness! It cannot be.

ALICE. And how I longed and waited for my marriage-hour!

EDMUND. For me, each minute seemed a century, till then.

ALICE. At last the hour was here!

EDMUND. At last she married him!

ALICE. And love, its one hope lost, instead of fleeing from our breast . . .

EDMUND. Arose therein, with outcries like a wild beast at bay.

ALICE. Silent we, still silent.

EDMUND. In spite of Yorick's prayers and tears, I would no longer live with him.

ALICE. Yet here he often had to come.

EDMUND. So Yorick bade.

ALICE. We saw each other daily—silent.

EDMUND. Hour after hour we passed alone together—silent.

ALICE. At last one day while playing Romeo and Juliet . . .

EDMUND. Animated by the flame of the beautiful fiction . . .

ALICE. Mingling with the flame of the fiction the burning flame of reality . . .

EDMUND. With all eyes fixed on us . . .

ALICE. And all ears hanging on our words . . .

EDMUND. Then my lips—nay, my heart—asked her gently, very gently : 'Dost thou love me?'

ALICE. And my lips—nay, my heart—softly, very softly, answered : 'Yes.'

EDMUND. Such is our guilt.

ALICE. Our punishment, at every hour to dread and tremble.

EDMUND. A cankering remorse.

ALICE. Without a single solace.

EDMUND. One remedy alone.

ALICE. To die.

EDMUND. There's nothing more to tell you.

ALICE. We swear it.

EDMUND. By the soul of Yorick!

ALICE. By his soul!

EDMUND. This is what has come to pass.

ALICE. Just this.

SHAKESPEARE. Poor human nature! In thee the noble enterprise begun with strength unequal to the task, becomes a well of evil. Poor human nature. Thou dost recoil before the smaller bar, and dost leap o'er the greater. You love each other; 'Tis imperative you shall not love.

EDMUND. Who says so knows not that the soul enslaved by love cannot free itself from its tyrant.

SHAKESPEARE. Who says so knows the soul is free, as being the child of God.

ALICE. Explain it to me, in the name of pity! What must be done when one who loves would cease to love?

SHAKESPEARE. *Will.*

EDMUND. To will is not enough.

SHAKESPEARE. 'Tis enough, if the willing be not feigned.

ALICE. Who assures that?

SHAKESPEARE. A witness not to be denied.

EDMUND. What witness?

SHAKESPEARE. Your conscience. If it were not responsible for the guilt, why these starts, these tears, and this remorse. You will flee from Alice forever.

EDMUND. That thought has come to me a thousand times already. Don't demand the impossible.

SHAKESPEARE. On the downward slope of sin one must advance, or make retreat; you will retreat despite yourself.

EDMUND. You'll force me to go away?

SHAKESPEARE. If 'tis the only means, by force must right prevail.

ALICE. Edmund will obey you. At last with some one to protect us, you shall see how faith and courage are reborn in our hearts.

EDMUND. Ah, yes: with you to aid, no deed can seem impossible. We are soldiers of duty.

ALICE. You, our captain.

EDMUND. Lead us to victory!

SHAKESPEARE. Could I but bring to pass this one good deed, I'd laugh at my Othello and Macbeth and all that foolery. (*With inner joy.*) I trust in the promise of a man. (*Taking* Edmund's *hand.*) And in the promise of a woman (*Taking hers.*)

EDMUND and ALICE. Yes!

SHAKESPEARE. Now then, until the day shall come when Edmund leaves us, you must not be alone; never in the presence of others look at each other, not even by a glance. Duty asks this, necessity demands it. I thought myself the sole possessor of the secret . . . fool that I was! Love never could stay hidden.

ALICE. What say you?

EDMUND. Explain yourself!

SHAKESPEARE. This awful secret's known as well by one quite capable of villainy.

EDMUND. What's he?

SHAKESPEARE. By getting his assignment in the new drama, Yorick has maddened Walton.

EDMUND. (*With terror.*) Walton!

SHAKESPEARE. I have it from the author of the piece, who came just now from Walton's house to mine, and told me of their recent discourse. He saw not Walton's thoughts, but he did echo certain words of his, as these : 'The rôle of outraged husband divinely fits this Yorick, and no one should dispute his having it.'

ALICE. God of my soul!

SHAKESPEARE. 'If now neglect or blindness should make him miss the fine points of the rôle, 'tis I shall open his eyes.'

ALICE. Ah, 'tis certain. That man's a wicked wretch; he'll ruin us!

EDMUND. (*With profound anxiety.*) Yes, Alice, we are ruined, ruined utterly.

SHAKESPEARE. Not yet. I go at once in search of him, and finding him—there is no longer anything to fear. (*Going toward the rear.*)

EDMUND. (*Going to her, seizing her hand.*) Alice! Alice!

ALICE. What is it? Why so moved?

SHAKESPEARE. (*From the rear.*) Courage, Edmund. I shall return at once to calm you both.

EDMUND. Leave us not, for God's sake!

SHAKESPEARE. (*Taking a few steps toward the front.*) Not leave you? What's the reason?

EDMUND. Walton's no longer there—not at his house.

SHAKESPEARE. (*Coming to* Edmund's *side.*) How know you this?

EDMUND. 'Tis I who say to you, Courage! (*To* Shakespeare.) Courage, poor girl! (*To* Alice.)

ALICE. Nay, end this horrible suspense.

SHAKESPEARE. Where is he?

EDMUND. Here.

SHAKESPEARE. Heavens!

ALICE. With him?

EDMUND. With him!

SHAKESPEARE. You have seen him, then?

EDMUND. Even in my presence he began to explain the object of his coming.

ALICE. Ah! what shall I do now—my God, what shall I do?

EDMUND. Earth hates me, else would she open at my feet!

SHAKESPEARE. Ill fortune!

ALICE. Do not abandon me; defend me, shield me. . . .

EDMUND. In pity's name, a way, a hope!

SHAKESPEARE. If we lose our heads . . . Calm . . . quiet. . . . (*Pondering.* Yorick *appears in the door at right, followed by* Walton; *he gives* Walton *the manuscript that he holds in his hand, and with joyous countenance, makes signs for him to keep silence, putting his finger on his lips. He then approaches his wife rapidly on tip-toe.*)

EDMUND. (*With great anxiety, to* Shakespeare.) What make you of it?

ALICE. Speak.

YORICK. (*Seizing his wife with one arm, with a tragically affected attitude, and declaiming with exaggerated emphasis.*) 'Tremble, thou faithless spouse! thou ingrate . . .'

ALICE. Christ! (*Shuddering with fright.*) Pardon! (*Falling to the floor in a faint.*)

YORICK. Eh? . . .

EDMUND. (*Trying to hurl himself at* Walton.) Damned villain!

SHAKESPEARE. (*In a low tone to* Edmund, *holding him back.*) Fool!

YORICK. (*Confused and stunned.*) 'Pardon!'

WALTON. (*Aside, ironically.*) Such a coincidence!

YORICK. 'Pardon!' . . . (*Trying to explain to himself what has happened.* Shakespeare *goes to help* Alice.)

JOHN D. FITZGERALD and THACHER GUILD

RAMÓN DE CAMPOAMOR
[1817–1901]

Ramón de Campoamor, an extremely popular poet in his own day, has not been treated kindly by many recent critics. Few dispute, however, the deftness of his wit or the wisdom of his observations. These qualities are most evident in the series which he called humoradas *(epigrams in verse) and* doloras *(poetic vignettes expressing a simple truth or philosophy). In the latter group,* Quién supiera escribir *is his best-known poem.*

DOLORAS

BOREDOM

Grievous is the hermit's plight;
Lone, he know not love's delight :
But Solitude's more dreadful far,
When two together lonely are.

J. D. M. FORD

AFTER TWENTY YEARS

Now after twenty years have passed; again he's here,
And meeting, they exclaim, both she and he :
Good Lord ! is this the man I once held dear?
Good God ! and can this woman here be she?

J. D. M. FORD

THE GREAT BANQUET

Cast from a rush, into a running stream
    A worm once chanced to fall;
And then a trout, darting with silvery gleam,
    Seized it and ate it all.

The bird king-fisher came and caught the trout,
    Its appetite to sate;
And then this bird, after a savage bout,
    A hawk o'ercame and ate.

Such carnage to avenge, a hunter shot,
    With his unerring aim,
The hawk that with rapacious claw had got
    King-fisher as his game.

Alas! the luckless hunter who had slain
    The hawk, with cunning wont,
A guard now killed, for failing to obtain
    A privilege to hunt.

To other worms his corpse will soon give life,
    As it must rot away;
And now again this circle fierce of strife
    Will have its ceaseless play.

And love? and happiness? and all men born,
    What other end have they?
Unless to eat, and in their turn adorn
    Earth's cruel banquet on their fated day.

J. D. M. FORD

IF ONLY I COULD WRITE!

I

'I pray you, reverend Sir, this letter write.'
    'To whom then? Ah, I know.'
'You know, because that dark and starless night
    You saw us meet?' 'E'en so.'

'O Sir, forgive us.' 'Nay, 'twas no great sin,
    The hour to love did lend;
Give me a pen and paper, I'll begin :
    Raymond, beloved friend!'

'Beloved? Well, 'tis written.' 'You're not vext?
    Do you approve it?' 'Yes.'
'*I am so sad alone.* (Should that come next?)
    More sad than you can guess.

Such sorrow fills me since we two did part!'
    'How do you know my pain?'
'To these old eyes is every young maid's heart
    Like crystal, free from stain.

What without you is life? A vale of woe.
    With you? The promised land.'
'Ah, Señor Cura! Make your writing so
    That he may understand.'

'The kiss I gave you when you left me, sweet—'
'What! Know you of my kiss?'
'Ever when lovers part, and when they meet—
   Oh, take it not amiss.

Oh, if your love should never bring you more,
   How should I grieve and sigh!'
'What grieve, and nothing more? Nay, good Señor,
   Say, I were like to die.'

'To die! My child, such word were blasphemy.'
   'Yet die full well I might.'
'I'll not put "die".' 'Your heart is ice. Ah me!
   If only I could write!'

II

'Ah, Señor Cura, 'tis in vain you seek
   My sorrow thus to still;
Unless, indeed, to make my whole heart speak
   These pen-strokes have the skill.

For God's sake write, my soul would fain be free
   From all its weary grief,
Which day by day would even stifle me,
   But that tears bring relief.

Tell him these rosy lips he loved, that met
   His own dear lips erewhile,
Are now for ever closed, and fast forget
   Even what 'tis to smile.

Tell him, these eyes, that won from him such praise,
   Are drooping and dejected,
Even because therein his well-loved face
   No longer is reflected.

Tell him, of all the torments life can bring,
   Be absence my last choice;
Tell him, that ever in my ears will ring
   The echo of his voice.

Yet say, that since for him so sad I stay,
   I count my sorrow light,
O God, how many are the things I'd say,
   If I could only write!

END *

Now Sir, 'tis done. I trace these words for end :
   "*To Raymond*", and bestow
Upon it this my mark, the which to send,
   Small Latin need I know.'

IDA FARNELL

HUMORADAS

You wave your fan with such a graceful art,
You brush the dust off from the oldest heart.

The children of the mothers I loved, ah see,
They kiss me as though they kissed a saint in me!

No woman yet, since they were made all
Has ever got quite outside of the cradle.

   If too easy she should be,
     I, beholding, quit her;
   If the thing's too hard for me,
     Trying proves too bitter.
   Girls, now see,
   Best it is to love with easy
     Difficulty.

Have I not seen you? Yes, but where and when?
Ah, I remember : I was dreaming then.

She's faithless, and you love her? As you will :
Hope I adore, and hope is faithless still.

ARTHUR SYMONS

---

* A more precise translation of the epilogue would show a change of speaker and that it is the priest who says the last four lines. The editors offer the following substitution :

   'Well, now, I'll copy what you've said and add
     To Raymond . . . for you speak
   More clearly with love's fire than if you had
     All my Latin and my Greek.'

GUSTAVO ADOLFO BÉCQUER
[1836–1870]

A poverty-stricken orphan, dogged by poor health, unhappily married, Gustavo Adolfo Bécquer spent the few years of his life in a stranglehold of financial and emotional difficulties. But from the depths of his personal grief, Bécquer composed lyric poetry of such breath-taking artistry and bittersweet sentiment that his name is today immortal in Spanish literature. Hardly a Spaniard exists who cannot recite at least one of his seventy-six Rimas, *the exquisite poems for which he is most famous.*

Besides the small collection of Rimas *and other short poems, Bécquer wrote a brief series of literary letters, and twenty-two* leyendas. *The latter are dream-like legends of Spain, especially of Toledo, written in prose as haunting and delicate as his poetry.*

THE GOLDEN BRACELET

I

She was beautiful, beautiful with that beauty which turns a man dizzy; beautiful with that beauty which in no wise resembles our dream of the angels, and yet is supernatural; a diabolical beauty that the devil perchance gives to certain things to make them his instruments on earth.

He loved her—he loved her with that love which knows not check nor bounds; he loved her with that love which seeks delight and finds but martyrdom; a love which is akin to bliss, yet which Heaven seems to cast on mortals for the expiation of their sins.

She was wayward, wayward and unreasonable, like all the women of the world.

He, superstitious, superstitious and valiant, like all the men of his time.

Her name was Maria Antúnez.

His, Pedro Alfonso de Orellana.

Both were natives of Toledo, and both had their homes in the city which saw their birth.

The tradition which relates this marvellous event, an event of many years since, tells nothing more of these two central actors.

I, in my character of scrupulous historian, will not add a single word of my own invention to describe them further.

II

One day he found her in tears and asked her:

'Why dost thou weep?'

She dried her eyes, looked at him searchingly, heaved a sigh and began to weep anew.

Then, drawing close to Maria, he took her hand, leaned his elbow on the fretted edge of the Arabic parapet whence the beautiful maiden was watching the river flow beneath, and again he asked her : 'Why dost thou weep?'

The Tajo, moaning at the tower's foot, twisted in and out amid the rocks on which is seated the imperial city. The sun was sinking behind the neighbouring mountains, the afternoon haze was floating a veil of azure gauze, and only the monotonous sound of the water broke the profound stillness.

Maria exclaimed : 'Ask me not why I weep, ask me not; for I would not know how to answer thee, nor thou how to understand. In the souls of us women are stifling desires which reveal themselves only in a sigh, mad ideas that cross the imagination without our daring to form them into speech, strange phenomena of our mysterious nature which man cannot even conceive. I implore thee, ask me not the cause of my grief; if I should reveal it to thee, perchance thou wouldst reply with peals of laughter'

When these words were faltered out, again she bowed the head and again he urged his questions.

The radiant damsel, breaking at last her stubborn silence, said to her lover in a hoarse, unsteady voice :

'Thou wilt have it. It is a folly that will make thee laugh, but be it so. I will tell thee, since thou dost crave to hear.

'Yesterday I was in the temple. They were celebrating the feast of the Virgin; her image, placed on a golden pedestal above the High Altar, glowed like a burning coal; the notes of the organ trembled, spreading from echo to echo throughout the length and breadth of the church, and in the choir the priests were chanting the *Salve, Regina*.

'I was praying; I was praying, all absorbed in my religious meditations, when involuntarily I lifted my head, and my gaze sought the altar. I know not why my eyes from that instant fixed themselves upon the image, but I speak amiss—it was not on the image; they fixed themselves upon an object which until then I had not seen—an object which, I know not why, thenceforth held all my attention. Do not laugh; that object was the golden bracelet that the Mother of God wears on one of the arms in which rests her divine Son. I turned aside my gaze and strove again to pray. Impossible. Without my will, my eyes moved back to the same point. The altar lights, reflected in the thousand facets of those diamonds, were multiplied prodigiously. Millions of living sparks,

rosy, azure, green and golden, were whirling around the jewels
like a storm of fiery atoms, like a dizzy round of those spirits of
flame which fascinate with their brightness and their marvellous
unrest.

'I left the church. I came home, but I came with that idea fixed
in imagination. I went to bed; I could not sleep. The night passed,
a night eternal with one thought. At dawn my eyelids closed and
—believest thou?—even in slumber I saw crossing before me,
dimming in the distance and ever returning, a woman, a woman
dark and beautiful, who wore the ornament of gold and jewel
work; a woman, yes, for it was no longer the Virgin, whom I
adore and at whose feet I bow; it was a woman, another woman
like myself who looked upon me and laughed mockingly. "Dost
see it?" she appeared to say, showing me the treasure. "How it
glitters! It seems a circlet of stars snatched from the sky some
summer night. Dost see it? But it is not thine, and it will be thine
never, never. Thou wilt perchance have others that surpass it,
others richer, if it be possible, but this, this which sparkles so
piquantly, so bewitchingly, never, never." I awoke, but with the
same idea fixed here, then as now, like a red-hot nail, diabolical,
irresistible, inspired beyond a doubt by Satan himself.—And what
then?—Thou art silent, silent, and dost hang thy head.—Does not
my folly make thee laugh?'

Pedro, with a convulsive movement, grasped the hilt of his
sword, raised his head, which he had, indeed, bent low and said
with smothered voice :

'Which Virgin has this jewel?'

'The Virgin of the Sagrario,' murmured Maria.

'The Virgin of the Sagrario!' repeated the youth, with accent
of terror. 'The Virgin of the Sagrario of the cathedral!'

And in his features was portrayed for an instant the state of his
mind, appalled before a thought.

'Ah, why does not some other Virgin own it?' he continued,
with a tense, impassioned tone. 'Why does not the archbishop bear
it in his mitre, the king in his crown, or the devil between his
claws? I would tear it away for thee, though its price were death
or hell. But from the Virgin of the Sagrario, our own Holy
Patroness,—I—I who was born in Toledo! Impossible, impossible!'

'Never!' murmured Maria, in a voice that scarcely reached the
ear. 'Never!'

And she wept again.

Pedro fixed a stupefied stare on the running waves of the river

—on the running waves, which flowed and flowed unceasingly before his absent-thoughted eyes, breaking at the foot of the tower amid the rocks on which is seated the imperial city.

III

The cathedral of Toledo! Imagine a forest of colossal palm trees of granite, that by the interlacing of their branches form a gigantic, magnificent arch, beneath which take refuge and live, with the life genius has lent them, a whole creation of beings, both fictitious and real.

Imagine an incomprehensible fall of shadow and light wherein the coloured rays from the ogive windows meet and are merged with the dusk of the nave; where the gleam of the lamps struggles and is lost in the gloom of the sanctuary.

Imagine a world of stone, immense as the spirit of our religion, sombre as its traditions, enigmatic as its parables, and yet you will not have even a remote idea of this eternal monument of the enthusiasm and faith of our ancestors—a monument upon which the centuries have emulously lavished their treasures of knowledge, inspiration and the arts.

In the cathedral-heart dwells silence, majesty, the poetry of mysticism, and a holy dread which guards those thresholds against worldly thoughts and the paltry passions of earth.

Consumption of the body is stayed by breathing pure mountain air; atheism should be cured by breathing this atmosphere of faith.

But great and impressive as the cathedral presents itself to our eyes at whatsoever hour we enter its mysterious and sacred precinct, never does it produce an impression so profound as in those days when it arrays itself in all the splendours of religious pomp, when its shrines are covered with gold and jewels, its steps with costly carpeting and its pillars with tapestry.

Then, when its thousand silver lamps, aglow, shed forth a flood of light, when a cloud of incense floats in air, and the voices of the choir, the harmonious pealing of the organs, and the bells of the tower make the building tremble from its deepest foundations to its highest spires, then it is we comprehend, because we feel, the ineffable majesty of God who dwells within, gives it life with His breath and fills it with the reflection of His glory.

The same day on which occurred the scene we have just described, the last rites of the magnificent eight-day feast of the Virgin were held in the cathedral.

The holy feast had attracted an immense multitude of the

faithful; but already they had dispersed in all directions; already the lights of the chapels and of the High Altar had been extinguished, and the mighty doors of the temple had groaned upon their hinges as they closed behind the last departing worshipper, when forth from the depth of shadow, and pale, pale as the statue of the tomb on which he leant for an instant, while he conquered his emotion, there advanced a man, who came slipping with the utmost stealthiness toward the screen of the central chapel. There the gleam of a lamp made it possible to distinguish his features.

It was Pedro.

What had passed between the two lovers to bring him to the point of putting into execution an idea whose mere conception had lifted his hair with horror? That could never be learned.

But there he was, and he was there to carry out his criminal intent. In his restless glances, in the trembling of his knees, in the sweat which ran in great drops down his face, his thought stood written.

The cathedral was alone, utterly alone, and drowned in deepest hush.

Nevertheless, there were perceptible from time to time suggestions of dim disturbance, creakings of wood maybe or murmurs of the wind, or—who knows?—perchance illusion of the fancy, which in its excited moments hears and sees and feels what is not; but in very truth there sounded, now here, now there, now behind him, now even at his side, something like sobs suppressed, something like the rustle of trailing robes, and a muffled stir as of steps that go and come unceasingly.

Pedro forced himself to hold his course; he reached the grating and mounted the first step of the chancel. All along the inner wall of this chapel are ranged the tombs of kings, whose images of stone, with hand upon sword-hilt, seem to keep watch night and day over the sanctuary in whose shade they take their everlasting rest.

'Onward!' he murmured under his breath, and he strove to move and could not. It seemed as if his feet were nailed to the pavement. He lowered his eyes, and his hair stood on end with horror. The floor of the chapel was made of wide, dark burial slabs.

For a moment he believed that a cold and fleshless hand was holding him there with strength invincible. The dying lamps, which sparkled in the hollow aisles and transepts like lost stars in the dark, wavered before his vision, the statues of the sepulchres wavered and the images of the altar, all the cathedral wavered, with its granite arcades and buttresses of solid stone.

'Onward!' Pedro exclaimed again, as if beside himself; he approached the altar and climbing upon it, he reached the pedestal of the image. All the space about clothed itself in weird and frightful shapes, all was shadow and flickering light, more awful even than total darkness. Only the Queen of Heaven, softly illuminated by a golden lamp, seemed to smile, tranquil, gracious and serene, in the midst of all that horror.

Nevertheless, that silent, changeless smile, which calmed him for an instant, in the end filled him with fear, a fear stranger and more profound than what he had suffered hitherto.

Yet he regained his self-control, shut his eyes so as not to see her, extended his hand with a spasmodic movement and snatched off the golden bracelet, pious offering of a sainted archbishop, the golden bracelet whose value equalled a fortune.

Now the jewel was in his possession; his convulsed fingers clutched it with superhuman force; there was nothing left save to flee—to flee with it; but for this it was necessary to open his eyes, and Pedro was afraid to see, to see the image, to see the kings of the sepulchres, the demons of the cornices, the griffins of the capitals, the blotches of shadow and flashes of light which, like ghostly, gigantic phantoms, were moving slowly in the depths of the nave, now filled with confused noises, unearthly and appalling.

At last he opened his eyes, cast one glance about him, and from his lips escaped a piercing cry.

The cathedral was full of statues, statues, which, clothed in strange, flowing raiment, had descended from their niches and were thronging all the vast compass of the church, staring at him with their hollow eyes.

Saints, nuns, angels, devils, warriors, great ladies, pages, hermits, peasants surrounded him on every side and were massed confusedly in the open spaces and about the altar. Before it there officiated, in presence of the kings who were kneeling upon their tombs, the marble archbishops whom he had seen heretofore stretched motionless upon their beds of death, while a whole world of granite beasts and creeping things, writhing over the paving-stones, twisting along the buttresses, curled up in the canopies, swinging from the vaulted roof, quivered into life like worms in a giant corpse, fantastic, distorted, hideous.

He could resist no longer. His brows throbbed with terrible violence; a cloud of blood darkening his vision; he uttered a second scream, a scream heart-rending, inhuman, and fell swooning across the altar.

When the sacristans found him crouching on the altar steps the

16—SA

next morning, he still clutched the golden bracelet in both hands and on seeing them draw near, he shrieked with discordant yells of laughter :

'Hers ! hers !'

The poor wretch had gone mad.

CORNELIA FRANCES BATES

and KATHARINE LEE BATES

RIMA II

Flitting arrow, speeding onward,
   To the air at random cast,
Ne'er divining where now trembling
   It shall fix itself at last.

Leaf which from the branch now withered
   By the wind is snatched away,
And no one can mark the furrow
   Where at last it falls to stay.

Giant wave urged by a tempest,
   Curling, tumbling o'er the sea,
Rolling, passing, never knowing
   Of what strand its quest must be.

Light in wavering circles gleaming,
   To exhaustion nearing now,
And each circle all unwitting
   Which shall be the last to glow.

This am I, who, aimless roving,
   O'er this earth my way must wend;
Ne'er reflecting whence I came, nor
   To what goal my footsteps tend.

J. D. M. FORD

RIMA IV

Say not that, its treasure exhausted,
   The lyre is mute, lacking a melody :
There may be no poets, but forever
   Poesy will be.

As long as the waves quiver glowingly
   At dawning's caress;
As long as the sun doth, with fire and gold,
   The flying clouds dress;

As long as the breezes are laden with
   Fragrance and harmony;
As long as the springtide comes to the earth,
   Poesy will be!

As long as by science the well of life
   Has not been found,
And in seas or in heavens an abyss remains
   That men cannot sound;

While ignorant whither, but forward yet,
   Goes humanity;
As long as one mystery remains for man,
   Poesy will be!

As long as the soul joys and yet no smile
   Without doth appear;
As long as there's sorrow when from the eye
   There falls no tear;

As long as mankind is still left with hope
   And memory;
As long as the heart and head battle still,
   Poesy will be!

As long as eyes mirror the tender gaze
   Of other eyes;
As long as a sighing mouth still responds
   To a mouth that sighs;

As long as two souls in a kiss can feel
   One unity;
As long as one beautiful woman is . . .
   Poesy will be!

                YOUNG ALLISON

RIMA VII

In the room, in a corner all darkened,
By its owner perhaps now forgotten,
Mute-voiced and covered over with dust,
   The harp was seen.

What notes lay slumbering in its chord-strings—
As the bird sleeps in the branches—
Awaiting the snow-white fingers
   Which know how to wake them!

Oh ! thought I—how often does genius
Thus sleep in the deep of soul's vault,
And, like Lazarus, a voice await, anxious,
That will bid it : 'Arise and walk !'

JEANNE PASMANTIER

RIMA X

The particles invisible of air
  Around me quiver and vehemently glow;
The heavens burst forth in rays of golden light;
  All earth doth tremble in a joyous throe.
Floating in waves of harmony I hear
  A stir of kisses and of wings on high;
Mine eyelids close themselves. . . . What passes now?
  ' 'Tis love goes by!'

YOUNG ALLISON

RIMA XI

I am black and comely; my lips are glowing;
I am passion; my heart is hot;
The rapture of life in my veins is flowing.
For me thou callest?—I call thee not.

Pale is my forehead and gold my tresses;
Endless comforts are locked in me,
Treasure of hearthside tendernesses.
'Tis I whom thou seekest?—Nay, not thee.

I am a dream, afar, forbidden,
Vague as the mist on the mountain-brow,
A bodiless glory, haunting, hidden;
I cannot love thee.—Oh, come ! come thou !

KATHARINE LEE BATES

RIMA XXI

What is poetry, you say,
Holding my eyes with yours of blue,
What is poetry? . . . *You* ask that?
Poetry . . . It is you !

INA DUVALL SINGLETON

RIMA XXXVIII

Sighs are air, and go to the air.
    Tears are water, and to the sea flow.
Tell me, woman : when love's forgot,
    Knowest where it doth go?

YOUNG ALLISON

RIMA LII

O waves gigantic that roaring break
And hurl yourselves on a desert strand,
Wrapt in a sheet of the foam you make
    Drag me below with you, bear me on high.

O hurricane, driving with whips of wind
The faded leaves from the forest grand,
Dragged along by the whirlwind blind
    Goad me to go with you, prone as I lie.

O clouds of the tempest, by lightning kiss'd,
Your edges shot with the fire of its love,
Whirled along in the sombre mist
    Bear me away with you, bear me above.

O bear me away with you, bear me away
Where frenzied with vertigo mad I may slay
My reason and memory, for I fear
    To be left all alone with my sorrow here.

MASON CARNES

RIMA LIII

The dusky swallows will hang their nests
In your balcony once again,
And with their wings they will lightly tap,
As they flit past your window-pane;
But those who paused in their eager flight
And lingered our names to learn,
That viewed your beauty and my delight. . . .
Ah! these will not return!

Dense honeysuckle will scale the walls
Of your garden, and there once more
Will show its blossoms when evening comes,
Even lovelier than before;

But those, dew-laden, whose drops we watched
Now tremble and fall, alack !
That we saw fall like the tears of day. . . .
Ah ! these will not come back !

   The burning passionate words of love
Once again in your ears will sound;
And then your heart will perhaps awake,
Will be roused from its sleep profound;
But as one kneels at His altar, mute,
Adoring, with head bent low,
As I have loved you . . . be undeceived,
Ah ! they'll not love you so !

MRS. W. S. HENDRIX

RIMA LXXIII

They closed her eyes
That were still open;
They hid her face
With a white linen,
And, some sobbing
Others in silence,
From the sad bedroom
All came away.

The nightlight in a dish
Burned on the floor;
It threw on the wall
The bed's shadow,
And in that shadow
One saw sometime
Drawn in sharp line
The body's shape.

The dawn appeared.
At its first whiteness
With its thousand noises
The town awoke.
Before that contrast
Of light and darkness,
Of life and strangeness
I thought a moment.

My God, how lonely
The dead are!

On the shoulders of men
To church they bore her,
And in a chapel
They left her bier.
There they surrounded
Her pale body
With yellow candles
And black stuffs.

At the last stroke
Of the ringing for the Souls,
An old crone finished
Her last prayers.
She crossed the narrow nave,
The doors moaned,
And the holy place
Remained deserted.

From a clock one heard
The measured ticking,
And from a candle
The guttering.
All things there
Were so dark and mournful,
So cold and rigid,
That I thought a moment :
My God, how lonely
The dead are!

From the high belfry
The tongue of iron
Clanged, giving out
A last farewell.
Crêpe on their clothes,
Her friends and kindred
Passed in a line
In homage to her.

In the last vault
Dark and narrow,
The pickaxe opened
A niche at one end;

They laid her away there.
Soon they bricked the place up,
And with a gesture
Bade grief farewell.

Pickaxe on shoulder
The gravedigger,
Singing between his teeth,
Passed out of sight.
The night came down,
It was all silent.
Alone in the darkness
I thought a moment,—
My God, how lonely
The dead are!

In the dark nights
Of bitter winter,
When the wind makes
The rafter creak,
When the violent rain
Lashes the windows,
Lonely I remember
That poor girl.

There falls the rain
With its noise eternal,
There the northwind
Fights with the rain.
Stretched in the hollow
Of the damp bricks,
Perhaps her bones
Freeze with the cold.

Does the dust return to dust?
Does the soul fly to heaven?
Or is all vile matter,
Rottenness, filthiness?
I know not, but
There is something—something—
Something which gives me
Loathing, terror,—
To leave the dead
So alone, so wretched.

                              JOHN MASEFIELD

GASPAR NÚÑEZ DE ARCE
[1834–1903]

The poetry of Gaspar Núñez de Arce, an important figure in the politics of his day, often reflects his activities. Gritos del combate (*1875*) *contains some of his most impressive verses, generally on social, political and philosophical themes. He also wrote a number of plays; the best is* El haz de leña, *an historical drama in verse which deals with the imprisonment and death of Prince Don Carlos in the sixteenth century.*

DEJECTION

Whene'er my mind the dawn of life recalls,
How once within the walls
Of our cathedrals, lost in prayer, I knelt,
And, kneeling, saw the blessed Rood before me,
While God's own peace came o'er me,
And dreams of Paradise within dwelt;

My heavy brow I beat, and all aflame
With feverish desire
Would seek the vanished bliss of childhood tender;
To hold once more that faith without alloy
Alas, with what great joy
This weary length of life I would surrender!

Ah me! The ardent love I mind me now,
Wherewith I bent my brow
E'en to the flagstones of the holy shrine,
Steeping, the while I prayed, my fantasy
In light and poetry,
Mingled with reverent awe for things divine.

The soaring arches, that to heaven raised
My spirit as I gazed,
Their majesty serene, sublime, and grave,
The slow and cadenced psalm, that, mounting high,
Seeming half groan, half sigh,
Reverberated in the spacious nave;

The splendour dimly seen in twilight gloom
Of many an ancient tomb,
Whose art austere the infinite proclaims,
The light that set the painted windows glowing,
Which, soft reflections throwing,
Lit up grey columns with their coloured flames;

Those clustered shafts, from whence in graceful flight
To build the arch aright,
United yet apart, each branch ascends,
As when the multitude in prayer is found,
And from one wave of sound
Each heart distinct its own petition sends;

The Gothic altar with the Cross above,
Whereon in wondrous love
Hangs the Redeemer—Christ the Crucified,
Wresting in agony, with failing breath,
'Gainst sin, our foe, and Death,
His arms to all that sorrow opening wide;

And the wild clamour of the pealing bell,
That to the soul would tell
Its heavenly story from the belfry-tower,
While strange, sweet promises appear to float
Around each winged note
To all who sigh in dark and lonely hour;

These bore me upwards into regions fair,
Where in serener air
Religion fed my soul with rapture mute,
All, all, that in the sanctuary I saw,
Made me with holy awe
To tremble like the strings of harp or lute.

Led by that voice that he alone can hear
Who with a holy fear
And fervent faith and love is all aflame,
Arrayed in floating garments, dazzling white,
Up to the zenith's height
My infant prayer like some pure virgin came.

.   .   .

O breath that givest life to all our being!
O glory past our seeing!
O thirst unquenchable, divine and pure!
O heaven, whose azure vault in days of old
Meseemed o'erlaid with gold,
But now hangs shrouded, gloomy, and obscure!

My inner heart Thou dost no longer chasten,
No longer do I hasten
As once in childhood to Thy holy altar;

Alas! to reach Thee I have lost the way,
And, miserably astray,
Ever in darkness and despair I falter.

Onward I go 'mid bitter tears and sighs,
I call, no voice replies,
Distractedly I cast mine eyes around,
Yet may not pierce the gloom, so, reft of hope,
Full timorously I grope
Along a weary path where thorns abound.

Child of the age, I strive, O Christ, in vain
Against its impious reign;
Its demoniac greatness lays me low;
An age it is of wonders and of fears,
That amid ruin rears
Its god of dull dejection, doubt, and woe.

Not such art Thou, for with Thy gracious face
Vain terrors dost Thou chase;
Thou to the wanderer art light and guide;
But this one is a god from the Unknown,
Chaos his only throne,
His law supreme, blind chance and naught beside.

.   .   .

A helmless, broken vessel is this Age!
Round it the billows rage,
The lightning burns, the furious tempests beat,
As, drifting on a wide and heaving sea,
In its immensity
It flames resplendent 'mid devouring heat.

Ah me! The mystic shore so distant seems,
And wondrously it gleams,
As the great Sun sinks sadly in the West;
The vessel burns, above the storm-winds pass,
Too late, too late, alas,
To reach the far-off haven of our rest!

What then is Science when our faith is cold?
A war-horse none may hold,
That, by delirium seized, outstrips the wind,
Till, plunging into thick and tangled brakes,
His random course he takes,
And struggling ever, still no goal may find.

.   .   .

Save us, O Christ, who once for men didst bleed,
Oh, save us in our need !
Haply less guilty than infirm our race;
O'erwhelmed by very pride, a heavy weight,
We rush upon our fate,
Saviour, if yet Thou livest, grant us grace.

When science rashly from Thy way departs,
It plants within our hearts
Full many an evil germ of hidden powers;
E'en as the insect, when it takes its flight,
Leaves, like a poisonous blight,
Its larva in the calyx of the flowers.

If in this dreary maze, profound and dark,
Dwell yet the enkindling spark,
Source of all life and hope—Thy holy Word,
Speak to our faith long dead, and cry aloud :
'Awake, put off thy shroud,'
E'en as when Lazarus Thy summons heard.

IDA FARNELL

JOSÉ MARÍA DE PEREDA
[1833–1906]

José María de Pereda, native of the province of Santander, is a leading author among the great realist-regionalist novelists of the nineteenth century. His first publication, a collection of sketches and poems, was entitled Escenas montañesas *(1864). With its realistic descriptions of character types and landscapes of the Montaña region, the work forecast the pattern of his numerous novels.*

Throughout his writings, Pereda defends the conservative, traditional viewpoint in religious, political and social doctrines. His language and style are vigorous, enriched by an abundance of regional expressions.

La leva ('The Conscription'), part of which is presented here, is taken from Escenas montañesas, *and is regarded as one of the best short stories of the century.*

THE CONSCRIPTION

TUERTO'S FAMILY LIFE

. . . So now we continue.

Tuerto ('Cross-Eyes') enters his house. He tosses off his sou'-wester, or serviceable tarpaulin hat, throws down upon an old chest his duck waterproof, which he had carried on his shoulder, and hangs up on a nail a basket with an oilskin covering, and full of fishing-tackle. His wife dishes up in an old broken pan a mess of beans and cabbage, badly cooked and worse seasoned, sets it on the chest, and puts alongside it a big piece of coarse brown bread. Tuerto, without letting fall a word, waits till his children have got around the board also, and then begins to eat the mess with a pewter spoon. His wife and children accompany him, taking turns with another spoon, of wood. The beans and cabbage are finished. Tuerto has the air of expecting something next, which does not come; he looks at the dish, then into the bottom of the empty stew-pan, then finally at his wife. The woman turns pale.

'Where is the meat?' he at length inquires, with the chronic hoarse voice of the fisherman.

'The meat?' stammers his wife. 'As the butcher's shop was closed when I went to get it, I did not bring any.'

'That's a lie. I gave you the two reals and a half to buy it yesterday noon, and the butcher's doesn't close till four. What have you done with the money?'

'The money?—the money?—It's in my pocket.'

'You thieving jade, if you've been drinking again, I swear I'll let daylight through you,' roared the enraged Tuerto, on observing the continually increasing confusion of his wife. 'Let me see that money, and be quick about it, I say.'

The woman pulls forth tremblingly a few small coins from her pocket, and holds them out to her husband, without fully opening her hand.

'It's only eight coppers you've got there, and I gave you twenty-one. Where's the rest?'

'I must have lost—have lost them. I had twenty-one this morning.'

'Don't tell me such a thing as that; the two reals I gave you were in silver.'

'Yes, but I changed them at the market.'

'What has your mother done this morning?' quickly demands Tuerto, clutching his eldest child by the arm.

The child trembles in affright, looks alternately at father and mother, and remains silent.

'Speak out, I say.'

'Mother will go and beat me if I do,' replies the poor little brat, snivelling.

'And if you don't answer me, I'll give you a crack that will spoil your face.'

The boy, who knows by hard experience that his father never deals in vain threats, now, despite the signals his mother makes him to keep still, shuts his eyes, and speaking as rapidly as if he feared the words would burn his mouth, says :

'Mother brought home a pint of brandy this morning, and has the bottle hidden in the straw mattress.'

Tuerto no sooner hears these words than he fells his culprit spouse to the floor with a resounding whack, rushes to the bed, rummages amid the contents of the poor mattress, pulls out from it a small bottle which contains the remainder of the contraband liquor, and returning with it towards his wife, hurls it at her head at the moment when she is just getting up from the floor. It knocks her down anew, and the children are sprinkled with the flying spirits. The wretched woman, sorely hurt, laments and groans; the frightened children weep; and the irate mariner sallies forth to the balcony, cursing his wife and the day that he was ever born.

Uncle Tremontorio, who arrived from the sea at the same time with his mates Bolina and Tuerto, had been on his balcony knitting away at his fishing-nets (his customary occupation when at home) from the beginning of the dispute between his neighbours. From time to time he would take a bite out of a hunk of bread, and another of dried codfish, the provision that constituted his usual dinner. Though he is perfectly well posted about what has just taken place, it is not his way to mix himself up in what does not concern him. But the furious husband, who needs an outlet for the venomous rage that still half chokes him, calls to his neighbour, and the pair shout from one balcony to the other the following dialogue :

'Uncle Tremontorio, I can't stand this devil of a woman any longer. One of these days you'll hear of some desperate deed on my part; I suppose that's the way it will all end.'

'I have told you that it was your own fault, from the beginning. She tacked your way a little, and you let her go your whole cable and thought your voyage was over.'

'What could I do? I thought then she was one of heaven's own saints.'

'What could you do? Do? Why, what I've always told you : haul her taut, and make fast with a double turn. Rough wind astern? All right, ahead you go.'

'But there's not a bone in her body I haven't already tinkered at with a cudgel, as you might mend the ribs of a boat.'

'You waited till the wood was rotten, my friend.'

'As God is my witness she's the worst villain unhung. What is going to become of those poor brats of mine when I am taken away from them? . . . for the devil will never take that woman : he has no place to put her. Last week I handed her twenty-four reals to dress the children with. Have you laid eyes on that money? Well, neither have I. The drunkard spent them for drink. I gave her a walloping that left her for dead, and yet what does she do? Three days after that she sells a sheet from our bed for a quart of rum. Yesterday I gave her twenty-one cents for meat, and she drank them also. And with all this the young ones are naked, I haven't a shirt to my back, and I never dare think of treating myself to an honest glass of wine of a fête-day.'

'Why don't you get an exorcism said over her? Maybe she's bewitched by evil spirits, and that's the cause of it.'

'I've spent a small fortune in those very tomfooleries, Tremontorio. I took her to more than three leagues from here, to get a parson that they said had the gift of such things, to chuck the gospels at her. Well, he did; then he gave me a little card he had said a prayer over, and a sprig of rue, sewed it all up in a bag, hung it round her neck, charged me nearly four dollars for it, and that was all the good it did—not the first blessed thing. The very next day she had a jag on worse than ever, and wanted to paint the town red. I've given her brandy with gunpowder in it,—a thing, they say, that creates a distaste for liquor,—but that beast, did it affect her that way? Not much! She seemed to like the drink after that better than ever. I've laid out a treasure in candles alone, setting them up before the Holy Martyrs, to see if they'd rid her of the vice; and it was just the same as if I had not spent a farthing. I swear to you, I don't know what to do, Uncle Tremontorio, unless it is to kill her; there are no bounds to this vice of hers. Just tell me what you say of this : When I gave her the brandy with powder in it, she was taken with such a colic I thought she'd burst. I had heard that flannels soaked in spirits, applied good and hot, was a cure for that sort of pains in the stomach; so I heated up about half a pint of liquor in a saucepan. When it was blazing hot, I took it over to the bedside, where the thief of the world was writhing about in contortions. I had to leave the saucepan with her a minute while I went to the chest to get out some rags; I turned around, and, man, what do you think I saw? She was just swallowing down the last drops of the spirits from the saucepan, almost ablaze as it was. Man, man, was there ever a worse curse of God?'

'Well, friend—in regard to that—ahem! what can I say to you? When a woman chooses to take the crooked path, like yours, give her the stick, and plenty of it. If with that she doesn't mend her ways and float off in good style, then either sink her to the bottom, once for all, or string yourself up to a yard-arm.'

'I've told you already—what's the matter with you?—that I've covered every inch of her body with the welts of a stick, and I've decorated her face all over with bruises till there's hardly room for another.'

'Then go hang yourself, and leave me in peace to finish these meshes. And you may as well know that the reason I never married is to keep out of the devil's own scrape that you are in.'

WILLIAM HENRY BISHOP

PEDRO ANTONIO DE ALARCÓN
[1833–1891]

*An inspired and skilful teller of tales, the Andalusian Pedro Antonio de Alarcón wrote what has been termed the most perfect short story in all Spanish literature—*El sombrero de tres picos (1874). *Closer to a novelette in length, it is based on the popular legend of the mayor and the miller's wife. The picaresque story is related in graceful, humorous style against a glowing Andalusian background; its characters are so vividly delineated that they seem alive.*

Besides the charming Sombrero de tres picos, *Alarcón wrote many excellent short stories and a number of long novels, of which the best is* El escándalo.

THE THREE-CORNERED HAT

CHAPTER XI

THE BOMBARDMENT OF PAMPELUNA

'God save you, Frasquita,' said the Corregidor, in a low tone, appearing under the grapevine and walking on tip-toe.

'Oh, Señor Corregidor, how good of you,' she replied in her usual tone of voice, making a deep curtsy. 'You Honour here at this time of day, and when it is so very warm! Well, well, please sit down here, Your Honour. It is cool here; why did not your Lordship wait for the other gentlemen. I have their seats all ready for them. We expect the Lord Bishop himself this afternoon, who has promised my Luke to come to taste some of the first grapes off the vine. And how do you do? and how is your lady?'

The Corregidor was confused. He did desire to find Frasquita alone, but it seemed to him now like a dream, or else a snare spread by treacherous fate to decoy him into a yawning gulf of deception. He therefore only answered:

'It is not so early as you imagine it is. It is certainly half-past three.' Just then the parrot squawked the hour.

'It is exactly a quarter-past two!' said the Navarrese, staring at the Corregidor full in the face.

He kept silent like a convicted criminal who renounces his defence.

'And Luke? is he asleep?' he inquired after a short pause.

Now just at this point, we must tell you that the Corregidor, like all who have no teeth, spoke with a drivelling, hissing sound, as though he were chewing his own lips.

'Of course,' replied Señá Frasquita, 'usually at this time he falls asleep, wherever he may be, even if it were on the edge of a precipice.'

'Well, just let him sleep on,' exclaimed the Corregidor, turning even paler than usual. 'And you, my dear Frasquita, listen to me; hark ye, come here. Sit down by my side. I have a great deal to say to you.'

'There now, I'm ready,' replied the miller's wife, bringing a low chair, and putting it in front of the Corregidor at a very short distance from his own.

As soon as she was seated, Frasquita crossed one leg over the other, leaned forward, resting her elbow on her knee, which she kept trotting up and down; and leaning her fresh and lovely face on one of her hands; and so with her head bent a little to one side, a smile on her lips, her bodice provocatively gaping, the five dimples in full play, and her clear eyes fixed on the Corregidor, she waited to hear what he would say. You might have compared her, figuratively, to Pampeluna waiting for the bombardment.

The poor man tried to speak, but remained dumbfounded, with his mouth wide open, before the superb beauty of that formidable woman, with her exuberant charms, her alabaster-like complexion, her magnificent form, her overwhelming bosom, her lovely smiling lips, her deep, unfathomable blue eyes, and looking altogether like one of Rubens' creations.

'Frasquita,' the King's Delegate murmured at last in a faint voice, while his wrinkled face, covered with perspiration rising above his hump, expressed the greatest anguish, 'Frasquita.'

'That's my name,' replied the daughter of the Pyrenees. 'Well, what is it?'

'Whatever you like,' replied the old man most tenderly.

'Well, your Honour already knows what I want. I want you to appoint my nephew in Estella as Secretary of the City Corporation, so that he may get away from those mountains where he is having such a hard time of it.'

'I told you, Frasquita, that it is quite impossible. The Secretary who now holds that office——'

'Is a thief, a drunkard, and a beast!'

'Yes, I know it, but he has a good hold on the Perpetual Alderman, and I cannot appoint a new one without the sanction of the City Corporation. If I did, I would run the risk of——'

'Would run the risk of! Would run the risk of! What wouldn't we risk for your Honour? yes, even to the cats in the house.'

'Would you like me at that price?' stuttered the old Corregidor.

'No, sir, for I love your Lordship gratis.'

'Child, do not treat me with so much formality, say simply—you—do not say your Lordship. Call me what you please. So you will like me? Say now.'

'Have I not already told you that I like you?'

'But.'

'But—there's no but worth a button. You'll see how handsome my nephew is, what an honest fellow he is !'

'You, indeed, are handsome, Frasquita.'

'Do you really like me?'

'Do I like you? There is no woman equal to you.'

'Well, see here, there's nothing false here,' replied Frasquita, rolling up her sleeve of her bodice, and displaying to the Corregidor the rest of her arm whiter than a lily, and a fit model for a sculptor.

'Do I like thee?' continued the Corregidor. 'By day and by night, at all hours, wherever I may be, I am thinking of thee.'

'How's that? Don't you like the Lady Mayoress?' inquired Señá Frasquita, with such poorly feigned compassion that it would have moved even a hypochondriac to mirth. 'What a pity! My Luke says that he had the pleasure of meeting her and talking with her, when he went to regulate the clock in your sleeping chamber, and that she is very beautiful, very good, and has very sweet manners.'

'Not quite, not quite,' murmured the Corregidor, with a certain degree of bitterness.

'On the other hand, some say,' added the miller's wife, 'that she has a bad temper, and is very jealous, and that you fear her more than a green switch.'

'Not quite, my girl,' replied Don Eugene de Zuñiga Ponce de Leon, turning red. 'Not so much, nor so little. My lady has her whims, it's true, but that she makes me quake with fear is a very different matter. I am the Corregidor.'

'But, in short, do you love her or not?'

'I'll tell you the truth. I love her a great deal, or I should say, I did before I knew you. But since I saw you I don't know what is the matter with me, and she herself knows that something ails me. You must know, for instance, to caress my wife's face would not affect me more than if I touched my own. So you see, I cannot like her more, nor feel less, while just to touch your hand, your arm, your waist, I would give what I have not got.'

So saying the Corregidor attempted to seize the bare arm which Frasquita was actually rubbing into his eyes, but she, without losing her self-possession in the least, extended her hand, just touched his Lordship's chest with the pacific force and incomparable rigidity of an elephant's trunk, and threw him sprawling on the ground, chair and all.

'*Ave Maria Purisima!*' exclaimed the Navarrese, laughing until she could laugh no longer. 'It seems that chair must have been broken.'

'What's going on down there?' just at this moment exclaimed Uncle Luke, with his homely face looming out among the leaves and the tendrils of the grapevine. The Corregidor was still lying on his back on the ground, and looked up with unutterable fear at the man who now appeared suspended in the air face downward. One might say that his Honour was the devil conquered not by St. Michael, but by some fiend from the infernal regions.

'What's going on?' answered Frasquita briskly. 'Why, the Señor Corregidor went to balance his chair on nothing, went to rock on it, and over he fell!'

'Jesus, Mary and Joseph!' piously exclaimed the miller. 'And has his Honour hurt himself? Do you want some vinegar and water?'

'Oh, no, I have not hurt myself,' said the Corregidor, getting up as well as he could, while he added in a low tone, but so that Frasquita could hear him:

'You'll pay for this.'

'But, then, on the other hand, his Honour saved my life,' added the miller, without moving from his perch, 'Just imagine, wife, I was seated up here, gazing at the grapes, when I fell asleep on a network of twigs and stalks, which left an opening big enough for my body to fall through. So if you had not awakened me by your fall, just as you did, I might have broken my head against those stones.'

'Is that so? Eh,' replied the Corregidor; 'well, I am glad of it, I assure you. I am really glad that I fell down.'

'I'll pay you up for this,' he added immediately after, addressing the miller's wife.

He pronounced these words with such an expression of concentrated rage that Frasquita immediately became serious. She perceived that the Corregidor had got frightened at first, thinking that the miller had overheard all, but since he was convinced now that he had not, for Uncle Luke's dissimulation would have disarmed the most suspicious being, he began to give way to his passion and try to devise some means of revenging himself.

'Come now, get down from there and help me brush his Honour, for he is covered with dust,' exclaimed Frasquita.

While Uncle Luke was getting down from the trellis, she remarked to the Corregidor, brushing his coat with her apron and, in her zeal, occasionally giving him some hard cuffs over the ears :

'The poor fellow did not hear anything. He was as sound asleep as a log.' The very fact that she uttered these words in a low tone, more than the words themselves, pretending to have a secret understanding with him, produced a most marvellous effect.

'You rogue, you sly kitten,' stammered Don Eugene de Zuñiga, with his mouth watering, but still grunting.

'Do you still feel angry with me?' asked Frasquita coaxingly.

As the Corregidor noticed that his severity produced a good effect, he tried to look at her with anger; but when he met her bewitching smile, her heavenly eyes gazing at him so imploringly, his ire melted at once, and he said with a drivelling and hissing accent, displaying more than ever his total lack of teeth :

'It all depends on you, my darling—' Now at this particular moment, down dropped Uncle Luke from the grapevine trellis.

CHAPTER XX

DOUBT AND REALITY

It was now open, and yet when he left he had heard his wife close and fasten it with key, bolt, and bar. Consequently only his own wife could have opened it. But how? Why? When? Had it been the result of some treachery? Or was it in consequence of a command? Or had she opened it deliberately and voluntarily by virtue of a previous understanding with the Corregidor? What was he about to see? What awaited him at home? Had Frasquita eloped? Had she been carried off? Was she dead, or was she in the arms of his rival? 'The Corregidor was sure that I could not possibly get back tonight,' said Uncle Luke gloomily, 'and the village Alcalde had orders even to chain me up before letting me come home, without doubt. Was Frasquita aware of all this? Was she in the plot? Or has she been the victim of some deceit, some violent act of villainy?'

The time it took for these cruel reflections to pass through the wretched man's brain was just while he was crossing the square under the grapevine. The front door of the house was also open, and the front room was the kitchen as in all rustic dwellings. There was no one in the kitchen. Nevertheless an enormous fire of faggots blazed away in the fireplace—the fireplace which he had left bare; for they never built a fire until way into the middle of December. Lastly, on one of the hooks on the rack a lighted lamp was hanging.

What was the meaning of all this? And how could such a sign of company and watchfulness tally with the death-like stillness which reigned in the house? What had become of his wife?

Then and only then did uncle Luke notice that some clothes were hanging on the backs of two or three chairs placed around in front of the hearth.

He fixed his gaze on the apparel and then gave a hoarse cry, as though it strangled in his throat and was turned into a dumb and suffocating sob. The unhappy man thought that he was choking, and put his hand to his throat, while pale, convulsed, with his eyes starting from their sockets, he gazed at the apparel, filled with as much horror as a criminal about to be executed, to whom they bring the black shroud of death. Because what he beheld was the red cloak, the three-cornered hat, the dove-coloured coat and waistcoat, the black silk breeches, the white stockings, the shoes with buckles, and even the cane, the small sword, and the gloves of the execrable Corregidor. What he saw there was the robe of his ignominy, the shroud of his honour, the winding sheet of his happiness.

The formidable blunderbuss was in the same corner still, where the Navarrese had left it two hours ago.

Uncle Luke gave a leap like a tiger and seized it. He tried the barrel with the ramrod, and found that it was loaded. He looked at the flint and found it in its proper place. Then he turned toward the staircase which led to the bedroom which he and his wife had shared so many years together, while he murmured hoarsely : 'They are there !' He advanced a step in that direction, but immediately stopped to look round about him to see whether anyone was watching him. 'Nobody,' he murmured mentally, 'only my Heavenly Father—God—and He has allowed this to happen !'

The sentence thus pronounced, he was going to advance a step forward, when his wandering gaze alighted on a document which was lying on the table. To see it, fall on it, and seize it in his grasp, was but the work of a second.

That document was the appointment of Frasquita's nephew, signed by Don Eugene de Zuñiga Ponce de Leon.

'So this was the price of the transaction,' muttered Uncle Luke, stuffing the paper into his mouth in order to stifle his cries and to feed his rage. 'I always feared that she cared more for her family than for me! Alas, we never had any children! This is the cause of it all!'

And the unhappy man almost burst into tears again. But he again became infuriated, and expressed it by a terrible gesture, but without words.

'Up, up!' and he began to creep up the stairway on all fours, feeling around with one hand, while carrying the blunderbuss in the other, and the infamous paper between his teeth. To corroborate his reasonable suspicions, on arriving at the door of the room, which was closed, he saw some rays of light issuing through the cracks in the door, and through the keyhole.

'There they are!' he repeated, stopping a moment as though to swallow this new dose of bitterness.

Then he went on until he reached the very door of the bedroom; no noise was to be heard from within.

'Suppose that there is nobody there!' hope suggested timidly, but at that very moment the unfortunate man heard someone cough in the room.

It was the Corregidor's asthmatic cough!

There was no longer any doubt about it! No plank was left on which to save himself from the wreck.

The miller smiled in the darkness in a horrible manner. How is it that such lightning flashes do not shine out in the dark? what is all the fire of the infernal regions compared to that which sometimes rages in the heart of man?

Notwithstanding, Uncle Luke's temperament was so peculiar, as we have already stated that as soon as he heard his enemy's cough he became calmer. Reality did him less harm than doubt. As he had told Frasquita that afternoon, from the very moment and the hour that he lost the faith which was the very life of his soul, he was transfigured into another man. Like the Moor of Venice, with whom we compared him at the beginning of this tale in describing his peculiar temperament, disenchantment killed his love at one blow, causing him to look on the world like a strange region in which he had just arrived. The only difference was that Uncle Luke's temperament was less tragic, less austere, and more selfish than that of Desdemona's stupid destroyer.

It was very singular, indeed, but the natural result of such situations!

Doubt, or hope, which in that case is perchance the same, began to torment him again, for a moment. 'Suppose I was mistaken,' he thought. 'Suppose it were Frasquita who coughed.'

But, in the midst of his unfortunate tribulation, he forgot for a moment that he had seen the Corregidor's apparel in front of the hearthstone, that he had found the door of the mill open, and that he had read the credential of his dishonour. Then, stooping down, he peered through the keyhole, trembling with doubt and anxiety. But his visual range could only discern a small corner of the couch, just by the headpost, and exactly within that limited range he saw one end of the pillows, and resting there was the Corregidor's head!

Another diabolical smile disfigured the miller's face. It might be said that he was beginning to be happy again.

'I have mastered the truth,' he said. 'Let me think,' he added, drawing himself up proudly.

And he descended the stairs as cautiously as he had ascended, and while he went on his way, he reflected, 'This is a delicate affair, but I have time and to spare for all!'

When he reached the kitchen, he sat down in the middle of the room, and covered his face with his hands. He remained so for some time, till he was startled from his meditation by a slight blow on his foot. It was the blunderbuss, which had slipped off his knees and made him this sort of signal.

'No, I tell you no!' murmured Uncle Luke, facing the weapon. 'You don't suit me! All the world would pity them, and they would hang me! This affair treats with a mayor, and it is still an unpardonable offence in Spain to kill a mayor. They would say that I killed him for unfounded jealousy, and afterward undressed him, and put him in my bed. Furthermore they'd say that I killed my wife on simple suspicion—and they'd hang me! Of course they'd hang me! Besides, I'd be very mean-spirited if the end of my life should inspire pity! Everybody would laugh at me! They'd say that my misfortune was only natural, I being a humpback and Frasquita a beauty! No, indeed! what I need is to avenge myself, and, after I have avenged myself, to triumph over them, loathe them, and laugh, laugh till I can laugh no longer; laugh at all of them; and so prevent anyone from ever making sport of this hump, which I have succeeded in making even enviable, and which would look so grotesque on the scaffold!'

Thus reasoned Uncle Luke, and perhaps unconsciously; and as the result of his pondering he put the weapon in its place, and commenced to pace up and down, with his head bowed, and his hands behind his back, as though seeking for some means of vengeance, on the floor, in the earth, in the baseness of life; for some way of inflicting a ludicrous and ignominious vengeance on his wife and the Corregidor, far from seeking redress from the law, or in a duel, in forgiveness, or in heaven; as some other man, less rebellious against the restraints of nature and society, or his own sentiments, might have done in his place.

Suddenly his eyes alighted on the Corregidor's clothes. Then his face began to express, little by little, joy, pleasure, and an inexpressible triumph, until at last he began to laugh in a frightful manner; that is, shaking with uncontrollable laughter, but without making any noise. So none should overhear him upstairs, he held on to his sides as though not to split, shaking all over as if with an epileptic fit; and at last threw himself into a chair, until this sardonic burst of merriment passed off. It was like the satanic glee of Mephistopheles.

As soon as he became calmer, he began to undress with feverish haste, and put all his clothes on the same chairs where the Corregidor's were. Then he put on all his apparel, from the shoes with buckles to the three-cornered hat; buckled on the small sword; wrapped himself in the red cloak, took the cane and gloves and left the mill, going toward the city with the very same swaggering gait characteristic of Don Eugene de Zuñiga, and muttering once in a while these words, which gave an inkling to his purpose :

'The mayor's wife is very luscious also.'

CHAPTER XXXI

LEX TALIONIS

'Mercedes !' exclaimed the Corregidor, appearing before his wife, 'I must know immediately——'

'Ah, Uncle Luke! so you are here?' interrupted the mayoress. 'Has anything happened at the mill?'

'Madame, I am in no mood for jesting !' replied the infuriated Corregidor. 'Before entering into explanations on my part, I must know what has become of my honour.'

'That is not my affair. Did you perchance leave it in my keeping?'

'Yes, madame, in yours,' replied Don Eugene. 'The wife is the keeper of her husband's honour.'

'Well, then, my dear Uncle Luke, ask your wife there; she is listening to us now.'

Señá Frasquita, who was standing at the door of the apartment, gave a sort of hoarse cry.

'Come in, madame, and sit down,' continued the mayoress, addressing the miller's wife with queenly dignity, and going toward the sofa herself. The generous and high-minded Navarrese knew how to understand all the grandeur of the wronged wife's attitude, doubly wronged, perchance. Thus raising herself to the same level, and restraining her natural impetuosity, she preserved a decorous silence; all the more so, as Dame Frasquita, sure of her own innocence and strength, was in no haste to defend herself.

She was most certainly prepared to make accusations, and heavy ones too, but not against the mayoress. The person with whom she wanted to settle accounts was Uncle Luke, and Uncle Luke was not there !

'Señá Frasquita,' repeated the noble dame, perceiving that the miller's wife had not moved from her place, 'I have told you that you might come in and sit down.'

This second invitation was given in a kinder and more affectionate manner than the first. It appeared as though the mayoress instinctively perceived, on looking at that woman's noble beauty, that she was not about to deal with a vulgar and despicable being; but perchance another as unfortunate as herself; unfortunate, surely, in the mere fact of having known the Corregidor.

So those two delectable ladies, who considered each other as rivals, doubly so, exchanged peaceful and forgiving looks and were surprised to feel that their souls seemed to soothe each other, like two sisters meeting again. Somewhat in this fashion do the chaste snows of lofty mountains salute each other from afar.

In the enjoyment of these sweet emotions the miller's wife entered the room majestically, and sat down on the edge of the chair.

When she passed by the mill, foreseeing that she would have to make some important visits in the city, she had arranged her toilet a little, and put on a black flannel mantelet, trimmed with broad fringe, which was very becoming to her, so she looked just like a lady.

As for the Corregidor, he had not opened his lips during this episode. Mistress Frasquita's hoarse cry of rage, and her appearance on the scene, had startled him. He was more afraid of that woman than of his own wife.

'So now, Uncle Luke,' continued Donna Mercedes, addressing her husband. 'There you have Señá Frasquita. You may repeat your charge to her. You can now ask her about that little affair of your honour.'

'Mercedes, by the blood of Christ!' shouted the Corregidor, 'take care; you do not know of what I am capable! I again command you to stop joking, and tell me all that has transpired here during my absence! Where is that man?'

'Who, my husband? My husband is getting up and will soon be here.'

'Getting up!' roared Don Eugene.

'Are you surprised? Well, where would you expect an honest man to be at this hour of the night but in his own home, in his own room, with his own lawful wife, as God has commanded.'

'Mercedes, take care what you say! Remember that they are listening to us! Recollect that I am the Corregidor!'

'Don't dare to raise your voice to me, Uncle Luke; or I shall tell the alguazils to march you off to prison,' replied the mayoress, starting to her feet.

'Take me to jail? Me, the Corregidor of the city?'

'The Corregidor of the city, the representative of justice, the King's Delegate,' replied the noble lady with energetic severity, which drowned the voice of the fictitious miller, 'came home at the usual hour, to rest from the arduous duties of his noble office, in order to be able to continue tomorrow to protect the honour and the lives of our citizens, the sanctity of their homes, and the purity of their women, so that no one, disguised as a corregidor, or in any other disguise, shall be able to penetrate into the apartments of his neighbour's wife; that nobody shall overcome her virtue when resting secure in slumber, nor take advantage of her chaste repose.'

'Mercedes, what are you saying?' hissed the Corregidor between his lips and gums. 'If it is true that such a thing has happened in my dwelling, I shall say that you are a sly, perfidious, and abandoned woman!'

'To whom is that man talking?' burst forth the mayoress disdainfully, looking all around at the assembled company. 'Who is that lunatic? Who is that tippler? I cannot believe that he is an honest miller like Uncle Luke, in spite of his wearing a peasant's garb.

'Don Juan Lopez, believe me,' she said, facing the country alcalde, who was stupefied with fear. 'My husband, the Corregidor of the city, came home two hours ago, with his three-cornered hat, his red cloak, his knightly sword and his official staff; the alguazils and the servants, who are listening to me now, arose, and saluted him as he passed through the portico, went upstairs, and through the ante-chamber. All the doors were immediately closed, and since then, no one else has entered my dwelling, until your arrival. It is not so? Answer, all of you.'

'It is true, very true!' replied the nurse, the servants, and the attendants, who were all grouped around the door of the salon, witnessing this most extraordinary scene.

'Get out of here, every one of you!' cried Don Eugene, foaming at the mouth with rage. 'Garduña, Garduña, come and arrest all these scoundrels who are insulting me! Off to jail with them! Off to the scaffold!'

But Garduña did not make his appearance.

'Furthermore, sir,' continued Donna Mercedes, changing her tone, and condescending to look at her husband and consider him as such once more, afraid that the joke might be carried too far; 'Let us suppose that you are Don Eugene de Zuñiga y Ponce de Leon.'

'So I am!'

'Let us suppose, in addition, that I might be slightly to blame in having mistaken for you the man who entered my apartment, dressed as the Corregidor.'

'Vile wretches!' cried the old man, attempting to draw his sword, and finding only the miller's sash in place of it.

The Navarrese covered her face with one end of her mantilla, in order to conceal her jealous rage. 'Let us suppose that all you say may be true,' continued Donna Mercedes, with inexplicable calmness.

'But, answer me now, sir, would you have a right to complain? Could you accuse me as a prosecutor, could you condemn me as a judge? Do you happen to come from mass? Do you come from confession? Do you come from hearing a sermon? Or where do you come from, in that garb? Whence do you come with that lady? Where have you passed half of the night?'

'With your permission!' exclaimed Frasquita, jumping up as though moved by springs, and coming proudly between the mayoress and her husband.

The latter, who was just about to speak, remained with his mouth wide open on seeing the Navarrese open the attack. But Donna Mercedes forestalled her by saying:

'Madame, do not trouble yourself to explain anything to me. I do not require any explanations at all. Here comes the proper person to demand them, armed with the rights of a husband. Explain yourself to him.'

At the same moment, the door of the boudoir opened, and Uncle Luke made his appearance, dressed like the Corregidor, from head to foot, with his cane, gauntlets, and small sword; just as he used to present himself in the Hall of the Corporation.

CHAPTER XXXII

FAITH MOVES MOUNTAINS

'Good evening, gentlemen and ladies,' said the newcomer, taking off his three-cornered hat, and talking with his mouth drawn in, as Don Eugene de Zuñiga had the habit of doing.

Immediately afterward he advanced into the salon with his swaggering gait and proceeded to kiss the mayoress's hand.

All were astounded. The resemblance of Uncle Luke to the real Corregidor was truly marvellous, so that even the servants and Don Juan Lopez could not restrain their mirth. Don Eugene felt this new insult keenly, and sprang upon Uncle Luke like a serpent.

But Dame Frasquita came to the rescue, and with her robust arm pulled the Corregidor away, and his Honour, to avoid toppling over again and the subsequent derision this would involve, made no effort to defend himself, neither saying yea nor nay. It was plain to see that this woman was destined to be the tamer of the poor old man.

Uncle Luke turned paler than death, on seeing that his wife drew near him; but afterward restrained himself, while with a burst of laughter, so violent that he was obliged to put his hand on his heart, so that it should not burst, he said, mimicking the Corregidor:

'God keep you, Frasquita, have you already sent the appointment to your nephew?'

The Navarrese was then a sight to behold. She threw back her mantilla, raised her head as proudly as a lioness, and fixing her eyes like two daggers on the false Corregidor, thrusting her face close to his, said:

'I despise you, Luke!'

All thought that she had spat on him, for her gesture, her attitude, and her tone of voice gave force to her words.

On hearing his wife, the miller's face become transfigured. A sort of inspiration, like that of a religious belief, had penetrated his soul, inundating it with light and joy. For a moment he forgot all that he had seen, or thought he had seen in the mill, while he exclaimed with tears in his eyes and sincerity on his lips :

'So you are my own Frasquita still?'

'No !' replied the Navarrese, beside herself. 'I am not any longer your Frasquita ! I am—— You may ask your exploits of tonight who I am, and they will tell you what you have done to the woman who loved you so dearly !'

So saying, she burst into tears—and seemed like an iceberg when it begins to melt, and is about to sink.

The mayoress advanced toward her, no longer able to restrain herself, throwing her arms around her with the greatest affection. Señá Frasquita began to kiss her, without being conscious either of what she was doing; saying in the midst of her sobs, like a child who seeks for shelter in her mother's arms :

'Madame, madame, how unhappy I am !'

'Not so much as you fancy you are !' answered the mayoress, shedding tears of sympathy.

'I am the unhappy one !' blubbered Uncle Luke, ramming his fists into his eyes, which were overflowing with tears, as though he were ashamed to shed them.

'Well then, and I ?' burst forth at length Don Eugene, feeling himself moved by the contagious grief of the rest, and hoping to save himself also by giving full play to his lachrymal glands. 'Alas, I am a scamp, a monster, a hot-headed man who has only got what he deserved !'

And he began to bellow mournfully, clasping the ponderous waist of Don Juan Lopez, while the latter and the servants likewise cried, and it looked as though everything had ended, but notwithstanding no one had made any kind of an explanation whatever.

CHAPTER XXXV

AN IMPERIAL EDICT

Just then the Corregidor and Uncle Luke returned to the room, each dressed in his own clothes.

'It is my turn now !' said the arrogant Don Eugene de Zuñiga as he entered.

After thumping the floor with his cane, as though to regain his energy, like unto an official Antaeus, who did not feel his strength till his Indian reed touched the earth, he said emphatically to the mayoress :

'Mercedes, I am waiting to hear your explanations.'

Meanwhile the miller's wife had risen and given Uncle Luke such a playful pinch as a token of peace, that it made him see stars, although she looked at him at the same time with happy and bewitching eyes.

The Corregidor, who observed this pantomime, was bedazzled, without being able to comprehend a reconciliation which seemed so senseless to him. He therefore addressed his wife again, saying in a tone as sour as vinegar :

'Madame, they all understand one another except you and I. Relieve me of my doubts. I command you to do so as your husband and as the Corregidor.'

So saying, he thumped again on the floor with his cane.

'So you are going!' exclaimed Donna Mercedes, drawing near Mistress Frasquita, without paying any attention whatever to Don Eugene. 'Well, rest assured that all this disturbance will have no further result. Rosa, light the way for these gentlefolks, who say that they are going. Good-bye, Uncle Luke.'

'Oh, no!' cried Zuñiga, thrusting himself in the way. 'As for Uncle Luke, he shall not go! Uncle Luke is under arrest until I discover the truth! Here, ho! alguazils. In the King's name!'

Not a soul stirred to obey Don Eugene. All looked at the mayoress.

'Come now, man, clear the way!' added she, passing almost over her husband, and dismissing everybody with the greatest politeness; that is, with her head bent to one side, catching up her skirt with the tips of her fingers, and stooping down gracefully to complete the courtesy in vogue at that time, called *la pompa*.

'But I—but you—but we—but they!' cried the old man, mumbling his words, pulling at his wife's dress, and spoiling her best courtesies.

Useless labour. Nobody paid any attention to his Honour.

As soon as all had gone away, and the discordant couple were left alone, the mayoress deigned to remark to her husband at last, in a tone with which a Russian Czarina might have fulminated upon a fallen Minister the order of perpetual banishment to Siberia :

'If you live a thousand years, you shall never know what transpired tonight in my apartment. If you had been there in your proper place you would have no need to ask anybody. As for my part, there is no longer, nor never will be, any reason to oblige me to give you satisfaction; because I despise you so thoroughly that, if you were not the father of my children, I would throw you over the balcony, at once; as I now cast you out from my apartment forever. So, good night, sir!'

After pronouncing these words, which Don Eugene heard without winking, because, when he found himself alone with his wife, he dared not cope with her, the mayoress passed into her boudoir, and from that to her bedroom, closing the door behind her; while the wretched old man was left standing in the middle of the drawing-room, mumbling with unparalleled cynicism between his gums, for he had no teeth :

'Well, sir ! I did not expect to get off so well. Garduña will find me another one !'

CHAPTER XXXVI

CONCLUSION, MORAL, AND EPILOGUE

The birds were saluting the dawn of day when Uncle Luke and Frasquita left the city on their way to the mill.

The married pair went afoot, while the coupled donkeys trotted on ahead.

'Sunday you must go to confession,' said the miller's wife to her husband, 'because you must clear your conscience of all your bad conclusions and wicked purposes of tonight.'

'You are right,' replied the miller. 'But, meanwhile, you must do me a favour, and that is to give away to the poor the mattress and all the bedclothes in our room, and get everything new. I will not lie down where that venomous beast has lain !'

'Don't speak of him, Luke !' replied his wife. 'Let us talk of something else. I want you to do me another favour.'

'Open your mouth and ask.'

'Next summer you must take me to the baths at the Solanillos.'

'What for?'

'To see whether we may have any children.'

'Most happy thought ! I will certainly take you, if God spares our lives.'

Just then they arrived at the mill, while the rising sun was just gilding the mountain-tops.

That afternoon, much to the surprise of the worthy couple, who did not expect any distinguished visitors to come there again after a scandal like that of the preceding night, more people of rank came to the mill than ever before, the venerable prelate, a number of canons, the advocate, two priors from the convent, and several other dignitaries; and later on they found out that all had been summoned to meet there by His Grace the Bishop; and they quite filled the square in the grapevine arbour.

Only the Corregidor was wanting. When the company were all

assembled the worthy bishop took the floor, saying that for the very reason that certain things had happened in that dwelling, his canons and he would continue to frequent it the same as ever, so that neither the honest miller, nor any of the other people gathered there, should suffer from public censure, only merited by the one who had profaned by his wicked conduct, a reunion so circumspect and so orderly. He exhorted Mistress Frasquita, in a fatherly way, to be less provocative and coquettish in her sayings and doings in future; and to endeavour to wear her bodice cut higher in the neck, and to cover her arms more. He advised Uncle Luke to show more disinterestedness, greater circumspection and reserve in his demeanour toward his superiors; and concluded by bestowing his blessing on all, and adding that, as he was not fasting on that day, he would eat a couple of clusters of grapes with great gusto.

All agreed with him regarding this last point, so that the grape-vine was left in a trembling condition that afternoon; and Uncle Luke calculated the cost to him at fifty pounds of grapes.

MARY J. SERRANO

JUAN VALERA
[1824–1905]

Juan Valera combined a distinguished diplomatic career with that of a dedicated littérateur. An exponent of 'art for art's sake', he excelled in the field of literary criticism. But he is most famous for his penetrating psychological novel, Pepita Jiménez *(1874).*

The first part of the novel consists of letters from a young seminary student, Don Luis, to his uncle. The youth's character reveals itself in the course of these letters, and Valera masterfully depicts his hero's panic as he becomes aware of his perilous situation. Valera's prose is faultless; his style, almost classic in feeling.

PEPITA JIMÉNEZ

LETTERS FROM DON LUIS TO HIS UNCLE

May 19th.

I return thanks to Heaven and to you for the letters and the counsels you have lately sent me. Today I need them more than ever.

The mystical and learned St. Theresa is right in dwelling upon the suffering of timid souls that allow themselves to be disturbed by temptation; but a thousand times worse than that suffering is the awakening from error of those who, like me, have permitted themselves to indulge in arrogance and self-confidence.

Our bodies are the temples of the Holy Spirit; but when fire is set to the walls of the temple, though they do not burn, yet they are blackened.

The first evil thought is the head of the serpent; if we do not crush it with firm and courageous foot, then will the venomous reptile climb up and hide himself in our bosom.

The nectar of earthly joys, however innocent they be, is sweet to the taste; but afterward it is converted into gall, and into the venom of the serpent.

It is true—I can no longer deny it to you—I ought not to have allowed my eyes to rest with so much complacency on this dangerous woman.

I do not deem myself lost; but I feel my soul troubled.

Even as the thirsty hart desires and seeks the water-brooks, so does my soul still seek God. To God does it turn that He may give it rest; it longs to drink at the torrent of His delights, whose gushing waters rejoice Paradise, and whose clear waves can wash us whiter than snow; but deep calleth unto deep, and my feet have stuck fast in the mire that is hidden in their abysses.

Yet have I still breath and voice to cry out with the psalmist: 'Arise, my joy! If thou art on my side, who shall prevail against me?'

I say unto my sinful soul, full of the chimerical imaginings and sinful desires engendered by unlawful thoughts: 'Oh, miserable daughter of Babylon! happy shall he be who shall give thee thy reward! Happy shall he be that dasheth thy little ones against the stones!'

Works of penance, fasting, prayer, and penitence, are the weapons wherewith I shall arm myself to the combat, and, with the Divine help, to vanquish.

It was not a dream, it was not madness; it was the truth. She lets her eyes rest upon me at times with the ardent glance of which I have told you. There is in her glance an inexplicable magnetic attraction. It draws me on, it seduces me, and I cannot withdraw my gaze from her. On such occasions my eyes must burn, like hers, with a fatal flame, as did those of Ammon when he turned them upon Tamar, as did those of the prince of Shechem when they were fixed upon Dinah.

When our glances thus meet, I forget even God. Her image rises up within my soul, the conqueror of everything. Her beauty outshines all other beauty; the joys of heaven seem to me less desirable than her affection. An eternity of suffering would be little in exchange for a moment of the infinite bliss with which one of those glances which pass like lightning inundates my soul.

When I return home, when I am alone in my room, in the silence of the night, I realize all the horror of my position, and I form good resolutions, only to break them again.

I resolve to feign sickness, to make use of any pretext so as not to go to Pepita's on the following night, and yet I go.

My father, confiding to the last degree, says to me when the hour arrives, without any suspicion of what is passing in my soul:

'Go to Pepita's; I will go later, when I have finished with the overseer.'

No excuse occurs to me; I can find no pretext for not going, and instead of answering, 'I cannot go,' I take my hat and depart.

On entering the room I shake hands with Pepita, and as our hands touch she casts a spell over me; my whole being is changed; a devouring fire penetrates my heart, and I think only of her. Moved by an irresistible impulse, I gaze at her with insane ardour, and at every instant I think I discover in her new perfections. Now it is the dimples in her cheeks when she smiles, now the roseate whiteness of her skin, now the straight outline of her nose, now the smallness of her ear, now the softness of contour and the admirable modelling of her throat.

I enter her house against my will, as though summoned there by a conjurer, and no sooner am I there than I fall under the spell of her enchantment. I see clearly that I am in the power of an enchantress whose fascination is irresistible.

Not only is she pleasing to my sight, but her words sound in my ears like the music of the spheres, revealing to my soul the harmony of the universe; and I even fancy that a subtle fragrance emanates from her, sweeter than the perfume of the mint that grows by the brookside, or the woodlike odour of the thyme that is found among the hills.

I know not how, in this state of exaltation, I am able to play *ombre*, or to converse rationally, or even to speak, so completely am I absorbed in her.

When our eyes meet, our souls rush forth in them and seem to join and interpenetrate each other. In that meeting a thousand feelings are communicated that in no other way could be made known; poems are recited that could be uttered in no human tongue, and songs are sung that no human voice could sing, and no guitar accompany.

Since the day I met Pepita by the Pozo de la Solana I have not seen her alone. Not a word has passed between us, yet we have told each other everything.

When I withdraw myself from this fascination, when I am again alone at night in my chamber, I set myself to examine coolly the situation in which I am placed; I see the abyss that is about to engulf me yawning before me; I feel my feet slip from under me, and that I am sinking into it.

You counsel me to reflect upon death—not on the death of this woman, but on my own. You counsel me to reflect on the instability, on the insecurity of our existence, and on what there is beyond it. But these considerations, these reflections neither terrify nor daunt me. Why should I, who desire to die, fear death? Love and death are brothers. A sentiment of self-abnegation springs to life within me, and tells me that my whole being should be consecrated to and annihilated in the beloved object. I long to merge myself in one of her glances; to diffuse and exhale my whole being in the ray of light shot forth from her eyes; to die while gazing on her, even though I should be eternally lost.

What is still to some extent efficacious with me against this love is not fear, but love itself. Superior to this deep-rooted love with which I now have evidence that Pepita inspires me, Divine love exalts itself in my spirit in mighty uprising. Then everything is changed within me, and I feel that I may yet obtain the victory. The object of my higher love presents itself to my mental vision, as the sun that kindles and illuminates all things, and fills all space with light; and the object of my inferior love appears but as an atom of dust floating in the sunbeam. All her beauty, all her splendour, all her attractions are nothing but the reflection of this uncreated sun, the brilliant, transitory, fleeting spark that is cast off from that infinite and inexhaustible fire.

My soul, burning with love, would fain take itself wings and rise to that flame, in order that all that is impure within it might be consumed therein.

My life, for some days past, is a constant struggle. I know not how it is that the malady which I suffer does not betray itself in my countenance. I scarcely eat, I scarcely sleep; and if by chance sleep closes my eyelids, I awake in terror, as from a dream in which rebel angels are arrayed against good angels, and in which I am one of the combatants. In this conflict of light against darkness I do battle for the right, but I sometimes imagine that I have gone over to the enemy, that I am a vile deserter; and I hear a voice from Patmos saying, 'And men loved darkness rather than light'; and then I am filled with terror, and I look upon myself as lost.

No recourse is left me but flight. If, before the end of the month, my father does not go with me, or consent to my going alone, I shall steal away like a thief, without a word to any one.

May 23rd.

I am a vile worm, not a man; I am the opprobrium and disgrace of humanity. I am a hypocrite.

I have been encompassed by the pangs of death, and the waters of iniquity have passed over me.

I am ashamed to write to you, and yet I write. I desire to confess everything to you.

I can not turn away from evil. Far from abstaining from going to Pepita's, I go there each night earlier than the last. It would seem as if devils took me by the feet and carried me there against my will!

Happily, I never find Pepita alone; I do not desire to find her alone. I almost always find the excellent vicar there before me, who attributes our friendship to similarity of feeling in religious matters, and bases it on piety, like the pure and innocent friendship he himself entertains for her.

The progress of my malady is rapid. Like the stone that is loosened from the mountain-top and gathers force as it falls, so is it with my spirit.

When Pepita and I shake hands, it is not now as at first. Each one of us, by an effort of the will, transmits to the other, through the handclasp, every throb of the heart. It is as if, by some diabolical art, we had effected a transfusion and a blending together of the most subtle elements of our blood. She must feel my life circulate through her veins, as I feel hers in mine.

When I am near her, I love her; when I am away from her, I hate her. When I am in her presence she inspires me with love; she draws me to her; she subjugates me with gentleness; she lays upon me a very easy yoke.

But the recollection of her undoes me. When I dream of her, I dream that she is severing my head from my body, as Judith slew the captain of the Assyrians; or that she is driving a nail into my temple, as Jael did to Sisera. But when I am near her, she appears to me the Spouse of the Song of Songs, and a voice within me calls to her and I bless her, and I regard her as a sealed fountain, as an enclosed garden, as the flower of the valley, as the lily of the fields, my dove and my sister.

I desire to free myself from her, and I cannot. I abhor, yet I almost worship her. Her spirit enters into me and takes possession of me as soon as I behold her; it subjugates me, it abases me.

I leave her house each night, saying, 'This is the last night I shall return here'; and I return there on the following night!

When she speaks, and I am near, my soul hangs, as it were, upon her words. When she smiles, I imagine that a ray of spiritual light enters into my heart and rejoices it.

It has happened, when playing *ombre*, that our knees have touched by chance, and then I have felt a thrill run through me impossible to describe.

Get me away from this place. Write to my father and ask him to let me return to you. If it be necessary, tell him everything. Help me! Be my refuge!

May 30th.

God has given me strength to resist, and I have resisted.

It is now many days since I have been in the house of Pepita, many days since I have seen her.

It is scarcely necessary that I should feign sickness, for I am in reality sick. I have lost my colour, and dark circles begin to show themselves under my eyes; and my father asks me, full of affectionate anxiety, what the cause of my suffering is, and manifests the deepest concern.

The kingdom of Heaven is said to yield to violence, and I am resolved to conquer it. With violence I call at its gates that they may open to me.

With wormwood am I fed by the Lord, in order to prove me; and in vain do I supplicate Him to let this cup of bitterness pass away from me. But, as I have passed and still pass many nights in vigil, delivered up to prayer, a loving inspiration from the Supreme Consoler has come to sweeten the bitterness of my cup.

I have beheld with the eyes of the soul the new country; and the new song of the heavenly Jerusalem has resounded within the depths of my heart.

If in the end I should conquer, glorious will be the victory; but I shall owe it to the Queen of Angels, under whose protection I place myself. She is my refuge and my defence; the tower of the house of David, on whose walls hang innumerable shields and the armour of many valiant champions; the cedar of Lebanon, which puts the serpent to flight.

The woman who inspires me with an earthly love, on the contrary, I endeavour to despise and abase in my thoughts, remembering the words of the sage, and applying them to her.

'Thou art the snare of the hunter,' I say of her; 'thy heart is a net of deceit, and thy hands are bands that imprison; he who fears God will flee from thee, and the sinner shall be taken captive by thee.'

In my meditations on love I find a thousand reasons for loving God, and against loving her.

I feel, in the depths of my heart, an indescribable enthusiasm that convinces me that for the love of God I would sacrifice all things—fame, honour, power, dominion. I feel myself capable of imitating Christ, and if the Tempter should carry me off to the mountain-top, and should there offer me all the kingdoms of earth if I consented to bow the knee before him, yet would I not bend it. But were he to offer me this woman if I should do so, I feel that I should waver, that I could not reject his offer. Is this woman, then, worth more in my eyes than all the kingdoms of the earth? More than fame, honour, power, and dominion?

Is the virtue of love, I ask myself at times, always the same, even when applied to divers objects? Or are there two species and qualities of love? To love God seems to me to be the giving up of self and selfish interest. Loving Him, I desire to love, and I can love, all things through Him, and I am not troubled or jealous because of His love toward all things. I am not jealous of the saints, or of the martyrs, or of the blessed, or even of the seraphim. The greater I picture to myself to be the love of God for His creatures, and the graces and gifts He bestows upon them, the less am I troubled by jealousy; the more I love Him, the nearer to me do I feel Him to be, and the more loving and gracious does He seem toward me. My brotherhood, my more than brotherhood, with all creatures, stands forth then in a most pleasing light. It seems to me that I am one with all things, and that all things are bound together in the bonds of love, through God and in God.

Very different is it when my thoughts dwell upon Pepita, and on the love with which she inspires me. This love is a love full of hatred, that separates me from everything but myself. I love her for myself, altogether for myself, and myself altogether for her. Even devotion to her, even sacrifices made for her sake, partake of the nature of selfishness. To die for her would be to die of despair at not being able to possess her in any other manner— from the fear of not enjoying her love completely, except by dying and commingling with her in an eternal embrace.

By these reflections I endeavour to render the love of Pepita hateful to me. I envest my love in my imagination with something diabolical and fatal; but, as if I possessed a double soul, a double understanding, a double will, and a double imagination, in contra- diction to this thought, other feelings rise up within me in its train, and I then deny what I have just affirmed, and insanely endeavour to reconcile the two loves. Would it not be possible, I ask myself, to fly from Pepita, and yet continue to love her, without ceasing therefore to consecrate myself with fervour to the love of God? For, as the love of God does not exclude love of country, love of humanity, love of learning, love of beauty in Nature and in Art, neither should it exclude another love, if it be spiritual and immaculate. I will make of her, I say to myself, a symbol, an allegory, an image of all that is good, of all that is beautiful. She shall be to me, as Beatrice was to Dante, the image and the symbol of country, of knowledge, and of beauty.

This intention suggests to me a horrible fancy, a monstrous thought. In order to make of Pepita this symbol, this vaporous and ethereal image, this sign and epitome of all that I can love under God, in God, and subordinate to God, I picture her to myself dead, as Beatrice was dead when Dante made her the subject of his song.

If I picture her to myself among the living, then I am unable to convert her into a pure idea; and if I convert her into a pure idea, I kill her in my thoughts.

Then I weep; I am filled with horror at my crime, and I draw near to her in spirit, and with the warmth of my heart I bring her back to life again; and I behold her, not errant, diaphanous, floating in shadowy outline among roseate clouds and celestial flowers, as the stern Ghibelline beheld his beloved in the upper sphere of Purgatory; but coherent, solid, clearly defined in the pure and serene air, like the masterpieces of Greek art, like Galatea already animated by the love of Pygmalion, and descending from her pedestal of marble, full of fire, exhaling love, rich in youth and beauty.

Then I exclaim in the depths of my perturbed heart : 'My virtue faints! My God, do not Thou forsake me! Hasten to my help; show Thy countenance, and I shall be saved!'

Thus do I recover strength to resist temptation. Thus again does the hope spring to life within me, that I shall regain my former tranquillity when I shall have left this place.

The Devil longs with ardour to swallow up the pure waters of Jordan, by which are symbolized the persons who are consecrated to God. Hell conspires against them, and lets loose all her monsters upon them. St. Bonaventure says : 'We should not wonder that these persons have sinned, but rather that they have not sinned.'

Notwithstanding, I shall be able to resist and not sin. The Lord will protect me.

June 6th.

Pepita's nurse—now her housekeeper—is, as my father says, a good bag of wrinkles; she is talkative, gay, and skilful, as few are. She married the son of Master Cencias, and has inherited from the father what the son did not inherit—a wonderful facility for the mechanical arts, with this difference : that while Master Cencias could set the screw of a wine-press, or repair the wheels of a wagon, or make a plough, this daughter-in-law of his knows how to make sweetmeats, conserves of honey, and other dainties. The father-in-law practised the useful arts; the daughter-in-law those that have for their object pleasure, though only innocent, or at least lawful pleasure.

Antoñona—for such is her name—is permitted, or assumes, the greatest familiarity with all the gentry here. She goes in and out of every house as if it were her own. She uses the familiar 'thou' to all young people of Pepita's age, or four or five years older; she calls them 'child', and treats them as if she had nursed them at her breast.

She behaves toward me in this way; she comes to visit me, enters my room unannounced, has asked me several times already why I no longer go to see her mistress, and has told me that I am wrong in not going.

My father, who has no suspicion of the truth, accuses me of eccentricity; he calls me an owl, and he, too, is determined that I shall resume my visits to Pepita. Last night I could no longer resist his repeated importunities, and I went to her house very early, as my father was about to settle his accounts with the overseer.

Would to God I had not gone!

Pepita was alone. When our glances met, when we saluted each other, we both turned red. We shook hands with timidity and in silence.

I did not press her hand, nor did she press mine, but for a moment we held them clasped together.

In Pepita's glance, as she looked at me, there was nothing of love; there was only friendship, sympathy, and a profound sadness.

She had divined the whole of my inward struggle; she was persuaded that Divine love had triumphed in my soul—that my resolution not to love her was firm and invincible.

She did not venture to complain of me; she had no reason to complain of me; she knew that right was on my side. A sigh, scarcely perceptible, that escaped from her dewy, parted lips, revealed to me the depth of her sorrow.

Her hand still lay in mine; we were both silent. How was I to tell her that she was not destined for me, nor I for her; that we must part forever?

But though my lips refused to tell her this in words, I told it to her with my eyes; my severe glance confirmed her fears; it convinced her of the irrevocableness of my decision.

All at once her gaze was troubled; her lovely countenance, pale with a translucent pallor, was full of a touching expression of melancholy. She looked like Our Lady of Sorrows. Two tears rose slowly to her eyes, and began to steal down her cheeks.

I know not what passed within me, nor how to describe it, even if I knew.

I bent toward her to kiss away her tears and our lips met.

Rapture unspeakable, a faintness full of peril, invaded us both. She would have fallen, but that I supported her in my arms.

Heaven willed that we should at this moment hear the step and the cough of the reverend vicar, who was approaching, and we instantly drew apart.

Recovering myself, and summoning all the strength of my will, I brought to an end this terrible scene, that had been enacted in silence, with these words, which I pronounced in low and intense accents :

'The first and the last !'

I made allusion to our profane kiss; but, as if my words had been an invocation, there rose before me the vision of the Apocalypse in all its terrible majesty. I beheld Him who is indeed the First and the Last, and with the two-edged sword that proceeded from His mouth He pierced my soul, full of evil, of wickedness, and of sin.

All that evening I passed in a species of frenzy, an inward delirium, that I know not how I was able to conceal.

I withdrew from Pepita's house very early.

The anguish of my soul was yet more poignant in solitude.

When I recalled that kiss and those words of farewell, I compared myself with the traitor Judas, who made use of a kiss to betray; and with the sanguinary and treacherous assassin Joab, who plunged the sharp steel into the bowels of Amasa while in the act of kissing him.

I had committed a double treason; I had been guilty of a double perfidy. I had sinned against God and against her.

I am an execrable wretch.

June 11th.

Everything may still be remedied.

Pepita will in time forget her love and the weakness of which we were guilty.

Since that night I have not returned to her house. Antoñona has not made her appearance in ours.

By dint of entreaties I have obtained a formal promise from my father that we shall leave here on the 25th, the day after St. John's day, which is here celebrated with splendid feasts, and on the eve of which there is a great vigil.

Absent from Pepita, I begin to recover my serenity and to think that this first beginning of love was a trial of my virtue.

All these nights I have prayed, I have watched, I have performed many acts of penance.

The persistence of my prayers, the deep contrition of my soul, have found favour with the Lord, who has manifested to me His great mercy.

The Lord, in the words of the prophet, has sent fire to the stronghold of my spirit; He has illumined my understanding, He has kindled my resolution, and He has given me guidance.

The working of the Divine love which animates the Supreme Will has had power, at times, without my deserving it, to lead me to that condition of prayerful contemplation in which the soul enjoys repose. I have cast out from the lower faculties of my soul every image—even her image; and I am persuaded, if pride does not deceive me, that, in perfect peace of mind and heart I have known and enjoyed the Supreme Good that dwells within the depths of the soul.

Compared with this good all else is worthless—compared with this beauty all else is deformity—compared with these heights all else is vile. Who would not forget and scorn every other love for the love of God?

Yes; the profane image of this woman shall depart finally and forever from my soul. I shall make of my prayers and of my penance a sharp scourge, and with it I will expel her therefrom, as Christ expelled the moneylenders from the Temple.

June 18th.

This is the last letter I shall write to you. On the 25th I shall leave this place without fail.

I shall soon have the happiness of embracing you. Near you I shall be stronger. You will infuse courage into me, and lend me the energy in which I am wanting.

A tempest of conflicting emotions is now raging in my soul. The disorder of my ideas may be known by the disorder of what I write.

Twice I returned to the house of Pepita. I was cold and stern. I was as I ought to have been, but how much did it cost me!

My father told me yesterday that Pepita was indisposed, and would not receive.

The thought at once assailed me that the cause of her indisposition might be her ill-requited love.

Why did I return her glances of fire? Why did I basely deceive her? Why did I make her believe I loved her? Why did my vile lips seek hers with ardour, and communicate the ardour of an unholy love to hers?

But no; my sin shall not be followed, as its unavoidable consequence, by another sin!

What has been, has been, and can not be undone; but a repetition of it may be avoided—shall be avoided in future.

On the 25th, I repeat, I shall depart from here without fail.

The impudent Antoñona has just come to see me. I hid this letter from her, as if it were a crime to write to you.

Antoñona remained here only for a moment.

I arose, and remained standing while I spoke to her, that the visit might be a short one.

During this short visit she gave utterance to a thousand mad speeches, which disturbed me greatly. Finally, as she was going away, she exclaimed, in her half-gipsy jargon :

'You deceiver ! You villain ! My curse upon you ! You have made the child sick, and now you are killing her by your desertion. May witches fly away with you, body and bones !'

Having said this, the fiendish woman gave me, in a coarse and vulgar fashion, six or seven ferocious pinches below the shoulders, as if she would like to tear the skin from my back in strips, and then went away, looking daggers at me.

I do not complain. I deserve this brutal jest, granting it to be a jest. I deserve that fiends should tear my flesh with red-hot pincers.

Grant, my God, that Pepita may forget me ! Let her, if it be necessary, love another, and be happy with him !

Can I ask more than this of Thee, oh, my God?

My father knows nothing, suspects nothing. It is better thus.

Farewell for a few days, till we see and embrace each other again.

How changed will you find me ! How full of bitterness my heart ! How soiled my purity ! How bruised and wounded my soul !

MARY J. SERRANO

BENITO PÉREZ GALDÓS
[1843–1920]

The great master of the modern Spanish novel is Benito Pérez Galdós, born in the Canary Islands. He delved into painting and law as a young man, but soon dedicated himself entirely to writing, publishing his first novel at the age of twenty-seven. Until his death in 1920 he wrote unceasingly and prodigiously, despite blindness in his later years.

The universal appeal of his works combined with their brilliant execution has given Pérez Galdós a place unique in contemporary Spanish literature. No other modern novelist has been so widely read by all classes of people and at the same time been so admired by critics. His voluminous production includes thirty novels, forty-six episodios nacionales (semi-historical novels which range in period from the battle of Trafalgar, 1805, to the end of the nineteenth century), twenty-two dramas and numerous short stories.

A crusading reformer, Galdós consistently defends the liberal side of social problems. One of his best novels, Doña Perfecta, depicts the evils of religious fanaticism, personified by the character of a strong and ruthless woman.

DOÑA PERFECTA

The Disagreement Continued to Increase and Threatened to Become Discord

... Doña Perfecta and Señor Don Cayetano at this moment made their appearance.

'What a beautiful evening!' said the former. 'Well, nephew, are you getting terribly bored?'

'I am not bored in the least,' responded the young man.

'Don't try to deny it. Cayetano and I were speaking of that as we came along. You are bored, and you are trying to hide it. It is not every young man of the present day who would have the self-denial to spend his youth, like Jacinto, in a town where there are neither theatres, nor opera bouffe, nor dancers, nor philosophers, nor athenaeums, nor magazines, nor congresses, nor any other kind of diversions or entertainments.'

'I am quite contented here,' responded Pepe. 'I was just now saying to Rosario that I find this city and this house so pleasant that I would like to live and die here.'

Rosario turned very red and the others were silent. They all sat down in a summer-house, Jacinto hastening to take the seat on the left of the young girl.

'See here, nephew, I have a piece of advice to give you,' said Doña Perfecta, smiling with that expression of kindness that seemed to emanate from her soul, like the aroma from the flower. 'But don't imagine that I am either reproving you or giving you a lesson —you are not a child, and you will easily understand what I mean.'

'Scold me, dear aunt, for no doubt I deserve it,' replied Pepe, who was beginning to accustom himself to the kindnesses of his father's sister.

'No, it is only a piece of advice. These gentlemen, I am sure, will agree that I am in the right.'

Rosario was listening with her whole soul.

'It is only this,' continued Doña Perfecta, 'that when you visit our beautiful cathedral again, you will endeavour to behave with a little more decorum while you are in it.'

'Why, what have I done?'

'It does not surprise me that you are not yourself aware of your fault,' said his aunt, with apparent good humour. 'It is only natural; accustomed as you are to enter athenaeums and clubs, and academies and congresses without any ceremony, you think that you can enter a temple in which the Divine Majesty is in the same manner.'

'But excuse me, señora,' said Pepe gravely, 'I entered the cathedral with the greatest decorum.'

'But I am not scolding you, man; I am not scolding you. If you take it in that way I shall have to remain silent. Excuse my nephew, gentlemen. A little carelessness, a little heedlessness on his part is not to be wondered at. How many years is it since you set foot in a sacred place before?'

'What I assure you is—— There, if you are going to be offended I won't go on. What I assure you is that a great many people noticed it this morning. The Señores de González, Doña Robustiana, Serafinita—in short, when I tell you that you attracted the attention of the bishop—— His lordship complained to me about it this afternoon when I was at my cousin's. He told me that he did not order you to be put out of the church only because you were my nephew.'

Rosario looked anxiously at her cousin, trying to read in his countenance, before he uttered it, the answer he would make to these charges.

'No doubt they mistook me for some one else.'

'No, no! it was you. But there, don't get angry! We are talking here among friends and in confidence. It was you. I saw you myself.'

'You saw me!'

'Just so. Will you deny that you went to look at the pictures, passing among a group of worshippers who were hearing mass? I assure you that my attention was so distracted by your comings and goings that—well, you must not do it again. Then you went into the chapel of San Gregorio. At the elevation of the Host at the high altar you did not even turn around to make a gesture of reverence. Afterward you traversed the whole length of the church, you went up to the tomb of the Adelantado, you touched the altar with your hands, then you passed a second time among the group of worshippers, attracting the notice of every one. All the girls looked at you, and you seemed pleased at disturbing so finely the devotions of those good people.'

'Good Heavens! How many things I have done!' exclaimed Pepe, half angry, half amused. 'I am a monster, it seems, without ever having suspected it.'

'No, I am very well aware that you are a good boy,' said Doña Perfecta, observing the canon's expression of unalterable gravity, which gave his face the appearance of a pasteboard mask. 'But, my dear boy, between thinking things and showing them in that irreverent manner, there is a distance which a man of good sense and good breeding should never cross. I am well aware that your ideas are—— Now, don't get angry! If you get angry, I will be silent. I say that it is one thing to have certain ideas about religion and another thing to express them. I will take good care not to reproach you because you believe that God did not create us in his image and likeness, but that we are descended from the monkeys; nor because you deny the existence of the soul, asserting that it is a drug, like the little papers of rhubarb and magnesia that are sold at the apothecary's——'

'Señora, for Heaven's sake!' exclaimed Pepe, with annoyance. 'I see that I have a very bad reputation in Orbajosa.'

The others still remained silent.

'As I said, I will not reproach you for entertaining those ideas. And, besides, I have not the right to do so. If I should undertake to argue with you, you, with your wonderful talents, would confute me a thousand times over. No, I will not attempt any thing of that kind. What I say is that these poor and humble inhabitants of Orbajosa are pious and good Christians, although they know nothing about German philosophy, and that, therefore, you ought not publicly to manifest your contempt for their beliefs.'

'My dear aunt,' said the engineer gravely, 'I have shown no contempt for any one, nor do I entertain the ideas which you attribute to me. Perhaps I may have been a little wanting in reverence in the church, I am somewhat absent-minded. My thoughts and my attention were engaged with the architecture of the building and, frankly speaking, I did not observe—— But this was no reason for the bishop to think of putting me out of the church, nor for you to suppose me capable of attributing to a paper from the apothecary's the functions of the soul. I may tolerate that as a jest, but only as a jest.'

The agitation of Pepe Rey's mind was so great that, notwithstanding his natural prudence and moderation, he was unable to conceal it.

'There! I see that you are angry,' said Doña Perfecta, casting down her eyes and clasping her hands. 'I am very sorry. If I had known that you would have taken it in that way, I should not have spoken to you. Pepe, I ask your pardon.'

Hearing these words and seeing his kind aunt's deprecating attitude Pepe felt ashamed of the sternness of his last words, and he made an effort to recover his serenity. The venerable Penitentiary extricated him from his embarrassing position, saying with his accustomed benevolent smile:

'Señora Doña Perfecta, we must be tolerant with artists. Oh, I have known a great many of them! Those gentlemen, when they have before them a statue, a piece of rusty armour, a mouldy painting, or an old wall, forget everything else. Señor Don José is an artist, and he has visited our cathedral as the English visit it, who would willingly carry it away with them to their museums, to its last tile, if they could. That the worshippers were praying, that the priest was elevating the Sacred Host, that the moment of supreme piety and devotion had come—what of that? What does all that matter to an artist? It is true that I do not know what art is worth, apart from the sentiments which it expresses, but, in fine, at the present day, it is the custom to adore the form, not the idea. God preserve me from undertaking to discuss this question with Señor Don José, who knows so much, and who, reasoning with the admirable subtlety of the moderns, would instantly confound my mind, in which there is only faith.'

'The determination which you all have to regard me as the most learned man on earth annoys me exceedingly,' said Pepe, speaking in his former hard tone. 'Hold me for a fool; for I would rather be regarded as a fool than as the possessor of that Satanic knowledge which is here attributed to me.'

Rosarito laughed, and Jacinto thought that a highly opportune moment had now arrived to make a display of his own erudition.

'Pantheism or panentheism,' he said, 'is condemned by the Church, as well as by the teachings of Schopenhauer and of the modern Hartmann.'

'Ladies and gentlemen,' said the canon gravely, 'men who pay so fervent a worship to art, though it be only to its form, deserve the greatest respect. It is better to be an artist, and delight in the contemplation of beauty, though this be only represented by nude nymphs, than to be indifferent and incredulous in every thing. The mind that consecrates itself to the contemplation of beauty, evil will not take complete possession of. *Est Deus in nobis. Deus,* be it well understood. Let Señor Don José, then, continue to admire the marvels of our church; I, for one, will willingly forgive him his acts of irreverence, with all due respect for the opinions of the bishop.'

'Thanks, Señor Don Inocencio,' said Pepe, feeling a bitter and rebellious sentiment of hostility springing up within him toward the canon, and unable to conquer his desire to mortify him. 'But let none of you imagine, either, that it was the beauties of art, of which you suppose the temple to be full, that engaged my attention. Those beauties, with the exception of the imposing architecture of a portion of the edifice and of the three tombs that are in the chapel of the apse, I do not see. What occupied my mind was the consideration of the deplorable decadence of the religious arts; and the innumerable monstrosities of which the cathedral is full, caused me not astonishment, but disgust.'

The amazement of all present was profound.

'I cannot endure,' continued Pepe, 'those glazed and painted images that resemble so much—God forgive me for the comparison —the dolls that little girls play with. And what am I to say of the theatrical robes that cover them? I saw a St. Joseph with a mantle whose appearance I will not describe, out of respect for the holy patriarch and for the church of which he is the patron. On the altar are crowded together images in the worst possible taste; and the innumerable crowns, branches, stars, moons, and other ornaments of metal or gilt paper have an air of an ironmongery that offends the religious sentiment and depresses the soul. Far from lifting itself up to religious contemplation, the soul sinks, and the idea of the ludicrous distracts it. The great works of art which give sensible form to ideas, to dogmas, to religious faith, to mystic exaltation, fulfil a noble mission. The caricatures, the aberrations of taste, the grotesque works with which a mistaken piety fills the churches, also fulfil their object; but this is a sad one enough : They encourage superstition, cool enthusiasm, oblige the eyes of the believer to turn away from the altar, and, with the eyes, the souls that have not a very profound and a very firm faith turn away also.'

'The doctrine of the iconoclasts, too,' said Jacinto, 'has, it seems, spread widely in Germany.'

'I am not an iconoclast, although I would prefer the destruction of all the images to the exhibition of buffooneries of which I speak,' continued the young man. 'Seeing it, one may justly advocate a return of religious worship to the august simplicity of olden times. But no; let us not renounce the admirable aid which all the arts, beginning with poetry and ending with music, lend to the relations between man and God. Let the arts live; let the utmost pomp be displayed in religious ceremonies. I am a partisan of pomp.'

'An artist, an artist, and nothing more than an artist !' exclaimed the canon, shaking his head with a sorrowful air. 'Fine pictures, fine statues, beautiful music; pleasure for the senses, and let the devil take the soul !'

'Apropos of music,' said Pepe Rey, without observing the deplorable effect which his words produced on both mother and daughter, 'imagine how disposed my mind would be to religious contemplation on entering the cathedral, when just at that moment, and precisely at the offertory at high mass, the organist played a passage from "Traviata".'

'Señor de Rey is right in that,' said the little lawyer emphatically. 'The organist played the other day the whole of the drinking song and the waltz from the same opera, and afterward a rondeau from the "Grande Duchesse".'

'But when I felt my heart sink,' continued the engineer implacably, 'was when I saw an image of the Virgin, which seems to be held in great veneration, judging from the crowd before it and the multitude of tapers which lighted it. They have dressed her in a puffed-out garment of velvet, embroidered with gold, of a shape so extraordinary that it surpasses the most extravagant of the fashions of the day. Her face is almost hidden under a voluminous frill, made of innumerable rows of lace, crimped with a crimping-iron, and her crown, half a yard in height, surrounded by golden rays, looks like a hideous catafalque erected over her head. Of the same material, and embroidered in the same manner, are the trousers of the Infant Jesus. I will not go on, for to describe the Mother and the Child might perhaps lead me to commit some irreverence. I will only say that it was impossible for me to keep from smiling, and for a short time I contemplated the profaned image, saying to myself : "Mother and Lady mine, what a sight they have made of you !" '

As he ended Pepe looked at his hearers, and although, owing to the gathering darkness, he could not see their countenances distinctly, he fancied that in some of them he perceived signs of angry consternation.

'Well, Señor Don José !' exclaimed the canon quickly, smiling with a triumphant expression, 'that image, which to your philosophy and pantheism appears so ridiculous, is Our Lady of Help, patroness and advocate of Orbajosa, whose inhabitants regard her with so much veneration that they would be quite capable of dragging any one through the streets who should speak ill of her. The chronicles and history, Señor Don José, are full of the miracles which she has wrought, and even at the present day we receive constantly incontrovertible proofs of her protection. You must know also that your aunt, Doña Perfecta, is chief lady in waiting to the Most Holy Virgin of Help, and that the dress that to you appears so grotesque—well, the dress, I repeat, which, to your impious eyes, appears so grotesque—went out from this house, and that the trousers of the Infant are the work of the skilful needle and the ardent piety combined of your cousin Rosarito, who is now listening to us.'

Pepe Rey was greatly disconcerted. At the same instant Doña Perfecta rose abruptly from her seat, and, without saying a word, walked toward the house, followed by the Penitentiary. The others rose also. Recovering from his stupefaction, the young man was about to get his cousin's pardon for his irreverence, when he observed that Rosarito was weeping. Fixing on her cousin a look of friendly and gentle reproof, she said :

'What ideas you have !'

The voice of Doña Perfecta was heard crying in an altered accent :

'Rosario ! Rosario !'

The latter ran toward the house.

MARY J. SERRANO

EMILIA PARDO BAZÁN
[1851–1921]

*The erudite Countess of Pardo Bazán is one of the major figures of
modern Spanish literature. An incisive literary critic, she was, in her later
years, a professor of literature at the University of Madrid.*

*She is credited with the introduction of French naturalism into Spain.
Although she later tended away from this school of writing, her masterpiece
is a naturalistic novel,* Los Pazos de Ulloa *(1886). Set typically in
Galicia, pervaded by an atmosphere of gloom and foreboding, the work
adheres uncompromisingly to realism in action, detail and dialogue; on this
basis are constructed striking descriptions and powerful character portraits.*

*In addition to some twenty novels, the Countess of Pardo Bazán wrote
scores of short stories; she is considered among the best Spanish* cuentistas.
Indulto *('The Pardon') is an example of her skill in this field.*

THE PARDON

Of all the women busily engaged in lathering soiled linen in
the public laundry of Marineda, their arms stiff with the biting
cold of a March morning, Antonia the charwoman was the most
bowed down, the most disheartened, the one who wrung the clothes
with the least energy, and rinsed them with the greatest lassitude.
From time to time she would interrupt her work in order to pass
the back of her hand across her reddened eyelids; and the drops
of water and soapy bubbles glistened like so many tears upon
her withered cheeks.

Antonia's companions at the tubs eyed her compassionately,
and every now and again, in the midst of the confusion of gossip
and of quarrels, a brief dialogue would ensue in lowered tones,
interrupted by exclamations of astonishment, indignation, and
pity. The entire laundry knew, down to the smallest details, the
poor washerwoman's misfortunes, which furnished occasion for
unending comment. No one was unaware that, after her marriage
a few years ago with a young butcher, she had kept house together
with her mother and husband in one of the suburbs outside the
town wall, and that the family lived in comfortable circumstances,
thanks to Antonia's steady industry, and to the frugal savings of
the older woman in her former capacity of huckster, second-hand
dealer, and money-lender.

Still less had anyone forgotten the tragic evening when the old
woman was found assassinated, with nothing but splinters left

of the lid of the chest in which she kept her money and a few ear-rings and trinkets of gold; still less, the horror that spread through the neighbourhood at the news that the thief and assassin was none other than Antonia's husband, as she herself declared, adding that for some time past the guilty man had been tormented with a desire for his mother-in-law's money, with which he wished to set up a butcher's shop of his own. The accused, to be sure, attempted to establish an alibi, relying on the testimony of two or three boon companions, and so far confused the facts that, instead of going to the gallows, he got off with twenty years in prison.

Public opinion was less indulgent than the law; in addition to the wife's testimony, there was one overwhelming piece of evidence, namely, the wound itself which had caused the old woman's death, an accurate, clean-cut wound, delivered from above downward, like the stroke used in slaughtering hogs, evidently with a broad, keen blade, like that of a meat knife. Among the people, there was no question but that the culprit should have paid for his deed upon the scaffold. And Antonia's destiny began to evoke a holy horror when the rumour was circulated that her husband had *sworn to get even with her*, on the day of his release, for having testified against him. The poor woman was expecting soon to have a child; yet none the less, he left her with the assurance that, as soon as he should come back, she might count herself among the dead.

When Antonia's son was born, she was unable to nurse him, because of her enfeebled and wasted condition, and the frequent attacks of prostration from which she had suffered since the commission of the crime. And since the state of her purse did not permit her to pay for a nurse, the women of the neighbourhood who had nursing children took turns in caring for the poor little thing, which grew up sickly, suffering the consequences of all its mother's anguish. Before she had fully got back her strength, Antonia was hard at work again, and although her cheeks continually showed that bluish pallor which is characteristic of a weak heart, she recovered her silent activity and her placid manner.

Twenty years of prison! In twenty years, she told herself, either he might die, or she might die, and from now until then was, in any case, a long time. The idea of a natural death did not disturb her; but the mere thought of her husband's return filled her with horror. In vain her sympathetic neighbours tried to console her, suggesting the possibility that the guilty wretch might repent and mend his ways, or, as they expressed themselves, 'think better of it'; but Antonia would only shake her hand, murmuring gloomily :

'What, he? Think better of it? Not unless God Himself came down from Heaven to tear his dog's heart out of him and give him another !'

And at the mere mention of the criminal, a shudder would run throughout Antonia's body.

After all, twenty years contain a good many days, and time alleviates even the cruelest pain. Sometimes it seemed to Antonia as though all that had happened was a dream, or that the wide gates of the prison, having once closed upon the condemned man, would never again reopen; or that the law, which in the end had inflicted punishment for the first crime, would have the power to prevent a second. The law! that moral entity, of which Antonia formed a mysterious and confused conception, was beyond doubt a terrible force, yet one that offered protection; a hand of iron that would sustain her upon the brink of an abyss. Accordingly she added to her illimitable fears a sort of indefinable confidence, founded chiefly upon the time that had already elapsed and that which remained before the expiration of the sentence.

Strange, indeed, is the conception of human events ! Certainly it would never have occurred to the king, when, clad in the uniform of general-in-chief and with his breast covered over with decorations, he gave his hand to a princess before the altar, that this solemn act would cost pangs beyond number to a poor washerwoman in the capital of a distant province. When Antonia learned that her husband had been one of the convicts singled out for royal clemency, she spoke not a word; and the neighbours found her seated on the sill of her doorway, with her fingers interlocked and her head drooping forward on her breast; while the boy, raising his sad face, with its stamp of chronic invalidism, kept moaning :

'Mother, mother, warm me some soup, for God's sake, for I am starving !'

The kind-hearted and chattering chorus of neighbours swooped down upon Antonia; some busied themselves in preparing the child's dinner; others tried as best they could to instil courage into the mother. She was very foolish to distress herself like this ! Holy Virgin ! It wasn't as though the brute had nothing to do but just walk in and kill her ! There was a government, God be thanked, and the law courts, and the police; she could appeal to the authorities, to the mayor——

'The mayor's no good !' she answered, with a gloomy look in a hopeless tone.

'Or to the governor, or the regent, or the chief of the city council; you ought to go to a lawyer and find out what the law says.'

One kind-hearted girl, married to a policeman, offered to send for her husband, 'to give the scoundrel a good scare'; another, a swarthy, dauntless sort of woman, insisted on coming every night to sleep at the charwoman's house; in short, so many and so varied were the signs of interest shown by her neighbours that Antonia made up her mind to take a bold step, and without waiting for her counsellors to adjourn, decided to consult a lawyer and find out what he advised.

When Antonia returned from the consultation, paler even than usual, from every basement and ground floor dishevelled women emerged to hear the news, and exclamations of horror arose. Instead of protecting her, the law required the daughter of the murdered woman to live under the same roof with the assassin, as his wife!

'What laws, divine Lord of Heaven! That's how the brigands who make them carry them out!' clamoured the indignant chorus. 'And is there no help for it, my dear, no help at all?'

'He says that I could leave him after I got what they call a divorce.'

'And what is a divorce, my dear?'

'It's a lawsuit that takes a long time.'

All the women let their arms fall hopelessly. Lawsuits never came to an end, or if they did it was all the worse, because they were always decided against the innocent and the poor.

'And to get it,' continued the charwoman, 'I should have to prove that my husband had ill-treated me.'

Lord of mercy! Hadn't the beast killed her own mother? And if that wasn't ill treatment, then what was? And didn't the very cats in the street know that he had threatened to kill her too?

'But since no one heard him—The lawyer says the proof has to be very clear.'

Something akin to a riot ensued. Some of the women insisted that they would certainly send a petition to the king himself, asking to have the pardon revoked; and they took turns at spending the night at the charwoman's house, so that the poor thing could get a chance to sleep. Fortunately, it was only three days later that the news arrived that the pardon was only a partial remission of the sentence, and that the assassin still had some years to drag his chains behind prison bars. The night after

Antonia had learned this was the first that she did not suddenly start up in bed, with her eyes immeasurably wide open, and scream for help.

After this first alarm, more than a year passed, and the char-woman recovered her tranquillity and was able to devote herself to her humble labours. One day the butler in one of the houses where she worked thought that he was doing a kindness to the poor, white-faced thing who had a husband in prison, by telling her that there was soon to be an heir to the throne, and that this would undoubtedly mean some more pardons.

The charwoman was in the midst of scrubbing the floor, but on hearing this announcement she dropped her scrubbing-brush and, shaking down her skirt, which had been gathered up around her waist, she left the house, moving like an automaton, as cold and silent as a statue. To all inquiries from her various employers, she replied that she was ill; although, in reality, she was merely suffering from a sort of general prostration, and inability to raise her arms to any work whatever. On the day of the royal birth, she counted the number of salutes, whose reverberations seemed to jar through to the centre of her brain; and when someone told her that the royal child was a girl, she began to take heart at the thought that a male child would have been the occasion of a larger number of pardons.

Besides, why should one of the pardons be for her husband? They had already remitted part of his sentence once, and his crime had been a shocking one. To kill a defenceless old woman, just for the sake of a few wretched pieces of gold! The terrible scene once more unrolled itself before her eyes. How did they dare to pardon the beast who had inflicted that fearful knife-thrust? Antonia remembered that the lips of the wound were livid, and it seemed as though she could still see the coagulated blood at the foot of the narrow bed.

She locked herself into her house, and passed the hours seated in a low chair before the hearth. Bah! If they were bound to kill her, they might as well come and do it!

Nothing but the plaintive voice of the little boy aroused her from her self-absorption.

'Mother, I am hungry! Mother, who is at the door? Who is coming?'

But at last, on a beautiful, sunny morning, she roused herself and, taking a bundle of soiled clothing, made her way towards the public washing place. To the many affectionate inquiries she answered only in slow monosyllables, and her eyes rested in unseeing absorption on the soapy water that now and again splashed in her face.

Who was it that brought to the laundry the unlooked-for news? It happened just as Antonia was gathering up her washing and preparing to start for home. Did someone invent the story, meaning to be kind, or was it one of those mysterious rumours, of unknown origin, which on the eve of momentous happenings, whether personal or public, palpitate and whisper through the air? The actual facts are that poor Antonia, upon hearing it, raised her hand instinctively to her heart and fell backward upon the wet flooring of the laundry.

'But is he really dead?' demanded the early comers of the more recent arrivals.

'Indeed he is!'

'I heard it in the market-place.'

'I heard it in the shop.'

'Well, and who told you?'

'Me? Oh, I heard it from my husband.'

'And who told your husband?'

'The captain's mate.'

'Who told the mate?'

'His foster-father.'

At this point the matter seemed to be sufficiently authenticated, and no one sought to verify it further, but assumed that the news was valid and beyond question. The culprit dead, on the eve of pardon, and before completing the term of his sentence! Antonia, the charwoman, raised her head, and for the first time her cheeks took on the colour of health, and the fountain of her tears was opened. She wept to her heart's content, and of all who saw her, there was no one that blamed her. It was she who had received her release, and her gladness was justified.

The tears chased each other from the corners of her eyes, and as they flowed her heart expanded; because, from the day of the murder she had been under a weight too heavy for relief in tears. Now once more she could breathe freely, released from her nightmare fear. The hand of Providence had so plainly intervened that it never even occurred to the poor charwoman that the news might be false.

That evening, Antonia returned home later than usual, because she stopped at the primary school for her boy, and bought him some spice cakes and other dainties that he had long been wanting; and the two wandered from street to street, lingering before the shop windows. She forgot the dinner hour, and thought of nothing but of drinking in the air, and feeling herself alive, and little by little taking possession of herself.

So great was Antonia's self-absorption that she did not notice that her outer door was unlatched. Still holding the child by the hand, she entered the narrow quarters that served as parlour, kitchen, and dining-room all in one, then recoiled in amazement at seeing that the candle was lighted. A huge, dark bulk raised itself from the table, and the scream which rose to the charwoman's lips was strangled in her throat.

It was he. Antonia, motionless, riveted to the ground, stared unseeingly at him, although the sinister image was mirrored in her dilated pupils. Her rigid body was for the moment paralysed; her icy hands relaxed their hold upon the boy, who clung in terror to her skirts. The husband spoke :

'You were not counting on me today!' he murmured in a hoarse but tranquil tone; and at the sound of that voice, in which Antonia fancied that she could hear the echo of maledictions and threats of death, the poor woman, waking from her doze, came to life, emitted one shrill wail, and snatching her boy up in her arms, started to run to the door. The man intercepted her.

'Come, come! Where are you off to, my lady?' he asked her, with harsh irony. 'Rousing the neighbourhood at this time of night? Stay home and stop your noise!'

The last words were spoken without any accompanying gesture of intimidation, but in a tone that froze Antonia's blood. Her first stupefaction had by this time given place to fever, the lucid fever of the instinct of self-preservation. A sudden thought flashed through her mind : she would appeal to him through the child. The father had never seen him, but after all he was his father. Catching the boy up, she carried him over to the light.

'Is that the kid?' murmured the convict, and taking up the candle he held it close to the boy's face. The latter, dazzled, blinked his eyes and covered his face with his hands, as if trying to hide from this unknown father whose name he had never heard pronounced excepting with universal fear and condemnation. He shrank back against his mother, and she at the same time nervously held him close, while her face grew whiter than wax.

'What an ugly kid!' muttered the father, setting the candle down again. 'He looks as if the witches had sucked him dry.'

Antonia, still holding the boy, leaned against the wall, half fainting. The room seemed to be circling around her, and the air was full of tiny flecks of blue light.

'Look here, isn't there anything to eat in the house?' demanded her husband. Antonia set the boy on the floor in a corner, where he sat, crying from fear and stifling his sobs, while she proceeded to hurry about the room, setting the table with trembling hands; she brought out some bread and a bottle of wine, and removed the pot of codfish from the fire, making herself a willing slave in the hope of placating the enemy. The convict took his seat and proceeded to eat voraciously, helping himself to repeated draughts of wine. She remained standing, staring in fascination at the hard, parchment-like face, with close-clipped hair, and the unmistakable prison pallor. He filled his glass again and reached it towards her.

'No, I don't want it,' stammered Antonia, for the wine, where the candlelight fell upon it, seemed to her imagination like a pool of blood.

He drank it himself, with a shrug of his shoulders, and replenished his plate with the codfish, which he consumed, greedily, feeding himself with his fingers and devouring huge slices of bread. His wife watched him as he ate, and a faint hope began to dawn in her heart. As soon as he had finished his meal, he might go out without killing her; in that case, she would lock and bar the door, and if he tried to come back to kill her, it would rouse the neighbours and they would hear her screams. Only it was quite likely that she would find it impossible to scream! She hawked repeatedly in order to clear her voice. Her husband, having eaten his fill, drew a cigar from his pocket, pinched off the tip with his finger nail, and tranquilly lighted it with the candle.

'Here, where are you going?' he called, seeing that his wife made a furtive movement towards the door. 'Let's enjoy ourselves in peace.'

'I must put the boy to bed,' she answered, scarcely knowing what she said, and she took refuge in the adjoining room, carrying the child in her arms. She felt sure that the murderer would not dare to enter there. How could he have the dreadful courage to do so? It was the room where the crime was committed, her mother's room; the room that she had shared before her marriage. The poverty that followed the old woman's death had forced Antonia to sell her own bed and use that of the deceased. Believing herself in security, she proceeded to undress the child, who now ventured to sob aloud, and with his face buried on her breast. All at once the door opened and the ex-convict came in.

Antonia saw him cast a side glance around the room; then he proceeded tranquilly to remove his shoes, to undress, and finally stretch himself in the murdered woman's bed. The charwoman felt that she must be dreaming; if her husband had drawn a knife, he would have frightened her less than by this horrible show of tranquillity. He meanwhile stretched and turned between the sheets, sighing with the contentment of a weary man who has obtained the luxury of a soft, clean bed.

'And you?' he exclaimed, turning towards Antonia, 'what are you sitting there for, as dumb as a post? Aren't you coming to bed?'

'No, I—I am not sleepy,' she temporized, with her teeth chattering.

'What if you aren't sleepy? Are you going to sit up all night?'

'No,—no,—there isn't room. You go to sleep. I'll get on here, some way or other.'

He uttered two or three coarse words.

'Are you afraid of me, do you hate me, or what on earth is the trouble? We'll see whether you aren't coming to bed! If you don't——'

He sat up, reached out his hands, and prepared to spring from the bed to the floor. But Antonia, with the fatalistic docility of a slave, had already begun to undress. Her hurrying fingers broke the strings, violently tore off the hooks and eyes, ripped her skirts and petticoats. In one corner of the room could still be heard the smothered sobbing of the boy.

It was the boy who summoned the neighbours the following morning by his desperate cries. They found Antonia still in bed, stretched out as if dead. A doctor, summoned in haste, declared that she was still alive, and bled her, but he could not draw from her one drop of blood. She passed away at noon, by a natural death, for there was no mark of violence upon her. The boy insisted that the man who had passed the night there had called her several times to get up, and seeing that she didn't answer, had gone away, running like a madman.

ANONYMOUS

LEOPOLDO ALAS
[1852–1901]

Leopoldo Alas, who used the pen name Clarín, *is best known for his discerning literary criticism. He also wrote two novels and numerous short stories. His best work, the novel* La Regenta (*1885*), *is a lengthy, detailed, naturalistic study of life in a provincial town. From his short stories, the touching* Adiós, Cordera! *is here presented.*

ADIÓS, CORDERA!

There were three; always the three! Rosa, Pinin and Cordera.

The Somonte meadow was a triangular cutting of velvety green, stretched like a tapestry, down hill across the mountains. The railroad from Oviedo to Gijon cut off one of its corners, the lower one. A telegraph pole, planted there like a standard of conquest, with its little white cups, and it parallel wires to right and left, represented to Rosa and Pinin the wide world, unexplored, mysterious, awful, forever unknown. Pinin, after thinking a good deal about it, and seeing the post day after day, quiet, inoffensive, neighbourly, with resolution, without doubt, accustoming itself to its surroundings and looking exactly like a dry tree, by force of habit got used to it, and his confidence led him to embrace the trunk and to climb up to the wires. But he never reached the porcelain cups aloft, for they reminded him of the little chocolate cups which he had seen in the rectory of Puao. When he realized he was so near the sacred mystery, a panic of veneration overwhelmed him, and he hastened to slip down until he touched the sward with his feet.

Rosa, less bold, but more enchanted with the unknown, was content to press her ear against the telegraph pole, and she passed minutes and even quarters of an hour listening to the tremendous metallic noises which the wind wrested out of the fibres of dry pine in contact with the wires. These vibrations, intense as those of a tuning fork held to the ear, sounded like a conflagration with their rhythmical pulsations, and to Rosa the messages which were passing seemed letters written over the wires in an incomprehensible language which unknown talked with unknown. What did it matter? Her interest was in the noise, for the sake of the noise itself, its tone and its mystery.

La Cordera, much more sedate than her companions, true it is, of an age much more mature, kept away from all communication with the civilized world, and looked from afar at the telegraph pole, as at something which was, in her mind, certainly a dead thing and useless, answering no good purpose unless it were to scratch her back against. She was a cow who had lived much. Reposing hours after hours, experienced in pastures, she knew how to make good use of her time. She meditated more than she ate, she enjoyed the pleasure of living in peace, beneath the grey and tranquil heaven of her native land, and peace nourishes the soul which the brutes have also, as well as we. And if it shall not be thought a profanation, one might say that the thoughts of the matron cow appear very similar to the soothing and bucolic odes of Horace.

She was present at the sports of the little shepherds, whose duty it was to guard her, as a grandmother might. If she could, she would have smiled at the idea that Rosa and Pinin should have as their mission in life to look after her in the meadow, her, Cordera, and to see that she did not go out of bounds, nor put herself in the way of the railroad train, nor jump into the neighbour's farm. What had she to do with jumping? What had she to do with going astray!

To graze each day for a while without losing time in raising her head through idle curiosity, cropping without hesitating the best mouthfuls, and afterwards to recline upon her haunches, either contemplating life or enjoying the delight of not suffering, or allowing herself to exist, that was her task.

Xatu (the bull) with the wide leaps through the pasture ground higher up. That was so long ago! and all the other dangerous adventures. Now, she could not remember when the last fly had bitten her!

The only thing which had disturbed that peace was the opening of the railroad. The first time Cordera saw the trains go by she was crazy. She jumped the hedge on the highest part of Somonte, ran through the neighbouring meadows, and her fright lasted many days, renewing itself more or less violently each time the machine began to appear in the neighbouring cut. Little by little she became accustomed to the harmless din. When she began to convince herself that it was a danger which would pass by, a catastrophe which was threatening without striking, she reduced her precautions to getting upon her feet, and to looking straight forward at the formidable monster, with her head raised. Later she did nothing but look without getting up, with antipathy and lack of confidence; she finished by not paying any attention to the trains at all.

In Pinin and Rosa the novelty of the railroad produced impressions more persistent and agreeable. If in the beginning it was an exhilaration, a mixture of superstitious fear and nervous excitement which caused them to break into screams, and to make gestures and absurd grimaces, afterwards it was a peaceful recreation, sweet, renewed several times a day. It was slow to wear out, that emotion of looking on at the dizzy progress, swift as the wind, of the great iron serpent which carried along within itself so great noise and so many unknown foreign persons.

But telegraph or railroad was of little account—a passing chance which was drowned in the sea of solitude which encircled the Somonte meadow, from whence no human habitation could be seen, and no noises of the world arrived except the passing of the train.

Mornings without end, beneath the passing of the sun, sometimes, amid the humming of the insects, the cow and the children awaited the approach of midday to go to the house. And finally eternal afternoons of sweet, silent sadness, in the same meadow, before the coming of the night, with the evening star as a mute witness on high. The clouds rolled there overhead. The shadows of the trees and of the rocks lengthened on the hill and in the dale; the birds went to bed; some stars began to shine in the darkest part of the blue sky, and Pinin and Rosa, the twins, the children of Anton de Chinta, their souls possessed by the sweet, dreamy serenity of the solemn and serious Nature, were quiet for hours and hours, after their games, never very noisy, seated near Cordera, who accompanied the august silence with the soft sound of her lazy bell. '

In this quiet, in this inactive calm, there was love. The brother and sister loved each other like the two halves of a green fruit, united by the same life, with a bare consciousness of that in which they were distinct and of what separated them. Pinin and Rosa loved Cordera, their large, dun-coloured grandmother cow, whose udder appeared to be a foundling hospital. Cordera will remind a poet of the 'Zavala' of Rabayana, the holy cow. She resembled her in the amplitude of her form, in the solemn serenity of her slow and noble movements; the airs and graces of a dethroned idol, fallen but content with her lot, better satisfied to be a true cow than a false god. One might say that Cordera, as well as it is possible to guess those things, also loved the twins, whose duty it was to look after her. She had little gift of expression, but the patience with which she suffered them to use her as a hiding place, and for a mount, and for other things which caught the fancy of the shepherds, tacitly showed the affection of the pacifist and thoughtful animal.

In hard times Pinin and Rosa had given to Cordera the very

limit of solicitude and care. Anton de Chinta had not always had the Somonte meadow. That luxury was comparatively new. Years before Cordera had to go out on the Common, that is, to graze as she could upon mouthfuls of scant herbage along the roads and lanes, which served as both highway and pasturage. Pinin and Rosa in those days of want spied out the best croppings in the neighbourhood, the least disturbed, and guarded her from the thousand ills which cattle that must get their food on public roads are subject to. In the days of hunger in the stable where hay was scarce, and straw to make a warm bed for the cow was not to be had, Cordera owed to the labours of Pinin and Rosa the alleviation of her misery. And in the heroic days of maternity, when her calf arrived, and when the inevitable struggle ensued between the feeding and prosperity of the little one and the nourishing of the Chintas, which consisted of robbing from the mother cow every drop which was not necessary for the life of the new born calf! Rosa and Pinin, in this struggle, were always on the side of Cordera.

Anton de Chinta knew that he had been born to poverty, when he realised the impossibility of accomplishing that gilded dream of keeping a corral of his own with a yoke of oxen, at least. He owned, thanks to a thousand economies, which caused rivulets of sweat and purgatories of privation—yes, he owned one cow, Cordera; and he never got beyond that. Before he was able to buy another, he found himself in arrears to the overseer, who was the landlord of the cottage which he rented, and to pay him he was obliged to take to the market, though it wrung his heart, Cordera, the darling of his children. Chinta's wife had died two years after Anton had brought Cordera to their home. The stable and the marriage bed had a partition wall between, if you can call a web of chestnut branches and cornstalks a wall. Chinta's wife, the muse of economy, in that humble hovel, looking at the cow through a chink in the broken wall of branches, pointed her out as the salvation of her family.

'Take care of her. She is your support,' appeared to say the eyes of the poor, dying woman, who perished, exhausted by hunger and work. The love of the twin children had been centred on Cordera. As the lap of a mother, which the father could not replace, was the warmth of Cordera in the stable and there in Somonte. All this Anton understood in his own way, confusedly. Of the sale that was necessary he need not say a word to the children.

On Saturday, at dawn of day, in bad humour, Anton began

to walk toward Gijon, driving Cordera ahead of him, without more gear than her bell collar. Pinin and Rosa were asleep. On other days he used to wake them at daybreak. When they got up, they found themselves without Cordera. When at dusk Anton and Cordera came up the lane, fretful, tired and covered with dust, the father gave no explanations but the children guessed that there was danger.

He had not sold her because no one was willing to give the price he had put on her head—a price made excessive by a sophistry of affection; he asked much so that no one might dare bid. Those who had come near to try their luck had soon taken their departure, swearing at him while he looked with eyes of hate and distrust on any one who dared to insist on going near the price fixed. Up to the last moment Anton de Chinta stood in the market place of Humedal defying fate.

'They can't say I do not want to sell, only I cannot get for Cordera what she is worth.' Thus he deceived himself, and finally sighing, as though not quite satisfied, he took his way for the high road to Candas, amidst the confusion and noise of pigs and bullocks, oxen and cows which the country people of many parishes were driving with greater or lesser trouble, depending on how old the relationship between master and beast was.

In Natahoyo, at the crossing of two roads, Chinta again ran the risk of losing Cordera; a neighbour of Carrió who had hung around all day offering only a little less than Chinta asked, made a final attack; somewhat drunk he raised his bid higher and higher, struggling between covetousness and desire to get the cow.

They stood motionless, their hands clasped in the middle of the highway, stopping the traffic. At last covetousness won the day; the small amount of fifty centimos kept them apart, like an abyss; they let go their hands, and each went his way, Anton by a little lane which led through honeysuckles which were not in bloom and flowering bramble berries to his home.

From the day on which they suspected danger, Pinin and Rosa were never at ease. In the middle of the week the superintendent came himself to the corral of Anton. He was a countryman of the same parish, ill tempered and cruel to tenants who were in debt. The landlord would not wait any longer. The cow would have to be sold at a low price. He must pay or get out into the street. On the Saturday following, Pinin went to Humedal with his father. The boy looked with horror at the meat contractors, tyrants of the market. Cordera was sold at a fair price to the highest bidder, a man from Castile. They made a brand on her skin, and sent her back to her stable at Puao, mournfully tinkling her bell. Behind her walked Anton de Chinta in silence and Pinin, with eyes like fists. When Rosa heard of the sale, she threw her arms around the neck of Cordera, who submitted to her embraces as she used to do to the yoke.

'We're losing our old friend,' thought the despondent Anton. She was only a dumb animal, but his children had no other mother or grandmother.

Some days afterwards, in the green field of Somonte, the silence was funereal. Cordera, who was ignorant of her fate, was resting and eating *sub specie aeternitatis*, as she would rest and eat until the moment the cruel blow would strike her dead. But Rosa and Pinin remained desolate, stretched on the grass, useless in the future. They looked with anger at the trains which passed and at the telegraph wires. It was that unknown world, on the one side and on the other, which was taking their beloved Cordera away from them.

Friday at dusk was the time of departure. There came an agent of the buyer of Castile for the cattle. He paid; Anton and the agent had a drink and Cordera was led out to the road. Anton had been plying the bottle, and was excited. Also the weight of the money in his purse enlivened him. He wanted to rattle on. He talked much, praised the excellences of the cow. The other smiled, for the praises of Anton were of no concern to him. The cow gave so many quarts of milk? She was obedient under the yoke? Strong under a burden? What did it matter, if in a few days she would be cut up into steaks and other savoury bits? Anton did not like to think of that. He imagined her alive and working, serving some other farmer, forgetful of him and his children, but alive and happy.

Pinin and Rosa, seated on a mound, thinking of nothing but Cordera and her troubles, their hands clasped, looked at the enemy with terror-stricken eyes. At the last moment they threw themselves upon their friend with kisses and hugs, and would not let go of her; while Anton, overcome by the excitement of the wine, looked as if he had suffered a paralytic stroke. He crossed his arms and went into the dark corral. The children followed for quite a distance through the lane of high hedges Cordera and the agent, the former going against her will with a stranger, and at such an unusual hour. At last they had to separate. Anton called from the house.

'Bah, children, come here; I tell you there has been enough of trifles,' he called, with tears in his voice.

Night was falling, and the long lane was growing dark beneath the vault of high hedges. The form of Cordera became black in the distance. Then there remained nothing but the slow tinkle of the bell, vanishing in the distance amidst the melancholy chirrups of countless crickets.

'Adiós, Cordera,' cried Rosa in tears. 'Good-bye, Cordera of my soul!'

'Good-bye, Cordera!' repeated Pinin, as excited as Rosa.

'Good-bye,' answered last of all the bell, in its own way, until its sad lament was lost among the many sounds of a July evening in a country village.

On the following morning at the usual hour, very early, Pinin and Rosa were at the Somonte meadow. That lonely spot never before had seemed desolate to them, but that day, Somonte without Cordera was like the desert.

Suddenly a locomotive whistled, steam appeared, an instant later the train. In an inclosed box car with tall, narrow windows or air vents, were dimly seen the heads of the cows who, bewildered, were looking through the openings.

'Adiós, Cordera,' shouted Rosa, guessing that her friend, the grandmother cow, was there.

'Adiós, Cordera,' shrieked Pinin, in the same belief, shaking his fist at the train which was flying by on its way to Castile. And weeping, the lad cried out, more acquainted than his sister with the ways of the world :

'They are taking her to the slaughter house so that rich gentlemen may eat meat.'

'Adiós, Cordera.'

'Adiós, Cordera.'

Both Rosa and Pinin looked with anger at the railway and the telegraph, the symbols of that enemy, the world, which was carrying off and would devour the companion of so many lonely hours, the sharer of tenderness so great, so silent, in order to convert her into tid-bits for rich gluttons.

'Adiós, Cordera; Adiós, Cordera.'

.   .   .

There passed many years. Pinin grew to be a young man, and was taken as a conscript by the King. The Carlist war was raging. Anton de Chinta was a workman for a boss of the beaten side. He had no influence to get Pinin declared unfit for service. To tell the truth, the young man was like a young oak tree.

And one dreary afternoon in October, Rosa, in the Somonte

meadow, alone, was waiting for the passing of the local train for Gijon, which was taking away from her her only love, her brother. The engine whistled in the distance, the train appeared in the cut, passed like a flash of lightning. Rosa, almost ground by the wheels, could see for an instant in a third-class coach a multitude of heads of poor conscripts who shouted and made gestures, saluting the trees, the soil, the fields, all the familiar country and the humble homes of those who were going to die in fratricidal struggles of the great fatherland in the service of a King, and for ideas of which they knew nothing.

Pinin, with half his body out the window, stretched his arm out to his sister. They almost touched each other, and Rosa could hear amidst the noise of the wheels and the clamour of the recruits, the distant voice of her brother, who cried out as though inspired by a recollection of a far away grief :

'Adiós, Rosa ! . . . Adiós, Cordera !'

'Adiós, Pinin, Pinin of my soul !'

He was going away like the other, like the grandmother cow, The world was taking him away. The cow had been meat for gluttons; her own flesh and blood was to be cannon fodder, on account of the madness of the world, for the ambitions of others.

Amidst the confusion of grief and of ideas, thus thought the poor sister, as she saw the train lose itself in the distance, whistling mournfully, with a whistle which shook the chestnut trees, the open plains and the huge rocks. How all alone she was left; and now the Somonte meadow seemed like a desert.

'Adiós, Pinin ! Adiós, Cordera !'

With what hatred Rosa looked at the road-bed, smirched with dead coals, with what anger at the telegraph wires. Oh, Cordera was right not to go near them. Such was the world, the unknown, which was taking everything away from her. And without thinking, Rosa leaned her head against the telegraph pole, rising like a standard on the promontory of Somonte, and listened to its inward chant. And now she understood it. It was the tune of tears, of leave-taking, of loneliness, of death.

In the swift vibrations, almost lamentations, she seemed to hear a far away voice which was sobbing along the track :

'Adiós, Rosa ! Adiós, Cordera !'

CHARLES B. McMICHAEL
(Revised by the Editors)

ARMANDO PALACIO VALDÉS
[1853–1938]

One of Spain's most popular novelists, both in that country and abroad, Armando Palacio Valdés is noted for the readability of his works. His style is easy and uncluttered; his tone, good-humoured; his characterizations, interesting. In particular he is adept at the art of description, drawing word-pictures of such compelling charm that the reader feels almost literally transported into the scene.

Among his best-known novels are La hermana San Sulpicio (*1889*), José (*1885*) *and* Marta y María (*1883*). La hermana San Sulpicio *concerns the courtship of an Andalusian novice by a Galician poet.* José *tells a tale of life among Asturian fishermen.* Marta y María *deals with two sisters, one of whom becomes fanatically steeped in mysticism.*

MARTA AND MARIA

HOW THE MARQUIS OF PEÑALTA BECAME THE DUKE OF THURINGEN

'*Mi Queridisimo Ricardo,—*

'For some time I have been anxious to tell you a thought that has filled my mind, but I have not had the courage. I know your nature well : you are extremely impetuous, and thus many times, instead of reflecting on my words and trying to understand their meaning, you would flare up like gunpowder, spoil everything, and frighten me terribly, as on the evening when we celebrated mamma's fête-day. Accordingly, after much vacillation, I have decided to tell you by letter and not by word of mouth.

'The thought that disturbs me of late is to ask you to postpone our wedding still a little longer. Don't get angry, Ricardo *mio*, and read on calmly. I am sure that the first thought that will occur to your mind is that I don't love you. How mistaken you would be to think such a thing ! If you could read in my soul, you would see that your love holds my conscience in its sway, and this I deplore bitterly. But that is not the question now.

'Are you sure, Ricardo, that you and I are properly trained to enter upon a state which entails so many and such serious responsibilities? Have you thought well of what the sacrament of marriage means? Is there not in our hearts rather an unreflecting inclination, mixed, perhaps, with carnal impulses, than a serious desire to undertake an austere, religious life, becoming in a Christian family, educating our children in the fear of God and in the practice of virtue? If you reflect a little on how frivolous hitherto our love has been, and on the sins which we are constantly committing, you cannot but agree with me that two young people, so wanting in gravity and genuine virtue, are not authorized by God to bring up and direct a family. I should feel a great smiting of the conscience if I were married now (and you ought to feel the same), and I believe that God could not bless or make our union happy. If it is to be blessed, we must make ourselves worthy of celebrating it, by leaving forever behind us our frivolous, worldly manner of loving, for another, more lofty and spiritual, by refraining absolutely from certain earthly manifestations to which we are impelled by our great love, and by making preparations for it, during a few months at least, by a virtuous and devout life, by performing a few sacrifices and works of charity, and by constantly imploring God to illumine our minds, and give us power to fulfil the duties imposed upon us by the new state.

'There is an example in history which ought to encourage us greatly in doing what I propose. The beloved Saint Isabel of Hungary had been betrothed from early youth to the Duke Luis of Thuringen, but the nuptials were not celebrated until both reached the proper age. After the betrothal was celebrated, Isabel and Luis did not separate, but lived in the same palace, as though they had been brother and sister, until, by the will of God, they became husband and wife. The pious sentiments of the lovers, together with the austere education which was given them, made their affection always pure and upright, founding the unchangeable union of their hearts, not on the ephemeral sentiments of a purely human attraction, but on a common faith and the stern observance of all the virtues inculcated by this faith. Until they were united by the indissoluble bond of matrimony, they always called each other brother and sister; and even after they were married, they frequently used to apply this sweet name to each other.

'I confess, Ricardo, that the spectacle of those noble and holy young people has an unspeakable attraction for me. Love sanctified in such a way is a thousand times more beautiful, and bestows upon the heart purer and loftier pleasures. Why should we not follow, as far as possible, the steps of that illustrious husband and wife, the pattern of abnegation and tenderness, as well as of purity and fidelity? Why should you not imitate, my beloved Ricardo, the stern virtue of the young Duke of Thuringen, the nobleness and dignity of all his actions, the innocence and modesty of his soul, never found guilty of falsehood,—virtues which in no respect were opposed to the valour and boldness of which he always gave eminent proofs? For my part, I promise you to imitate, according to the measure of my feeble strength, the tenderness, the obedience, and the faithfulness of his saintly spouse Isabel, living subject to the law of God, within the affection which I profess for you.

'This is what I propose to you, and desire to do. Don't get angry, for God's sake, dear Ricardo. Reflect over what I have just said, and you will see how right I am. Doubt not that I love you much, much,—I, who am, for the time being,

'Your sister,
'Maria.'

THE ROAD TO PERFECTION

The letter which we have just read led to a very important crisis in the lives of our lovers. Ricardo at first was furious, and wrote a long answer to his betrothed, announcing the end of their acquaintance, but he did not send it. Then he held a consultation with her in which he overwhelmed her with recriminations and insults, saying that all she had written in her letter was nothing but a tissue of follies and absurdities, manufactured on purpose to hide her treachery; that she might have dismissed him in some way not so grotesque; that although he had no claim upon her love, at least he might and ought to demand the frankness and loyalty which he had always shown; that for a long time back he had noticed her coldness and indifference, but he could never have believed that she would make use of a pretext so ridiculous and so absurd for breaking the tie that united them, etc., etc. Maria received this storm of contumely with great humility, assuring him with gentle words of persuasion, when he left her a moment's chance to speak, that she still loved him with all her soul; that he might put her love to the test as often as he pleased, since she was ready to make whatever sacrifice he demanded, except what went against her conscience; that his suspicions of her untruth and treachery cut her to the heart, but she forgave him because she was aware of his excited state of mind; that she likewise felt it keenly that he should call the motives of her resolution grotesque and ridiculous when she found them so worthy; and, in fine, that she begged him to calm himself.

After the young marquis had thoroughly vented his ill-feeling without result, he began to get off his high horse and try the effect of skilful reasoning, and then he changed to entreaties, but without any better results. He employed all the devices of genius and all the tender and expressive words dictated by his honourable heart, in order to convince her that neither of them was fortunately under the necessity of mourning for their sins like two criminals; since if they were not better than the average of humanity, they were at least as good; and as for their skill and judgment in governing themselves and their children in matrimony, he believed that they were no less fitted than the rest, and that in the end they would come out as well as other people. All was useless. The young woman met argument with argument, and her lover's prayers, sprinkled with endearments, with a firm and obstinate silence. Ricardo, in a state of tribulation . . . went straight to Don Mariano, whom he loved like a father, to tell him the state of things, and ask his aid and advice. The latter was highly surprised and disturbed when he read his daughter's letter. He read it over many times as though he could not get the key of it, and at each new reading he found it more obscure and inexplicable. Finally he handed it back with a gesture of dismay, signifying that his daughter must have lost her wits, for he could not understand any such nonsense. . . .

. . . It is easy to imagine the effect made upon him by his daughter's letter. He looked upon it as one of those many extravagant hobbies which she had passed through in her life, and he solemnly promised Ricardo to make her desist from such folly. But after he had called her to his room and spent about two hours closeted with her, he began to suspect that the thing was not so easy as it appeared at first sight. Neither by turning her austere plan into ridicule by his jests, nor by showing that he was annoyed, nor by descending to entreaties, was our worthy *caballero* able to accomplish anything. Maria met these attacks like her lover's, with a humble but resolute attitude impossible to overcome. No other way was left them but to resign themselves, and this they both did perforce with the secret hope that the girl would very soon change of her own accord when once her caprice was satisfied. Accordingly the wedding was indefinitely postponed, and poor Ricardo began to play his part as Duke of Thuringen almost as ill as a Spanish actor.

From that time forth his interviews with Maria became less frequent and familiar. The girl seemed to shun him and to avoid opportunities of talking confidentially with him as she used. Ricardo eagerly sought them, sometimes employing them in bitter expostulations, at others in softly whispering a thousand passionate phrases. She always appeared sweet and affectionate, but endeavoured to turn the conversation to serious subjects. Ricardo still caressed her whenever he had an opportunity, but he no longer obtained from her the usual reciprocation in spite of the incredible efforts which he made to obtain it. And not only he did not obtain this grace, but little by little the girl came to avoid his familiarities by always talking with him in the presence of others. One day when he found her alone in the dining-room, he said to himself with inward delight, 'She is mine.' And creeping up behind her carefully, he gave her a ringing kiss on her neck. Maria sprang suddenly from her chair and said, with a certain sweetness not free from severity,

'Ricardo, don't do that again!'

'Why not?'

'Because I don't like it.'

'How long since?'

'I never did; don't be foolish.' She said these words with asperity, and another unpleasant stage in Ricardo's love was signalized. Almost absolutely ceased those happy moments of fond raptures, sweet and delicious as the pleasures of the angels in which the poesy of spirit and matter is indistinguishable, the prospect of which kindles and stirs the deepest roots of our being, and their remembrance throws over all our lives, even for the most prosaic of men, a vague and poetic melancholy helping us to endure the rebuffs of existence and to contemplate without envy the felicity of others. The most that the young marquis obtained grudgingly from his sweetheart was the permission to give her a brotherly kiss on the forehead from time to time. And there is no need of telling my experienced readers, for they must be able to imagine it, that with this enforced fast the young man's love far from growing less, increased and became violent beyond all power of words.

Maria was able fully to devote herself to the life of perfection toward which she had felt such vehement aspiration. The hours of the day seemed to her too few for her prayers, both at church and at home, and for the repentance of her sins. She attended the sacraments more and more, and she was present and assisted with her sympathy and money in all the religious solemnities which were celebrated in the town. The time left free from her prayers she spent in reading books of devotion, which, in a short time, formed a library almost as numerous as her novels. The lives of the saints pleased her above all, and she soon devoured a multitude of them, paying most attention, as was logical, to the lives of those who reached the greatest glory and brough the greatest splendour to the Church,—the life of Saint Teresa, that of Saint Catalina of Siena, of Saint Gertrudis, of Saint Isabel, Saint Eulalia, Saint Monica, and many others who, without having been canonized, were celebrated for their piety and for the spiritual grace which God bestowed upon them, like the holy Margarita of Alacoque, Mademoiselle de Melun, and others. These works made a very profound impression on our young lady's ardent and enthusiastic mind, driving her farther and farther along the road to perfection. The incredible and marvellous powers of those heroic souls, who, through love and charity, succeeded in lifting themselves to heaven, and in enjoying through anticipation, while still on earth, the delights reserved for the blessed, filled her with deep, fervent admiration. She felt an ecstasy over the most insignificant incidents in the lives of the saints, where God often showed them that He held them as His chosen ones, and would not let the world entice them away, as, for example, the scene of the miraculous toad which Saint Teresa saw talking in the garden with a *caballero* toward whom she felt a drawing; the sudden death of Buenaventura, Saint Catalina's sister, who was leading that holy woman along the worldly path of bodily adornments and pleasures; and many others which filled the books aforesaid. Maria regarded these notable heroines of religion with the same emotion and astonishment as one regards the phenomena and marvels of Nature. A long time passed before she dared to lift her eyes toward them in the way of imitation; she contented herself with beseeching them, through interminable prayers, to intercede with God to pardon her sins. She bought the finest effigies that she found and, when she had caused them to be richly framed, she hung them up on the walls of her room. To do this she had to take down Malec-Kadel and many other warriors of the Middle Ages which had invaded them. She was especially carried away by the scenes of their infancy, and by the first steps which these blessed women had taken along the road to perfection; but when she reached that part of their lives which marked the apogee of their glory on earth, when God, overcome by their steadfast love, their fidelity, and the wonderful penances imposed upon themselves, began to grant them favours and spiritual gifts by means of ecstasies and visions, she remained somewhat disturbed and even cast down. She did not as yet comprehend the mystic delight of direct communication through the senses between the soul and God, and she confessed with great compunction that if one of these miraculous visions were to be vouchsafed her, she should feel much greater fear than pleasure.

Nevertheless, before long, the desire to imitate them sprang up in her heart. It is always a short step from admiration to imitation. She began where it was proper, that is, by imitating their humility. Hitherto she had been modest, but not to such a degree as not to enjoy being flattered and applauded; but from this time forth she not only carefully avoided all praise, but she repelled those who offered it, and even tried to hide her talents so as to give her friends no chance to praise her. She began to talk as little as possible with friends or members of the family, and to do on the instant whatever they asked her to, lamenting in her heart that they did not give her harsh commands. She managed to have the servants help her at table after all the rest, and always give her stale bread instead of fresh. To conquer the natural impulses of selfishness she showed those who had offended her more affability than others, and anyone had only to offend her pride more or less for her immediately to overwhelm them with attentions, as though she owed them gratitude. On the other hand, to those who, as she knew, loved and admired her, she took delight in seeming peevish, so that they might not think her better than she really was.

Having started out on this pious path, which had been travelled by all the saints for the glory of God and of the human race, since the virtue of humility raises man above his own nature, conquering the passion deepest rooted in the human heart, and, of all virtues is the one that best proves the power of the spirit, and inspires respect even in the most unbelieving of men; having started out, I say on this pious path, and being aided by vivid imagination, she performed a number of strange deeds, well-nigh incomprehensible to those whose attention is turned to the world and not to religious things, deeds which the illustrious biographers of Saint Isabel call *secret and holy fancies*, serving as the mystic steps whereby the soul mounts to perfection and communicates with God. One day, for example, it came into her mind to eat humbly with the servants as though she were one of them. In order to do this, when dinner-time came, she pretended to have a headache, and kept in her chamber; but when the family were gathered in the dining-room, she softly ran downstairs to the kitchen, and there she stayed all through the dinner-hour, helping herself to the remains of the food, to the surprise and admiration of the servants. Another day, when it seemed to her that she had not answered her father with sufficient respect, she suddenly presented herself in his office, fell on her knees, and begged his pardon. Don Mariano lifted her from the floor, with startled eyes :

'But, my daughter, suppose you have not offended me or committed any fault? And even if you had, there is no need of going to these extremes. What nonsense! Come, give me a kiss, and go and sew with your sister, and don't frighten me again with such absurdities!'

Maria did not meet with the contrarieties in the bosom of her family that she would have liked, in the way of test. Her father and sister, though they did not encourage her in her devotions, said nothing to oppose her; and each day they showed her more and more affection, which was the natural consequence of the growing sweetness and gentleness of her character. Her mother adored her with foolish frenzy, blindly applauded all her acts of piety, and never wearied of praising to the skies the virtue and talent of her first-born. The servants likewise joined their voices in a chorus of flatteries, spreading all over town the fame of her virtues, and crowning her with a halo of respect and sanctity. As far as such things influenced her salvation, our maiden would have preferred a cruel, tyrannical father, who laid harsh commands upon her, or a disagreeable mother or an envious sister, who would not let her live in peace, since, according to the biographies which she read, no saint had been free from suffering persecutions in her own family. She grieved inwardly at the ease and comfort which she enjoyed at home, and she thought that she suffered nothing for the God who had redeemed us with His blood. She would have liked it had a calumny been breathed about her, such as Palmerina caused Saint Catalina of Siena to suffer, so that she might be scorned and maltreated; but no one in the house or out of it dreamed of doing such a thing.

To compensate for this absence of persecutions, she mortified her flesh with fasting and penances, always performing those which were more unpleasant to her. Some dish on the table was distasteful to her; then she imposed upon herself the penance of eating it, leaving others, of which she was extremely fond, untouched. She went so far as to put aloes in some, in imitation of what was done by Saint Nicolas of Tolentino. On Fridays she fasted rigorously on bread and water, performing miracles of shrewdness to prevent her father from discovering it; for she felt certain that if he knew it, he would not give his consent.

She always wore a locket around her neck, containing the picture of her betrothed. One day, when he had succeeded in having a moment's conversation alone with her, she said to him,

'Listen, Ricardo; if you would not be vexed, I would tell you something.'

'What is it?' hastily asked the young man, with the sudden alarm of one who is always afraid of some misfortune.

'I see that I am going to offend you—but I will tell you. I have taken your picture out of the locket.'

Ricardo's face expressed amazement.

'And the worst is, that I have put another in its place.'

The expression of amazement changed into one of such pain, that Maria, on looking in his contracted and grief-stricken face, could not refrain from breaking out into a fresh, ringing peal of merry laughter, such as in former times used to ripple from her lips all the time, and which little by little had decreased, as though the fire of light and joy from which they came had died down.

'Good heavens! what a long face! Wait! Now I'll show your substitute, so as to make you suffer more.'

And taking the locket from her neck she showed it to him. It held the effigy of Jesus crowned with thorns. Ricardo, half satisfied and half vexed, answered with a smile.

'Now kiss it!'

The young man obeyed instantly, placing his lips on the picture of the Lord, and at the same time touching the rosy fingers that held it out to him. Maria withdrew them and ran away.

NATHAN HASKELL DOLE

JOSÉ ECHEGARAY
[1832–1916]

A remarkable man who had been a brilliant mathematician, engineer and politician before turning to the theatre, José Echegaray wrote his first drama after the age of forty. During the next thirty years he poured out more than sixty plays.

They are for the most part exaggerated, moralizing melodramas. But Echegaray was Spain's most popular dramatist during the last quarter of the nineteenth century, and in 1904 he was awarded the Nobel Prize for literature, thus becoming the first Spaniard to be so honoured.

His masterpiece, El gran Galeoto (1881), *is a powerful drama whose theme is the destruction of a happy home by the consuming force of slander. It is written in verse, with a prose prologue.*

THE GREAT GALEOTO

PROLOGUE

Ernesto's *study. To the left, a french window; to the right, a door.—Nearly in the centre, a table on which are books, papers, and a lighted lamp.—To the right is a sofa. It is evening.* Ernesto *is seated at the table, as though about to write.*

ERN. There's no use. I can't do it. It is impossible. I am simply contending with the impossible. The idea is here; it is stirring in my brain; I can feel it. Sometimes a light from within illumines it and I see it with its shifting form and vague contours, and suddenly there sound in the hidden depths voices that give it life; cries of grief, sighs of love, sardonic, mocking laughter—a whole world of living, struggling passions. They break from me, and spread out, and fill the air all about me! Then, then, I say to myself, the moment has come, and I take up my pen, and with eyes gazing into space, with straining ears, with fast-beating heart, I bend over my paper.—But oh, the irony of impotence! The contours become blurred, the vision disappears, the shouts and sighs die away, and nothingness, nothingness surrounds me! The desolation of empty space, of meaningless thought, of deadly weariness! More than all that, the desolation of an idle pen and a barren page—a page bereft of all life-giving thought. Ah, how many forms has nothingness, and how it mocks, dark and silent, at creatures of my sort! Many, many forms :—the colourless canvas, the shapeless piece of marble, the discordant sound, but none more irritating, more mocking, more blighting, than this worthless pen and this blank paper. Ah, I cannot cover you, but I can destroy you, vile accomplice in my wrecked ambitions and my everlasting humiliation!—So, so,—smaller, still smaller. (*Tearing the paper—then, a pause.*) Well, it's fortunate that no one saw me, for at best such ranting is foolish, and it's all wrong. No—I will not give in; I will think harder, harder, until I conquer or blow up in a thousand pieces. No, I will never admit I am beaten. Come, let's see whether now——

(*Enter* Don Julian, *right, wearing a frock coat and carrying his overcoat on his arm. He looks in at the door but doesn't come in.*)

JUL. Hello, Ernesto!

ERN. Don Julian!

JUL. Still working? Am I disturbing you?

ERN. Disturbing me? Indeed, no. Come in, come in, Don Julian. Where's Teodora?

JUL. We've just come from the opera. She went up to the third floor with my brother and his wife to see some purchases of Mercedes, and I was on my way to my own room, when I saw a light in yours and looked in to say good night.

ERN. Were there many people there?

JUL. A good many—as usual. All my friends were asking for you. They were surprised at your not going.

ERN. How kind of them!

JUL. Not so very, considering all that you deserve. But how about you? Have you made good use of these three hours of solitude and inspiration?

ERN. Solitude, yes; inspiration, no. That would not come to me, though I called upon it desperately and with passion.

JUL. It wouldn't obey the summons?

ERN. No, and this was not the first time. But I did make a profitable discovery, though I accomplished nothing.

JUL. What?

ERN. Simply this—that I am a poor good-for-nothing.

JUL. Good-for-nothing! Well, that's a profitable discovery, indeed.

ERN. Precisely.

JUL. And why so disgusted with yourself? Isn't the play you told about the other day going well?

ERN. I'm the one who is going—out of my mind!

JUL. And what is all this trouble that inspiration and the play together are making for my Ernesto?

ERN. The trouble is this : when I conceived it I thought the idea a good one; but when I give it form and dress it out in the proper stage trappings the result is extraordinary; contrary to all laws of the drama; utterly impossible.

JUL. But why impossible? Come, tell me about it. I am curious.

ERN. Imagine, then, that the principal character, the one who creates the drama, who develops, who animates it, who brings about the catastrophe, and who thrives upon that catastrophe and revels in it—that person cannot appear on the stage.

JUL. Is he so ugly? Or so repulsive? Or so wicked?

ERN. It's not that. He is no uglier than any one else—than you or I. Nor is he bad. Neither bad nor good. Repulsive? No indeed. I am not such a sceptic, nor such a misanthrope, nor so at odds with the world that I would say such a thing or commit such an injustice.

JUL. Well, then, what is the reason?

ERN. Don Julian, the reason is that there probably wouldn't be room on the stage for the character in question.

JUL. Good heavens, listen to the man! Is this a mythological play, then, and do Titans appear on the stage?

ERN. They are Titans; but a modern variety.

JUL. In short?

ERN. In short this character is—*Everybody*.

JUL. *Everybody!* Well, you are right! There's not room in the theatre for everybody. That is an indisputable fact that has often been demonstrated.

ERN. Now you see how right I was.

JUL. Not altogether. *Everybody* can be condensed into a certain number of types, or characters. I don't understand these things myself, but I have heard that authors have done it more than once.

ERN. Yes, but in my case, that is, in my play, it can't be done.

JUL. Why not?

ERN. For many reasons that it would take too long to explain; especially at this time of night.

JUL. Never mind, let's have some of them.

ERN. Well then, each part of this vast whole, each head of this thousand-headed monster, of this Titan of today whom I call *Everybody*, takes part in my play only for the briefest instant, speaks one word and no more, gives one glance; perhaps his entire action consists in the suggestion of one smile; he appears for a moment and goes away again; he works without passion, without guile, without malice, indifferently, and absently—often *by* his very abstraction.

JUL. And what then?

ERN. From those words, from those fleeting glances, from those indifferent smiles, from all those little whispers, from all those peccadilloes; from all these things that we might call insignificant rays of dramatic light, when brought to a focus in one family, result the spark and the explosion, the struggle and the victims. If I represent the whole of mankind by a given number of types or symbolic characters, I have to ascribe to each one that which is really distributed among many, with the result that a certain number of characters must appear who are made repulsive by vices that lack verisimilitude, whose crimes have no object. And, as an additional result, there is the danger that people will believe I am trying to paint society as evil, corrupt, and cruel, when I only want to show that not even the most insignificant acts are really insignificant or impotent for good or evil; for, gathered together by the mysterious agencies of modern life, they may succeed in producing tremendous results.

JUL. Come, stop, stop! That is all dreadfully metaphysical. I get a glimmering, but the clouds are pretty thick. In fact, you understand more than I do about these things. Now, if it were a question of drafts, of notes, of letters of credit, of discount, it would be another matter.

ERN. Oh, no, you have common sense, which is the main thing.

JUL. Thanks, Ernesto, you are very kind.

ERN. But are you convinced?

JUL. No, I'm not. There must be some way of getting round the difficulty.

ERN. If only there were!

JUL. Is there something more?

ERN. I should say so! Tell me, what is the moving force of the drama?

JUL. I don't know exactly what you mean by the moving force of the drama, but I will say that I don't find any pleasure in plays in which there are no love-affairs; preferably unhappy love-affairs, for I have plenty of happy love-making in my own house with my Teodora.

ERN. Good. Splendid! Well, in my play there is hardly any love-making at all.

JUL. Bad, very bad indeed, I say. Listen, I don't know what your play is about, but I am afraid that it won't interest anybody.

ERN. That's just what I told you. Still, love-making might be put in, and even a little jealousy.

JUL. Well, with that, with an interesting and well-developed intrigue, with some really striking situation . . .

ERN. No, señor, certainly not that. Everything must be quite commonplace, almost vulgar. This drama can have no outward manifestation. It goes on in the hearts and minds of the characters; it progresses slowly; today it is a question of a thought; tomorrow of a heartbeat; gradually the will is undermined . . .

JUL. But how is all this shown? How are these inner struggles expressed? Who tells the audience about them? Where are they seen? Are we to spend the whole evening in pursuit of a glance, a sigh, a gesture, a word? My dear boy, that is no sort of amusement. When a man wants to meddle with such abstractions he studies philosophy.

ERN. That's it, exactly. You repeat my thoughts like an echo.

JUL. I don't want to discourage you, however. You probably know what you are doing. And, even though the play may be a little colourless, even though it may seem a bit heavy and uninteresting, so long as it has a fine climax and the catastrophe . . . eh?

ERN. Catastrophe—climax! They have hardly come when the curtain falls.

JUL. You mean that the play begins when the play ends?

ERN. I'm afraid so—though, of course, I shall try to put a little warmth into it.

JUL. Come now, what you ought to do is write the second play, the one that begins when the first ends; for the first, judging by what you say, isn't worth the trouble—and plenty of trouble it's bound to give you.

ERN. I was convinced of that.

JUL. And now we both are—thanks to your cleverness and the force of your logic. What is the title?

ERN. Title! Why, that's another thing. It has no title.

JUL. What! What did you say? No title, either?

ERN. No, señor.

JUL. Well, Ernesto, you must have been asleep when I came in— you were having a nightmare and now you are telling me your dreams.

ERN. Dreaming? Yes. A nightmare? Perhaps. And I am telling you my dreams, good and bad. You have common sense, and you always guess right in everything.

JUL. It didn't take much penetration to guess right in this case. A play in which the principal character doesn't appear, in which there is almost no love-making, in which nothing happens that doesn't happen every day, which begins as the curtain falls on the last act, and which has no title.—Well, I don't see how it can be written, how it can be acted, or how any one can be found to listen to it,—or, indeed, how it is a play at all.

ERN. Ah, but it is a play. The only trouble is that I must give it form, and *that* I don't know how to do.

JUL. Do you want my advice?

ERN. Your advice? The advice of my friend, my benefactor, my second father! Oh, Don Julian!

JUL. Come, come, Ernesto, let us not have a little sentimental play of our own here in place of yours which we have pronounced impossible. I only asked you whether you wanted to know my advice.

ERN. And I said, Yes.

JUL. Well, forget all about plays—go to bed—go to sleep—go shooting with me tomorrow, kill any number of partridges instead of killing two characters, and perhaps having the audience kill you —and when all is said and done, you'll be thankful to me.

ERN. That can't be: I must write the play.

JUL. But, my dear fellow, you must have thought of it by way of penance for your sins.

ERN. I don't know why it happened, but think of it I did. I feel it stirring in my mind, it begs for life in the outer world, and I am bound to give it that.

JUL. Can't you find some other plot?

ERN. But what about this idea?

JUL. Let the devil take care of it.

ERN. Ah, Don Julian, do you think that when an idea has been hammered out in our minds, we can destroy it and bring it to naught whenever we choose? I should like to think of another play, but this accursed one won't let me until it has been born into the world.

JUL. There's no use talking, then. I only hope you get some light on the subject.

ERN. That is the question, as Hamlet says.

JUL. (*In a low voice, with mock mystery.*) Couldn't you put it in the literary orphanage for anonymous works?

ERN. Don Julian, I am a man of conscience. My children, good or bad, are legitimate, and shall bear my name.

JUL. I'll say no more. It must be—it is written.

ERN. I only wish it were. Unfortunately it is not written, but no matter, if I don't write it, someone else will.

JUL. Well, to work! Good luck, and don't let any one get ahead of you.

TEO. (*Without.*) Julian! Julian!

JUL. There's Teodora!

TEO. Are you here, Julian?

JUL. Yes, here I am. Come in !

(*Enter* Teodora.)

TEO. Good evening, Ernesto.

ERN. Good evening, Teodora. Did they sing well?

TEO. As usual. Have you done a lot of work?

ERN. As usual; nothing.

TEO. Why, you might better have gone with us. All my friends were asking for you.

ERN. It seems that everybody is taking an interest in me.

JUL. I should say so; since you are going to make *Everybody* the principal character in your play, naturally it is to his interest to have you for his friend.

TEO. A play?

JUL. Hush, it's a great mystery; you mustn't ask anything about it. It has no title, no actors, no action, no catastrophe! Oh, how sublime! Good night, Ernesto.—Come, Teodora.

ERN. Good-bye, Julian.

TEO. Until tomorrow.

ERN. Good night.

TEO. (*To* Julian.) How preoccupied Mercedes seemed !

JUL. And Severo was in a rage.

TEO. I wonder why.

JUL. I'm sure I don't know. Pepito, on the other hand, was lively enough for both.

TEO. He always is—and speaking ill of every one.

JUL. A character for Ernesto's play.

(Teodora *and* Julian *go out, right*.)

ERN. Let Julian say what he likes, I am not going to give up my undertaking. It would be rank cowardice. No, I will not retreat. Forward! (*He rises and walks up and down in agitation. Then he goes over to the french window*.) Night, lend me your protection, for against your blackness the luminous outlines of my inspiration are defined more clearly than against the blue cloak of day. Lift up your roofs, ye thousands of houses in this mighty city; for surely you should do as much for a poet in distress as for that crooked devil who mischievously lifted your tops off. Let me see the men and women coming back to your rooms to rest after the busy hours of pleasure-seeking. As my ears become more sensitive, let them distinguish the many words of those who were asking Julian and Teodora about me; and as a great light is made from scattered rays when they are gathered into a crystal lens, as the mountains are formed from grains of sand and the sea from drops of water, so from your chance words, your stray smiles, your idle glances, from a thousand trivial thoughts which you have left scattered in cafés, in theatres, in ball-rooms, and which are now floating in the air, I shall shape my drama, and the crystal of my mind shall be the lens that brings to a focus the lights and shadows, so that from them shall result the dramatic spark and the tragic explosion. My drama is taking shape. Now it has a title, for there in the lamp-light I see the work of the immortal Florentine poet, and in Italian it has given me the name which it would be madness or folly to write or speak in plain Spanish. Paolo and Francesca, may your love help me! (*Sitting down at the table and beginning to write*.) The play! the play begins! The first page is no longer blank. (*Writing*.) Now it has a title. (*Writes madly*.) *The Great Galeoto*!

(*Curtain*.)

ELEANOR BONTECOU

TWENTIETH CENTURY

VICENTE BLASCO IBÁÑEZ
[1867–1928]

Vicente Blasco Ibáñez began his prolific writing career as a regionalist, vividly portraying scenes from his native Valencia. To this early period belong his best novels: La barraca *(1898) and* Cañas y barro *('Reeds and Mud') (1902). There followed a number of novels on social themes in which Blasco Ibáñez projects his own attitudes. The best known are the anti-clerical* La catedral *(1903), set in Toledo, and* Sangre y arena *('Blood and Sand'), depicting the brutality of bullfighting, set in Seville. Blasco Ibáñez finally undertook novels of international scope, and one of them,* Los cuatro jinetes del Apocalipsis *('The Four Horsemen of the Apocalypse') (1916), a war novel favouring the Allies, brought him great fame and fortune. His style is vigorous and he is a master of realistic description. Blasco Ibáñez was extremely popular in his own country, and he is no doubt one of the most translated of all Spanish authors.*

THE CABIN

BATISTE'S TRIAL

It was Thursday, and according to a custom which dated back for five centuries, the Tribunal of the Waters was going to meet at the doorway of the Cathedral named after the Apostles.

The clock of the Miguelete pointed to a little after ten, and the inhabitants of the *huerta* were gathering in idle groups or seating themselves about the large basin of the dry fountain which adorned the *plaza*, forming about its base an animated wreath of blue and white cloaks, red and yellow handkerchiefs, and skirts of calico prints of bright colours.

Others were arriving, drawing up their horses, with their rush-baskets loaded with manure, satisfied with the collection they had made in the streets; still others, in empty carts, were trying to persuade the police to allow their vehicles to remain there; and while the old folks chatted with the women, the young went into the neighbouring café, to kill time over a glass of brandy, while chewing at a three-centime cigar.

All those of the *huerta* who had grievances to avenge were here, gesticulating and scowling, speaking of their rights, impatient to let loose the interminable chain of their complaints before the syndics or judges of the seven canals.

547

The bailiff of the tribunal, who had been carrying on this contest with the insolent and aggressive crowd for more than fifty years, placed a long sofa of old damask which was on its last legs within the shadow of the Gothic portal, and then set up a low railing, thereby closing in the square of sidewalk which had to serve the purpose of an audience-chamber. . . .

The bailiff finished arranging the Tribunal, and placed himself at the entrance of the enclosure to await the judges. The latter arrived solemnly, dressed in black, with white sandals, and silken handkerchiefs under their broad hats, they had the appearance of rich farmers. Each was followed by a cortège of canal-guards, and by persistent supplicants who, before the hour of justice, were seeking to predispose the judges' minds in their favour.

The farmers gazed with respect at these judges, come forth from their own class, whose deliberations did not admit of any appeal. They were the masters of the water : in their hands re-maimed the living of the families, the nourishment of the fields, the timely watering, the lack of which kills a harvest. And the people of these wide plains, separated by the river, which is like an impass-able frontier, designated the judges by the number of the canals.

A little, thin, bent, old man, whose red and horny hands trembled as they rested on the thick staff, was Cuart de Faitanar; the other, stout and imposing, with small eyes scarcely visible under bushy white brows, was Mislata. Soon Roscaña arrived; a youth who wore a blouse that had been freshly ironed, and whose head was round. After these appeared in sequence the rest of the seven : Favara, Robella, Tornos and Mestalla.

Now all the representatives of the four plains were there; the one on the left bank of the river; the one with the four canals; the one which the *huerta* of Rufaza encircles with its roads of luxuriant foliage ending at the confines of the marshy Albufera; and the plain on the right bank of the Turia, the poetic one, with its strawberries of Benimaclet, its *cyperus* of Alboraya and its gardens always overrun with flowers.

The seven judges saluted, like people who had not seen each other for a week; they spoke of their business beside the door of the Cathedral : from time to time, upon opening the wooden screens covered with religious advertisements, a puff of incense-laden air, somewhat like the damp exhalation from a subterranean cavern, diffused itself into the burning atmosphere of the *plaza*.

At half-past eleven, when the divine offices were ended and only some belated devotee was still coming from the temple, the Tribunal began to operate.

The seven judges seated themselves on the old sofa; then the people of the *huerta* came running up from all sides of the *plaza*, to gather around the railing, pressing their perspiring bodies, which smelled of straw and coarse sheep's wool, close together, and the bailiff, rigid and majestic, took his place near the pole topped with a bronze crook, symbolic of aquatic majesty.

The seven syndics removed their hats and remained with their hands between the knees and their hats upon the ground, while the eldest pronounced the customary sentence :

'Let the Tribunal begin.'

Absolute stillness. The crowd, observing religious silence, seemed here, in the midst of the *plaza,* to be worshipping in a temple. The sound of carriages, the clatter of tramways, all the din of modern life passed by, without touching or stirring this most ancient institution, which remained tranquil, like one who finds himself in his own house, insensible to time, paying no attention to the radical change surrounding it, incapable of any reform.

The inhabitants of the *huerta* were proud of their tribunal. It dispensed justice; the penalty without delay, and nothing done with papers, which confuse and puzzle honest men.

The absence of stamped paper and of the clerk of court who terrifies, was the part best liked by these people who were accustomed to looking upon the art of writing of which they were ignorant with a certain superstitious terror. Here were no secretary, no pens, no days of anxiety while awaiting sentence, no terrifying guards, nor anything more than words.

The judges kept the declarations in their memory, and passed sentence immediately with the tranquillity of those who know that their decisions must be fulfilled. On him who would be insolent with the tribunal, a fine was imposed; from him who had refused to comply with the verdict, the water was taken away forever, and he must die of hunger.

Nobody played with this tribunal. It was the simple patriarchal justice of the good legendary king, coming forth mornings to the door of his palace in order to settle the disputes of his subjects; the judicial system of the Kabila chief, passing sentences at his tent-entrance. Thus are rascals punished, and the honourable triumph, and there is peace.

And the public, men, women, and children, fearful of missing a word, pressed close together against the railing, moving, sometimes, with violent contortions of their shoulders, in order to escape from suffocation.

The complainants would appear at the other side of the railing, before the sofa as old as the tribunal itself.

The bailiff would take away their staffs and shepherds' crooks, which he regarded as offensive arms incompatible with the respect due the tribunal. He pushed them forward until with their mantle folded over their hands they were planted some paces distant from the judges, and if they were slow in baring their head, the handkerchief was wrested from it with two tugs. It was hard, but with this crafty people it was necessary to act thus.

The line filing by brought a continuous outburst of intricate questions, which the judges settled with marvellous facility.

The keepers of the canals and the irrigation-guards, charged with the establishment of each one's turn in the irrigation, formulated their charges, and the defendants appeared to defend themselves with arguments. The old men allowed their sons, who knew how to express themselves with more energy, to speak; the widow appeared, accompanied by some friend of the deceased, a devoted protector, who acted as her spokesman.

The passion of the south cropped out in every case.

In the midst of the accusation, the defendant would not be able to contain himself. 'You lie! What you say is evil and false! You are trying to ruin me!'

But the seven judges received these interruptions with furious glances. Here nobody was permitted to speak before his own turn came. At the second interruption, he would have to pay a fine of so many *sous*. And he who was obstinate, driven by his vehement madness, which would not permit him to be silent before the accuser, paid more and more *sous*.

The judges, without giving up their seats, would put their heads together like playful goats, and whisper together for some seconds; then the eldest, in a composed and solemn voice, pronounced the sentence, designating the fine in *sous* and pounds, as if money had suffered no change, and majestic Justice with its red robe and its escort of plumed crossbow-men were still passing through the centre of the *plaza*.

It was after twelve, and the seven judges were beginning to show signs of being weary of such prodigious outpouring of the stream of justice, when the bailiff called out loudly to Bautista Borrull, denouncing him for infraction and disobedience of irrigation-rights.

Pimentó and Batiste passed the railing, and the people pressed up even closer against the bar.

Here were many of those who lived near the ancient land of Barret.

This trial was interesting. The hated newcomer had been denounced by Pimentó, who was the *'atandador'** of that district.

The bully, by mixing up in elections, and strutting about like a fighting cock all over the neighbourhood, had won this office which gave him a certain air of authority and strengthened his prestige among the neighbours, who made much of him and treated him on irrigation days.

Batiste was amazed at this unjust denunciation. His pallor was that of indignation. He gazed with eyes full of fury at all the familiar mocking faces, which were pressing against the rail, and at his enemy Pimentó, who was strutting about proudly, like a man accustomed to appearing before the tribunal, and to whom a small part of its unquestionable authority belonged.

'Speak,' said the eldest of the judges, putting one foot forward, for according to a century-old custom, the tribunal, instead of using the hands, signalled with the white sandal to him who should speak.

Pimentó poured forth his accusation. This man who was beside him, perhaps because he was new in the *huerta*, seemed to think that the apportionment of the water was a trifling matter, and that he could suit his own blessed will.

He, Pimentó, the *atandador,* who represented the authority of the canals in his district, had set for Batiste the hour for watering his wheat. It was two o'clock in the morning. But doubtless the señor, not wishing to arise at that hour, had let his turn go, and at five, when the water was intended for others, he had raised the flood-gate without permission from anybody (the *first* offence), and attempted to water his fields, resolving to oppose, by main force, the orders of the *atandador,* which constituted the *third* and last offence.

The thrice-guilty delinquent, turning all the colours of the rainbow, and indignant at the words of Pimentó, was not able to restrain himself.

'You lie, and lie doubly!'

The tribunal became indignant at the heat and the lack of respect with which this man was protesting.

If he did not keep silent he would be fined.

But what was a fine for the concentrated wrath of a peaceful man! He kept on protesting against the injustice of men, against the tribunal which had, as its servants, such rogues and liars as Pimentó.

The tribunal was stirred up; the seven judges became excited.

* One in charge of the *tanda,* or turn in irrigating.

Four *sous* for a fine!

Batiste, realizing his situation, suddenly grew silent, terrified at having incurred a fine, while laughter came from the crowd and howls of joy from his enemies.

He remained motionless, with bowed head, and his eyes dimmed with tears of rage, while his brutal enemy finished formulating his denunciation.

'Speak,' the tribunal said to him. But little sympathy was noted in the looks of the judges for this disturber, who had to trouble the solemnity of their deliberations with his protests.

Batiste, trembling with rage, stammered, not knowing how to begin his defence because of the very fact that it seemed to him perfectly just.

The court had been misled; Pimentó was a liar and furthermore his declared enemy. He had told him that his time for irrigation came at five, he remembered it very well, and was now affirming that it was two; just to make him incur a fine, to destroy the wheat upon which the life of his family depended. . . . Did the tribunal value the word of an honest man? Then this was the truth, although he was not able to present witnesses. It seemed impossible that the honourable syndics, all good people, should trust a rascal like Pimentó!

The white sandal of the president struck the square tile of the sidewalk, as if to avert the storm of protests and the lack of respect which he saw from afar.

'Be silent.'

And Batiste was silent, while the seven-headed monster, folding itself up again on the sofa of damask, was whispering, preparing the sentence.

'The tribunal decrees . . .' said the eldest judge, and there was absolute silence.

All the people around the roped space showed a certain anxiety in their eyes, as if they were the sentenced. They were hanging on the lips of the eldest judge.

'Batiste Borrull shall pay two pounds for penalty, and four *sous* for a fine.'

A murmur of satisfaction arose and spread, and one old woman even began to clap her hands, shouting 'Hurrah! hurrah!' amid the loud laughter of the people.

Batiste went out blindly from the tribunal, with his head lowered as though he were about to fight, and Pimentó prudently stayed behind.

If the people had not parted, opening the way for him, it is certain that he would have struck out with his powerful fists, and given the hostile rabble a beating on the spot. . . .

FRANCIS HAFFKINE SNOW
and BEATRICE M. MEKOTA

RAMÓN DEL VALLE-INCLÁN
[1869–1936]

The most polished stylist of the modernist novelists is probably Ramón María del Valle-Inclán. Endowed with a fantastic imagination and exquisite sensitivity, he creates a moody, exotic atmosphere for the many novels set in his native Galicia. His style is musical and poetic (he was a poet and dramatist, as well as a novelist) and is flavoured by numerous literary, archaic and popular expressions.

Valle-Inclán's most famous novels are the four Sonatas (1902–1905), one for each season of the year, symbolizing the four phases of man's amatory life as seen in the memoirs of a sentimental Don Juan, the Marquis de Bradomín. Some of Valle-Inclán's novels deal with the Carlist wars, and in his later writings he developed a satirical, grotesque style—the esperpento—reminiscent of Quevedo.

SONATA OF SPRING

CHAPTER XVI

That night the daughters of the Princess gathered in the moonlight on the terrace; they were like sprites in the fairytales as they surrounded a beautiful young friend who from time to time gazed on me in curiosity. In the salon the older ladies were carrying on a discreet conversation, smiling at the sound of the young voices that came in eddies with the perfume of lilies from the openings on the terrace. The garden stretched out motionless in the moonlight which wove magic over the pallid tops of the cypresses and the balconies, where a peacock was spreading his fantastic fan of feathers.

I tried at various times to approach Maria Rosario. It was useless; she divined my intentions and cautiously and noiselessly defeated them with her eyes lowered and her hands crossed on the conventual scapular she was already wearing. The sight of her timidity so aroused, flattered my pride as a Don Juan, and sometimes merely to torment her I would pass from one side to another. The poor child prepared for flight on the instant. I would pass apparently without seeing her. I had all the impetuosity of my twenty years. Again I would enter the salon and approach the old ladies who received my intentions with the timidity of damsels. I remember I was once talking with the devout old Marquise de Téscara when intuitively I turned my head toward the white form of Maria Rosario, and suddenly found my saint had gone.

A cloud of gloom came over me; I left the elderly lady and hurried to the terrace. I remained a long time leaning on the marble baluster, gazing on the garden. A nightingale was singing amid the silent perfume and its voice seemed to harmonize with the fountains. The moon shone down the path of roses I had followed the night before; the breeze was light and soft as though it carried sighs and would murmur them far among the myrtle groves and over the stirring waters of the pool. With Maria Rosario's face in my memory I incessantly asked myself : 'What does she think? What does she think of me?'

Light clouds gathered about the moon and followed her on her fantastic journey; suddenly in a heap they blinded her and left the garden in darkness. The pool lost its gleam among the still myrtles; only the tops of the cypresses held the light. As if to harmonize with the darkness a breeze arose and swept in a great gust across the scene, bringing the scent of scattered roses. I returned to the Palace; one of the windows was lighted up and a strange presentiment caused my heart to palpitate. The window was raised only a little above the terrace and the wind was waving its curtains. It seemed to me that a pale shadow crossed the room. I wished to draw closer but the sound of steps on the avenue of the cypresses held me back; it was the old major-domo walking in his dreams of art. I stood still in the depths of the garden. Gazing on her lighted window, my heart repeated : 'What does she think? What does she think of me?'

Poor Maria Rosario! I believe she was in love and yet her heart forewarned her of some strange confused adventure. I wished to lose myself in my amorous dreams but the croak of a frog, monotonously sounding under the arching cypresses, distracted and disturbed my thoughts. I remember that as a child I had read many times in my grandmother's prayerbook that the devil used to take the form of a frog to interrupt the devotions of a holy monk. It seemed natural that the same thing should occur to me. I, the calumniated and misunderstood, was just such another mystical gallant as Saint John of the Cross! In the flower of my youth I would gladly have given up all other early glories to be able to inscribe on my cards: 'The Marquis de Bradomín, Confessor of Princesses.'

CHAPTER XXIV

What a sad memory that day has become to me! Maria Rosario was filling the flower-jars of the chapel at the end of the salon; when I entered she stood undecided for a moment. With a timid, ardent light her eyes looked in fear on the door and back again at me. As she was filling the last jar, a rose broke over her hand. I smiled and said to her: 'Even the roses die in kissing your hands.'

She also smiled, seeing the petals between her fingers, and gave a slight sigh as they drifted away. We remained silent. It was nightfall, and the sun shone in its last golden glow upon the window. The cypresses lifted their pensive points in the twilight azure below. Within, one could hardly make out the arrangement of things; throughout the salon the roses scattered a perfume as light as the light words that died away with the sun. My eyes sought the eyes of Maria Rosario with the hope of imprisoning them in the shadows. She sighed heavily as though for want of air, and drawing back her locks with both hands from her forehead she took refuge by a window. I was afraid to assist her, and without following her merely said after a long silence: 'Are you not going to give me a rose?'

She turned and answered softly: 'Would you like one?'

I hesitated a moment and then drew nearer. I managed to appear calm, but I could see her hands trembling over the jars as she selected the flower. With a sorrowful smile she said: 'I shall give you the most beautiful one.'

She continued to search among the roses. I sighed romantically: 'The loveliest would be your lips.'

She drew back and looked at me in pain: 'You are not kind. Why do you say such things to me?'

'To see your anger.'

'And that delights you? Sometimes I think you are the devil.'

'The devil does not know what love is.'

Silence fell again. I could hardly make out her face in the dying light, and I only knew from her soft sobs that she wept. I came closer to console her: 'Oh! forgive my faults.'

My voice was tender and passionate. I myself as I heard it felt its strange seductive power. The supreme moment had arrived; my heart was seized with anxiety over the great adventure that faced me. Maria Rosario closed her eyes in dread, as though she were on the brink of an abyss. Her colourless lips expressed a painful voluptuousness. I seized her hands, which were lying inert. She abandoned them to me, sobbing in her grief : 'Why do you take pleasure in making me suffer? You know that everything is impossible!'

'Impossible! I know I shall never obtain your love! I know I do not deserve it! Only I want you to pardon me and to know that you will pray for me when I am far away.'

'Silence! Silence!'

'I regard you as so high, so far above me, so ideal, that I want your prayers as I should want those of a saint.'

'Silence! Silence!'

'My heart suffers, without a single hope. Perhaps I may learn to forget you, but your love will always be a purifying fire.'

'Silence! Silence!'

There were tears in my eyes and I knew that with tears the hands may show some boldness. Poor Maria Rosario seemed pale as death and I thought she was about to faint in my arms. This maiden was really a saint; seeing the extremity of my grief she did not wish to show me any more cruelty. She closed her eyes and murmured in agony : 'Leave me! Leave me!'

I whispered to her : 'Why do you abhor me so?'

'Because you are the devil!'

She gazed at me in terror, and as if the sound of my voice were awakening her she broke from my arms and fled toward the window, which was golden with the sunset. She leaned her forehead against the glass and sobbed. From the garden came the song of the nightingale, stirring in the twilight some innocent memory of holiness.

MAY HEYWOOD BROUN
and THOMAS WALSH

PÍO BAROJA
[1872–1956]

The Basque Pío Baroja was a doctor and baker before he turned to writing as his exclusive occupation. He is one of the most original and unorthodox of modern authors. His numerous novels cover a wide variety of themes, but he has a penchant, in particular, for writing about the lower classes of society, and reflects in his novels a sceptical and pessimistic view of our civilization. His style is careless and abrupt, perhaps deliberately so, and his plots are, by design, often incomplete.

A number of Baroja's novels deal with the Carlist wars. The swift-moving Zalacaín el aventurero (1909) *belongs in this category, as well as some of the twenty-two novels of the series* Memorias de un hombre de acción. *Among the works in which Baroja best reveals his iconoclastic ideas are* Camino de perfección (1902), Paradox Rey (1906) *and* El árbol de la ciencia (1911). *Baroja has termed the latter 'probably my most finished and complete book'.*

THE TREE OF KNOWLEDGE

UNIVERSAL CRUELTY

Andrés felt a great desire to comment philosophically on the lives of these lodgers in Lulu's house; but his friends were not interested in these comments or philosophies, and one morning, a holiday, he resolved to pay a visit to his Uncle Iturrioz.

When he first knew him—he had not met him till he was about fifteen—Iturrioz seemed to him a dry and selfish man who looked on everything with indifference; later, without exactly knowing how far his dryness and egoism went, he found he was one of the few persons with whom one could discuss transcendental subjects.

Iturrioz lived on the fifth floor of a house in the Argüelles quarter, a house with a fine flat roof.

He was attended by a servant who had been a soldier when Iturrioz was an army doctor.

Between them they had set the house-top in order, painted the tiles with pitch to make them waterproof, and set up steps for the wooden boxes and tubs full of earth in which they kept their plants.

The morning on which Andrés paid him a visit, Iturrioz was having his bath, and the servant took Andrés up to the roof.

Between two tall houses one had a view of the Guadarrama

Mountains; to the west the roof of the Montaña barracks concealed the hills of the Casa del Campo; and on one side of the barracks appeared the Torre de Móstoles and the highroad to Extremadura with some windmills near it. Farther to the south shone in the April sun the green patches of the cemeteries of San Justo and San Isidro, the two towers of Getafe, and the hermitage of the Cerrillo de los Angeles.

After a little Iturrioz came out on to the house-top.

'Well, is anything the matter?' he asked, when he saw his nephew.

'Nothing; I came to have a talk with you.'

'Very good. Sit down; I am going to water my flower-pots.'

Iturrioz opened a tap at a corner of the terrace and filled a tub with water, and then with a piece of pot began to throw water on to the plants.

Andrés spoke of Lulu's neighbours and of the scenes at the hospital as strange things requiring a commentary, of Manolo the Buffoon, Old Skinflint, Don Cleto, and Doña Virginia.

'What inference can one draw from all these lives?' he asked.

'For me the inference is easy,' answered Iturrioz, waterpot in hand : 'that life is a constant struggle, a cruel carnage in which we devour one another. Plants, microbes, animals.'

'Yes,' answered Andrés, 'the same idea occurred to me, but I do not think it will hold water. In the first place the conception of life as a struggle among animals, plants and even minerals is an anthropomorphic idea; and then what kind of a struggle for life is that of Don Cleto, who refuses to fight, or of Brother Juan, who gives his money to the poor?'

'I will answer the two questions separately,' said Iturrioz, setting down his watering-pot, for such questions were his delight. 'You say the idea of a struggle is an anthropomorphic idea. Well, of course, we give to all the various conflicts the name of a struggle because it is the human idea best fitted to express the relations which with us produce a victor and a vanquished. If that were not, essentially, what we meant we would not speak of a struggle. The hyena picking clean the bones of a carcass, the spider sucking the life out of a fly, is acting precisely in the same way as the kindly tree which takes from the earth the moisture and salts necessary to its life. An indifferent spectator like myself watches the hyena, the spider, and the tree and understands them; a man with a sense of justice shoots the hyena, crushes the spider under his foot, and sits down under the shade of the tree, imagining that he has done a good deed.'

'Then you consider there is no struggle and no justice?'

'In an absolute sense there is none; in a relative sense there is. Every living thing has first to gain possession of space, of a place to exist, and then of the means to grow and multiply; this process carried on by the energy of the living against the obstacles which surround it is what we call a struggle. As to justice I think that, essentially, it is what happens to suit us. Suppose, for instance, that the hyena, instead of being killed, kills the man, or that the tree falls upon him and kills him, or that the spider gives him a poisonous bite; nothing in all that seems to us just, because it does not suit us. Yet, although essentially it is no more than a question of utilitarian interest, who can doubt that the idea of justice and equity is a tendency which exists in us? But how are we to put it into practice?'

'That's what I ask myself, how put it into practice?'

'Are we to grow indignant because a spider kills a fly?' went on Iturrioz. 'What are we to do—kill the spider? If we kill it, that will not prevent spiders from devouring flies. Are we to cure mankind of these ferocious instincts to which you object? Are we to erase the Latin writer's verdict that man is a wolf to man : *homo homini lupus*? Very well; in four or five thousand years we shall be able to do so. Man has converted a carnivorous animal like the jackal into an omnivorous animal like the dog; but it requires centuries to effect this. You may have read that Spallanzini taught a dove to eat meat, and an eagle to eat and digest bread. That is the case of these great religious and lay apostles : they are eagles eating bread instead of raw meat; they are wolves turned vegetarians. Brother Juan for instance.'

'I don't think he's an eagle, nor a wolf.'

'He may be an owl or a martin, a perverted one.'

'Possibly,' answered Andrés, 'but I think we have wandered from the point; I don't see what inference is to be drawn.'

'The inference that I wished to draw is this : that a man of clear mind confronted with life has but two practical courses open, either to abstain from action and contemplate everything with indifference, or to limit his action to a small area; in other words one may be quixotic in an anomalous case but to be so as a general rule is absurd.'

'Then you think that a man of action must limit his love of justice within narrow bounds?'

'Of course he must; you may include in your view your house, your town, your region, society, the world, every dead and living thing; but if you attempt to act, and to act in a spirit of justice, you must restrict yourself more and more, even perhaps within your own conscience.'

'That is the beauty of philosophy,' said Andrés bitterly. 'It convinces one that it is best to do nothing.'

Iturrioz walked up and down the house-top and then said : 'That is the only objection you can bring against me, and it's not my fault.'

'I know it.'

'To entertain an idea of universal justice is fatal,' continued Iturrioz. 'Adapting Fritz Müller's principle that the embryology of an animal reproduces its genealogy, or, as Haeckel says, that ontogenesis is but a recapitulation of phylogenesis, one may say that human psychology is but a synthesis of animal psychology. Thus we find in man all the forms of struggle and development : that of the microbe, the insect, the wild beast. How many incarnations cannot zoology show of that usurer you have described to me, Old Skinflint ! We see the acinetids sucking the protoplasm from other infusoria; and the various animals that fatten on decaying matter. And the mutual antipathy of those people : is it not seen perfectly in the obstinate antagonism of a certain bacillus for certain bacteria ?'

'Possibly,' murmured Andrés.

'And among the insects how many Old Skinflints and Victorios ! How many Manolos ! There is the ichneumon which lays its eggs in a worm and gives it an injection of a substance which acts like chloroform; there is the sphex which takes small spiders, holds them down, winds thread round them and places them alive in the cells of its larvae for their food; there are the wasps which do the same thing with other insects which they paralyse with their sting; there is the estafilino which treacherously hurls itself upon another individual of its own species, holds it down, wounds it and sucks out its life; there is the insect which penetrates surreptitiously into the honeycomb of the bees, enters the queen's cell, eats its fill of honey, and then devours the queen's larva; there is——'

'Yes, yes, you need say no more : life is a horrible carnage.'

'It is characteristic of Nature that when it intends to ruin you, it does so thoroughly. Justice is a human illusion : essentially everything is destruction and creation. Hunting, war, digestion, breathing are instances of simultaneous creation and destruction.'

'But what must one do ?' murmured Andrés. 'Become indifferent ? Digest, fight, and hunt with the serenity of a savage ?'

'You believe in the serenity of the savage ? What an illusion !

That is another of our inventions. The savage has never been serene.'

'Is there no possible plan to live with a certain decency?' asked Andrés.

'Only if one invents one for one's own use. And, today, I believe that whatever is spontaneous and natural is bad, that only the artificial, man's creation, is good. If I could I would live in a London club; I would never go into the country except to a park; the water I drank would be filtered, the air sterilized——'

But Andrés was no longer listening to Iturrioz, who had begun to follow the bent of his fancy. He got up and leant upon the balustrade running around the roof.

Some doves were flying above the neighbouring roofs; on a large gutter cats were running and playing.

In front, separated by a high wall, were two gardens; one belonged to a girls' college, the other to a monastery.

The convent garden was surrounded by shady trees; that of the college had nothing but plots of grass and flowers; and it was a strange thing, not without a certain impression of allegory, to see at one and the same time the girls running and shouting and the friars walking silently round their court, in rows of five or six.

'Both the one and the other are life,' said Iturrioz philosophically, and began to water his plants.

Andrés went out into the street.

What should he do? How order his life? he asked himself searchingly. And with this problem in his mind the people he met, the things he saw, the sun itself seemed to lack reality.

AUBREY F. G. BELL

MIGUEL DE UNAMUNO
[1864–1936]

In the opinion of many scholars Miguel de Unamuno was the outstanding Spaniard of the twentieth century. Professor, philosopher, essayist, poet and novelist, he exerted an important influence upon Spanish intellectuals.

His most famous work, Del sentimiento trágico de la vida (*1913*), *develops one of the author's main themes, the struggle between faith and reason. Since his novels do not conform to conventional novelistic requirements, Unamuno invented the term 'nivolas'. One of his most popular 'nivolas' is* Niebla (*1914*), *from which our excerpt comes. It is of unusual interest for it presents a lively argument between the author and one of his characters.*

MIST

AUGUSTO HAS AN INTERVIEW WITH THE AUTHOR

The storm in the soul of Augusto ended in a terrible calm : he had resolved to kill himself. He wanted to put an end to that self which had been the cause of all his misery. But before carrying out his plan it occurred to him, like a drowning sailor who grasps at a straw, to come and talk it over with me, the author of this whole story. Augusto had read an essay of mine in which I made a passing reference to suicide and this, together with some other things of mine that he had read, had evidently made such an impression upon him that he did not wish to leave this world without having met me and talked with me for a while. Accordingly, he came here to Salamanca, where I have been living for twenty years past, to pay me a visit.

When his call was announced I smiled enigmatically, and I had him come into my study. He entered like a ghost. He looked at a portrait of me in oil which presides over the books of my library, and then at a sign from me he took a seat opposite me.

He began by speaking of my literary works, in particular of those that were more or less philosophical, showing that he knew them very well; which, of course, did not fail to please me. Then he began to tell me of his life and of his misfortunes. I interrupted him by telling him to spare himself the trouble; I was as familiar with the vicissitudes of his life as he himself; and this I demonstrated to him by citing some of the most intimate details, and in particular some things that he thought to be utterly hidden. He looked at me with genuine terror in his eyes, as one looks at some incredible being. I seemed to see a change in the colour and in the lines of his face, and I saw that he even trembled. I had him fascinated.

'It hardly seems true,' he kept repeating, 'it hardly seems true. I shouldn't believe it if I had not seen it. I don't know whether I am awake or dreaming——'

'Neither awake nor dreaming,' I replied.

'I can't explain it—I can't explain it,' he went on. 'But since you seem to know as much about me as I know myself, perhaps you guess my purpose in coming.'

'Yes,' I said. 'You'—and I gave to this 'you' the emphasis of authority—'you, oppressed by the weight of your misfortunes, have conceived the diabolical idea of killing yourself; and before doing it, impelled by something you have read in one of my last essays, you have come to consult me about it.'

The poor man shook like a drop of mercury and looked at me with the stare of one possessed. He tried to rise, perhaps with the idea of flight, but he could not. He could not summon the strength.

'No, don't move,' I commanded him.

'Do you mean—do you mean——' he stammered.

'I mean that you cannot commit suicide even if you wish to do so.'

'What!' he cried, finding himself so flatly opposed and contradicted.

'Yes, if a man is going to kill himself what is the first thing that is necessary?' I asked him.

'That he should have the courage to do it,' he replied.

'No,' I said, 'that he should be alive.'

'Of course!'

'And you are not alive.'

'Not alive! What do you mean? Do you mean that I have died?' And without clearly knowing what he was doing he began to pass his hands over his body.

'No, my man, no!' I replied. 'I told you before that you were neither waking nor sleeping; now I tell you that you are neither alive nor dead.'

'Tell me all of it at once; God, tell me all,' he begged me in terror. 'With what I am seeing and hearing this afternoon I am afraid of going mad.'

'Very well, then. The truth is, my dear Augusto,' I spoke to him the softest of tones, 'you can't kill yourself because you are not alive; and you are not alive—or dead either—because you do not exist.'

'I don't exist! What do you mean by that?'

'No, you do not exist except as a fictitious entity, a character of fiction. My poor Augusto, you are only a product of my imagination and of the imagination of those of my readers who read this story which I have written of your fictitious adventures and misfortunes. You are nothing more than a personage in a novel, or a *nivola*, or whatever you choose to call it. Now, then, you know your secret.'

Upon hearing this the poor man continued to look at me for a while with one of those perforating looks that seem to pierce your own gaze and go beyond; presently he glanced for a moment at the portrait in oil which presides over my books, then his colour returned and his breathing became easier, and gradually recovering, he was again master of himself. He rested his elbows on the arm of the sofa opposite me, against which he was leaning; and then with his face in the palms of his hands he looked at me with a smile and he said slowly :

'Listen to me, Don Miguel—it can't be that you are mistaken, and that what is happening is precisely the contrary of what you think and of what you have told me?'

'And what do you mean by the contrary?' I asked, rather alarmed to see him regaining his self-possession.

'May it not be, my dear Don Miguel,' he continued, 'that it is you and not I who are the fictitious entity, the one that does not really exist, who is neither living nor dead? May it not be that you are nothing more than a pretext for bringing my history into the world?'

'Really this is too much!' I cried, now becoming irritated.

'Please don't get so excited, Señor de Unamuno,' he replied. 'Keep calm. You have expressed doubts about my existence——'

'Doubts? No!' I interrupted. 'Absolute certainty that you do not exist outside of the novel that I have created.'

'Very well; then please don't be disturbed if I in turn doubt your existence rather than my own. Let us come to the point. Are you not the person who has said, not once but several times, that Don Quixote and Sancho are not only real persons but more real than Cervantes himself?'

'I can't deny it, but the sense in which I said it was——'

'Very well, never mind in what sense. Let us come to another point. When a man who is lying asleep in his bed dreams of something, which is it that more truly exists, he as the consciousness that dreams or the dreams themselves?'

'And what if the dreamer dreams that he himself exists?'—I turned the question on him.

'In that case, friend Don Miguel, my own question would be, in what fashion does he exist? As the dreamer who dreams of himself or as something dreamed by himself? And note this, moreover: in entering this discussion with me you are already recognizing me as an existence independent of yourself.'

'Not at all. Not at all,' I said quickly. 'In entering this discussion I am merely satisfying a private need of my own. Apart from discussion and contradiction I am never alive; and when there is no one outside of me to question and contradict me I invent some one to do it within me. My monologues are dialogues.'

'And perhaps the dialogues that you fabricate are nothing more than monologues.'

'It may be. But in any case I tell you, and I wish to repeat it, that you do not exist outside of me——'

'And I will again suggest this to you, namely, that you do not exist outside of me and of the other characters that you think you have invented. I am certain that Don Avito Carrascal would be of my opinion and the great Don Fulgencio——'

'You needn't mention them——'

'Very well, then, I won't; but you shouldn't make fun of them. And now let us see; what do you really think about my suicide?'

'I think, then, that since you do not exist except in my imagination—as I tell you again—and since you neither ought nor are you able to do anything but just what I please, and since it does not really suit me that you should kill yourself—well, you are not going to kill yourself. And that settles it.'

'Your saying that "it does not really suit me" is very Spanish, Señor de Unamuno, but it is far from edifying. Moreover, even granting your strange theory that I do not really exist and that you do, that I am nothing but a character of fiction, the product of your imagination as a novelist—or as a "nivolist"—even so there is no reason why I should submit to "what really suits you", that is, to your caprice. For even those whom we call characters of fiction have their own inwrought logic——'

'Yes, I know that song.'

'But, really, it is a fact that neither a novelist nor a playwright is at all able to do anything that happens to occur to him, to a character that he creates. That a fictitious character in a novel should do that which no reader would ever expect him to do, is forbidden by all of the established principles of art——'

'Doubtless a character in a novel——'

'Well, then?'

'But a character in a *nivola*—a "nivolistic" character——'

'Let us drop these buffooneries. They are offensive, and they wound me where I am most sensitive. Whether of myself, as I think, or because you have given it to me, as you suppose, I have my own character, my own manner of being, my own inwrought logic, and this logic demands that I kill myself——'

'You may think so, but you are wrong.'

'Let us see. Why am I wrong? And where am I wrong? Show me where my mistake lies. Since the most difficult knowledge that there is, is knowing yourself, I may easily be mistaken and it may be that suicide is not the logical solution of my problem. But prove it to me. For though this self-knowledge be difficult, Don Miguel, there is another kind of knowledge that seems no less difficult——'

'And that is?——' I asked.

He looked at me with a smile that was shrewd and enigmatic and then he said slowly :

'Well, that which is more difficult than self-knowledge is this : that a novelist or a playwright should know the characters that he creates or thinks he creates.'

These sallies of Augusto were beginning to make me uneasy and I was losing my patience.

'And I insist,' he added, 'that even granting you have given me my being—a fictitious being, if you please—even so, and because it is so, you cannot prevent me from killing myself just because, as you say, it does not really suit you.'

'Very well, that will do—enough!' I cried, bringing my fist down on the sofa. 'Hold your tongue! I don't wish to hear any more impertinence! And from a creature of mine, too! And since I have had enough of you and I don't know, moreover, what more to do with you, I have now decided, not that you may not now kill yourself, but that I shall kill you. You are to die, then, but soon! Very soon!'

Augusto was horror-struck. 'What!' he cried. 'Do you mean that you are going to let me die, make me die—you are going to kill me?'

'Yes, I am going to cause you to die.'

'Oh, never! never! never!' he shrieked.

'Ah!' I said, looking at him with mingled pity and rage. 'And so you were ready to kill yourself, but you don't want me to kill you? And you were about to take your own life, but you object to my taking it?'

'Yes, it is not the same thing——'

'To be sure, it is not. I have heard of cases of that kind. I heard of a man who went out one night armed with a revolver, intending to take his own life, when some thieves undertook to rob him. They attacked him, he defended himself, killed one of them and the others fled. And then, seeing that he had bought his life at the cost of another's, he renounced his intention.'

'One can understand that,' observed Augusto. 'It was a matter of taking the life of somebody, of killing a man; and after he had killed another, what was the use of killing himself? Most suicides are frustrated homicides; men kill themselves because they have not the courage to kill others——'

'Ah! now I understand you, Augusto, I understand. You mean that if you had had the courage to kill Eugenia* or Mauricio, or both, you would not be thinking of killing yourself, isn't that so?'

'Let me tell you, it is not precisely of them that I am thinking—no!'

'Of whom, then?'

'Of you'—and he looked me straight in the eye.

'What!' I cried, rising to my feet. 'What! Have you conceived the idea of killing me? You? And of killing me?'

'Sit down and keep cool. Do you think, Don Miguel, that it would the first case in which a fictitious entity, as you call me, had killed him whom he believed to have given him his being—his fictitious being, of course?'

'This is really too much,' I said, walking up and down my study. 'This passes all limits. This couldn't happen except——'

'Except in *nivolas*,' Augusto completed with a drawl.

'Very well, enough! enough! enough! This is more than I can stand. You came here to consult me—me, you understand—and you? You begin by disputing my own existence, forgetting that I have the right to do with you anything that suits me—yes, just what I say, anything that may happen to occur to——'

'Don't be so Spanish, Don Miguel——'

'And now this too, you idiot! Well, yes, I am indeed a Spaniard, Spanish by birth, by education, by profession and occupation; Spanish above everything and before everything. Spanishism is my religion, the heaven in which I wish to believe is a celestial and eternal Spain, and my God is a Spanish God, the God of our Lord Don Quixote, a God who thinks in Spanish and who said in Spanish, Let there be light! *Sea luz!*—His word was a Spanish word——'

* Augusto's fiancée, who ran off with Mauricio just before the wedding day.

'Well, and what of it?' he interrupted, recalling me to reality.

'And now you have conceived the idea of killing me. Of killing me—*me?* And you? Am I to die at the hands of one of my creatures? I'll stand no more of it. And so to punish you for your insolence, and to put an end to these disintegrating, extravagant, and anarchistic ideas with which you have come to me, I hereby render judgment and pass the sentence that you are to die. As soon as you reach home you shall die. You shall die, I tell you, you shall die.'

'But—for God's sake!' cried Augusto, now in a tone of supplication, pale and trembling with fear.

'There is no God that can help you. You shall die.'

'Yes, but I want to live, Don Miguel, I want to live—I want to live——'

'Weren't you just now thinking of killing yourself?'

'Oh! if that is why, Don Miguel, then I swear to you that I will not kill myself, I will not take away this life which God, or yourself, has given me; I swear it to you—now that you wish to kill me I myself want to live—to live—to live——'

'What a life!' I exclaimed.

'Yes, whatever it may be. I want to live even though I am again to be mocked at, even though another Eugenia and another Mauricio tear my heart out. I wish to live—live—live——'

'Now it cannot be—it cannot be——'

'I want to live—live—I want to be myself, myself, myself.'

'But what if that self is only what I wish to be——?'

'I wish to be myself—to be myself! I wish to live!' and his voice was choked with sobs.

'It cannot be—cannot be——'

'Listen, Don Miguel, for the sake of your children, of your wife, of whatever is dearest to you! Remember that you will then cease to be yourself—that *you* will die——'

He fell on his knees at my feet, begging and imploring me : 'Don Miguel, for God's sake! I want to live. I want to be myself.'

'It cannot be, my poor Augusto,' I said, taking him by the hand and lifting him up. 'It cannot be. I have now decreed it—it is written—and irrevocably; you can live no longer. I no longer know what to do with you. God, when he does not know what to do with us, kills us. And I do not forget that there passed through your mind the idea of killing me——'

'But, Don Miguel, if I——'

'It makes no difference. I know where I stand. And really I

am afraid that if I do not kill you soon, you will end by killing me.'

'But are we not agreed that——?'

'It cannot be, Augusto, it cannot be. Your hour has come. It is now written, and I cannot now recall it. And for all that your life can now be worth to you——'

'But——good God!'

'There is neither "but" nor "God" that can avail you. Go!'

'And so you won't?' he said. 'You refuse? You are unwilling to let me be myself, come out of the mist and live, live, live; to see myself, hear myself, touch myself, feel myself, feel my own pain, be myself—you are unwilling, then? And so I am to die as a fictitious character? Very well, then, my lord creator Don Miguel, you too are to die, you too! And you will return to that nothing from which you came! God will cease to dream you! You are to die, yes, you are to die, even though you do not wish to; and die shall all of those who read my story, all of them, all, all, without a single exception. Fictitious entities like myself—just like myself! All of them are to die; all, all. And it is I who tell you this—I, Augusto Pérez, a fictitious entity, a "nivolistic" entity, and your readers are "nivolistic" entities, just like me, just the same as Augusto Pérez, your victim——'

'Victim!' I cried.

'Victim, yes! To create me only to let me die! Well, you too are to die! He who creates creates himself, and he who creates himself dies. You will die, Don Miguel, you will die, and all those who think me, they are to die too! To death, then!'

This supreme effort of the passion for life—of the thirst for immortality—left poor Augusto utterly weak.

I pushed him towards the door. He walked out with his eyes fixed upon the ground, passing his hands wonderingly over himself as if he were uncertain of his own existence. I wiped away a furtive tear.

WARNER FITE

AZORÍN
[b. 1874]

José Martínez Ruiz, who wrote under the pseudonym Azorín, is one of the foremost essayists and prose stylists of the twentieth century. Although Azorín has tried his hand at the novel and drama, it is as a sensitive essayist and impressionistic critic that he is most important. As a leader of the Generation of '98 he blames some of Spain's shortcomings on the past. Yet no one better than Azorín can evoke wistful and whimsical reminiscences of Spain's history, geography and literature. His style is highly personal, but clear and precise. Nubes ('Clouds') comes from the collection Castilla (1912).

CLOUDS

Calisto and Melibea were married, as the reader will know (if he has read *La Celestina*) a few days after the discovery of their stolen interviews in the garden. Calisto had become enamoured of the maiden, who was destined to be his wife, on a certain day when he entered her garden in pursuit of a falcon. Eighteen years ago it was. Twenty-three had been Calisto then. The two are living now as man and wife in Melibea's ancestral mansion; a daughter has been born to them, named like her grandmother, Alisa. From the broad verandah in the rear of the dwelling is to be seen the whole of the garden, wherein Melibea and Calisto had held their sweet colloquies of love. The house is large and stately; a carved staircase of stone ascends from the far end of the vestibule. Above are spacious retiring-rooms, silent and secluded bed-chambers, dimly-lighted galleries, and in the rear a small doorway with squares of glass in its upper part, giving a glimpse, as in *Las Meninas* of Velasquez, of an inner court bathed in light. A carpet of green branches and yellow fir-cones, worked on a crimson ground, is stretched over the floor of the chief drawing-room, where, on silken cushions, noble dames may sit at ease. Here and there are small divans covered with red leather, or folding-chairs with Moorish inlaid-work. A sculptured cabinet with painted and soft-lined drawers contains papers and jewels. In the centre of the apartment, on a walnut table with carved legs and framework, and with bars of wrought-iron, lies a delicately-fashioned box of chessmen with reliefs of ivory, mother-of-pearl, and silver; while in the crystal border of a broad mirror are reflected from a background of gold the elongated faces of a painting on wood, hanging on the wall that fronts the door of entrance.

All is peace and silence in the house. Melibea moves gently from room to room, sees to all things, thinks of all things. The presses are full of smooth and sweet-smelling linen, redolent of juicy quinces. In the pantry a sunbeam lights up a row of capacious and glazed Talaveran bowls. In the kitchen the brazen pots and pans hanging upon the dresser are as mirrors, and canakins and pitchers wrought by the hands of a craftsman of the potteries near by, display their round, smooth, and shining bellies. Over all things watches Melibea with untiring diligence; nothing escapes those soft green eyes of hers.

Ever and again, breaking upon the silence of the house is heard the sweet and languorous sound of a harpsichord; it is Alisa, who is making music. Ere long upon the garden-paths is seen in gentle movement a maiden's tall and slender figure; it is Alisa walking amid the trees.

The garden is sweet to look upon and full of verdure. Oleanders and jasmine-plants grow side by side. At the foot of the never-changing cypresses rose-bushes lay their offering, fleeting as life itself, of their yellow, white, and crimson flowers. Three colours meet the eye where'er it turns : the intense blue of the sky, the white coating of the walls, and the green of the trees and shrubs. In the silence is heard, like diamond upon crystal, the shrill note of the swallows in their rapid flight through the deep indigo of the firmament. From the marble basin of a fountain trickles the water peacefully into the trough below. In the air rises the penetrating fragrance of the jasmines, roses and magnolias. 'Climb over my garden wall,' said Melibea in soft tones to Calisto, eighteen years ago.

Calisto is basking in the sun near one of the balconies, his elbow is on the arm of his chair, and his chin is in his hand. In his house are beautiful pictures; if he has a mind for music, his daughter, Alisa, delights his ear with sweet melodies, or if it is poetry that his soul desires, from his book-shelves he can cull the choicest poets of Spain and Italy. His fellow citizens love him well; the careful hands of Melibea tend him; he sees his race continued, though not by a son, yet for the present by a lovely girl of bright intelligence and gentle heart. Nevertheless, Calisto sits lost in thought, with his head resting in his hand. Juan Ruiz, Archpriest of Hita, wrote in his book :

. . . 'Et crei la fabrilla
Que dis : Por lo pasado no estés mano en mejilla.'

'And I believed the saying which says : Do not for that which is past sit with your cheek in hand.'

Calisto has indeed small need to mourn the past; past and present are for him alike rich in blessings. Nothing exists to trouble or to sadden him; and yet Calisto, chin in hand, gazes thoughtfully at the distant clouds, drifting over the blue sky.

Clouds inspire us with a feeling of instability, and of eternity. Clouds are, like the sea, ever changing yet ever the same. While watching their flight we feel that our life and all things earthly are hastening into nothingness, while they, fugitive though they be, are yet eternal. The clouds, which we now see above us, were seen five hundred, one thousand, three thousand years ago by other men with the passions and the carking cares that we find in ourselves. When in a moment of happiness we would fain make time our captive, we find weeks, months, and years already slipping away from us. But the clouds, the same yet not the same, each moment and each day are chasing one another over the heavens. Clouds there are, round, and full and dazzling white of colour, that in spring mornings float over the translucent sky. Others, like delicate gauze, spread themselves horizontally over a milky background; others are grey and veil grey distances; others, again, are crimson and gold in those sunsets of the great plains, sunsets interminable, full of deep melancholy. Others there are, like little fleeces, countless in number, and alike in form, revealing through some break in their midst a fragment of blue sky. Some go their way slowly and solemnly, some course along swiftly. Some again, ashy in colour, darken the whole face of the sky, casting upon the earth beneath a certain grey, opaque, and subdued light that lends a charm of its own to the autumnal landscape.

Hundreds of years after the day when Calisto is sitting chin in hand, a great poet, Campoamor, will dedicate to the clouds a canto in one of his poems named *Columbus*. 'Clouds', says the poet, 'mirror our own existence. What is existence but the sporting of clouds? . . . Life consists in seeing that which passes.' Yes, to live is to see things passing, passing as above the clouds up yonder. Rather might we say; 'To live is to see things returning, for ever returning, griefs, joys, and hopes, even as these clouds, distinct yet ever one, fugitive yet unchangeable.' Clouds are the image of Time. Can there be sensation more tragic than that of the fleetingness of Time, as when one sees in the present the past, and in the past the future?

In the garden, full of silence, is heard the shrill note of the swallows in their rapid flight. The water of the fountain peacefully trickles from the marble basin; at the foot of the cypresses short-lived roses, white, yellow, and crimson, open their petals to the light. The heavy fragrance of jasmine and magnolia perfumes the air. The green of the foliage contrasts with the white walls, and above both green and white is seen the indigo blue of the sky. Alisa is seated in the garden book in hand; her little feet peep from beneath her skirt of finest cloth. They are shod in black velvet slippers, trimmed with lace-edging and with buckles of burnished silver. Alisa's eyes are green, like those of her mother, her face is long rather than round. Who could find words for the softness and delicacy of her hands? Who could praise as it deserves the sweetness of her speech?

In the garden all is peace and silence. Above, in the sunshine, leaning against a balustrade, Calisto watches his daughter with a fond delight. Suddenly he sees a falcon, circling in rapid and frenzied movement amidst the trees. In hot pursuit of him appears an excited youth. Brought face to face with Alisa, he halts, lost in contemplation of her, smiles and begins to speak.

Calisto sees him from the verandah, and guesses his words. Far above him a few round, white clouds pass slowly over the blue sky.

IDA FARNELL

JOSÉ ORTEGA Y GASSET
[1883–1955]

Professor of metaphysics for many years at the University of Madrid, José Ortega y Gasset was Spain's leading contemporary philosopher. With brilliant, forceful style, he attacked and analysed Spain's many problems—usually from a pessimistic point of view. His most famous essays are included in España invertebrada *(1922) and* La rebelión de las masas *(1930).*

INVERTEBRATE SPAIN
THE INCREASING MENACE OF SOCIETY

Ever since the middle of the last century, life in Europe has become more and more public, and in these last few years that tendency has increased at a rate that is positively dizzy. A life which is private, hidden, solitary, closed to public view, becomes more difficult every day.

The situation has certain characteristics which are obvious to the senses. Noise in the street, for instance—the street has become stentorian. One of the privileges which man used to take for granted was silence. Now his right to a certain amount of silence is recognized no more. The street penetrates into our own private corners and fills them with public clamour. He who wishes to meditate must get used to doing it submerged in the midst of a public racket, a diver in an ocean of collective noise. Man is never left alone by himself. Whether he likes it or not, he must be with others. The public square and the avenue force their anonymous clamour in through the very walls of his home.

Confronted with unlimited public invasion, everything that used to signify reverence has become less and less important. Especially the theory that a man's house is his castle. Family life, that society in miniature erected outside of and opposed to society in the large, is reduced to a minimum. The more advanced a country is, the less important the family.

The immediate cause of its disappearance is curious. It has always been recognized that the heart of the family was the hearth. But then, as usual, man began surrounding it with an aura of romance. The hearth was altar as well as cooking place; the haven of the family, of fatherhood, of the lares. But the fact is that just as soon as it began to be difficult to get domestic servants, the lares, fatherhood, and the family altar commenced to disappear. One began to realize that in the last analysis the cornerstone of the family was not the household gods, nor the paterfamilias, but the hired girl. It became possible to reduce the fact to a formula almost as exact as a functional law—in every country, family life today is important in direct ratio to the available amount of domestic service. In the United States, where it is harder to keep a good maid than to keep a giraffe, family life has contracted to a minimum. And so has the size of the house. Why have a large house if you cannot stay in it? Without servants, some simplification of domestic existence is essential, and when you simplify it you make it uncomfortable. The complicated, semi-religious rite of seasoning food—the rite of the kitchen-altar—was reduced to a minimum. Man was thrust out of domestic seclusion into public life. The real god Lar was the soup kettle.

The modern family tends to fly apart. There is a vast difference between the hours that used to be passed at home and those that are passed there now. In those long, slow hours of another day, man used to assist in the crystallization of a part of himself which was private, non-public and which easily became anti-public.

The physical change in the thickness of walls since the Middle Ages could be shown by a diagram. In the 14th century each house was a fortress. Today, each many-storied house is a bee-hive. It is a city in itself, and its walls are thin partitions which barely shut us off from the street. Even as late as the 18th century, houses were still spacious and deep. Man spent the major portion of his day in them, in secret and well-defended solitude. That solitude, working on the soul hour after hour, forged it, like a transcendent blacksmith, into a compact and forceful character. Under its treatment, man consolidated his individual destiny and sallied forth with impunity, never yielding to contamination from the public. It is only in isolation that we gain, almost automatic-ally, a certain discrimination in ideas, desires, longings, that we learn which are ours, and which are anonymous, floating in the air, falling on us like dust in the street.

No one knows what the end of this process will be. Until very recently the whole of European development was focused on the education and encouragement of the individual. With increasing intensity it insisted that life should take individual form. That is to say, that by the very act of living each one should feel himself unique. Unique in joy, as in duty and in sorrow. And is this not the truth, the pure transcendental truth about human life? Whether humble or magnificent, to live is to be alone—to have this consciousness of the singleness, the exclusiveness of man's own individual destiny, a destiny which he alone possesses. Life is not lived in company. Each must live his own life by himself, taste it with his own lips, whether the cup be full of bitter or of sweet. Some of us find ourselves with partners, but this does not mean that we allow another to participate in the secret life which is ours and only ours.

Yet, today, there is no doubt that the direction of social evolution has changed. For the last two generations, life in Europe has tended to be less and less individual. Everything forces man to lose that sense of being unique and to make himself less com-pact. Just as the house has been opened up, made more porous and better ventilated, so people and ideas, tastes, opinions blow back and forth across us until each one of us begins to think that perhaps he is someone else.

Is this just a phase, a passing change, a step backwards in order to make a still higher leap toward greater intensifying of the individual? No one knows; but it is a fact that right now a great number of Europeans are feeling a sense of luxurious fruition in ceasing to be individuals and dissolving themselves into the mass.

There is a delicious epidemic of feeling oneself part of the mass, of ceasing to have any individual destiny. Man is becoming part of society.

Throughout the long course of human history there is no novelty in this. It has been the thing that has happened with the greatest frequency. The unusual was the opposite—the desire to be individual, non-transferable, unique. What is happening now, clarifies the situation of man in the good old days of Greece and Rome. Liberty to live by and for oneself was not conceded then. The State had a right to the whole of one's existence. When Cicero wanted to retire to his Tuscan villa and devote himself to the reading of Greek books, he had to justify himself publicly, and to obtain pardon for momentarily seceding from the collective body. The great crime which cost Socrates his life was the pretension that he possessed a particular and private daemon; that is, an inspiration which was individual.

The process of making man a social animal is terrifying. It is not content with demanding of me that what is mine be given to others—an excellent idea which causes me no annoyance whatever—but it also insists that what is theirs be mine. For example, that I adopt their tastes and their ideas. Everything private and apart is forbidden, including the right of having convictions for one's own exclusive use.

The abstract divinity of 'the collective' is coming back to exercise its tyranny; indeed it is already creating havoc in Europe. The press believes it has the right to publicize our private lives, to judge them, to condemn them. Day by day the government forces us to give a larger part of our existence to society. Man is left no corner to retire to, no solitude for himself. The masses protest angrily against any reserve which we hold back for ourselves.

Probably the origin of this anti-individual fury lies in the fact that in their inmost hearts the masses feel themselves weak and defenceless in the face of their destiny. On a bitter and terrible page Nietzsche notes how, in primitive societies which were weak when confronted with the difficulties of existence, every individual and original act was a crime, and the man who tried to lead a solitary life was a malefactor. He must in everything comport himself according to the fashion of the tribe.

Now, apparently, many men are again feeling homesick for the herd. They devote themselves passionately to whatever there is left in them of the sheep. They want to march through life together, along the collective path, shoulder to shoulder, wool rubbing wool, and the head down. This is the reason why so many European peoples are looking for a shepherd and a sheep dog.

Hatred of liberalism comes from this and nothing else. For liberalism, before it becomes a question of this or that in politics, is a fundamental idea about life. It is believing that every human being ought to be free to fulfil his individual and non-transferable destiny.

MILDRED ADAMS

JACINTO BENAVENTE
[1866–1954]

When Jacinto Benavente began to write, towards the end of the nineteenth century, the exaggerated melodramas of José Echegaray dominated the Spanish stage. Benavente's art was a radical and refreshing change. Most of his plays fall into the category of social satire and deal mainly with the upper classes of his native Madrid. The dialogue, in prose, is calm and sophisticated, with frequent ironic and sceptical overtones.

Benavente's masterpiece, Los intereses creados (1907), takes its stock characters from the old Italian commedia dell'arte. Two of Benavente's powerful dramas have a rural setting: Señora ama (1908) and La malquerida (1913). The latter, translated for the American stage as The Passion Flower, is the gripping story of a stepfather's illicit love for his beautiful stepdaughter.

One of the most prolific of modern dramatists, Benavente received the Nobel Prize in 1922. Many of his plays have been translated into English by John Garrett Underhill.

THE BONDS OF INTEREST

ACT I

SCENE I

A plaza in a city. The façade of an Inn is at the right, having a practicable door, with a knocker upon it. Above the door is a sign which reads Inn.

(Leander *and* Crispin *enter from the left.*)

LEANDER. This must be a very great city, Crispin. Its riches and its power appear in everything.

CRISPIN. Yes, there are two cities. Pray God that we have chanced upon the better one!

LEANDER. Two cities do you say, Crispin? Ah! Now I understand —an old city and a new city, one on either side of the river.

CRISPIN. What has the river to do with it, or newness or age? I say two cities just as there are in every city in the world; one for people who arrive with money and the other for persons who arrive like us.

LEANDER. We are lucky to have arrived at all without falling into the hands of Justice. I should be heartily glad to stop here awhile and rest myself, for I am tired of this running about the world so continually.

CRISPIN. Not I! No, it is the natural condition of the freeborn subjects of the Kingdom of Roguery, of whom am I, not to remain seated long in any one place, unless it be through compulsion, as to say in the galleys, where, believe me, they are very hard seats. But now since we have happened upon this city, and to all appearances it is a well-fortified and provisioned one, let us like prudent captains map out our plan of battle beforehand, if we are to conquer it with any advantage to ourselves.

LEANDER. A pretty army we shall make to besiege it.

CRISPIN. We are men and we have to do with men.

LEANDER. All our wealth is on our backs. You were not willing to take off these clothes and sell them, when by doing so we could easily have obtained money.

CRISPIN. I would sooner take off my skin than my good clothes. As the world goes nothing is so important as appearances, and the clothes, as you must admit, are the first things to appear.

LEANDER. What are we going to do, Crispin? Hunger and fatigue have been too much for me. I am overcome; I cannot talk.

CRISPIN. There is nothing for us to do but to take advantage of our talents and our effrontery, for without effrontery talents are of no use. The best thing, as it seems to me will be for you to talk as little as possible, but be very impressive when you do, and put on the airs of a gentleman of quality. From time to time then I will permit you to strike me across the back. When anybody asks you a question, reply mysteriously, and if you open your mouth upon your own account, be sure that it is with dignity, as if you were pronouncing sentence. You are young; you have a fine presence. Until now you have known only how to dissipate your resources; this is the time for you to begin to profit by them. Put yourself in my hands. There is nothing so useful to a man as to have some one always at his heels to point out his merits, for modesty in one's self is imbecility, while self-praise is madness, and so between the two we come into disfavour with the world. Men are like merchandise; they are worth more or less according to the skill of the salesman who markets them. I tell you, though you were but muddy glass, I will so contrive that in my hands you shall pass for pure diamond. And now let us knock at the door of this inn, for surely it is the proper thing to have lodgings on the main square.

LEANDER. You say at this inn? But how are we going to pay?

CRISPIN. If we are to be stopped by a little thing like that, then we had better search out an asylum or an almshouse or else beg on the streets, if so be that you incline to virtue. Or if to force, then back to the highway and cut the throat of the first passer-by. If we are to live upon our means, strictly speaking, we have no other means to live.

LEANDER. I have letters of introduction to persons of importance in this city, who will be able to lend us aid.

CRISPIN. Then tear those letters up; never think of such baseness again. Introduce yourself to no man when you are in need. Those would be pretty letters of credit indeed! Today you will be received with the greatest courtesy; they will tell you that their houses and their persons are to be considered as yours. The next time you call, the servant will tell you that his master is not at home. No, he is not expected soon . . . and at the next visit nobody will trouble so much as to open the door. This is a world of giving and taking, a shop, a mart, a place of exchange, and before you ask you have to offer.

LEANDER. But what can I offer when I have nothing?

CRISPIN. How low an opinion you must have of yourself! Is a man in himself, then, worth nothing? A man may be a soldier, and by his valour win great victories. He may be a husband or a lover, and with love's sweet, oblivious medicine, restore some noble dame to health, or some damsel of high degree, who has been pining away through melancholy. He may be the servant of some mighty and powerful lord, who becomes attached to him and raises him up through his favour, and he may be so many other things besides that I have not the breath even to begin to run them over. When one wants to climb, why, any stair will do.

LEANDER. But if I have not even that stair?

CRISPIN. Then accept my shoulders, and I will lift you up. I offer you the top.

LEANDER. And if we both fall down upon the ground?

CRISPIN. God grant that it may be soft! . . .

ACT III

SCENE IX

(Leander *and* Crispin *enter.*)

CRISPIN. What is this sadness, this dejection? I expected to find you in better spirits.

LEANDER. I was never unfortunate till now; at least it never mattered to me whether or not I was unfortunate. Let us fly, Crispin, let us fly from this city before any one can discover us and find out who we are.

CRISPIN. If we fly it will be after every one has discovered us and they are running after us to detain us and bring us back in spite of ourselves. It would be most discourteous to depart with such scant ceremony without bidding our attentive friends good-bye.

LEANDER. Do not jest, Crispin; I am in despair.

CRISPIN. So you are. And just when our hopes are under fullest sail.

LEANDER. What could you expect? You wanted me to pretend to be in love, but I have not been able to pretend it.

CRISPIN. Why not?

LEANDER. Because I love—I love in spirit and in truth!

CRISPIN. Silvia? Is that what you are complaining about?

LEANDER. I never believed it possible a man could love like this. I never believed that I could ever love. Through all my wandering life along the dusty roads, I was not only the one who passed, I was the one who fled, the enemy of the harvest and the field, the enemy of man, enemy of sunshine and the day. Sometimes the fruit of the wayside tree, stolen, not given, left some savour of joy on my parched lips, and sometimes, after many a bitter day, resting at night beneath the stars, the calm repose of heaven would invite and soothe me to a dream of something that might be in my life like that calm night sky, brooding infinite over my soul— serene! And so tonight, in the enchantment of this fête, it seemed to me as if there had come a calm, a peace into my life—and I was dreaming! Ah! How I did dream! But tomorrow it will be again the bitter flight with justice at our heels, and I cannot bear that they should take me here where she is, and where she may ever have cause to be ashamed at having known me.

CRISPIN. Why, I thought that you had been received with favour! And I was not the only one who noticed it. Doña Sirena and our good friends, the Captain and the poet, have been most eloquent in your praises. To that rare excellent mother, the Wife of

Polichinelle, who thinks of nothing but how she can relate herself by marriage to some nobleman, you have seemed the son-in-law of her dreams. As for Signor Polichinelle . . .

LEANDER. He knows . . . he suspects. . . .

CRISPIN. Naturally. It is not so easy to deceive Signor Polichinelle as it is an ordinary man. An old fox like him has to be cheated truthfully. I decided that the best thing for us to do was to tell him everything.

LEANDER. How so?

CRISPIN. Obviously. He knows me of old. When I told him that you were my master, he rightly supposed that the master must be worthy of the man. And upon my part, in appreciation of his confidence, I warned him not to permit you under any circumstances to come near to or speak with his daughter.

LEANDER. You did? Then what have I to hope?

CRISPIN. You are a fool! Why, that Signor Polichinelle will exert all his authority to prevent you from meeting her.

LEANDER. I do not understand.

CRISPIN. In that way he will become our most powerful ally, for if he opposes it, that will be enough to make his wife take the opposite side, and the daughter will fall in love with you madly. You have no idea what a young and beautiful daughter of a rich father, who has been brought up to the gratification of her every whim, can do when she finds out for the first time in her life that somebody is opposing her wishes. I am certain that this very night, before the fête is over, she will find some way of eluding the vigilance of her father at whatever cost, and return to speak with you.

LEANDER. But can't you see that Signor Polichinelle is nothing to me, no, nor the wide world either? It is she, only she! It is to her that I am unwilling to appear unworthy or mean, it is to her—to her that I cannot lie.

CRISPIN. Bah! Enough of this nonsense! Don't tell me that. It is too late to draw back. Think what will happen if we vacillate now and hesitate in going on. You say that you have fallen in love? Well, this real love will serve us better than if it were put on. Otherwise you would have wanted to get through with it too quickly. If insolence and effrontery are the only qualities which are of use elsewhere, in love a faint suggestion of timidity is of advantage to a man. Timidity in a man always makes the woman bolder. If you don't believe it, here is the innocent Silvia now, skulking in the shadows and only waiting for a chance to come near until I retire or am concealed.

LEANDER. Silvia, do you say?

CRISPIN. Hush! You may frighten her. When she is with you, remember, discretion—only a few words, very few. Adore her, admire her, contemplate her, and let the enchantment of this night of pallid blue speak for you, propitious as it is to love, and whisper to her in the music whose soft notes die away amid the foliage and fall upon our ears like sad overtones of this festival of joy.

LEANDER. Do not trifle, Crispin! Do not trifle with my love! It will be my death.

CRISPIN. Why should I trifle with it? I know, too, it is not always well to grovel on the ground. Sometimes we must soar and mount up into the sky better to dominate the earth. Mount now and soar —and I will grovel still. The world lies in our hands!

(He goes out to the right.)

JOHN GARRETT UNDERHILL

ANTONIO MACHADO
[1875–1939]

Antonio Machado, though born in Seville, is intimately associated with Castile, where he spent most of his life. His verse, small in quantity, is serious, intense and restrained. His most characteristic work is contained in Campos de Castilla (*1912*), *in which he exalts the austere beauty of the plains of Castile. Some critics believe him to be Spain's greatest poet of the twentieth century.*

FIELDS OF SORIA
III

An undulating country, where the roads
Do now conceal the travellers, astride
Their dusky-coated asses,
Now, in the crimson light of dying day,
Uplift in full relief their rustic forms,
Darkening the golden canvas of the West.
Climb now yon mount, and from those jagged peaks
Where dwells the eagle, gaze upon the scene;
And see the leaden plains and silvery slopes
All bathed in carmine, shot with steely grey,
Circled by mountains of deep violet,
With snowy summits blushing like the rose.

IV

Lo, these are they that move 'twixt land and sky;
Two oxen, slowly ploughing
Upon a hillside, touched by Autumn's breath,
The while between their sturdy heads, low bent
Beneath the heavy yoke,
A basket hangs woven of reeds and broom—
An infant's rustic cradle;
And, following the team,
A man, who bows him down towards the earth,
Likewise a woman, who in the gaping furrows
Scatters the precious seed.
Beneath a cloud of crimson and of flame
See in the West, all liquid gold and green,
Their shadows slowly lengthen as they pass.

IDA FARNELL

TO DON FRANCISCO GINER DE LOS RIOS

Now, when the Master left us,
There came that morning's light,
Whispering : 'Three days have fled,
And lo, my brother Francis worketh not!
Died he?' We only know
That he went hence upon a shining path,
And spake : 'Mourn me with works,
Mourn me with hopes, I would no dole of tears;
Only be good. Be, as I strove to be
While in this life—a soul.
Live on, life hath no end;
The dead alone shall die, and shadows pass;
Who sowed is reaping now, who lived yet liveth;
Let the good anvils sound, let bells be dumb !'
Then to a purer light
The brother of the light of dawn went forth,
Forth from the scene of toils
That bright and glad old man of saintly life.

... Yea, comrades, let us bring
His body to the mountains,
Up to those azure heights
Where Guadarrama towers.

Yonder are shadowy gorges
With pine-trees, where the winds make melody.
Let his great heart repose
Beneath this sacred oak,
Where beds of thyme scatter their fragrance sweet,
And golden butterflies play.
'Tis there of old our Master
Dreamt his sweet dream of Spain's new blossoming.

IDA FARNELL

COUNSELS

Learn how to hope, to wait the proper tide—
    As on the coast a bark—then part without a care;
He who knows how to wait wins victory for bride;
    For life is long and art a plaything there.
But should your life prove short
    And never come a tide,
    Wait still, unsailing, hope is on your side,
Art may be long or, else, of no import.

THOMAS WALSH

SONGS OF SEVERAL LANDS

I

By the sierra gardens
The wide seas break in foam,
And grains of salt I find
Within the honeycomb.

II

By waters in darkness flowing—
Night over Málaga—
Sea foam and jasmine blowing.

III

Suddenly—spring is here!
No one saw her appear.

IV

Now comes the spring.
Blossoms of briers upon the air
White hosannas fling!

V

Full moon, full moon,
Glory-crowned, so very round,
In this peaceful, springtime night,
White bees are building you,
A honeycomb of light !

VI

Castilian evening . . .
The music will begin,
Or better, cease to sing.
To the window will I come
When all are slumbering.

VII

Singing and keeping time,
River willow and green
Almond bough sing a rhyme.

They sing of grey oak tree
With branch for axe to fell,
And flowers none may see.

White flowers of the pear,
Pink flowers of the peach,
In gardens everywhere.

And of this perfume
By winged, wet winds carried
From bean fields in bloom.

VIII

Above the little square
The sun no longer burns.
With the four acacias
To dusk the fountain turns.
O happy afternoon !
Sing, nightingale, thy rue !
In my heart this hour
It is twilight too.

IX

On whitewashed walls
Of traveller's cell,
My shadow falls !

XIII

In meadows green they dance
To sound of fifes and drums.
With sandals gold and crook
In bud, a shepherd comes.

From hills in haste came I,
Only to dance with her;
Back to the hills I'll hie.

Among the garden trees
There is a nightingale.
By night and day, to sun
And moon he tells his tale.
The bird in garden close
Is hoarse with song. The maid
Will come to pluck a rose.

Among the oak trees black
There is a fountain stilled,
A little jar of clay
That never has been filled.

With the white moon
Through groves of oak,
She will come soon.

XV

While you dance in a ring,
Maidens, sing.
Now green the meadows are,
Now comes the wooing spring.

Among the oak trees black,
By river murmuring,
Where tread his sandalled feet,
The silver traces cling.
Now green the meadows are,
Now comes the wooing spring.

FLORENCE LEWIS MAY

MANUEL MACHADO
[1874–1947]

Manuel Machado, born in Seville but brought up in Madrid, retains in his poetry the lyricism of his native Andalusia. Though neither as deep nor as original as his brother Antonio, Manuel Machado is one of the outstanding modernist poets of Spain, following the path of Rubén Darío. Alma (1902), Apolo (1911) and Cante hondo (1912) are among his best works.

ADELPHOS

I am kindred to those people who made this land their own;
I spring from the Moorish race, born lovers of the sun.
A scion of that nation who won and lost a throne,
My soul like the Spanish Arab's is a pale sweet-scented one.

My failing will died in me beneath the moonlight's spell—
Sweet the release from reason and from love's tyrant claim;
My joy to lie at ease where no illusions dwell—
From time to time embraces or the music of a name.

In my soul as in the twilight, all shapes inconstant change,
And the rose which is a symbol of my one abiding passion
Shall be a flower opened in distant lands and strange
And have no certain perfume, no colour, nor rightful fashion.

Kisses—but not to give them. Glory—what the world owes,
Let all this like an aura descend around my head.
May the tide still bear me with it as it softly ebbs and flows,
And never need I choose the road which I must tread.

Ambition I have none, and love I have not known;
I never burned with faith nor glowed with gratitude.
I had towards art vague yearnings, now forever flown;
I am not swayed by vice, with virtue not imbued.

In loftiness of lineage to no man need I yield;
Innate and not acquired are breeding and blazon proud.
But the emblem of my house, the device upon my shield
Is a futile sun half-hidden in a faint uncertain cloud.

I ask nought, love nor hate, only by going now
Can you grant to me the boon that I to you would give.
And let life take the trouble to kill, I care not how,
Since I'll not bestir myself to take the pains to live.

My failing will died in me beneath the moonlight's spell—
Sweet the release from reason and rest from love to earn;
From time to time a kiss, where no illusions dwell,
The kind and generous kiss that asks for no return.

BEATRICE GILMAN PROSKE

FIGURINES

With loveliness the little princess
Fairly seems to glow,
Completely charming,
Small, disarming,
The princess of Watteau!

When the princess is before me,
I admire, I adore!
If she is sighing,
I am crying,
If she smiles, I laugh once more.

At times, as now, she smiles on me,
And oh, her smile is gay!
Her eyes are dancing,
Roguish, glancing,
Then lost in thought she looks away.

The little princess of Watteau,
She really seems to live!
All who view her
Find allure there,
Those who know her their love give.

Her sweet face echoes each emotion,
There I can divine
Sorrow blending
With love, ending
In death, her fate like mine.

ALICE JANE MᶜVAN

PHILIP THE FOURTH

None could more gracious nor more courtly be
Than our King Philip, may God keep him well!
With raven night his sombre clothes agree.
Pallid his face as is the twilight's spell;

Heavy his hair with golden ringlets drest;
In furtive eyes faint sapphire shadows dwell.
Above his generous and noble breast
No flash of gems nor clink of littering chains
Disturbs the hush where folds of velvet rest.
The sceptre laid aside, he now sustains,
With languid grace, a single glove within
His ivory hand enlaced with frail blue veins.

BEATRICE GILMAN PROSKE

JUAN RAMÓN JIMÉNEZ
[b. 1881]

At first a follower of the modernist innovations of Rubén Darío, the Andalusian Juan Ramón Jiménez soon developed a highly personal and original style. His numerous poems, contained in more than twenty volumes, are notable for their imagery, delicate romanticism and musicality. His earlier poems were inspired by Nature and beauty; more recently Jiménez sought to achieve 'pure poetry'. He is also the author of a number of prose works, among them the delightful tale about a child and his pet donkey, Platero y yo (1914). Juan Ramón Jiménez has exerted a tremendous influence on the younger poets of Spain and Spanish America. He was awarded the Nobel Prize for Literature in 1956.

GREEN

Green was the maiden, green, green!
Green her eyes were, green her hair.

The wild rose in her green wood
was neither red nor white, but green.

Through the green air she came.
(The whole earth turned green for her.)

The shining gauze of her garment
was neither blue nor white, but green.

Over the green sea she came.
(And even the sky turned green then.)

My life will always leave unlatched
a small green gate to let her in.

J. B. TREND

AUTUMNAL ARIA

XVIII

Idly sings the shepherd,
Trusty crook in hand,
And eyes the veiled horizon
Where dim the pine trees stand.

The sheep in drowsy flock
Raise dusty clouds and soon
Their little bells are crying
Beneath the golden moon.

Over the town in the valley
Trembles a cloud of white;
All that was gay in the sun
Dreams of lost love by night.

If lovers sad should pass
There where the river lies,
There would be warm salt tears
And secrets in their eyes.

The countryside would tell them,
Sweet are the pangs of love,
Within the shadow, gilded
By the autumn moon above.

The smoke cloud lifts; alone
And sad the vale is lying;
Beneath the golden moon
The little bells are crying.

ALICE JANE McVAN

ONE NIGHT

The ancient spiders with a flutter spread
    Their misty marvels through the withered flowers,
The windows, by the moonlight pierced, would shed
    Their trembling garlands pale across the bowers.

The balconies looked over to the South;
    The night was one immortal and serene;
From fields afar the newborn springtime's mouth
    Wafted a breath of sweetness o'er the scene.

How silent! Grief had hushed its spectral moan
　　Among the shadowy roses of the sward;
Love was a fable—shadows overthrown
　　Trooped back in myriads from oblivion's ward.

The garden's voice was all—empires had died—
　　The azure stars in languor having known
The sorrows all the centuries provide,
　　With silver crowned me there, remote and lone.

THOMAS WALSH

DREAM NOCTURNE

The earth leads by the earth.
But, sea,
You lead by the heavens.
With what security of gold and silver light
Do the stars mark the road for us!
One would think
That the earth was the road
Of the body,
That the sea was the road
Of the soul.
Yes. It seems
That the soul is the only traveller
Of the sea; that the body, alone,
Remains behind, on the beach,
Without her, saying goodbye,
Heavy, cold, as though dead.
How like
Is a journey by sea
To death,
To eternal life!

THOMAS McGREEVY

I WOULD THAT ALL MY VERSES

I would that all my verses
could be such as the sky is in the night-time :
truth of the moment—now—without history.

20*—SA

That, like the sky, they would yield at every instant
all things, with all their streaming stars, and
neither childhood, nor youth, nor age could rob them,
nor cast a spell on the immensity of their beauty.

A thrill, a bright flash, music,
before my eyes and upon me!
The thrill, the bright flash, the music, right between my eyes,
—the whole sky in my heart—the naked book!

J. B. TREND

PEDRO SALINAS
[1892–1951]

*One of the finest of the newer poets was the cultured professor and critic,
Pedro Salinas. His poetry is intimate and intellectual; his style, simple and
lyric. From 1940 until his untimely death, Salinas was Professor of Spanish
at Johns Hopkins University. Many of his poems have been translated into
English by Eleanor L. Turnbull.*

IT MIGHT BE ÁVILA

Walls unbroken rise
In undisputed reign
And gaze in still surprise
Upon the lonely plain.
And the foe?

The towered height commands
The quiet roads below
Where sheep in dusty bands
Pass humbly to and fro.
And the foe?

Beneath the valiant arch
Now comes the farmer's spoil;
In dreary legions march
Wine casks, wheat bags, and oil.
And the foe?

Where stands the battlement
The winds a refuge take,
And storks on nesting bent
A peaceful murmur make.
And the foe?

Towers that from the height
A faithful vigil keep
While centuries take flight
And farms in stillness sleep,
And thy foe?

ANNE SAWYER DURAND

SOIL

Soil. Nothing more.
Soil. Nothing less.
And let that suffice you.
Because on the soil the feet are planted,
on the feet body erect,
on the body the head firm,
and there, in the lee of the forehead,
pure idea and in the pure idea
the tomorrow, the key
tomorrow of the eternal
Soil. No more no less.
And let that suffice you.

ELEANOR L. TURNBULL

HOW GENTLY YOU ROCK MY CHILD
TO SLEEP

How gently you rock my child to sleep,
enormous cradle of the world,
cradle of the August night!
The wind caresses his cheeks for me
and that which sings in the tree-tops
has the soothing sound of a lullaby
which quiets and puts him to sleep.
Tranquil stars watch over him,
from too much light and darkness
they guard and protect his eyes.
The earth seems to turn very slowly,
I feel it revolve on its axis
with no more motion than needful
to lull the child to sleep,
son of mine and son of yours.

ELEANOR L. TURNBULL

SWIMMER OF NIGHT

Swimmer of night, swimmer between
waves and shadows.
White arms submerging and rising
with a rhythm
governed by unknown designs,
you advance 'gainst
the double, silent resistance
of darkness and sea, world of gloom.
At the shipwreck of day,
you, voyager
crossing through April and May,
wished to save, are saving yourself,
not from death, from resignation.
The waves break over you, their fierceness gone,
their war repented of,
their wonder turned to foam,
when you offer them as a pact,
your strong, virgin breast.
The broad, dense billows of the night
break against
that desire for light that you seek,
by uplifting arms, that raises
in the heavens a great foaming;
a foam of lights, yes, of stars,
which sprinkle your face
with a riot of constellations,
of worlds. By your bare
innocence, seas of centuries defied,
centuries of shadows.
Your rhythmic bodily motion
supports, impels and saves
much more than your flesh. Thus your triumph
will be your end, and at last, sea,
night and conventions passed over,
on the far side of the black world,
on the shore of the day which breaks,
you will die in the dawn you have won.

ELEANOR L. TURNBULL

JORGE GUILLÉN
[*b.* 1893]

Jorge Guillén is regarded by many critics as the initiator of 'pure poetry' in the intellectual manner. His verse is of classic perfection and great lyric beauty—his one volume of poetry, Cántico *(1928, and expanded several times), sings the joy and wonder of life. Guillén is at present Professor of Spanish at Wellesley College.*

NAMES

It is dawn. The horizon
Peeps between its eyelashes,
And begins to see. What?
Names written on the surface,

The patina of things.
The rose is still called rose
Today, and the memory
Of its passing is haste.

Haste to be living more.
To abundant love we are
Raised by that unripe power
Of the Moment, so nimble

That on reaching its goal
It hastes to impose the Aftermath.
Be alert, on your guard!
I shall be, I shall be!

And the roses? Eyelashes
Fast closed : final horizon.
If perchance there is nothing?
But the names still remain.

ELEANOR L. TURNBULL

PERFECTION

The firmament, a dense blue,
Is overarching the day.
'Tis the rounding out of splendour,
Midday. All is curving dome.

At the centre lies, unwilling,
The rose, subject to a sun
At its zenith. And the present
So yields itself up that the
Foot that is moving now feels
The completeness of the planet.

ELEANOR L. TURNBULL

SLENDER SPRING

When the formless infinite enshrouds
                    With the clouds
Its vast uncertainty and drifting soars . . .
                    To what shores,

While the river curving as it goes
                    Ever flows
Pursuing then with etched, oblique caprice
                    Its release,

While the water hides in folds of green
                    Fish unseen
Below the deep reflections trembling there
                    Of the air . . .

When morning lingers on her misty way
                    All the day
Along a silver wake which glimmering weaves
                    Among the leaves,

Then sinuous spring unites in her design
                    The smooth line
Of clouds wind-borne that swaying in the sky
                    Circle by

With bubbles which a pointed pattern make
                    And crystal break . . .
For a moment seen in the oars that flashing swing—
                    Slender spring.

ANNE SAWYER DURAND

FEDERICO GARCÍA LORCA
[1899–1936]

Undoubtedly the most popular Spanish writer of this century was the brilliant and versatile Andalusian, Federico García Lorca. A spontaneous and gifted poet and dramatist, whose works have been widely translated, Lorca was in addition an excellent painter and musician. His tragic death at the outbreak of the Civil War cut short a truly remarkable career.

In the traditions and folk songs of Andalusia Lorca found his main inspiration. (Libro de poemas, *1921;* Canciones, *1927;* Romancero Gitano, *1928;* Poema del cante jondo, *1931.*) *His favourite metre is the traditional ballad, but he also wrote extensively in the modernistic style, notably the surrealistic* Poeta en Nueva York (*1929*). *His dramatic production includes light, lyric pieces as well as gripping tragedies.*

RIDER'S SONG

Cordoba.
Distant and lonely.

Black my pony, full the moon
and olives stowed in my saddle-bags.
Though well I may know the way
I'll never arrive at Cordoba.

Across the plain, through the wind,
black my pony, red the moon,
stark death is staring at me
from the tall towers of Cordoba.

Alas, how long is the way!
Alas, for my brave black pony!
Alas, stark death awaits me
before I arrive at Cordoba!

Cordoba.
Distant and lonely.

ELEANOR L. TURNBULL

SIX STRINGS

The guitar
makes the dreams weep.

The sobbing of souls
that are lost
escapes from its round
open mouth.
And like the tarantula
it weaves a great star
to catch the sighs
that float on its dark
pool of wood.

ELEANOR L. TURNBULL

THE GUITAR

Now begins the cry
Of the guitar,
Breaking the vaults
Of dawn.
Now begins the cry
Of the guitar.
Useless
To still it.
Impossible
To still it.
It weeps monotonously
As weeps the water,
As weeps the wind
Over snow.
Impossible
To still it.
It weeps
For distant things,
Warm southern sands
Desiring white camelias.
It mourns the arrow without a target,
The evening without morning.
And the first bird dead
Upon a branch.
O guitar!
A wounded heart,
Wounded by five swords.

ELIZABETH DU GUÉ TRAPIER

SOMNAMBULE BALLAD

Green, how I want you green.
Green wind. Green branches.
The ship upon the sea
and the horse in the mountain.
With the shadow on her waist
she dreams on her verandah,
green flesh, hair of green,
and eyes of cold silver.
Green, how I want you green.
Beneath the gipsy moon,
all things look at her
but she cannot see them

Green, how I want you green.
Great stars of white frost
come with the fish of darkness
that opens the road of dawn.
The fig-tree rubs the wind
with the sand-paper of its branches,
and the mountain, a filching cat,
bristles its bitter aloes.
But who will come? And from where?
She lingers on her verandah,
green flesh, hair of green,
dreaming of the bitter sea.
—Friend, I want to change
my horse for your house,
my saddle for your mirror,
my knife for your blanket.
Friend, I come bleeding,
from the harbours of Cabra.
—If I could, young man,
this pact would be sealed.
But I am no more I,
nor is my house now my house.
—Friend, I want to die
decently in my bed.
Of iron, if it be possible,
with sheets of fine holland.
Do you not see the wound I have
from my breast to my throat?

—Your white shirt bears
three hundred dark roses.
Your pungent blood oozes
around your sash.
But I am no more I,
nor is my house now my house.
—Let me climb at least
up to the high balustrades :
let me come ! let me come !
up to the green balustrades.
Balustrades of the moon
where the water resounds.

Now the two friends go up
towards the high balustrades.
Leaving a trail of blood,
Leaving a trail of tears.
Small lanterns of tin
were trembling on the roofs.
A thousand crystal tambourines
were piercing the dawn.
Green, how I want you green,
green wind, green branches.
The two friends went up.
The long wind was leaving
in the mouth a strange taste
of gall, mint and sweet-basil.
Friend ! Where is she, tell me,
where is your bitter girl?
How often she waited for you !
How often did she wait for you,
cool face, black hair,
on this green verandah !

Over the face of the cistern
the gipsy girl swayed.
Green flesh, hair of green,
with eyes of cold silver.
An icicle of the moon
suspends her above the water.
The night became as intimate
as a little square.
Drunken civil guards
were knocking at the door.

Green, how I want you green.
Green wind. Green branches.
The ship upon the sea.
And the horse in the mountain.

J. L. GILI and STEPHEN SPENDER

RAFAEL ALBERTI
[*b.* 1902]

Like Lorca, Rafael Alberti is a talented Andalusian who has cultivated both popular and modern themes. His first book of verse, Marinero en tierra, *was awarded the National Prize for Literature in 1925. In 1929 he published the Gongoristic* Cal y canto *and the surrealistic* Sobre los ángeles. *He has written some dozen volumes of poetry; his work is characterized by perfection of form.*

THE SEA

The sea, the sea,
the sea, only the sea!

Father, oh why to the city
did you drag me?

Why, oh why, did you pull me
out of the sea?

In dreams, the swell of the sea
tugs at the strings of my heart,
and away with it would flee.

here from the sea?
Father, why did you drag me

ELEANOR L. TURNBULL

STREET CRY UNDER SEA

How happy now would I be
with you, my fair young gardener,
in a garden under sea!

In a cart of cockle-shell,
drawn by a trout, oh what glee
for me, love, your wares to sell
under the salty blue sea!

—Fresh seaweed here from the sea,
seaweed, seaweed!

ELEANOR L. TURNBULL

STREET CRY

I sell clouds of many colours :
dark clouds to cool heat of summers!

I sell fleecy clouds of violet,
clouds that rosy flush at dawning,
gilded clouds of evening sunset!

Buy the yellow star of morning,
plucked from green boughs still dew-wet,
the heavenly peach tree adorning!

I sell snow and flames of fire,
and the call of the street crier!

ELEANOR L. TURNBULL

THE ANGEL OF NUMERALS

Virgins with T-squares
and compasses, guarding
celestial blackboards.

And the angel of numerals
pensively flying
from 1 to 2, from 2
to 3, from 3 to 4.

Dull chalk and wet sponges
erased and crossed out
the light of spaces.

Neither sun, moon, nor stars,
nor the sudden green
of flash of lightning,
nor air. Only mist.

Virgins without squares
and compasses, weeping.

And on the blurred blackboards
the angel of numerals,
lifeless, shrouded, lying
on 1 and on 2,
on 3 and on 4.

ELEANOR L. TURNBULL

BIBLIOGRAPHY

I. Histories of Spanish Literature in English

Aubrey F. G. Bell, *Castilian Literature*, Oxford, 1938.

——, *Contemporary Spanish Literature*, New York, 1933.

Gerald Brenan, *The Literature of the Spanish People*, Cambridge, 1952.

James Fitzmaurice-Kelly, *Chapters on Spanish Literature*, London, 1908.

——, *A History of Spanish Literature*, New York, 1898.

J. D. M. Ford, *Main Currents of Spanish Literature*, New York, 1919.

Ernest Mérimée and S. Griswold Morley, *A History of Spanish Literature*, New York, 1930.

Maxim Newmark, *Dictionary of Spanish Literature*, New York, 1956.

George Tyler Northup, *An Introduction to Spanish Literature*, Chicago, 1936.

George Ticknor, *History of Spanish Literature*, 3 vols., New York, 1849.

II. Spanish Literature in English Translation

John Bowring, *Ancient Poetry and Romances of Spain*, London, 1824.

Barrett H. Clark, *Masterpieces of Modern Spanish Drama*, New York, 1917.

Harriet de Onís, *Spanish Stories and Tales*, New York, 1954.

Ida Farnell, *Spanish Prose and Poetry*, Oxford, 1920.

Angel Flores, *Great Spanish Stories*, New York, 1956.

——, *Spanish Literature in English Translation: a bibliographical syllabus*, New York, 1926.

Mildred E. Johnson, *Spanish Poems of Love*, New York, 1955.

Willis Knapp Jones, *Spanish One Act Plays in English*, Dallas, 1934.

James Kennedy, *Modern Poets and Poetry of Spain*, London, 1852.

John Gibson Lockhart, *Ancient Spanish Ballads*, London, 1841.

Henry Wadsworth Longfellow, *The Poets and Poetry of Europe*, Philadelphia, 1845.

Charles B. McMichael, *Short Stories from the Spanish*, New York, 1920.

Paul T. Manchester, *Joyas Poéticas: Spanish and Spanish-American Poetry*, New York, 1951.

Remigio U. Pane, *English Translations from the Spanish, 1484–1943: a bibliography*, New Brunswick, 1944.

Samuel Putnam, *The European Caravan*, New York, 1931.

Thomas Roscoe, *The Spanish Novelists*, London, 1832.

605

Tales from the Italian and Spanish, New York, 1920.
Susette M. Taylor, *The Humour of Spain*, London, 1894.
Translations from Hispanic Poets, New York, 1938.
J. B. Trend, *Spanish Short Stories of the 16th Century in Contemporary Translation*, London, 1928.
Eleanor L. Turnbull, *Contemporary Spanish Poetry*, Baltimore, 1945.
——, *Ten Centuries of Spanish Poetry*, Baltimore, 1955.
J. F. Vingut, *Selections from the Best Spanish Poets*, New York, 1856.
Thomas Walsh, *Hispanic Anthology: Poems Translated from the Spanish by English and North American Poets*, New York, 1920.
Warre B. Wells, *Great Spanish Short Stories*, New York, 1932. (Published in England as *The Spanish Omnibus*, London, 1932.)

III. A Brief English Bibliography of Spanish-American Literature

Germán Arciniegas, *The Green Continent*, New York, 1944.
Alice Stone Blackwell, *Some Spanish-American Poets*, Philadelphia, 1937.
Alfred Coester, *The Literary History of Spanish America*, New York, 1928.
G. Dundas Craig, *The Modernist Trend in Spanish-American Poetry*, Berkeley, 1934.
Harriet de Onís, *The Golden Land*, New York, 1948.
Dudley Fitts, *Anthology of Contemporary Latin-American Poetry*, Norfolk (Conn.), 1942.
Isaac Goldberg, *Studies in Spanish-American Literature*, New York, 1920.
Pedro Henríquez-Ureña, *Literary Currents in Hispanic America*, Cambridge (Mass.), 1945.
E. Herman Hespelt and others, *An Outline History of Spanish-American Literature*, New York, 1942.
Jefferson Rea Spell, *Contemporary Spanish-American Fiction*, Chapel Hill, 1944.
Arturo Torres-Ríoseco, *New World Literature*, Berkeley and Los Angeles, 1949.

INDEX

[AUTHORS AND MAJOR ANONYMOUS WORKS]